Lecture Notes in Computer Science 8806

Commenced Publication in 1973
Founding and Former Series Editors:
Gerhard Goos, Juris Hartmanis, and Jan van Leeuwen

T0212876

Luís Lopes et al. (Eds.)

Euro-Par 2014: Parallel Processing Workshops

Euro-Par 2014 International Workshops
Porto, Portugal, August 25-26, 2014
Revised Selected Papers, Part II

 Springer

Volume Editor

Luís Lopes
University of Porto
CRACS/INESC-TEC and FCUP
Rua do Campo Alegre, 1021, 4169-007 Porto, Portugal
E-mail: lblopes@dcc.fc.up.pt

Workshop Editors *see next page*

ISSN 0302-9743   e-ISSN 1611-3349
ISBN 978-3-319-14312-5   e-ISBN 978-3-319-14313-2
DOI 10.1007/978-3-319-14313-2
Springer Cham Heidelberg New York Dordrecht London

Library of Congress Control Number: 2014957415

LNCS Sublibrary: SL 1 – Theoretical Computer Science and General Issues

Typesetting: Camera-ready by author, data conversion by Scientific Publishing Services, Chennai, India

Printed on acid-free paper

Springer is part of Springer Science+Business Media (www.springer.com)

Workshop Editors

APCI&E
Julius Žilinskas
Vilnius University, Lithuania
julius.zilinskas@mii.vu.lt

BigDataCloud
Alexandru Costan
Inria Rennes, France
alexandru.costan@inria.fr

DIHC
Roberto G. Cascella
Inria Rennes, France
roberto.cascella@inria.fr

FedICI
Gabor Kecskemeti
MTA SZTAKI, Budapest, Hungary
kecskemeti.gabor@sztaki.mta.hu

HeteroPar
Emmanuel Jeannot
Inria Bordeaux Sud-Ouest, France
emmanuel.jeannot@inria.fr

HiBB
Mario Cannataro
University Magna, Catanzaro, Italy
cannataro@unicz.it

LSDVE
Laura Ricci
University of Pisa, Italy
ricci@di.unipi.it

MuCoCoS
Siegfried Benkner
University of Vienna, Austria
siegfried.benkner@univie.ac.at

OHMI
Salvador Petit
University of Valencia, Spain
spetit@disca.upv.es

PADABS
Vittorio Scarano
University of Salerno, Italy
vitsca@dia.unisa.it

PROPER
José Gracia
High Performance Computing Center
Stuttgart (HLRS), Germany
gracia@hlrs.de

REPPAR
Sascha Hunold
Vienna University of Technology,
Austria
hunold@par.tuwien.ac.at

Resilience
Stephen L. Scott
Tennessee Tech University, Cookeville,
USA
sscott@tntech.edu

ROME
Stefan Lankes
RWTH Aachen, Germany
SLankes@eonerc.rwth-aachen.de

SPPEXA
Christian Lengauer
University of Passau, Germany
lengauer@fim.uni-passau.de

TASUS
Jesus Carretero
University Carlos III of Madrid, Spain
jesus.carretero@uc3m.es

UCHPC
Jens Breitbart
Technical University Munich, Germany
j.breitbart@tum.de

VHPC
Michael Alexander
Vienna University of Technology,
Austria
michael.alexander@tuwien.ac.at

Preface

Euro-Par is an annual series of international conferences dedicated to the promotion and advancement of all aspects of parallel and distributed computing. Euro-Par 2014, held in Porto, Portugal, was the 20th edition of the series. The conference covers a wide spectrum of topics from algorithms and theory to software technology and hardware-related issues, with application areas ranging from scientific to mobile and cloud computing. Euro-Par conferences host a set of technical workshops, with the goal of providing a space for communities within the field to meet and discuss more focused research topics. The coordination of the workshops was in the hands of Workshop Chairs Luc Bougé, also with the Euro-Par Steering Committee, and Luís Lopes, with the local organization. In the coordination process, we were kindly assisted by Dieter an Mey, one of the workshop chairs for the Euro-Par 2013 event at Aachen, to whom we wish to express our warm thanks for his availability, expertise, and advice. In early January 2014, a call for workshop proposals was issued, and the proposals were reviewed by the co-chairs, with 18 workshops being selected for the 2-day program:

APCI&E – First Workshop on Applications of Parallel Computation in Industry and Engineering

BigDataCloud – Third Workshop on Big Data Management in Clouds

DIHC – Second Workshop on Dependability and Interoperability in Heterogeneous Clouds

FedICI – Second Workshop on Federative and Interoperable Cloud Infrastructures

HeteroPar – 12th International Workshop on Algorithms, Models and Tools for Parallel Computing on Heterogeneous Platforms

HiBB – 5th Workshop on High-Performance Bioinformatics and Biomedicine

LSDVE – Second Workshop on Large-Scale Distributed Virtual Environments on Clouds and P2P

MuCoCoS – 7th International Workshop on Multi-/Many-Core Computing Systems

OMHI – Third Workshop on On-chip Memory Hierarchies and Interconnects: Organization, Management and Implementation

PADABS – Second Workshop on Parallel and Distributed Agent-Based Simulations

PROPER – 7th Workshop on Productivity and Performance – Tools for HPC Application Development

Resilience – 7th Workshop on Resiliency in High-Performance Computing with Clouds, Grids, and Clusters

REPPAR – First International Workshop on Reproducibility in Parallel Computing

ROME – Second Workshop on Runtime and Operating Systems for the Many-Core Era

SPPEXA – Workshop on Software for Exascale Computing - Project Workshop
TASUS – First Workshop on Techniques and Applications for Sustainable
   Ultrascale Computing Systems
UCHPC – 7th Workshop on UnConventional High-Performance Computing
VHPC – 9th Workshop on Virtualization in High-Performance Cloud
   Computing

Furthermore, collocated with this intensive workshop program, two tutorials
were also included:

Heterogeneous Memory Models – Benedict R. Gaster (Qualcomm, Inc.)
High-Performance Parallel Graph Analytics – Keshav Pingali
   (UT Austin) and Manoj Kumar (IBM)

Paper submission deadlines, notification dates, and camera-ready submission
deadlines were synchronized between all workshops. The new workshop coordination procedures, established with the 2012 edition, turned out to be very
helpful for putting together a high-quality workshop program. After the conference, the workshop organizers delivered a workshop management report on the
key performance indicators to the Workshop Advisory Board and the Steering
Committee. These reports will help to improve the procedures for, and the quality of, the workshop program of future Euro-Par conferences. Special thanks are
due to the authors of all the submitted papers, the members of the Program
Committees, the reviewers, and the workshop organizers. We had 173 paper
submissions, with 100 papers being accepted for publication in the proceedings.
Given the high number of papers, the workshops proceedings were divided into
two volumes with the following distribution:

LNCS 8805 – APCI&E, BigDataCloud, HeteroPar, HiBB, LSDVE, PADABS,
   REPPAR, Resilience
LNCS 8806 – DIHC, FedICI, MuCoCoS, OMHI, PROPER, ROME, TASUS,
   UCHPC, VHPC, SPPEXA

We are grateful to the Euro-Par general chairs and the members of the Euro-
Par Steering Committee for their support and advice regarding the coordination
of workshops. We would like to thank Springer for its continuous support in
publishing the workshop proceedings.
   It was a great pleasure and honor to organize and host the Euro-Par 2014
workshops in Porto. We hope all the participants enjoyed the workshop program
and benefited from the ample opportunities for fruitful exchange of ideas.

October 2014   Luís Lopes

Organization

Euro-Par Steering Committee

Chair

Christian Lengauer   University of Passau, Germany

Vice-Chair

Luc Bougé   ENS Rennes, France

European Representatives

Marco Danelutto	University of Pisa, Italy
Emmanuel Jeannot	LaBRI-Inria, Bordeaux, France
Christos Kaklamanis	Computer Technology Institute, Greece
Paul Kelly	Imperial College, UK
Thomas Ludwig	University of Hamburg, Germany
Emilio Luque	Autonomous University of Barcelona, Spain
Tomàs Margalef	Autonomous University of Barcelona, Spain
Wolfgang Nagel	Dresden University of Technology, Germany
Rizos Sakellariou	University of Manchester, UK
Henk Sips	Delft University of Technology, The Netherlands
Domenico Talia	University of Calabria, Italy
Felix Wolf	GRS and RWTH Aachen University, Germany

Honorary Members

Ron Perrott	Oxford e-Research Centre, UK
Karl Dieter Reinartz	University of Erlangen-Nuremberg, Germany

Observers

Fernando Silva	University of Porto, Portugal
Jesper Larsson Träff	Vienna University of Technology, Austria

Euro-Par 2014 Organization

Conference Co-chairs

Fernando Silva	University of Porto, Portugal
Inês Dutra	University of Porto, Portugal
Vítor Santos Costa	University of Porto, Portugal

Local Organizing Committee

Luís Lopes   University of Porto, Portugal
Pedro Ribeiro   University of Porto, Portugal

Workshop Co-chairs

Luc Bougé   ENS Rennes, France
Luís Lopes   University of Porto, Portugal

Workshop Introduction and Organization

First Workshop on Applications of Parallel Computation in Industry and Engineering (APCI&E 2014)

Workshop Description

The APCI&E minisymposium/workshop series started in 2008 at the Workshop on State of the Art in Scientific and Parallel Computing (PARA) and continued at the International Conference on Parallel Processing and Applied Mathematics (PPAM). Since PARA was held on even years and PPAM on odd years, the APCI&E minisymposium alternated between these two conference series on parallel computing. The minisymposium was held at PARA 2008 in Trondheim (Norway), PPAM 2009 in Wroclaw (Poland), PPAM 2011 in Torun (Poland), PARA 2012 in Helsinki (Finland), and PPAM 2013 in Warsaw (Poland). This year the minisymposium was renamed as workshop and was held at the International European Conference on Parallel Processing (Euro-Par).

The Workshop APCI&E provided a forum for researchers and practitioners using parallel computations for the solution of complex industrial and engineering applied problems. Topics discussed included application of parallel numerical methods to engineering and industrial problems, scientific computation, parallel algorithms for the solution of systems of PDEs, parallel algorithms for optimization, solution of data and computation-intensive real-world problems, and others.

Organizers

Raimondas Čiegis	Vilnius Gediminas Technical University, Lithuania
Julius Žilinskas	Vilnius University, Lithuania

Program Committee

Jesus Carretero	Carlos III University of Madrid, Spain
Raimondas Čiegis	Vilnius Gediminas Technical University, Lithuania
Francisco Gaspar	University of Zaragoza, Spain
Jacek Gondzio	University of Edinburgh, UK
Mario Guarracino	CNR, Italy
Pilar Martínez Ortigosa	University of Almería, Spain
Antonio J. Plaza	University of Extremadura, Spain
Mindaugas Radziunas	Weierstrass Institute for Applied Analysis and Stochastics, Germany

Vadimas Starikovičius	Vilnius Gediminas Technical University, Lithuania
Roman Wyrzykowski	Czestochova University of Technology, Poland
Julius Žilinskas	Vilnius University, Lithuania

Additional Reviewers

| Algirdas Lančinskas | Vilnius University, Lithuania |
| Natalija Tumanova | Vilnius Gediminas Technical University, Lithuania |

Third Workshop on Big Data Management in Clouds (BigDataCloud 2014)

Workshop Description

The Workshop on Big Data Management in Clouds was created to provide a platform for the dissemination of recent research efforts that explicitly aim at addressing the challenges related to executing big data applications on the cloud. Initially designed for powerful and expensive supercomputers, such applications have seen an increasing adoption on clouds, exploiting their elasticity and economical model. While Map/Reduce covers a large fraction of the development space, there are still many applications that are better served by other models and systems. In such a context, we need to embrace new programming models, scheduling schemes, hybrid infrastructures and scale out of single data centers to geographically distributed deployments in order to cope with these new challenges effectively.

In this context, the BigDataCloud workshop aims to provide a venue for researchers to present and discuss results on all aspects of data management in clouds, as well as new development and deployment efforts in running data-intensive computing workloads. In particular, we are interested in how the use of cloud-based technologies can meet the data-intensive scientific challenges of HPC applications that are not well served by the current supercomputers or grids, and are being ported to cloud platforms. The goal of the workshop is to support the assessment of the current state, introduce future directions, and present architectures and services for future clouds supporting data-intensive computing.

BigDataCloud 2014 followed the previous editions and the successful series of BDMC / CGWS workshops held in conjunction with EuroPar since 2009. Its goal is to aggregate the data management and clouds/grids/p2p communities built around these workshops in order to complement the data-handling issues with a comprehensive system / infrastructure perspective. This year's edition was held on August 25 and gathered around 40 enthusiastic researchers from academia and industry. We received a total of ten papers, out of which four were selected for presentation. The big data theme was strongly reflected in the keynote given this year by Dr. Toni Cortes from Barcelona Supercomputing Center. The talk introduced the idea of self-contained objects and showed how third party enrichment of such objects can offer an environment where the data providers keep full control over data while service designers get the maximum flexibility.

We wish to thank all the authors, the keynote speaker, the Program Committee members and the workshop chairs of EuroPar 2014 for their contribution to the success of this edition of BigDataCloud.

Program Chairs

Alexandru Costan   IRISA/INSA Rennes, France
Frédéric Desprez   Inria ENS Lyon, France

Program Committee

Gabriel Antoniu   Inria, France
Luc Bougé   ENS Rennes, France
Toni Cortes   Barcelona Supercomputing Center, Spain
Kate Keahey   University of Chicago/ANL, USA
Dries Kimpe   Argonne National Laboratory, USA
Olivier Nano   Microsoft Research ATLE, Germany
Bogdan Nicolae   IBM Research, Ireland
Maria S. Pérez   Universidad Politecnica De Madrid, Spain
Leonardo Querzoni   University of Rome La Sapienza, Italy
Domenico Talia   University of Calabria, Italy
Osamu Tatebe   University of Tsukuba, Japan
Cristian Zamfir   EPFL, Switzerland

Second Workshop on Dependability and Interoperability in Heterogeneous Clouds (DIHC 2014)

Workshop Description

The DIHC workshop series started in 2013 with the aim of bringing together researchers from academia and industry and PhD students interested in the design, implementation, and evaluation of services and mechanisms for dependable cloud computing in a multi-cloud environment. The cloud computing market is in rapid expansion due to the opportunities to dynamically allocate a large amount of resources when needed and to pay only for their effective usage. However, many challenges, in terms of interoperability, performance guarantee, and dependability, still need to be addressed to make cloud computing the right solution for companies, research organizations, and universities.

This year's edition consisted of three sessions and focused on heterogeneous cloud platforms and aspects to make cloud computing a trustworthy environment addressing security, privacy, and high availability in clouds. The accepted papers address issues to manage complex applications and facilitate the seamless and transparent use of cloud platform services, including computing and storages services, provisioned by multiple cloud platforms. The workshop also covered HPC applications with the need of a new generation of data storage, management services and heterogeneity-agnostic programming models for a better utilization of heterogeneous cloud resources for scientific and data-intensive applications while dealing with performance and elasticity issues. Privacy and security aspects in cloud computing from theory to practical implementations were presented and discussed.

In addition to the presentation of peer-reviewed papers, the 2014 edition of the DIHC workshop includes a presentation on "Identities and Rights in e-Infrastructures" by the invited keynote speaker Jens Jensen. The keynote presented lessons from the state-of-the art technology used to identify management in clouds and took a look into standards and the future solutions for federated identity management.

Program Chairs

Roberto G. Cascella	Inria, France
Miguel Correia	INESC-ID/IST, Portugal
Elisabetta Di Nitto	Politecnico di Milano, Italy
Christine Morin	Inria, France

Program Committee

Vasilios Andrikopoulos	University of Stuttgart, Germany
Alvaro Arenas	IE Business School, Spain
Alysson Bessani	University of Lisbon, Portugal
Lorenzo Blasi	HP, Italy
Paolo Costa	Imperial College London, UK
Beniamino Di Martino	University of Naples, Italy
Federico Facca	Create-Net, Italy
Franz Hauck	University of Ulm, Germany
Yvon Jégou	Inria, France
Jens Jensen	STFC, UK
Paolo Mori	CNR, Italy
Dana Petcu	West University of Timisoara, Romania
Paolo Romano	INESC-ID/IST, Portugal
Louis Rilling	DGA-MI, France
Michael Schöttner	University of Düsseldorf, Germany
Thorsten Schütt	ZIB Berlin, Germany
Stephen Scott	ORNL/Tennessee Technological University, USA
Gianluigi Zavattaro	University of Bologna, Italy

Additional Reviewer

Ferrol Aderholdt	Tennessee Technological University, USA

Second Workshop on Federative and Interoperable Cloud Infrastructures (FedICI 2014)

Workshop Description

Infrastructure as a service (IaaS) cloud systems allow the dynamic creation, destruction, and management of virtual machines (VM) on virtualized clusters. IaaS clouds provide a high level of abstraction to the end user that allows the creation of on-demand services through a pay-as-you-go infrastructure combined with elasticity. As a result, many academic infrastructure service providers have started transitions to add cloud resources to their previously existing campus and shared grid deployments. To complete such solutions, they should also support the unification of multiple cloud and/or cloud and grid solutions in a seamless, preferably interoperable way. Hybrid, community, or multi-clouds may utilize more than one cloud system, which are also called cloud federations. The management of such federations raises several challenges and open issues that require significant research work in this area.

The Second Workshop on Federative and Interoperable Cloud Infrastructures (FedICI 2014) aimed at bringing together scientists in the fields of high-performance computing and cloud computing to provide a dedicated forum for sharing the latest results, exchanging ideas and experiences, presenting new research, development, and management of interoperable, federated IaaS cloud systems. The goal of the workshop was to help the community define the current state, determine further goals, and present architectures and service frameworks to achieve highly interoperable federated cloud infrastructures. Priority was given to submissions that focus on presenting solutions to interoperability and efficient management challenges faced by current and future infrastructure clouds.

The call for papers for the FedICI workshop was launched early in 2014, and by the submission deadline we had received six submissions, which were of good quality and generally relevant to the theme of the workshop. The papers were swiftly and expertly reviewed by the Program Committee, each of them receiving at least three qualified reviews. The program chair thanks the whole Program Committee and the additional reviewers for the time and expertise they put into the reviewing work, and for getting it all done within the rather strict time limit. Final decision on acceptance was made by the program chair and co-chairs based on the recommendations from the Program Committee. Being half-day event, there was room for only four of the contributions, resulting in an acceptance ratio of 66%. All the accepted contributions were presented at the workshop yielding an interesting discussion on the role that federated management may play in the broad research field of cloud computing. Presentations were organized in two sessions: in the former, two papers discussed performance analysis issues of interoperating clouds, while in the later session, two papers were presented on the topic of elastic management of generic IaaS and MapReduce-based systems in interoperable and federated clouds. These proceedings include the final versions of the presented FedICI papers, taking the feedback from the reviewers and workshop audience into account.

The program chairs sincerely thank the Euro-Par organizers for providing the opportunity to arrange the FedICI workshop in conjunction with the 2014 conference. The program chairs also warmly thank MTA SZTAKI for its financial support making it possible to organize the workshop. Finally, the program chairs thank all attendees at the workshop, who contributed to a successful scientific day. Based on the mostly positive feedback, the program chairs and organizers plan to continue the FedICI workshop in conjunction with Euro-Par 2015.

Program Chairs

Gabor Kecskemeti	MTA SZTAKI, Hungary
Attila Kertesz	MTA SZTAKI, Hungary
Attila Marosi	MTA SZTAKI, Hungary
Radu Prodan	University of Innsbruck, Austria

Program Committee

Jameela Al-Jaroodi	United Arab Emirates University, UAE
Salvatore Distefano	Politecnico di Milano, Italy
Eduardo Huedo Cuesta	Universidad Complutense de Madrid, Spain
Philipp Leitner	University of Zurich, Switzerland
Daniele Lezzi	Barcelona Supercomputing Center, Spain
Nader Mohamed	United Arab Emirates University, UAE
Zsolt Nemeth	MTA SZTAKI, Hungary
Ariel Oleksiak	Poznan Supercomputer and Networking Center, Poland
Anne-Cecile Orgerie	CNRS, Myriads, IRISA, France
Simon Ostermann	University of Innsbruck, Austria
Dana Petcu	Western University of Timisoara, Romania
Ivan Rodero	Rutgers the State University of New Jersey, USA
Matthias Schmidt	1&1 Internet AG, Germany
Alan Sill	Texas Tech University, USA
Gergely Sipos	European Grid Infrastructure, The Netherlands
Massimo Villari	University of Messina, Italy

Additional Reviewers

Matthias Janetschek	University of Innsbruck, Austria
Weiwei Chen	University of Southern California, USA

12th International Workshop on Algorithms, Models and Tools for Parallel Computing on Heterogeneous Platforms (HeteroPar 2014)

Workshop Description

Heterogeneity is emerging as one of the most profound and challenging characteristics of today's parallel environments. From the macro level, where networks of distributed computers, composed by diverse node architectures, are interconnected with potentially heterogeneous networks, to the micro level, where deeper memory hierarchies and various accelerator architectures are increasingly common, the impact of heterogeneity on all computing tasks is increasing rapidly. Traditional parallel algorithms, programming environments, and tools, designed for legacy homogeneous multiprocessors, will at best achieve a small fraction of the efficiency and the potential performance that we should expect from parallel computing in tomorrow's highly diversified and mixed environments. New ideas, innovative algorithms, and specialized programming environments and tools are needed to efficiently use these new and multifarious parallel architectures. The workshop is intended to be a forum for researchers working on algorithms, programming languages, tools, and theoretical models aimed at efficiently solving problems on heterogeneous platforms.

Program Chair

Emmanuel Jeannot   Inria, France

Steering Committee

Domingo Giménez   University of Murcia, Spain
Alexey Kalinov   Cadence Design Systems, Russia
Alexey Lastovetsky   University College Dublin, Ireland
Yves Robert   Ecole Normale Supérieure de Lyon, France
Leonel Sousa   INESC-ID/IST, Technical University of
                            Lisbon, Portugal
Denis Trystram   LIG, Grenoble, France

Program Committee

Rosa M. Badia   BSC, Spain
Jorge Barbosa   University of Porto, Portugal
Olivier Beaumont   Inria, France
Paolo Bientinesi   RWTH Aachen, Germany
Cristina Boeres   Fluminense Federal University, Brazil
George Bosilca   University of Tennessee, USA
Louis-Claude Canon   Université de Franche-Comté, France
Alexandre Denis   Inria, France
Toshio Endo   Tokyo Institute of Technology, Japan
Edgar Gabriel   University of Houston, USA

Rafael Mayo Gual	Jaume I University, Spain
Toshihiro Hanawa	University of Tokyo, Japan
Shuichi Ichikawa	Toyohashi University of Technology, Japan
Helen Karatza	Aristotle University of Thessaloniki, Greece
Hatem Ltaief	KAUST, Saudi Arabia
Pierre Manneback	University of Mons, Belgium
Loris Marchal	CNRS, France
Ivan Milentijevič	University of Nis, Serbia
Satoshi Matsuoka	Tokyo Institute of Technology, Japan
Wahid Nasri	ESST de Tunis, Tunisia
Dana Petcu	West University of Timisoara, Romania
Antonio Plaza	University of Extremadura, Spain
Enrique S. Quintana-Ortí	Jaume I University, Spain
Thomas Rauber	University of Bayreuth, Germany
Vladimir Rychkov	University College Dublin, Ireland
Erik Saule	University of North Carolina at Charlotte, USA
H. J. Siegel	Colorado State University, USA
Pedro Tomás	INESC-ID/IST, University of Lisbon, Portugal
Jon Weissman	University of Minnesota, USA

Additional Reviewers

Jose Antonio Belloch	Jaume I University, Spain
Adrián Castelló	Jaume I University, Spain
Ali Charara	KAUST, Saudi Arabia
Vladimir Ciric	University of Nis, Serbia
Diego Fabregat-Traver	RWTH Aachen, Germany
João Guerreiro	University of Lisbon, Portugal
Francisco D. Igual	Jaume I University, Spain
Samuel Kortas	KAUST, Saudi Arabia
Lídia Kuan	University of Lisbon, Portugal
Emina Milovanovic	University of Nis, Serbia
Aline Nascimento	Fluminense Federal University, Brazil
Elmar Peise	RWTH Aachen, Germany
Alexandre Sena	Fluminense Federal University, Brazil
Paul Springer	RWTH Aachen, Germany
François Tessier	University of Bordeaux, France

5th International Workshop on High-Performance Bioinformatics and Biomedicine (HiBB 2014)

Workshop Description

The HiBB workshop series started in 2010 and its first edition was held at Ischia (Italy) in conjunction with the Euro-Par conference. Since then, the workshop has been held, always in conjunction with Euro-Par, at Bordeaux (France), Rhodes (Greece), Aachen (Germany), and Porto (Portugal), respectively, in 2011, 2012, 2013, and 2014.

Since 2010, the HiBB workshop series has included 25 regular papers, two invited talks, two panels, and one tutorial on several aspects of parallel and distributed computing applied to bioinformatics, health informatics, biomedicine, and systems biology.

The main motivation for the HiBB workshop is the increasing production of experimental and clinical data in biology and medicine, and the needs to provide efficient storage, preprocessing, and analysis of these data to support biomedical research.

In fact, the availability and large diffusion of high-throughput experimental platforms, such as next-generation sequencing, microarray, and mass spectrometry, as well as the improved resolution and coverage of clinical diagnostic tools, such as magnetic resonance imaging, are becoming the major sources of data in biomedical research, and the storage, preprocessing, and analysis of these data are becoming the main bottleneck of the biomedical analysis pipeline.

Parallel computing and high-performance infrastructures are increasingly used in all phases of life sciences research, e.g., for storing and preprocessing large experimental data, for the simulation of biological systems, for data exploration and visualization, for data integration, and for knowledge discovery.

The current bioinformatics scenario is characterized by the application of well-established techniques, such as parallel computing on multicore architectures and grid computing, as well as by the application of emerging computational models such as graphics processing and cloud computing. Large-scale infrastructures such as grids or clouds are mainly used to store in an efficient manner and to share in an easy way the huge amount of experimental data produced in life sciences, while parallel computing allows the efficient analysis of huge data. In particular, novel parallel architectures such as GPUs and emerging programming models such as MapReduce may overcome the limits posed by conventional computers to the analysis of large amounts of data.

The fifth edition of the HiBB workshop aimed to bring together scientists in the fields of high-performance computing, bioinformatics, and life sciences, to discuss the parallel implementation of bioinformatics algorithms, the deployment of biomedical applications on high-performance infrastructures, and the organization of large-scale databases in biology and medicine.

These proceedings include the final revised versions of the HiBB papers taking the feedback from the reviewers and workshop audience into account. The program chair sincerely thanks the Program Committee members and the additional reviewers, for the time and expertise they put into the reviewing work, the Euro-Par organization, for providing the opportunity to arrange the HiBB workshop in conjunction with the Euro-Par 2014 conference, and all the workshop attendees who contributed to a lively day.

Program Chair

Mario Cannataro   University Magna Græcia of Catanzaro, Italy

Program Committee

Pratul K. Agarwal	Oak Ridge National Laboratory, USA
Ignacio Blanquer	Universidad Politecnica de Valencia, Spain
Daniela Calvetti	Case Western Reserve University, USA
Werner Dubitzky	University of Ulster, UK
Ananth Y. Grama	Purdue University, USA
Concettina Guerra	Georgia Institute of Technology, USA
Pietro H. Guzzi	University Magna Græcia of Catanzaro, Italy
Vicente Hernandez	Universidad Politecnica de Valencia, Spain
Salvatore Orlando	University of Venice, Italy
Horacio Perez-Sanchez	University of Murcia, Spain
Omer F. Rana	Cardiff University, UK
Richard Sinnott	University of Melbourne, Australia
Fabrizio Silvestri	Yahoo Labs, Barcelona, Spain
Erkki Somersalo	Case Western Reserve University, USA
Paolo Trunfio	University of Calabria, Italy
Albert Zomaya	University of Sydney, Australia

Additional Reviewers

Giuseppe Agapito	University Magna Græcia of Catanzaro, Italy
Barbara Calabrese	University Magna Græcia of Catanzaro, Italy
Nicola Ielpo	University Magna Græcia of Catanzaro, Italy
Alessia Sarica	University Magna Græcia of Catanzaro, Italy

Second Workshop on Large-Scale Distributed Virtual Environments on Cloud and P2P (LSDVE 2014)

Workshop Description

The LSDVE workshop series started in August 2013, in Aachen, where the first edition of the workshop was held in conjunction with Europar 2013. LSDVE 2014, the second edition of the workshop, was held in Porto, in August 2014, again in conjunction with Europar.

The focus of this edition of the workshop was on cooperative distributed virtual environments. The recent advances in networking have determined an increasing use of information technology to support distributed cooperative applications. Several novel applications have emerged in this area, like computer-supported collaborative work (CSCW), large-scale distributed virtual worlds, collaborative recommender and learning systems. These applications involve several challenges, such as the definition of user interfaces, of coordination protocols, and of proper middle-ware and architectures supporting distributed cooperation.

Collaborative applications may benefit greatly also from the support of cloud and P2P architectures. As a matter of fact, with the emergence of readily available cloud platforms, collaborative applications developers have the opportunity of deploying their applications in the cloud, or by exploiting hybrid P2P/cloud architectures with dynamically adapting cloud support. This brings possibilities to smaller developers that were reserved for the big companies until recently. The integration of mobile/cloud platforms for collaborative applications is another challenge for the widespread use of these applications.

The LSDVE 2014 workshop aim was to provide a venue for researchers to present and discuss important aspects of P2P/cloud collaborative applications and of the platforms supporting them. The workshop's goal is to investigate open challenges for such applications, related to both the application design and to the definition of proper architectures. Some important challenges are, for instance, collaborative protocol design, latency reduction/hiding techniques for guaranteeing real-time constraints, large-scale processing of user information, privacy and security issues, state consistency/persistence. The workshop presented assessment of current state of the research in this area and introduced further directions.

LSDVE 2014 was opened by the invited talk "Decentralization: P2P and Personal Clouds" by Prof. Pedro Garcia Lopez, Universitat Rovira i Virgili. The program of the workshop included two sessions, "Cooperative Distributed Environments" and "Architectural Supports." The papers presented in the first session regard novel cooperative distributed applications, like social networks and massively multi player games, while those of the second session present architectural supports, both cloud and P2P based, for these applications.

We remark that the number of submissions to LSDVE 2014 has almost doubled over the previous edition. Finally, the extended version of selected papers accepted and presented at the workshop will be published in a special issue of the Springer journal *Peer-to-Peer Networking and Applications* (PPNA).

We wish to thank all who helped to make this second edition of the workshop a success: Prof. Pedro Garcia Lopez who accepted our invitation to present a keynote, authors submitting papers, colleagues who refereed the submitted papers and attended the sessions, and finally the Euro-Par 2014 organizers whose invaluable support greatly helped in the organization of this second edition of the workshop.

Program Chairs

Laura Ricci	University of Pisa, Italy
Alexandru Iosup	TU Delft, Delft, The Netherlands
Radu Prodan	Institute of Computer Science, Innsbruck, Austria

Program Committee

Michele Amoretti	University of Parma, Italy
Ranieri Baraglia	ISTI CNR, Pisa, Italy
Emanuele Carlini	ISTI CNR, Pisa, Italy
Massimo Coppola	ISTI CNR, Pisa, Italy
Patrizio Dazzi	ISTI CNR, Pisa, Italy
Juan J. Durillo	Institute of Computer Science, Innsbruck, Austria
Kalman Graffi	University of Düsseldorf, Germany
Alexandru Iosup	TU Delft, The Netherlands
Dana Petcu	West University of Timisoara, Romania
Andreas Petlund	Simula Research Laboratory, Norway
Radu Prodan	Institute of Computer Science, Innsbruck, Austria
Duan Rubing	Institute of High Performance Computing, Singapore
Laura Ricci	University of Pisa, Pisa, Italy
Alexey Vinel	Tampere University of Technology, Finland

7th International Workshop on Multi-/Many-Core Computing Systems (MuCoCos 2014)

Workshop Description

The pervasiveness of homogeneous and heterogeneous multi-core and many-core processors, in a large spectrum of systems from embedded and general-purpose to high-end computing systems, poses major challenges to the software industry. In general, there is no guarantee that software developed for a particular architecture will run on another architecture. Furthermore, ensuring that the software preserves some aspects of performance behavior (such as temporal or energy efficiency) across these different architectures is an open research issue.

Therefore, a traditional focus of the MuCoCos workshop is on language level, system software and architectural solutions for performance portability across different architectures and for automated performance tuning.

The topics of the MuCoCoS workshop include but are not limited to:

- Programming models, languages, libraries and compilation techniques
- Run-time systems and hardware support
- Automatic performance tuning and optimization techniques
- Patterns, algorithms and data structures for multi-/many-core systems
- Performance measurement, modeling, analysis and tuning
- Case studies highlighting performance portability and tuning.

Besides the presentation of selected technical papers, MuCoCos 2014 featured a keynote talk on "Execution Models for Energy-Efficient Computing Systems" by Philippas Tsigas, Chalmers University, Sweden.

Previous workshops in the series were: MuCoCoS 2008 (Barcelona, Spain), MuCoCoS 2009 (Fukuoka, Japan), MuCoCoS 2010 (Krakow, Poland), MuCoCoS 2011 (Seoul, Korea), MuCoCoS 2012 (Salt Lake City, USA), and MuCoCoS 2013 (Edinburgh, UK).

Program Chairs

Siegfried Benkner	University of Vienna, Austria
Sabri Pllana	Linnaeus University, Sweden

Program Committee

Beverly Bachmayer	Intel, Germany
Eduardo Cesar	Universitat Autonoma de Barcelona, Spain
Milind Chabbi	Rice University, USA
Jiri Dokulil	University of Vienna, Austria
Franz Franchetti	Carnegie Mellon University, USA
Michael Gerndt	TU Munich, Germany

Joerg Keller	FernUniversität Hagen, Germany
Christoph Kessler	Linkoping University, Sweden
Shashi Kumar	Jönköping University, Sweden
Erwin Laure	KTH, Sweden
Renato Miceli	Irish Centre for High-End Computing, Ireland
Lasse Natvig	NTNU Trondheim, Norway
Beniamino Di Martino	Seconda Università di Napoli, Italy
Samuel Thibault	University of Bordeaux, France
Philippas Tsigas	Chalmers University, Sweden
Josef Weidendorfer	TU Munich, Germany

Additional Reviewers

Pasquale Cantiello	Seconda Università di Napoli, Italy
Antonio Esposito	Seconda Università di Napoli, Italy
Francesco Moscato	Seconda Università di Napoli, Italy
Kameswar Rao Vaddina	NTNU Trondheim, Norway
Tomas Margalef	Universitat Autonoma de Barcelona, Spain
Tilman Kuestner	TU Munich, Germany
Terry Cojean	University of Bordeaux, France
Jens Breitbart	TU Munich, Germany
Minh Le	TU Munich, Germany
Luka Stanisic	University of Grenoble, France
Toni Espinosa	Universitat Autonoma de Barcelona, Spain
Rocco Aversa	Seconda Università di Napoli, Italy

Third International Workshop on On-chip Memory Hierarchies and Interconnects (OMHI 2014)

Workshop Description

The gap between processor and memory performances has been growing for more than four decades since the first commercial microprocessor was built by Intel in 1971. To avoid the memory access times caused by this gap, manufacturers implemented cache memories on-chip. Moreover, as the memory latency became larger, more cache levels were added to the on-chip memory hierarchy, and, as a consequence, on-chip networks were also integrated to interconnect the different cache structures among the different levels.

Nowadays, commercial microprocessors include up to tens of processors sharing a memory hierarchy with about three or four cache levels. In the lowest levels of the on-chip memory hierarchy, the cache structures can store hundreds of megabytes, requiring alternative memory technologies (such as eDRAM or STT-RAM) as well as new microarchitectural techniques to limit energy consumption and power dissipation. In addition, advanced on-chip networks are needed to cope with the latency and bandwidth demands of these complex memory hierarchies.

Finally, new manufacturing techniques, such as 3D integration is considered to enlarge even more the capacity and complexity of these memory hierarchies and interconnection networks.

In this context, the synergy between the research on memory organization and management, interconnection networks, as well as novel implementation technologies becomes a key strategy to foster further developments. With this aim, the International Workshop on On-chip Memory Hierarchy and Interconnects (OMHI) started in 2012 and continued with its third edition that was held in Porto, Portugal. This workshop is organized in conjunction with the Euro-Par annual series of international conferences dedicated to the promotion and advancement of all aspects of parallel computing.

The goal of the OMHI workshop is to be a forum for engineers and scientists to address the aforementioned challenges, and to present new ideas for future on-chip memory hierarchies and interconnects focusing on organization, management and implementation. The specific topics covered by the OMHI workshop have been kept up to date according to technology advances and industrial and academia interests.

The chairs of OMHI were proud to present Prof. Manuel E. Acacio as keynote speaker, who gave an interesting talk focusing on the key topics of the workshop entitled "Increased Hardware Support for Efficient Communication and Synchronization in Future Manycores," which jointly with the paper sessions finally resulted in a nice and very exciting one-day program.

The chairs would like to thank the members of the Program Committee for their reviews, the Euro-Par organizers, Manuel E. Acacio and the high number of attendees. Based on the positive feedback from all of them, we plan to continue the OMHI workshop in conjunction with Euro-Par.

Program Chairs

Julio Sahuquillo	Universitat Politècnica de València, Spain
Maria Engracia Gómez	Universitat Politècnica de València, Spain
Salvador Petit	Universitat Politècnica de València, Spain

Program Committee

Manuel Acacio	Universidad de Murcia, Spain
Sandro Bartolini	Università di Siena, Italy
João M. P. Cardoso	University of Porto, Portugal
Marcello Coppola	STMicroelectronics, France
Giorgos Dimitrakopoulos	Democritus University of Thrace, Greece
Pierfrancesco Foglia	Università di Pisa, Italy
Crispín Gómez	Universidad de Castilla-La Mancha, Spain
Kees Goossens	Eindhoven University of Technology, The Netherlands
David Kaeli	Northeastern University, USA
Sonia López	Rochester Institute of Technology, USA
Pierre Michaud	Inria, France

Iakovos Mavroidis   Foundation for Research and Technology –
                                 Hellas, Greece
Tor Skeie   Simula Research Laboratory, Norway
Rafael Ubal   Northeastern University, USA

Second Workshop on Parallel and Distributed Agent-Based Simulations (PADABS 2014)

Workshop Description

The Parallel and Distributed Agent-Based Simulations workshop series started in 2013.

Agent-based simulation models are an increasingly popular tool for research and management in many fields such as ecology, economics, sociology, etc..

In some fields, such as social sciences, these models are seen as a key instrument to the generative approach, essential for understanding complex social phenomena. But also in policy-making, biology, military simulations, control of mobile robots and economics, the relevance and effectiveness of agent-based simulation models has been recently recognized.

The computer science community has responded to the need for platforms that can help the development and testing of new models in each specific field by providing tools, libraries, and frameworks that speed up and make massive simulations.

The key objective of the workshop is to bring together researchers who are interested in getting more performances from their simulations, by using:

- Synchronized, many-core simulations (e.g., GPUs)
- Strongly coupled, parallel simulations (e.g., MPI)
- Loosely coupled, distributed simulations (distributed heterogeneous setting).

Program Chairs

Vittorio Scarano   Università di Salerno, Italy
Gennaro Cordasco   Seconda Università di Napoli, Italy
Rosario De Chiara   Poste Italiane, Italy
Ugo Erra   Università della Basilicata, Italy

Program Committee

Maria Chli   Aston University, UK
Claudio Cioffi-Revilla   George Mason University, USA
Biagio Cosenza   University of Innsbruck, Austria
Nick Collier   Argonne National Laboratory, USA
Rosaria Conte   CNR, Italy
Andrew Evans   University of Leeds, UK
Bernardino Frola   The MathWorks, Cambridge, UK
Nicola Lettieri   Università del Sannio and ISFOL, Italy

Sean Luke	George Mason University, USA
Michael North	Argonne National Laboratory, USA
Mario Paolucci	CNR, Italy
Paul Richmond	The University of Sheffield, UK
Arnold Rosenberg	Northeastern University, USA
Flaminio Squazzoni	Università di Brescia, Italy
Michela Taufer	University of Delaware, USA
Joanna Kolodziej	Cracow University of Technology and University of Science and Technology, Poland

Additional Reviewers

Carmine Spagnuolo	Università di Salerno, Italy
Luca Vicidomini	Università di Salerno, Italy

7th Workshop on Productivity and Performance – Tools for HPC Application Development (PROPER 2014)

Workshop Description

The PROPER workshop series started at Euro-Par 2008 in Gran Canarias, Spain. Since than it has been held at every Euro-Par conference. It is organized by the Virtual Institute – High Productivity Supercomputing (VI-HPS), an initiative to promote the development and integration of HPC programming tools.

Writing codes that run correctly and efficiently on HPC computing systems is extraordinarily challenging. At the same time, applications themselves are becoming more complex as well, which can be seen in emerging scale-bridging applications, the integration of fault-tolerance and uncertainty quantification, or advances in algorithms. Combined, these trends place higher and higher demands on the application development process and thus require adequate tool support for debugging and performance analysis. The PROPER workshop serves as a forum to present novel work on scalable methods and tools for high-performance computing. It covers parallel program development and analysis, debugging, correctness checking, and performance measurement and evaluation. Further topics include the integration of tools with compilers and the overall development environment, as well as success stories reporting on application performance, scalability, reliability, power and energy optimization, or productivity improvements that have been achieved using tools.

This year's keynote on "Rethinking Productivity and Performance for the Exascale Era" was given by Prof. Allen D. Malony, Department of Computer and Information Science, University of Oregon. The talk discussed directions for parallel performance research and tools that target the scalability, optimization, and programmability challenges of next-generation HPC platforms with high productivity as an essential outcome. Further, Prof. Malony stated that it is becoming more apparent that in order to address the complexity concerns unfolding in the exascale space, we must think of productivity and performance in a more connected way and the technology to support them as being more open, integrated, and intelligent.

Program Chairs

José Gracia	High-Performance Computing Center Stuttgart, Germany

Steering Committee

Andreas Knüpfer (Chair)	Technische Universität Dresden, Germany
Michael Gerndt	Technische Universität München, Germany
Shirley Moore	University of Texas at El Paso, USA
Matthias Müller	RWTH Aachen, Germany
Martin Schulz	Lawrence Livermore National Laboratory, USA
Felix Wolf	German Research School for Simulation Sciences, Germany

Program Committee

José Gracia (Chair)	HLRS, Germany
Denis Barthou	Inria, France
David Böhme	German Research School for Simulation Sciences, Germany
Karl Fürlinger	LMU München, Germany
Michael Gerndt	TU München, Germany
Kevin Huck	University of Oregon, USA
Koji Inoue	Kyushu University, Japan
Andreas Knüpfer	TU Dresden, Germany
Ignacio Laguna	Lawrence Livermore National Laboratory, USA
John Mellor-Crummey	Rice University, USA
Matthias Müller	RWTH Aachen, Germany
Shirley Moore	University of Texas at El Paso, USA
Martin Schulz	Lawrence Livermore National Laboratory, USA
Nathan Tallent	Pacific Northwest National Laboratory, USA
Jan Treibig	RRZE, Friedrich-Alexander-Universität Erlangen-Nürnberg, Germany
Felix Wolf	German Research School for Simulation Sciences, Germany
Brian Wylie	Jülich Supercomputing Centre, Germany

First International Workshop on Reproducibility in Parallel Computing (REPPAR)

Workshop Description

The workshop is concerned with experimental practices in parallel computing research. We are interested in research works that address the statistically rigorous analysis of experimental data and visualization techniques of these data. We also encourage researchers to state best practices to conduct experiments and papers that report experiences obtained when trying to reproduce or repeat experiments of others. The workshop also welcomes papers on new tools for experimental computational sciences, e.g., tools to archive large experimental data sets and the source code that generated them. This includes (1) workflow systems for defining the experimental structure of experiments and their automated execution as well as (2) experimental testbeds, which may serve as underlying framework for experimental workflows, e.g., deploying personalized operating system images on clusters.

Program Chairs

Sascha Hunold	Vienna University of Technology, Austria
Arnaud Legrand	CNRS, LIG Grenoble, France
Lucas Nussbaum	CNRS, LORIA, France
Mark Stillwell	Cranfield University, UK

Program Committee

Henri Casanova	University of Hawai'i, USA
Olivier Dalle	University of Nice - Sophia Antipolis, France
Andrew Davison	CNRS, France
Georg Hager	University of Erlangen-Nuremberg, Germany
James Hetherington	University College London, UK
Olivier Richard	LIG Grenoble, France
Lucas M. Schnorr	Universidade Federal do Rio Grande do Sul, Brazil
Jesper Larsson Träff	Vienna University of Technology, Austria
Jan Vitek	Purdue University, USA

Second Workshop on Runtime and Operating Systems for the Many-core Era (ROME 2014)

Workshop Description

Since the beginning of the multicore era, parallel processing has become prevalent across the board. However, in order to continue a performance increase according to Moore's Law, a next step needs to be taken: away from common multi-cores toward innovative many-core architectures. Such systems, equipped with a significant higher amount of cores per chip than multi-cores, pose challenges in both hardware and software design. On the hardware side, complex on-chip networks, scratchpads, and memory interfaces as well as cache hierarchies, cache-coherence strategies and the building of coherency domains have to be taken into account.

However, the ROME workshop focuses on the software side because without complying system software, runtime and operating system support, all these new hardware facilities cannot be exploited. Hence, the new challenges in hardware/software co-design are to step beyond traditional approaches and to wage new programming models and OS designs in order to exploit the theoretically available performance as effectively and power-aware as possible.

This focus of the ROME workshop stands in the tradition of a successful series of events originally hosted by the Many-core Applications Research Community (MARC). Such MARC symposia took place at the Hasso Plattner Institute in Potsdam in 2011, at the ONERA Research Center in Toulouse in 2012 and at the RWTH Aachen University in 2012. This successful series was then continued by the 1st ROME workshop (*R*untime and *O*perating Systems for the *M*any-core *E*ra) at the Euro-Par 2013 conference in Aachen as a thematically related follow-up event for a broader audience.

This year, this tradition was again pursued by holding the Second ROME workshop in conjunction with the Euro-Par 2014 conference in Porto. The organizers were very happy that Prof. Norbert Eicker from Jülich Supercomputing Centre (JSC) volunteered to give an invited keynote for this workshop with the title "Running DEEP – Operating Heterogeneous Clusters in the Many-core Era."

Program Chairs

Stefan Lankes   RWTH Aachen University, Germany
Carsten Clauss   ParTec Cluster Competence Center GmbH,
                            Germany

Program Committee

Carsten Clauss   ParTec Cluster Competence Center GmbH,
                            Germany
Stefan Lankes   RWTH Aachen University, Germany
Timothy Mattson   Intel Labs, USA

Jörg Nolte	BTU Cottbus, Germany
Eric Noulard	ONERA, France
Andreas Polze	Hasso Plattner Institute, Germany
Michael Riepen	IAV GmbH, Germany
Bettina Schnor	University of Potsdam, Germany
Oliver Sinnen	University of Auckland, New Zealand
Christian Terboven	RWTH Aachen Univeristy, Germany
Carsten Trinitis	TU München, Germany
Theo Ungerer	Universität Augsburg, Germany
Josef Weidendorfer	TU München, Germany

Additional Reviewers

Christian Bradatsch	Universität Augsburg, Germany
David Büttner	TU München, Germany
Steffen Christgau	University of Potsdam, Germany
Ralf Jahr	Universität Augsburg, Germany
Tilman Küstner	TU München, Germany
Simon Pickartz	RWTH Aachen University, Germany
Randolf Rotta	BTU Cottbus, Germany
Roopak Sinha	University of Auckland, New Zealand
Vincent Vidal	ONERA, France

7th Workshop on Resiliency in High-Performance Computing in Clusters, Clouds, and Grids (Resilience 2014)

Workshop Description

Clusters, clouds, and grids are three different computational paradigms with the intent or potential to support high performance computing (HPC). Currently, they consist of hardware, management, and usage models particular to different computational regimes, e.g., high-performance cluster systems designed to support tightly coupled scientific simulation codes typically utilize high-speed interconnects and commercial cloud systems designed to support software as a service (SAS) do not. However, in order to support HPC, all must at least utilize large numbers of resources and hence effective HPC in any of these paradigms must address the issue of resiliency at large scale.

Recent trends in HPC systems have clearly indicated that future increases in performance, in excess of those resulting from improvements in single-processor performance, will be achieved through corresponding increases in system scale, i.e., using a significantly larger component count. As the raw computational performance of these HPC systems increases from today's tera- and peta-scale to next-generation multi-peta-scale capability and beyond, their number of computational, networking, and storage components will grow from the ten-to-one-hundred thousand compute nodes of today's systems to several hundreds of thousands of compute nodes and more in the foreseeable future. This substantial growth in system scale, and the resulting component count, poses a challenge for HPC system and application software with respect to fault tolerance and resilience.

Furthermore, recent experience in extreme-scale HPC systems with non-recoverable soft errors, i.e., bit flips in memory, cache, registers, and logic added another major source of concern. The probability of such errors not only grows with system size, but also with increasing architectural vulnerability caused by employing accelerators, such as FPGAs and GPUs, and by shrinking nanometer technology. Reactive fault-tolerance technologies, such as checkpoint/restart, are unable to handle high failure rates due to associated overheads, while proactive resiliency technologies, such as migration, simply fail as random soft errors cannot be predicted. Moreover, soft errors may even remain undetected resulting in silent data corruption.

The goal of this workshop is to bring together experts in the area of fault tolerance and resilience for HPC to present the latest achievements and to discuss the challenges ahead. The program of the Resilience 2014 workshop included one keynote and six high-quality papers. The keynote was given by Ives Robert from ENS Lyon with the title "Algorithms for Coping with Silent Errors."

Workshop Chairs

Stephen L. Scott   Tennessee Technological University and Oak
                                          Ridge National Laboratory, USA
Chokchai (Box) Leangsuksun   Louisiana Tech University, USA

Program Chairs

Patrick G. Bridges   University of New Mexico, USA
Christian Engelmann   Oak Ridge National Laboratory, USA

Program Committee

Ferrol Aderholdt   Tennessee Institute of Technology, USA
Vassil Alexandrov   Barcelona Supercomputer Center, Spain
Wesley Bland   Argonne National Laboratory, USA
Greg Bronevetsky   Lawrence Livermore National Laboratory, USA
Franck Cappello   Argonne National Laboratory, USA
Zizhong Chen   University of California at Riverside, USA
Nathan DeBardeleben   Los Alamos National Laboratory, USA
Kurt Ferreira   Sandia National Laboratory, USA
Cecile Germain   Université Paris-Sud, France
Larry Kaplan   Cray Inc., USA
Dieter Kranzlmueller   Ludwig Maximilians University of Munich,
                                            Germany
Sriram Krishnamoorthy   Pacific Northwest National Laboratory, USA

Scott Levy	University of New Mexico, USA
Celso Mendes	University of Illinois Urbana-Champaign, USA
Kathryn Mohror	Lawrence Livermore National Laboratory, USA
Christine Morin	Inria Rennes, France
Mihaela Paun	Louisiana Tech University, USA
Alexander Reinefeld	Zuse Institute Berlin, Germany
Rolf Riesen	Intel Corporation, USA

Workshop on Software for Exascale Computing (SPPEXA 2014)

Workshop Description

SPPEXA is a priority program of the German Research Foundation (DFG). It targets the challenges of programming for exascale performance, which have been recognized in recent years and are being addressed by national and international research initiatives around the world. Exascale computing promisses performance in the range of 10^{18} floating-point operations per second. Today's fastest supercomputers are just a factor of 30 away from this mark. Software technology faces extreme challenges, mainly because of the massive on-chip parallelism necessary to reach exascale performance, and because of the expected complexity of the architectures that will be able to deliver it.

The DFG runs close to 100 priority programs at any one time, each lasting up to six years. SPPEXA started in January 2013 and will run through to the end of 2018. It consists of two three-year funding periods. In the first period, 13 projects were chosen from 67 proposals. Each project is being run by a multi-site consortium with between three and five funded research positions. The overall funding amounts to roughly 3.7 million Euro per year. Each project addresses at least two and concentrates on at most three of the following six challenges:

- Computational algorithms
- System software
- Application software
- Data management and exploration
- Programming
- Software tools

The program is more than the sum of the individual projects. There are inter-project collaborations and program-wide activities like an annual *SPPEXA Day* and an annual *Coding Week* devoted each year to a specific theme.

This workshop started with a keynote by Rosa Badia from the Barcelona Supercomputing Center and then continued with the initial results of the following six of the 13 projects:

- EXA-DUNE: Flexible PDE Solvers, Numerical Methods and Applications
- DASH: Data Structures and Algorithms with Support for Hierarchical Locality
- ExaStencils: Advanced Stencil-Code Engineering
- EXAHD: An Exa-Scalable Two-Level Sparse Grid Approach for Higher-Dimensional Problems in Plasma Physics and Beyond
- ESSEX: Equipping Sparse Solvers for Exascale
- Catwalk: A Quick Development Path for Performance Models

For more information on the program and the individual projects, please consult the website: http://www.sppexa.de.

Program Chairs

Christian Lengauer	University of Passau, Germany
Wolfgang Nagel	Technical University of Dresden, Germany

Program Committee

Christian Lengauer	University of Passau, Germany
Wolfgang Nagel	Technical University of Dresden, Germany
Christian Bischof	Technical University of Darmstadt, Germany
Alexander Reinefeld	Humboldt University of Berlin, Germany
Gerhard Wellein	Friedrich Alexander University, Germany
Ramin Yahyapour	University of Göttingen, Germany

First Workshop on Techniques and Applications for Sustainable Ultrascale Computing Systems (TASUS 2014)

Workshop Description

The TASUS workshop series started in 2014 to join researchers on ultrascale computing systems (UCS), envisioned as a large-scale complex system joining parallel and distributed computing systems, perhaps located at multiple sites, that cooperate to provide solutions to the users. As a growth of two or three orders of magnitude of today's computing systems is expected, including systems with unprecedented amounts of heterogeneous hardware, lines of source code, numbers of users, and volumes of data, sustainability is critical to ensure the feasibility of these systems. Due to these needs, currently there is an emerging cross-domain interaction between high-performance computing in clouds or the adoption of distributed programming paradigms, such as Map Reduce, in scientific applications, the cooperation between HPC and distributed system communities still poses many challenges toward building the ultrascale systems of the future. Especially in unifying the services to deploy sustainable applications portable to HPC systems, multi-clouds, data centers, and big data.

The TASUS workshop focuses specially on the software side, aiming at bringing together researchers from academia and industry interested in the design, implementation, and evaluation of services and system software mechanisms to improve sustainability in ultrascale computing systems with a holistic approach, including topics like scalability, energy barrier, data management, programmability, and reliability.

Program Chairs

Jesus Carretero	Carlos III University of Madrid, Spain
Laurent Lefevre	Inria, ENS of Lyon, France
Gudula Rünger	Technical University of Chemnitz, Germany
Domenico Talia	Universitá della Callabria, Italy

Program Committee

Francisco Almeida	Universidad de la Laguna, Spain
Angelos Bilas	ICS, FORTH, Greece
Pascal Bouvry	University of Luxembourg, Luxembourg
Harold Castro	Universidad de los Andes, Colombia
Alok Choudhary	Northwestern University, USA
Michele Colajanni	Università di Modena e Reggio Emilia, Italy
Toni Cortes	BSC, Spain
Raimondas Ciegis	Vilnius Gediminas Technical University, Lithuania
Georges DaCosta	Université Paul Sabatier, Tolouse 3, France
Jack Dongarra	University of Tennessee, USA
Skevos Evripidou	University of Cyprus, Cyprus
Thomas Fahringer	University of Innsbruck, Austria
Sonja Filiposka	University of Ss Cyril and Methodius, FYR Macedonia
Javier Garcia-Blas	University Carlos III of Madrid, Spain
Jose D. Garcia	University Carlos III of Madrid, Spain
Florin Isaila	Argonne National Labs, USA
Emmanuel Jeannot	Inria Bordeaux Sud-Ouest, France
Helen Karatza	Aristotle University of Thessaloniki, Greece
Alexey Lastovetsky	University College Dublin, Ireland
Dimitar Lukarski	Uppsala University, Sweden
Pierre Manneback	University of Mons, Belgium
Svetozar Margenov	Bulgarian Academic of Sciences, Bulgaria
Attila Marosi	Hungarian Academy of Sciences, Hungary
M. José Martín	University of Coruña, Spain
Anastas Mishev	University of Ss Cyril and Methodius, FYR Macedonia
Ricardo Morla	Universidade de Porto, Portugal
Maya Neytcheva	Uppsala University, Sweden

Ariel Oleksiak	Poznan Supercomputing Center, Poland
Dana Petcu	West University of Timisoara, Romania
Jean Marc Pierson	Université Paul Sabatier, Tolouse 3, France
Radu Prodan	University of Innsbruck, Austria
Gudula Ruenger	Technische Universität Chemnitz, Germany
Enrique S. Quintana-Orti	Universitat Jaume I, Spain
Thomas Rauber	University of Bayreuth, Germany
Karolj Skala	Ruder Boskovic Institute, Croatia
Victor J. Sosa	CINVESTAV, Mexico
Leonel Sousa	INESC, Portugal
Roman Trobec	Jozef Stefan Institute, Slovenia
Trinh Anh Tuan	Budapest University of Technology and Economics, Hungary
Eero Vainikko	University of Tartu, Estonia
Roman Wyrzykowski	Czestochowa University of Technology, Poland
Laurence T. Yang	St. Francis University, Canada
Julius Žilinskas	Vilnius University, Lithuania
Albert Zomaya	University of Sydney, Australia

7th Workshop on UnConventional High-Performance Computing (UCHPC 2014)

Workshop Description

Recent issues with the power consumption of conventional HPC hardware resulted in new interest in both accelerator hardware and low-power mass-market hardware. The most prominent examples are GPUs, yet FPGAs, DSPs, and other embedded designs may also provide higher power efficiency for HPC applications. The so-called dark silicon forecast, i.e., that not all transistors can be active at the same time, may lead to even more specialized hardware in future mass-market products. Exploiting this hardware for HPC can be a worthwhile challenge.

As the word "UnConventional" in the title suggests, the workshop focuses on usage of hardware or platforms for HPC that are not (yet) conventionally used today, and may not be designed for HPC in the first place. Reasons for its use can be raw computing power, good performance per watt, or low cost. To address this unconventional hardware, often, new programming approaches and paradigms are required to make best use of it. A second focus of the workshop is on innovative, (yet) unconventional new programming models.

To this end, UCHPC tries to capture solutions for HPC that are unconventional today, but could become conventional and significant tomorrow, and thus provide a glimpse into the future of HPC.

This year was the seventh time the UCHPC workshop took place, and it was the fifth time in a row that it was co-located with Euro-Par (each year since 2010). Before that, it was held in conjunction with the International Conference on Computational Science and Its Applications 2008 and with the ACM International Conference on Computing Frontiers 2009. However, UCHPC is a perfect addition to the scientific fields of Euro-Par, and this is confirmed by the continuous interest we see among Euro-Par attendees for this workshop.

While the general focus of the workshop is fixed, the topic is actually a moving target. For example, GPUs were quite unconventional for HPC a few years ago, but today a notable portion of the machines in the Top500 list are making use of them. Currently, the exploitation of mobile processors for HPC – including on-chip GPU and DSPs – are a hot topic, and we had a fitting invited talk on the EU Mont-Blanc project given by Axel Auweter, LRZ, Germany.

These proceedings include the final versions of the papers presented at UCHPC and accepted for publication. They take the feedback from the reviewers and workshop audience into account.

The workshop organizers want to thank the authors of the papers for joining us in Porto, the Program Committee for doing the hard work of reviewing all submissions, the conference organizers for proving such a nice venue, and last but not least the large number of attendees this year.

Program Chairs

Jens Breitbart	Technische Universität München, Germany
Dimitar Lukarski	Uppsala University, Sweden
Josef Weidendorfer	Technische Universität München, Germany

Steering Committee

Lars Bengtsson	Chalmers University of Technology, Sweden
Jens Breitbart	Technische Universität München, Germany
Anders Hast	Uppsala University, Sweden
Josef Weidendorfer	Technische Universität München, Germany
Jan-Philipp Weiss	COMSOL, Sweden
Ren Wu	Baidu, USA

Program Committee

Michael Bader	Technische Universität München, Germany
Denis Barthou	Université de Bordeaux, France
Alex Bartzas	National Technical University of Athens, Greece
Lars Bengtsson	Chalmers University of Technology, Sweden
Jens Breitbart	Technische Universität München, Germany
Giorgos Dimitrakopoulos	Democritus University of Thrace, Greece
Karl Fürlinger	LMU Munich, Germany
Dominik Goeddeke	TU Dortmund University, Germany
Frank Hannig	Friedrich-Alexander-Universität Erlangen-Nürnberg, Germany
Anders Hast	Uppsala University, Sweden
Rainer Keller	Hochschule für Technik, Stuttgart, Germany

Gaurav Khanna	University of Massachusetts Dartmouth, USA
Harald Köstler	Friedrich-Alexander-Universität Erlangen-Nürnberg, Germany
Dimitar Lukarski	Uppsala University, Sweden
Manfred Mücke	Sustainable Computing Research, Austria
Andy Nisbet	Manchester Metropolitan University, UK
Ioannis Papaefstathiou	Technical University of Crete, Greece
Bertil Schmidt	University of Mainz, Germany
Ioannis Sourdis	Chalmers University of Technology, Sweden
Josef Weidendorfer	Technische Universität München, Germany
Jan-Philipp Weiss	COMSOL, Sweden
Stephan Wong	Delft University of Technology, The Netherlands
Ren Wu	Baidu, USA
Yunquan Zhang	Chinese Academy of Sciences, Beijing, China
Peter Zinterhof Jr.	University of Salzburg, Austria

Additional Reviewers

Vlad-Mihai Sima	Delft University of Technology, The Netherlands

9th Workshop on Virtualization in High-Performance Cloud Computing (VHPC 2014)

Workshop Description

Virtualization technologies constitute a key enabling factor for flexible resource management in modern data centers, and particularly in cloud environments. Cloud providers need to dynamically manage complex infrastructures in a seamless fashion for varying workloads and hosted applications, independently of the customers deploying software or users submitting highly dynamic and heterogeneous workloads. Thanks to virtualization, we have the ability to manage vast computing and networking resources dynamically and close to the marginal cost of providing the services, which is unprecedented in the history of scientific and commercial computing. Various virtualization technologies contribute to the overall picture in different ways: machine virtualization, with its capability to enable consolidation of multiple underutilized servers with heterogeneous software and operating systems (OSes) and its capability to live-migrate a fully operating virtual machine (VM) with a very short downtime, enables novel and dynamic ways to manage physical servers; OS-level virtualization, with its capability to isolate multiple user-space environments and to allow for their co-existence within the same OS kernel, promises to provide many of the advantages of machine virtualization with high levels of responsiveness and performance and I/O virtualization allowing physical NICs/HBAs to take traffic from multiple VMs.

The workshop series on Virtualization in High-Performance Cloud Computing (VHPC) – originally the Workshop on Xen in High-Performance Cluster and Grid Computing Environments – started in 2006. It aims to bring together researchers and industrial practitioners facing the challenges posed by virtualization. VHPC provides a platform that fosters discussion, collaboration, mutual exchange of knowledge and experience, enabling research to ultimately provide novel solutions for virtualized computing systems of tomorrow.

VHPC 2014 was again successfully co-located with Euro-Par. We would like to thank the organizers of this year's conference and the invited speakers: Helge Meinhard, CERN, and Ron Brightwell, Sandia National Laboratories, for their very well received talks.

Program Chairs

Michael Alexander	Vienna University of Technology, Austria
Anastassios Nanos	National Technical University of Athens, Greece
Tommaso Cucinotta	Amazon, Ireland

Program Committee

Costas Bekas	IBM, Switzerland
Jakob Blomer	CERN, Switzerland
Roberto Canonico	University of Naples Federico II, Italy
Piero Castoldi	Sant'Anna School of Advanced Studies, Italy
Paolo Costa	MS Research Cambridge, UK
Jorge Ejarque Artigas	Barcelona Supercomputing Center, Spain
William Gardner	University of Guelph, Canada
Balazs Gerofi	University of Tokyo, Japan
Krishna Kant	George Mason University, USA
Romeo Kinzler	IBM, Switzerland
Nectarios Koziris	National Technical University of Athens, Greece
Giuseppe Lettieri	University of Pisa, Italy
Jean-Marc Menaud	Ecole des Mines de Nantes, France
Christine Morin	Inria, France
Dimitrios Nikolopoulos	Foundation for Research and Technology – Hellas, Greece
Herbert Poetzl	VServer, Austria
Luigi Rizzo	University of Pisa, Italy
Josh Simons	VMware, USA
Borja Sotomayor	University of Chicago, USA
Yoshio Turner	HP Labs, USA
Kurt Tutschku	Blekinge Institute of Technology, Sweden
Chao-Tung Yang	Tunghai University, Taiwan

Table of Contents – Part II

7th International Workshop on Multi-/Many-core Computing Systems (MuCoCoS 2014)

Third Workshop on On-chip Memory Hierarchies and Interconnects (OMHI 2014)

7th Workshop on Productivity and Performance Tools for HPC Application Development (PROPER 2014)

Second Workshop on Runtime and Operating Systems for the Many-Core Era (ROME 2014)

First Workshop on Techniques and Applications for Sustainable Ultrascale Computing Systems (TASUS 2014)

7th Workshop on UnConventional High-Performance Computing (UCHPC 2014)

9th Workshop on Virtualization in High-Performance Cloud Computing (VHPC 2014)

Workshop on Software for Exascale Computing (SPPEXA 2014)

Table of Contents – Part I

12th International Workshop on Algorithms, Models and Tools for Parallel Computing on Heterogeneous Platforms (HeteroPar 2014)

5th Workshop on High-Performance Bioinformatics and Biomedicine (HiBB 2014)

Second Workshop on Large-Scale Distributed Virtual Environments on Clouds and P2P (LSDVE 2014)

Second Workshop on Parallel and Distributed Agent-Based Simulations (PADABS 2014)

First International Workshop on Reproducibility in Parallel Computing (REPPAR 2014)

7th Workshop on Resiliency in High-Performance Computing with Clouds, Grids, and Clusters (Resilience 2014)

On the Role of Ontologies in the Design of Service Based Cloud Applications

Fotis Gonidis[1], Iraklis Paraskakis[1], and Anthony J.H. Simons[2]

[1] South-East European Research Centre (SEERC),
City College – International Faculty of the University of Sheffield,
24 Proxenou Koromila Street, 54622 Thessaloniki, Greece
{fgonidis,iparaskakis}@seerc.org
[2] Department of Computer Science, University of Sheffield,
Regent Court, 211 Portobello Street,
Sheffield S1 4DP, United Kingdom
A.Simons@dcs.shef.ac.uk

Abstract. The wide exploitation of cloud resources has been hindered by the diversity on the provision of these resources and thus resulting in heterogeneity between them. Research efforts on the design of cloud applications, leveraging resources form heterogeneous cloud environments, have been concentrated on traditional cloud platform resources such as deployment capabilities and data stores. However, the emergence of the cloud application platforms has made available a wide range of platform basic services (e.g. e-mail, message queue and authentication service) that can drastically decrease the application development time. Our work focuses on eliminating the heterogeneity among the providers offering those services. To this end we propose an ontology-driven framework, which facilitates the seamless and transparent use of platform basic services provisioned by multiple clouds environments. Ontologies are leveraged to enable the homogeneous description of the functionality of the service providers.

Keywords: Multi-Cloud, Ontologies, Cloud platform service description.

1   Introduction

Cloud application platforms [1] are becoming increasingly popular and have the potential to change the way applications are developed, involving compositions of platform basic services. A platform basic service, in the Platform as a Service level (PaaS), can be considered as a piece of software which offers certain functionality and is reusable. Examples of such services are authentication mechanisms, logging mechanisms, message queues and email service. Such services are considered to be interwoven in the creation of many applications running from a cloud application platform and thus using the service instead of creating the corresponding code is of great benefit to the application developer. A service can be offered natively by the platform, such as the e-mail service offered by Google App Engine [2] and Amazon Elastic Beanstalk [3]. Alternatively, Independent Software Vendors (ISVs) can offer added-value services for a given platform, such as Heroku [4].

L. Lopes et al. (Eds.): Euro-Par 2014 Workshops, Part II, LNCS 8806, pp. 1–12, 2014.

The cloud application platforms have the potential to lead to a new paradigm of designing service-based cloud applications. Applications rather than being developed from the ground up, they can be synthesised from services offered by multiple clouds. This way developers can drastically increase their productivity and significantly shorten the time to market of the product.

However, an impediment for the wide exploitation of the available platform basic services constitutes the heterogeneity among the offered solutions. The heterogeneity mainly arises from (i) the variability in the workflow required to complete an operation [5] and (ii) the differences in the web API through which the service providers provision their services. This paper focuses on the latter variability point. For developers to leverage the full capabilities of services provided by multiple platforms should not be forced to develop an application directly against proprietary APIs, but rather should use either (i) standard and widely adopted technologies; or (ii) abstraction layers which decouple standard end-user APIs from the platform specific APIs. To this end, this paper proposes an ontology-driven framework, which promotes the uniform access to platform basic services via the use of an abstract reference cloud API.

The use of ontologies is primarily motivated by their ability to support separation of concerns [6], that is enable the development of an application where the logic is separated from the data upon which it operates. This allows for data to be altered as much as it is required without altering the code related to the logic that operates on the data. In our case the data are the descriptions of the platform basic services that could be consumed by the various applications. Therefore, future service providers can be supported on the fly through an ontological description of their service. The framework is capable of reading the description and generating automatically the provider specific source code.

The rest of the paper is organised as follows. The next Section attempts to contextualise the scope of the proposed framework by defining the cluster of cloud platforms that it will focus on. Established work on the field related to the proposed solution is reviewed in Section 3. Thereafter, the main components of the framework are described namely, the ontologies and the core engine, which is responsible for generating the provider specific code.

2   Clustering of Cloud Platforms

Before stepping into the details of the proposed solution, the application scope of the approach needs to be defined. Particularly, we attempt a high-level clustering of the cloud platforms environments and subsequently we state the focus of our research. The clustering of the cloud platforms has been primarily based upon the adopted technologies and the provisioning of additional platform services either natively or via a service marketplace. From earlier surveys and reports [7], [8], [9], [10], [11], [12], [13] we find that cloud platform solutions can be clustered into three broad categories:

The first category includes platforms, which adopt standard and widely used technologies, such as popular programming languages and databases. They provide basic development resources only, such as an application server and a database, and do not offer further cloud platform services or a service marketplace. An example platform in this category is CloudBees [14].

The second category includes platforms, which offer additional services via APIs such as e-mail service, image manipulation service and a message queue service. The services are offered natively by the platform such as the Google App Engine [2]. Alternatively the platforms may offer additional services via a marketplace such as the Heroku [4] add-ons.

The third category includes platforms, which adopt a native application development paradigm, where developers are expected to use bespoke visual tools and graphical interfaces to create the applications. Additional services can be offered by ISVs via marketplaces. However, those services are tightly integrated to the platform and no programming library or web interface is exposed. Platforms in this category include Zoho Creator [15].

Regarding the provisioning of services, platforms in the first category offers only deployment capabilities without any additional services. On the other edge of the spectrum, platforms in the third category are characterised by proprietary development tools and technologies. The lack of programming APIs makes them intractable when it comes to abstracting the offered services. Consequently, this paper focuses on platforms in the second category. Specifically, we are interested in the proprietary APIs that the services expose and the way these APIs can be abstracted in order to enable uniform and transparent access to the services.

3   Related Work

The constant increase in the offering of platform basic services has resulted in a growing interest in leveraging services from multiple clouds. Significant work has been carried out on the field, which can be grouped into three high-level categories: middleware platforms, Model-driven Engineering techniques and library based solutions. Representative work on each of the three categories is listed.

Library-based solutions such as jclouds [16] and LibCloud [17] provide an abstraction layer for accessing specific cloud resources such as compute, storage and message queue. While, library-based approaches efficiently abstract those resources, they have a limited application scope which makes it difficult to reuse them for accommodating additional services.

Middleware platforms constitute middle layers, which decouple applications from directly being exposed to proprietary technologies and deployed on specific platforms. Rather, cloud applications are deployed and managed by the middleware platform, which has the capacity to exploit multiple cloud platform environments. mOSAIC [18] is such a PaaS solution which facilitates the design and execution of scalable component-based applications in a multi-cloud environment. mOSAIC offers an open source API in order to enable the applications to use common cloud resources offered by the target environment such as virtual machines, key value stores and message queues.

Initiatives that leverage MDE techniques present meta-models, which can be used for the creation of cloud platform independent applications. The notion in this case is that cloud applications are designed in a platform independent manner and specific technologies are only infused in the models at the last stage of the development. MODAClouds [19] and PaaSage [20] aim at cross-deployment of cloud applications. Additionally, they offer monitoring and quality assurance capabilities. They are based on CloudML, a modelling language which provides the building blocks for creating applications deployable in multiple IaaS and PaaS environments. Hamdaqa et al. [21] have proposed a reference model for developing applications which leverage the elasticity capability of the cloud infrastructure. Cloud applications are composed of CloudTasks which provide compute, storage, communication and management capabilities. MULTICLAPP [22] is a framework leveraging MDE techniques during the software development process. Cloud artefacts are the main components that the application consists of. A transformation mechanism is used to generate the platform specific project structure and map the cloud artefacts onto the target platform. Additional adapters are generated each time to map the application's API to the respective platform's resources.

The solutions listed in this Section focus mainly on eliminating the technical restrictions that each platform imposes, enabling this way multi-cloud deployment of applications. Additionally, they offer monitoring and quality assurance capabilities as well as the creation of elastic applications. On the contrary, the vision of the authors is to facilitate the use of platform services, such as e-mail service, authentication service etc. and concrete providers from heterogeneous clouds in a seamless manner. To this end, we envision the creation of a framework, which enables the uniform description of the API of the services and the concrete providers. In turn, this will facilitate the design of applications, which leverage services from multiple cloud application platforms without being bound to the specific proprietary APIs.

4   Ontology Driven Framework

Towards enabling the design of service-based cloud applications, we present our solution approach, which is based on an ontology driven framework. With respect to the classification of the cloud platforms performed in Section 2, the proposed solution targets the platforms in the second category, namely the ones who offer platform services either natively or via a marketplace through a web API. The framework receives a description of the service functionality and subsequently generates automatically the client adapter to map onto the abstract reference API for the specific service.

In order to evaluate the effectiveness of the framework we apply the solution approach to the cloud e-mail service. The e-mail service allows a cloud application to send and receive e-mails without the need for the developer to set up and maintain an e-mailing server. Instead the service is offered by the cloud provider via a web interface.

The choice of the e-mail service was motivated primarily by the need for enabling cloud applications to leverage services from multiple clouds. The emergence of the cloud application platforms and the service marketplaces has made available a wide range of services which the cloud application should be capable of exploiting. To this end, the role of ontologies is explored as enablers for vendor specific API abstraction. The concrete provider's API is captured in an ontology and subsequently is mapped to the abstract reference API which is exposed to the cloud developers.

4.1   Benefits of Using Ontologies

Ontologies are the novel aspect of the framework. They are used in order to allow a uniform description of the platform basic services. According to Gruber [23], they are formal knowledge over a shared domain that is standardized or commonly accepted by certain group of people.

The advantages here are two-fold. First, ontologies allow to define clearly the domain model of our interest; in our case the domain model is the cloud platform services offered by multiple platforms. The fact that an ontology is shared and commonly accepted description of a service, contributes towards the homogenisation of the latter. The cloud vendors can adhere to and publish the description of their service based on the common and shared ontology.

Moreover, ontologies can be reused and expanded if necessary. Thus, an ontology describing a platform basic service may not be constructed from the ground up but may be based on an existing one such as USDL (Unified Service Description Language) [24].

The reasoning capabilities that ontologies offer may be exploited for consistency check of the service descriptions.

Furthermore, mature tools are available in order to create and manipulate an ontology. Specifically, Protégé [25] is a well-established tool that allows users to create and edit ontologies, whereas the OWL API [26] and Jena framework [27] are among the popular Java frameworks that enable developers to manipulate ontologies using the Java language.

It is not the first time that ontologies are used in the cloud computing domain to enable service description. mOSAIC [28] ontology is used to enable service discovery and brokerage. This further motivates our choice of using ontologies for enabling service description. However, while the mOSAIC ontology focuses on describing the general and quality characteristics of a service, our ontology aims at the concrete functionality and the API of the services.

4.2   Architecture of the Ontology Driven Framework

Figure 1 depicts the high-level overview of the abstraction framework. The developer initiates the development of the application using a popular development environment such as Eclipse and a programming language such as Java. When the application requires a platform basic service that is supported by the framework, the API description of the service is inserted into the framework. Consequently, the service description is parsed and the source code for the particular service is generated. The proposed cloud abstraction framework consists of two main parts: the models that represent the supported platform basic services and the core engine of the framework.

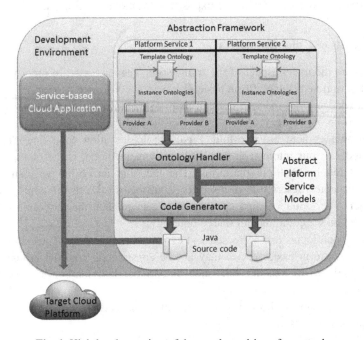

Fig. 1. High-level overview of the ontology-driven framework

Platform Service Models. The models represent the services that the framework supports. As mentioned in the previous Section, ontologies are used in order to build the models. The models, as seen in Figure 2 are structured into three levels. Inspiration has been gained by the Meta-Object-Facility (MOF) standard [29] defined for the Model Driven Engineering domain. Specifically, the hierarchy of the ontologies resembles the bottom three levels of the MOF structure, namely the meta-models, the models and the instances of the models.

The level 2 Ontology (O2) includes the description of the abstract platform services. Common concepts that define the platform basic services are captured at this level. Information about the configuration settings and the authentication mechanisms of the service are included. The O2 level also contains concepts, such as Operations and Attributes, required to describe an API.

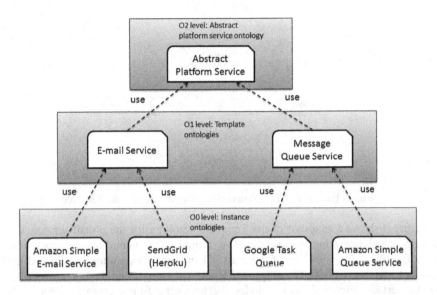

Fig. 2. The three levels of the ontology hierarchy

The level 1 Ontologies (O1) includes the concrete description of each of the platform basic services, which are supported by the framework. A dedicated ontology corresponds to each of the services and captures information about the functionality that they expose. For example, in the case of the cloud e-mail service, information that is captured in the O1 ontology describes the functionality for performing actions related to sending, receiving and manipulating e-mails. The ontologies in the O1 level are also referred to as Template ontologies.

The level 0 Ontologies (O0) include the description of the specific platform service providers. A dedicated ontology corresponds to each of the service providers and describes the native vendor specific API. For example, in the case of the e-mail service, an O0 ontology describes the concrete operations and attributes that a provider specific API exposes. The ontologies in the O0 level are also referred to as Instance ontologies. The users of the framework can form the Instance ontologies after reading the service providers` API. Alternatively, the Instance ontologies are created and published by the service providers and are automatically discovered by the framework.

In order to further clarify the use of the three levels of ontologies and the relationships among them, a simple description of a vendor specific API is constructed. The example that follows serves only illustrative purposes. Therefore, for the sake of simplicity only the necessary amount of information has been included. The example focuses on the cloud e-mail service and particularly on the description of the operation, which allows the users to send e-mails.

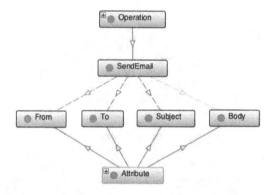

Fig. 3. Example of Template ontology for the cloud e-mail service

Figure 3 shows a snapshot of the Template ontology for the e-mail service, which describes the operation for sending an e-mail. The name of the operation is "SendEmail". It is a subclass of the class "Operation". "Operation" is defined in the Abstract Platform Service Ontology (O2 level) and includes all the operations offered by the service. Figure 3 also includes the following four elements: "From", "To" "Subject" and "Body". "From" denotes the sender of the e-mail, while "To" refers to the recipient. "Subject" refers to the title of the e-mail and "Body" holds the content. All four elements are subclasses of the class "Attribute". The class "Attribute" is defined in the Abstract Platform Service Ontology and includes all the attributes that are used for the execution of the operations. An attribute is linked to a specific operation with a property. Specifically, the four afore mentioned attributes are linked to the "SendEmail" operation with the following properties respectively: "hasFrom", "hasTo", "hasSubject" and "hasBody".

Figures 4 and 5 show how the service providers can describe their service and their specific API by creating their own ontology (Instance ontology), which is based on the publicly available Template ontology (Figure 3). Particularly, two Instance ontologies are shown which correspond to the Amazon Simple E-mail Service (SES) [30] and to SendGrid [31], a cloud E-mail service offered as add-on via Heroku.

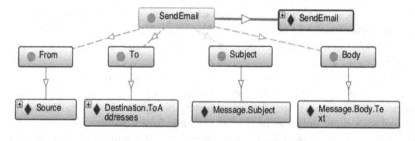

Fig. 4. Example of Instance ontology for the Amazon SES service

Figure 4 shows the parameters required to send an e-mail as defined in the API of the Amazon SES service. Individuals are created to express each of the specific elements of the provider's API. An individual, in ontologies, can be considered a member of a class. Specifically, the "send" individual denotes the operation name, which is equivalent to the "SendEmail" operation of the Template ontology. This justifies the fact that "send" individual is of type "SendEmail". The individual "Source" denotes the sender of the e-mail and is equivalent to the "From" attribute. Thus, it is defined of type "From". Likewise the individual "Destination.ToAddresses" is of type "To", the "Message.Subject" is of type "Subject" and the "Message.Body.Text", which holds the content of the e-mail, is of type "Body".

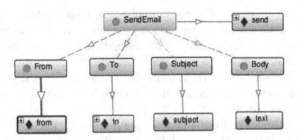

Fig. 5. Example of Instance ontology for the SendGrid (Heroku)

In the same way an Instance ontology can be created (Figure 5) to describe the API of the "SendGrid" E-mail service provider offered via Heroku. The individual "SendEmail" identifies the operation of sending an e-mail and is equivalent to the "SendEmail" of the Template ontology. Therefore it is of type "SendEmail". Likewise, the individuals "from", "to", "subject" and "text" are of type "From", "To", "Subject" and "Body" respectively.

In the same way the rest of the functionality of a platform basic service can be described. At the same time, the differences in the APIs between the various providers can be captured. The e-mail service has been used as an example. The proposed structure of the three levels of ontologies can be used to describe any platform basic services, offered natively by the platforms or via marketplaces through a web API, such as message queue service, authentication service and payment service. Initially, a Template ontology is required to describe the functionality of each of the services. Consequently the Instance ontologies are created to capture the vendor specific APIs.

Core Engine of the Framework. The second part of the cloud abstraction framework comprises the core engine. It receives as input the service description of the platform basic services and generates the source code for the target cloud provider. As seen from Figure 1, the core engine can further be decomposed into the following three high–level components: The Ontology Handler, the Abstract Platform Service Models and the Code Generator.

The Ontology Handler is responsible for manipulating the ontologies which contain a platform service description. It first discovers the published Instance ontologies, which describe a particular service provider. Alternatively, the Instance ontologies can be fed manually to the Ontology Handler. Then, it performs a consistency check to reassure that the Instance ontology conforms to the respective Template ontology. For that reason the capabilities of reasoning in ontologies may be exploited. Consequently, the ontology is parsed and an object representation is created in memory. The object representation of the ontology is then forwarded to the Code Generator.

The Abstract Platform Service models contain a collection of abstract models, which correspond to the Template ontology and describe the service. They can be considered as the scaffold of the service. They are later enriched with the provider's specific API information.

The Code Generator, as the name implies, is responsible for generating the concrete source code for the target service provider. It receives as input the object representation of the parsed Instance ontology and the abstract service models. Then it enriches the abstract models with the provider specific information and outputs the provider specific source code. Thus, while the developer uses a single common API to access a platform service, internally the source code is adjusted to map each time to the concrete service provider API.

In order to illustrate the functionality of the proposed framework, the example of the cloud e-mail service has been used. However, the generic nature of the framework enables the support of any platform basic service offered via a web API. As described in Section 4, the Template and Instance ontologies are required. The former captures the reference functionality that is exposed to the developers. The latter includes the provider specific API and the mapping to the reference functionality.

The proposed solution is capable of abstracting efficiently the heterogeneities among the cloud providers' APIs and thus eliminating the exposure of the application to proprietary APIs. However, the approach is inherently limited to the abstraction of the common functionality offered by the cloud providers. This means that specific functionality that is provided only by one vendor is not included in the Template ontologies and therefore not mapped to the abstract reference API. In order to allow developers to use the provider specific functionality, the latter is described directly in the Instance ontologies. Then, additional client adapters can be generated and used by the developers. In case the functionality is adopted by additional providers it can be also included in the Template ontology. Therefore, the proposed framework rather than being static, it is continuously updated to accommodate new features offered by the platform basic services.

5   Conclusions

In this paper, we addressed the issue of the design of service-based cloud applications capable of leveraging services offered by multiple cloud environments. To this end, we presented an ontology driven framework, which facilitates: (i) the description of the functionality of concrete service providers, (ii) the provisioning of a common platform service API to be used independently of the target provider and (iii) the automatic generation of the client adapters required to consume the target services. The proposed solution comprises two main parts: the ontological description of the services and the core engine. The first one includes the Template and Instance ontologies, which contain the abstract and the provider specific service description respectively. The second part reads the Instance ontology and generates the source code for the target provider. Thus, the use of the ontology driven framework facilitates the design of applications exploiting services from multiple platforms using provider independent API rather than being bound to proprietary technologies.

Acknowledgment. The research leading to these results has received funding from the European Union Seventh Framework Programme (FP7/2007-2013) under grant agreement n°264840, the RELATE project (http://www.relate-itn.eu).

References

1. Kourtesis, D., Bratanis, K., Bibikas, D., Paraskakis, I.: Software Co-development in the Era of Cloud Application Platforms and Ecosystems: The Case of CAST. In: Camarinha-Matos, L.M., Xu, L., Afsarmanesh, H. (eds.) Collaborative Networks in the Internet of Services. IFIP AICT, vol. 380, pp. 196–204. Springer, Heidelberg (2012)
2. Google App Engine (2014), https://developers.google.com/appengine
3. Amazon Elastic Beanstalk (2014), http://aws.amazon.com/elasticbeanstalk/
4. Heroku (2014), http://heroku.com
5. Gonidis, F., Paraskakis, I., Simons, A.J.H.: A Development Framework Enabling the Design of Service-Based Cloud Applications. In: 2nd International Workshop on Cloud Service Brokerage. Springer, Manchester (2004) (in press)
6. Kourtesis, D., Paraskakis, I., Simons, A.J.H.: Policy-driven governance in cloud application platforms: an ontology-based approach. In: Proceedings of the 4th International Workshop on Ontology-Driven Information Systems Engineering, Graz (2012)
7. Badger, L., Grance, T., Patt-Corner, R., Voas, J.: NIST Cloud Computing Synopsis and Recommendations. Technical Report, National Institute of Standards and Technology (2012)
8. Kourtesis, D., Bratanis, K., Bibikas, D., Paraskakis, I.: Software Co-development in the Era of Cloud Application Platforms and Ecosystems: The Case of CAST. In: Camarinha-Matos, L.M., Xu, L., Afsarmanesh, H. (eds.) Collaborative Networks in the Internet of Services. IFIP AICT, vol. 380, pp. 196–204. Springer, Heidelberg (2012)
9. Khan, N., Noraziah, A., Ismail, E.I., Deris, M.M., Herawan, T.: Cloud Computing: Analysis of Various Platforms. Int. J. E-Entrep. Innov. 3(2), 9 (2012)
10. Pastaki Rad, M., Sajedi Badashian, A., Meydanipour, G., Ashurzad Delcheh, M., Alipour, M., Afzali, H.: A Survey of Cloud Platforms and Their Future. In: Gervasi, O., Taniar, D., Murgante, B., Laganà, A., Mun, Y., Gavrilova, M.L. (eds.) ICCSA 2009, Part I. LNCS, vol. 5592, pp. 788–796. Springer, Heidelberg (2009)
11. Ried, S., Rymer, J.R.: The Forrester WaveTM: Platform- As-A-Service For Vendor Strategy Professionals, Q2 2011. Technical Report, Forrester (2011)
12. Development in the Cloud: A Framework for PaaS and ISV Flexibility, Saugatuck Technology Inc. (2010)

13. Gonidis, F., Paraskakis, I., Simons, A.J.H., Kourtesis, D.: Cloud Application Portability. An Initial View. In: 6th Balkan Conference in Informatics, pp. 275–282. ACM, Thessaloniki (2013)
14. CloudBees (2014), http://www.cloudbees.com
15. Zoho Creator (2014), http://www.zoho.com/creator
16. jclouds (2014), http://www.jclouds.org
17. Apache LibCloud (2014), https://libcloud.apache.org/index.html
18. Petcu, D.: Consuming Resources and Services from Multiple Clouds. Journal of Grid Computing 10723, 1–25 (2014)
19. Ardagna, D., Di Nitto, E., Casale, G., Petcu, D., Mohagheghi, P., Mosser, S., Matthews, P., Gericke, A., Ballagny, C., D'Andria, F., Nechifor, C.S., Sheridan, C.: MODAClouds: A model-driven approach for the design and execution of applications on multiple Clouds. In: Workshop on Modeling in Software Engineering, pp. 50–56. IEEE, Zurich (2012)
20. Jeffery, K., Horn, G., Schubert, L.,: A vision for better cloud applications. In: Proceedings of the 2013 International Workshop on Multi Cloud Applications and Federated Clouds, pp. 7–12. ACM, Prague (2013)
21. Hamdaqa, M., Livogiannis, T., Tahvildari, L.: A reference model for developing cloud applications. In: 1st International Conference on Cloud Computing and Services Science, pp. 98–103. Noordwijkerhout (2011)
22. Guillén, J., Miranda, J., Murillo, J.M., Cana, C.: Developing migratable multicloud applications based on MDE and adaptation techniques. In: 2nd Nordic Symposium on Cloud Computing & Internet Technologies, pp. 30–37. ACM, Oslo (2013)
23. Gruber, T.R.: A translation approach to portable ontology specifications. Knowledge Acquisition 5(2), 199–220 (1993)
24. Pedrinaci, C., Cardoso, J., Leidig, T.: Linked USDL: A Vocabulary for Web-Scale Service Trading. In: Presutti, V., d'Amato, C., Gandon, F., d'Aquin, M., Staab, S., Tordai, A. (eds.) ESWC 2014. LNCS, vol. 8465, pp. 68–82. Springer, Heidelberg (2014)
25. The Protégé Ontology Editor and Knowledge Acquisition System (2014), http://protege.stanford.edu/
26. OWL API (2014), http://owlapi.sourceforge.net/
27. Jena Framework (2013), http://jena.apache.org
28. Moscato, F., Aversa, R., Di Martino, B., Fortis, T., Munteanu, V.: An analysis of mOSAIC ontology for Cloud resources annotation. In: Federated Conference on Computer Science and Information Systems, pp. 973–980. IEEE, Szczecin (2011)
29. Gardner, T., Griffin, C., Koehler, J., Hauser, R.: A review of OMG MOF 2.0 Query / Views / Transformations Submissions and Recommendations towards the final Standard. In: Workshop on Metamodeling for MDA, York, pp. 179–197 (2003)
30. Amazon Simple E-mail Service (2014), http://aws.amazon.com/ses/
31. SendGrid (2014), http://www.sendgrid.com

Sharing Files Using Cloud Storage Services

Tiago Oliveira, Ricardo Mendes, and Alysson Bessani

Universidade de Lisboa, Faculdade de Ciências, LaSIGE, Portugal
{toliveira,rmendes}@lasige.di.fc.ul.pt, bessani@di.fc.ul.pt

Abstract. The widespread use of cloud storage in the last few years can be attributed to the existence of appealing applications such as file backup, data archival and file sharing. File sharing in particular, is implemented in different ways by distinct cloud storage services. These differences can appear at the offered permission types and in the form they are applied. We present a survey of these differences for several popular cloud storage services. We also show how to realize secure data sharing using these services, allowing the implementation of equivalent data sharing features in different clouds, an important requirement for secure multi-cloud systems.

1 Introduction

With more people accessing their files online, an important part of file sharing today is done by taking advantage of cloud storage. This can be done through personal file synchronization services like Dropbox [4], Google Drive [6], Microsoft OneDrive [13], Box [3] or Ubuntu One [18], which store users' data in the cloud. These services have been extremely successful, as attested by the success of DropBox, which has announced last April that it reached 275 million users [5].

These systems perform file sharing through dedicated application servers which are responsible for controlling access to the files as well as user groups management, data deduplication, etc. It means that the security of the file sharing requires trusting not only the storage service (for instance, Dropbox is built on top Amazon S3 [4]), but also these application servers.

An alternative for using these services is to mount the cloud storage (e.g., Amazon S3) in a user-level file system and access it directly. S3QL [17], BlueSky [26] and SCFS [24] are examples of this kind of systems.

BlueSky uses a proxy that acts as a network file server, which is accessed by the clients in order to store their data. This proxy is responsible for sending the users' data to the storage clouds. Nonetheless, as in synchronization services, clients need to trust this component and the cloud storage provider.

On the other hand, S3QL and SCFS allow clients to share data without a proxy. In S3QL, the clients just mount the file system to access the storage service objects as files, with no concurrency control. SCFS, on the other hand, offers controlled file sharing where concurrent updates and file version conflicts are avoided through the use of locks. Moreover, in SCFS clients are able to take advantage of DepSky [23] to store data in a multiple cloud providers, i.e., a

L. Lopes et al. (Eds.): Euro-Par 2014 Workshops, Part II, LNCS 8806, pp. 13–25, 2014.

cloud-of-clouds. DepSky and SCFS ensure the privacy, integrity and availability of the data stored in the clouds as long as less then a third of the cloud providers are faulty.

SCFS uses the *pay-per-ownership* model, in which each user pays for the files he/she creates. A more simple model where all the clients use the same cloud account could be used, and automatically share all the data stored by the system. This alternative raises some problems. First, all users could access all data stored in the clouds. In this way, each client must trust all the system users since they can access, delete or corrupt all stored data. Second, just one organization will be charged for all the data stored in the system.

In this paper we present a survey of the access-control techniques provided by some popular cloud storage services. We also show how to implement secure data sharing using these services, allowing the implementation of equivalent data sharing features in different clouds, a fundamental requirement for multi-cloud systems.

In summary, we contribute with (1) a study of several cloud storage services' access control models (i.e., Amazon S3 [1], Google Storage [7], Window Azure Storage [19], RackSpace Cloud Files [15], HP Public Cloud [9], and Luna Cloud [11]), i.e, a study of the techniques used by these services to apply the permissions they provided and (2) a set of protocols that allow the sharing of files between clients according with pre-defined access control patterns for each of the studied storage clouds.

2   Access Control on Storage Clouds

To allow users to share their data, all cloud storage services provide some mechanisms that enable data owners (users) to grant access over their resources to other principals.

In all these storage services, the resources can be either *buckets* or *objects*. A bucket, or *container*, represents a root directory where objects must be stored. There could be several buckets associated with a single cloud storage account.[1] However, in most of the services, buckets must have unique names. Objects are stored in a bucket and can be either files or directories.

On the other hand, the cloud storage services differ in the techniques they provide to allow users to grant access over their resources, and also in the permission types that users are able to specify. In this paper these techniques will be called *access-granting* and the permission types that can be specified with them will be named *permissions*.

Access-granting Techniques. These are the techniques provided by cloud storage services to allow users to give others access to their resources. The users are able to specify a set of permissions in each technique. To apply these permissions over the resources, different storage clouds could offer different techniques.

---

[1] Some storage clouds has a limited number of buckets. For instance, an Amazon S3 account can have at most 100 buckets.

In this paper we cover three of them: *Per Group Predefined Permissions*, *Temporary Constraints* and *Access Control Lists* (ACLs).

In the first one the users are able to make their stored data accessible to some predefined group. The second technique allows users to give other users a ticket that grant access for a resource by a predefined period of time. The last one, ACLs, permits to associate with each resource a list of grantees that are able to access it.

Permissions. When a user wants to share some resource with another user, i.e., with a different account/user, he/she needs to specify what are the capabilities of this other user with respect to the shared resource(s). Permissions are specified in the access-granting techniques. Each permission has a semantic that specifies the capabilities of the grantees of some resource.

However, different storage clouds provide a different set of specifiable permissions. For example, Amazon S3's users cannot grant WRITE permission to specific objects. On the other hand, RackSpace Cloud Files users can do that [15] (see Section 3).

Moreover, equal permissions could have different semantics. As an example, in Amazon S3 [1] when a READ permission over a bucket is given, grantees can list objects inside it. On the other hand, the same permission in Windows Azure [19] does not allow grantees to list the objects in a bucket, instead it grants the permission to read all the objects it contains.

3   Permissions

To allow users to define the grantees' capabilities over a shared resource, all clouds provide a set of permissions with documented semantics. As explained before, the same permission could have different semantics in different clouds. Table 1 shows the available permissions for buckets and objects in several cloud storage providers.

As can be seen, Amazon S3 [1] and LunaCloud [11] provide the largest set of permissions among all the services studied. They permit users to give READ, WRITE, READ_ACP, WRITE_ACP and FULL_CONTROL permissions [2,12] over both buckets and objects. Google Storage [7] have almost the same set of permissions. The difference is that Google Storage does not allow users to apply READ_ACP and WRITE_ACP permissions separately [8]. Instead, it put together these two permissions into the FULL_CONTROL one. This means that if a user wants to give other users the capability of read some resource's ACL, he/she is forced to also grant the capability to write or update that ACL.

Interestingly, in most clouds the READ permission over a bucket does not allow a grantee to read an object inside it. Instead, it only allows grantees to list the objects inside the bucket. To grant read access, a READ permission need to be applied on the desired objects. On the other hand, the WRITE permission on the bucket allows a grantee to write, overwrite or delete any object inside that bucket. In this case, the same permission is not applicable to objects. Given that,

Table 1. Storage services available permissions

	Available Permissions	
	On bucket:	**On object:**
Amazon S3	•READ: List the objects in the bucket. •WRITE: Create, overwrite, and delete any object in the bucket. •READ_ACP: Read the bucket ACL. •WRITE_ACP: Write the ACL for the applicable bucket. •FULL_CONTROL: READ, WRITE, READ_ACP, and WRITE_ACP permissions on the bucket.	•READ: Read the object data and its metadata. •WRITE: Not applicable. •READ_ACP: Read the object ACL. •WRITE_ACP: Write the ACL for the applicable object. •FULL_CONTROL: READ, READ_ACP, and WRITE_ACP permissions on the object.
Google Storage	•READ: List a bucket's contents. •WRITE: List, create, overwrite, and delete objects in a bucket. •FULL_CONTROL: READ and WRITE permissions on the bucket. It also lets a user READ and WRITE bucket ACLs and other metadata.	•READ: Download an object. •WRITE: Not applied. •FULL_CONTROLL: READ access. It also lets a user READ and WRITE object ACLs and other metadata.
HP Public Cloud	•READ: Read and list any object in the bucket. •WRITE: Create, overwrite and delete any object in the bucket.	•READ: Read the specified object. •WRITE: Write in the object.
RackSpace	•READ: Read any object in the bucket. •WRITE: Create, overwrite and delete any object in the bucket.	•READ: Read the specified object. •WRITE: Write in the object.
Windows Azure	•READ: Read any object in the bucket. •WRITE: Write and overwrite any object in the bucket. •DELETE: Delete any object in the bucket. •LIST: List the objects in the bucket.	•READ: Read the specified object. •WRITE: Write the specified object. •DELETE: Delete specified object.
LunaCloud	•READ: List the objects in the bucket. •WRITE: Create, overwrite, and delete any object in the bucket. •READ_ACP: Read the bucket ACL. •WRITE_ACP: Write the ACL for the applicable bucket. •FULL_CONTROL: READ, WRITE, READ_ACP, and WRITE_ACP permissions on the bucket.	•READ: Read the object data and its metadata. •WRITE: Not applicable. •READ_ACP: Read the object ACL. •WRITE_ACP: Write the ACL for the applicable object. •FULL_CONTROL: READ, READ_ACP, and WRITE_ACP permissions on the object.

it is impossible to grant WRITE access to a subset of the objects inside a bucket. This means that there is no way to grant write access over objects individually.

Another important thing to highlight is that those clouds allow users to give others the right to read or write a resource's ACL through the READ_ACP, WRITE_ACP and FULL_CONTROL permissions. It is also important to notice that when a grantee have the permission to update an ACL, he/she is able to grant access over it to other users without being the resource owner.

HP Public Cloud [9] and RackSpace Cloud Files [15] available permissions are more simple [10,14]. These two services only provide two different permissions, either for buckets and objects: READ and WRITE. The only difference between these two storage clouds is that the READ permission on the bucket for Hp Public cloud allow grantees to list and read its objects (contrary to Amazon S3, Luna-Cloud and Google Storage), while for RackSpace only allow grantees to read the objects inside it. Also different of Amazon S3, LunaCloud and Google Storage, in these two clouds is impossible give other users the right to read/update the bucket permissions.

The Windows Azure Storage's [19] set of permissions [20] differs from all other studied cloud storage services. Basically, the WRITE and DELETE permissions are separated, as well as the READ and the LIST. In the other clouds these permissions are grouped in one permission, i.e., when the WRITE access is granted, grantees have also the capability to delete resources. Similarly with HP Public Cloud and RackSpace, a grantee cannot update/read the bucket permissions.

4 Access-granting Techniques

4.1 Per Group Predefined Permissions

Using Per Group Predefined Permissions, the users are able to apply permissions on buckets or objects granting access for two kinds of groups: *All Users* and *Authenticated Users*. The All Users group refers to anyone in the internet. In turn, the Authenticated Users group represents all users that have an account in the cloud provider. However, to give permissions to these groups, the owners must use some predefined permissions that the storage clouds provide. For instance, Amazon S3 and LunaCloud call this technique *Canned ACLs*, while Google Storage name it *Predefined ACLs*.

The first column of Table 2 shows the available predefined permissions for each group, as well as the type of access that each one grants. As we can see, Amazon S3 and Google Storage provide the same Per Group Predefined Permissions [2,8].[2] These default permissions allow users to make their resources public for the All Users group, for both READ and WRITE. For the Authenticated group, the storage clouds only allow the users to grant READ permission over buckets or objects. Notice that the *bucket-owner-read* and *bucket-owner-full-control* predefined permissions over objects for Amazon S3 and Google Storage, only grant access permissions to resources owners (not for the Authenticated Group). These predefined permissions are provided because the bucket owner could not be the object owner. In these two clouds, each user is the owner of the objects he uploads, even if the uploads are made to a bucket owned by other user. Thus, they are useful to give access rights to the bucket owner when a user uploads an object to a bucket that is not owned by him. The LunaCloud's predefined permissions are similar to the Amazon S3 and Google Storage (see Table 2), with the exception that they do not have the *bucket-owner-read* and *bucket-owner-full-control* permissions over the objects.

Windows Azure differs from the previous clouds in two ways. First, there is no predefined permissions to the Authenticated Users group. Second, it provides no way to give WRITE permissions over buckets or objects, allowing only users to grant READ access to the All Users group [21].

Although not shown in the table, all the clouds that provide predefined permissions also provide a special permission that gives FULL_CONTROL to the bucket/object owner, with no one else getting any access to it. In fact, this is the default predefined permission for a resource on its creation.

HP Public Cloud and RackSpace Cloud Files do not provide Per Group Predefined Permissions. However they allow users to make their buckets public through different techniques.

---

[2] There are some other predefined permissions for this two storage clouds that are not shown in the figure.

4.2   Temporary Constraints

Temporary Constraints is another way to give access permissions to other users. However, using this technique, the access will be temporary. The second column of Table 2 shows the studied clouds that implement this access-granting technique. As can be seen, only three of the studied clouds have this feature. RackSpace and HP Public Cloud provide *Temporary URLs* [16,10], while Windows Azure provide *Shared Access Signatures* [22]. Temporary URLs are used to support the sharing of objects (and only objects), whereas Shared Access Signature allows the sharing of both buckets and objects. These temporary constraints work as a capability given by resource owners to other users in order for them to access to the specified resource. In this case the ticket that proves the right to access the object is the URL. This URL contains information about the period of time that the access will be valid, the path to the resource over which the access is being granted, the permissions granted, and a signature. This signature, not to be confused with a digital signature [25], is different from cloud to cloud:

Table 2. Storage services access-granting techniques

	Per Group Predefined Permissions		Temporary Constraints	ACLs
	All Users	**Authenticated Users**		
Amazon S3	•public-read (bucket and object): Owner gets FULL_CONTROL. The All Users group gets READ access. •public-read-write (bucket and object): Owner gets FULL_CONTROL. The All Users group gets READ and WRITE access.	•authenticated-read (bucket and object): Owner gets FULL_CONTROL. The Authenticated Users group gets READ access. •bucket-owner-read (object): Object owner gets FULL_CONTROL. Bucket owner gets READ access. •buclet-owner-full-control (object): Both the object owner and the bucket owner get FULL_CONTROL over the object.	✗	✔
Google Storage	•public-read (bucket and object): Owner gets FULL_CONTROL. The All Users group gets READ access. •public-read-write (bucket and object): Owner gets FULL_CONTROL. The All Users group gets READ and WRITE access.	•authenticated-read (bucket and object): Owner gets FULL_CONTROL. The Authenticated Users group gets READ access. •bucket-owner-read (object): Object owner gets FULL_CONTROL. Bucket owner gets READ access. •buclet-owner-full-control (object): Both the object owner and the bucket owner get FULL_CONTROL over the object.	✗	✔
HP Public Cloud	✗	✗	TempURL	✔
RackSpace	✗	✗	TempURL	✔
Windows Azure	•full-public-access: All Users group gets READ and LIST access. •public-read-access-for-blobs-only: All Users gets READ access .	✗	Shared Access Signature	✗
LunaCloud	•public-read (bucket and object): Owner gets FULL_CONTROL. The All Users group gets READ access. •public-read-write (bucket and object): Owner gets FULL_CONTROL. The All Users group gets READ and WRITE access.	•authenticated-read (bucket and object): Owner gets FULL_CONTROL. The Authenticated Users group gets READ access.	✗	✗

- RackSpace Cloud Files: SHA-1 HMAC computed over the URL information and a key.
- HP Public Cloud: SHA-1 HMAC computed over the URL information and a key.
- Windows Azure Storage: SHA-256 HMAC computed over the URL information and a key.

In the first case, the key is a sequence of letters chosen by the user, while in the others, it is the secret key used to access the account. This signature ensures (with high probability) that the URL cannot be guessed or changed by an attacker even if he knows the other fields of the URL.

4.3   Access Control Lists – ACLs

As shown in Table 2, Amazon S3 [2], Google Storage [8], HP Public Cloud [10] and RackSpace Cloud Files [14] are the clouds that allow users to specify access rights to other users through ACLs. Contrary to the use of Temporary Constraints, by using ACLs, the user does not need to give to grantees a capability (a URL like described in Section 4.2). In this case the user who wants to share data needs to create an ACL and include the names or ids (depending on the cloud) of the clients whom he want to give access together with the corresponding permissions and associate it with the shared objects.

However, there are some differences among the storage clouds that provide ACLs. One difference between Amazon S3 and Google Storage, and RackSpace and HP Public Cloud is that in the last two, the users can only manage ACLs for containers. This means that it is impossible for a user to associate an ACL with an object. Another difference is that, while Amazon S3 and Google Storage allow users to grant access to a user from a different account, RackSpace and HP Public Cloud only allow they to set an ACL for sub-users.[3]

All clouds that allow sharing across different accounts through ACLs, do not permit buckets to have the same name, even if they belong to different accounts.

5   Setting Per User Permissions

Table 3 summarizes which clouds implement mechanisms for securely sharing buckets and objects between different users (which is a requirement for implementing the cloud-of-clouds models of DepSky [23] and SCFS [24]). Among the studied clouds, LunaCloud is the only one that does not provide enough features for this, since it only provides Per Group Predefined Permissions. In the remaining clouds, the per user sharing can be done through ACLs or Temporary Constraints. However, none of these clouds provide mechanisms for securely sharing a bucket in a simple way.

To clarify what we mean by "securely" and "simple", we define a minimum set of rules to share a bucket in a secure way:

---

[3] A sub-user is a user within an account owned by other user. Such users can be associated to an account by associating with him a username and a password.

- **Rule A**: the permissions on the bucket allow a grantee to list, delete, create, read and write any object inside it.
- **Rule B**: only grantees and the bucket owner can operate on the bucket.
- **Rule C**: a grantee cannot delegate access rights to other users.

Sharing a container using a cloud storage service that satisfies these rules and support ACL as access-granting technique would be very simple. First, the bucket owner gathers the ids of the accounts he wants to grant access to, and then he creates/associates a bucket with an ACL granting the desired permissions for those accounts.

Unfortunately, as described before, this simple protocol cannot be applied to any cloud we are aware of. However, equivalent functionalities can be implemented in most clouds, albeit using additional steps. In the following subsections we present the steps required for sharing a bucket with specific users in the different clouds in which this is possible.

Table 3. Per user permissions in storage services

		Amazon S3	Google Storage	HP Public Cloud	RackSpace	Windows Azure	LunaCloud
Per User Permission	**on bucket:**	ACL	ACL	ACL	ACL	Temp. Constraints	✖
	on object:	ACL	ACL	Temp. Constraints	Temp. Constraints	Temp. Constraints	✖

5.1   Sharing with Amazon S3 and Google Storage

Sharing a bucket among specific users in Google Storage and Amazon S3 is quite similar. In the following we describe a protocol (illustrated in Figure 1) for sharing a bucket in these storage clouds.

1. The bucket owner needs to gather the ids of the users he want to share with. In the case of Amazon S3, this is the *Canonical User ID* while for Google Storage this is the email associated with the account.
2. The bucket owner must create the bucket and associate with it an ACL with the ids of grantee X and Y granting READ and WRITE permissions. The bucket owner can always get the bucket ACL from the cloud, add more or remove users to it, and update it again.
3. All the ids, including the id of the bucket owner, must be sent to all grantees.
4. When a grantee or the bucket owner uploads an object, it needs to associate an ACL granting READ access to the other grantees (including the bucket owner).

The permissions provided by these two clouds are different from the set of permissions we defined in Section 5, therefore, this protocol is more costly than the protocol exemplified in that section. For instance, *Rule A* is not respected

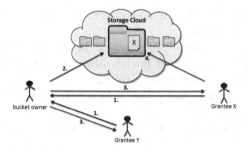

Fig. 1. Sharing a bucket with Amazon S3 and Google Storage

in the second step: there is no permission on the bucket that allows grantees to read all objects inside it. This leads to the third and fourth step described above: when an object is uploaded to the shared bucket we need to associate an ACL with it to ensure READ access to all grantees.

Assuming that all grantees are trusted, this algorithm fulfill all the requirements present in the set of rules we defined in Section 5. However, if any of them deviate from the protocol, some new issues can arise. In these clouds each user is the owner of the objects he uploads, consequently, he/she can grant READ access over his objects to other users without the knowledge of bucket owner, or even give no access to other grantees. The first case does not respect *Rule C*, while the last case contradicts *Rule A*. Notice that it is impossible to the grantee to give write access to others because these two clouds provide no WRITE permission for objects. If the bucket owner detect these situations, it can always delete the objects the grantee uploaded and revoke his access permissions.

5.2 Sharing with HP Public Cloud and RackSpace Cloud Files

HP Public Cloud and RackSpace are the only two clouds, of the five we studied, that allow per user permissions and that provide ACLs and Temporary Constraints to share resources. However, their temporary URLs only allow users to share objects, not buckets (see Section 4.2). Figure 2 illustrates the steps required for sharing a container using ACLs.

1. The bucket owner needs to get the grantees' names and emails. This is the information needed to add a sub-user. Notice that the grantees do not need to have an HP Public Cloud or RackSpace account.
2. The bucket owner adds the grantees as sub-users of its account. By default, a sub-user cannot access any service until the account owner allows it.
3. After that, the bucket should be created and an ACL with READ and WRITE permissions granting access for the previous added users must be associated with it. For RackSpace in particular, there is no way to update an ACL already associated with a bucket in the cloud, only to replace it. This means that if the bucket owner updates an ACL only granting access to grantee X,

when updating the ACL for giving access to grantee Y, the access to grantee X must be granted again.

4. The next step is to provide to grantees the credentials they need to get authenticated as sub-users. The bucket owner can get these credentials after adding the grantees to its account (step 2).
5. From now on, the grantees can authenticate themselves with cloud service using the referred credentials.
6. Thereafter, they can operate in the bucket that was granted access.

Since RackSpace do not allow grant list access to grantees (see Section 3), in this case *Rule A* is not respected. However, in the case of HP Public Cloud all rules that we specify in Section 5 are covered. Despite that, in both cases, *Rule B* and *Rule C* are only respected as long as all grantees are trusted. Otherwise, a non-trusted grantee can provide non authorized users with the access credentials, making them able to read, write, delete and list on the bucket. This contradicts *Rule C*. However, the bucket owner can revoke grantees permissions just by deleting them from the bucket ACL, or even by removing their sub-users.

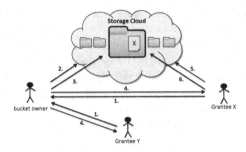

Fig. 2. Sharing a bucket with HP Public Cloud and RackSpace Cloud Files

Another issue is that these two clouds do not allow sharing across different accounts. This increase the number of necessary steps of the protocol. More specifically, there is the need of steps 2, 4 and 5. It is important that the step 4 is executed over a secure connection to ensure that no one can read the access credentials from the network.

5.3 Sharing with Windows Azure

The only way to share a container with other users using Windows Azure is through a Temporary Constraint. Figure 3 illustrates the required steps.

1. The bucket owner creates the bucket he wants to share.
2. Generate the Shared Access Signature to this bucket with all the permissions that Windows Azure provide: READ, WRITE, DELETE and LIST.
3. Disseminate the URL among the grantees.

4. Once the grantee have the URL, he can use it to access the bucket for READ, WRITE, DELETE and LIST until its expiration.

As in the previous protocols, there is the need to assume that the grantees are trusted. The second step of the protocol allows the creation of a URL with the rules we define in Section 5. However, using a Temporary Constraint as an access-granting technique raises some issues. Firstly, step 3 should be done via a secure connection. The second one relates to the fact that a grantee can give to others the URL, thus breaking *rule C*. This means that other users can access the bucket for read, write, list and delete. Finally, there is the inconvenience of repeating the process (with the exception of step 1) every time the URL expires.

5.4 Suggestions for Improvements

In each cloud service there are some aspects that can be modified in order to make secure sharing easier. Here they are summarized.

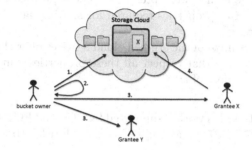

Fig. 3. Sharing a bucket with Windows Azure

Amazon S3 and Google Storage. As explained above, when a user wants to give the capability of read the content of the files inside a bucket, it needs to give the READ permission to each object inside that bucket. This obviously does not scale in applications with a large number of objects. To solve this problem, these services should provide bucket permissions that give users read access to all objects inside that bucket. In order to prevent grantees to give others access to files they upload, these clouds just need to use a model where the bucket owner is the owner of all objects inside the buckets it pays for, instead of the model where the owner of an object is the user who uploads it.

RackSpace Cloud Files and HP Public Cloud. These clouds require additional steps for defining the credentials for grantees to have access to the shared data. These steps are needed because neither of these services allow cross-account sharing, and could be avoided if this was supported. Specially for RackSpace Cloud Files, a permission to grant list access to grantees should be provided.

Windows Azure Storage. With Shared Access Signatures a malicious grantee is always able to give others the URL allowing anyone to access the shared resources. To solve this issue, Windows Azure just need to provide other access-granting technique, such as ACLs, allowing users to share data between accounts.

6   Conclusion

This paper presents a study of the access control capabilities of some storage cloud services that permit users to share data using the unmodified clouds directly and assuming a model where each user pays for the storage of the objects he/she creates. The storage clouds studied were Amazon S3, Google Storage, HP Public Cloud, RackSpace Cloud Files, Windows Azure Storage and Luna Cloud

We described the permissions provided by the services, their semantics, and the different access-granting techniques that are used to apply these permissions to specific users. Additionally, a set of protocols for sharing data securely in several public storage clouds were presented. These protocols were defined by extending an ideal set of properties required for sharing data between different users of a cloud service.

We concluded that none of the studied cloud services offer the tools to implement an optimal solution that respect all these properties, but it is possible to implement sharing in most of them.

Acknowledgments. This work is supported by EC's and FCT through projects BiobankCloud (FP7-317871) and LaSIGE (PEst-OE/EEI/UI0408/2014).

References

1. Amazon s3, http://aws.amazon.com/s3/
2. Amazon s3 documentation,
   http://docs.aws.amazon.com/AmazonS3/latest/dev/ACLOverview.html
3. Box, https://www.box.com/
4. Dropbox, https://www.dropbox.com/
5. Dropbox number of users announcement, http://techcrunch.com/2014/04/09/dropbox-hits-275m-users-and-launches-business-product-to-all/
6. Google drive, https://drive.google.com/
7. Google storage, https://developers.google.com/storage/
8. Google storage documentation,
   https://developers.google.com/storage/docs/accesscontrol
9. HP public cloud, http://www.hpcloud.com/products-services/storage-cdn
10. HP public cloud documentation,
    https://docs.hpcloud.com/api/object-storage#general_acls-jumplink-span
11. Lunacloud, http://www.lunacloud.com/pt/cloud-storage
12. Lunacloud predefined permissions documentation,
    http://www.lunacloud.com/docs/tech/storage-restful-api.pdf
13. Microsoft onedrive, https://onedrive.live.com/about/pt-br/

14. Rackspace acls documentation, http://www.rackspace.com/blog/create-cloud-files-container-level-access-control-policies/
15. Rackspace cloud files, http://www.rackspace.co.uk/cloud/files
16. Rackspace temporary urls documentation, http://docs.rackspace.com/files/api/v1/cf-devguide/content/TempURL-d1a4450.html1
17. S3QL - a full-featured file system for online data storage, http://code.google.com/p/s3ql/
18. Ubuntu one, https://one.ubuntu.com/
19. Windows azure, http://www.windowsazure.com/pt-br/solutions/storage-backup-recovery/
20. Windows azure permissions documentation, http://msdn.microsoft.com/en-us/library/windowsazure/dn140255.aspx
21. Windows azure predefined permissions documentation, http://msdn.microsoft.com/en-us/library/windowsazure/dd179354.aspx
22. Windows azure shared access signature documentation, http://azure.microsoft.com/en-us/documentation/articles/storage-dotnet-shared-access-signature-part-1/
23. Bessani, A., Correia, M., Quaresma, B., Andre, F., Sousa, P.: DepSky: Dependable and secure storage in cloud-of-clouds. ACM Transactions on Storage 9(4) (2013)
24. Bessani, A., Mendes, R., Oliveira, T., Neves, N., Correia, M., Pasin, M., Verissimo, P.: SCFS: a shared cloud-backed file system. In: Proceedings of the 2014 USENIX Annual Technical Conference – ATC 2014 (2014)
25. Rivest, R.L., Shamir, A., Adleman, L.: A method for obtaining digital signatures and public-key cryptosystems. Communications of the ACM 21(2) (1978)
26. Vrable, M., Savage, S., Voelker, G.M.: BlueSky: A cloud-backed file system for the enterprise. In: Proceedings of the 10th USENIX Conference on File and Storage Technologies, FAST 2012 (2012)

Next Generation HPC Clouds: A View for Large-Scale Scientific and Data-Intensive Applications

Dana Petcu[1], Horacio González–Vélez[2], Bogdan Nicolae[3],
Juan Miguel García–Gómez[4], Elies Fuster–Garcia[5], and Craig Sheridan[6]

[1] West University of Timişoara, Romania
[2] National College of Ireland, Ireland
[3] IBM Research, Ireland
[4] Universitat Politècnica de València, Spain
[5] Veratech for Health SL, Spain
[6] Flexiant, UK

Abstract. In spite of the rapid growth of Infrastructure-as-a-Service offers, support to run data-intensive and scientific applications large-scale is still limited. On the user side, existing features and programming models are insufficiently developed to express an application in such way that it can benefit from an elastic infrastructure that dynamically adapts to the requirements, which often leads to unnecessary over-provisioning and extra costs. On the provider side, key performance and scalability issues arise when having to deal with large groups of tightly coupled virtualized resources needed by such applications, which is especially challenging considering the multi-tenant dimension where sharing of physical resources introduces interference both inside and across large virtual machine deployments. This paper contributes with a holistic vision that imagines a tight integration between programming models, runtime middlewares and the virtualization infrastructure in order to provide a framework that transparently handles allocation and utilization of heterogeneous resources while dealing with performance and elasticity issues.

Keywords: heterogeneous clouds, cloud storage, HPC, data analytics.

1 Introduction

Data analytics and data-intensive scientific applications are undoubtedly a major driving force behind scientific advancement and business insight. Over the years, the increasing complexity of such applications has led to a rapid evolution of the computational infrastructure, to the point where massive computational facilities and data-centers are necessary in order to satisfy the computing and data storage needs. In a ceaseless quest for performance, a large variety of hardware devices and software stacks were developed to catch up with the increasing requirements. Unsurprisingly, such infrastructures are prohibitively expensive to own and maintain for the vast majority of users, which makes infrastructure clouds particularly appealing as an alternative, thanks to their pay-as-you-go model.

However, current usage patterns of clouds are mostly concentrated on long-running scale-out deployments that exhibit little dependencies between the virtual machines

L. Lopes et al. (Eds.): Euro-Par 2014 Workshops, Part II, LNCS 8806, pp. 26–37, 2014.

(VMs) or data sharing constraints: most large commercial cloud providers, such Amazon AWS and Rackspace, follow a philosophy of "throwing" more VMs at an application in order to deal with scalability issues. While this scale-out solution works for workloads that are loosely coupled, in the context of scientific and enterprise applications, there is a need to introduce support for closer coordination between virtualized resources in order to enable a tighter coupling in an efficient fashion.

These patterns were long ago acknowledged as difficult to deal with at large scale in the HPC (high performance computing) community, with decades of efforts dedicated to overcome them. In this context, the introduction of IaaS clouds as an alternative to high-end, privately-owned infrastructure presents a new challenges that calls for disruptive solutions, because the whole viewpoint needs to be changed: instead of optimizing the application to make the best out of a fixed physical infrastructure, we need to adopt the opposite: adapt the infrastructure to the dynamic needs of the application in order to satisfy performance requirements while incurring minimal costs. Thus, we cannot simply "port" techniques developed in the HPC community for IaaS clouds: novel approaches need to be developed that are designed to adopt the viewpoint from scratch. This has consequences across the whole IaaS software stack, from low level virtualization technologies up to the programming models exposed directly at application level.

More specifically, there are several important dimensions to this problem, related both to functional and non-functional aspects. With respect to functional aspects, application developers need programming models and tools to *automate resource allocation*. This aspect is non-trivial due to increasing complexity of cloud offers, which overwhelm not only new but also existing users: for example, if they opt to use Amazon EBS [2], they have to choose from 36 services, 20 instance types, 6 instance families, 2 generations of instances, 3 types of billing models and 2 types of block storage options. This level of complexity is already present for a single provider, not to mention the scenario of leveraging multiple at the same time, which in addition to increased complexity, also introduces the need to address *interoperability*. Furthermore, once the application is up and running, *elasticity* is an issue: programming models need to expose the right abstractions to let applications express their needs to grow and shrink dynamically in an easy way, while hiding the complexity of resource allocation.

With respect to non-functional aspects, *performance* and *optimal resource utilization* are key concerns. In particular, the problem of efficient resource sharing under concurrency to improve both performance and resource utilization is more difficult in IaaS clouds, considering they are multi-tenant and thus susceptible to more system noise and jitter compared to bare-bone architectures, for which this is already a problem [12]. On the other hand, the multi-tenant aspect also introduces new exploitable avenues, since common access patterns and synergies between different users can be detected and leveraged to improve both performance and resource utilization (e.g. data deduplication can be used to find common data between users and store only a single copy).

We argue in this paper for the need to provide a framework of tightly integrated layers that enables seamless access to high-performance heterogeneous resources by exposing the right programming models and abstractions at user level, while optimizing the performance and cost effectiveness of the infrastructure specifically for tightly coupled scientific and data-intensive applications running at large scale. As the target users of such applications are mostly domain-experts and do not necessarily have a deep understanding of the technical details of the infrastructure, *transparency* is crucial: we propose to hide the functional and non-functional challenges as much as possible from the users, such that they can leverage simplified programming models that enable them to focus on the domain-specific aspects without giving up on performance, while at the same time enabling cloud providers to maximize infrastructure utilization and introduce competitive targeted offers with reduced costs.

2   High Priority Areas of Improvement

On the road to materialize our vision, we identified several high priority areas listed below.

2.1   Virtualization and Storage

Large scale scientific and data-intensive applications are often tightly coupled, which introduces the need for frequent synchronization and data sharing under a high degree of concurrency. Naturally, this leads to intense communications and exchanges of data, putting a high pressure on the networking infrastructure. Network virtualization overhead in this context was known to be a major barrier [9], however it is gradually improving thanks to wider adoption of single root I/O virtualization [6]. On the other hand, two major areas still remain open: scalable data storage and management, and access to accelerators.

Scalable Data Storage and Management. In an IaaS cloud, data storage is typically achieved by manually provisioning raw virtual disks that are then attached to running VM instances. All details related to the management of such raw disks, including what size or type to pick, how to use it (e.g., with what file system) and when to attach/detach a virtual disk are the responsibility of the user, which greatly increases complexity and leads to several issues. First, there is limited support to address *sharing under concurrency*: users have to manage sharing themselves or deploy a higher level abstraction (e.g. parallel or distributed file system) on top of their VMs, which is a solution that suffers from performance penalties in cloud environments. Second, there is limited potential to leverage *elasticity*: to avoid the complexity of manually managing disks, user often over-provision storage to cover the worst-case scenario, which leads to unnecessary tied-up resources that generate costs. Thus, it is important to introduce novel storage abstractions that can handle these aspects transparently to reduce application complexity while addressing the aforementioned issues.

Access to Accelerators. There are a few technologies to enable access to accelerators within a VM (e.g. pass-through [20]). However, these often force exclusive access to the accelerator, which negates any resource optimization opportunities due to multi-tenancy. Although there is progress in this direction especially in the context of GPUs [3], general purpose accelerators beyond GPUs were not explored so far from this perspective. Furthermore, several advanced virtualization features that are crucial on IaaS clouds (such as live migration) are not yet supported. Besides multi-tenancy support, *elasticity* is also an important issue: users cannot dynamically turn on/off accelerators and easily move between general purpose CPUs and accelerators in order to optimize utilization and reach their goals with minimal costs. Thus, it is important to introduce novel abstractions that overcome these limitations and hide the complexity of accelerator management and sharing from the upper layers.

2.2   Provider Heterogeneity

Cloud Service Providers (CSPs) typically have their own Application Programming Interfaces (APIs) that allow customers to deploy and manage their cloud resources. However, users accessing multiple CSPs face the challenge of adapting their applications to a multiplicity of cloud environments with mostly incompatible APIs. Besides this drive, the multi-cloud migration is necessary for backup purposes when a CSP becomes unavailable at a certain point [24]. Moreover, the financial argument is another motivation for approaching the portability challenge as it enables seamless switching between CSPs when economic factors change [10]. Further reasons for using multiple Clouds have been identified in [21].

The Open Cloud Computing Interface (OCCI) [8] initiative aims to circumvent the vendor locks-in problem by engaging with a several initiatives such as SLA@SOI [7] and OpenNebula/OpenStack. The OCCI aims to standardize the RESTful APIs for task management. The standardization was started for the IaaS and now is extensible for SaaS and PaaS. However, OCCI fails to exhibit common platform for vendor APIs to define VM and their operations [14].

The application requirements are currently only partially taken into account in the application deployment and execution phases. By combining the benefits of SLA@SOI [7] and RESERVOIR [23], Metsch et. al. [13] have delivered a framework working with OCCI and providing a proof-of-concept of inter-operation between clouds. For scalable provisioning of resources and services, Buyya et. al. [5] have proposed an architecture for federated cloud environments. Similarly, the Contrail project used a Virtual Execution Platform (VEP) [11] to provide the virtual distribution of the resources and deploy the users applications independently. Enhanced with a proprietary Cloud broker, the mOSAIC project [22] provided an open-source deployable platform as a service that allows code portability between major IaaS providers.

However, the above mentioned approaches do not necessarily take into account the structure of a given application when elastically expanding and contracting resources in a widely distributed environment with heterogeneous resources. Thus, there is a need to *automate elasticity across cloud providers given specific application requirements and fine resource granularity that goes beyond VMs.*

2.3   Automation

Automation is a current challenge which requires to be adopted across cloud computing services, in order to increase efficiency and to facilitate the interaction of users with cloud services. An automation tool should arguably provide full automation with little or no human interaction. Automation solutions such as Chef, Puppet Labs, and CFEngine are currently tested. The Chef configuration management system can be used in order to automate the installation and configuration of the applications. If the OVF format is used, the flexibility is therefore increased and the creation of a specific Chef recipes is not required for each cloud middleware [4].

There are a number of proprietary and open-source commercial tools such as Right-Scale, Amazon's CloudFormation and AutoScaling, SlipStream, Dell Cloud Manager, and Scalr which automate the access, deployment, and/or management of resources. Several research initiatives have been also recently initiated. PANACEA (www.pana-cea-cloud.eu) is currently developing solutions for a proactive autonomic management of cloud resources, based on a set of machine learning techniques and virtualization. CELAR (www.celarcloud.eu) intends to provides automatic resource allocation for applications that activates a right amount of resources based on application demands.

However, the work is still incomplete. Additional features should be made available to the current tools such as: *automated configuration and deployment of applications, automated user management, auto-scaling, automated recovery, automated backup, or automated governance.*

2.4 Ubiquitous Access

The design of a well-structured and optimized access layer is mandatory for a cloud computing platform focused on high demanding data analytics applications. An access layer should be responsible for making the applications available from a wide variety of devices including smart-phones, tablets or workstations, as well as available from the main operative systems. It must not only collect the data needed for the computation (even if the data is stored externally), but also prepare the acquired data and to send it to the computational platform in order to be processed. The way the access layer has to communicate with external data sources depends largely on the data analytics application. In case of the application described in Section 3, the images are collected from healthcare information systems; to do so, clinical information guidelines developed by Integrating the Healthcare Enterprise need to be followed.

Interoperability becomes an important issue when mobile users need to interact and communicate with the cloud. The current interface between mobile users and cloud are mostly based on the web interfaces. The rapid advances in HTML5 have resulted in a much more mobile friendly version of the best-known Web language, which has paved the way for web applications to work on any HTML5-compliant web browser.

Finally, in order to define and implement all the required functionalities of the access layer, a standard language could be used to describe a topology of cloud based web services, their components, relationships, and the processes that manage them. Nowadays one of the most used solutions is the Amazon AWS CloudFormation Template [1], a JSON data standard that allow cloud application administrators to define a collection of related AWS resources. However, platforms such OpenStack that includes Heat orchestrator are migrating from the AWS proprietary solution to a neutral, native Heat Template format/DSL. The Topology and Orchestration Specification for Cloud Applications (TOSCA [19]) is an emerging standard language that includes specifications to describe processes that create or modify web services. TOSCA is expected to interoperate with the upcoming Heat Native DSL. An access layer can use a generic definition of the services architecture based on standard languages such as the TOSCA. This allows the adaptability of the access layer capabilities to fit the requirements of future applications. Moreover, such an approach will allow the reusability of common web services facilitating the easy deployment of new applications.

3   Case Study: Multi-biomarker Profile Imaging

In what follows we describe an case study and in the next section we reveal how an advance of the state-of-the-art is possible.

Problem Description. The next generation of medical imaging will provide patient-specific images relative to the biological-processes underlying the tissues as a non-invasive tool for the diagnosis, prognosis, treatment and follow-up of complex diseases, such as cancer and neurological disorders. The current medical imaging techniques enhance anatomical and functional aspects of the human body in three-dimensional spaces. Nevertheless, the characterization of the underlying biological processes at voxel level requires the combination of complementary biomarker images that enhance different characteristics from the tissues. The typical input of these studies is a 5-dimensional structure for each patient where each voxel has a set of biomarkers' values positioned in a 3D space at a specific moment of a time series. The calculation of multi-biomarker profile images is therefore computational and space-demanding, as it involves several phases over a stack of images from different acquisitions and protocols of the same patient or even of several patients. Each case typically takes more than 900 minutes on a state-of-the-art workstation.

The computation of the multi-biomarker profile images can be divided in five sequential phases: pre-processing, quantification, feature extraction, feature reduction and classification. The pre-processing phase is composed by seven steps that may be applied to each independent image of the study: denoising, inhomogeneity correction, super-resolution, registration, skull strepping and intensity range normalization. This phase can arguably be done concurrently for each image. Next, the quantification step calculated derived biomarkers' images relative to the underlined biological processes of the tissues from the functional images. Those functional images are usually sequences of images, hence, this step can be done concurrently at the acquisition level. After the pre-processing and quantification steps, additional features are extracted from the anatomical images and biomarkers' images. Those features, such as first-order central moments (mean, variance, skewness, and kurtosis), increase the information extracted from the patient. This phase can be parallelized at the image level. After the feature extraction, the number of features for each voxel may be high (e.g. from 20 to 100). Hence, linear and non-linear reduction techniques are applied to obtain a non-redundant representation of the data. This phase can be parallelized at patient level. Afterwards, the supervised or non-supervised classification using structured or unstructured algorithms receive the reduced 5D structure of data to classify each voxel into a biological-relative label. When unsupervised methods are applied, a post-processing step may be required to construct the final biological relative labels. This phase can be done concurrently at patient level.

Expected Benefits and Challenges of Moving to IaaS Clouds. As described above, the computation involves a high degree of parallelism not only per-patient but also from the perspective of handling multiple patients independently in parallel. Thus, moving to a cloud infrastructure has the potential to speed up not only the number of cases that can be handled at the same time, but also each individual case itself. However, such a move is difficult for a domain expert that has limited knowledge about IaaS cloud infrastructures. Specifically, there are several difficulties: (1) how to parallelize the various computational phases and orchestrate the I/O between them for the purpose of speeding up individual cases; (2) how to interleave and pipeline the individual cases together in order to process as many cases in parallel with as little computational and storage resources as possible; (3) how to elastically grow and shrink the computational and storage capability to match the needs of the hospital; (4) how to enforce quality-of-service constraints and priorities (e.g. some cases have tight deadlines). Thus, it is important to come up with a programming model and runtime that focuses on the requirements and the description of the workflow, while hiding all details about parallelization, resource provisioning and elasticity from the domain expert.

4   Towards an Integrated Framework

Figure 1 explains our vision in a nutshell: users write their applications using specialized programming models that enable simple ways to determine and attain goals on parallelism, elasticity, task dependencies, functional requirements, and performance-cost optimization.

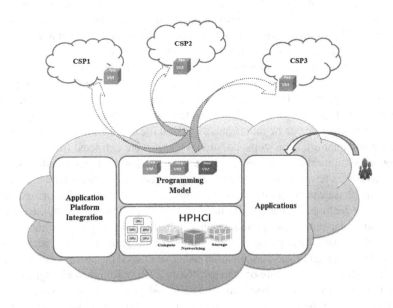

Fig. 1. General schema of the proposed framework

A specialized runtime environment is expected to interpret the user requirements (expressed through the programming models) and automates the provisioning and orchestration of lower-level resources. The key here is to enable autonomic elasticity and data sharing, potentially over multiple clouds, in order to minimize resource usage and cost, whilst preserving functional and non-functional constraints (e.g. performance requirements, SLAs, security etc.). Lower-level resources are exposed by the high performance heterogeneous cloud infrastructure (HPHCI) layer. They include data storage and management services and accelerator-enabled computational capabilities that are specifically designed to deliver high performance at large scale while enabling efficient sharing and transparent elasticity. The programming model runtime and the HPHCI layer integrate into the overall cloud ecosystem through a dedicated application platform integration layer that is responsible to ensure inter-operability through standardized APIs, effectively enabling our approach not only to co-exist with other cloud building blocks and tools, but also to span multiple cloud providers. Furthermore, an additional ubiquitous access layer is responsible to provide easy access and control to jobs to users of the software stack from a variety of devices, both static and mobile.

4.1 High Performance Heterogeneous Cloud Infrastructure

The framework intends to provide cloud infrastructure building blocks. These blocks are specifically targeted at data analytics applications which use advanced programming models in order to take advantage of both the cloud elasticity and the heterogeneous hardware. In this context, we propose several approaches to handle the two directions identified in Section 2.1.

Data Storage and Management. Build a lightweight storage layer that is centred around the idea of "storage neighbourhoods." Such neighbourhoods encompass groups of VMs that share storage resources based on interest, access patterns, resilience, and high availability requirements. The key in this context is that the VMs can help each other out to meet these sharing requirements for tightly coupled application without the need for a heavyweight repository that enables sharing at global level (e.g. parallel file system) while at the same time increasing the scalability and elasticity potential thanks to the focus on locality. Preliminary work [15,16,18,17] undertaken so far shows interesting potential for this avenue.

Access to Accelerators. Introduce virtualization techniques that enable sharing of accelerators between VMs at scale and consolidation in a multi-tenant environment. Similar to the storage neighbourhood concept, VM can cooperate to achieve elasticity and improve the utilization of the CPUs and accelerators by offloading work remotely or migrate on-the-fly as a whole to different physical nodes altogether.

Starting from these two high-priority areas, building higher level data abstractions on top of them specifically designed to enhance the potential of data-intensive applications is essential. In this context, the idea is to enrich raw data with metadata and active storage aspects that optimize the application and the programming model runtime with respect to high level data processing requirements, such as graph analytics or NoSQL.

4.2   Programming Model Runtime

A programming model is needed to enable the user to express functional and non-functional requirements (e.g. performance requirements, SLAs, security) and the provisioning and orchestration of low-level resources.

One important aspect to consider in this context is heterogeneity of multiple clouds and how to avoid vendor lock-in. We propose to create generic deployment templates based on different IaaS providers by deconstructing the complete description regarding an instance running in a standardized form. Based on the OVF, such deployment templates will be based on architectural patterns and forwarded to instantiate the pre-configured virtual machines on the specific IaaS platform. Moreover, the automated installation of applications onto the deployment template will be executed through open-source tools such as Chef cookbooks. Application programmers will not need to know the specifics of different APIs of the underlying IaaS from different vendors. New optimization mechanisms are needed to support transparent elasticity of resources between heterogeneous cloud platforms through the programming model.

Elasticity is intended to provide targeted performance constraints and on-demand provisioning and de-provisioning of cloud resources between heterogeneous cloud platforms, driven by usage policies, availability, and costs. Consequently, the efficiency of deployment and configuration of computationally-demanding and/or data demanding applications across multiple cloud providers will be arguably improved by the automation framework. At current state-of-the-art, the application developers not only need to have expertise in both areas (i.e. application domain and cloud services), but also need to manually implement the complex workflows, a time consuming error prone process. This will allow the realization of a seamless inter-operability in a multi-target environment, which is currently perceived as a drawback of adopting the cloud services.

4.3   Ubiquitous Access

The development and deployment of an access and visualization platform is necessary to allow seamless access to the computational resources of the high-performance heterogeneous cloud infrastructure from a multiplicity of devices. We propose to focus on three main features: (1) the cross-platform compatibility and rich interaction environment, (2) the capability of collecting and preparing the data needed for the computation, even if the data is stored in external data sources, and (3) the capability of interchanging heterogeneous data with the computational resources. In the development and deployment of the seamless access and visualization platform an effort will be done to enhance the reusability of the modules and services developed.

Methodology-wise, an approach as described above is experimental in nature. It systematically leverages a set of standardized, and representative applications, in order to study their access patterns and identify the functional and non-functional limitations and weaknesses to formulate best practices and software products that can be confidently used by industry practitioners and academics. Once we have obtained the desired performance levels, we can build the higher level data abstractions closely aligned to the infrastructure building blocks. Their design will be based on the results and lessons learned from the prototyping, and will include again an iterative improvement phase to make sure desired performance and resource utilization levels are satisfied. Once the higher level data abstractions are complete, they will be integrated into the programming model runtime via standardized APIs and open data formats, integrated vertically to the application which will then be ubiquitously accessible.

4.4 How the Proposed Framework Enhances the Multi-biomarker Use Case

A cloud-based service can be developed to generate multi-biomarker profile images from the combination of a set of anatomical and functional images that can be seamlessly accessed and that agrees with the security constrains of medical information. Specifically, this approach can be applied to perfusion-weighted images to segment the tumoral, peritumoral, and edema regions of primary glioblastoma tumours in biological signatures relative to the aggressiveness of the tumour, such as the neoangiogenesis and microvascular proliferation. The development of this cloud computing technology can provide support in the decision-making to clinical centres, medical image analysis SMEs, and expert radiologists, with independence of their computational capabilities, infrastructures, location and devices. The cloud-based system should provide access to these services through mobile devices and low performance computers optimizing available resources by the institutions involved in this process. The services can be used in a flexible and scalable manner, establishing the necessary resources based on demand. Several alternatives will be implemented for the computer-intensive modules to take advantages of heterogeneous computing infrastructures, such as those composed by CPUs and GPUs. Finally, the use of a cloud-based service allows the easy update of the analysis algorithms and fast inclusion of new features.

5   Conclusions

In this paper we insisted on several challenges that result from the change in the way we reason about large scale scientific and data intensive computations on IaaS clouds, which involves adapting the infrastructure dynamically to the needs of the application in order to satisfy performance requirements while incurring minimal costs. In this context, *automated resource allocation, interoperability, elasticity, performance* and *optimal resource utilization* are key goals that are difficult to achieve with existing approaches, both because of the complexity introduced by specific IaaS aspects (such as multi-tenancy), as well as the fact that previous work was mostly designed to leverage a fixed infrastructure.

To this end, we advocated for a new generation of data storage and management services, accelerator-enabled computational capabilities, parallel pattern-oriented and heterogeneity-agnostic programming models in order to achieve the aforementioned goals in a *transparent* fashion, ultimately enabling users to easily adopt the advantages of IaaS clouds without sacrificing performance, while at the same time enabling cloud providers to maximize infrastructure utilization and introduce competitive targeted offers with reduced costs. We suggested several high priority areas that range from low-level virtualization and storage capabilities to high level abstractions that facilitate ubiquitous access. We believe that the key to enable such high priority areas to best contribute to a new disruptive approach that specifically addresses the needs of large scale scientific and data-intensive applications on IaaS clouds in an efficient fashion is an integrated co-design that guides all software layers according to the unified goals and the feedback from domain-experts that come with real-life use cases.

Acknowledgment. The research of the first author is partially supported by the grant FP7-REGPOT-CT-2011-284595 (HOST).

References

1. Amazon Web Services (AWS), http://aws.amazon.com/
2. Amazon Elastic Block Storage (EBS), http://aws.amazon.com/ebs/
3. Becchi, M., Sajjapongse, K., Graves, I., Procter, A., Ravi, V., Chakradhar, S.: A virtual memory based runtime to support multi-tenancy in clusters with gpus. In: HPDC 2012: Proceedings of the 21st International Symposium on High-Performance Parallel and Distributed Computing, pp. 97–108. ACM, Delft (2012)
4. Boob, S., González-Vélez, H., Popescu, A.: Automated instantiation of heterogeneous Fast Flow CPU/GPU parallel pattern applications in clouds. In: PDP 2014, pp. 162–169. IEEE, Torino (2014)
5. Buyya, R., Ranjan, R., Calheiros, R.N.: InterCloud: Utility-oriented federation of cloud computing environments for scaling of application services. In: Hsu, C.-H., Yang, L.T., Park, J.H., Yeo, S.-S. (eds.) ICA3PP 2010, Part I. LNCS, vol. 6081, pp. 13–31. Springer, Heidelberg (2010)
6. Dong, Y., Yang, X., Li, J., Liao, G., Tian, K., Guan, H.: High performance network virtualization with sr-iov. J. Parallel Distrib. Comput. 72(11), 1471–1480 (2012)
7. Edmonds, A., Metsch, T., Papaspyrou, A., Richardson, A.: Open cloud computing interface: Open community leading cloud standards. ERCIM News 2010(83), 23–24 (2010)
8. Edmonds, A., Metsch, T., Papaspyrou, A., Richardson, A.: Toward an open cloud standard. IEEE Internet Computing 16(4), 15–25 (2012)
9. Expósito, R.R., Taboada, G.L., Ramos, S., Touriño, J., Doallo, R.: Performance analysis of HPC applications in the cloud. Future Generation Computer Systems 29(1), 218–229 (2013)
10. Grozev, N., Buyya, R.: Inter-cloud architectures and application brokering: taxonomy and survey. Software: Practice and Experience 44(3), 369–390 (2014)
11. Harsh, P., Jegou, Y., Cascella, R.G., Morin, C.: Contrail virtual execution platform challenges in being part of a cloud federation. In: Abramowicz, W., Llorente, I.M., Surridge, M., Zisman, A., Vayssière, J. (eds.) ServiceWave 2011. LNCS, vol. 6994, pp. 50–61. Springer, Heidelberg (2011)
12. Hoefler, T., Schneider, T., Lumsdaine, A.: Characterizing the influence of system noise on large-scale applications by simulation. In: SC 2010, pp. 1–11. ACM/IEEE (2010)
13. Metsch, T., Edmonds, A., Bayon, V.: Using cloud standards for interoperability of cloud frameworks. A technical RESERVOIR report (2010)
14. Metsch, T., Edmonds, A., Nyrén, R., Papaspyrou, A.: Open cloud computing interface–core. In: Open Grid Forum, OCCI-WG, Specification Document (2010), http://www.ogf.org/documents/GFD.183.pdf
15. Nicolae, B.: Understanding Vertical Scalability of I/O Virtualization for MapReduce Workloads: Challenges and Opportunities. In: BigDataCloud 2013: 2nd Workshop on Big Data Management in Clouds, Aachen, Germany (2013)

16. Nicolae, B., Rafique, M.M.: Leveraging Collaborative Content Exchange for On-Demand VM Multi-Deployments in IaaS Clouds. In: Wolf, F., Mohr, B., an Mey, D. (eds.) Euro-Par 2013. LNCS, vol. 8097, pp. 305–316. Springer, Heidelberg (2013)
17. Nicolae, B., Riteau, P., Keahey, K.: Bursting the Cloud Data Bubble: Towards Transparent Storage Elasticity in IaaS Clouds. In: IPDPS 2014: Proc. 28th IEEE International Parallel and Distributed Processing Symposium, Phoenix, USA (2014)
18. Nicolae, B., Riteau, P., Keahey, K.: Transparent Throughput Elasticity for IaaS Cloud Storage Using Guest-Side Block-Level Caching. In: UCC 2014: 7th IEEE/ACM International Conference on Utility and Cloud Computing, London, UK (2014)
19. OASIS Open: Topology and orchestration specification for cloud applications version 1.0. OASIS Standard. Version 1.0 (November 2013), http://docs.oasis-open.org/tosca/TOSCA/v1.0/os/TOSCA-v1.0-os.html
20. Ou, W.S., et al.: On implementation of GPU virtualization using PCI pass-through. In: CloudCom 2012, pp. 711–716. IEEE, Taipei (2012)
21. Petcu, D.: Consuming resources and services from multiple clouds. Journal of Grid Computing, 1–25 (in press, 2014), doi:10.1007/s10723-013-9290-3
22. Petcu, D., Martino, B., Venticinque, S., Rak, M., Mahr, T., Lopez, G., Brito, F., Cossu, R., Stopar, M., Sperka, S., Stankovski, V.: Experiences in building a mosaic of clouds. Journal of Cloud Computing: Advances, Systems and Applications 2(1), 12 (2013)
23. Rochwerger, B., et al.: The Reservoir model and architecture for open federated cloud computing. IBM Journal of Research and Development 53(4), 4:1–4:11 (2009)
24. Rodero-Merino, L., Vaquero, L.M., Gil, V., Galán, F., Fontán, J., Montero, R.S., Llorente, I.M.: From infrastructure delivery to service management in clouds. Future Generation Computer Systems 26(8), 1226–1240 (2010)

One Click Cloud Orchestrator: Bringing Complex Applications Effortlessly to the Clouds*

Gabor Kecskemeti, Mark Gergely, Ádám Visegrádi,
Zsolt Nemeth, Jozsef Kovacs, and Péter Kacsuk

Institute for Computer Science and Control, Hungarian Academy of Sciences.
1111 Budapest, Kende u. 13-17, Hungary
kecskemeti.gabor@sztaki.mta.hu

Abstract. Infrastructure cloud systems offer basic functionalities only for managing complex virtual infrastructures. These functionalities demand low-level understanding of applications and their infrastructural needs. Recent research has identified several techniques aimed at enabling the semi-automated management and using applications that span across multiple virtual machines. Even with these efforts however, a truly flexible and end-user oriented approach is missing. This paper presents the One Click Cloud Orchestrator that not only allows higher level of automated infrastructure management than it was possible before, but it also allows end-users to focus on their computational problems instead of the complex cloud infrastructures needed for their execution. To accomplish these goals the paper reveals the novel building blocks of our new orchestrator from the components closely related to infrastructure cloud to the ways virtual infrastructures are modeled. Finally, we show our initial evaluation and study on how the orchestrator fulfills the high level requirements of end-users.

1 Introduction

Infrastructure as a service (IaaS) cloud systems allow automated construction and maintenance of virtual infrastructures [2]. Such infrastructures exploit the concept of virtualization and use virtual machines (VMs) as the smallest building block. Thus, IaaS systems enable the creation, management and destruction of VMs through a convenient and machine accessible API as their core functionalities. Their reliability and the possibility of virtually infinite sized infrastructure of commercial IaaSs lead to their fast adoption and widespread use.

Unfortunately, even with these IaaS functionalities, setting up and using complex virtual infrastructures is the privilege of a few due to several reasons: (*i*) current IaaS APIs barely manage more than single VMs, but (*ii*) even if they do so, they are mostly focused on network management among user controlled VMs.

---

* The research leading to these results has received funding from the European Community's Seventh Framework Programme FP7/2007-2013 under grant agreement no. 608886 (CloudSME)

L. Lopes et al. (Eds.): Euro-Par 2014 Workshops, Part II, LNCS 8806, pp. 38–49, 2014.

Thus, IaaS systems have severely limited applicability because they require deep knowledge of system administration. This highlights the need for techniques capable of automating the creation and management of large-scale applications deployed over potentially thousands of virtual machines without knowing how particular virtual machines or their networking are set up [17].

Recent research answered these needs with the cloud orchestrator concept [3,8] that shifts the center of attention from sole VMs to the required functionalities. To reduce the needed networking knowledge, orchestrators also expect the description of dependencies between the different functional blocks of a large-scale application. Although this description greatly reduces the expertise needed to operate complex infrastructures, there are still several outstanding issues (e.g., VM creation conforming to required functionalities, cross VM or cross-cloud error resilience, autonomous scaling techniques that not only consider application load but other properties – like cost, energy – as well, high level user interfaces).

In this paper, we propose a new orchestrator technique – called the One Click Cloud Orchestrator (OCCO) – that targets these issues with novel approaches. Our technique is based on a virtual machine management technique independent of infrastructures. Next, OCCO encompasses several software delivery approaches from custom and on-the-fly virtual machine construction (e.g., with Chef) to supporting user built virtual machine images that are optimized for a particular purpose. The proposed orchestrator also incorporates a unified infrastructure state model (which allows the system to determine what functionalities are missing or perform below expectations). Finally, on top of these components, OCCO offers customizable techniques for automated infrastructure maintenance (ranging from simple multi-VM infrastructure creation, to highly available and scalable application management).

To reveal OCCO's capabilities, we have investigated several academic use case scenarios that presumably require such advanced orchestrators. We have selected a scenario that is capable to run parametric study based scientific workflow applications in a built-to-order virtual infrastructure. Afterwards, we implemented a prototype system to evaluate the applicability of our findings. We showed that the prototype is capable of hiding the details of the infrastructure and can manage scientific workloads automatically while it also increased the productivity of scientists with no experience in management of computing infrastructure.

The rest of the paper is organized as follows. First, in Section 2, we shortly overview the currently available orchestrator solutions. Afterwards, Section 3 provides a discussion on the architecture devised for our One Click Cloud Orchestrator. Later, we reveal a prototype implementation of the new orchestrator in Section 4. Then, the last section provides a conclusion with our closing thoughts and future plans to enhance our orchestrator.

2   Related Works

One type of orchestration tools covers development and operations aspects. Such tools, also called as configuration management tools, are aimed at automating development and system administration tasks such as delivery, testing and maintenance releases to improve reliability and security but these mechanisms can also perform orchestration activities such as creating, deploying and managing virtual machines. These are well known and are briefly listed here: Saltstack [15], Puppet [14], Chef [4], Docker [7], Juju [16] and Cloudify [5]. These provide lower level, basic functionalities in comparison to OCCO, but OCCO may include some of them in its VM Reshaper (a Chef example is provided in Section 3.)

Beyond these general-purpose utilities there is another category of orchestration tools with specific aims. Liu et al. [11] propose a data-centric approach (Data-centric Management Framework, DMF) to cloud orchestration where cloud resources are modeled as structured data that can be queried by a declarative language, and updated with well-defined transactional semantics. This data centric approach is further advanced by an additional Cloud Orchestration Policy Engine (COPE) in [12]. COPE takes policy specifications (of system wide constraints and goals) and cloud system states and then optimizes compute, storage and network resource allocations within the cloud such that provider operational objectives and customer SLAs can be better met. In contrast to OCCO, this solution is focused on global policies and system-wide optimisation. In other words, it is data-center oriented as opposed to the application centered OCCO.

Dynamic orchestration obviously appear in mobile and volatile environments. Orchestrator [9] is aimed at sensor-rich mobile platforms where it enables multiple, context aware applications that simultaneously run and share highly scarce and dynamic resources. Applications submit high-level context specifications and comply with Orchestrator's resource allocation. Resource selection and binding is postponed until resources' availability is sufficiently explored. The major innovation of Orchestrator, the notion of active resource use orchestration, is explored in [10]. Where resource needs are decoupled from the actual binding to physical resources and can be changed dynamically at runtime. Opposed to passive resource use orchestration, where the resource needs are programmed in the application, this approach provides adaptivity via demand based, selective use of alternative plans for application requests. Merwe at al. define a Cloud Control Architecture for a ubiquitous cloud computing infrastructure [6]. The Cloud Control Architecture has a layered design where orchestration is in a separate layer and connects the Service Abstraction (presents service logic to users) and Intelligence (gathers information about the cloud infrastructure) and derives abstract knowledge. The Orchestration layer collects both the requests from Service Abstraction and actual data from Intelligence and makes decision about initial placements, resource allocation, resource adjustment and movement of resources. In all these approaches the key idea is to provide fair resource provisioning in a limited and competitive environment, which is not the case for OCCO.

Lorincz et al. present a very different way or resource orchestration in Pixie: resource tickets [13]. A ticket is an abstraction for a certain part (capacity) of a resource and all orchestration actions are mediated via the tickets. Tickets are generated by resource allocators and managed by resource brokers. A ticket provides information about the resource, the allocated capacity and the timeframe.

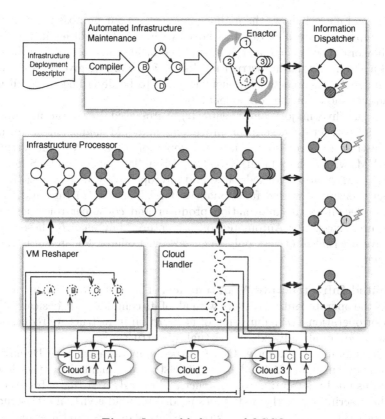

Fig. 1. Internal behavior of OCCO

Resources can be manipulated by operations on tickets such as join (increasing resource capacity), split (sharing), revoke or redeem (collecting specific tickets for a certain operation) just to mention a few. This approach also decouples actual resources from resource requests and gives a great flexibility in planning, advance requests and adaptation. The ticketing scheme provides a logic control of resource orchestration. Due to the entirely different approach, such global coordination is not applicable in OCCO.

3   Architecture

3.1   The View of an Infrastructure Maintainer

This sub-section reveals the internal components of our architecture and how these components interact to automatically operate a virtual infrastructure described by an infrastructure maintainer. In the scope of this paper, the term *infrastructure maintainer* refers to those users of OCCO who have the capabilities to describe a virtual infrastructure and its expected behavior. To understand the design considerations of OCCO and the required knowledge of infrastructure maintainers, Figure 1 shows the main components of our proposed orchestrator. These components are illustrated as boxes with gray boundaries in the figure. The behavior of each component is exemplified inside the box through the operation of a simple virtual infrastructure. In the following we give an overview of the components, then each component is going to be described in detail using the examples shown in the component's boxes.

OCCO has five major components: (*i*) Automated Infrastructure Maintenance – infrastructure descriptor processing and VM management initiator; (*ii*) Infrastructure Processor – internal depiction of a virtual infrastructure (groups VMs with a shared aim); (*iii*) Cloud Handler – abstracts IaaS functionality (e.g., VM creation) for federated and interoperable use of clouds; (*iv*) VM Reshaper – ensures awaited functionalities for VMs; and (*v*) Information Dispatchor – decouples the information producer and consumer roles across the architecture. Except for Automated Infrastructure Maintenance, these compo nents have internal interfaces only (e.g., not even offered for an infrastructure maintainer).

Automated Infrastructure Maintenance. This component is the only one that sees the operated infrastructure with all of its complexity. It basically allows two major operations: (*i*) submission of new virtual infrastructure requests and (*ii*) destruction of already existing virtual infrastructures.

For the submission interface, OCCO expects an Infrastructure Deployment Descriptor as an input. Defined by an infrastructure maintainer, the descriptor contains vital information to construct and operate a virtual infrastructure. First, the descriptor lists the node types needed to build a virtual infrastructure (in Figure 1 types, such as an Apache server, are shown as capital letters in the range of $A–D$). Then, it specifies the functional dependencies (that also imply ordering) between these types of nodes (*directed edges* between nodes in the figure). These dependencies allow the Automated Infrastructure Maintenance component to determine which node types need to be instantiated first – in cases when there is a loop in the dependency graph, the infrastructure maintainer should specify node types that could be deployed earlier than others. Finally, the descriptor also includes rules for error resolution (e.g., what to do when nodes are failing, under- or over-provisioned).

After the submission interface receives the descriptor, it is immediately *compiled* into an internal representation (in Figure 1 shown as a white graph with annotated node types). In case of compilation failure immediate feedback is provided to the infrastructure maintainer allowing easy development and debugging of deployment descriptors. On the other hand, successful compilation leads to the enactment of the virtual infrastructure.

The *enactor* subcomponent is the fundamental component within the orchestrator. During infrastructure construction, the enactor pushes node requests to the Infrastructure Processor in the sequence determined by dependencies (the figure shows this sequence as numbers in the nodes within the enactor). After the sequence is pushed and the requested infrastructure is created, the enactor continuously monitors the state of the infrastructure to detect errors and resolve them according to the rules specified in the descriptor. As an example, rules could define the necessary actions – like node re-instantiation, dependency re-evaluation – when a particular kind of node becomes inaccessible. Such error resilience is exemplified through the node type D (in Figure 1 step 4 is a faulty node and step 5 re-instantiates it). The rules also allow the scaling of the de- scribed virtual infrastructure. Scaling rules define the number of necessary node instances depending on the state of the virtual infrastructure, expressed as a function of some properties of a node type (e.g., the CPU load of all instances of a node) or time (e.g., on workdays we need more resources than on holidays). Scaling is exemplified in Figure 1 with the node type C (see the multi instance node configuration behind step 3). It is easy to conceive that such simple condi- tion – action rules may easily lead to unstable or oscillating states. The enactor eradicates this behavior via complex rules, i.e. ones that involve some global parameters in their conditions such as "stop asking for more instances unless some time has passed since last changing the number of instances".

The enactor maintains the virtual infrastructure completely autonomously unless a change is needed in the Infrastructure Deployment Descriptor. In such case, first, the infrastructure maintainer updates the descriptor, and then the Automated Infrastructure Maintenance component compiles a new internal rep- resentation and finally, the enactor switches to a transitional mode. In this mode, the enactor checks the differences between the old and the new internal repre- sentation. If it finds new error resolution rules only, then the enactor ensures the infrastructure's conformance with them (e.g., if a new scaling rule needs fewer instances for the same load then the excess instances are terminated via the Infrastructure Processor) and it returns to normal operation. If the evaluation finds new node types and dependencies also, then the currently operated virtual infrastructure is restructured according to the new deployment descriptor.

Finally, one can order the destruction of a virtual infrastructure. During de- struction, the enactor pushes node destruction requests for previously created nodes to the Infrastructure Processor. The request order is reversed compared to node creation so every node can use its dependencies during its existence.

Infrastructure Processor. OCCO creates an abstraction for virtual infras- tructures with this component. As discussed before, the Infrastructure Processor receives node creation or destruction requests from the enactor. When the first creation request is received for a virtual infrastructure, this component prepares an *administrative group* for the future virtual infrastructure. Nodes of the virtual infrastructure can share information between each other through this administra- tive group (e.g., allowing newly created nodes to retrieve the dynamic properties – like IP addresses – of existing ones). Depending on the underlying systems uti- lized by the implementation these administrative groups can be mapped to lower level concepts (e.g., if Chef is used behind the VM Reshaper component, then administrative groups can be implemented through Chef's `environments`).

Node creation requests are processed as follows. First, the processor ensures that the VM Reshaper knows the node type that is going to be instantiated. Fol- lowing the example above, if Chef is behind the VM Reshaper, then the processor checks for the presence of the type's recipe. If the recipe is not present, then the processor pushes the recipe of the type to the reshaper. The pushed recipe could be retrieved either from another Chef server or from the extended node type definition of the Infrastructure Deployment Descriptor. Once the reshaper knows the node type, the Infrastructure Processor sends a contextualized VM request to the Cloud Handler component. Within the contextualization information the processor places a reference to the previously created administrative group and the expected node type of the future VM. Figure 1 exemplifies processed requests for creation with gray shaded circles. The example shows various stages of a virtual infrastructure's operation (from the initial phases on the left, to the final developments in the right side of the Infrastructure Processor's box). These stages show how an infrastructure is constructed and how it is adopted to errors and problematic situations identified by the enactor.

In contrast to node creation, *node destruction* requests are directly sent to the Cloud Handler. If the last node is destructed in a virtual infrastructure then the Infrastructure Processor also destroys its administrative group automatically.

Cloud Handler. As its basic functionality, this component provides an abstraction over IaaS functionalities and allows the creation, monitoring and destruction of virtual machines. For these functionalities, it offers a plugin architecture that can be implemented with several IaaS interfaces (currently we aim at supporting at least OCCI and EC2 interfaces). These plugins are expected to serve all concurrently available requests as soon as they can manage. To increase the throughput and flexibility of the deployed virtual infrastructure, the Cloud Handler also offers VM scheduling across multiple clouds. If this functionality is used, cloud selection criteria can be either specified by the infrastructure maintainer – e.g., as a guideline – or by the user who initiated the virtual infrastructure. The Cloud Handler always expects some selection criteria for each VM (e.g., a static cloud mapping has to be specified in every deployment descriptor).

Our example in Figure 1 shows VM requests arriving at the handler, ordered bottom-up (first at the bottom, last at the top, parallel requests side by side). Cloud to VM request association is shown as arrows between requests and clouds. At the end of arrows, little squares represent the actual VMs created in the clouds. Each VM shows its contextualized node type with gray letters (A–D).

VM Reshaper. This component manages the deployed software and its configuration on the node level. This functionality is well developed and even commercial tools are available to the public. Our VM Reshaper component therefore offers interfaces to these widely available tools – e.g., [4, 5, 7, 14, 15]. These software tools use their proprietary node type definitions (e.g., so called `recipes` in Chef and `manifests` in Puppet). The VM Reshaper allows the reuse of these proprietary definitions for node types already described, even if stored at external – but accessible – locations (thus, regular node type definitions are just references to these proprietary definitions). On the other hand, new node types can be defined in the infrastructure deployment descriptor in the extended node type definition. The form of these definitions allows the Infrastructure Processor to select a VM

Reshaper with matching node management tools behind (e.g., in case a recipe is given as an extended node type definition then Chef will be the tool used). It is expected that advanced infrastructure maintainers could create such node type definitions for custom applications.

Returning to our example in Figure 1, node type definitions are presented as dotted circles within the VM Reshaper. With arrows between the VMs and type definitions, the figure also shows how VMs contact the VM Reshaper to retrieve and apply node type definitions. These activities ensure the presence and correct configuration of the software components needed VMs to fulfill their role.

Information Dispatcher. In order to make accurate decisions based on the state of the ordered virtual infrastructure, our proposed architecture has a common interface to reach the diverse information sources from which the state can be composed. In order to reduce redundancy and structural bottlenecks, requests to our dispatcher component are directly forwarded to relevant information sources. The minimal processing done inside the dispatcher is limited to two activities: (i) request transformation and (ii) information aggregation. For the first activity, the dispatcher transforms the – sometimes abstract or conceptual – requests to the actual information pieces accessible from the various components and underlying clouds of the OCCO (e.g., request for node D load can be translated to the CPU utilization of the VM hosted in Cloud 1 or Cloud 3 in Figure 1). The second activity happens when the dispatcher receives requests to information that is available only as a composite. In such cases, the dispatcher forwards the request to all relevant OCCO components and if necessary to the virtual infrastructure. Upon receiving their response, the dispatcher calculates an aggregated value of the responses and presents this as a response to the original request. For example, using our running example of Figure 1, a request for node C load will be computed as an average of the CPU utilization of all VMs hosting node type C in Cloud 2 and 3. In OCCO, generic transformation and aggregation rules can be specified by the deployer of the Information Dispatcher while specific rules for the particular kind of virtual infrastructure are given in the Infrastructure Deployment Descriptor by the infrastructure maintainer.

In Figure 1, within the box of Information Dispatcher, we show by three scenarios how querying this component can help with understanding the state of the operating virtual infrastructure. We expect that the enactor regularly queries the dispatcher. In the top graph within the dispatcher's box, we see that a query to the dispatcher is sent to check the availability of each node in the virtual infrastructure. This query is then forwarded to all participating virtual machines. Unfortunately, in this scenario, the dispatcher is not receiving node D's response, thus it is reported unavailable (represented as striped circle D). As this would render the virtual infrastructure unusable, the enactor will immediately request a new node for type D through the Infrastructure Processor. Similarly, in the middle two graphs we see requests for load of node type C. When a single VM performs this type, the dispatcher transforms this request to CPU load request on that VM. If the load is too high (shown with an exclamation mark in the respective node of the figure) and it is expected that a single VM

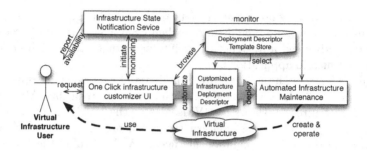

Fig. 2. User's relation to OCCO

cannot handle the anticipated load, the enactor will increase the node count for type C. This will make later requests to the dispatcher as composite. In the third graph it is also shown that even a composite request reports unmanageably high loads and thus the enactor will again increase the node count of type C.

3.2   The View of a Virtual Infrastructure User

After infrastructure maintainers complete an infrastructure deployment descriptor, they can publish it in OCCO's template store. The published infrastructure templates are going to be available for regular cloud users with the need of deploying complex but easily maintainable virtual infrastructures. Figure 2 reveals the interfaces and the use case OCCO offers for these regular users.

The figure shows that regular users are expected to interface with OCCO through a graphical user interface that allows browsing and customizing deployment descriptors. This interface supports the user in the selection of the appropriate kind of virtual infrastructure based on textual descriptions accompanied with templates in the store. Once a template is selected, users receive a list of customization options that were added as hints for the GUI in the deployment descriptor by the infrastructure maintainer. These hints could range from the supported IaaS providers to the possibility to specify an initial size of the custom infrastructure, but hints could also include pricing and cost allowances.

When the customization is done, users can request the deployment of their virtual infrastructure via the GUI. After the request is made, the monitoring of the requested infrastructure is initiated at the notification service. This service has two purposes: (i) let the user know when the requested infrastructure is completely available and (ii) monitor the changes – introduced by the infrastructure maintainer – of the deployment template and propagate them to the Automated Infrastructure Maintenance component. The first purpose allows users to immediately use the prepared infrastructure when it is ready. The notification service can trigger automated actions (so the user's application can react to infrastructure availability immediately) or it can also send emails to interested parties. The second purpose ensures that infrastructures are updated transparently to their latest, most secure and stable versions the particular maintainer can produce.

4 Evaluation

In order to test the concept of the new orchestrator, to perform analysis of the internal operation and to provide a demonstration platform, we have implemented a prototype of OCCO. It is currently limited to a single Infrastructure Deployment Descriptor template, and it is publicly available[1] for users.

The infrastructure template is aimed at providing a distributed computing infrastructure (DCI) with a science gateway attached as a front-end. The DCI is implemented by a BOINC [1] based Desktop Grid project with a molecular docking simulator called autodock. As an extra functionality, the BOINC project is associated with a public IP address, therefore the user can attach his/her own BOINC client to the server. Using automatically deployed and configured BOINC clients in virtual machines, computational resources are automatically attached to this BOINC project. Our descriptor template allows the customization of the number of computational resources. Computing jobs arrive to the BOINC project as work units with the help of the WS-PGRADE/gUSE science gateway (also automatically deployed as a node of the virtual infrastructure). Overall, the prototype shows how a complete gateway plus DCI with resources can be deployed by OCCO and how the components attach to each other. Detailed description of a similar infrastructure is shown at http://doc.desktopgrid.hu/doku.php?id=scenario:unidg with a different application.

In the prototype's welcome- and request submission page (see Figure 3) the user is requested to fill in the list of customization options, and he/she also must provide some details for identification and justifying the use of the infrastructure. After a request is submitted, the prototype first asks for approval by the SZTAKI cloud administrators (due to local regulations) then initiates the infrastructure's creation with the Automated Infrastructure Maintenance component. Once the infrastructure is created the notification service generates an email with all the authentication and access details to the new infrastructure (e.g., url of the science gateway and of the BOINC project plus user/password for login). With these details, users just need to login to the gateway, submit a prepared autodock workflow with their inputs and inspect the operation (i.e. how the jobs are flowing through the infrastructure and processed by the BOINC clients). To prevent SZTAKI's IaaS from overloading, virtual infrastructures created by OCCO have a limited lifetime. Our notification service sends an email to the infrastrucure's user before the shutdown procedure is initiated.

As the aim of the prototype implementation is to demonstrate and test the OCCO concept, we implemented the most crucial components with basic functionalities only. The current Automated Infrastructure Maintenance component provides virtual infrastructure creation and termination facilities only. The simple VM Reshaper can handle prepared VM images with pre-installed applications and expects these applications to be configurable through IaaS contextualization methods. Our Cloud Handler is already capable to support multiple IaaS clouds as long as they offer EC2 interfaces.

---

[1] http://desktopgrid.hu/oc-public

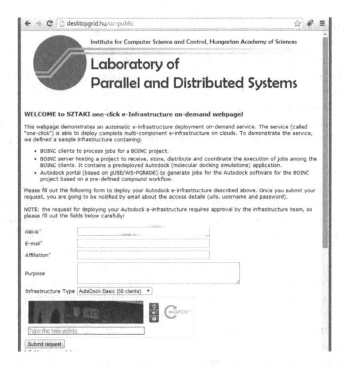

Fig. 3. Request submission page of the OCCO prototype

5   Conclusions and Future Work

Through the analysis of this paper we have found several issues with currently existing scientific and commercial cloud orchestrators. Namely, recent solutions lack support to functionality oriented VM creation, error resilience across VMs or even clouds and high level user orientation with such advanced but hidden features like automatic scaling of entire virtual infrastructures. To remedy these issues, we have proposed the OCCO architecture that builds on the strengths of past solutions (e.g. Chef). We have shown the behavior of OCCO from the point of view of both a regular cloud user and also a maintainer of the virtual infrastructure template. In the discussions we have shown the way maintainers can describe virtual infrastructures. Finally, we have presented our initial prototype implementation of the architecture which already shows the high potential of the architecture and available as a public service for the scientific community with access to the SZTAKI cloud infrastructure.

Other than implementing a more complete and openly downloadable version of OCCO, we also identified several future research areas. First, error resilience and scaling are only based on simple reactive rules, in the future we plan to incorporate proactive approaches combined with learning techniques. Next, decisions on cloud use are made on a per VM request basis. However, in some cases (e.g. expected significant network activities between particular nodes), it would be beneficial to make decisions considering more information about the operating virtual infrastructure. Finally, we are planning to increase the reliability and failure handling of the internal components by introducing atomic operations and cross-component transactions.

References

[1] Anderson, D.P.: Boinc: A system for public-resource computing and storage. In: Proceedings of the 5th International Workshop on Grid Computing (GRID 2004), Pittsburgh, PA, USA, pp. 4–10. IEEE Computer Society (November 2004)

[2] Bhardwaj, S., Jain, L., Jain, S.: Cloud computing: A study of infrastructure as a service (iaas). International Journal of engineering and information Technology 2(1), 60–63 (2010)

[3] Caballer, M., Blanquer, I., Molto, G., de Alfonso, C.: Dynamic management of virtual infrastructures. Journal of Grid Computing, 1–18 (2014), doi:10.1007/s10723-014-9296-5

[4] Chef, http://www.getchef.com/

[5] Cloudify, http://www.cloudifysource.org/.

[6] Van der Merwe, J., Ramakrishnan, K., Fairchild, M., Flavel, A., Houle, J., Lagar-Cavilla, H.A., Mulligan, J.: Towards a ubiquitous cloud computing infrastructure. In: Proceedings of the IEEE Workshop on Local and Metropolitan Area Networks, LANMAN (2010)

[7] Docker, https://www.docker.io/.

[8] Dukaric, R., Juric, M.B.: Towards a unified taxonomy and architecture of cloud frameworks. Future Generation Comp. Sys. 29(5), 1196–1210 (2013)

[9] Kang, S., et al.: Orchestrator: An active resource orchestration framework for mobile context monitoring in sensor-rich mobile environments. In: IEEE International Conference on Pervasive Computing and Communications (2010)

[10] Lee, Y., Min, C., Ju, Y., Kang, S., Rhee, Y., Song, J.: An active resource orchestration framework for pan-scale sensor-rich environments. IEEE Transactions on Mobile Computing 13(3) (2014)

[11] Liu, C., et al.: Cloud resource orchestration: A data-centric approach. In: Proceedings of the Biennial Conference on Innovative Data Systems Research, CIDR (2011)

[12] Liu, C., Loo, B.T., Mao, Y.: Declarative automated cloud resource orchestration. In: 2nd ACM Symposium on Cloud Computing (2011)

[13] Lorincz, K., Chen, B.-R., Waterman, J., Werner-Allen, G., Welsh, M.: Resource aware programming in the pixie os. In: SenSys, pp. 211–224 (2008)

[14] Puppet, http://puppetlabs.com/.

[15] SaltStack, http://www.saltstack.com/.

[16] Ubuntu. Juju, http://juju.ubuntu.com.

[17] Wettinger, J., Behrendt, M., Binz, T., Breitenbücher, U., Breiter, G., Leymann, F., Moser, S., Schwertle, I., Spatzier, T.: Integrating configuration management with model-driven cloud management based on tosca. In: 3rd International Conference on Cloud Computing and Service Science, pp. 437–446 (2013)

Towards Autonomous Data Sharing
Across Personal Clouds

Roland Tornyai[1] and Attila Kertesz[1,2]

[1] University of Szeged, Department of Software Engineering
H-6720 Szeged, Dugonics ter 13, Hungary
tornyai.roland@gmail.com
[2] MTA SZTAKI Computer and Automation Research Institute
H-1518 Budapest, P.O. Box 63, Hungary
kertesz.attila@sztaki.mta.hu

Abstract. Cloud Computing has reached a maturity state and high
level of popularity that various Cloud services have become a part of our
lives. Mobile devices also benefit from Cloud services: the huge data users
produce with these devices are continuously posted to online services,
which may require the use of several Cloud providers at the same time
to efficiently store these data. Using Cloud-based storage services such
as Personal Clouds for these purposes are free for certain amount of
data; therefore uniting these separate storages can provide a suitable
solution for these user needs. In this paper we propose a novel solution
for autonomous data management among Personal Clouds. Our approach
applies a continuous monitoring component to track the performance of
the managed Cloud providers, and based on this measured historical
information it manages user data across the interconnected providers in
an autonomous way.

1 Introduction

Nowadays Cloud Computing has reached a maturity state and high level of
popularity that various Cloud services have become a part of our lives. These
services are offered at different Cloud deployment models ranging from the lowest
infrastructure level to the highest software or application level. Within Infrastructure as a Service (IaaS) solutions we can differentiate public, private, hybrid
and community Clouds according to recent reports of standardization bodies [8].
The previous two types may utilize more than one Cloud system, which is also
called as a Cloud federation [9]. One of the open issues of such federations is the
interoperable management of data among the participating systems. Another
popular family of Cloud services is called Cloud storage services or Personal
Clouds. With the help of such solutions, user data can be stored in a remote
location, in the Cloud, and can be accessed from anywhere. Mobile devices can
also benefit from these Cloud services: the enormous data users produce with
these devices are continuously posted to online services, which may require the
use of several Cloud providers at the same time to efficiently store and retrieve

L. Lopes et al. (Eds.): Euro-Par 2014 Workshops, Part II, LNCS 8806, pp. 50–61, 2014.

these data. The aim of our research is to develop a solution that unites and manages separate Personal Clouds in an autonomous way to provide a suitable solution for these user needs.

In this paper we address the open issue of data interoperability in Clouds, and propose a novel solution for interoperable personal data management in storage Clouds. Our approach applies a continuous monitoring component to track the performance of the managed Cloud providers, and based on this measured historical information it manages user data across the interconnected providers in an autonomous way. Therefore the main contributions of this paper are: (i) envisioning a solution for autonomous data management among Personal Clouds, (ii) the development of an application that is able to measure the performance of the interconnected providers and use this information to distribute user data among them, and (iii) the evaluation of our proposed approach with four providers.

The remainder of this paper is as follows: Section 3 presents an overview of the addressed Cloud storage providers and introduces our motivation for this work; Section 4 describes our approach for autonomous data management and presents our proposed application. Finally, Section 5 discusses the performed evaluations, and the contributions are summarized in Section 6.

2   Related Works

Regarding related works, the need for data interoperability and the extensive use of Cloud storage services have been identified by various research and expert groups (eg. [8,5,1]). Managing user data in the Cloud also raises privacy issues [10,6] that need to be taken into account during data processing. Nevertheless in this paper we refrain from legal issues and focus on interoperability problems. Dillon et. al [2] gathered several interoperability issues that need to be considered in Cloud research, and named a new category called Data Storage as a Service to draw attention to the problem of data management in Clouds.

Drago et al. [3] have already analysed the usage of Dropbox on the Internet, and showed that it is the most popular provider of Cloud-based storage services. They presented an extensive characterization of Dropbox in terms of system workload and typical usage scenarios. They concluded that the performance of Dropbox is highly impacted by the distance between the clients and datacenters. They also identified a variety of user behaviours, e.g. taking full advantage of its functionalities by actively storing and retrieving files. In a later work [4] they continued this investigation for comparing 5 providers. Their results showed that all considered provider services suffer from some limitations, and in some scenarios the upload of the same set of files can take much more time, so they also acknowledged performance differences among these providers.

Garcia-Tinedo et al. [7] have also addressed performance issues of Personal Clouds. They developed a tool for actively measuring three providers: Dropbox, Box.com and SugarSync. They performed measurements for two months with various data transfer load models to search for interdependency among data sizes, transfer quality and speed. They published their measurement data and concluded that these providers have different service levels, and they often limit the speed of downloading. This work also served as a motivation for our research, but we decided to develop a more lightweight and easily extendible measuring tool to support our further research goal of autonomous data sharing among these providers.

3   An Approach for Autonomous Data Management among Personal Clouds

Besides IaaS Cloud solutions the largest amount of user provided data are stored at Cloud storage services also called as Personal Clouds [8,5]. Their popularity is accounted for easy access and sharing through various interfaces and devices, synchronization, version control and backup functionalities. The freemium nature [11] of these services maintain a growing user community, and their high number of users also implies the development of other higher level services that make use of their cloud functionalities. To overcome the limits of freely granted storage, users may sign up to services of different providers, and distribute their data manually among them, which situation leads to a provider selection problem – see Figure 1. In this situation tracking the amount and location of the already uploaded files and splitting larger files can be a difficult task for everyday users, which leads to the problem of Cloud provider selection – not to mention their different capabilities concerning data transfer speeds. These facts serve as a motivation for our research, and the main goal of this work is to propose a higher level service that helps users to better manage their data by providing automated access to a unified storage over these Clouds.

In this paper we addressed four providers, namely Dropbox [15], Google Drive [14], SugarSync [17] and Box.com [18]. Their main properties are shown in Table 1. The foundation of Dropbox is originated in a problem we still face nowadays.

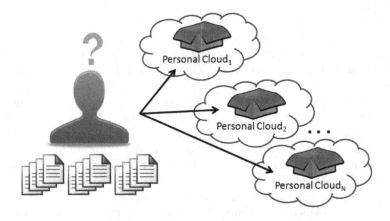

Fig. 1. Cloud provider selection problem

Drew Houston, one of the founders of the company, kept on leaving his pen-drive at home during attending courses at MIT. Since he used several computers simultaneously, he had to email necessary files to stay updated at all devices, which he got tired of soon. Hence no suitable online data sharing solution existed by that time, he invented one. In 2007 he founded Dropbox Inc, and their service was kicked off in 2008. By 2011 it reached 14% market share by having 50 million registered users. According to the latest figures, this number exceeded 200 million in 2013 [16]. Its freemium model grants 2 GBs storage for a new registration that can be extended up to 8 GBs by inviting others or performing certain tasks. Concerning the main properties of the service, it is written in Python, supports version control, and applies the so called "delta encoding" technique, which only uploads the newly changed parts of a previously uploaded file. It supports a wide range of APIs and has several SDKs, as shown in Table 1.

Google Drive is a Personal Cloud solution of Google. It was initiated in 2012, but it has several predecessors such as Google Docs since 2006. It also serves as an in-house data store for several other Google services, therefore it provides 15 GBs freely for a new user. Thanks to the coupled services of Google, its web interface is capable of previewing numerous file formats in a browser. SugarSync was launched in 2009, but its predecessor Sharpcast Photos dates back to 2006. It provided 5 GBs free storage for a newly registered user till December 2013, when the owners announced to close freemium services till February 2014. Since then its free service is only valid for 30 days trial period. Box.com was founded as a startup company in 2005. Since 2010 it has a built-in file preview functionality. It provides 10 GBs of free storage for a new user.

Table 1. The main properties of the managed providers

Provider	Initial Storage (GB)	Bonus (GB)	Max. Storage (GB)	Supported OS	Mobile Platforms
Google Drive [14]	15	-	15	Win, Mac	iOS, Android
Dropbox [15]	2	0.5	8	Win, Mac, Linux	iOS, Android
SugarSync [17]	5	-	5	Win, Mac	iOS, Android
Box.com [18]	10	-	10	Win, Mac	iOS, Android

Provider	Version Control	Encryption	Num. of devices	API	SDK
Google Drive [14]	+	-	-	+	Java, Python, PHP, .NET, Ruby
Dropbox [15]	+	+	-	+	iOS, Android, Python, Ruby, Java, OS X
SugarSync [17]	+	+	1	+	Java
Box.com [18]	+	+	-	+	iOS, Android, Python, Ruby, Win, Java, C#

4   The Proposed Solution

Now that we have stated our motivation and introduced the considered Cloud providers in the previous section, we describe our proposed solution shown in Figure 2.

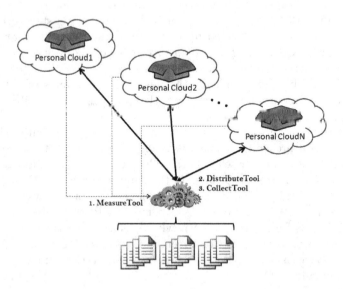

Fig. 2. The proposed solution

Our approach is demonstrated with an application written in Java, which uses the OAuth [12] standard to authenticate users. By using this protocol, client tools can act on behalf of certain users to access certain files without knowing their passwords, they use so called tokens instead with limited lifetime. Its version 2.0 is the latest since 2012. It is only a framework not a clearly defined protocol so it can be regarded as a guideline, therefore different providers have slightly different implementations. The application consists of three components:

- the MeasureTool component for performing monitoring processes,
- the DistributeTool component for splitting and distributing files,
- and the CollectTool component for retrieving splitted parts of a required file.

4.1   The MeasureTool Component

This component implements three basic functions: connecting to a user account at a certain provider, uploading and downloading certain files to and from the storage of this account. It has a plugin-based structure to separate methods for different providers and to enable further provider support.

A monitoring process for measuring the performance of a provider consists of generating a file of a predefined size with randomized content, uploading this file to the provider's storage under a given user account, then downloading this file back to the host of the application. The monitoring results and the measured performance data for the mentioned providers are shown and discussed later in Section 5.

4.2   The DistributeTool Component

The main task of this component is to apply certain policies for splitting up and packaging files to be distributed among the participating Cloud providers in an efficient way.

The file to be uploaded to the providers' storages is first split to a predefined number of files, what we call chunks, with equal sizes (large files are also supported, since only parts of a file are in memory at a time using buffering). The second step decides where to upload these file chunks. Once it has been determined and a chunk is uploaded, the DistributeTool component stores chunk identifiers (e.g. name, user token, file ID) to a local meta-data cache file. By using this meta-data file, the CollectTool component can later fetch the required chunk files from the different providers.

The provider selection in the second step is made upon the information gathered by the MeasureTool component. Historical performance values are also stored and taken into account, and it is the role of the application administrator to set the relevance (i.e. ratio) of historical and latest performance results for provider selection. The measured performance values are converted to the following format (denoting percentage shares – the sum of these values represent 100%) taking into account the aggregated historical performance values (h), the latest performance values (l) and their ratio (r) by evaluating ($h + l * r$), e.g.:

$$\{ \text{"googledrive"} : 5392, \text{"dropbox"} : 1615, \text{"box"} : 1085, \text{"sugarsync"} : 292 \}$$

According to these configuration numbers, the DistributeTool component takes the sum of these values (sum) and generates a random number independently drawn from the range $\{0, sum\}$ for each chunk by using Gaussian distribution. The given number will determine the provider to be used for the actual chunk (e.g. the randomly generated number 4537 denotes Google Drive, while 7509 selects Box.com according to the example above ($5392 + 1615 + 502$)). This selection criteria can be easily expanded later if needed, e.g. incorporating the experienced number of failures during the measurements. Our further goal is to support scenarios, where not only freemium storages are considered. In this way provider selection could be optimized by payment minimization.

4.3   The CollectTool Component

As mentioned in the previous subsection, this component is able to collect the previously uploaded user files from the Cloud providers by using the meta-data

description file. Once the chunks of a required file are retrieved, they are unified
with an optimized buffering technique.

5   Evaluation

We have performed our evaluations on a private IaaS Cloud based on Open-
Nebula. It has been developed by a national project called SZTAKI Cloud [13],
which was initiated in 2012 to perform research in Clouds, and to create an
institutional Cloud infrastructure for the Computer and Automation Research
Institute of the Hungarian Academy of Sciences. Since 2013 it operates in experimental state, and since 2014 it is in production state available for all researchers
associated with the institute. It runs OpenNebula 4.4 with KVM, and controls
over 440 CPU cores, 1790 GBs of RAM, 66 TBs shared and 35 TBs local storage
for serving an average of 250 Virtual Machines (VM) per day for the last month.

The application consisting of the previously discussed components has been
deployed in a VM started at SZTAKI Cloud. The evaluation architecture is
depicted in Figure 3.

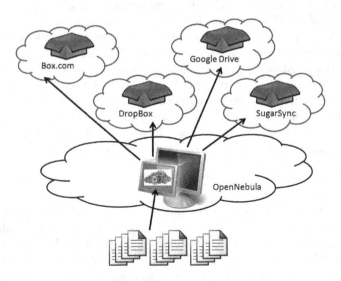

Fig. 3. Evaluation architecture

5.1   MeasureTool Evaluation

For users, the most important metric for measuring provider performance is the
data transfer speed. Therefore we used this metric to monitor the providers, and
to use as a base for autonomous file sharing. To perform an evaluation of the
MeasureTool component, we up- and downloaded files to each Personal Cloud
with the following data sizes: 5, 10, 50 and 100 MBs, considering the following

scenarios: (i) transferring two 5 MBs file or a 10 MBs file, (ii) transferring five 10 MBs file or a 50 MBs file, and (iii) transferring ten 10 MBs file or a 100 MBs file.

In this way we arrived to 6 different cases, and we could also measure data transfer performance for handling many small and few big files. We went through all cases systematically, and performed the same measurements several times (at least 5 for each case). Once the limit of the freemium storage of a provider got exceeded, we halted the measurement and deleted all files on that storage to start following tests. We performed the same measurements on different periods of a week, i.e. on weekdays and at weekends. For measuring failures, we omitted failed transactions caused by server-side errors. Finally, the measured time taken to upload and download the files incorporates the writing of the files to the storage discs at the providers' side (in case of Google Drive we could have omitted this interval, if we wanted to).

In the following diagrams we show the experienced performance values and provide a discussion on these results. Figure 4 shows detailed values concerning average, minimal and maximal transfer speeds. From these results we can see that Google Drive has the best performance values followed by Dropbox and Box.com, while SugarSync has the worst values, which is further acknowledged by detailed results shown in Figure 5.

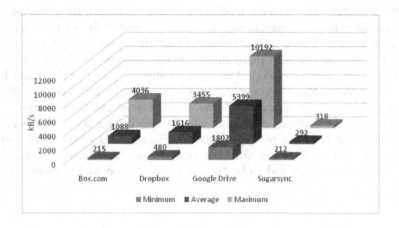

Fig. 4. Measured speed of the utilized Cloud providers

While the difference between Google Drive and SugarSync is obvious, it is not easy to compare Box.com and Dropbox. As this figure suggests, many small files are better handled by Dropbox, while bigger files are transferred faster by Box.com. It is also an interesting observation that transfer speeds are accelerating for larger files. This is caused by the fact that during transferring a small file the connection won't "speed-up" in time, but for bigger files it can utilize most of the available bandwidth. As mentioned before, the evaluation has been

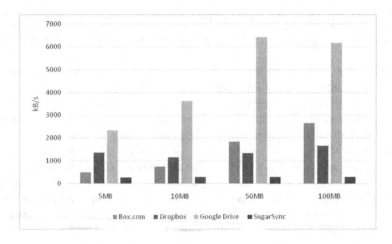

Fig. 5. Speed of providers for different amount of data

performed at different days of a week, but we experienced no major differences in these cases.

Table 2 depicts the amount of data transferred to and from the utilized providers. Of course, the same cases have been executed for all providers, the differences among them lies in transaction restarts caused by failures or storage limit exceeding (though "delta encoding" and similar techniques could save some amount of data transfers). The total amount of data moved to and from these providers for the whole evaluation was more than 100 GBs by utilizing freemium storages. Regarding reliability of the considered Cloud services, we also measured the number of failures experienced during up- and downloading the files. For Box.com we experienced a relatively high number of failures by downloading big files resulted in abortion of the transactions. On the other hand, SugarSync was proved to be the most reliable provider without a single failure.

Table 2. Data movements (in MBs) by Personal Cloud providers

Provider	Num. of Transactions	Num. of Failures	Uploaded	Downloaded	Sum
Google Drive [14]	1072	4	12100	12090	24190
Dropbox [15]	1106	8	11800	11800	23600
SugarSync [17]	567	0	4420	4415	8835
Box.com [18]	1014	120	14520	6570	21090

5.2 Data Distribution Evaluation

Based on the results of the evaluation of the MeasureTool component, our initial hypothesis that service quality levels differ for various Cloud providers has been proven. Now we continue with the evaluation of our proposed autonomous file distribution solution.

In Section 4 we have introduced how the DistributeTool component works for a sample configuration based on aggregated historical performance values, latest performance values and their predefined ratio. In this subsection we evaluate the performance of our proposed application with 4 different configurations (i.e. $r = 0, 0.1, 0.5, 0.9$) for user data distribution for the same set of files represented by the 6 cases introduced in the previous section, spread over the interconnected Personal Clouds. The computed values for these configurations are depicted in Figure 6.

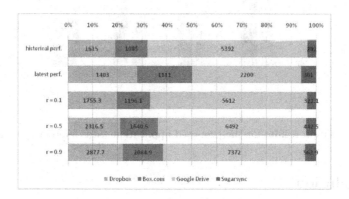

Fig. 6. Configurations for data distribution

During these measurements the DistributeTool component performed the splitting and packaging of the user files, selecting providers for the created file chunks based on the performance values and configurations, and uploading the files to these providers. The retrieval of the files was performed by the CollectTool component by using the meta-data description file created by the DistributeTool component. The average transfer speeds during the evaluation for the considered providers is shown in Figure 7 – which correlates to the ones gathered in the previous subsection. Furthermore we can also observe that transfer speeds achieved by our application by utilizing all providers are faster than single utilization of three providers (only Google Drive performs better alone).

The final evaluation results for the different configurations are shown in Figure 8. As we can see on this diagram, slight modifications on the ratio of historical and latest performance values (e.g. changing r from 0 to 0.1) do not imply big differences, but relying more on the latest performance values (i.e. using $r = 0.5$) results in faster uploading times for the overall user data.

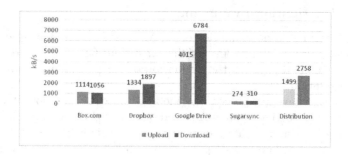

Fig. 7. The measured speed of Cloud providers during the evaluation

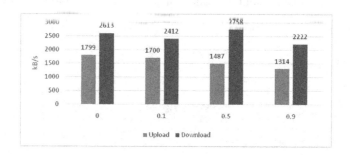

Fig. 8. Evaluation results for the proposed application with different configurations

6   Conclusion

The enormous data users produce with mobile devices are continuously posted to online services, may require the use of several Cloud storage providers at the same time to efficiently store and retrieve these data. The aim of our research in this paper was to develop a solution that unites and manages separate Personal Clouds in an autonomous way to provide a suitable solution for these needs. We have introduced our proposed application consisting of three components responsible for monitoring providers, managing and distributing user data to these providers, and retrieving user files in an autonomic way. Finally we evaluated our approach by utilizing four real Cloud providers, and concluded that our solution is capable of managing user data in a unified storage over these providers in an autonomous way, and still provides a good performance as well.

Our future work aims at further examining the configuration capabilities of our proposed application, and extending it with other service quality metrics, and investigating replication mechanism to eliminate dependability, and incorporate additional provider plugins to widen provider support.

Acknowledgment. The research leading to these results has received funding from the CloudSME FP7 project under grant agreement 608886.

References

1. Bozman, J.: Cloud Computing: The Need for Portability and Interoperability. IDC Executive Insights (August 2010)
2. Dillon, T., Wu, C., Chang, E.: Cloud Computing: Issues and Challenges. In: Proc. of the 24th IEEE International Conference on Advanced Information Networking and Applications, pp. 27–33 (2010)
3. Drago, I., Mellia, M., Munafo, M.M., Sperotto, A., Sadre, R., Pras, A.: Inside Dropbox: Understanding Personal Cloud Storage Services. In: Proceedings of the 2012 ACM Conference on Internet Measurement Conference (IMC 2012), pp. 481–494. ACM, New York (2012)
4. Drago, I., Bocchi, E., Mellia, M., Slatman, H., Pras, A.: Benchmarking personal cloud storage. In: Proceedings of the 2013 Conference on Internet Measurement Conference (IMC 2013), pp. 205–212. ACM, New York (2013)
5. Fraunhofer Institute for Secure Information Technology. On THE Security of Cloud Storage Services, SIT Technical reports (March 2012), http://www.sit.fraunhofer.de/content/dam/sit/en/documents/Cloud-Storage-Security_a4.pdf
6. Gagliardi, F., Muscella, S.: Cloud Computing – Data Confidentiality and Interoperability Challenges. In: Cloud Computing. Computer Communications and Networks, pp. 257–270. Springer, London (2010)
7. Garcia-Tinedo, R., Sanchez-Artigas, M., Moreno-Martinez, A., Cotes, C., Garcia-Lopez, P.: Actively Measuring Personal Cloud Storage. In: The 6th IEEE International Conference on Cloud Computing (Cloud 2013), pp. 301–308 (2013)
8. Jeffery, K., Neidecker-Lutz, B.: The Future of Cloud Computing, Opportunities for European Cloud Computing beyond 2010. Expert Group Report (January 2010)
9. Kertesz, A.: Characterizing Cloud Federation Approaches. In: Mahmood, Z. (ed.) Cloud Computing - Challenges, Limitations and R&D Solutions. Springer Series on Computer Communications and Networks (accepted in 2014)
10. Kertesz, A., Varadi, S.: Legal Aspects of Data Protection in Cloud Federations. In: Nepal, S., Pathan, M. (eds.) Security, Privacy and Trust in Cloud Systems. Springer, Signals & Communication, pp. 433–455 (2014)
11. Wikipedia, Freemium (2014), http://en.wikipedia.org/wiki/Freemium
12. Wikipedia, OAuth (April 2014), http://en.wikipedia.org/wiki/Oauth
13. The SZTAKI Cloud project website (May 2014), http://cloud.sztaki.hu/en/home
14. Google Drive (May 2014), https://drive.google.com/
15. Dropbox (May 2014), https://www.dropbox.com/
16. Wikipedia – Dropbox (April 2014), http://en.wikipedia.org/wiki/Dropbox_%28service%29
17. SugarSync (May 2014), https://www.sugarsync.com/
18. Box.com (May 2014), https://www.box.com/

Privacy-Preserving Search in Data Clouds Using Normalized Homomorphic Encryption

Mohanad Dawoud[1] and D. Turgay Altilar[2]

Department of Computer Engineering, Istanbul Technical University, Istanbul, Turkey
{dawoud,altilar}@itu.edu.tr

Abstract. By the rapid growth of computer systems, many IT applications that rely on cloud computing have appeared; one of these systems is the data retrieval systems, which need to satisfy various requirements such as the privacy of the data in the cloud. There are many proposed Privacy-Preserving search (PPS) techniques that uses homomorphic encryption to process the data after encryption, but these techniques did not take into account the possibility of repetition of some values of the features table (especially zero), even after the encryption, which makes them vulnerable to frequency attacks. On the other hand, the non-inclusion of these values may lead to the ability to infer some statistical information about the data. In this paper, we took the advantages of homomorphic encryption to encrypt the data as well as preventing any ability to infer any kind of information about the data by normalizing the histogram of the features table while maintaining the quality of the retrieval. The results showed that the proposed technique gave better retrieval efficiency than the previously proposed techniques while preventing frequency attacks.

Keywords: data clouds, security, homomorphic encryption, normalization, frequency attacks, data retrieval.

1 Introduction

Recently, and with the quick production of the enterprise systems and the need for competition with highly supported and resource-allocated systems, clouds became essential in the IT industry. Cloud was defined by Buyya in [2] as a type of parallel and distributed system consisting of a collection of interconnected and virtualized computers that are dynamically provisioned and presented as one or more unified computing resources based on service-level agreements established through negotiation between the service provider and consumers. By this way, any new or small system can has the same capabilities of the resources (computing, storage, etc) as the enterprise systems in a cheap and scalable way, also the enterprise systems can benefit from the clouds by increasing capacity or adding capabilities, by pay-per-use service, according to their current needs. Nowadays, there are many platforms for the cloud computing that are opened for the users, such as Amazon's EC2, IBM's Smart Business cloud offerings, Microsoft's Azure and Google's AppEngine. Rad et al. surveyed many platforms

L. Lopes et al. (Eds.): Euro-Par 2014 Workshops, Part II, LNCS 8806, pp. 62–72, 2014.

by comparing their arrangements, foundation and infrastructure services and their main capabilities used in some leading software companies [10]. To realize the cloud, many requirements should be satisfied as shown by Dikaiakos in [4], suitable software/hardware architecture, data management, cloud interoperability, security, privacy, service provisioning and cloud economics are the main requirements; these requirements can be extended into many more specific requirements. Despite the advantages of using clouds and the ability to reduce costs and to improve the productivity, security issues should be handled carefully; they may inhibit wide adoption of the cloud model [1]. Jansen and Grance provided an overview of the security and privacy challenges pertinent to public cloud computing, they pointed out considerations that organizations should consider when they outsource their data, applications and infrastructure to a public cloud environment [7]. According to Zhang et al. [15], the security and integrity of the cloud images are the foundation of the overall security of the cloud. One of the new security related research problems is the Privacy-Preserving Search (PPS) over encrypted data. The importance of this problem comes from being the cloud server untrusted or curious. Fig. 1 shows a simple model of data cloud comprising of three actors: Data Owner, Cloud Server (or simply Cloud) and Client. The Owner is the one who has a large set of data to be searched, she encrypt the data and outsource it with the querying services to the Cloud, the Cloud is responsible of storing and processing the data, while the Client will query the data stored in the cloud using the trapdoors that are given by the Owner, therefore, the following requirements need to be satisfied to achieve the Privacy-Preserving search in such a model:

1. Neither the cloud nor the data owner is allowed to know or to be able to deduce anything about the client's queries.
2. The cloud should process the client's queries.

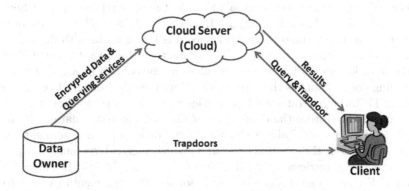

Fig. 1. A simple Model of Data Clouds

Gopal and Singh [5] proposed a technique for Privacy-Preserving search that uses Gentry's Fully Homomorphic encryption [13]. The technique uses the Homomorphic encryption to encrypt the number of occurrences of each keyword in the documents (by the owner) and the query (by clients) using the same key, so, if the cloud does not know the key, it will do calculations using the encrypted data and query without being able to know what they mean. Cao et al. [3] proposed a multi-keyword ranked search technique. The idea depends on encrypting these vectors by some operations that includes adding dummy keywords, splitting of the vectors and multiplication by the key (the key consists of one vector and two matrices). On the other side, the client will also apply the same operations (with some changes) on the query vector using the same key before sending it to the cloud, which in turn processes the encrypted vectors (the query and index) to generate the similarity vector. Li et al. [9] proposed a technique for fuzzy keyword search over encrypted data; In this technique, the data owner builds an index by constructing a fuzzy keyword set then computing trapdoor set with a secret key shared between data owner and authorized users, the data owner sends this index to the cloud. To search in the dataset, the authorized user computes the trapdoor set for the query keyword using the same secret key shared between her and the data owner then sends it to the cloud. Upon receiving the search request, the cloud compares them with the index table and returns all the possible encrypted file identifiers according to fuzzy keyword definition explained in their paper. For such techniques, deterministic encryption is needed to give the right matches.

2   Problem Statement

In data mining, Term Frequency (TF) table is used to get feature vectors for the documents (especially text documents). In this paper, we consider a dataset D consists of N documents where $D=(d_1, d_2, ..., d_N)$, and the set of all the ID's of these documents is $ID=(id_1, id_2, ..., id_N)$, the total number of the unique keywords in the entire documents is M, therefore, the set of all the unique keywords is $W=(w_1, w_2, ..., w_M)$. For a TF table, the rows represents ID while the columns represents W, so, $\text{TF}=[\ x_{n,m} \mid 1{\leq}n{\leq}N \text{ and } 1{\leq}m{\leq}M]$, the value of $x_{n,m}$ represents how many times the m'th keyword is found in the n'th document. If the value of an entity $x_{n,m}$ is zero, this means that the n'th document doesn't has the m'th keyword, also, any equal values in one column means that the corresponding documents has the same keyword with equal number of occurrences. Creating TF table generates a lot of entities with zero value; to show that, stopwords are removed from the documents of the "uw-can-data" dataset [6] using three lists of stopwords, Table 1 shows that the ratio of the non-zero entities to the zero entities in the TF table is 1.41%, which means large number of zeros in the table. For retrieval efficiency, Term Frequency–Inverse Document Frequency (TF-IDF) table [11] is used. Also, for security, these entities need to be encrypted. In most efficient Privacy-Preserving Search techniques, the entities of the comparable parts of the index need to be encrypted individually, therefore,

Table 1. Statistics of the keywords in the "uw-can-data" dataset

The total number of keywords in the documents	The total number of different keywords in the documents	The number of non-zero's in the table	The number of zero's in the table	The ratio of the non-zero's to the zero's in the table (non-zeros/ zero's)
91923	21014	91923	6506473	1.413%

if the encryption has to be deterministic, the values in the TF-IDF table will be mapped to new values in the encrypted TF-IDF table, which means a new table with the same statistics but different values, this make the dataset vulnerable to frequency analysis attacks, whatever the value that appears with largest number of times in the encrypted TF-IDF table, it will be considered to represent the zero's in the TF table. During this paper we will call this "zero's attack".

2.1 Zero's Attack

The matrix multiplication, as in Cao et al. [3] technique, may handle the zero's attack problem since each element in the vector will depend on the other elements in the same vector and the corresponding vector in the key matrix, so, elements with zero or high frequently occurred values will have different values after encryption according to the randomness of the key. But, this is not the case with the techniques similar to Gopal et al. [5] since the entities of the features table is encrypted using the same key. Also, for techniques similar to Li et al. [9], where the encrypted keywords are compared to find the matches, it will need the similar keywords before encryption keep similar after encryption which makes it vulnerable to frequency analysis attacks. Therefore the proposed technique has to be developed to prevent this frequency analysis attacks keeping in mind not to affect the properties of homomorphic encryption and the retrieval efficiency.

2.2 Relations between Documents

Technique to be developed should not allow the cloud to deduce any relation between documents from the encrypted index. Including only the keywords with values greater than zero can also give an idea about which keywords are not found in specific documents, which can be considered as threat as in [9] where the index consists of the unique keywords and the document ID's for only the documents that include each of these keywords.

2.3 Retrieval Efficiency

Data retrieval quality depends on many different factors; one of these factors is the way of choosing feature vectors for the documents. According to [12], binary term vectors give lower efficiency than weighted term vectors. Note that Cao used the binary vectors while Gopal used the weighted vectors in their techniques.

3 Suggested Technique

As mentioned before, Cao et al. [3] can hide zero's and high frequently occurred values. However, because of using the binary vectors (beside the dummy keywords), the retrieval efficiency will be lower than weighted term vector algorithms. Therefore, Gopal technique [13] has to be improved to be able to handle the three issues mentioned in Section 2. With reference to Fig. 1, the suggested model is working as follows:

1. Data owner creates the TF table; the keywords in this table are hashed.
2. The names of the documents and the documents themselves are encrypted separately using symmetric or asymmetric key (K_s).
3. TF-IDF is created from the TF table.
4. TF-IDF table is normalized using the technique which will be explained later in this section.
5. The entities of the normalized TF-IDF table are encrypted individually using homomorphic encryption with the same key (K_h), the encrypted TF-IDF table is the index that will be outsourced to the cloud (encrypted data & querying services).
6. K_h and K_s are sent from the data owner to the client (the trapdoors).
7. The client applies the same operations on the query using K_h before sending it to the cloud.
8. The cloud calculates the similarity between the query and the documents using operations on the encrypted data without revealing them.
9. The similarity vector is sent to the client to decrypt it using K_h and find the best matches to be retrieved.
10. The client sent the names to the cloud and the cloud sends the encrypted file that will be decrypted by the client using the secret key K_s.

Prior to explaining the suggested normalizing technique, the need of including zero's as well as hiding these zero's and highly frequented values have to be discussed. Assume that:

1. $Keyword_1$ found in documents 1, 3 and 8 for 5, 12 and 6 times respectively.
2. $Keyword_2$ found in documents 1, 3 and 9 for 3, 1 and 13 times respectively.
3. $Keyword_3$ found in documents 4, 5 and 10 for 7, 9 and 2 times respectively.

Even the keywords, document names and frequencies are encrypted; one can end up with some deductions such as:

1. Document 1 and document 3 are related (contain two common keywords)
2. Document 8 and document 4 are not related (have no common keywords)
3. Document 1 does not contain $Keyword_3$

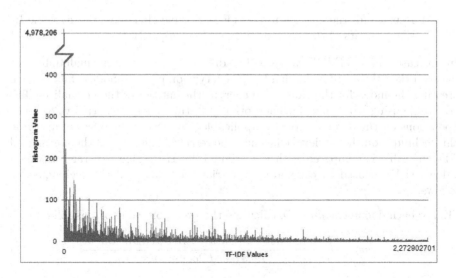

Fig. 2. Histogram for the TF-IDF table of uw-can-data dataset

Even though such a simple example, it is seen that including zeros is necessary to prevent such deductions. Fig. 2 shows the histogram for the TF-IDF table of uw-can-data dataset [6], some TF-IDF values have frequencies more than others, which can be considered as indicators to them in the frequency analysis attacks even after encryption. So, the goal is to normalize these values before encrypting them.

Consider the number of the unique values in the TF-IDF table is Q, then $U = (u_1, u_2, ..., u_Q)$ where U is the set of unique values in the TF-IDF table, in this case, the histogram will be $H = (h_1, h_2, ..., h_Q)$ where h_q represents the number of times that u_q appeared in the TF-IDF table for $1 \leq q \leq Q$. To normalize these values, the following steps are done:

1. Order U increasingly in $V = (v_1, v_2, ..., v_Q)$. Values of H will be ordered corresponding to V in $HV = (hv_1, hv_2, ..., hv_Q)$.
2. For each $v_q \in V$, calculate $e_q = (v_{q+1} - v_q)/(hv_q \times k)$, where k is scaling factor that determines the size of difference between the original value and the normalized values (will be discussed later in Section 4). For e_Q, minimum e_q value is taken to be its value.
3. For each $v_q \in V$:

    (a) Define $S_q = hv_q - 1$

    (b) Generate new set $v_q' = (v_q'_0, v_q'_1, ..., v_q'_{S_q})$ where $0 \leq s \leq S_q$ as follows:

    – For $s = 0$ to (S_q)

        • $v_q'_s = v_q + s \times e_q$

(c) Replace all the entities in the TF-IDF table that have the v_q value by the elements of the v_q' randomly without repetition.

In this case all the TF-IDF values will be different. Also, even in small difference between the values will be hidden by the encryption process. So, the final step in creating the index for the cloud is to encrypt the entities of the normalized TF-IDF table using Homomorphic encryption [13]; this hides the actual values, but operations on these values are still applicable. To discuss the effect of applying this technique on the retrieval efficiency, the retrieval efficiency of the normalized TF-IDF table is compared with the original TF-IDF table. Average precision value (APV) is used to calculate the retrieval efficiency of the techniques as follows:

1. For each document $d_n \in n$, calculate the precision value pr_n as follows:

$$pr_n = \frac{RetrievedDocuments \cap RelatedDocuments}{RetrievedDocuments} \tag{1}$$

Where the number of retrieved documents is equal to the size of the cluster containing the document d_n in the original dataset

2. Calculate the APV as follows:

$$APV = \frac{\sum\limits_{n} pr_n}{Number of Documents} \tag{2}$$

4 Simulations and Results

In order to test the suggested technique, we used three different datasets: uw-can-data [6], mini-classicdocs [14] and mini-20newsgroups [8]. Table 2 shows some details about these three datasets. The datasets are prepared before being used by the following steps:

1. html documents are parsed using htmlparser-1.6 to extract the data from them.
2. Stopwords are removed using three different lists of stopwords: Long list, Short list and Google list.
3. Porter stemmer is used to stem the keywords.
4. The datasets are classified using k-means classification with cosine similarity distance.

Using the normalization technique will make all the histogram values of the normalized TF-IDF table equal one. The number of different numbers of the TF-IDF table will be equal to: number of unique keywords × number of documents To know the effect of normalization on the retrieval efficiency, different values of the factor k are used. As mentioned before, the factor k determines the size of the difference between the original value (v_q) and the expanded set of values (v_q') in the normalization process. The technique was applied on the uw-can-data, mini-20newsgroups and mini-classicdocs datasets separately as follows:

- For $z=1$ to 10000 increasing by 5:
  - Calculate $APV_z=$ the APV where $k=z$.
  - Calculate $AV=$ Average of APV_z over all z values.

Table 2. Details of the three datasets (uw-can-data, mini-20newsgroups and mini-classicdocs) used in the evaluation of the suggested technique

Dataset	Number of Documents	Number of Classes	Description
uw-can-data	314	10	web pages from various web sites at the University of Waterloo, and some Canadian websites
mini-20newsgroups	400	20	20 Newsgroups data set is a collection of approximately 20,000 newsgroup documents, partitioned (nearly) evenly across 20 different newsgroups, the number of documents is minimized to 400 documents with the same number of classes
mini-20newsgroups	800	10	Consists of 4 different document collections: CACM, CISI, CRAN, and MED. the number of documents is minimized to 800 documents clustered in 10 classes

Table 3 shows the APV's using the original TF-IDF tables (without normalization) for the three datasets in the first column, which is the case in Gopal et al. [5] technique. The second column represents the APV's for the binary term tables also for the three datasets, which is the case in Cao et al. [3] technique, Finally, the third column represents the average APV's (AV's) for the normalized TF-IDF tables with $k = 1$ to 10000 increased by 5 for the three datasets, which is the case in the suggested technique in this paper.

5   Analysis

The effectiveness of proposed technique is discussed in this section with regard to the results given in Section 4.

Table 3. Comparison between normalized and unnormalized TF-IDF tables according to *AVP* and *AV* values

Dataset	APV without normalization (Gopal Technique)	APV With binary term tables (Cao Technique)	AV value for the normalized TF-IDF tables
uw-can-data	0.175935689	0.150279841	0.183681939
mini-20newsgroups	0.110836309	0.101195467	0,114799958
mini-20newsgroups	0.110236005	0.107274797	0.111710287

Table 4. Comparison between the three discussed techniques

Problem	Gopal Technique	Cao Technique	Suggested Technique
Hiding Zero's	Doesn't hide Zero's	Hides zero's	Hides zero's
Relations Between Documents	Can be deduced	Hard to deduce	Hard to deduce
Retrieval Efficiency	Higher than Cao	Lower than Gopal	Higher than both

5.1 The Effects of the Used Normalization on Privacy

Using normalization gave different values with the same number of appearance in the TF-IDF table which prevents any kind of frequency attacks (discussed in 2.1 and 2.2 subsections). Although the difference between the values may be small before encryption, the Homomorphic encryption will map them to different values.

5.2 The Effects of the Normalization on Retrieval Efficiency

Results show that the retrieval efficiency does not decrease after normalization of the TF-IDF tables. As shown in Table 3, the average of the *APV*'s (*AV*) after normalization are higher than the precision values before normalization for the three datasets.

5.3 The Effects of this Technique on the Time and Memory Costs

Time cost: The normalization technique will be done once in the setup of the system (which is offline process), all the steps can be done using parallel processors, ordering the histogram increasingly according to the TF-IDF values is O(n log$n$) for n unique keywords. Memory cost: Storing the different values after normalization will be: (number of unique keywords × number of documents × size of each unit). Table 4 summarizes the comparison between the two discussed techniques with the proposed technique with regard to the first three problems have been introduced in Section 2.

6   Conclusion

We started with three problems: Zero's attack, hiding relations between documents and conserving retrieval efficiency. We proposed a technique that normalizes the TF-IDF tables; this technique hides the large number of zeros (or any highly frequented values) in the tables as well as any other relation between documents since it keeps the zeros. The technique was applied on three different datasets; results show that the technique improves the retrieval efficiency even with small values. The next step is to find a technique to retrieve only the chosen documents without giving any information about them to both the client and the cloud, or in the case of sending the similarity vector to the client, she will not be able to know anything about the unchosen documents, the technique should also prevent the cloud from guessing any relation between the document lists and the previous queries on the same dataset; this technique should integrate with the suggested technique in this paper to satisfy the needs of a "Privacy-Preserving Search in Data Clouds"

References

1. Armbrust, M., Fox, A., Griffith, R., Joseph, A.D., Katz, R., Konwinski, A., Lee, G., Patterson, D.A., Rabkin, A., Stoica, I., Zaharia, M.: Above the clouds: A berkeley view of cloud computing (February 2009)
2. Buyya, R.: Market-oriented cloud computing: Vision, hype, and reality of delivering computing as the 5th utility. In: 9th IEEE/ACM International Symposium on Cluster Computing and the Grid, CCGRID 2009, p. 1 (May 2009)
3. Cao, N., Wang, C., Li, M., Ren, K., Lou, W.: Privacy-preserving multi-keyword ranked search over encrypted cloud data. IEEE Transactions on Parallel and Distributed Systems 25(1), 222–233 (2014)
4. Dikaiakos, M.D., Katsaros, D., Mehra, P., Pallis, G., Vakali, A.: Cloud computing: Distributed internet computing for it and scientific research. IEEE Internet Computing 13(5), 10–13 (2009)
5. Gopal, G.N., Singh, M.P.: Secure similarity based document retrieval system in cloud. In: 2012 International Conference on Data Science Engineering (ICDSE), pp. 154–159 (July 2012)
6. Hammouda, K., Kamel, M.: Web mining data - uw-can-dataset (June 2013), http://pami.uwaterloo.ca/~hammouda/webdata
7. Jansen, W., Grance, T.: Sp 800-144. guidelines on security and privacy in public cloud computing. Technical report, Gaithersburg, MD, United States (2011)
8. Lang, K.: Newsweeder: Learning to filter netnews. In: Proceedings of the Twelfth International Conference on Machine Learning, pp. 331–339 (1995)
9. Li, J., Wang, Q., Wang, C., Cao, N., Ren, K., Lou, W.: Fuzzy keyword search over encrypted data in cloud computing. In: 2010 Proceedings IEEE INFOCOM, pp. 1–5 (March 2010)
10. Pastaki Rad, M., Sajedi Badashian, A., Meydanipour, G., Ashurzad Delcheh, M., Alipour, M., Afzali, H.: A survey of cloud platforms and their future. In: Gervasi, O., Taniar, D., Murgante, B., Laganà, A., Mun, Y., Gavrilova, M.L. (eds.) ICCSA 2009, Part I. LNCS, vol. 5592, pp. 788–796. Springer, Heidelberg (2009)

11. Rajaraman, A., Ullman, J.D.: Data Mining: Mining of Massive Datasets. Cambridge University Press (November 2011) Number 978-1107015357
12. Salton, G., Buckley, C.: Term-weighting approaches in automatic text retrieval. In: Information Processing and Management, pp. 513–523 (1988)
13. van Dijk, M., Gentry, C., Halevi, S., Vaikuntanathan, V.: Fully homomorphic encryption over the integers. In: Gilbert, H. (ed.) EUROCRYPT 2010. LNCS, vol. 6110, pp. 24–43. Springer, Heidelberg (2010)
14. Volkan, T.: Data mining research - classic3 and classic4 datasets (January 2012), http://www.dataminingresearch.com/index.php/2010/09/classic3-classic4-datasets
15. Wei, J., Zhang, X., Ammons, G., Bala, V., Ning, P.: Managing security of virtual machine images in a cloud environment. In: Proceedings of the 2009 ACM Workshop on Cloud Computing Security, CCSW 2009, pp. 91–96. ACM, New York (2009)

Integrated Management of IaaS Resources

Fernando Meireles[1,2] and Benedita Malheiro[1,2]

[1] School of Engineering, Polytechnic Institute of Porto, Porto, Portugal
[2] INESC TEC, Porto, Portugal
{fmdms,mbm}@isep.ipp.pt

Abstract. This paper proposes and reports the development of an open
source solution for the integrated management of Infrastructure as a Service (IaaS) cloud computing resources, through the use of a common API
taxonomy, to incorporate open source and proprietary platforms. This
research included two surveys on open source IaaS platforms (OpenNebula, OpenStack and CloudStack) and a proprietary platform (Parallels
Automation for Cloud Infrastructure - PACI) as well as on IaaS abstraction solutions (jClouds, Libcloud and Deltacloud), followed by a thorough
comparison to determine the best approach. The adopted implementation reuses the Apache Deltacloud open source abstraction framework,
which relies on the development of software driver modules to interface
with different IaaS platforms, and involved the development of a new
Deltacloud driver for PACI. The resulting interoperable solution successfully incorporates OpenNebula, OpenStack (reuses pre-existing drivers)
and PACI (includes the developed Deltacloud PACI driver) nodes and
provides a Web dashboard and a Representational State Transfer (REST)
interface library. The results of the exchanged data payload and time
response tests performed are presented and discussed. The conclusions
show that open source abstraction tools like Deltacloud allow the modular and integrated management of IaaS platforms (open source and proprietary), introduce relevant time and negligible data overheads and, as
a result, can be adopted by Small and Medium-sized Enterprise (SME)
cloud providers to circumvent the vendor lock-in problem whenever service response time is not critical.

Keywords: IaaS, Deltacloud PACI Driver, Multiple IaaS Interoperable
Management.

1 Introduction

The provisioning of the Infrastructure as a Service (IaaS) concept, initiated by
the Elastic Compute Cloud (EC2) [1] as part of Amazon Web Services (AWS)
[2], was rapidly adopted by other well-known technology enterprises with large
computing resources, that launched their own IaaS platforms. As a result, the
Research & Development (R&D) community as well as the involved enterprises
concentrated efforts on the development of new IaaS platforms. However, since
Cloud Computing was a recent concept, lacking pre-defined standards and a con-
sensual definition, the resulting platforms were highly heterogeneous in terms of

L. Lopes et al. (Eds.): Euro-Par 2014 Workshops, Part II, LNCS 8806, pp. 73–84, 2014.
© Springer International Publishing Switzerland 2014

functionalities, architecture and interface libraries. This diversity hinders the selection of an IaaS platform and, above all, constitutes an obstacle to the interoperability among cloud service providers.

To overcome this problem, this paper proposes and presents an open source solution that promotes the interoperability and standardization between heterogeneous IaaS platforms. This work involved the research, proposal and development of an interoperable open source solution with standard interfaces (both Web and application programming interfaces) for the integrated management of IaaS cloud computing resources based on new as well as existing abstraction libraries or frameworks. The research consisted of two surveys covering existing open source and a proprietary IaaS platforms as well as open source IaaS abstraction solutions.

The approach proposed and adopted, which was supported on the conclusions of the carried surveys, reuses an existing open source abstraction solution - the Apache Deltacloud framework [3]. Deltacloud relies on the development of software driver modules to interface with different IaaS platforms, officially provides and supports drivers to sixteen IaaS platform, including OpenNebula and OpenStack, and allows the development of new provider drivers. The latter functionality was used to develop a new Deltacloud driver for PACI. Furthermore, Deltacloud provides a Web dashboard and REpresentational State Transfer (REST) API interfaces. To evaluate the adopted solution, a test bed integrating OpenNebula, OpenStack and PACI nodes was assembled, deployed and the time response and data payload via the Deltacloud framework and via direct IaaS platform API calls was measured. The Deltacloud framework behaved as expected, i.e., introduced additional delays, but no substantial overheads. The Web and the REST interfaces produced identical results.

The developed interoperable solution for the seamless integration and provision of IaaS resources from PACI, OpenNebula and OpenStack IaaS platforms fulfils the specified requirements, i.e., enables IaaS cloud providers to expand the range of adopted IaaS platforms and offers a Web dashboard and REST API for integrated management. The contributions of this work include the surveys and comparisons made, the selection of the abstraction framework and, last, but not the least, the PACI driver developed.

2   IaaS Platforms

The IaaS platforms surveyed include the OpenNebula [4], OpenStack [5] and CloudStack [6] open source frameworks and the PACI [7] proprietary solution.

OpenNebula is the only European IaaS platform studied. This platform manages virtual resources from public and hybrid clouds. It presents a layered architecture, which enables the centralised management of data-centres, and provides a detailed level of customization. At the top of the stack, it exposes multiple API to communicate with AWS EC2 [1] and the OpenGrid Forum (OGF) Open Cloud Computing Interface (OCCI) solutions [8][9].

OpenStack is a highly dynamic platform, presenting several new functionalities with each software release. However, it is fragmented into multiple software modules (OpenStack projects) with dedicated interface libraries [10]. This fragmentation hardens the installation process, the management of the platform and increases the complexity of the system. On the other hand, it interacts with several third-party applications, uses RESTful interfaces and offers OCCI [11], AWS EC2 [1] and S3 [12] interface libraries.

Apache CloudStack uses a modular architecture for the automation and centralised management of data-centres, which is organized in zones, pods and clusters. It uses a Query API as well as an API translator so that applications written for CloudStack can also run in AWS EC2 [1]. Although the studied version of CloudStack (4.2.1) does not provide official OCCI support, it is available via a third-party contribution [13].

PACI includes various proprietary products to enable the creation, management, monitoring and billing of public or hybrid (if the PACI platform is used) IaaS platforms. It exposes an open interface (RESTful API) to enable the development of third-party applications for the interaction with the system. However, PACI is a platform without software modules to support directly the interaction with other IaaS platforms. This behaviour is common among proprietary solutions in order to generate the user lock-in phenomenon.

Table 1 compares the authentication, hypervisors, management, interfaces, network, storage and governance features of the studied IaaS platforms. The main differences among the open source IaaS platforms are related to the architecture, interface libraries and governance models. This diversity is caused by

Table 1. IaaS platforms comparison

Features	OpenNebula	OpenStack	CloudStack	PACI
Author./Authen.	Password, SSH RSA keypair, X509, LDAP	In-memory Key-Value Store, PAM, LDAP, X509	Password, LDAP, SSH RSA keypair	Password, LDAP
Hypervisors	XEN, KVM, VMware vSphere	KVM, LXC, UML, VMWare vSphere, Xen, PowerVM, Hyper-V	VMware vSphere, KVM, Citrix Xen	Parallels hypervisor, KVM
Management	Centralized	Scattered	Centralized	Centralized
Interfaces	XML-RPC API; AWS EC2, OCCI, OCA	RESTful API; AWS EC2, S3, EBS and OCCI	Query API; AWS EC2, OCCI, Plug-in API	RESTful API
Network	Virtual router, Contextualization	Nova-network, Newtron	Virtual router	POA
Storage	Volume Storage	Volume and Object storage (Glance, Swift, Cinder)	Volume Storage	System DB
Governance Model	Benevolent Dictator	Foundation	Technical Meritocracy	Proprietary

the absence of well defined architectural standards for the commoditization of IaaS systems. Every IaaS platform tends to provide distinct functionalities and be compatible with specific third-party services in order to monopolize the market and impose its technologies as standards. OpenStack is a good example of an IaaS platform that tries to monopolize the market. On the other hand, the proprietary IaaS platform PACI has a limited set of features and no interoperable mechanisms to interact with other platforms, which may purposely lead to a vendor lock-in problem. There are also significant differences regarding the type and number of interfaces, the level of customization, the organization of the groups of operations as well as the structure of the request and response messages provided by the four IaaS platform interface libraries. OpenStack and PACI rely on RESTful interfaces, while OpenNebula and CloudStack use natively XML-RPC and Query (RESTlike) interfaces, respectively.

3   Abstraction Solutions

Interface abstraction libraries provide a collection of implementations for the development of middleware systems that abstract the peculiarities of the underlying IaaS platform and offer a standard and unique API for the management of multiple IaaS clouds. Deltacloud [3], jClouds [14] and Libcloud [15] are examples of existing cloud abstraction solutions.

Deltacloud is an open source framework from the Apache Software Foundation [16] that aims to abstract differences between IaaS cloud platform interface libraries. It is written in Ruby and contains a Web dashboard, a group of IaaS provider drivers [17] (including OpenNebula and OpenStack) and multiple API – the Deltacloud RESTful API, the Distributed Management Task Force (DMTF) open standard Cloud Infrastructure Management Interface (CIMI) REST API [18] and the AWS (EC2 [1] and S3 [12]) API. Each driver exposes the list of implemented Ruby collections. These collections describe the abstractions offered by the Deltacloud API [19] and each collection represents an entity in the back-end provider node.

Apache jClouds and *Libcloud* are open source libraries, developed by Apache Software Foundation [16] in Java and Python, that abstract the differences among multiple cloud provider interface libraries. jClouds offers both portable abstractions and cloud-specific features, which enable the management of buckets (BlobStore) and compute operations (ComputeService), and has a list of compatible cloud providers and IaaS platforms, including OpenStack and CloudStack [20]. The Libcloud library supports an extensive group of IaaS platforms [21], including OpenNebula, CloudStack and OpenStack and allows users to manage compute, storage and network cloud resources.

Deltacloud, jClouds and Libcloud are among the most representative cloud IaaS abstraction solutions and are used in several R&D cloud interoperability related projects, *e.g.*, Aeolus and mOSAIC [22][23]. Deltacloud, which provides by default three different service API (native RESTful Deltacloud, CIMI and AWS EC2 API), is a framework that includes a Ruby client, a Web dashboard and a driver development environment to support the integration of further IaaS platforms. jClouds and Libcloud are standard programming libraries and, unlike Deltacloud, do not integrate additional development tools. In terms of IaaS platform support, Libcloud provides official integration with the studied open source IaaS platforms (OpenNebula, OpenStack and CloudStack), jClouds supports CloudStack and OpenStack while Deltacloud supports OpenNebula and OpenStack. None of these abstraction solutions provides support for PACI. Table 2 presents the comparison between these open source abstraction solutions.

Table 2. Open-source abstraction solutions comparison

Features	Deltacloud	jClouds	Libcloud
Type	Framework	Library	Lybrary
Programming language	Ruby	Java	Python
Supported providers	17 cloud providers	30 cloud providers	38 cloud providers
Supported operations	Compute, Storage, Network	Compute, Storage	Compute, Storage, Network
Platform integration	Drivers	Maven dependencies	Drivers
API	REST, CIMI, AWS		
Other interfaces	Web dashboard, Ruby client		

Although Libcloud provides official support for the analysed open source IaaS platforms, there are also third-party drivers that integrate CloudStack with Deltacloud [24]. Thus, the Deltacloud abstraction framework was adopted because it provides additional development tools and Web services (*e.g.*, the Ruby Command Line Interface and Web Dashboard), exposes broadly used interface libraries (CIMI and AWS EC2) and provides documentation for the development of Deltacloud drivers to integrate new IaaS platforms that can be used for the development of the PACI driver.

4   Interoperable Service Proposal and Development

The Interoperable Service uses the Deltacloud abstraction framework as a middleware between cloud users and IaaS platforms, permitting the management of multiple IaaS platforms via a single service. The architecture of this Interoperable Service is composed by the back-end driver modules (OpenNebula, OpenStack, CloudStack and PACI driver), the software daemon `deltacloudd` and the Graphical User Interface (GUI) and API services. Figure 1 illustrates the architecture of the Interoperable Service.

The back-end driver modules, composed of the OpenNebula, OpenStack, CloudStack and PACI drivers, are integrated and developed to enable the abstraction and interaction with the respective back-end IaaS platforms. These drivers define, through method instantiation and implementation, the Deltacloud operations that the IaaS platform provides. The software daemon `deltacloudd` is included in the deltacloud-core component and is responsible for the start-up and deployment of the front-end interface services (the GUI and API services). The GUI

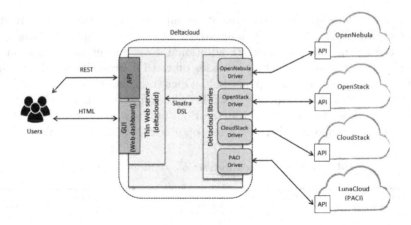

Fig. 1. Interoperable Service architecture

service presents a simple Web dashboard containing the driver implemented collections and operations. The API service has a RESTful implementation that uses the Deltacloud defined collections and operations to expose the cloud resources of the IaaS platforms [19].

Depending on the configuration of the Deltacloud daemon, two different deployments modes can be adopted: (*i*) the single tenant configuration where a single Deltacloud daemon loads a pre-defined YAML file containing the credentials and the cloud provider URL endpoint for each driver module; and (*ii*) the multiple tenant configuration where multiple server instances, containing each the GUI and API services, are defined by individual back-end driver modules, *i.e.*, each Deltacloud server instance contains a specific driver, port and cloud provider endpoint URL to access the respective back-end IaaS platform.

5   Tests and Results

In order to test the developed Interoperable Service, a test bed containing Open-Nebula, OpenStack, CloudStack nodes and Internet access to a PACI cloud provider was assembled – Figure 2. This test bed is not intended to test the individual properties and capabilities of each IaaS system.

The OpenNebula, OpenStack, CloudStack and PACI driver modules were tested and evaluated in terms of functionality and interoperability performance using this test bed. The experiments compared the Deltacloud API calls with the direct IaaS platform API calls in terms of response time per operation (*i.e.*, the total amount of time required to perform a HTTP request and obtain the response) as well as the HTTP request packet length and HTTP response content length. The execution of the API operations (via the Deltacloud API and via the IaaS platform API) and the measurement of the corresponding response time was performed with the cURL command line tool [25]. The HTTP request packet

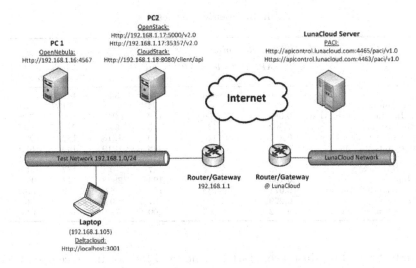

Fig. 2. Test bed platform

length and response payload were measured using the Wireshark software [26]. For the sake of these tests, the HTTP Secure Sockets Layer (SSL) encryption security procedure was purposely discarded.

Problems were detected with the OpenNebula, OpenStack and CloudStack drivers. The OpenNebula driver supplied with the Deltacloud framework had two minor bugs related with an id argument mismatch in the `destroy_image` method (included in the `opennebula_driver.rb` file) and the instantiation of an unused `xmlfile` argument in the delete method of the `occi_client.rb` file. Both problems were corrected and reported. The OpenStack driver, although fully functional, lacked the start and stop VM operations in the OpenStack rubygem. Moreover, the `delete_instance` method was defined as an alias of the `stop_instance` method, causing the destruction of the VM whenever the Stop Instance operation is invoked. The third party CloudStack driver, added to Deltacloud in order to integrate the CloudStack IaaS platform, did not work. From the analysis of the driver implementation, it was possible to conclude that the driver is incomplete and, thus, non functional.

The results obtained for OpenNebula are presented in Table 3. The interaction via the Deltacloud API, which relies on the OpenNebula driver module, increases the operation response time, particularly in the listing operations, _e.g._, the List Instances, List Images and List Hardware Profiles operations. It is also possible to observe that the Delete Image and Create Instance operations have almost the same average response time.

The HTTP request packet length and returned payload per operation reinforce the interpretation of the response time results from Table 3. The HTTP request packets length of the OpenNebula OCCI API operations are slightly bigger than the ones of the Deltacloud API operations. This can be observed mainly in the

Table 3. OpenNebula results

	Time Response (s)		Data (B)			
	OCCI API	Deltacloud API	OCCI API		Deltacloud API	
			Request	Response	Request	Response
List Collections	0.010	0.030	174	348	172	654
List Instances	0.130	0.582	194	6585	181	7376
Show Instance Information	0.089	0.150	183	1219	183	729
Create Instance	0.462	0.482	515	591	298	592
Stop Instance	0.295	0.426	349	1218	189	907
Start Instance	0.203	0.396	348	1219	190	639
Reboot Instance	0.194	0.359	348	1218	191	907
Delete Instance	0.323	0.361	187	0	187	0
List Images	0.105	0.529	194	2828	178	10 966
Show Image Information	0.071	0.133	183	287	180	1101
Delete Image	0.220	0.234	187	0	184	0
List Hardware Profiles	0.012	0.067	200	720	189	1232

Create Instance, Stop Instance, Start Instance and Reboot Instance operations. On the other hand, the length of the HTTP response payload varies and is bigger for the responses of Deltacloud API List Collections, List Instances, List Images, Show Image Information and List Hardware Profiles operations (being the List Instances and List Images the responses containing the larger values), identical in the Create Instance operation and larger for the responses of the OpenNebula OCCI API Show Instance, Stop Instance, Start Instance and Reboot Instance operations. In the case of the Delete Instance and Delete Image operations, the returned payload length is nil since they are silent.

The OpenStack response time as well as the HTTP request packet length and returned payload (using the Deltacloud API and the OpenStack services API) are presented in the Table 4. Since the authentication request is performed in each Deltacloud API operation when using the OpenStack driver, the average HTTP authentication request response time was added to the average of the OpenStack services (Nova and Glance) API operations time response. As expected, the response time of the Deltacloud API operations is significantly higher than the response time of the OpenStack services API (Keystone, Nova

Table 4. OpenStack results

	Time Response (s)		Data (B)			
	OpenStack API	Deltacloud API	OpenStack API		Deltacloud API	
			Request	Response	Request	Response
List Instances	0.131	1.196	2605	16 522	157	13 608
Show Instance Information	0.064	0.387	2635	2371	194	1346
Create Instance	0.380	0.848	2748	665	290	931
Reboot Instance	0.198	1.025	2721	0	202	1346
Delete Instance	0.244	0.947	2670	0	200	1346
List Images	0.095	0.508	2604	7050	154	16 547
Show Image Information	0.070	0.445	2634	967	191	1378
Delete Image	0.194	0.412	2669	0	194	0
List Hardware Profiles	0.024	0.216	2598	1356	165	2177

and Glance) operations. This occurs for all listed operations except for the Delete Image and List Hardware Profiles operations. In fact, the average response time of operations like the List Instances, Create Instance and Reboot Instance Deltacloud API operations reached values higher than the operations performed via the Deltacloud API using the OpenNebula driver.

The authentication procedure (authentication token) used by OpenStack is reflected in the values of the HTTP request packet length of the OpenStack API operations, which is substantially bigger than the values of the corresponding Deltacloud API operations. On the other hand, the HTTP response payload varies. The OpenStack API List Instance and Show Instance Information operations return bigger payloads than the corresponding Deltacloud API operations, the Delete Image operation returns the same payload in both cases (a void HTTP response body) and the remaining operations return a smaller payload than the Deltacloud API counterparts. The Reboot Instance and Delete Instance operations are silent. Usually, the HTTP response of the Delete Instance operation defined by the Deltacloud API is also silent. However, since the OpenStack driver defined the `stop_instance` method as an alias of the `destroy_instance` method, the pause of an OpenStack instance with the Deltacloud API deletes the instance. In fact, it sends the Delete Instance operation, but returns the Stop Instance operation result.

Contrary to the open source IaaS platforms (OpenNebula, OpenStack and CloudStack), which were in the same test network as the laptop used to perform the tests, the PACI IaaS platform was in an external network. This way, the latency of the network was taken in consideration in the results presented in Table 5. The analysis of the results shows that, despite the registered latency, the time response values of the PACI API operations are lower than the values registered for the OpenNebula OCCI API and OpenStack API operations, with the exception of the List Images operation. Although, the List Image operation lists 103 Images in comparison with the 10 images that were listed by the same

Table 5. PACI results

	Time Response (s)		Data (B)			
	PACI API	Deltacloud API	PACI API		Deltacloud API	
			Request	Response	Request	Response
List Instances	0.032	1.385	180	726	177	10 276
Show Instance Information	0.033	0.124	188	938	185	1128
Create Instance	0.374	0.647	675	165	343	932
Stop Instance	0.078	0.278	193	17	191	939
Start Instance	0.064	0.280	194	18	192	1126
Delete Instance	0.078	0.186	191	19	188	0
List Images	0.655	3.235	186	46 029	174	153 680
Show Image Information	0.042	0.094	206	449	194	1508
List Load Balancers	0.035	2.483	191	818	182	9592
Show Load Balancer Information	0.033	1.717	195	1063	186	947
Create Load Balancer	0.393	0.520	203	167	355	610
Delete Load Balancer	0.075	0.081	198	21	189	0
Associate Instance with LB	0.076	0.463	204	131	284	947
Dissociate Instance from LB	0.081	0.286	206	28	286	610

operations of the OpenNebula OCCI API and OpenStack API. In comparison, the results of the interaction with the Deltacloud API, using the PACI driver, show a significantly response time increase, mainly with the List Instances, List Images, List Load Balancers and Show Load Balancers Information operations. The List Images operation presents the highest time response value, since the driver has to process the information of 103 returned images. On the other hand, the response time results for the remaining operations is justified by the need to perform additional calls to the back-end PACI API and to process the returned information. The refinement of this methodology may improve the measured response time. Other Deltacloud API operations, *e.g.*, Show Instance Information, Stop Instance, Start Instance, Delete Instance and Show Image Information present lower response time than the corresponding operations via the OpenNebula and OpenStack drivers.

The length of the HTTP request packets is larger for the PACI API operations with the exception of the Create Load Balancer, Associate Load Balancer and Dissociate Load Balancer operations. These Deltacloud API operations require more parameters than the corresponding PACI API operations. The Deltacloud API operations return a larger payload than the direct API calls with the exception of the Show Load Balancer Information, Delete Instance and Delete Load Balancer operations. In the case of the last two operations, the Deltacloud API does not send a HTTP response body.

6   Conclusions

In order to propose and develop an interoperable service for the integrated management of cloud resources provisioned by different IaaS platforms, a survey was conducted to compare the features of the most popular open source IaaS platforms - OpenNebula, OpenStack and CloudStack - and of a proprietary IaaS platform - PACI. This survey concluded that, although the open-source IaaS platforms expose similar functionalities, the architecture, interface library operations and governance models are significantly different. The proprietary solution does not support directly the interaction with other IaaS platforms and originates, on purpose, the vendor lock-in problem to monetize new products and paid support services. Additionally, the proprietary IaaS platform has a smaller group of functionalities in comparison with the open source IaaS platforms studied. Regarding the interface libraries, the OpenNebula, OpenStack, CloudStack and PACI client API showed significant differences in terms of type and number of interfaces, level of customization, organization of the groups of operations and structure of the request/response messages.

A second survey on existing IaaS abstraction solutions compared the Deltacloud framework and the jClouds and Libcloud libraries. The result was the selection of the Deltacloud framework since it provides many of the desired functionalities (Web dashboard, multiple API, a Ruby client application), includes several IaaS platform driver modules and integrates new IaaS platforms through the development of new dedicated driver modules.

To evaluate the proposed solution, a test bed was assembled, deployed and used to determine the time response and data payload via the Deltacloud framework and via direct IaaS platform API calls. In terms of driver functionalities, these experiments showed that the new PACI driver was fully functional, the OpenNebula and OpenStack drivers were fully operational after minor corrections and improvements and the CloudStack driver module was incomplete and non functional. In terms of driver performance, the results showed that the use of Deltacloud drivers to access the IaaS platform resources introduces an expected response time delay when compared with the direct platform API calls. In the majority of the operations, the HTTP request packet length of the Deltacloud API was lower and the results of the HTTP response payload were substantially higher in the case of the Deltacloud API listing operations. In general, the Deltacloud abstraction framework reduces the HTTP request and response detail to the essential information. The PACI platform, despite being located at an external network, presented the lowest time response of the tested platforms.

The solution adopted for the integrated management and provision of IaaS resources from PACI, OpenNebula and OpenStack IaaS platforms fulfils the specified requirements, *i.e.*, integrates multiple IaaS platforms and offers a Web dashboard and a REST API for user management. The contributions of this work include the surveys made, the selection of the abstraction framework, the assembled test bed platform and, last, but not the least, the developed PACI driver. Although the PACI driver performed well, it can be refined to enhance the response time of certain operations. Future improvements to the Deltacloud API may also enhance the performance of the included drivers. The PACI driver was shared with the Deltacloud community and the detected OpenNebula and OpenStack driver malfunctions were also reported.

Acknowledgements. This work was partially supported by the ERDF – European Regional Development Fund through the COMPETE Programme (operational programme for competitiveness) and by National Funds through the FCT – Fundação para a Ciência e a Tecnologia (Portuguese Foundation for Science and Technology) within project «FCOMP – 01-0124-FEDER-022701».

References

1. Amazon: Amazon Web Services: Amazon EC2 (April 2014),
   http://aws.amazon.com/ec2
2. Amazon: Amazon Web Services (April 2013), http://aws.amazon.com
3. Deltacloud: Deltacloud Framework (May 2014), http://deltacloud.apache.org
4. C12G Labs: Open–Source Enterprise Cloud Simplified (April 2014),
   http://opennebula.org
5. OpenStack Foundation: Open source software for building private and public clouds
   (April 2014), http://www.openstack.org
6. Apache Software Foundation: Apache CloudStack: Open Source Cloud Computing
   (April 2014), http://cloudstack.apache.org

7. Parallels: Parallels Automation for Cloud Infrastructure (May 2014),
   http://sp.parallels.com/products/paci
8. Open Grid Forum (OGF): Open Forum - Open Standards (April 2014),
   https://www.ogf.org/dokuwiki/doku.php
9. OGF: OCCI: About (April 2014),
   http://occi-wg.org/about/
10. OpenNebula: OpenStack Programs (May 2014),
    https://wiki.openstack.org/wiki/Programs
11. OpenStack: OCCI (April 2014),
    https://wiki.openstack.org/wiki/Occi#Summary
12. AWS: Amazon S3 (April 2014), https://aws.amazon.com/s3
13. Isaac Chiang: rOCCI Server – A Ruby OCCI Server (June 2014),
    https://github.com/isaacchiang/rOCCI-server
14. jClouds: The Java Multi-Cloud Toolkit (May 2014), http://jclouds.apache.org
15. Apache Libcloud: One Interface To Rule Them All (May 2014),
    http://libcloud.apache.org
16. Apache: The Apache Software Foundation (April 2014),
    http://www.apache.org/foundation
17. Deltacloud: Deltacloud drivers (May 2014),
    http://deltacloud.apache.org/drivers.html#drivers
18. DMTF: Cloud Management Initiative (May 2014),
    http://dmtf.org/standards/cloud
19. Deltacloud: Deltacloud API (May 2014),
    https://deltacloud.apache.org/rest-api.html#rest
20. jClouds: Providers (May 2014),
    http://jclouds.apache.org/reference/providers
21. Libcloud: Supported Providers (May 2014),
    http://libcloud.apache.org/supported_providers.html
22. Aeolus: Manage Your Cloud Deployments with Ease (May 2014),
    https://github.com/aeolusproject/aeolusproject.github.com/wiki
23. mOSAIC: Open source API and platform for multiple clouds (May 2014),
    http://www.mosaic-cloud.eu
24. Childers, C.: CloudStack Driver for Deltacloud (May 2014),
    https://github.com/chipchilders/deltacloud/tree/
    cloudstack-driver/server/lib/deltacloud/drivers/cloudstack
25. Stenberg, D.: cURL (May 2014), http://curl.haxx.se
26. Wireshark Foundation: Wireshark (May 2014), http://www.wireshark.org

Performance Investigation and Tuning in the Interoperable Cloud4E Platform

Steffen Limmer[1], Maik Srba[2], and Dietmar Fey[1]

[1] Friedrich-Alexander University Erlangen-Nürnberg (FAU),
Computer Architecture, Martensstr. 3, 91058 Erlangen, Germany
{steffen.limmer,dietmar.fey}@informatik.uni-erlangen.de
[2] GWDG, Am Fassberg 11, 37077 Göttingen, Germany
maik.srba@gwdg.de

Abstract. The paradigm of Software as a Service (SaaS) offers an interesting option to vendors of simulation software for providing their applications to a wide circle of customers. However, this imposes a challenge to vendors whose applications exist only as classical desktop tools, so far: Interfaces for the remote control have to be provided which are as independent from the underlying cloud infrastructure as possible in order to avoid vendor lock-ins. We present an interoperable platform developed in the project Cloud4E (Trusted Cloud Computing for Engineering), which allows the provisioning of existing simulation software in form of a service in a cloud. The interoperability of the platform and of the services is achieved by the usage of the Open Cloud Computing Interface (OCCI) together with the Advanced Message Queuing Protocol (AMQP) where OCCI is not only used as interface to Infrastructure as a Service (IaaS) but also as interface to SaaS. Hence, the OCCI server plays a central role within the platform and can quickly become a bottleneck, which degrades the performance of the whole platform. We present detailed performance investigations and suggest options to improve the performance. The investigations were performed on the widely used OCCI server implementation called rOCCI server connected to the OpenNebula cloud middleware.

Keywords: Cloud4E, OCCI, rOCCI server, OpenNebula, CAE, cloud.

1 Introduction

Today, the design of technical systems usually requires computer simulations like for example finite element method (FEM) computations. These computer-aided engineering (CAE) simulations are frequently very compute intensive and thus require an appropriate amount of computational power. Furthermore, are the licenses for professional simulation software usually very cost-intensive. In the publicly funded project Cloud4E [1] a platform was developed, which allows vendors of such simulation software to provide their software as a service in a cloud. This can be beneficial for the user as well as the software provider. The user is able to use the soft- and hardware on a pay-per-use basis, which can yield

L. Lopes et al. (Eds.): Euro-Par 2014 Workshops, Part II, LNCS 8806, pp. 85–96, 2014.

significant cost savings and the simulation software provider is able to make its tools available to users who were previously not able to use them due to cost reasons.

In order to increase the user's trust, it is envisaged that primarily regional compute centers act as providers of the cloud resources on which the Cloud4E services are deployed. Hence, it has to be ensured that the Cloud4E platform and services are portable between different cloud middlewares. This is achieved by the usage of OCCI [2,3], which is not only used as interface to IaaS but also as interface to the services.

Since regional compute centers have only limited resources available, it has to be possible to outsource computations to resources of other cloud providers if necessary and if the user agrees. Thus, hybrid or federated clouds have to be supported. This is enabled by the employment of OCCI together with AMQP [4,5]. Since the communication via AMQP is done over a central server, VMs or services can communicate, which can not directly reach each other. This makes it possible to distribute tasks or services over VMs of multiple clouds, without restricting the communication between them.

The Cloud4E platform was already used successfully to build services for the CAE simulation software SimulationX [6] and the free FEM solver UNA [7]. Although the platform is intended for the provisioning of simulation software as service, it can be used for the provisioning of other types of services as well. For example, there are services for the parameter sweep tool GridWorker [8] and the evolutionary algorithm framework FrogEA [8,9], which were both initially developed for the usage in grids.

The OCCI server is besides the AMQP server a central component of the Cloud4E platform, which acts as link among multiple service instances and between clients and services. In the project an open source Ruby implementation named rOCCI server [10], which was adapted to the needs of Cloud4E, is used. Experience has shown that the rOCCI server has a crucial impact on the performance of the Cloud4E platform. This has been investigated in detail in order to improve the performance. This manuscript presents the results of these investigations and describes possibilities to improve the performance.

But first, in Section 2 related work is discussed before Section 3 gives an overview of the complete Cloud4E platform. Then in Section 4 the rOCCI server and the functional adaptions we made to it in Cloud4E are described more in detail. Section 5 covers the performance investigation and tuning and finally, Section 6 gives a short summary and conclusion.

2   Related Work

A number of simulation tools can already be used in form of cloud services. Rescale [11] provides more then 30 simulation tools in form of services running on their own infrastructure. A lot of CAE tools from Autodesk [12] can also be used as cloud services.

Tsai et al. [13] developed SimSaaS – a framework and runtime environment that allows the execution of simulations in service-oriented architectures. The framework is based on the description of simulations with PSML (Process Spec-ification and Modeling Language) [14] combined with automatic code generation. Thus, it is not suitable for integrating existing simulation software. The Euro-pean projects CloudSME (Cloud based Simulation platform for Manufacturing and Engineering) [15] and Fortissimo [16] have a similar scope like Cloud4E but at the time of writing they were not started, yet.

OCCI is also used in other interoperable platforms than the Cloud4E platform. Lezzi et al. [17] use the rOCCI server in order to execute applications over the COMP Superscalar programming framework (COMPS) [18] in a federated cloud operated by the EGI (European Grid Infrastructure). But in contrast to Cloud4E, they use OCCI only for the control of IaaS. In the project BonFIRE [19] the specification of OCCI was extend in order to use it for the monitoring in federated clouds. They do not use an existing OCCI server. Instead, they use the OCCI API of the cloud middleware if available or self-implemented servers, otherwise. To the best of our knowledge there are no publications on performance investigations related to OCCI, yet.

3 Overview of the Cloud4E Platform

The Cloud4E platform consists of several components that allow to easily create and control portable simulation services. Figure 1 illustrates all the components and their communication over OCCI. The components are able to communicate with each other over an AMQP bus. Running instances of a simulation service are connected over AMQP, as well.

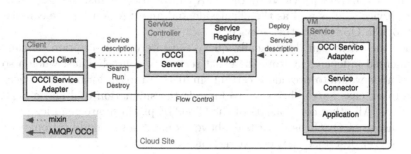

Fig. 1. The Cloud4E architecture

Heart of the Cloud4E platform is a so called *Service Controller*. This is a node where the following tools are running: A rOCCI server, which is reachable over AMQP (see Section 4), a service registry, which stores all simulation services available in the platform and an AMQP server (RabbitMQ in the project in-frastructure). The Service Controller can be a physical host of the cloud, a VM running in the cloud or even a host at the client side.

With help of the rOCCI client library a client can start VMs in the cloud over the rOCCI server of the Service Controller. In OCCI a VM is represented in form of an *OCCI compute resource*. Such a compute resource contains attributes providing information about the VM like the number of physical cores or the state of the VM. Additionally, a compute resource provides actions that can be triggered by a client – e.g. a restart- or a stop-action. Over these actions and attributes an OCCI client can control running VMs. A compute resource can be extended by a so called *OCCI mixin* which defines additional actions and/or attributes.

In a VM a service stored in the service registry can be deployed. A service consists of three components. One component is the simulation application provided by the service. Another component is the *OCCI Service Adapter (OSA)* developed in Cloud4E. The OSA provides an OCCI interface to the simulation tool in form of actions and attributes. It registers the interface in form of a mixin to the rOCCI server and listens at an AMQP queue for incoming OCCI requests.

Since different simulation tools require different interfaces, there is a third component named *Service Connector*. This is a Ruby (or JRuby) class which defines the attributes and actions of the interface with help of a domain-specific language and implements the actions in form of usual Ruby methods. This Service Connector is used by the OSA to handle incoming OCCI requests. Thus, the OSA forms a generic OCCI wrapper around a service connector, which in turn forms a service dependent Ruby interface to the simulation software.

A client can query the interface description from the rOCCI server and can control the service over the actions and attributes defined in the interface description. It can send an OCCI request either directly to the OSA of the service or to the rOCCI server which forwards the request to the OSA. For the control of a service a library provided by the OSA can be used. Thus, the OSA is used at the service side as well as the client side and an OSA of a service can act as client for the OSA of another service.

Since the client can dynamically query the interface description, it can be implemented independent from the exact service to control. Thus, when a software vendor wants to provide a certain simulation tool in form of a service, in the simplest case he/she has only to provide the simulation tool and a Service Connector. All other components of the Cloud4E platform are generic.

The usage of OCCI as described above required some modifications to the rOCCI server described in the next section.

4   The rOCCI Server in Cloud4E

The rOCCI server has a modular design: A frontend is responsible for the communication with a client while a backend acts as interface between the server and the cloud middleware. More precisely, the backend is responsible for monitoring and controlling the middleware as required. There are different backends for different cloud middlewares. The rOCCI server provides four backends: a dummy backend for testing purposes, backends for OpenNebula and OpenStack and an EC2 backend. Further backends can be added by the user if required.

In order to use OCCI not only as interface to IaaS but also as interface to services, the following adaptions to the rOCCI server were made in Cloud4E:

- The frontend was extended in order to support communication over AMQP and not only over HTTP. This AMQP support will be adopted in future official releases of the server.
- The actions and attributes that are offered by a service, which is running on a certain VM are linked with the OCCI compute resource representing this VM in form of an OCCI mixin. And the AMQP queue to which the service is connected is linked as OCCI link to the compute resource. The backend was appropriately extended to support this functionality: When a link/mixin is registered to a compute resource, the link/mixin is stored in a database. In subsequent queries of the compute resource the link/mixin is added to that compute resource by the backend. Before adding the mixin, the current values of the attributes stored in that mixin are retrieved from the service over AMQP and are inserted into the mixin in order to ensure that they are always up to date.
- When a client triggers an action on a service over the rOCCI server the request is forwarded to the service over AMQP. Also this functionality was added to the backend.

The described adaptions which concern the backend are integrated into the backends for OpenNebula and for OpenStack since these two cloud middlewares are used in Cloud4E.

5   Performance Investigations and Tuning

Initially, performance problems occurred during the test of Service Connectors in the described infrastructure. These issues related to performance were investigated thoroughly and could be solved to the greatest extent. They are mainly caused by the rOCCI server and the cloud middleware and thus do not solely affect the platform used in Cloud4E. Therefore, in the following the results of the investigations are presented and options to improve the performance are described.

The performance problems particularly occur when worker services are started over a master service. The master-worker principle is a convenient method to distribute work over multiple VMs or services: One service acts as a master, which controlls multiple worker services and is responsible for distributing the work over them. The master is also responsible for the start of the workers (the worker VMs along with the worker services running on them). With the current Cloud4E service connectors this is done in the following way: The user or client triggers an action start_workers on the master service and passes the desired number of workers to start as parameter to the action. Then the master starts the specified number of worker VMs and periodically queries their state from the rOCCI server until the VMs and the services on them are running (the services start automatically after the boot of the VMs). When the worker VMs and services are running, the master is ready to distribute the work over them.

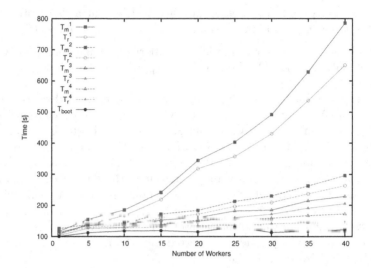

Fig. 2. Start times for different numbers of workers during different stages of performance improvement measured over the master service (T_m) and over the rOCCI server (T_r) together with the time T_{boot} to start and boot the worker VMs over OpenNebula.

We measured the times it takes to start different numbers of workers from 1 to 40 without any performance optimizations. These times are shown as T_m^1 in Figure 2. The times are measured over the master service and represent the timespan between triggering the **start_workers** action and the moment when the master recognizes that all workers are running. All values are averaged over five measurements. The measurements are done in the following testbed: Version 0.5 of the rOCCI server is used, running over Ruby 2.0.0 and connected to OpenNebula 4.0.1 (ON) as cloud middleware. The rOCCI server and ON are running on the cloud frontend (with two AMD Opteron 2435 hex-cores) with Debian as operating system. QEMU 1.1.2 is used as hypervisor and the physical hosts (with two AMD Opteron 2216HE dual-cores, each) connected to ON are running with Debian as well. After the master service has started the worker VMs, it queries their states from the rOCCI server in intervals of five seconds until all the started VMs are in the ON state **running**. From that moment on it queries their states in intervals of 15 seconds until all worker services are started. The worker VMs run Windows XP as operating system. During the measurements, attribute updates were deactivated in order to omit their influence on the start times of the workers.

The measurements show that T_m^1 is increasing rapidly with an increasing number of workers to start. While the start of one worker takes around 115 s, the start of 40 workers takes ca. 13 min. It can be assumed that in practice frequently far more than 40 workers are demanded – e.g. 100 workers. Based on the increase of T_m^1, start times way beyond 30 min can be expected for 100 workers. Hence, it is necessary to investigate the reasons for such long start times.

One might argue that the reason is that the times required to start the worker VMs over ON and to boot them rise with an increasing number of worker VMs. That is quite possible since the workers are started with help of the ON qcow transfer driver from overlay images that all depend on the same base-image, which is shared over NFS (Network File System). Thus, it is possible that VMs interfere with each other during boot. In order to figure out if this is the case, we measured the times required to start different numbers of worker VMs directly over ON. The VMs are started with the ON command line tool `onetemplate`. In the VMs a small program is started automatically after boot which connects via a socket to the cloud head node. We measured the times between creating the VMs with `onetemplate` and the moment when all VMs have notified the head node. The times are shown as T_{boot} in Figure 2 and they are averaged over 10 measurements. It has to be mentioned that we do not use the scheduler of ON for the scheduling of the VMs to physical hosts. Instead, we use a self-implemented scheduler [20] which delegates the scheduling to a cluster batch system (Oracle Grid Engine) in order to better integrate the cloud infrastructure in our existing cluster. The scheduling interval of this scheduler was set to 10 s. Thus, 10 to 20 seconds of the start times arise from the scheduling. As it can be seen in Figure 2, there is a certain increase of T_{boot} when the number of VMs is increased from 1 to 5. The reason for that is most likely that the VMs are configured with one virtual CPU (VCPU) and thus, up to 4 VMs are scheduled to the same physical host where they slightly interfere with each other. From 5 to 40 VMs T_{boot} is only marginally increasing and it is much less than T_m^1. Thus, the reason for the high start times of the workers is not that the worker VMs take too long to start/boot.

Since the master has to query periodically the states of the worker services, there is a certain delay between the moment when all worker services are started and the moment when this is recognized by the master. In order to investigate if that delay is responsible for the strong increase of T_m^1, we did not only measure the start times of the workers over the master but simultaneously over the rOCCI server. The times measured over the rOCCI server do not contain the delay, thus representing the "real" start times. They are shown as T_r^1 in Figure 2. It can be seen that the gap between T_r^1 and T_m^1 increases with increasing number of workers. For 20 workers it takes the master around 25 s to recognize that the worker services are started. For 40 workers this time increases to around 135 s. But nevertheless, T_r^1 increases similarly strong as T_m^1. For 40 workers it amounts to ca. 11 min.

Thus, it can be stated that the strong increase of T_m^1 with increasing number of workers is partly caused by an increase of the boot times of the VMs and the increasing time it takes the master to recognize that the worker services are running. But these are definitely not the main reasons. Hence, there has to be a performance problem with the start of the worker services after the worker VMs are booted. During the start of a worker service it sends five requests to the rOCCI server in order to register its interface to the server. Along with each request, authentication information for the cloud middleware is send to the server. Thus, a service acts as a certain cloud user (for example the account of the service provider or of the end user). For each request the rOCCI server uses the authentication information for querying all relevant information from the cloud middleware (per XML-RPC calls with help of the Ruby OCA gem in the case of OpenNebula) that is accessible by the authenticated user, like VM templates, VM images and so on. Especially, all running VMs are queried from the cloud middleware. The obtained information about running VMs is then parsed and converted into the internal OCCI format (OCCI compute resources). It turned out that the time the rOCCI server requires to handle a request, strongly depends on the number of VMs that are currently running for the user. Figure 3 shows the times we measured for different numbers of running VMs. All values are averaged over 10 measurements and the times are split up into the time it takes the server to query all running VMs from ON, the time it takes to parse the VM information and the rest of time it takes to handle the request.

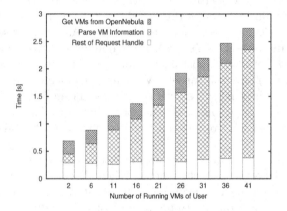

Fig. 3. Time required by the rOCCI server without any performance improvements to handle a request when different numbers of VMs of the requesting user are running.

The time to query all VMs from ON slightly increases with an increasing number of running VMs. The time to parse the VMs increases very strong and the rest of time stays almost constant. With two running VMs the time to handle a request takes ca. 0.69 *s*. With 41 running VMs it takes ca. 2.7 *s*. When 40 workers are started, 41 VMs are running (the 40 workers VMs and the master VM) and as already stated each worker service sends five requests to the server. The requests of all worker services are send almost simultaneously and the server handles all requests sequentially. Additionally to the requests of the worker services, there are requests of the master in order to query the states of the workers. This explains the long start times of the workers – the rOCCI server becomes a bottleneck and so the worker services interfere each others start. This would also be the case when the workers are started directly over the user client and not over the master service.

In order to improve the performance of the rOCCI server, we removed tasks from it that are done during handling a request and that are either redundant or not required for the Cloud4E infrastructure: During the parsing of a VM the information about the VM is again queried from ON. This was removed since it is not necessary. Additionally, the parsing of all information that is not relevant for the Cloud4E infrastructure, like the used virtual network or the IP address of the VM, was removed. We also removed the query of all VM images and all virtual networks from ON.

This yielded a significant reduction of the start times of the workers. The start times measured after the improvement of the performance of the rOCCI server are shown as T_m^2 and T_r^2 in Figure 2. T_m^2 are the times measured over the master and T_r^2 the times measured over the rOCCI server. It can be seen that the increase of T_m^2 and T_r^2 is less strong than that of T_m^1 and T_r^1. By the described performance improvements the start time for 40 workers could be reduced from about 13 min to 5 min. Additionally, the gap between T_m^2 and T_r^2 is less than that between T_m^1 and T_r^1.

But the start times are still unsatisfying. For 40 workers T_m^2 is more than twice as much as T_{boot}. Hence, we were looking for further possibilities to improve the performance. By the described improvements of the rOCCI server the time to parse the VMs is reduced and thus, the time to query the VMs from ON accounts for a bigger portion of the total time required to handle a request. Measurements yielded that the time required to query all running VMs from ON does not only depend on the number of running VMs but also on the VMs accessible by the user that are stored in the database of ON. For accounting purposes VMs, even those that are already shutdown, are kept in a database. As configured per default, we use a SQLite database for ON. During the measurements so far, between 21,000 and 23,000 VMs of the user as which the worker services authenticated themself to the rOCCI server were stored in the ON database. Figure 4 shows how long it takes the rOCCI server to query all running VMs of a user from ON for different numbers of running VMs and different numbers of VMs of the user in the ON database. The values are averaged over 10 measurements. When 40 VMs are running the time to query the running VMs with 25,000 VMs in the database (0.4 s) is about 3 times as high as with 1,000 VMs in the database (0.14 s). If only one VM is running the time with 25,000 VMs in the database (0.26 s) is about 16 times as high as with 1,000 VMs (0.016 s). Although the absolute differences in time are small, they sum up to a notable amount when regarded over multiple requests to the rOCCI server. This can be seen from T_m^3 and T_r^3 in Figure 2. These are the start times of the workers after deleting already shutdown VMs from the ON database. For 40 workers the start time could be reduced by more than one minute to 228 s only by deleting shutdown VMs from the ON database.

But it is still ca. 100 s higher than T_{boot}. Hence, we tried to further improve the performance by parallelizing the rOCCI server so that multiple requests can be

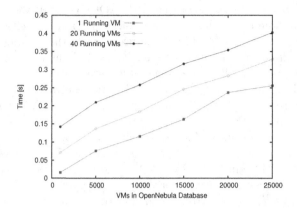

Fig. 4. Time it takes the rOCCI server to query all running VMs of a user from OpenNebula for different numbers of running VMs of the user and different numbers of VMs of the user in the OpenNebula database.

handled in parallel. A parallelization on the thread level would yield no benefit since Ruby threads do not run in parallel. But since we use AMQP as transport protocol the server can be easily parallelized by starting multiple processes of the server, which are all connected to the same AMQP queue. The requests arriving on that queue are automatically distributed by the AMQP server per round-robin among the multiple processes. A consequence of the parallelization is that it can theoretically not be ensured that requests are finished in the same order as they are send by a client. But usually clients wait for a response of the server before sending a subsequent request and thus a fixed order is ensured. The effect of the parallelization on the start times of the workers can be seen from T_m^4 and T_r^4 in Figure 2. These are the times measured when the rOCCI server runs with 4 processes. By the parallelization the start times of 40 workers could be further reduced by 50 s and it can be seen that T_r^4 is close to T_{boot}. Figure 5 shows the start times of 40 workers with different numbers of processes used by the rOCCI server (averaged over 10 measurements). As it can be seen, starting with 4 processes an increase of the number of processes has no effect on the start times. But for higher numbers of workers it can be assumed that an increase of the number of processes would be beneficial. After all the described performance improvements the "real" start time T_r of 40 workers is about 20 s higher than the pure start time T_{boot} of the worker VMs and there is a delay of about 30 s between T_r and the start time T_m measured over the master. Thus, there might be further potential for improvements but the start times are now in an acceptable range. T_m^4 and T_r^4 increase only slightly with an increasing number of workers, leading to a much better scalability compared to the infrastructure before the improvements. And although the performance investigations and tuning focused on the start of workers because here the performance issues are most obvious, the whole OCCI communication in the Cloud4E platform is affected by the performance improvements.

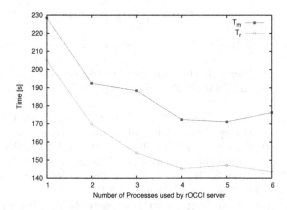

Fig. 5. Start time of 40 workers measured over the master (T_m) and over the rOCCI server (T_r) for different numbers of processes used by the rOCCI server.

6   Conclusion

The Cloud4E platform allows simulation software vendors to provide their existing applications in form of a cloud service. The employment of the open standards OCCI and AMQP ensures interoperability and avoids vendor lock-ins. Integration tests yielded that the rOCCI server has a significant impact on the performance of the whole platform. It can quickly become a bottleneck, especially during the start of multiple services. In order to improve the performance of the rOCCI server, it can be beneficial to remove unneeded features from it. Adaptions to the cloud middleware, like deleting VMs from the database of OpenNebula, can increase the performance as well. The usage of AMQP as transport protocol for the OCCI communication provides an easy way to parallelize the rOCCI server, yielding an additional performance improvement. Thus, we were able to enhance the performance of the rOCCI server connected to Open-Nebula to an acceptable niveau. The next steps are to do analogous performance improvements with OpenStack as cloud middleware and to enable EC2 based middlewares in the Cloud4E platform by appropriate adjustments of the EC2 backend of the rOCCI server.

Acknowledgment. The Cloud4E project is supported by the German Federal Ministry for Economic Affairs and Energy (BMWI) as part of the Trusted Cloud initiative.

References

1. Cloud4E, http://www.cloud4e.de/ (retrieved May 2014)
2. Open Cloud Computing Interface, http://occi-wg.org/ (retrieved May 2014)
3. Edmonds, A., Metsch, T., Papaspyrou, A., Richardson, A.: Toward an Open Cloud Standard. IEEE Internet Computing 16(4), 15–25 (2012)

4. Advanced Message Queueing Protocol, http://www.amqp.org/ (retrieved May 2014)
5. Vinoski, S.: Advanced Message Queuing Protocol. IEEE Internet Computing 10(6), 87–89 (2006)
6. SimulationX, http://www.simulationx.com/ (retrieved May 2014)
7. UNA – Finite Element Analysis Program, http://www.una-fem.com/ (retrieved May 2014)
8. Limmer, S., Schneider, A., Boehme, C., Fey, D., Schmitz, S., Graupner, A., Sülzle, M.: Services for numerical simulations and optimisations in grids. International Journal of Parallel, Emergent and Distributed Systems, 1–23 (2013)
9. Limmer, S., Fey, D.: Framework for Distributed Evolutionary Algorithms in Computational Grids. In: Cai, Z., Hu, C., Kang, Z., Liu, Y. (eds.) ISICA 2010. LNCS, vol. 6382, pp. 170–180. Springer, Heidelberg (2010)
10. rOCCI server at GitHub, https://github.com/gwdg/rOCCI-server (retrieved May 2014)
11. Rescale, http://www.rescale.com/ (retrieved May 2014)
12. Autodesk, http://www.autodesk.com/ (retrieved May 2014)
13. Tsai, W.-T., Li, W., Sarjoughian, H., Shao, Q.: SimSaaS: Simulation Software-as-a-service. In: Proceedings of the 44th Annual Simulation Symposium, pp. 77–86. Society for Computer Simulation International, San Diego (2011)
14. Tsai, W.-T., Wei, X., Cao, Z., Paul, R., Chen, Y., Xu, J.: Process Specification and Modeling Language for Service-Oriented Software Development. In: 11th IEEE International Workshop on Future Trends of Distributed Computing Systems, pp. 181–188 (2007)
15. CloudSME: http://cloudsme.eu/ (retrieved May 2014)
16. Fortissimo, http://www.fortissimo-project.eu/ (retrieved May 2014)
17. Lezzi, D., Lordan, F., Rafanell, R., Badia, R.M.: Execution of Scientific Workflows on Federated Multi-cloud Infrastructures. In: an Mey, D., Alexander, M., Bientinesi, P., Cannataro, M., Clauss, C., Costan, A., Kecskemeti, G., Morin, C., Ricci, L., Sahuquillo, J., Schulz, M., Scarano, V., Scott, S.L., Weidendorfer, J. (eds.) Euro-Par 2013. LNCS, vol. 8374, pp. 136–145. Springer, Heidelberg (2014)
18. Tejedor, E., Badia, R.M.: COMP Superscalar: Bringing GRID Superscalar and GCM Together. In: 8th IEEE International Symposium on Cluster Computing and the Grid, CCGRID, pp. 185–193 (2008)
19. García-Pérez, D., et al.: Cloud and Network Facilities Federation in BonFIRE. In: an Mey, D., et al. (eds.) Euro-Par 2013. LNCS, vol. 8374, pp. 126–135. Springer, Heidelberg (2014)
20. Ditter, A., Limmer, S., Fey, D.: i3sched – Ein OpenNebula Scheduler für die Oracle Grid Engine. In: Proceedings of Grid4Sys 2013, pp. 1–4 (2013)

Cloud Federation to Elastically Increase MapReduce Processing Resources

Alfonso Panarello, Maria Fazio, Antonio Celesti,
Antonio Puliafito, and Massimo Villari

DICIEAMA, University of Messina, Contrada di Dio, S. Agata, 98166 Messina, Italy
apanarello{mfazio,acelesti,apuliafito,mvillari}@unime.it

Abstract. MapReduce is a programming model that allows users the parallel processing of large data sets into a cluster. One of its major implementation is the Apache Hadoop framework that couples both big data storage and processing features. In this paper, we aim to make Hadoop Cloud-like and more resilient adding a further level of parallelization by means of cooperation of federated Clouds. Such an approach allows Cloud providers to elastically scale up/down the system used for parallel job processing. More specifically, we present a system prototype integrating the Hadoop framework and CLEVER, a Message Oriented Middleware supporting federated Cloud environments. In addition, in order to minimize overhead of data transmission among federated Clouds, we considered a shared memory system based on the Amazon S3 Cloud Storage Provider.Experimental results highlight the major factors involved for job deployment in a federated Cloud environment.

Keywords: Cloud Computing, Federation, Big data, MapReduce, Hadoop.

1 Introduction

MapReduce is a programming model for the parallel processing of large data sets. Hadoop MapReduce is one of the major implementation of the MapReduce paradigm developed and maintained by the Apache Hadoop project, that works in tandem with the parallel Hadoop File System (HDFS). Parallelization capabilities of a system strongly depends on available resources into the cluster. To fulfill several requests from many different users, an elastic approach for resource management is required. Cloud computing, offers such a feature. By means of virtualization resources can elastically scale up/down. However for each Cloud Provider (CP) the number of available virtual resources depends on its own physical assets. In order to overcame such a limit, CPs can rent Virtual Machines (VMs) from big commercial provider or they can establish a federation relationship. The latter approch allows small-medium provider to cooperate in order borrow/lend resources according to particular agreements. In this manner, Cloud federation also offers to small/medium CPs new business opportunities, guaranteeing high flexibility in service provisioning in a transparent way for end

L. Lopes et al. (Eds.): Euro-Par 2014 Workshops, Part II, LNCS 8806, pp. 97–108, 2014.

users. We chose to use CLEVER because, although it arises as middleware for the management of IAAS, it has been designed looking to the future and keeping an eye to the federation issues [1]. In fact, all communications, both inter-domain that intra-domain, use the technology XMPP, which in our opinion is a powerful solution to manage and to support the Cluod federation. So, our work aims to provide a Platform as a Service (PaaS) for a MapReduce processing of big data in a federated Cloud scenario. In particular, the solution we propose integrates the Hadoop functionalities into the the above mentioned CLEVER. Whenever a client submits a job to a Cloud, it, which may be not able to meet the client's request for computational tasks, processes the job exploiting resources distributed across different administrative domains. Each CP offers its processing resources according to the policies of the federation agreements and the provider that receives a commitment from the client manages the available pool of resources in the federation till the job processing ends. Our work, therefore, by exploiting the federated system potentialities, aims to add another parallelization layer to Hadoop Framework, thus making it elastic, scalable and cloud-like.

The rest of the paper is organized as follows. In Section 2, we provide a brief overview of current works on the topics dealt in the paper. Section 3 presents the proposed distributed processing service and one of many possible use cases. In Section 4, we introduce the technologies adopted in this work to arrange a real federated environment, i.e., Hadoop, CLEVER which is a Message Oriented Middleware (MOM) exploiting the Extensible Messaging and Presence Protocol (XMPP) technologies to handle the communication among the different administrative domains. Architectural details on how to integrate Hadoop and CLEVER are discussed in Section 4.3. In Section 5, we present experimental results highlighting the major factors involved for job deployment in a federated Cloud environment arranged by means of Hadoop and CLEVER. Section 6 concludes the paper.

2   Related Works

In the near future, the heavy penetration of sensing devices into Internet applications will cause the explosion of the amount of data to be stored and processed. This problem, well known as Big Data issue, is becoming the new buzzword in ICT world, involving both IoT and Cloud Computing, [2] technologies. Cloud Computing is already a consolidated technology useful for spreading massive computations on heterogeneous environments. In this perspective Cloud is becoming even more the basis for Big Data computation needs. At the Infrastructure as a Service (IaaS) level, Big Data can leverage the Computation capabilities of Clouds where the computation relying onVMs. Such an example is given in [3], where Hadoop is installed into VMs exploiting the Public Cloud as Amazon EC2. Here the authors re-modeled the resource provisioning of the VMs in public cloud platforms for big data applications. In particular the authors relied only on modifying the configuration of two types of EC2 VM instances that is Small instance and Extra Large (XLarge) instance for optimizing the processing of Big Data. Our work uses a similar approach of this ([3]), but we believe is much more challenging to setup a Hadoop environment in Federated Clouds. Cloud Federation [4] [5] represents a compelling opportunity in which IaaS Cloud Operators might achieve great business benefits, renting to others cloud operators the computation resources on-demand (see [6]). The well-know Hadoop platform can represent an appealing opportunity in this way because its architecture is well consolidated and widely used. Any Cloud Operator might offer Hadoop computation resources on-fly joining a federated cloud environment. Hadoop uses MapReduce paradigm, an high-level programming model for data-intensive applications using transparent fault detection and recovery, widely adopted in cloud datacenters such as Microsoft, Google, Yahoo, and Facebook. Hadoop is an opensource implementation firstly developed by Yahoo [7]. In our work it is possible to setup a high-level programming model even in Federated and Heterogeneous Clouds. Deploying VMs in federated scenarios with Hadoop nodes inside, is a challenge as shown in [8].Many works are trying to optimize Hadoop computations in heterogeneous environment like shown in LATE [9], TARAZU [10], Cross-Phase Optimization [11] and PIKACHU [12].These works look at the paradigm attempting to optimize all processing tasks, in particular the three main phases: *map, shuffle and reduce.* At the first stage of our solution, we are looking at the possibility to elastically increase the computation resources leveraging even more VMs. A step over we should also consider similar approach in which to organizer all MapReduces phases and tasks in a federated way, that is selecting federated providers and deploying suitable VMs. Another example of Big Data processing in the Cloud is presented in [13]. In this work the computation framework used is Sailfish, a new MapReduce environment similar to Hadoop. Sailfish was conceived for improving the disk performance for large scale MapReduce computations. Hence it is possible to make the selection of federated contributors based on types of MapReduce paradigms.

3   Distributed Processing Service in Cloud Federation

In a federated Cloud environment, a CP can benefit of the storage and computational resources other CPs acting on other administrative domains. To satisfy client's requests, each CP in the federation asks for available resources to the other members of the federation, which offer their unused resources at that time. Of course, the amount of resources offered for each request can be regulated by specific federation agreements, but such issue is out of the scope of this paper. A CP can require to establish a partnership with other CPs for multiple reasons: it has saturated its own resources and it needs external assets, it wants to perform software consolidation in order to save energy cost, it want to move part of processing into other providers for improving security or performance in order to respect particular Service Level Agreements (SLAs). In particular, in this paper, we focus on a federated Cloud scenario offering MapReduce processing service. MapReduce can take the advantages of data location, processing it on closer storage assets in order to reduce data trasmission delay. Thus, in our scenario,

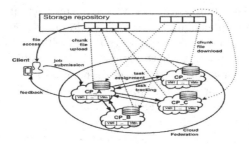

Fig. 1. Processing service management

CPs hold their internal storage system where deploying data sets they have to process. Since each CP stores a portion of data for local processing, we assume that big files that have to be processed are stored in an external Cloud Storage Providers (CSPs), such as Amazon S3, Google Drive, Dropbox, etc. The choise to rely on external public CSP was made to minimize the overhead associated to the data transmission between the federated domains. They, in this manner, have to exchange, each other, only coordination and sincronization messages. The idea behind such a service is shown in Figure 1. When a user requests to run a job, he contacts his Cloud Provider (CP_A in the example in Figure 1) and sends an input file (Xml file) containing the parameters nedeed to the job to be executed. CP_A involves all (or just a part of, depending on the job requirements) the CPs in the federation, giving them directives on the task they have to process. Supposing that the input data to process is memorized in a CSP that supports multipart download (i.e., the CSP splits the file in several blocks that clients are able to download), each involved CP to accomplish its task has to download only particular blocks of file. It is important to say that the system can scale both horizontally and vertically. It scales horizontally when a CP_A (Home CP) dynamically forwards the user task request to the federated domains (Foreign CP). But the system can also scales vertically when a chosen foreign CP, for some reason, cannnot longer fully meet the forwarded request by the home CP. So the foreign CP may in turn forward the sub-request to others available foreign CP. In this case, therefore, the CP plays both the role of foreign CP, towards the CP that initially sent the request, and the role of home cloud towards the new CPs to which it is forwarding the sub-request. Once each CP have download their respective blocks of data from CSP, it has to parallel process them by means of pieces of parallel processing middleware running on VMs. Each downloaded blocks is further divided in smaller chunks by the middleware used for parallel processing running on the Cloud domain. For simplicity, we assume that each CP in the scenario has an image of the VM including the piece of middleware for processing the task. However, additional mechanisms for VM image provisioning can be implemented to improve the flexibility of the offered service. At the end of the task, each CP uploads the results of the processing into the repository system and it notifies that to CP_A. As soon as all the CP end their work, CP_A

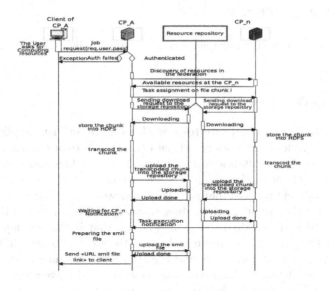

Fig. 2. Processing service management

informs the client about the result of the processing. To better understand the benefits of this scenario, let us consider a video transcoding job as possible use case. A user would like to enjoy a movie that is available on a remote storage repository by using his mobile device. Unfortunately, the movie is stored as HD file and the user device is not able to play it. Thus, the user needs an on-fly video transcoding to convert the file to another format. The steps accomplished to obtain the transcoded video are shown in Figure 2. A client submits to his provider (CP_A) the job together with his credentials to access the service. If the authentication process has success, CP_A starts a resources discovery into the federated environment to look for available resources. The generic CP_n offers its storage and computational resources, if possible, and waits for instruction on the task to carry on and the chunks of file to process. The Hadoop framework at CP_A, exploiting the MapReduce features, parallelizes the transcoding process of the video file thus to involve as much resources as possible. As soon as CP_n receives the file localization information, it starts the download of the file chunks and put them (uploads) in its HDFS cluster for local processing. At the end of the processing step, CP_n stores the result of its processing in the CSP and sends to CP_A an end task notification. Once CP_A has received all the end task notifications from all the involved CPs, it generates a *SMIL* file, i.e., an XML file used to play the video avoiding to merge all the processed chunks. Also the SMIL file is uploaded into the CSP and it provides the base location of the video chunks and the necessary information for the client player to rebuild the whole video file. Finally, CP_A notifies its client about the end of job execution and provides him the location of the SMIL file.

4   Reference Scenario

In this Section, we describe our reference scenario including CLEVER, Hadoop, and Amazon S3.

4.1   Hadoop Overview

Hadoop MapReduce is a software framework to write and run applications in processing in parallel huge amounts of data (e.g. terabyte of datasets) on large clusters in a reliable, fault tolerant manner. A MapReduce job usually splits the input data set into independent chunks, which are processed by the map tasks in a completely parallel manner. The framework sorts the outputs of the maps, which are then input to the reduce tasks. Both the input and the output of the job are stored in a distributed file system, that is the Hadoop File System (HDFS).Typically the compute nodes and the storage nodes are the same, that is, the MapReduce framework and the HDFS are running on the same set of nodes. This configuration allows the framework to effectively schedule tasks on the nodes where data is already present, resulting in very high aggregate bandwidth across the cluster. The Hadoop framework has a Master/Slave architecture. MapReduce components consist of a single master JobTracker and one slave TaskTracker per cluster-node. The master is responsible for scheduling the jobs' component tasks on the slaves, monitoring them and re-executing the failed tasks. The slaves execute the tasks as directed by the master. The master node of the HDFS is called *NameNode*. It manages the namespace file system by maintaining a file metadata image that includes file name, location and replication state. DataNodes manage storage resources into the host they run on and allow read/write accesses. A typical Block size is 64 MB. Thus, a HDFS file is chopped up into 64 MB chunks, and, if possible, chunks are located at different DataNodes.

4.2   CLEVER Overview

The CLoud-Enabled Virtual EnviRonment (CLEVER) is a Message-Oriented Middleware for Cloud comptuting (MOM4C), able to support several Cloud-based services [14]. Each CLEVER Cloud includes several distributed hosts organized in a cluster. Each Phisical Machine (PM) is controlled by a management module, called Host Manager (HM), and only one host runs a cluster management module, called Cluster Manager (CM) that acts as interface between Cloud and clients. CM receives commands from clients, gives instructions to HMs, elaborates information and finally sends back results to clients. It also performs tasks for cluster orchestration. A CLEVER Cloud makes use of XMPP to exchange all communication messages and presence information in a near-real time fashion. A Jabber/XMPP server provides basic messaging, presence, and XML routing features within the Cloud. All the PMs in the Cloud are connected via a Multi User Chat (MUC) and cooperate according to the CM orchestration directives. In CLEVER, CM and HMs implements software *Agents* communicating through XMPP. Hence, it is easy to include new modules and functionalities to the CLEVER environment by adding new Agents and updating the CM and HMs configurations for the correct delivering of messages.

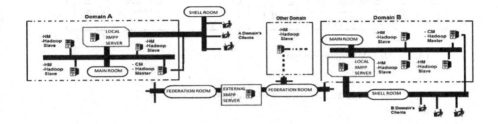

Fig. 3. CLEVER Federation Management

With CLEVER, each Cloud involved in the federation is identified by a *Jabber ID* (JID). As shown in Figure 3, in order to set up a federation, CMs belonging to different administrative domains exchange messages through the MUC with the unique room ID *Federation*, and only the authenticated, by the XMPP server itself or by external third party entities [15], ACTIVE CMs of federated Clouds can access it.

4.3 Integration of Hadoop in CLEVER

To make the Hadoop functionalities cloud like, we make use of a virtual infrastructure provided by CLEVER. VMs run on HMs and work as slaves of the Hadoop cluster. Virtual Hadoop slaves are coordinated by the Hadoop Master arranged at the CLEVER CM. The first advantage of the integration of Hadoop in CLEVER is that, typically, Hadoop uses the TCP/IP layer for communication, and it is a problem during the inter-domain comunication due to heavy usage of firewalls by each domain which take part to federation. Infact firewalls can block inter-domain communication. So, integrating Hadoop in CLEVER, federation messages can be sent on port 80 thanks to XMPP technology.The second one is that the system can automatically scale according to real time requirements. The two main software agents enabling CLEVER to integrate Hadoop are the *Hadoop Master Node (HMN) Agent* and *Hadoop Slave Node (HSN) Agent*. In the following, we discuss their activities and synchronization processes. Figure 4.a shows the software components at the CM. Through the *HMs interface*, the CC communicates with all the HMs in the cluster, exchanging information on available resources, running tasks, work specifications and offered services. The CC makes use of the *Client interface* to interact with Cloud clients, in order to receive client requests, and to give back inquired services. The Client interface allows service provisioning to clients exchanging XML messages into the

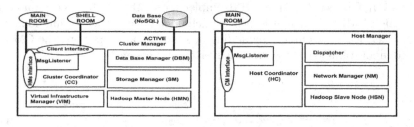

(a) Cluster Manager design.   (b) Host Manager design.

Fig. 4. Integration of Hadoop in CLEVER

Shell Room. The VIM is the agent designed for managing virtual infrastructures. Moreover, the CM makes use of an internal NoSQL database for storing current system configurations, which is properly updated by the Data Base Manager (DBM). Figure 4.b shows the software components at the HM. The agent specifically designed to support the Hadoop activities in the Cloud is the *HMN Agent*. It provides the configuration settings to all the virtual nodes in the Hadoop cluster. The CLEVER HMN works as master for Hadoop cluster. Specifically, it implements the Hadoop functionalities to manage the hadoop system. At the startup, the *HMN Agent* reads the Hadoop configuration setup and then the CC subscribes this new Agent in the list of all the active agents of CLEVER, in order to make it reachable from the agents instantiated in the HMs. After the early registration, the *HMN Agent* can receive Notifications from the agents at the HMs.

4.4 Amazon S3

Amazon S3 is Cloud storage service. It is designed to make web-scale computing easier for developers. Amazon S3 provides a simple web-services interface that can be used to store and retrieve any amount of data, at any time, from anywhere on the web. It gives any developer access to the same highly scalable, reliable, secure, fast, inexpensive infrastructure that Amazon uses to run its own global network of web sites. The service aims to maximize benefits of scale and to pass those benefits on to developers.

5 Experiments

In this Section, we discuss several experiments, we conducted on a real testbed involving four CLEVER/Hadoop administrative domains (i.e., A, B, C, and D) acting as federated Cloud providers and Amazon S3 acting as real Cloud storage provider. The objective of the experiments described in this Section consists to know what are the main factors needed for the job submission in a federated

Cloud environments and demonstrating, considering a real testbed, how Cloud federation can enable Cloud providers to take the advantages of parallel distributed processing. it is important to emphasize that integrating Hadoop in CLEVER we are adding a second livel of parallelization. In order to test the whole environment, we considered a parallel video transcoding use case involving several federated cloud providers. In particular, we arranged the testbed considering four physical servers (one per Cloud domain) running in total 10 VMs and Amazon S3. Experiments were conducted with the following hardware configuration: CPU: Intel(R) Core(TM)2 CPU 6300; 1.86GHz, 3GB RAM, running Linux Ubuntu 12.04 x86_64 OS and VirtualBox. Each experiment was repeated 50 times in order to consider mean values and a low confidence intervals.In the following, we summarize the main phases involved in our experiments. The process starts at time t_0 when a Cloud client sends a video transcoding request to a particular CLEVER domain. At time t_1 the CLEVER cloud that receives the request decides to establish a federation with the other CLEVER domains, retrieving domains information. For simplicity, in this paper, we have not treated how this process can be accomplished in autonomic fashion, but we a priori arranged the environment using the CLEVER commands. At t_2, the Cloud provider, that has initiated the federation establishment process, performs a task assignment involving the whole federated environment. Supposing that the Cloud that has started the process uses an external Cloud storage service provided by Amazon S3, each involved federated CLEVER Cloud will download only a particular number of video chunks for processing using the multipart download mechanism. In the end, t_4 indicates the time taken by each CLEVER Cloud to upload the previously downloaded video chunks in HDFS of the local domain, so that the Hadoop task tracker slave node, controlled by means of CLEVER, can process them. Figure 5.a shows the average time required for the accomplishment of phase 1 ($t_1 - t_0$). It is possible to observe that, independently from the number of external administrative domains, the time for retrieving domain information remains constant taking roughly 5 seconds. We attribute this overhead at the access operation to the local database needed to CLEVER to

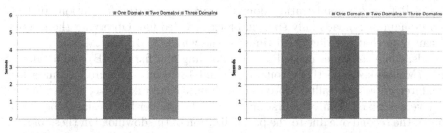

(a) Average time required to retrieve domain information on Clouds.

(b) Average time required to forward a request to federated Clouds.

Fig. 5. Retrieving information and forward request times

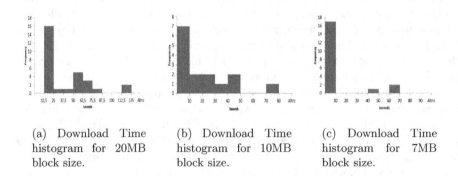

(a) Download Time histogram for 20MB block size.

(b) Download Time histogram for 10MB block size.

(c) Download Time histogram for 7MB block size.

Fig. 6. Download time from Amazon S3

retrieve the network parameters of the other domains. At phase 2, $t_2 - t_1$ interval indicates the time required to forward the video transcoding request to the external federated CLEVER Clouds domains. These times are shown in the Figure 5.b. After that the CLEVER Cloud that has started the process, obtained the network information regarding external Cloud domains, runs a new thread for each of them, sending the requests in parallel. Thus, the average time does not change if the number of the foreign domains does. Figure 5.a, 5.b, and 5.c show respectively the distribution of the download times of 1/3, 1/2, and the whole video files from Amazon S3. In our timing diagram, this time is represented by the $t_3 - t_2$ interval. Observing the Figure 6.a, 6.b, and 6.c, we can notice that, if there is only one domain which takes part to the federation, it has to download the whole video file(20MB), instead when there are other domains into the federetion, each of them has to retrive only a block of the original file. So, when the number of the federated domains increases, the download-time decreases. In particular Figure6.a, shows the download time when a single external CLEVER Cloud administrative domain takes part to the federation, so that, it has to download the whole video file(20MB) from Amazon S3. Figures 6.b and 6.c, instead, respectively show the download times when two and three external CLEVER Cloud administration domains take part to the federation. In fact, each domain downloads only specific block of video file. Observing the graphs, we can note that the download time for the whole 20MB file takes roughly 40 seconds, while the times needed for downloading half file (10MB) and a third of file (7MB) take respectively roughly 22 and 15 seconds. Figure 5 summarizes the aforementioned results. Moreover, each download takes place in parallel, so we have a double benefit, the first one due to the smaller blocks size to be downloaded, the second one due to the parallelization of the download in these blocks. The average download time is depicted in Figure 7.a. Instead, Figure 7.b shows how the average upload time of blocks of file in the HDFS of each domain. This time changes according to the number of active DataNodes and video file sizes. Observing the graph depicted in Figure 7.b, we can notice that increasing the number of Hadoop Data Nodes the upload time increases too. We can motivate

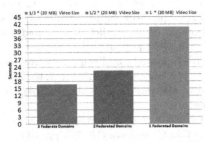

(a) Average download time of file blocks from Amazon S3.

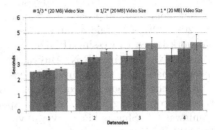

(b) Average Upload time of file blocks in Hadoop.

Fig. 7. Average download and upload

this trend remembering that the Hadoop has been configured with a redundancy parameter equal to 2. In fact with a single active DataNode, the upload time has a very low value, because the system does not have the need to replicate the file. Instead, due to Hadoop's data replication mechanisms, increasing the number of Data Nodes, we can notice a linear increase of the upload.

6   Conclusion

In this paper, we discussed how can be possible to apply the MapReduce paradigm in a federated Cloud environment. MapReduce allows to perform a parallel processing of large data set stored into a file system. The Hadoop framework couples the MapReduce algorithms with the HDFS storage system. The proposed solution integrates the Hadoop framework into CLEVER and uses Amazon S3 as external CSP. We deeply discussed the proposed processing service focusing on job submission.

References

1. Panarello, A., Celesti, A., Fazio, M., Villari, M., Puliafito, A.: A Requirements Analysis for IaaS Cloud Federation. In: 4th International Conference on Cloud Computing and Services Science, Barcelona, Spain (2014)
2. Petruch, K., Stantchev, V., Tamm, G.: A survey on it-governance aspects of cloud computing. IJWGS 7(3), 268–303 (2011)
3. Yuan, Y., Wang, H., Wang, D., Liu, J.: On interference-aware provisioning for cloud-based big data processing. In: 2013 IEEE/ACM 21st International Symposium on Quality of Service (IWQoS), pp. 1–6 (June 2013)
4. Rochwerger, B., Breitgand, D., Epstein, A., Hadas, D., Loy, I., Nagin, K., Tordsson, J., Ragusa, C., Villari, M., Clayman, S., Levy, E., Maraschini, A., Massonet, P., Muñoz, H., Tofetti, G.: Reservoir - when one cloud is not enough. Computer 44, 44–51 (2011)

5. Kertesz, A., Kecskemeti, G., Marosi, A., Oriol, M., Franch, X., Marco, J.: Integrated monitoring approach for seamless service provisioning in federated clouds. In: 2012 20th Euromicro International Conference on Parallel, Distributed and Network-Based Processing (PDP), pp. 567–574 (February 2012)

6. Toosi, A.N., Calheiros, R.N., Buyya, R.: Interconnected cloud computing environments: Challenges, taxonomy, and survey. ACM Comput. Surv. 47, 7:1–7:47 (2014)

7. The Apache Hadoop project: the open-source software for reliable, scalable, distributed computing, http://hadoop.apache.org/

8. Gahlawat, M., Sharma, P.: Survey of virtual machine placement in federated clouds. In: 2014 IEEE International Advance Computing Conference (IACC), pp. 735–738 (February 2014)

9. Zaharia, M., Konwinski, A., Joseph, A.D., Katz, R., Stoica, I.: Improving mapreduce performance in heterogeneous environments. In: 8th USENIX Conference on Operating Systems Design and Implementation, OSDI 2008, pp. 29–42. USENIX Association, Berkeley (2008)

10. Ahmad, F., Chakradhar, S.T., Raghunathan, A., Vijaykumar, T.N.: Tarazu. Optimizing mapreduce on heterogeneous clusters. SIGARCH Comput. Archit. News 40, 61–74 (2012)

11. Heintz, B., Wang, C., Chandra, A., Weissman, J.: Cross-phase optimization in mapreduce. In: Proceedings of the 2013 IEEE International Conference on Cloud Engineering, IC2E 2013, pp. 338–347. IEEE Computer Society, Washington, DC (2013)

12. Gandhi, R., Xie, D., Hu, Y.C.: Pikachu: How to rebalance load in optimizing mapreduce on heterogeneous clusters. In: USENIX Conference on Annual Technical Conference, USENIX ATC 2013, pp. 61–66. USENIX Association, Berkeley (2013)

13. Rao, S., Ramakrishnan, R., Silberstein, A., Ovsiannikov, M., Reeves, D.: Sailfish: A framework for large scale data processing. In: Proceedings of the Third ACM Symposium on Cloud Computing, SoCC 2012, pp. 4:1–4:14. ACM, New York (2012)

14. Fazio, M., Celesti, A., Puliafito, A., Villari, M.: A message oriented middleware for cloud computing to improve efficiency in risk management systems. Scalable Computing: Practice and Experience (SCPE) 14, 201–213 (2013)

15. Celesti, A., Fazio, M., Villari, M.: Se clever: A secure message oriented middleware for cloud federation. In: IEEE Symposium on Computers and Communications (ISCC), pp. 35–40 (July 2013)

A Novel Approach for Performance Characterization of IaaS Clouds

Sandor Acs[1,2], Nemeth Zsolt[1], and Mark Gergely[1]

[1] Computer and Automation Research Institute,
Hungarian Academy of Sciences, Hungary
acs.sandor@sztaki.mta.hu
[2] Obuda University, Hungary

Abstract. Infrastructure-as-a-Service (IaaS) clouds are widely used today, however there are no standardized or commonly used performance evaluation methods and metrics that can be used to compare the services of the different providers. Performance evaluation tools and benchmarks are able to grasp some aspects or details of performance but for various reasons are not capable to characterize cloud performance. Our aim is to collect these elementary or primitive facets of performance and derive high-level aggregated and qualitative performance characterization semantically far above the output of tools and benchmarks. We designed and implemented a framework that collects low-level raw performance data (in terms of CPU, disk, memory and network) of cloud providers based on standard benchmark tools and these data are aggregated and evaluated using a hierarchical fuzzy system. In this process performance characteristics are associated with symbolic values and fuzzy inference is applied to produce the normalized qualitative comparable and readable performance metrics. In this paper, we discuss the issues of cloud performance analysis, present the concept and implementation of our method, illustrate the proposed solution by comparing –in terms of performance– the general purpose medium instance type of the Amazon EC2 cloud (in Ireland) and the standard instance type of the OpenNebula installation at MTA SZTAKI.

Keywords: cloud computing, performance evaluation, fuzzy sets, hierarchical fuzzy inference.

1 Introduction

Cloud computing, from a user's perspective is a contract: the provider offers a service of negotiated quality and the consumer pays a negotiated fee. Just like in any other commercial scenario, the consumer is curious if the value vs price ratio is right and acceptable. Cloud vendors provide multi-tenant infrastructures and generally do not disclose the technical details of the services (e.g., overprovisioning rate) that makes it difficult for customers to anticipate cloud performance. Furthermore, cloud providers often use different terminologies for resource allocation. Albeit, Service Level Agreements (SLAs) declare the guaranteed level of

L. Lopes et al. (Eds.): Euro-Par 2014 Workshops, Part II, LNCS 8806, pp. 109–120, 2014.

services, these are typically just the lower limits that neither express what the consumer really gets nor make the services comparable to other providers. From the consumers' point of view the expected "performance" would be interesting so that it enables the comparison to other providers and to the costs. Albeit in this work we discuss "performance", it is worth mentioning that characterizing a service involves many other aspects that are quite related to performance such as Quality of Service (QoS), Quality of Experinece (QoE), in lesser extent robustness, fault tolerance, trust and many others.

Performance analysis of parallel computing environments has been studied extensively in the past (e.g., [7] [14] [8] [11] [2] just to mention a few.). Novel distributed paradigms obsolete parallel performance analysis models and new approaches and tools for characterizing large-scale inhomogeneous and dynamic distributed systems are required [4][9]. The advent of cloud computing introduced new features that rendered performance evaluation largely unsolved and target of intensive research.

The challenges of cloud performance analysis largely stem from virtualization, the complete separation of the physical and virtual entities. All former performance evaluation approaches were focusing on the physical infrastructure and the physical performance profile of resources. Virtualization, a characteristic and inherent feature of clouds however, introduces another dimension of complexity: the measured and evaluated performance, i.e. what a consumer gets, are *not of a physical machine*. This requires new approaches and potential, new definitions for performance evaluation for the following reasons. (i) Service providers may split or merge physical resources to accommodate virtual machines. Hence, performance measured at the physical level does not characterize the performance of virtual machines. (ii) Service providers may offer different instance types. Thus, performance of virtual machines is loosely coupled to physical machines: it is a characteristics of a hypothetical (volatile) infrastructure and potentially not characteristic to the entire or physical infrastructure. (iii) Multi-tenancy adds a large uncertainty factor. (iv) Due to all these reasons, for the time being, there are no widely accepted performance analysis techniques for cloud infrastructures. Performance itself is multi-dimensional, composed of many facets, performance metrics are not standardized, not comparable, sometimes even hard to interpret and cannot be measured at the physical level.

Our work is aimed at establishing a framework that enables the performance characterization of IaaS providers so that services of different providers or instance types of the same provider became comparable by metrics that are (i) symbolic for easy interpretation (ii) aggregated to cut down dimensions and data volume (iii) comparable to each other. Furthermore, our method is (iv) especially tailored for the virtualized machines. We apply logic and fuzzy inference to create the abstract, symbolic performance characterizations from raw performance data. The result is a readable, abstract yet precise and comparable description of virtual machines.

As it was stated we try to characterize and compare *cloud services* from performance point of view. This is not identical to the notion of performance analysis that typically refers to the *performance of an application*. On the other hand, it is not benchmarking either. Benchmarking is a comparison of the *performance of the infrastructure as a whole* to an established, industry-leading reference point (such as the TOP500 list) where performance tests are carried out in a standardised way in a closed environment (the number and specifications of the hardware elements are known and static) under controlled (preferably non-existent) loads and eliminating all intrusive effects. Hence, informally we call our approach as *performance characterization* as opposed to, and differentiate from, benchmarking or performance evaluation.

Furthermore, benchmarking is a questionable technique (as has been for grid computing [9]) due to the fact that performance figures cannot be representative to the *entire cloud*, just for some *services* — potentially a very small subset of the cloud — *actually utilized* in the experiment and virtualization adds another factor to unreproducible experiments. Hence, in our view, the traditional notion of benchmarking physical resources is not applicable for the entire cloud. On the other hand we do use benchmark tools but not for measuring the infrastructure rather, for providing raw data on the performance of a VM instance. Benchmarking in this setting is part of the process but not the process itself.

In the followings, in Section 2 the related work is intorduced, in Section 3 the concept, design principles and technical details of our proposed performance characterization method are presented. Test cases in Section 4 give a practical validation of the approach and Section 5 concludes the paper.

2 Related Work

An overview of grid performance analysis and its tools [4] already surveyed the difficulties of measuring any dynamic, heterogeneous computing infrastructure and pointed out that well-established methods of (parallel) benchmarking are not applicable where virtualization is present.

The primary goal of the CloudHarmony [1] is to make cloud services comparable, therefore they provide objective, independent performance comparisons between different cloud providers. Using these data, customers can quickly compare providers and have reasonable expectations for cloud performance. However, CloudHarmony can only provide quantitative performance data in a raw form produced by benchmark tools and can not present refined qualitative information created from processed benchmark results. As performance data are produced by multiple benchmark tools, they quite often contain discrepancies, contradictions or simply not easily interpretable by a human.

Garg et al. [3] also recognize the difficulty for customers to select service providers. In their paper, they propose a mechanism and a framework to measure the quality and prioritize Cloud services. This solution evaluates Cloud offerings and rank them based on their ability to meet the users Quality of Service (QoS) requirements. This work addresses slightly different aspects of characterizing a service than our work: less emphasis on the performance and more on the quality.

The notion of fuzzy inference for resource modeling appears in [18] in a different setting. The work is aimed at realizing a two-level resource management system with autonomic resource allocation. To this end, local and global controllers are using fuzzy logic to deal with the complexity of the virtualized data center and the uncertainties of the dynamically changing workloads. Virtual containers are treated as black boxes and their behaviour is modeled without any a priori knowledge using fuzzy logic. Ultimately, workload and related resource needs to meet QoS criteria are learned by the system. Albeit strongly related to our work, in this setting the fuzzy inference is used for resource control and not for performance characterisation — performance data are simply input to the mechanism.

Another aspect of fuzzy resource management appears in [17], namely fulfilling performance guarantees in the presence of interference of requests (especially, for non-partitionable resources) of co-hosted VMs. The aim of the fuzzy model is to detect the performance coupling of co-hosted VMs using a fuzzy a multi-input-multi-output model. The model quantifies the contention of competing resources and this information is used for VM placement and resource allocation. This approach is also similar to ours but analyses performance in a broader sense: capturing the relationship between resource allocations and the performance of the hosted applications.

The work presented in [13] applies the same mechanism to a different problem: trust and trust management but defines performance as a component of trust. Other factors are financial and agility and each such factor has many sub-metrics. The similarity to our work appears in unifying the diverse quantities into a single metrics of trust. They also propose a hierarchical (2-stage) fuzzy inference framework. This work differs mainly in the scope and the level of details of performance characterisation.

A.Vanitha et al., [16] investigate the cloud infrastructures as test bed environments for software developments. They presented a similar notion of fuzzy logic for performance evaluation. The most important difference to our work is in the fuzzy inference mechanism: they apply multidimensional inference whereas we propose hierarchical one. Their model uses a few input parameters only and they do not take the CPU performance into account in the procedure. This presumably could be the consequence of the complexity of multidimensional inference. Our solution is aimed at eliminating this obstacle by a hierarchy and hence, it can provide a generic framework for performance evaluation in cloud environments.

3   A Novel Approach to Cloud Performance Characterization

3.1   Principles

The theoretical and technical difficulties of performance characterization of a complex infrastructure were presented in Section 1. In this section we narrow the scope to processing, presenting and interpreting the performance metrics. We assume, raw performance data are gathered by some monitoring and/or benchmarking tool. Still, this data set is inappropriate due to its large dimensionality, incomparable and incompatible data types and lack of any structure. Common approaches apply statistical methods, noise filtering, feature extraction and similar numerical procedures to reduce the information to the most essential details and get readable and comparable performance figures. Performance characterisation has many dimensions and these are not independent. For instance, comparing two CPUs is possible but comparing two CPUs so that the memory is also taken into consideration is surprisingly complex: neither the CPU nor the memory speeds determine the performance but their interaction via subtle details in the actual application. These correlations are present in practically all dimensions of performance yet, their exact formulation is extremely hard analytically.

Fuzzy techniques have a vast range of features and potential application fields. We focus on their ability to transform quantitative information into qualitative one so that the resulted data is concise, readable, interpretable and comparable. Fuzzy techniques are based on the negation of the basic principle in set theory as 'a certain element is either element of a set or not'. Instead, fuzzy set theory assumes a metric, how much, or in what degree a certain element belongs to a set. This metric called *membership function* ranges between 0 (not element of the set) and 1 (element of the set). In such a way uncertain values, subjective measures can be captured and handled in a mathematical framework.

Fuzzy logic is a many-valued logic based on the fuzzy sets where logic variables have values between 0 (false) and 1 (true). It allows reasoning on uncertain or partial information where different degrees of 'true' is possible [20]. Fuzzy values may also be assigned symbolic or linguistic tags resembling intuitive classification. A fuzzy inference is a method where fuzzificated (values assigned to fuzzy sets) input variables are mapped onto output variables and the result is defuzzificated.

Recall the example above, a CPU of architecture A and frequency f_1 with memory of size M_1 and bandwidth b_1 is hardly comparable numerically to a CPU of architecture B and frequency f_2 with memory of size M_2 and bandwidth b_2; none of the numerical comparisons would yield a definite answer. However, after fuzzification – transforming the values into fuzzy sets – this question is reduced to a more comprehensible form of comparing an 'upper mediocre' processor with 'large and fast' memory to a 'lower top' processor with 'small and very fast' memory. The relationship between these sets can be precisely described by fuzzy rules resulting a similarly readable and easily comparable result.

A fundamental problem in a fuzzy inference system is that the number of rules increases exponentially with the system variables involved. The hierarchical fuzzy systems (HFS) [19] [6] have the advantage that the total number of rules is greatly reduced by a hierarchical structure, linear with the number of input variables [10]. A HFS divides the inference into stages so that a subset of input variables produce intermediate results and these results are taken as inputs in subsequent stages whereas, the intermediate results may also possess interpretable meaning.

The core of our concept is to build a hierarchical fuzzy system so that the stages of the hierarchy correspond to certain aspects of performance. We consider CPU, memory, disk and network as main determining factors. In an experimental setup these were captured by 157 parameters. In a flat fuzzy inference system the number of corresponding fuzzy rules would be in the magnitude of n^{157} where n is proportional to the number of fuzzy sets (i.e., granularity of rules, how finely the sets are described). We categorized the parameters according to the four main aspects and established sub-categories within each (cf. Figure 2.) In such a way input parameters to an inference stage do not exceed 7 and thus, the overall number of rules in the system is bounded by $c * n^7$ where c is the number of inference stages.

3.2   Framework Design

Figure 1 provides an architectural overview and presents the components of the proposed system. At the lowest level of hierarchy input data called "raw performance data" are produced by benchmarking probes. These probes are realised as virtual machines (VM instances) and executed on some cloud resources, involving steps of authentication, deployment, and VM control. On one hand the system core (depicted as Core & Valuator) provides a part of these essential functions. The Image Repository and the IaaS client/API interface (top right) are responsible for storing the disk image for the probes and handling (deploying, launching and stopping) VM instances. The disk image contains a preconfigured Phoronix Test Suite (PTS) application (a probe) for realizing the raw measurement procedures on the infrastructure. Images are deployed on target clouds (Cloud#1, Cloud#2, etc.) prepared and run as VM instances, called PerfVMs in the followings. PerfVMs execute the appropriately configured benchmark suite and push the raw results into the central object store. The Valuator part of the Core & Valuator component realises database handling as well as evaluating fuzzy results (to be described in details in Section 3.3).

3.3   Details of Valuator

The Valuator realizes the essential functionality of the performance characterization as it aggregates raw benchmark data and associates symbolic performance values with the IaaS clouds. It provides the fuzzy inferences systems and stores the results in a database. The corresponding fuzzy rules are described in a standardized control language [5].

Figure 2 presents the proposed three layered HFS. In the first layer (L0), the raw benchmark results produced by the probes of PerfVM are taken as inputs. These are already processed by the probes so that erroneous measurements and noise are filtered out and the deviation of the results are within limits. Data are grouped by benchmark tools such as compilation performance, database performance, disk write performance, numeric performance, etc. A fuzzy inference

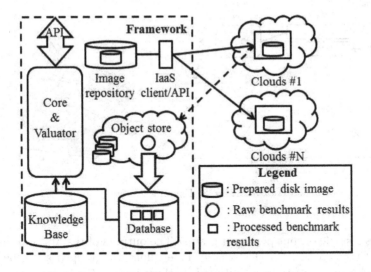

Fig. 1. Framework components

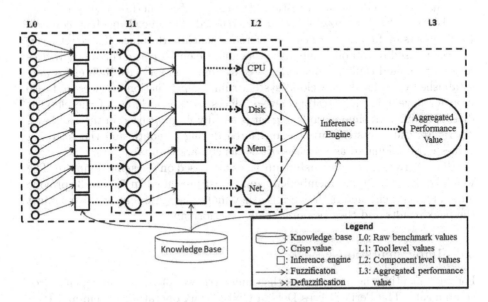

Fig. 2. Hierarchical fuzzy system

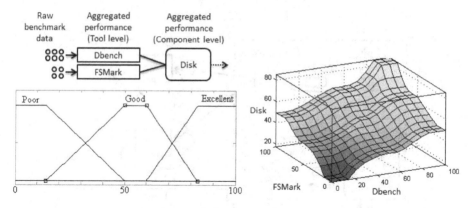

Fig. 3 Example

produces a single output per input groups. The outputs of the first layer are the inputs of the second layer (L1) where these values are grouped again by probe types and a fuzzy inference is initiated on these inputs. For instance, first level inputs are the execution times of three CPU benchmark tool. As an output, a single fuzzy metric is produced that represents the CPU performance. Similar tests are carried out for disk, memory and network. From the numerous raw data items four outputs are generated representing each categories.

The last layer groups the component level values and provides a single value (L3) that we consider characteristic to the cloud infrastructure in scope.

A key aspect is how fuzzy rules are constructed. The knowledge base contains the membership functions, rules and reference benchmark values. These reference values are used to establish the fuzzy sets and are empiric as a common practice for designing and tuning fuzzy logic based systems and services. References were established on a local IaaS cloud system running production services and also used for developing and testing new products so the workload of the cloud is diverse in different time periods (e.g., it is usually more utilized in the daytime). Therefore, the infrastructure was measured during a month and the reference values were calculated as averages of the benchmark results.

All fuzzy rules and membership functions are based on the same template. The weighted rules with the membership functions, presented in Figure 3, provide an appropriate characteristic, because they make the system insensitive against the peak results and they penalize the low performance.

3.4 Implementation

For implementing the prototype of the framework, we solely relied on open source components. The PerfVM uses Debian GNU/Linux operating system and PTS for producing benchmark data from the target clouds. These data are stored in central storage that is accessible via a Simple Storage Service (S3) compatible interface. The proposed framework is implemented in Python [15] and it uses the freely available draft version of Fuzzy Control Language (FCL) and pyfuzzy (a Python fuzzy library package). The FCLs describes (i) the requested input variables and their fuzzy membership functions; (ii) the output variables; (iii) the defuzzification method and rules. The system uses the Central of Gravity (CoG) defuzzification method. The fuzzy inference results are stored in a MySQL database. For the evaluation, the Fuzzy Toolbox of Matlab [12] was used.

4   Proof of Concept

In this section, we demonstrate the effectiveness of our proposed performance characterization method by explaining a part of the whole procedure, the disk performance process as an example. Experiments were carried out on raw performance data collected from the SZTAKI Cloud and from the European region of Amazon EC2. The experiment is a hypothetic performance (wrt. disk I/O) comparison of the two services running on the general purpose m1.medium instance type. We present the benchmark results both representing the 'common approaches' and the characterization produced by our method and contrast the two. They are examined in terms of correctness, comparability and readability.

Figure 3 shows our example, the disk evaluation sub-process composed of a two layered HFS.

DBench and fs_mark produce the raw benchmark data (L0). The tool uses I/O patterns that are similar to what a particular application performs. It can simulate concurrent clients in order to predict the robustness and I/O throughput of the underlying storage system. The fs_mark tool can test synchronous write workloads with different running options such as number of files, file size, directory depth or number of used threads (for instance the third column in Table 1, where the test wrote 5000 files through 4 threads with 1 MB size per file) that makes it adequate for benchmarking I/O performance. Both tools provide reliable information about the I/O system of the tested machines as presented in Tables 1 and 2. Recall our aim as it was put forward in Section 1: customers are curious if a service meet the expectations, if the performance of two services can be compared objectively. If one examines the figures in Tables 1 and 2, no clear conclusion can be drawn. For instance, raw performance figures in Table 1 suggest that SZTAKI Cloud is superior to Amazon EC2 yet, it is impossible to trace *how much* it is better (differences are not proportional); *in what measure* it exceeds the limits declared in SLAs. Roughly the same applies to measurements presented in Table 2. Hence, it is a difficult to infer the performance characteristic of clouds solely from the raw benchmark data at level L0. On the other hand, performance metrics at level L1 produced by our method (denoted as *Calculated value* in Tables 1 and 2) are a result of fuzzy inference, normalisation and defuzzification.

Understanding and analysing raw benchmark data requires domain knowledge whereas the calculated values are easily comprehensible: instead of a vector of metrics, a single aggregated value between 0 and 100 represents the

Table 1. fs_mark results

Args [Options]	1000 Files, 1MB size	5000 Files, 1MB Size, 4 Threads	4000 Files, 32 Sub Dirs, 1MB Size	1000 Files, 1MB Size, No Sync / FSync	Calculated value [0-100]
SZTAKI [Files/s]	58.55	93.87	68.33	132.63	62.55
Amazon [Files/s]	38.87	49.73	40.83	119.07	43.60

Table 2. Dbench results

Arguments [Client(s)]	1	6	12	48	128	256	Calculated value [0-100]
SZTAKI [MB/s]	113.385	225.64	242.08	220.02	185.53	134.38	72.16
Amazon [MB/s]	80.14	174.37	166.09	176.74	177.51	119.48	62.06

Table 3. Aggregated results

Tool	DBench	fs_mark	Calculated value
SZTAKI [0-100]	72.16	62.55	62.98
Amazon [0-100]	62.06	43.60	47.05

characterization. Hence, comparison is straightforward. Reference values (e.g., limits) can also be transformed into the [0-100] scale that makes it possible to compare the performance wrt. SLA minimums. In this particular example the reference value was set to 50. Furthermore, these performance metrics produced by a fuzzy calculation can be easily transformed to symbolic, easy-to-read values for human interpretation such "medium performance", "high performance", "upper medium performance" and similar tags in arbitrary details and resolution. Accordingly, if reference values are introduced into the system, one may compare symbolicaly as "above the reference point", "close to the reference point", etc. At the next level of hierarchy these calculated values at level L1 are taken as inputs and values for level 2 (component level in this example) are produced in a similar way, cf. Table 3 for the summary of L1 and L2 values.

Important to notice the properties of the raw and calculated performance metrics as compared in Table 3. While benchmark tools typicaly generate outputs by simply averaging the measurements, HFS is a more elaborate calculation that is able to highlight or dampen (reward or penalize) certain aspects or details of the performance characteristics. Observing the results and the generated level

L2 system output surface, presented in Figure 3, it can be seen that the HFS or its rules cannot be substituted by any linear approximation schemes.

In this particular experiment SZTAKI Cloud performed better than the reference system because both of the DBench and fs_mark resulted a score above than 50. In case of Amazon EC2, the DBench performance was better than the reference value, however the fs_mark was below. The introduced example and its results demonstrated that the fuzzy inference method generated a performance characterization that enabled the straightforward comparison or classification of services based on their performances and the created HFS meets the requirements set in Section 1.

5   Conclusion and Future Work

In this paper, we discussed the difficulties of the performance characterisation of IaaS clouds that originate mainly from virtualization. There is an evident need for consumers to compare the cloud services in terms of "performance" on the other hand, it is not easy to capture the notion of "cloud performance" and the conventional performance tools such as benchmarks deliver large sets of numeric data that are not necessarily consistent and hard to analyse or compare. We analysed the reasons and background of this issue. Our work is aimed at establishing a framework for normalized, comparable and readable performance analysis of IaaS providers so that services of the different providers become easily characterized.

Our method also builds on benchmark tools at the low level but performance data are processed in a hierarchical fuzzy systems. The fuzzy framework allows to transform multi-dimensional numeric (quantitative) values into symbolic (qualitative) metrics of lesser dimensionality. This transformation is based on fuzzy inference governed by fuzzy rules. The large number of variables may lead to unacceptable exponential complexity of rules. We alleviated this issue by a hierarchical fuzzy inference system that both reduces the complexity of a single inference stage and also classifies performance variables so that meaningful performance characterization can be established at different levels and different details of the system.

Finally, we evaluated the prototype by comparing the Amazon EC2 and SZTAKI IaaS clouds that confirmed the applicability of the framework. In the future, we plan to improve our framework by refining FCLs for more comprehensive evaluations. Moreover, we plan to extend the framework with the capability of assessing other aspects of performance (see Sections 1 and 2) such as Service Level Agreement (SLA) violations of IaaS providers.

Acknowledgment. The authors would like to thank KMR-12-2012-0055 – "Cloud accreditations service" for its financial support.

References

1. Cloudharmony.com (June 2014), http://cloudharmony.com
2. Crowl, L.A.: How to measure, present, and compare parallel performance. IEEE Parallel & Distributed Technology: Systems & Technology 2(1), 9–25 (1994)
3. Garg, S., Versteeg, S., Buyya, R.: Smicloud: A framework for comparing and ranking cloud services. In: 2011 Fourth IEEE International Conference on Utility and Cloud Computing (UCC), pp. 210–218 (2011)
4. Gerndt, M., Mohr, B., Träff, J.L.: Evaluating openMP performance analysis tools with the APART test suite. In: Danelutto, M., Vanneschi, M., Laforenza, D. (eds.) Euro-Par 2004. LNCS, vol. 3149, pp. 155–162. Springer, Heidelberg (2004)
5. International Electrotechnical Commission, Programmable controllers - Fuzzy control programming, IEC 61131-7 (2000)
6. Lee, M.L., Chung, H.Y., Yu, F.M.: Modeling of hierarchical fuzzy systems. Fuzzy Soto and Systems 138(2), 343–361 (2003)
7. Miller, B.P., Callaghan, M.D., Cargille, J.M., Hollingsworth, J.K., Irvin, R.B, Karavanic, K.L., Kunchithapadam, K., Newhall, T.: The paradyn parallel performance measurement tool. Computer 28(11), 37–46 (1995)
8. Nelson, R., Towsley, D., Tantawi, A.N.: Performance analysis of parallel processing systems. IEEE Transactions on Software Engineering 14(4), 532–540 (1988)
9. Németh, Z., Gombás, G., Balaton, Z.: Performance evaluation on grids: directions, issues, and open problems. In: Proceedings of the 12th Euromicro Conference on Parallel, Distributed and Network-Based Processing, pp. 290–297. IEEE (2004)
10. Raju, G., Zhou, J., Kisner, R.A.: Hierarchical fuzzy control. International Journal of Control 54(5), 1201–1216 (1991)
11. Shende, S.S., Malony, A.D.: The tau parallel performance system. International Journal of High Performance Computing Applications 20(2), 287–311 (2006)
12. Sivanandam, S.: Introduction to fuzzy logic using MATLAB. Springer (2007)
13. Supriya, M., Venkataramana, L., Sangeeta, K., Patra, G.K.: Article: Estimating trust value for cloud service providers using fuzzy logic. International Journal of Computer Applications 48(19), 28–34 (2012)
14. Truong, H.-L., Fahringer, T.: SCALEA: A performance analysis tool for distributed and parallel programs. In: Monien, B., Feldmann, R.L. (eds.) Euro-Par 2002. LNCS, vol. 2400, pp. 75–85. Springer, Heidelberg (2002)
15. Van Rossum, G., et al.: Python programming language. In: USENIX Annual Technical Conference (2007)
16. Vanitha, K.A., Alagarsamy, K.: Article: A fuzzy mathematical model for peformance testing in cloud computing using user defined parameters. International Journal of Software Engineering and Applications 4(4), 27–39 (2013)
17. Wang, L., Xu, J., Zhao, M.: Modeling vm performance interference with fuzzy mimo model. In: 7th International Workshop on Feedback Computing (Feedback-Computing, co-held with ICAC2012) (2012)
18. Xu, J., Zhao, M., Fortes, J.A.B., Carpenter, R., Yousif, M.S.: On the use of fuzzy modeling in virtualized data center management. In: ICAC, p. 25 (2007)
19. Yager, R.R.: On the construction of hierarchical fuzzy systems models. IEEE Transactions on Systems, Man, and Cybernetics, Part C: Applications and Reviews 28(1), 55–66 (1998)
20. Zadeh, L.A.: Fuzzy sets. Information and Control 8(3), 338–353 (1965)

ExaStamp: A Parallel Framework for Molecular Dynamics on Heterogeneous Clusters

Emmanuel Cieren[1], Laurent Colombet[1], Samuel Pitoiset[2],
and Raymond Namyst[2]

[1] CEA, DAM, DIF, F-91297 Arpajon, France
[2] Université de Bordeaux, INRIA, 351 Cours de la Libération,
33405 Talence Cedex, France

Abstract. Recent evolution of supercomputer architectures toward massively multi-cores nodes equipped with many-core accelerators is leading to make MPI-only applications less effective. To fully tap into the potential of these architectures, hybrid approaches – mixing MPI, threads and CUDA or OpenCL – usually meet performance expectations, but at the price of huge development and optimization efforts.

In this paper, we present a programming framework specialized for molecular dynamics simulations. This framework allows end-users to develop their computation kernels in the form of sequential-looking functions and generates multi-level parallelism combining vectorized and SIMD kernels, multi-threading and communications. We report on preliminary performance results obtained on different architectures with widely used force computation kernels.

Keywords: Molecular dynamics, MPI, threads, TBB, vectorization, OpenCL, object-oriented design, Lennard-Jones, EAM.

1 Introduction

Molecular dynamics (MD) is a method used to compute the dynamical properties of a particles system, widely spread in fields such as Materials Science, Chemistry and Biology. With its scalable structure, MD took a substantial step with the ever increasing computer capabilities: after starting at a few hundreds particles [1], MD simulations have successfully coped with million particles systems in the 90s [11], before reaching one billion particles in 2005 [9].

Parallelism in most MD codes is limited to classical domain-decomposition techniques, and the use of accelerators is still rare. In the same time, future processor architectures are expected to feature a large number of cores with a fair decrease of the available memory per core, and the use of a co-processor has become quite common. The Intel® Xeon Phi™ architecture illustrates this trend well.

Stamp is a classical molecular dynamics production code which has been developed at CEA for twenty years [18]. Its flat MPI architecture and the absence

L. Lopes et al. (Eds.): Euro-Par 2014 Workshops, Part II, LNCS 8806, pp. 121–132, 2014.

of vectorization will obviously not fit requirements of next generation processors. To the best of our knowledge, no existing MD program is able to exploit clusters of such hybrid nodes, potentially equipped with different accelerators, in a uniform way. The development of a new object-oriented framework ExaStamp, capable of fulfill these new needs, began in 2012.

Optimized for large scale simulations of solid-state materials and shock physics, this framework supports several levels of parallelization. Besides the classical hybrid programming model, we developed a tool which enable generation of efficient vectorized code and *OpenCL* kernels for modern CPUs, GPUs and Intel® Xeon Phi™ accelerators. The complexity of implementing different parallelisms has been hidden from the non-expert developer through its object-oriented design. For main algorithms, our framework contains parallelism in specific modules. In the case of compute-intensive parts, specific vectorized instructions can be instantiated from the same sequential-looking code. Furthermore, data structures and their associated algorithms were carefully designed so as to keep the memory footprint as low as possible, meeting the requirements of future many-core architectures.

This paper discusses the design, implementation and performance of ExaStamp framework. It is organized as follows: in Sect. 2 we introduce Molecular Dynamics simulations and present the classical parallelization approaches. The design and implementation of our approach are are presented in Sect. 3. Performance results on different computers architectures are detailed and analyzed in Sect. 4. Finally, some conclusions and perspectives are discussed.

2   Molecular Dynamics

The main principle of MD consists in numerically integrating Newton's equation of motion $f = m\,a$, where the force on a particle depends on the interactions with all others [2]. Among the multiple ways to solve this equation, the *Leapfrog* integrator and the *Verlet* integrator, which are equivalent, are the most used as they offer greater stability, as well as other properties, for a low computational cost [14].

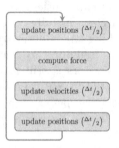

Fig. 1. Overview of a time-step in a MD simulation using the Leapfrog integrator

In most MD simulations, particles are treated as points and the interacting force between particles is approximated as a gradient of a potential that depends on the distance between those particles. The force computation is obviously the most challenging part: it contains all the physics of the simulation and can take up to 95% of the total time. When this potential comes from quantum mechanics principles, we talk about *ab initio* molecular dynamics; in the other case, the term *classical* molecular dynamics is used. Potentials from classical MD are empirical or semi-empirical; they are computed from an analytical formula, or they can be interpolated from tabulated values [22]. In this paper, we will focus on short-range interactions: it means that beyond a given distance r_c called the *cutoff* distance, interactions will be neglected. This approximation is completely justified for solid materials, since distant atoms are "screened" by nearer atoms. In case of systems with electrostatic or gravitational effects, long-range interactions cannot be omitted and special algorithms have been designed [10].

Although it was first designed to study gases, the *Lennard-Jones* potential (LJ) [13] has been used in a large part of material science, and became a standard benchmark for MD codes. The LJ potential is a pair potential, which means that it describes the interaction between a pair of particles (within the cutoff distance). For this potential, the expression of the energy on a particle i is given by

$$E_i = \frac{1}{2} \sum_j V(r_{ij}), \text{ with } V(r_{ij}) \overset{r_{ij} \leq r_c}{=} 4\varepsilon \left[\left(\frac{\sigma}{r_{ij}} \right)^{12} - \left(\frac{\sigma}{r_{ij}} \right)^6 \right], \quad (1)$$

where ε and σ are parameters which denotes respectively the well depth and the bond length.

Yet, pair potentials remain limited when it comes to bonded interactions: as an example, Stillinger and Weber developed a three-body potential for Silicon crystals [19]. For the study of metals and their alloys, effects from the electron charge density have a significant impact: the *Embedded Atom Method* (EAM) provides an accurate model and an acceptable computational cost [6,8,7].

$$E_i = \frac{1}{2} \sum_j \phi(r_{ij}) + F \left(\sum_j \rho_j(r_{ij}) \right), \quad (2)$$

where ϕ is a simple pair potential, ρ_j the contribution of the electron density near atom j, and F an embedding function representing the amount of energy required to place atom i in the electron cloud. Both ϕ and ρ are canceled beyond the cutoff distance. Common EAM potentials are for instance the Johnson potential, the *Sutton-Chen* (SC) and the Tersoff potentials [12,20,21].

3   A Framework for Molecular Dynamics Simulations

ExaStamp has been designed to replace the production code Stamp on the next generation of supercomputers. Targeting solid-state material and shock physics studies, it should be able to perform very large scale simulation of complex systems (a billion particles with many-body potentials) on a various range of architectures. As a future production code, all the programming refinement should be hidden from standard developers. To this end, we chose the C++ language and widely used C++11 standard features. With upcoming parallel architectures in mind, we also focused on minimizing memory footprint of our data structures, so as to handle large sets of particles.

There are three basic ways to parallelize work in a MD simulation: parallelization over particles, parallelization over pairs of particles and domain-decomposition. As explained in [16], the first two proved inefficient, as they require to many communications over the interconnection network, leaving the third one as the only possibility despite potential load-balancing issues.

The latter method is typically used in MPI implementations: the global domain is split and each process is assigned to a sub domain. To compute interactions on the edges, each sub-domain will be enclosed in a ghost layer, which consists in a copy of the boundaries with its neighboring sub-domains. In practice, the length of this ghost layer is generally the cutoff radius. The outline in Fig. 1 is hardly modified: everything is performed in parallel, one extra step is used to send and receive particles moving between sub-domains, and another one to update the ghost layer.

3.1   Overall Parallelization Strategy

In our approach, the global domain is *overdecomposed* with respect to the underlying cluster nodes (as illustrated in Fig. 2). Several domains can thus be assigned to a single node, each being treated either by regular CPU cores or by accelerators. We now present the main concepts and algorithms used in our framework.

Node and Communication Manager. A Node is the top structure of the code. We decided to use this terminology as we intend to use one Node structure per machine node in production mode, so that we can take advantage of shared-memory systems. Thus it contains the integration scheme, a list of one or several domains, and a communication manager. The Node is also responsible for IOs.

The Communication manager structure is an object-oriented framework for communications. It allows a developer to create its own custom types and provides wrappers to use these types in communication.

Integration Scheme. The family of integration schemes depicted in Fig. 1 reveals that they are basically made of the same elementary functions: updating a quantity (particles positions or velocities) with an explicit (first or second order) Euler scheme, or the force computation. Therefore we can define a NumericalScheme as an object with a function oneStep(), which contains a sequence of predefined elementary functions. Implementing a new scheme does not require the knowledge of lower classes implementation, as long as the requested elementary functions are implemented.

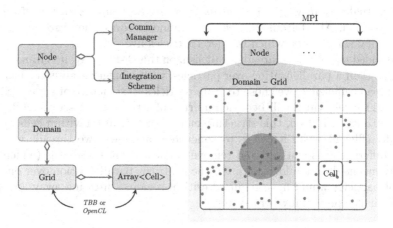

Fig. 2. Overview of ExaStamp architecture: pseudo-UML diagram with main classes of the code (left) with "physical" representation (right). The dark orange circle corresponds to the area of influence of a particle, whereas the light orange zone is the set of cells where neighbors will be looked for

Domain. Domain concept gathers an interface and its possible implementations. Domain interface contains basic accesses and elementary functions required by all `NumericalScheme` objects. A `Domain` proceeds to a reorganization and code factorization of these requirements for their implementation in lower-level classes.

Let us consider the force computation example. The code provides the possibility to overlap communication with computation: it means that it is possible to start updating ghost layers and compute forces inside the domain while communications are processing. Once the ghost layer update is over, we can start the force computation on the domain's edges. A `NumericalScheme` object does not need to know whether communication overlap has been enabled, it just asks for the forces computation. In the `Domain` class, two different functions handled by a strategy pattern are available.

Grid and Cells. When it comes to the force computation, each particle should get a list of its neighbors. Let us partition the domain with a virtual cubic mesh with a size slightly greater than the cutoff radius. Given a particle, we only have to look for its neighbors in the cell where it lives and its neighboring cells, which makes a total of 27 cells (in a three-dimensional space) to explore. This how the linked-list cell method [2] starts, reducing a naive pair search in $O(N^2)$ into a $O(N)$ algorithm.

Though we will not use this method (linked-cell list are not well suited neither for parallelism nor for vectorization), we will fully benefit from the cell partitioning. The task of `Grid` object is to implement all services required by the `Domain` class. In order to keep a high level of modularity without paying the cost of virtualization, we used a *curiously recurring template pattern* [5] in its implementation. Apart from this, we could almost reduce the `Grid` object into an array of `Cell` objects, which is where particles live.

We decided to focus the thread parallelism on this `Cell` array: it is roughly the same idea than a parallelization over particles, with a bigger grain-size. To maximize threads efficiency, we chose to store particles as structure of arrays (SOA) at the `Cell` level, which will become an array of structures of arrays (AOSOA) at the `Grid` level. Indeed, this structure enable vectorization within cells and is especially efficient when it comes to concurrent accesses: two threads working on two different cells can add and remove particles from those cells (which potentially means data reallocation). On the contrary, parallelization over one big array of particles would have required critical regions, throwing away any goal of performance on a many core system.

3.2 Code Specialization

Performing high performance molecular dynamics over hybrid machines requires to use highly optimized computation kernels combining threads/tasks and vectorization over CPU cores or Intel® Xeon Phi™accelerators, and highly parallel SIMD code for GPU accelerators. In our Framework, domains assigned to regular CPU cores are parallelized using Intel®'s *Threading Building Blocks* (TBB) [4], whereas domains assigned to GPU or Intel® Xeon Phi™accelerators rely on a series of OpenCL kernels which parallelize each step of an iteration loop.

Despite progress made by compilers regarding auto-vectorization, writing code to maximize the number of vectorization opportunities detected by the compiler remains a delicate process. Writing efficient OpenCL code is also a delicate task, and actually requires to perform target-specific (and even platform-specific) optimizations. Intel, AMD and NVIDIA programming guides, for instance, each suggest different optimizations which can actually lower performance on other platforms. For all these reasons, implementing a new particle interaction potential would normally require to develop and optimize multiple versions of the force computation kernel (Fig. 1), in multiple languages.

To solve this problem, our framework allows force computation steps to be written as a set of C++ sequential-looking functions, as illustrated on Fig. 3 for the LJ potential.

When instantiated on multi-core architectures, this code is transformed using C++ template classes to generate intrinsic vector functions instead of scalar operations, to guarantee that the force computation kernel is fully vectorized. A unique sequential-looking code is used, whatever the type of vectorization is performed (no vectorization, SSE, AVX, or IMCI[1]). The obtained vectorized kernel is used inside Cells and is called from within a sequential loop iterating over particles. At the upper level, each iteration step is parallelized using a TBB *parallel for* loop iterating over Cells (as described in Section 3.1).

---

[1] Intel® Initial Many Core Instructions, a set of vector instructions for the KNC.

```
void lennardJones ( double *ep_i,
    *fx_i, *fy_i, *fz_i,
    *rx_i, *ry_i, *rz_i ) {

    vector_t t0, t1, t2, t3, t4, t5;

    t0.load (rx_i);
    t1.load (ry_i);
    t2.load (rz_i);

    t3 = inv(t0*t0 + t1*t1 + t2*t2);

    t4 = t3 * _sigma2;
    t5 = t4 * t4 * t4;
    t4 = t5 * t5;

    t5 = t4 - t5;
    t4 = t5 + t4;

    t5 = _2epsilon  * t5;
    t4 = _24epsilon * t4 * t3;

    t0 = t0 * t4;
    t1 = t1 * t4;
    t2 = t2 * t4;

    t0.store (fx_i);
    t1.store (fy_i);
    t2.store (fz_i);
    t5.store (ep_i);

}
```

template<...> class vector_t →

(a)	double
(b)	__m128d
(c)	__m256d
(d)	__m512d

template<...> vector_t operator * (...)

(a)	t1 * t1
(b)	_mm_mul_pd(t1, t1)
(c)	_mm256_mul_pd(t1, t1)
(d)	_mm512_mul_pd(t1, t1)

$$t_5 = \left(\frac{\sigma}{\|r_i\|}\right)^6$$
$$t_4 = \left(\frac{\sigma}{\|r_i\|}\right)^{12}$$

$$t_5 = 2\varepsilon\left[\left(\frac{\sigma}{\|r_i\|}\right)^{12} - \left(\frac{\sigma}{\|r_i\|}\right)^6\right]$$
$$t_4 = 24\varepsilon\left[2\left(\frac{\sigma}{\|r_i\|}\right)^{12} - \left(\frac{\sigma}{\|r_i\|}\right)^6\right]\frac{1}{\|r_i\|^2}$$

Flags used to select right intrinsics instructions (at compile time):

(a)	<no flag>
(b)	__vectorize_sse
(c)	__vectorize_avx
(d)	__vectorize_mic

Fig. 3. Implementation of force and energy computation function using a LJ potential. If V denotes the potential as described in (1), we have to compute $e_i = \frac{1}{2}V(\|r_i\|)$ and $f_i = -\nabla_{\|r_i\|}V(\|r_i\|)$. Written in a C-like way (except for the function signature which contains templates and operator), it hides intrinsics functions enabled at compile-time with predefined flags.

When instantiated on accelerators, the sequential version of the code (see variant a on Fig. 3) is called from within an OpenCL force computation kernel. This kernel is executed by as many OpenCL *workitems* as the number of particles in the domain. The generic part of the kernel is optimized either for GPUs (coalesced memory accesses, bank conflicts avoidance, weak code divergence) or for Intel® Xeon Phi™accelerators (vectorization, cache reuse), but all these optimizations are hidden to the end-user. In the next Section, we present the performance achieved by our framework on various hardware platforms.

4   Performance Evaluation

All tests in this Section have been performed on CCRT's clusters[2] (see Table 1 for CPU specifications – the GPU used for OpenCL test is a NVIDIA Tesla K20c).

---

[2] Centre de Calcul Recherche et Technologie – http://www-hpc.cea.fr/en/complexe/ccrt.html

Table 1. Specifications of CPU used for our different tests. Cache size displayed are L3 sizes, except for the KNC which is L2. Airain's Ivybridge and Standard partitions are respectively made of 360 and 594 nodes connected with an Infiniband QDR network.

| | Airain | | Cirrus |
	Ivybridge	Standard	KNC
Model	Intel® Xeon® CPU E5-2680 v2	Intel® Xeon® CPU E5-2680	Intel® Xeon Phi™ Coprocessor 5120D
Max Freq. (GHz)	2.8	2.7	1.05
Number of cores	2×10	2×8	60
Cache Size (MB)	25.60	20.48	30.00
Vectorization	AVX	AVX	IMCI

Code was compiled using Intel® compiler (version 14.0.2) with O3 optimization and vectorization enabled. Simulations involve a FCC lattice (a=0.354 nm) of copper at 600 K, using either a LJ (ε=0.583 eV, σ=0.227 nm and r_c=0.227 nm) or an analytic Sutton-Chen potential (c=33.2, ε=2.25 · 10^{-2} eV, a_0=0.327 nm, n=9.05, m=5.01 and r_c=0.729 nm).

4.1 Vectorization

On a Single CPU Core. To compare compilers auto-vectorization capabilities against hand-vectorized code, we use the sample code presented in Fig. 3 and generate both a naive version (variant a) and a SIMD version (variant b, c or d). Results in Table 2 clearly exhibit that hand-vectorization is mandatory to get high performance on non-trivial computation kernels.

Fig. 4 presents vectorization performance over a full simulation, for two potentials: a light one (LJ) and an expensive one (SC, with analytical functions). As expected, the use of vector units is still quite efficient, especially for the SC potential (which is about 40% faster). Its vectorization has been made possible

Table 2. Performances of our "SIMD" wrapper against a naive version for a LJ potential. Here we compare execution times in seconds (average on a million runs with arrays of size 256) of both versions for different vectorization modes. Tests were performed on an Ivybridge (first three lines) and a Intel® Xeon Phi™ (last two lines).

Mode	Flags		Naive	Simd	Speedup
Default	-O3		2.42	2.26	1.07
SSE	-O3 -msse4.1	-D__vectorize-sse	2.41	1.06	2.27
AVX	-O3 -mavx	-D__vectorize-avx	2.48	0.73	3.39
Default	-O3		46.80	36.24	1.29
IMCI	-O3 -mmic	-D__vectorize-mic	46.79	5.10	9.17

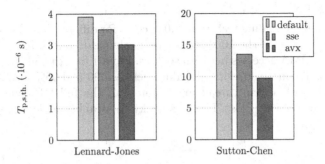

Fig. 4. Effect of vectorization for different potentials on Ivybridge (Airain). Simulations performed on 128 time-steps with one million atoms. $T_{\mathrm{p,s,th.}}$ represents the time per particle per iteration per thread.

thanks to Intel® Short Vector Math Library (SVML), which provides intrinsic instructions for advanced math functions. Issues between Intel® compiler and C++11 standard prevented us from performing full native code simulations on a Intel® Xeon Phi™.

4.2 Multithreading

In Fig. 3, we compared memory usage for different number of threads and MPI processes. Memory usage was measured with the `getrusage()` function given by the standard C library, and sum across processes when needed. If it remains constant for simulations using only TBB, we observe that those which use only MPI ones need up to 25% more memory. Differences are even more important on a larger runs: for 4.3 billion particles on 16,384 cores, simulations with respectively 1, 2 and 4 threads per MPI process need 11.5, 9.5, and 8.3 Terabytes of memory, which make the full MPI about 40% more expensive.

Table 3. Comparison of maximum memory usage (in GB) between MPI and threads simulations on one Ivybridge node. Simulations performed on 64 steps with a SC potential.

Total Num. Cores	1	10		20	
MPI × Threads	1×1	10×1	1×10	20×1	1×20
$2 \cdot 10^6$ atoms	3.82	4.35	3.85	4.80	3.87
$5 \cdot 10^6$ atoms	9.46	10.12	9.51	10.82	9.59
$10 \cdot 10^6$ atoms	18.86	19.77	18.97	20.90	19.06

4.3   Scalability

Results from a weak scaling test up to 2,048 cores for different number of threads are plotted on Fig. 5. If the 16 threads case is obviously out of touch, it can be explained by NUMA accesses between sockets. From 1 to 8 threads the efficiency drop is very well contained, with all values between 90 and 95% for 2,048 cores. Runs with more than one thread are faster than the full-MPI one, although efficiency values are very close. It seems tricky to establish a clear hierarchy.

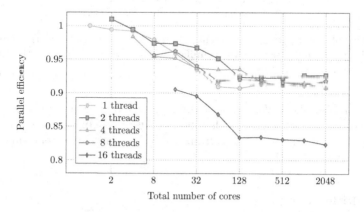

Fig. 5. Scaling tests of ExaStamp for different number of threads on Airain's Standard nodes. Simulations performed on 1,024 time-steps with $4.0 \cdot 10^5$ atoms per core using a SC potential.

4.4   Performances on Accelerators

Fig. 6 reports results obtained with the LJ potential on a Intel® Xeon Phi™ and a GPU. We observe that the GPU needs only five millions atoms to reach its peak performance, when the Intel® Xeon Phi™ requires around twenty. In single precision, the Intel® Xeon Phi™ gets slightly better performances (10% faster than the GPU), and this difference increases in double precision mode (+20%). Memory usage is perfectly linear with the number of atoms. As expected, the double precision mode requires twice the amount used for single precision one.

5   Related Work

Developed at Sandia National Laboratories, the LAMMPS [16] package has become a reference in MD. It can perform simulations up to a billion atoms on 64,000 cores (using mainly MPI), covering physics from solid-state materials to soft matter. Yet, its multithreads implementation is still limited to some modules, with no better performance than full MPI [17, Sect. 5]. Gromacs [3] and NAMD [15] are more recent high-performance oriented codes targeting biomolecular systems, which is far from condensed matter physics. As a result, these programs require a completely different coding approach than ours.

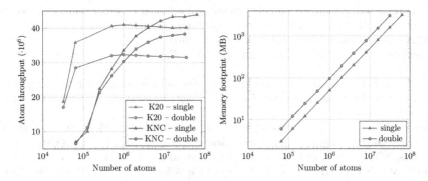

Fig. 6. Performance of OpenCL simulations on different accelerators, using LJ potential. For both single and double precision, we compare performance in term of atom throughput (number of atoms per second per iteration) and memory footprint.

6 Conclusion and Future Work

We presented ExaStamp, a classical molecular dynamics framework designed for production on new generation supercomputers. Its object oriented design allowed us to hide complexity introduced by multiple levels of parallelism. On that point, early returns by developers are very positive. Besides, performance results in terms of vectorization, scaling and memory usage are very promising.

We will soon be able to start testing on ExaStamp with native code on Intel® Xeon Phi™, which will undoubtedly be an important platform to achieve "real physics" simulations. On top of development of new potentials and numerical modules, we will also focus on the development of a dynamic load balancing capability on nodes level.

Acknowledgment. This work is integrated and supported by the PERFCLOUD project, a French FSN[3] cooperative project that associates academic and industrial partners to design and provide building blocks for new generations of HPC data-centers.

References

1. Alder, B.J., Wainwright, T.E.: Phase Transition for a Hard Sphere System. The Journal of Chemical Physics 27(5), 1208–1209 (1957)
2. Allen, M., Tildesley, D.: Computer Simulation of Liquids. Clarendon Press (1987)
3. Berendsen, H., van der Spoel, D., van Drunen, R.: GROMACS: A Message-passing Parallel Molecular Dynamics Implementation. Computer Physics Communications 91(1-3), 43–56 (1995)

---

[3] Fond pour la Société Numérique.

4. Contreras, G., Martonosi, M.: Characterizing and Improving the Performance of Intel Threading Building Blocks. In: IEEE International Symposium on Workload Characterization, IISWC 2008, pp. 57–66 (2008)
5. Coplien, J.O.: Curiously Recurring Template Patterns. C++ Rep. 7(2), 24–27 (1995)
6. Daw, M.S., Baskes, M.I.: Embedded-atom Method: Derivation and Application to Impurities, Surfaces, and other Defects in Metals. Phys. Rev. B 29, 6443–6453 (1984)
7. Daw, M.S., Foiles, S.M., Baskes, M.I.: The embedded-atom Method: a Review of Theory and Applications. Materials Science Reports 9(7-8), 251–310 (1993)
8. Foiles, S.M., Baskes, M.I., Daw, M.S.: Embedded-atom Method Functions for the FCC Metals Cu, Ag, Au, Ni, Pd, Pt, and their Alloys. Phys. Rev. B 33, 7983–7991 (1986)
9. Germann, T.C., Kadau, K., Swaminarayan, S.: 369 Tflop/s Molecular Dynamics Simulations on the Petaflop Hybrid Supercomputer 'Roadrunner', Concurrency and Computation: Practice and Experience 21(17), 2143–2159 (2009)
10. Greengard, L., Rokhlin, V.: A Fast Algorithm for Particle Simulations. Journal of Computational Physics 73(2), 325–348 (1987)
11. Hoover, W.G., De Groot, A.J., Hoover, C.G., Stowers, I.F., Kawai, T., Holian, B.L., Boku, T., Ihara, S., Belak, J.: Large-scale Elastic-plastic Indentation Simulations via Nonequilibrium Molecular Dynamics. Phys. Rev. A 42(10), 5844–5853 (1990)
12. Johnson, R.A.: Alloy Models with the Embedded-atom Method. Phys. Rev. B 39, 12554–12559 (1989)
13. Jones, J.E.: On the Determination of Molecular Fields. II. From the Equation of State of a Gas. Proceedings of the Royal Society of London. Series A 106(738), 463–477 (1924)
14. Leimkuhler, B.J., Reich, S., Skeel, R.D.: Integration Methods for Molecular Dynamics. In: Mesirov, J.P., Schulten, K., Sumners, D.W. (eds.) Mathematical Approaches to Biomolecular Structure and Dynamics. The IMA Volumes in Mathematics and its Applications, vol. 82, pp. 161–185. Springer, New York (1996)
15. Nelson, M.T., Humphrey, W., Gursoy, A., Dalke, A., Kalé, L.V., Skeel, R.D., Schulten, K.: NAMD: a Parallel, Object-oriented Molecular Dynamics Program. International Journal of High Performance Computing Applications 10(4), 251–268 (1996)
16. Plimpton, S.: Fast Parallel Algorithms for Short-range Molecular Dynamics. Journal of Computational Physics 117(1), 1–19 (1995)
17. Sandia National Laboratories: LAMMPS User Manual (2014), http://lammps.sandia.gov/doc/Manual.html
18. Soulard, L.: Molecular Dynamics Study of the Micro-spallation. The European Physical Journal D 50(3) (2008)
19. Stillinger, F.H., Weber, T.A.: Computer Simulation of Local Order in Condensed Phases of Silicon. Phys. Rev. B 31, 5262–5271 (1985)
20. Sutton, A.P., Chen, J.: Long-range Finnis-Sinclair Potentials. Philosophical Magazine Letters 61(3), 139–146 (1990)
21. Tersoff, J.: New Empirical Approach for the Structure and Energy of Covalent Systems. Phys. Rev. B 37, 6991–7000 (1988)
22. Wolff, D., Rudd, W.G.: Tabulated Potentials in Molecular Dynamics Simulations. Computer Physics Communications 120(1), 20–32 (1999)

Optimized Selection of Runtime Mode for the Reconfigurable PRAM-NUMA Architecture REPLICA Using Machine-Learning

Erik Hansson and Christoph Kessler

Dept. of Computer and Information Science
Linköpings universitet, Sweden
{eriha,chrke}@ida.liu.se

Abstract. The massively hardware multithreaded VLIW emulated shared memory (ESM) architecture REPLICA has a dynamically re-configurable on-chip network that offers two execution modes: PRAM and NUMA. PRAM mode is mainly suitable for applications with high amount of thread level parallelism (TLP) while NUMA mode is mainly for accelerating execution of sequential programs or programs with low TLP. Also, some types of regular data parallel algorithms execute faster in NUMA mode. It is not obvious in which mode a given program region shows the best performance. In this study we focus on generic stencil-like computations exhibiting regular control flow and memory access pattern. We use two state-of-the art machine-learning methods, C5.0 (decision trees) and Eureqa Pro (symbolic regression) to select which mode to use.We use these methods to derive different predictors based on the same training data and compare their results. The accuracy of the best derived predictors are 95% and are generated by both C5.0 and Eureqa Pro, although the latter can in some cases be more sensitive to the train-ing data. The average speedup gained due to mode switching ranges between 1.92 to 2.23 for all generated predictors on the evaluation test cases, and using a majority voting algorithm, based on the three best predictors, we can eliminate all misclassifications.

1 Introduction

In the multicore era we do not only face the problems that parallel programming brings; modern architectures and hardware platforms also expose the advantages and problems of managing heterogeneity. Today's computer systems usually have multicore processor chips and dedicated accelerators such as GPUs. To utilize these systems efficiently, boils down to selecting where and how to run a program. How to achieve high performance for real applications ist not straight forward, and predicting performance is even harder since aspects such as data locality and movement has to be considered.

In this study we use the VLIW massively hardware multithreaded emulated shared memory (ESM) architecture REPLICA. Each core has 512 hardware threads and the processor pipeline is designed so that the high number of threads

L. Lopes et al. (Eds.): Euro-Par 2014 Workshops, Part II, LNCS 8806, pp. 133–145, 2014.
© Springer International Publishing Switzerland 2014

effectively can hide the latency of accessing the emulated shared memory. Since it is realizes the PRAM (parallel random access machine) model [12] it is very convenient to program. To get full performance an ESM needs programs with large enough thread level parallelism (TLP). To solve the problem with low TLP REPLICA can be reconfigured at run time so that the time slot of several hardware threads are bunched together and access on-chip memory modules in NUMA mode such that the PRAM emulation is switched off and the overhead from plain ESM is removed [6,7]. Switching between PRAM and NUMA mode take only a moderate number of clock cycles as overhead.

For the programmer, NUMA mode means that there are fewer threads and the memory latency becomes "visible" and has to be taken care of manually to utilize the hardware fully. The main reason for having NUMA mode is to be able to accelerate execution of sequential legacy programs and programs with low thread level parallelism faster since they do not suit PRAM mode very well [8]. To switch to NUMA mode the programmer can join all the threads on a core at runtime, so each core becomes single threaded, and can execute faster. It is not always obvious which parallel programs will run faster in NUMA mode, one reason is that hashing of memory adresses is not exposed to the programmer. To tackle this we use state-of-the-art machine-learning methods.

We have in earlier work, for example in [8], introduced REPLICAs PRAM-NUMA programming model and given som basic examples and evaluations. We have also earlier done a preliminary evaluation of REPLICA PRAM capabilities [11], where one conclusion was that PRAM mode is very good for irregular memory access and control flow problems in contrast to commercially available state-of-the-art CPUs and GPUs. However, REPLICA PRAM mode was in several cases outperformed by cache based CPUs and GPUs when it comes to regular memory accesses and control computations [11].

The main goal of this paper is to define an initial model that predicts when to use NUMA mode and when to use PRAM mode in terms of performance.

Since PRAM mode already is very fast for irregular problems but possible suboptimal for regular [11], we here focus on regular data parallel problems namely, generic stencil computations. In [8] we also showed that locality and latency optimizations could be beneficial in NUMA mode, these optimizations suite of course regular problems well.

A secondary goal of this paper is to take two popular state-of-the-art machine learning tools, one based on decision trees and one on symbolic regression, to see if they can be used for modeling this kind of performance optimization problems of heterogeneous architectures. For both methods we use the same training and evaluation data sets. The accuracy of the best derived predictors are 95% and are generated by both C5.0 and Eureqa Pro, although the later can in some cases be more sensitive to the training data. The average speedup gained due to mode switching ranges between 1.92 to 2.23 for all generated predictors on the evaluation test cases. Using a majority voting algorithm, based on the three best predictors, we can eliminate all misclassifications on the evaluation test cases.

2   REPLICA Architecture

The REPLICA architecture is a *chip multiprocessor* (CMP) family of *configurable emulated shared memory machines* (CESM) [8] designed by VTT, Oulu, Finland[1]. Different configurations of the processor have different numbers of cores', arithmetical logical units (ALUs), and memory units (MUs). The processor cores memory modules are connected via a 2D multimesh network. In this study we use the cycle accurate REPLICA simulator, however a hardware prototype is under construction.

2.1   PRAM Mode

One main feature of the REPLICA architecture is PRAM mode. In PRAM mode, the programming model of the processor exposed to the programmer is the *Concurrent Read Concurrent Write* (CRCW) PRAM model. It gives a deterministic synchronous programming model that allows concurrent memory accesses and strict memory consistency [12]. To hide the memory latency each core has 512 hardware threads. Each REPLICA core is a VLIW architecture; in PRAM mode it supports chained functional units (FUs) which means that the result of one functional unit can be used as input to the next unit in the pipeline in the same step. This reduces the pressure on general purpose registers and we are not dependent on the same degree of instruction level parallelism (ILP) as ordinary VLIW architectures are to utilize all functional units. We have specific code generation support and an optimization phase in our LLVM based REPLICA compiler to support arbitrary numbers of chained functional units [13].

In PRAM mode REPLICA supports so called multiprefix instructions [5]. Threads in the same thread group that execute the same multiprefix instruction participate to calculate the result together. Multiprefix operations are considered important building blocks in parallel algorithms, see for example [12]. Programming PRAM mode is straight forward, but to get good performance out of PRAM mode the programmer should use the multiprefix operations if possible.

2.2   NUMA Mode

As mentioned before, the main motivation for NUMA mode is to be able to accelerate execution of sequential legacy programs and programs with low thread level parallelism faster than in PRAM mode. To switch to NUMA mode REPLICA has a specific assembly instruction JOIN that joins all threads in a thread group to a NUMA bunch. To switch back to PRAM mode we use the SPLIT instruction. In our C based REPLICA baseline language [8] we have a construct **numa(s)** that switches the processor to NUMA mode, executes the statement s, and switches back to PRAM mode. The construct also orchestrates setting up the stack pointers, thread ids etc. and restores them. The overhead of switching to NUMA and

---

[1]   REPLICA project site: http://www.vtt.fi/sites/replica/?lang=en

back is around 16000 clock cycles[2] [8]. When the processor runs in NUMA mode, no chaining of functional units is possible, the number of functional units is fixed to the ones given in Table 1 even though it can have more in PRAM mode. This is taken care of by the compiler [8]. Programming for NUMA mode is like programming for traditional NUMA multicore processor with global shared memory and private local memory.

In this paper we have selected a configuration (number of ALUs and MUs) in PRAM mode that looks most similar to the fixed one in NUMA mode, to be able to highlight the differences that comes from NUMA mode itself and not from having a fat PRAM. See Table 1 for the specific processor configurations.

Table 1. Configurations used in this paper

Mode	Cores	Threads per core	Pre memory ALU	MU	Post Memory ALU	Compare unit	Chained FU
PRAM	4	512	1	1	0	1	Yes
NUMA	4	1	1	1	0	1	No

There are three paradigms for accessing shared memory in NUMA mode [8]:
- Freeze processor: the whole processor freezes until the data has arrived.
- Freeze bunch: only the bunch freezes until data has arrived.
- Load with explicit receive (LER): After an asynchronous shared load, an explicit receive instruction RECO need to be issued; in between, other instructions can execute.

These paradigms are fixed and can not be selected at runtime. If a RECO is issued directly after a load the bunch will freeze until data has arrived just like int the case of "freeze bunch". It important to note that loding from shared memory with the LER paradigm occupies the memory unit twice, once for the load instruction (LDO) and once for the receive (RECO). With LER the result of the load will be stored in a register and used as an input to the receive. The used register will be kept alive until the receive is done. If we are short of the registers the compiler will insert spill code to local memory (stack) wich can reduce performance and it might have ben better to "freeze" the bunch instead. In this paper we still only focus on LER, since it gives more opportunities for optimizations.

3   Parameterized Benchmark

In earlier initial work we have shown that PRAM mode suits programs with irregular memory access and control flow very well, while regular problems do not benefit from PRAM mode [11]. In that study we only focused on PRAM

---

[2] About 11000 cycles for PRAM-NUMA switching and about 5000 vice versa. As there are 512 PRAM threads per core in PRAM mode, this corresponds to about 32 PRAM instructions executing per thread for switching back and forth again.

mode, still our experience is that in order to be able to make (any) practical use of NUMA the problems needs to be very regular in terms of memory accesses and control flow. We need to reduce loads and stores from shared memory, but also reading and writing to local memory is considered expensive in NUMA mode.

To explore when NUMA mode can be beneficial we introduce a parameterized benchmark that is very regular. It can be considered a stencil operation. Compared to other regular algorithms, such as vector and matrix operations, stencil operations are more generic especially regarding how much computation there is per data element. We apply register pipelining [4] in order to load each element once (recall that REPLICA has no caches), and obtain a typical software pipeline code structure consisting of prologue (filling the pipeline), computational kernel (steady state) and epilogue (draining the pipeline). We have the following parameters:

- N: Problem size (number of array elements to update)
- P: Prologue size
- C: Number of instructions for local computations with no memory access
- LLS: Number of local loads and stores.

P models how many times we run the prologue, eg. the prefetching of data in shared memory that we have to do before the kernel can start execute. The computational kernel loop run for N iterations, once for each data element. Inside the kernel we do LLS local loads and stores. Our experience shows that in order to be able to get any performance out of NUMA mode we can only access a shared memory data element once, otherwise the performance is ruined. If we need the same data again, we must keep it locally (in local memory but registers are preferred). The C parameter resembles the distance between the load and the receive (RECO instruction), and can be seen as how much local (register based) computation we need to do, to hide the latency of the shared memory access.

Optimizations done for NUMA, such as register pipelining [4] to avoid memory accesses (both shared and local) are in our experience often also useful in PRAM mode. To make a fair comparison between NUMA and PRAM mode we run the exactly same program with the same optimizations (locality, registers etc) for both NUMA and PRAM. The only difference is that we, of course, switch to NUMA and the back-end compiler compiles NUMA code to fit the NUMA pipeline (no chained FU). In NUMA mode we also access shared memory using the LER concept (loads with explicit receive instruction). In PRAM mode we also divide the work over all the available HW threads, e.g. 4×512. In NUMA mode we have joined all the threads per core, so we only have 4 cores (threads) to divide the work among.

4   Machine-Learning Models

Using a random number generator (with lower and upper limits on each parameter) we generated different training set and evaluation sets. The parameter space is well covered, see the distribution of the parameters for the evaluation set S_E in

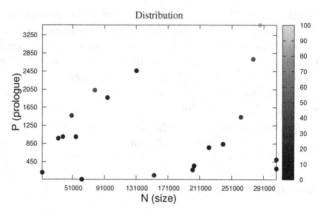

Fig. 1. Distribution of N (size), P (prologue) and LLS (local load store) parameters in the evaluation set S_E. LLS is shown in grayscale.

Figure 1. We generated programs in REPLICA baseline language (an extended version of C), compiled them and run them on the cycle accurate REPLICA simulator.

Initially we started with two training sets, S_1 and S_2 and their union S_3, where $|S_3| = 45$ and $|S_1| \approx |S_2|$. S_1 and S_2 are disjoint.

Using S_3 we derive formulas for both NUMA and PRAM execution times using the Eureqa Pro framework [18,17]. We assume that the execution time, t_n, for NUMA is $t_n = f_n(N, C, P, LLS)$ and t_p for PRAM in a similar way. Since we want to make a predictor for when to switch to NUMA mode it is natural to use the speedup, eg. only switch to NUMA if we get speedup larger than one, e.g. $\frac{t_p}{t_n} > 1$.

For C5.0 [16] we tried S_1, S_2 and S_3 as training sets, however the results were not good enough so we decided to increase the size of the training data. The new sets S_1', S_2' and $S_3' = S_1' \cup S_2'$ contains the old sets in the following way: $S_1 \subset S_1'$, $S_2 \subset S_2'$ where $S_3 \subset S_3'$, $|S_3'| = 98$ and $|S_1'| \approx |S_2'|$

For evaluation we use the set S_E, it is shown in Table 2. It is independent from the training sets and $|S_E| = 20$ [3]. Figure 1 depicts S_Es distribution of the parameters N (size), P (prologue) and LLS (local loads and stores) where LSS is shown with grayscale. Since C5.0 did not use the C parameter we do not show its distribution in the picture.

4.1   Eureqa Pro

A First Model Using S_3. With S_3 we got the following execution time models.
NUMA: $t_n = a_n * P + b_n * N + c_n * N * C + d_n * LLS^2$, where $a_n = 0$, $b_n = 9.65313889909994$, $c_n = 0.224715696133425$ and $d_n = 23005.0142108128$.

---

[3] Due to large simulation times, a significantly larger number of training and evaluation samples was not feasible.

PRAM: $t_p = a_p*P + b_p*N + c_p*N*C + d_p*LLS^2$ where $a_p = 3561.80442755642$, $b_p = 5.91351736227114$, $c_p = 0.232529731521942$ and $d_p = 8662.82648471137$.

As stated earlier we use the estimated speedup larger than one, $\frac{t_p}{t_n} > 1$, as a predictor. The generated expressions for the execution time, are quite similar for PRAM and NUMA, one interesting detail is that the P (prologue) is not used for NUMA and that $c_n \approx c_p$.

An Updated Model Using S_3'. When we double the training set size, adding more training cases, using S_3', we get different formulas for estimating the PRAM and NUMA execution times.

NUMA: $t_n = a_n * LLS + b_n * N + c_n * N * LLS * \sqrt{N} + d_n * S * LLS^2$ where $a_n = 44201.802640319$, $b_n = 8.01445073789093$, $c_n = 0.0765782960682957$ and $d_n = -0.000128963606572698$.

PRAM: $t_p = a_p*LLS + b_p*P + N*LLS + c_p*P*LLS + d_p*N*C + e_p*LLS^2$ where $a_P = 107691.057352967$, $b_P = 2919.18227717314$, $c_p = 107.696490731206$, $d_p = 0.26706472514021$ and $e_p = -1605.81303793423$. Note that the coefficient for $S * LLS$ is 1.

Binary Model Using S_3'. Deriving the execution times as functions of N, P, C and LLS seems unstable for Eureqa Pro, i.e. very depending on the specific training sets (see Table 4). However, we are only interested in relative performance. To handle this we introduced a binary model using Eureqa Pro and S_3'. It gives 1 as result if NUMA should be used and 0 for PRAM: $NUMA = P > 0.000905177867360653 * N + 0.055818680067241 * P * LLS$.

4.2   C5.0 Decision Trees

Running C5.0 on S_1' we get the following decision tree:

```
LLS > 8: PRAM
LLS<= 8:
:...P > 400: NUMA
    P <= 400:
    :...N <= 174851: NUMA
        N > 174851: PRAM
```

Running C5.0 on S_2' we get the following decision tree:

```
LLS > 15: PRAM
LLS <= 15:
:...N <= 177417: NUMA
    N > 177417:
    :...P <= 643: PRAM
        P > 643: NUMA
```

Running C5.0 on S_3' we get the following decision tree:

```
LLS > 8: PRAM
LLS <= 8:
:...N <= 210765: NUMA
    N > 210765:
    :...P <= 500: PRAM
        P > 500: NUMA
```

Note that no C5.0 model uses the C parameter and all the generated predictors are quite similar to each other.

4.3   Evaluation and Comparison of Eureqa Pro and C5.0 Models

Table 3 shows the results of evaluating the Eureqa Pro models based on S_3 and S_3' compared to actual results from test runs in the simulator. It might be interesting to note that the average speedup error is 15.1% for S_3 while it is 37.5% for the model based on S_3'. Table 4 shows the predicted mode for all cases in S_E for the models based on S_1', S_2', S_3' and S_3. The columns are sorted by the number of misclassifications and also show the average real speedup gained when using the corresponding predictors.

Table 2. The set of test cases, S_E, for evaluation and comparison

Case	N	C	P	LLS		Case	N	C	P	LLS
1	307200	104	300	4		11	202099	56	273	4
2	153600	12	150	24		12	240096	50	841	4
3	307300	16	500	8		13	131407	40	2463	8
4	38400	12	1000	8		14	277705	96	2720	44
5	38400	24	1000	16		15	55311	56	999	1
6	222401	16	765	8		16	12155	88	212	8
7	62709	72	59	1		17	203909	48	362	1
8	286382	16	3475	92		18	262394	80	1437	32
9	78714	56	2034	44		19	49693	80	1467	24
10	32431	88	966	4		20	94664	0	1871	1

For our problem and training sets Eureqa Pro using our first execution time based models seems to be some what unstable; it produces both their best and worst predictor depending on the training set, see Table 4. Eureqa Pro gives the best predictor with a smaller training set S_3 than the larger S_3'. With our binary Eureqa Pro predictor based on set S_3' we get only one misclassification, it seems as good as C5.0 for the same set. All predictors are very simple and can be implemented with a few instructions so the overhead of invoking them at runtime is very low.

All predictors give on average a speedup between 1.91 and 2.23. This is not a "magical range", it comes from the evaluation set S_E. In most cases misclassifications do not "hurt" so much since they are border cases and running in "wrong" mode will only affect performance marginally. If we remove the three worst predictors in terms of misclassifications and use the remaining predictors together with a majority voting algorithm we would eliminate all misclassifications in our evaluation set and get an average speedup of 2.23. In Table 4 the speedup for C5.0 on S_3' is also 2.23, even though it makes one misclassification, as this misclassification only changes the average speedup with 0.03% which can be explained by that there the PRAM and NUMA execution times are very similar. We also evaluated our different models on two different parallel 1D-average computations, the parameters and results are shown in Table 5. The only predictor that misclassifies is Eureqa on S_3'.

Table 3. Real speedup from simulator, estimated speedup for Eureqa Pro using S_3' and S_3 and the speedup error in % compared to the real speedup

Case	Real speedup	Eureqa S_3 speedup	Eureqa S_3 speedup error %	Eureqa S_3' speedup	Eureqa S_3' speedup error %
1	0.98	0.99	1.5	1.83	86.6
2	0.42	0.45	7.3	0.17	60.4
3	0.98	0.96	3.0	0.66	33.2
4	5.45	2.29	58.1	1.33	75.7
5	0.84	0.96	14.7	0.95	13.0
6	1.26	1.23	2.3	0.42	66.9
7	0.99	1.00	1.2	1.25	26.8
8	0.41	0.45	7.7	0.61	46.4
9	0.56	0.55	2.2	0.52	7.3
10	3.79	3.35	11.5	2.69	28.9
11	1.02	1.02	0.1	0.60	40.8
12	1.31	1.35	2.5	0.93	29.5
13	3.03	2.89	4.6	0.98	67.6
14	0.47	0.64	37.8	0.70	49.7
15	3.92	3.68	6.1	3.68	6.1
16	2.04	0.89	56.3	1.74	14.8
17	1.19	1.14	4.5	1.19	0.0
18	0.46	0.66	45.1	0.51	12.1
19	0.77	0.78	2.1	0.85	10.5
20	11.60	7.72	33.5	3.12	73.1

Table 4. Evaluation result using S_E. Misclassifications are marked in boldface. Average speedup for all 20 cases using the corresponding predictor.

Case	Correct	Eureqa S_3'	C5.0 S_2'	C5.0 S_1'	Eureqa S_3	C5.0 S_3'	Eureqa bin S_3'
1	PRAM	**NUMA**	PRAM	PRAM	PRAM	PRAM	PRAM
2	PRAM	PRAM	PRAM	PRAM	PRAM	PRAM	PRAM
3	PRAM	PRAM	**NUMA**	PRAM	PRAM	PRAM	PRAM
4	NUMA	NUMA	NUMA	NUMA	NUMA	NUMA	NUMA
5	PRAM	PRAM	PRAM	PRAM	PRAM	PRAM	**NUMA**
6	NUMA	**PRAM**	NUMA	NUMA	NUMA	NUMA	NUMA
7	PRAM	**NUMA**	**NUMA**	**NUMA**	PRAM	**NUMA**	PRAM
8	PRAM	PRAM	PRAM	PRAM	PRAM	PRAM	PRAM
9	PRAM	PRAM	PRAM	PRAM	PRAM	PRAM	PRAM
10	NUMA	NUMA	NUMA	NUMA	NUMA	NUMA	NUMA
11	NUMA	NUMA	**PRAM**	**PRAM**	NUMA	NUMA	NUMA
12	NUMA	NUMA	NUMA	NUMA	NUMA	NUMA	NUMA
13	NUMA	NUMA	NUMA	NUMA	NUMA	NUMA	NUMA
14	PRAM	**NUMA**	PRAM	PRAM	PRAM	PRAM	PRAM
15	NUMA	**PRAM**	NUMA	NUMA	NUMA	NUMA	NUMA
16	NUMA	**PRAM**	NUMA	NUMA	**PRAM**	NUMA	NUMA
17	NUMA	NUMA	**PRAM**	**PRAM**	NUMA	NUMA	NUMA
18	PRAM	PRAM	PRAM	PRAM	PRAM	PRAM	PRAM
19	PRAM	PRAM	PRAM	PRAM	PRAM	PRAM	PRAM
20	NUMA	NUMA	NUMA	NUMA	NUMA	NUMA	NUMA
	Misclassifications	**6**/20	**4**/20	**3**/20	1/20	1/20	1/20
	Average real speedup	1.92	2.21	2.21	2.01	2.23	2.22

Table 5. Parameters and evaluation results using a 1D average computation example. Misclassifications are marked in boldface.

Evaluation	N	C	P	LLS	Correct	Eureqa S_3'	C5.0 S_2'	C5.0 S_1'	Eureqa S_3	C5.0 S_3'	Eureqa bin S_3'
1	307200	60	8	1	PRAM	**NUMA**	PRAM	PRAM	PRAM	PRAM	PRAM
2	307200	80	8	1	PRAM	**NUMA**	PRAM	PRAM	PRAM	PRAM	PRAM

5   Related Work

The problem of selecting the best runtime mode for REPLICA is very related to the implementation selection problem for heterogenous systems such as CPU-GPU based systems; in both REPLICA and CPU-GPU case there are overhead costs of switching and data transfers costs. Similarities such as small local memory also exist.

The parallel programming language framework PetaBricks [1] uses auto tuning that effectively explores the search space to select from multiple user provided implementations the best one, depending on problem parameters [1]. Their compiler can generate OpenCL code that can execute on GPUs [15].

SkePU is a C++ skeleton programming library mainly for mapreduce problems with back-ends for both CPU and GPUS. It supports implementation selection using machine-learning methods to adopt skeletons to a given platform [3].

One example where C5.0 has been used for performance optimization of heterogeneous systems is [14], they use it to prune the search space when doing off-line tuning of component composition.

Danylenko et al. compared different machine-learning approches for context-aware composition in [2]. They consider decision tress, decision diagrams, naive bayes and suport vector machine classifiers. They evaluate their results on three different multicore machines.

In [10] Grewe and O'Boyle show how to select optimized mappings of OpenCL tasks on a heterogeneous CPU-GPU system to get good load balancing. They base their training on the support vector machine (SVM) model, and is based on static features (number of floating point operations etc) just like we do. However hybrid execution is not possible on REPLICA as the same hardware is used by both PRAM and NUMA mode.

Elastic computing is a framework that supports heterogenous computing, such multicore CPUs combined with FPGA accelerators. It separates functionality and implementations using elastic functions which can be executed with different parameters (input size etc) on different target architectures [20]. They use linear regression based to predict execution time based input size and other metrics captured by the specific performance model for each component.

As far as we know, Eureqa Pro has not been used before for performance prediction and implementation selection before, however in [9] Goel uses Eureqa for per-core power estimation and power aware scheduling for CMPs which is a related problem area.

6   Conclusion and Future Work

We used state-state-of-the-art machine-learning methods, decision trees and symbolic regression, and tools based on them, namely C5.0 and Eureqa Pro. Using the same training data we derive models to predict if to run the REPLICA architecture in PRAM or NUMA mode for a certain parameterized computation type (parallel stencil operation). Without machine-learning it had not been possible to derive predictors of when to use PRAM or NUMA mode.

The best predictors give a misclassification rate of 5%. Combining the three best ones using a majority voting algorithm misclassifications can be eliminated fully, at least on the test case. Average gained speedup over PRAM mode execution only ranges between 1.92 and 2.23 for all classifiers on the test cases.

For C5.0 it seems that adding more training data improves the accuracy while for Eureqa Pro more training data can generate more instable models. However, Eureqa Pro can be as good as C5.0 if the right training data is used and then it makes correct classification for the case where all other predictors are wrong. The derived formulas for PRAM and NUMA execution time are not accurate enough to predict the execution time, however they are accurate enough to be used for deciding if PRAM or NUMA mode should be used.

All the derived predictors are very simple, and can be implemented with a few computation and comparison instructions. The overhead of invoking them at runtime, if some parameters such as size are unknown statically, will be very small. As far as we know, Eureqa Pro has not been used for this type of performance predictions before.

Future work includes using the same methods on other problem types than stencil-like algorithms. It would als be interesting to test this on heterogeneous systems such as CPU-GPU based ones. Another interesting problem would be to derive parameterized models of algorithms using a pattern matching framework such as PRT [19] and combine it with machine learning. Each pattern could then be annotated with a predictor for the pattern implementations' best performance for specific parameters and for a given type of hardware.

Acknowledgments. This research is supported by SeRC. Thanks to Nutonian providing a free academic licence of Eureqa Pro. Thanks to Martti Forsell and Lu Li for their help and comments.

References

1. Ansel, J., Chan, C., Wong, Y.L., Olszewski, M., Zhao, Q., Edelman, A., Amarasinghe, S.: Petabricks: A language and compiler for algorithmic choice. In: ACM SIGPLAN Conference on Programming Language Design and Implementation, Dublin, Ireland (June 2009)
2. Danylenko, A., Kessler, C., Löwe, W.: Comparing machine learning approaches for context-aware composition. In: Apel, S., Jackson, E. (eds.) SC 2011. LNCS, vol. 6708, pp. 18–33. Springer, Heidelberg (2011)

3. Dastgeer, U., Enmyren, J., Kessler, C.W.: Auto-tuning SkePU: A multi-backend skeleton programming framework for multi-GPU systems. In: Proceedings of the 4th International Workshop on Multicore Software Engineering, IWMSE 2011, pp. 25–32. ACM, New York (2011)

4. Duesterwald, E., Gupta, R., Soffa, M.: Register pipelining: An integrated approach to register allocation for scalar and subscripted variables. In: Kastens, U., Pfahler, P. (eds.) CC 1992. LNCS, vol. 641, pp. 192–206. Springer, Heidelberg (1992)

5. Forsell, M.: Realizing multioperations for step cached MP-SOCs. In: Proc. SOC 2006 (2006)

6. Forsell, M.: Configurable Emulated Shared Memory Architecture for General Purpose MP-SoCs and NoC Regions. In: Proceedings of the 3rd ACM/IEEE International Symposium on Networks-on-Chip, San Diego, USA, May 10-13, pp. 163–172 (2009)

7. Forsell, M.: A PRAM-NUMA Model of Computation for Addressing Low-TLP Workloads. In: Proceedings of the 12th Workshop on Advances in Parallel and Distributed Computational Models (in conjunction with the 24th IEEE International Parallel and Distributed Processing Symposium, IPDPS 2010), Atlanta, USA, April 19, pp. 1–8 (2010)

8. Forsell, M., Hansson, E., Kessler, C., Mäkelä, J.M., Leppänen, V.: NUMA Computing with Hardware and Software Co-support on Configurable Emulated Shared memory Architectures. International Journal of Networking and Computing 4(1) (2014)

9. Goel, B.: Per-core Power Estimation and Power Aware Scheduling Strategies for CMPs, 70 (2011)

10. Grewe, D., O'Boyle, M.: A static task partitioning approach for heterogeneous systems using opencl. In: Knoop, J. (ed.) CC 2011. LNCS, vol. 6601, pp. 286–305. Springer, Heidelberg (2011)

11. Hansson, E., Alnervik, E., Kessler, C., Forsell, M.: A Quantitative Comparison of PRAM based Emulated Shared Memory Architectures to Current Multicore CPUs and GPUs. In: 2014 27th International Conference on Architecture of Computing Systems (ARCS), pp. 1–7 (February 2014)

12. Keller, J., Kessler, C., Träff, J.L.: Practical PRAM Programming. John Wiley & Sons, Inc., New York (2001)

13. Kessler, M., Hansson, E., Åkesson, D., Kessler, C.: Exploiting instruction level parallelism for REPLICA - a configurable VLIW architecture with chained functional units. In: Proc. PDPTA 2012 (July 2012)

14. Li, L., Dastgeer, U., Kessler, C.: Pruning strategies in adaptive off-line tuning for optimized composition of components on heterogeneous systems. Accepted for Proc. Seventh International Workshop on Parallel Programming Models and Systems Software for High-End Computing (P2S2) at ICPP (2014)

15. Phothilimthana, P.M., Ansel, J., Ragan-Kelley, J., Amarasinghe, S.: Portable performance on heterogeneous architectures. SIGPLAN Not. 48(4), 431–444 (2013)

16. Quinlan, R.: C5.0 release 2.07 GPL Edition [software], http://www.rulequest.com/download.html

17. Schmidt, M., Lipson, H.: Eureqa (version 0.99.5 beta) [software] (2014), http://www.nutonian.com

18. Schmidt, M., Lipson, H.: Distilling Free-Form Natural Laws from Experimental Data. Science 324(5923), 81–85 (2009)
19. Shafiee Sarvestani, A., Hansson, E., Kessler, C.: Extensible recognition of algorithmic patterns in DSP programs for automatic parallelization. International Journal of Parallel Programming, 1–19 (2012)
20. Wernsing, J.R., Stitt, G.: Elastic computing: A framework for transparent, portable, and adaptive multi-core heterogeneous computing. SIGPLAN Not. 45(4), 115–124 (2010)

A Study of the Potential of Locality-Aware Thread Scheduling for GPUs

Cedric Nugteren, Gert-Jan van den Braak, and Henk Corporaal

Eindhoven University of Technology, Eindhoven, The Netherlands
{c.nugteren,g.j.w.v.d.braak,h.corporaal}@tue.nl

Abstract. Programming models such as CUDA and OpenCL allow the
programmer to specify the independence of threads, effectively removing ordering constraints. Still, parallel architectures such as the graphics processing unit (GPU) do not exploit the potential of data-locality
enabled by this independence. Therefore, programmers are required to
manually perform data-locality optimisations such as memory coalescing
or loop tiling. This work makes a case for *locality-aware thread scheduling*: re-ordering threads automatically for better locality to improve the
programmability of multi-threaded processors. In particular, we analyse
the potential of locality-aware thread scheduling for GPUs, considering
among others cache performance, memory coalescing and bank locality.
This work does not present an implementation of a locality-aware thread
scheduler, but rather introduces the concept and identifies the potential.
We conclude that non-optimised programs have the potential to achieve
good cache and memory utilisation *when using a smarter thread scheduler*. A case-study of a naive matrix multiplication shows for example a
87% performance increase, leading to an IPC of 457 on a 512-core GPU.

1 Introduction

In the past decade, graphics processing units (GPUs) have emerged as a popular
platform for non-graphics computations. Through languages such as OpenCL
and CUDA, programmers can use these massively parallel architectures (and
other *accelerators*) for computational domains such as linear algebra, image processing and molecular science. The increased popularity of such accelerators has
made programming, maintainability, and portability issues of major importance.
Although accelerator programming models have partially addressed these issues,
programmers are still expected to tune their code for aspects such as (in the case
of GPUs) memory coalescing, warp size, core count and the on-chip memories.

To counter the imminent memory wall [3], recent GPUs have been equipped
with software-managed on-chip memories (scratch-pad) and hardware-managed
on-chip memories (cache). In particular for integrated solutions with general-
purpose memories (e.g. ARM Mali, AMD Fusion, XBox One) off-chip memory
bandwidth is scarce: using the on-chip memories efficiently is required to exploit
the GPU's full potential [13]. In fact, many GPU programs are memory bandwidth intensive: for an example set of benchmarks, this is as much as 18 out of

L. Lopes et al. (Eds.): Euro-Par 2014 Workshops, Part II, LNCS 8806, pp. 146–157, 2014.
© Springer International Publishing Switzerland 2014

31 [5]. Specific examples of cache optimisations include cache blocking for sparse matrix vector multiplication (5x speed-up) and *loop tiling* for a stencil computation (3x speed-up). Programmers of GPUs are therefore performing memory coalescing to maximise off-chip throughput or tiling to improve data-locality. Furthermore, programmers determine the allocation of threads to threadblocks, affecting scheduling freedom and cache performance.

With programming models such as CUDA and OpenCL, programmers create a large number of independent[1] threads that execute a single piece of program code (a *kernel*). Still, microprocessors such as the GPU do not exploit the potential of spatial and temporal data-locality enabled by this independence. Therefore, we propose locality-aware thread scheduling: changing the schedule of threads, warps and threadblocks with respect to a kernel's memory accesses.

This work does not aim to improve performance for already optimised (e.g. coalesced, tiled) code, but is instead motivated by non-optimised program code and the performance potential of locality-aware thread scheduling. This improves *programmability*, a metric intertwined with: 1) *portability*: the generality of program code when targeting different microprocessors, 2) *productivity*: the time it costs to design and maintain program code, and 3) *performance*: the speed or energy efficiency of a program. Although the focus of this work lies on GPUs, we make a note that the ideas are equally valid for other cache-based processors that are programmable in an SPMD-fashion.

This work demonstrates that locality-aware thread scheduling can significantly improve the programmability of GPUs. The main contributions are:

- **Section 5:** The potential of multi-level locality-aware thread scheduling for GPUs is identified and quantified for several non-optimised benchmarks.
- **Section 6:** Two example kernels are evaluated further, identifying the effects of thread scheduling on among others caches and memory bank locality.

2   Background

This section briefly introduces the GPU architecture and its execution model. Additional background can be found in the CUDA programming guide [10].

We use NVIDIA's Fermi architecture as an example in this paper. The Fermi architecture has up to 16 cores (also known as *streaming multiprocessors* or *compute units*). Each core contains 32 processing elements (or *CUDA cores*) and a 64KB on-chip configurable memory, combining scratchpad and L1 data cache (16/48KB or 48/16KB). All cores share a larger L2 cache (up to 768KB).

The CUDA and OpenCL programming models allow programmers to specify small programs (*kernels*) that are executed multiple times on different data. Each instance of a kernel (a *thread* in CUDA terminology, a *workitem* in OpenCL terminology) has its own unique identifier. Programmers furthermore divide all their threads in fixed-size blocks (*threadblocks* in CUDA terminology, *workgroups*

---

[1] Independent apart from explicit per-threadblock synchronisation barriers.

in OpenCL terminology). Threads within a block share an on-chip local memory and can synchronise. However, synchronisation is not possible among blocks.

In a Fermi GPU, a threadblock is mapped in its entirety onto a core. Together, threads from one or more threadblocks can form a set of *active* threads on a single core. For Fermi GPUs, this is limited to 8 threadblocks or 1536 threads, whichever limit is reached first [10]. Such a set of active threads executes concurrently in a multi-threaded fashion as *warps* (NVIDIA) or *wavefronts* (AMD). In Fermi, a warp is a group of 32 threads executing in an SIMD-like fashion on a single core, dividing the workload over processing elements [10].

3 Related Work

Locality-aware thread scheduling has been investigated for non-GPU microprocessors in earlier work. For instance, Philbin et al [11] formalise the problem of locality-aware thread scheduling for a single-core processor. In other work by Tam et al. [14], threads are grouped based on data-locality for multi-threaded multi-core processors, introducing a metric of *thread similarity*. Furthermore, Ding and Zhong [2] propose a model to estimate locality based on reuse distances. These approaches cannot be applied directly to GPUs, as they do not take into account aspects such as: scalability to many threads, cache sizes, the thread-warp-block hierarchy, nor the active thread count.

Recent work on GPUs has investigated the potential of scheduling less active threads to improve cache behaviour. Kayiran et al. [5] propose a compute/memory-intensity heuristic to select the active thread count. Furthermore, Rogers et al. [12] propose a hardware approach: the number of active threads is adapted at run-time based on *lost locality* counters. However, these works only consider active thread count reduction: they do not investigate thread scheduling.

Current scheduling research for GPUs is in the context of divergent control flow rather than data-locality. By dynamically regrouping threads into warps, those following the same execution path can be scheduled together. Dynamic warp formation in the context of memory access coalescing is discussed in e.g. [6,7]. Recent work has focussed on two-level warp scheduling to reduce the impact of memory latency [4,8]. Although we not address control flow, we note that an ideal scheduler takes both aspects (data-locality and control flow) into account.

4 Experimental Setup

The experiments in this work are performed with GPGPU-Sim 3.2.1 [1] using a GeForce GTX580 configuration (Fermi) with a 16KB L1 cache (128 byte cache-lines) and a 768KB L2 cache. The GTX580 has 16 SIMT cores (or SMs) for a total of 512 *CUDA cores*. From the simulation results we report IPC (higher is better)[2], cache miss rates (lower is better), and load balancing amongst off-chip memory banks (higher is better).

---

[2] IPC (instructions per cycle) is counted as the throughput of scalar operations and load/store instructions over all CUDA cores and load/store units in the GPU.

4.1   Implementation in GPGPU-Sim

The GPGPU-Sim simulator was modified to perform the thread scheduling experiments presented in this work. The run-time scheduling mechanism of a GPU (and of the simulator) is non-trivial, including multiple hierarchies and dynamic aspects (e.g. influenced by memory latencies). This mechanism is therefore kept intact in GPGPU-Sim. Instead, this work implements a pre-processing 'mapping' step to the thread and block identifiers. This mapping step takes thread identifiers t_i and block identifiers b_i and calculates new identifiers as $t'_i = f(t_i, b_i)$ and $b'_i = g(t_i, b_i)$. The functions $f()$ and $g()$ implement alternative thread schedules as will be further discussed in Sect. 5.1. Because the mapping is applied before the hardware run-time thread scheduling, the effect is equivalent to applying the $f()$ and $g()$ to the software thread and block identifiers - a task currently assigned to CUDA and OpenCL programmers.

4.2   Benchmark Selection

This paper includes results for 6 non-optimised CUDA benchmarks, i.e. suboptimal implementations rather than fine-tuned benchmarks (e.g. Parboil or Rodinia). The main reason for this choice is that this work aims to improve the programmability of the GPU rather than the maximum performance. In other words, if performance of these naive non-optimised benchmarks can be improved without having to change the program code, GPU acceleration is made available to a wider audience ('non-ninja programmers'). Even expert programmers can benefit from increased flexibility and require fewer optimisations to achieve the full potential of the GPU.

The benchmarks are: the computation of an integral image (row-major and column-major), a 2D convolution (11 by 11), a 2D matrix copy (each thread copies either a row or a column), and a naive matrix-multiplication. Image and matrix sizes are 512 by 512. Fig. 1 illustrates their memory access patterns:

1. **Integral image (row-wise):** Every thread at coordinates (x, y) in a 2D image produces a single output pixel at (x, y) by consuming all input pixels (x', y) for which $x' \leq x$. In the example, thread 0 consumes input 0 (red), thread 1 consumes inputs 0 and 1 (red and blue), and so on.
2. **Integral image (column-wise):** Equal to the row-wise version, but each thread instead consumes all input pixels (x, y') for which $y' \leq y$.
3. **11 by 11 convolution:** Each thread produces a single pixel in a 2D image by consuming an input pixel at the same coordinates (blue) and its neighbourhood of $(11 \cdot 11) - 1$ elements (green).
4. **Matrix-multiplication:** Each thread with coordinates (x, y) consumes a row $(*, y)$ of an input matrix and a column $(x, *)$ of another input matrix to produce a single element in an output matrix at (x, y).
5. **Matrix copy (per row):** Each thread consumes a row of an input matrix to produce the corresponding row in an output matrix.
6. **Matrix copy (per column):** As before, but now columns instead of rows.

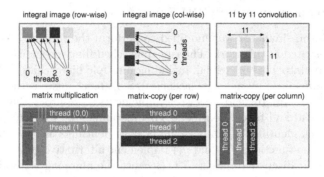

Fig. 1. Illustrating the memory access patterns of the 6 benchmarks

5   Quantifying the Potential

Many GPU programs contain a large number of independent threads that can be freely re-ordered. This re-ordering (changing the thread schedule) is motivated by the following data-locality performance optimisations: 1) multiple threads accessing a single cache-line must be grouped in a warp (memory coalescing), 2) threads having strong inter-thread locality must be grouped within a single threadblock (sharing a L1 cache), 3) threadblocks with data-locality must be executed either on a single core in temporal vicinity or simultaneously on different cores (sharing a L2 cache), 4) threads executing simultaneously must minimise pollution of the shared caches, and 5) threads executing simultaneously must spread their accesses as evenly as possible across the memory banks.

Consider an SPMD (single-program multiple-data) kernel with n threads $t_1, t_2, ..., t_n$, each referencing a number of data elements. This work assumes that all n threads are independent[3] and can be reordered as $r = n!$ distinct sequences $s_1, s_2, ..., s_r$. The problem of locality-aware thread scheduling is to find a sequence s_i of n threads such that execution time is minimal. On a GPU, thread scheduling influences execution time in terms of efficient use of the caches, memory coalescing, memory bank locality, and the number of active threads.

5.1   Candidate Thread Schedules

Various thread schedules are tested in GPGPU-Sim to quantify the potential of locality-aware thread scheduling. Because the number of threads n is typically large (e.g. 2^{20}), it is impractical to test all r orderings. Therefore, only a limited set of schedules is considered: schedules with regularity and structure, matching the target regular and structured programs. The selected schedules are illustrated in Fig. 2 and briefly discussed below. Note that these schedules represent the mapping step discussed in Sect. 4.1 and are still subject to the GPU's multi-level scheduling mechanism. The schedules are:

---

[3] Dependences (e.g. barriers) can be added as constraints on the thread ordering.

Fig. 2. Examples with 8 or 16 threads. The numbering shows the new sequence and the layout the original sequence (left-to-right, top-to-bottom).

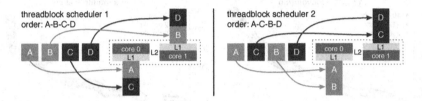

Fig. 3. Two schedulers for threadblocks A–D, assuming locality between A and B (red) and between C and D (purple). The results are L2 locality (left) or L1 locality (right). The arrows represent the GPU scheduler applied after our 'mapping' (or ordering).

1. **Sequential:** The unmodified original ordering, i.e. $f(x) = x$ and $g(x) = x$. Note that, although it is a sequential ordering from a pre-processing perspective, the actual ordering is still subject to the GPU's thread, warp, and block scheduling policies.
2. **Stride(a, b):** An ordering with a configurable stride (a) and granularity (b) (e.g. warp or threadblock granularity) with respect to the original ordering. Strided schedules have the potential to e.g. ameliorate bad choices of a 2D-coordinate to thread mapping [13].
3. **Zigzag(a, b):** An ordering assuming a 2D grid of threads, reversing the ordering of odd rows. The parameters are the row-length (a) and the granularity (b). Zigzag can exploit 2D locality, but might degrade coalescing for small granularities.
4. **Tile(a, b, c):** 2D tiling in a 2D grid. Tiling takes as parameter the length of a row (a) and the dimensions of the tile (b x c). It has been shown that tiling has potential to exploit locality on GPUs [13].
5. **Hilbert(a):** A space filling fractal for grids of size a by a with 2D locality.

Two threadblock-schedulers are implemented on top of the candidate schedules (Fig. 3): either schedule threadblocks over cores in a round-robin fashion (left) or allocate subsequent threadblocks to subsequent cores (right). In case threadblocks with locality are grouped close to each other, the first threadblock-scheduler can benefit from locality in the L2 cache (in space among cores), while the second can benefit from locality in L1 (in time among threadblocks).

Our experiments consider a subset of 2170 schedules. This includes a sweep over the 5 orderings, several small power-of-2 parameter values (e.g. stride-size), the two threadblock-schedulers, and 5 active thread counts (64, 128, 256, 512, 1024) to identify the trade-offs between cache contention and parallelism [5,12].

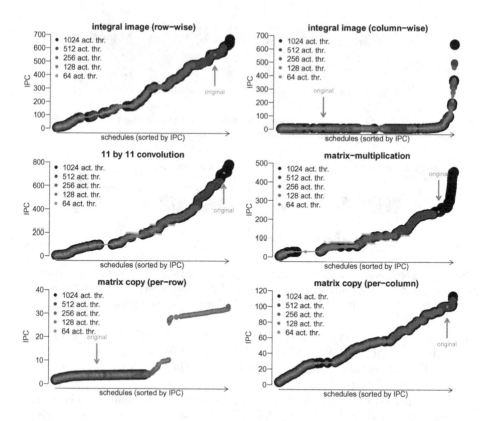

Fig. 4. Sorted IPC results (higher is better) from GPGPU-Sim for 2170 schedules per benchmark. The vertical red arrow identifies the original schedule (no changes applied to GPGPU-Sim). Darker and larger glyphs represent more active threads, lighter and smaller glyphs represent fewer active threads.

5.2   Experimental Results

Fig. 4 gives the IPC results when simulating all candidate schedules for the benchmarks with GPGPU-Sim. Each set of 2170 results is sorted by their achieved IPC. The original (unmodified) schedule is highlighted, its horizontal position indicating the performance potential for a particular benchmark. Note that these graphs are meant to identify the main shape of the '*landscape*', detailed results are presented in Sect. 6. We observe the following:

1. **Integral image (row-wise):** There is a wide performance variation among the different schedules: IPC ranges from 2 to 700. The default schedule is already performing well: it has coalesced memory accesses and uses the caches efficiently. Still, there is opportunity for a 20% performance improvement, achieved for example by using a 8 by 16 tiled schedule. The active thread count is not strongly correlated to performance. Even so, the best 5% schedules all use 1024 active threads.

2. **Integral image (column-wise):** The default schedule at an IPC of 7 is suffering from uncoalesced memory accesses and bad cache locality for this purposely poorly design kernel. Using a schedule with a stride equal to the width of the image resolves these problems, bringing performance back to the level of the row-wise integral image computation.
3. **11 by 11 convolution:** The overall results look similar to the row-wise integral image case at first glance. However, inspection of the results shows that the best candidates are zigzag as opposed to tiled schedules, achieving up to 10% improvement over the default.
4. **Matrix-multiplication:** The results show that there is up to 87% to gain over the default schedule in terms of performance (see Sect. 6.1 for details).
5. **Matrix copy (per row):** The active thread count is of significant importance, although the performance is in general low due to the cache and memory unfriendly assignment of work to threads. Schedules with 512 or 1024 active threads (including the default) yield an IPC of 5 at best, while schedules with 64, 128, or 256 active threads achieve an IPC of up to 34. This is the only test-case where more threads does not yield better performance.
6. **Matrix copy (per column):** Better overall performance compared to per-row copy. Sect. 6.2 analyses the results and the 12% potential in detail.

Note that in contrast to the two integral image cases, it is not possible to achieve equal performance for the two matrix copy cases. The reason is the integral image's flexibility: each thread computes a single result. In contrast, matrix copy processes (in our implementation) an entire row / column per thread, limiting the scheduling freedom: we do not consider changing the workload *within* a thread.

The same testing methodology was applied to several other naive benchmarks. An example is the computation of an 8 by 8 discrete cosine transform (DCT) on a 2048 by 2048 input using a nested for-loop in the kernel body with 64 iterations. A sweep through the different thread schedules led to a 3.2x speed-up (an increase from an IPC of 175 to 570) using a schedule with a stride of 512 at a granularity of 8, moving multiple groups of threads belonging to one 8 by 8 transform (64 threads) together into a single threadblock.

Similarly, a symmetric rank-k kernel from PolyBench shows a 3 times speedup. Several other tested benchmarks have not shown significant changes at all. This includes matrix-vector summation from the PolyBench benchmark and the breath-first-search and SRAD kernels from Rodinia. These results were expected, as closer inspection of these benchmarks shows already optimised code.

6   Two Case Studies

Sect. 5 illustrated that the performance potential varies from limited (e.g. 10% for the convolution benchmark) to significant (e.g. 87% for matrix-multiplication). We also saw different best schedules for different benchmarks and a varying correlation between performance and active thread count. To get additional insight, this section discusses two of the benchmarks in more detail. We only present a subset of the data due to the large quantity (schedules, benchmarks, metrics).

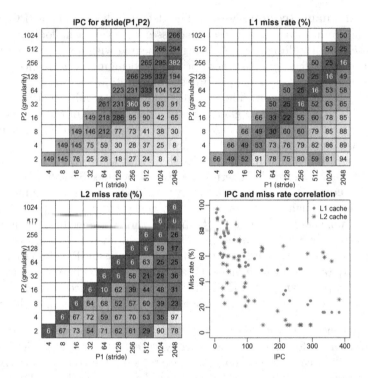

Fig. 5. Simulation results for the matrix-multiplication example for strided schedules. Shown are the IPC (higher is better) and the L1 and L2 miss rates (lower is better).

6.1 Matrix-Multiplication

Matrix-multiplication is one of the examples that shows a significant performance potential (up to 87%) from its default IPC of 245. To identify the reason why certain schedules perform better than others, we take a detailed look at the simulation results for the strided schedules. Because the stride ordering has two parameters (P1 for the stride and P2 for the granularity), the data can be visualised as a 2D heatmap. Fig. 5 shows the heatmaps for the IPC and the L1 and L2 cache miss rates, as well as their correlation.

Fig. 5 shows a high inverse correlation (-0.8) between the IPC and the L1 miss rate: the 4 best candidates (with IPC > 300) all have the lowest L1 miss rate (16%). Although a low L2 miss rate also contributes to a high IPC, Fig. 5 (bottom right) shows a lower correlation. The results of Fig. 5 can be explained after detailed investigation. First of all, schedules with a small granularity (P2 < 32) can reduce the amount of coalescing significantly, leading to a low IPC and high cache miss rates. Second, schedules with a large stride and a large granularity form small 'tiles' in the 2D space of the matrix, improving locality. Finding the best tile dimensions is non-trivial and dependent on among others matrix dimensions and cache configuration. In this case, a ratio of 8:1 for P1 and P2 yields the best results for L1 and 2:1 for the L2 cache.

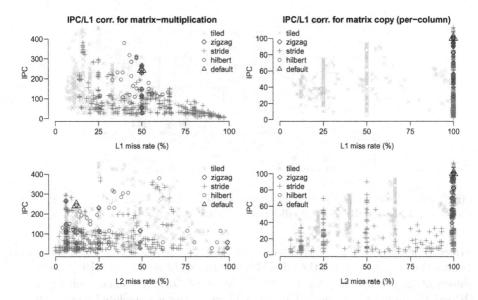

Fig. 6. Correlation plots for IPC (higher is better) and cache miss rates (lower is better) for the matrix-multiplication example (left) and the per-column matrix copy (right). Different colours/shapes represent different schedule types.

The left hand side of Fig. 6 shows the correlation plots of all the 2170 schedules for the matrix-multiplication example for 3 metrics: the top graph shows the correlation between IPC (y-axis) and L1 miss rate (x-axis), the bottom between IPC and L2 miss rate. From these results, we observe that the strided and tiled schedules have similar behaviour: they both cover the entire IPC and miss rate spectrum and show a high correlation between the IPC and L1 miss rate. We also observe a large amount of schedules with a L1 cache miss rate of around 50%, including the default and zigzag schedules. The best result uses 32x2 tiles with a width of 2048 and the first scheduler.

6.2 Per-column Matrix Copy

The correlation plots for the per-column matrix copy are shown on the right hand side of Fig. 6. From these plots, we observe that the IPC and cache miss rates are not as correlated as in the matrix-multiplication example. In fact, the best performing schedules have L1 and L2 cache miss rates of 100%. We furthermore observe that L1 cache miss rates only vary for tiled schedules and that most of them are distributed in a log_2 fashion: they have values of 100%, 50%, 25% and 12.5%. These 'improved' miss rates are cases where a lowered ($\frac{1}{2}$, $\frac{1}{4}$, $\frac{1}{8}$) memory coalescing rate results in additional cache hits.

Unlike the matrix-multiplication example, cache miss rates are not correlated with the IPC. Therefore, Fig. 7 focuses on other aspects: it shows the IPC and DRAM bank efficiency (the fraction of useful over theoretical accesses) for

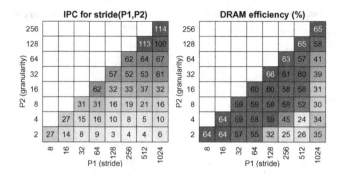

Fig. 7. Simulation results for the per-column matrix copy using strided schedules. Shown are IPC and DRAM bank efficiency (higher is better).

strided schedules. A low DRAM bank efficiency can be the cause of an uneven distribution of accesses over the DRAM banks (6 for the simulated GPU): certain phases of the benchmark access only a subset of DRAM banks, limiting the DRAM throughput. Although DRAM bank efficiency is correlated to the IPC, Fig. 7 also shows that it is not the only contributing effect. As with matrix-multiplication, memory access coalescing[4] also plays a role, explaining the low IPC for P2 < 32. DRAM efficiency can still be high in this case, as the number of accesses is increased as well.

7 Summary and Future Work

This work identified the potential for locality-aware thread scheduling on GPUs: re-ordering threads to increase data-locality and subsequently performance and energy efficiency. 2170 candidate schedules were simulated for 6 non-optimised CUDA benchmarks, showing a performance potential varying from 10% to multiple orders of magnitude. The benchmarks were explicitly chosen to be non-optimised: enabling competitive performance for such benchmarks will greatly improve the programmability. Our study has also identified aspects to consider: cache miss rates, coalescing, bank locality, and the number of active threads. An example is a straightforward implementation of matrix multiplication, which achieved a 87% performance increase by modifying the thread schedule.

Although this work has shown that locality-aware thread scheduling has the potential to improve programmability (better performance without changing the code), we have also shown that it is non-trivial to find the best thread schedule. This work can therefore be seen as a first step towards an investigation of how to find a good thread schedule: the ideas are presented, the potential has been shown, but an implementation has not been presented. A solution could potentially be found by evaluating schedules using a complete or partial performance model. This is motived by the detailed studies in this work, which have shown

---

[4] Coalescing is not visualised because GPGPU-Sim lacks the corresponding counters.

that performance is correlated to one or more metrics such as memory access coalescing or cache miss rate. An example of this is the use of the L1 cache model presented in [9]. Another possibility would be to iterate efficiently through all schedules, for example through auto-tuning (evaluating specific schedules on actual hardware), machine learning / neural networks (pre-training a model), or using hardware counters to dynamically change schedules (e.g. [12]).

References

1. Bakhoda, A., Yuan, G., Fung, W., Wong, H., Aamodt, T.: Analyzing CUDA Workloads using a Detailed GPU Simulator. In: ISPASS: International Symposium on Performance Analysis of Systems and Software. IEEE (2009)
2. Ding, C., Zhong, Y.: Predicting Whole-Program Locality through Reuse Distance Analysis. In: PLDI-24: Conference on Programming Language Design and Implementation. ACM (2003)
3. Fuller, S., Millett, L.: Computing Performance: Game Over or Next Level? IEEE Computer 44 (2011)
4. Gebhart, M., Johnson, D., Tarjan, D., Keckler, S., Dally, W., Lindholm, E., Skadron, K.: A Hierarchical Thread Scheduler and Register File for Energy-Efficient Throughput Processors. ACM Trans. on Computer Systems 30, 8:1–8:38 (2012)
5. Kayiran, O., Jog, A., Kandemir, M., Das, C.: Neither More Nor Less: Optimizing Thread-level Parallelism for GPGPUs. In: PACT-22: International Conference on Parallel Architectures and Compilation Techniques. IEEE (2013)
6. Lashgar, A., Baniasadi, A., Khonsari, A.: Dynamic Warp Resizing: Analysis and Benefits in High-Performance SIMT. In: ICCD-30: International Conference on Computer Design. IEEE (2012)
7. Meng, J., Tarjan, D., Skadron, K.: Dynamic Warp Subdivision for Integrated Branch and Memory Divergence Tolerance. In: ISCA-37: International Symposium on Computer Architecture. ACM (2010)
8. Narasiman, V., Shebanow, M., Lee, C., Miftakhutdinov, R., Mutlu, O., Patt, Y.: Improving GPU Performance via Large Warps and Two-level Warp Scheduling. In: MICRO-44: International Symposium on Microarchitecture. ACM (2011)
9. Nugteren, C., van den Braak, G.-J., Corporaal, H., Bal, H.: A Detailed GPU Cache Model Based on Reuse Distance Theory. In: HPCA-20: International Symposium on High Performance Computer Architecture. IEEE (2014)
10. NVIDIA. CUDA C Programming Guide 5.5 (2013)
11. Philbin, J., Edler, J., Anshus, O., Douglas, C., Li, K.: Thread Scheduling for Cache Locality. In: ASPLOS-7: International Conference on Architectural Support for Programming Languages and Operating Systems. ACM (1996)
12. Rogers, T., O'Connor, M., Aamodt, T.: Cache-Conscious Wavefront Scheduling. In: MICRO-45: International Symposium on Microarchitecture. IEEE (2012)
13. Stratton, J., Anssari, N., Rodrigues, C., Sung, I.-J., Obeid, N., Chang, L., Liu, G., Hwu, W.: Optimization and Architecture Effects on GPU Computing Workload Performance. In: INPAR: Workshop on Innovative Parallel Computing. IEEE (2012)
14. Tam, D., Azimi, R., Stumm, M.: Thread Clustering: Sharing-Aware Scheduling on SMP-CMP-SMT Multiprocessors. In: EuroSys-2: European Conference on Computer Systems. ACM (2007)

OpenCL Performance Portability for Xeon Phi Coprocessor and NVIDIA GPUs: A Case Study of Finite Element Numerical Integration

Krzysztof Banaś[1] and Filip Krużel[2]

[1] AGH University of Science and Technology
al. A. Mickiewicza 30, 30-059 Kraków, Poland
kbanas@agh.edu.pl
[2] Institute of Computer Modelling,
Cracow University of Technology, Warszawska 24, 31-155 Kraków, Poland

Abstract. We present the performance analysis of OpenCL kernels for three recently introduced many-core accelerator architectures: Intel Xeon Phi coprocessor and NVIDIA Kepler and Fermi GPUs. We use a case study of finite element numerical integration, a practically important and theoretically interesting algorithm used in scientific computing. We design a single parametrized kernel for all three architectures and test the performance obtained in numerical tests. We indicate possible further, architecture dependent, optimizations and draw conclusions on the performance portability for different accelerator architectures and OpenCL programming model.

Keywords: OpenCL, performance portability, performance analysis, Xeon Phi coprocessor, GPU, Kepler architecture, Fermi architecture, finite elements, numerical integration.

1 Introduction

1.1 New Processor Architectures

Accelerated computer hardware plays increasingly important role in scientific computing [18]. The most popular among recently introduced hybrid systems are those equipped with cards containing either graphics processors (mainly produced by NVIDIA) or new Intel Xeon Phi coprocessors [15]. New processor and accelerator architectures pose several problems when porting existing numerical codes. One of the most important, is the problem of programming efforts required to reach satisfactory performance levels on different platforms, the subject thoroughly investigated in [3]. It turns out that the "recompile and run" approach, used successfully for classical microprocessors during the last decades of the XXth century, either cannot be used at all, due to the differences in programming and execution models, as is the case of graphics processors, or does not bring expected results, as was reported for Intel Xeon Phi processors [16].

L. Lopes et al. (Eds.): Euro-Par 2014 Workshops, Part II, LNCS 8806, pp. 158–169, 2014.

Therefore, to reach the goal of efficiently exploiting new processor designs, at least several architecture characteristics has to be taken into account explicitly. These characteristics correspond to the development trends in microprocessor design, such as e.g.:

- the increasing number of processing cores
- the increasing role of SIMD scheduling
- the use of several levels of memory hierarchy
- the presence of vector registers and vector pipelines with increasing width

The first three development directions are well visible for massively multi-core architectures of GPUs. The last direction becomes more and more indispensable for getting the proper performance of not only special coprocessor cores [8], but also cores of standard processors [17]. It would be then advantageous to have a programming environment that would allow for exploiting all the mentioned above trends in microprocessor design. The environment should also allow for certain level of performance portability and eventually lead to performance levels in the range of several tens percent of the theoretical maximum for each considered hardware.

We choose OpenCL [6] as a programming model in order to reach the goals of our research. On one hand, it is based on CUDA model [12] designed specifically for GPUs and, thanks to this, capable of exploiting their possibilities. On the other hand, due to sufficiently broad support from hardware vendors, OpenCL software development kits exist for all popular processor and accelerator architectures, and offer opportunities for relatively easy porting of developed programs. The use of OpenCL as a tool for creating portable codes was investigated in the context of classical processors and GPUs (see e.g. [14]). We extend this research by considering the architecture of Xeon Phi and the problem of finite element numerical integration.

1.2 Finite Element Software

Finite element method is one of the most popular methods for approximating partial differential equations used in many application domains of science and engineering. For each new computing architecture, investigations are performed concerning the optimal mapping of finite element calculations.

Among the papers on finite elements on GPUs, several are of special interest when considering the general problem of code portability. The first group of papers is related to efforts to create optimized versions of codes, based on abstract specifications of weak formulations and suitable, sophisticated compilers that transform specifications into optimized procedures [10]. The research on mapping of algorithms to modern computer architectures has its own significance, as the basis for code development and further investigations concerning subsequent architectures and new development tools. One of the most important papers in the category of analysis of finite element solution procedures is [4], where several strategies for global linear system assembly are investigated and compared. Our approach is similar. We analyse the code and formulate design guidelines that can be further used in code design for particular hardware, but also for different approximation methods and problems solved.

1.3   Current Contribution

In the current paper we investigate the possibility of solving, at least partially, the problem of performance portability among different processor architectures, by using a generic OpenCL programming environment and a proper analysis and design of the code ported to new architectures.

As an algorithm for testing the development of portable OpenCL kernels we choose finite element numerical integration. We consider low order finite elements, the most popular in practical applications. The use of high order approximations was the subject of our papers [1] and [9] where investigations were conducted separately for GPUs and PowerXCell processor, respectively, the latter being a representative of architectures having specialized cores with extended vector capabilities.

In the current paper we perform an analysis of numerical integration algorithm and try to design a parametrized OpenCL kernel, that can be used for three recent accelerator architectures: Intel Xeon Phi coprocessor and NVIDIA Kepler and Fermi GPUs. We review briefly the OpenCL programming model and the finite element numerical integration algorithm. We describe the design of a parametrized kernel for numerical integration and analyse and test its performance in practical calculations. We draw some conclusions concerning further possible optimizations and porting to other processor architectures.

2   OpenCL Programming Model

We do not describe here the OpenCL programming model as it is defined in the specification [6]. Instead, we present a model that we adopt for designing the software, in some ways simplified, but including not only abstract specification of calculations, but also the characteristics of code execution on different processors.

We assume that each piece of OpenCL code for an accelerator is specified in the form of a kernel (a function written in a slightly modified variant of C99), that after compilation is run in the form of a single thread (we use the notion of "thread", as more intuitively obvious than "work-item" notion used in OpenCL).

In CUDA and OpenCL GPU programming models threads are grouped together into sets that are executed in a SIMD fashion (we do not discuss here the problem of thread divergence, the situation that we avoid in our designs). Threads in a single set are scheduled together and each thread is executed on a single SIMD lane and the whole group is scheduled for a single SIMD (vector) unit.

This model can be useful also for looking at the execution on CPU cores equipped with wide vector execution units. In fact, this is the perspective adopted by creators of the OpenCL compiler for Xeon Phi coprocessors (that contain modified Pentium CPU cores) [7]. Although the notions adopted in the compiler's description are different, in our derivations and analyses we will reserve the notion of a thread to a subsequent execution of instructions specified in the kernel code. Hence, in our model one vector instruction executed on a CPU core corresponds to a set of threads (contrary to a common perspective used e.g. in OpenMP model and the perspective in [7], where it corresponds to a single thread).

For both types of architectures, GPUs and Xeon Phi, we will use a notion of SIMD group of threads, for a set of threads forming a unit of scheduling, with individual threads executed on either separate scalar GPU cores or SIMD lanes of a vector unit in CPU cores. The notion of SIMD groups is absent in the OpenCL specification, however it is present in all CUDA and OpenCL performance considerations (as warps for NVIDIA GPUs, wavefronts for AMD GPUs and threads executing vector instructions for Xeon Phi).

Several SIMD groups form another level of thread organization, a workgroup. The role of a workgroup in our model, is to provide access to the fast memory, that is shared by all threads forming the workgroup. Apart from being units associated with shared memory allocation, workgroups in OpenCL are used for thread synchronization (mainly to arrange memory accesses).

The notion of fast shared memory (we use the notion of shared memory, as reflecting its role in OpenCL programs, instead of an OpenCL notion of local memory) is typical for GPU architectures. It is mapped to special memory modules on GPUs. The notion of shared memory does not play an important role in the Xeon Phi OpenCL model of execution. The documentation states that it is mapped to a part of global memory. Nevertheless, the memory in CPU-like architectures is cached and one may use OpenCL shared memory to rewrite the content of data structures in global memory, so that, when properly rewritten data are used by threads, the new data arrangement allow for lower access times than in original storage (assuming that caching takes place). This may resemble e.g. repackaging used for classical processors in high performance implementations of linear algebra routines [5].

The OpenCL specification assumes that the whole workgroup is scheduled for execution on a single compute unit. Compute units in GPUs are well defined hardware blocks (e.g. streaming multiprocessors for NVIDIA GPUs). For the OpenCL model of execution on Xeon Phi the hyperthreading capabilities of its cores are utilized. Each workgroup is treated as one classical thread and, hence, four workgroups are scheduled for concurrent execution on a single CPU core (since Xeon Phi cores have 4-way hyperthreading).

Finally, a set of workgroups forms the whole set of threads executing a single kernel on an OpenCL device. Workgroups are executed in a fully MIMD fashion and no dependencies can exist between different workgroups.

Apart from shared memory discussed above, we consider two other types of memory available to threads: registers and global memory. In OpenCL (and CUDA as well) there is a special type of variables (local variables) designed to be stored in registers, whenever it is possible. However, when the number of such variables exceeds the limits imposed by the hardware or programming model, the compiler may "spill" the variables to global memory. In the first generations of GPUs, such a situation resulted in serious performance deterioration, since global memory was not cached. In recent generations (and both architectures that we consider in our paper), the global memory is cached and one can expect lower penalties for register spilling.

The last aspect of programming and execution model that we mention in this brief description is the time of accesses to shared and global memory. In classical CPU programming, when creating a single thread code, the main design guideline is to increase spatial and temporal locality. For GPUs one more aspect appears, the proper organization of memory accesses for a SIMD group of threads. We try to use in our design the safest method leading to optimal memory performance (global as well as shared). Whenever threads access memory, the slowest memory present in the instruction is accessed in such a way that subsequent threads access subsequent memory locations (32 or 64-bit).

This method of accessing memory, should also work well for Xeon Phi architecture. When subsequent threads in a SIMD group access subsequent memory locations, their accesses can be grouped into a single vectorized memory access, that in turn should speed-up code execution.

3   Finite Element Numerical Integration

Finite element codes are based on integral weak statements of the problems solved [2]. To effectively solve the problems, finite element codes transform weak statements into systems of linear equations. Each entry in the system matrix is obtained as a sum of integrals, performed for individual finite elements. The most common way of calculating integrals is to use numerical integration. Hence, numerical integration forms one of indispensable parts of generic finite element codes in any application domain.

In the current paper we leave the problem of designing a generic numerical integration procedure for different approximation methods and problems solved and concentrate on two simple test cases for which we assess the performance of an OpenCL kernel on different processor architectures.

We assume that numerical integration is performed in a loop over finite elements and for each element a small dense matrix A^{iE} is created, that is further used in calculations. The algorithm of finite element numerical integration adopted for analysis in the current paper can be represented as Algorithm 1. Its essence lies in computing the entries to subsequent matrices A^{iE} (element stiffness matrices), based on the values stored, separately for each element, in arrays c (coefficients) and ψ (element shape functions with their derivatives).

Algorithm 1. The algorithm of numerical integration used in the study

1: read input data common to all elements processed by a thread
2: **for** $i_E = 1$ to N_E **do**
3:     read input data specific to a given element (including coefficients c)
4:     initialize element stiffness matrix, A^{i_E}
5:     **for** $i_Q = 1$ to N_Q **do**
6:         calculate derivatives of shape functions at a given integration point, $\psi[i_Q]$
7:         **for** $i_S = 1$ to N_S **do**
8:             **for** $j_S = 1$ to N_S **do**
9:                 **for** $i_D = 1$ to N_D **do**
10:                     **for** $j_D = 1$ to N_D **do**
11:                         $A^{i_E}[i_S][j_S] += c[i_D][j_D] \times \psi[i_D][i_S][i_Q] \times \psi[j_D][j_S][i_Q]$
12:                     **end for**
13:                 **end for**
14:             **end for**
15:         **end for**
16:     **end for**
17:     store A^{i_E} in global memory
18: **end for**

One of the most important characteristics of Algorithm 1 is the range of its loops. The parameters specifying the ranges are the following:

- N_E - the number of finite elements, assumed to be in the order of millions
- N_S - the number of element shape functions, in the order of several for low order approximations analysed in the current paper
- N_Q - the number of integration points within single element, in the order of several for low order approximations analysed in the current paper
- N_D - number of space dimensions plus one (in the algorithm it is assumed that arrays ψ contain the values of functions and the values of their spatial derivatives, index value 0 corresponds to the function itself, index values different from zero correspond to its derivatives). In our investigations for 3D problems, N_D is always equal to four.

Algorithm 1 takes as the input some data stored in global memory of the device performing calculations. In the current paper we do not consider the problem of transferring the input data from finite element data structures (that may reside in a different memory). For each element the main input data consist of parameters that describe the geometry of the element and the coefficients for computing matrix entries. The geometry parameters are used for calculating the derivatives of shape functions. In Algorithm 1 it is assumed that the input coefficient matrices c are used in calculations without changes.

The output of the algorithm is represented as a set of element stiffness matrices, that can be further assembled to the global matrix or used directly in matrix-free linear system solvers [13].

4   Computational Aspects of Numerical Integration Algorithm

From the computational point of view, the algorithm of finite element numerical integration is interesting as the one that combines relative simplicity with many ways for introducing different optimizations. The difficulty of optimizing it lies in the fact that PDE coefficients used in final calculations usually have different non-zero structure for different types of approximated problems and may be (e.g. for quasi-linear or non-linear problems) computed at each integration point based on input matrices c (the option not considered in the current paper). Moreover, the entries of arrays ψ are computed in different ways for different types of finite element approximations. All these facts influence significantly the optimizations that can be applied to the algorithm and the performance that can be achieved as a result [10,4].

4.1   Parallelization

In the form presented in Algorithm 1, the most suitable for parallelization is the loop over elements. The number of elements for large scale problems exceeds many times the number of threads necessary for optimal usage of computing resources (even for clusters with GPUs). When considering numerical integration alone, the algorithm is embarrassingly parallel with no dependencies between calculations for any two different elements (when considered as a part of finite element calculations, special techniques, such as colouring, has to be often applied to avoid dependencies).

In the current paper we consider only the parallelization of the loop over elements. The parallel code obtained from Algorithm 1 does not change at all, the only thing that changes is the range of element indices assigned to a thread. We pose the question how to design a portable OpenCL kernel for Algorithm 1, that would properly map to computing resources of different processor architectures. We test the performance obtained when the same, simple design guidelines are applied for different architectures.

These guidelines are the following: we try to limit the number of global memory accesses and maximize the use of registers in main calculations. We utilize the ability, offered by the OpenCL programming model, of explicitly managing the fast shared memory. However, we use shared memory with caution. For GPUs, despite the fact that it is usually one order of magnitude faster than global memory, it is several times slower than registers and, when its size for a single workgroup grows, it can limit the number of concurrently working SIMD groups and, in consequence, slow down execution by not allowing the concurrent execution of multiple SIMD groups to hide instruction and memory access latencies.

4.2   Arithmetic Operations and Register Accesses

In analysing the parallel version of Algorithm 1 we accept, in the usual way, the numbers of operations performed and the numbers of memory accesses, as the most important characteristics of code execution. The number of operations depends on the non-zero pattern of array c (with all optimizations that it induces taken into account) and the number of additional operations performed in line 6 of Algorithm 1. The number of global memory accesses, in the version adopted in our study, is related only to the operations in lines 1,3 and 17 of Algorithm 1 (assuming that there is no register spilling to global memory). The number of shared memory accesses depends on the details of operations in line 6 of Algorithm 1, as well as the ability of the hardware to store all the data used in main calculations in line 11 of Algorithm 1 in registers.

Typical for the situation when the number of required registers exceeds the limits of the GPU hardware, is to consider the use of shared memory for some of data used in calculations or even change the algorithm [1]. In the current study, for the purpose of analysing the portability of the code, we leave to further papers more elaborate investigations considering the optimal mapping of calculations for different architectures and design the code assuming that all the data in main calculations in line 11 of Algorithm 1 reside in registers and, in a manner typical for CPU programming, relying on the compiler for the optimization of register variable usage.

4.3 Memory Accesses

Reading input data in lines 1 and 3 of Algorithm 1 is assumed as reading from global memory to shared memory. The accesses to global memory from different threads in a SIMD group are organized in an optimal way with subsequent threads accessing subsequent memory locations. In a similar way, accesses to shared memory storing read data are organized during further calculations. The accesses to global memory when writing output data are also performed in the optimal manner. In that way, not optimal memory accesses are reduced to shared memory accesses during reading of input data from global memory.

4.4 Arithmetic Intensity

Table 1 presents arithmetic intensity parameters for executing Algorithm 1 for a single prismatic 3D finite element with linear approximation and two test cases selected for the paper, associated with two example forms of arrays c. The first case, corresponding to e.g. Laplace equations, has only 3 non-zero entries, all equal to one, for all 16 combinations of indices i_D and j_D and lead to 7 operations performed for calculations in lines 9–13 of Algorithm 1 (for off-diagonal stiffness matrix entries symmetry can be taken into account). The second case, corresponding e.g. to full convection-diffusion-reaction PDEs, has all 16 entries non-zero and results in more than two times more operations performed in loops over indices i_D and j_D in Algorithm 1. The relatively high ratios of the number of floating point operations to the number of global and fast memory accesses allow one to expect performance figures possible to obtain in the range of several tens of maximum performances for floating point operations.

Table 1. The ratio of the number of floating point operations to the number of global and fast (shared and constant) memory accesses for an implementation of Algorithm 1

	Type of problem:	
For single finite element:	Laplace	conv-diff
The number of floating point operations	2916	4806
The number of global memory accesses	60	74
The arithmetic intensity for global memory	≈48	≈65
The number of fast memory accesses	276	276
The arithmetic intensity for fast memory	≈10	≈17

However, the numbers in Table 1 are obtained assuming that there are no global memory accesses due to register spilling . Another factor that can limit the performance, especially in the case of GPUs, is the fact that large register and shared memory requirements, related to the optimal execution of individual statements, can induce low "processor occupancy", i.e. low number of concurrently executed SIMD groups, that in turn will not allow for fully hiding the latency of arithmetic and memory operations.

5   Numerical Experiments

5.1   Parametrized Implementation of Numerical Integration Algorithm

We design a single OpenCL kernel implementing a specific version of Algorithm 1, based on the OpenCL model of programming and the design guidelines and execution performance analysis described earlier. We parametrize the kernel with several parameters that are specified either at compile time or runtime. There are two parameters that adapt the kernel to processor architectures. The first is the size of workgroups. Based on recommendations in programming guides ([12,7]) we choose 64 threads for a single workgroup for NVIDIA GPUs and 16 threads for Xeon Phi. The second is the number of workgroups. We assume that at least 8 workgroups are assigned to each compute unit of GPUs, while there is only one workgroup for one compute unit for Xeon Phi (i.e. there are four workgroups for each of its cores).

5.2   Hardware Used for Testing

We performed numerical tests for Intel Xeon Phi coprocessor working in 5110P accelerator card and NVIDIA GPUs working in Tesla accelerator cards: Tesla M2075 for Fermi GPU and Tesla K20 for Kepler GPU. All cards are connected to systems running Linux with kernel 2.6.32. For OpenCL code development on NVIDIA GPUs, compilers and libraries from CUDA 5.5 SDK were used, while for Xeon Phi we employed compilers and libraries from Intel SDK for OpenCL

Table 2. Characteristics of accelerators used in computational experiments

OpenCL device	Fermi Tesla M2075	Kepler Tesla K20m	Xeon Phi 5110P
Number of compute units	14	13	236
Number of cores per comp. unit	32	192	1/4
Total number of cores	448	2496	59
Shared (local) memory size [KB]	48	48	32
Number of registers per comp. unit	32768x32bit	65536x32bit	32x512bit
Device memory size [MB]	5375	4800	5773
Global max alloc size [MB]	1343	1200	1924
Peak DP performance [TFlops]	0.515	1.17	1.01
Benchmark (DGEMM) performance	0.36	1.10	0.84
Peak SP performance [TFlops]	1.03	3.52	2.02
Benchmark (SGEMM) performance	0.51	2.61	1.74
Peak memory bandwidth [GB/s]	150	208	320
Benchmark (STREAM) bandwidth	105	144	165

Applications XE 3.0. Table 2 presents several characteristics of the accelerators used for testing[1].

5.3   Results

Table 3 presents the results of test runs for all three accelerators, single precision and double precision calculations and two problem types introduced above: Laplace and convection-diffusion-reaction. Several parameters are given for each run: execution time for a single finite element, performance in GFLOPS and as a percentage of the theoretical peak (the results are reported for the best of several executions). Additionally for GPUs the table contains the information provided by the *nvcc* compiler and concerning the number of registers used by each thread and the size of stack frame in global memory related to spilled loads and stores.

Several observations follow:

- the results vary significantly for both problems, different architectures and different precision of data
- for Fermi architecture, the resources are sufficient for single precision calculations (especially for Laplace test case, for which the calculated occupancy equals 33% and the performance reaches very high values around 60% of the theoretical peak), but the number of registers and the size of shared memory are too small to allow for high performance of the kernel for double precision calculations (where small occupancy and register spilling occurs)

---

[1] For Xeon Phi architecture the number of compute units reported by the OpenCL compiler is four times larger than the number of cores. This is related to the "hyperthreading" form of SMT for Intel x86 cores [11], where each core is seen as four "logical processors" (and each logical processor is considered as a compute unit).

Table 3. Finite element numerical integration execution characteristics and performance results for two test cases: Laplace equation and convection-diffusion PDE and three accelerator architectures: Fermi, Kepler and Xeon Phi. The same OpenCL kernel is used for all calculations, execution times are reported for one element .

	M2075 – Fermi		K20 – Kepler		5110P–Xeon Phi	
	SP	DP	SP	DP	SP	DP
Laplace						
Execution time [ns]	4.5	43.1	3.79	10.73	18.75	32.0
Performance [GFLOPS]	648	67	769	272	155	91
Performance [% of peak]	62.9	13.0	21.8	23.2	7.6	9.0
The number of registers used	63	63	92	158	–	–
The size of stack frame [B]	40	320	0	0	–	–
convection-diffusion						
Execution time [ns]	13.3	119.5	4.25	11.9	10.7	32.1
Performance [GFLOPS]	361	40	1131	404	257	150
Performance [% of peak]	35.0	7.7	32.1	34.5	12.7	14.8
The number of registers used	63	63	126	196	–	–
The size of stack frame [B]	120	616	0	0	–	–

- for Kepler architecture the results are consistent for single and double precision, while the performance is approximately 50% higher for the test case with higher arithmetic intensity (reaching more than 30% of the theoretical peak)
- the same observation holds for Xeon Phi, while the obtained performance, as the percentage of the peak, is more than two times lower than for the Kepler architecture
- the portable kernel used in the study, turned out to be the fastest for GPUs, but not the best for Xeon Phi, for which the kernel with no explicit usage of shared memory performed calculations approx. 20% faster

6   Conclusions

The analyses presented in the paper show how OpenCL notions can be used for designing a single code for such different architectures as NVIDIA GPUs and Xeon Phi. The same code, with only two parameters adapted to different architectures, was created for an example algorithm of finite element numerical integration. The performance results show that, using design process based on several simple, general optimization guidelines, it is possible to obtain for each architecture a reasonable performance, sometimes above 50% of its theoretical maximum. However, at the current stage, with the performance for several cases below 10% of the theoretical maximum, it cannot be concluded that full performance portability, if defined as obtaining high performance with a single code for all considered architectures, has been reached.

Acknowledgements. This work was supported by the Polish National Science Centre under grant no DEC-2011/01/B/ST6/00674.

References

1. Banaś, K., Płaszewski, P., Maciol, P.: Numerical integration on GPUs for higher order finite elements. Computers and Mathematics with Applications 67(6), 1319–1344 (2014)
2. Becker, E., Carey, G., Oden, J.: Finite Elements. An Introduction. Prentice Hall, Englewood Cliffs (1981)
3. Benkner, S., Pllana, S., Traff, J., Tsigas, P., Dolinsky, U., Augonnet, C., Bachmayer, B., Kessler, C., Moloney, D., Osipov, V.: Peppher: Efficient and productive usage of hybrid computing systems. IEEE Micro 31(5), 28–41 (2011)
4. Cecka, C., Lew, A.J., Darve, E.: Assembly of finite element methods on graphics processors. International Journal for Numerical Methods in Engineering 85(5), 640–669 (2011), http://dx.doi.org/10.1002/nme.2989
5. Goto, K., van de Geijn, R.A.: Anatomy of high-performance matrix multiplication. ACM Trans. Math. Softw. 34(3), 12:1–12:25 (2008), http://doi.acm.org/10.1145/1356052.1356053
6. Group, K.O.W.: The OpenCL Specification, version 1.1 (2010), http://www.khronos.org/registry/cl/specs/opencl-1.1.pdf
7. Intel: Intel SDK for OpenCL Applications XE 2013 R3. User's Guide (2013)
8. Jeffers, J., Reinders, J.: Intel Xeon Phi Coprocessor High Performance Programming, 1st edn. Morgan Kaufmann (2013)
9. Krużel, F., Banaś, K.: Vectorized OpenCL implementation of numerical integration for higher order finite elements. Computers and Mathematics with Applications 66(10), 2030–2044 (2013)
10. Markall, G.R., Ham, D.A., Kelly, P.H.: Towards generating optimised finite element solvers for gpus from high-level specifications. Procedia Computer Science 1(1), 1815–1823 (2010); iCCS 2010
11. Marr, D.T., Binns, F., Hill, D.L., Hinton, G., Koufaty, D.A., Miller, A.J., Upton, M.: Hyper-Threading Technology Architecture and Microarchitecture. Intel Technology Journal 6(1), 4–15 (2002)
12. NVIDIA: NVIDIA CUDA C Programming Guide Version 5.0 (2012)
13. Reguly, I., Giles, M.: Finite element algorithms and data structures on graphical processing units. International Journal of Parallel Programming, 1–37 (2013), http://dx.doi.org/10.1007/s10766-013-0301-6
14. Rul, S., Vandierendonck, H., D'Haene, J., De Bosschere, K.: An experimental study on performance portability of opencl kernels. In: Application Accelerators in High Performance Computing, 2010 Symposium, Papers, Knoxville, TN, USA, p. 3 (2010)
15. Top500, http://www.top500.org
16. Wienke, S., an Mey, D., Müller, M.S.: Accelerators for technical computing: Is it worth the pain? A TCO perspective. In: Kunkel, J.M., Ludwig, T., Meuer, H.W. (eds.) ISC 2013. LNCS, vol. 7905, pp. 330–342. Springer, Heidelberg (2013)
17. Williams, S., Waterman, A., Patterson, D.: Roofline: An insightful visual performance model for multicore architectures. Commun. ACM 52(4), 65–76 (2009), http://doi.acm.org/10.1145/1498765.1498785
18. Yuen, D., Wang, L., Chi, X., Johnsson, L., Ge, W., Shi, Y. (eds.): GPU Solutions to Multi-scale Problems in Science and Engineering. Springer (2013)

Eve: A Parallel Event-Driven Programming Language

Alcides Fonseca, João Rafael, and Bruno Cabral

University of Coimbra, Portugal
{amaf,bcabral}@dei.uc.pt, jprafael@student.dei.uc.pt

Abstract. We propose a model for event-oriented programming under shared memory based on access permissions with explicit parallelism. In order to obtain safe parallelism, programmers need to specify the variable permissions of functions. Blocking operations are non existent, and callback-based APIs are used instead, which can be called in parallel for different events as long as the access permissions are guaranteed. This model scales for both IO and CPU-bounded programs.

We have implemented this model in the Eve language, which includes a compiler that generates parallel tasks with synchronization on top of variables, and a work-stealing runtime that uses the epoll interface to manage the event loop.

We have also evaluated that model in micro-benchmarks in programs that are either CPU-intensive or IO-intensive with and without shared data. In CPU-intensive programs, it achieved results very close to multithreaded approaches. In the share-nothing IO-intensive benchmark it outperformed all other solutions. In shared-memory IO-intensive benchmark it outperformed other solutions with a more or equal value of writes than read operations.

Keywords: Event-oriented, Parallel Programming, IO performance.

1 Introduction

The high-performance of IO applications has become more important in the last decades as the Internet applications are required to handle a large number of clients with a high throughput and low latency. More recently, event-loop based models have become popular for high-performance applications.

However, it is not possible to assert whether event-loop models are better or worse than shared-memory multithreaded models. Event-loops have become popular because several applications using that model have shown to have a lower memory consumption, better performance and better scalability than equivalent programs written in a threaded model [1] [2]. The event-based model is also considered simpler than using threads, since threading requires proper synchronization and it is more difficult to debug[3]. A counter-argument against events is that reasoning about the control flow is difficult and with careful reengineering, threaded approaches can achieve similar performance values[4].

L. Lopes et al. (Eds.): Euro-Par 2014 Workshops, Part II, LNCS 8806, pp. 170–181, 2014.

The actor model has been a popular approach to unify both models, with each actor running on its own thread, each with its own event-loop [5]. This approach allows for an event-loop approach to scale across multiple processor cores with a composable interface. However, the actor model limits the memory access to the actor, which has less flexibility that threaded models for some applications.

The Eve language introduces a new model that supports the event-loop and task-based parallelism to allow for both IO and CPU bounded programs to achieve high concurrency. Unlike the actor model, the eve language is shared memory and any task can access data from any other task. But in order to reduce the complexity of handling all the synchronization necessary to avoid deadlocks and to guarantee data consistency, the language makes use of access permissions, which have to be specified in the program. From these access permissions, the program is automatically parallelized, and monitors are added when necessary to guarantee consistency. This works across the event loop, allowing for shared-memory task-based parallelism inside the event loop.

The main contributions of this paper are: A new model for shared-memory task parallelism within the event-loop; The definition of a language that supports that model; The implementation of a compiler for that language and a runtime library to support the execution; and an evaluation and comparison of that language against popular languages.

The rest of the paper is organized as follows: Section 2 explains the new programming model proposed; Section 3 details the implementation of the compiler and runtime; Section 5 compares our model to other state of the art approaches; finally Section 6 concludes the document and presents some future work.

2   Approach

We propose a model that combines the event loop and the shared-memory aspect of threaded programming. We will focus firstly on the programming model, and then on the execution aspect.

The three main differences between the programming model of Eve and those of mainstream object-oriented languages is the usage of tasks, permissions and event callbacks.

Eve allows programmers to execute methods and blocks of code as parallel tasks. This is expressed using the @ symbol. Program 1 is a parallel implementation of the Fibonacci function. Since the a and b assignment statement is prefixed with the @ symbol, they are executed in parallel. After the @, the programmer has to write the access permissions required to execute that block of code. As long as the access permissions are correct, tasks can be introduced in any part of the code.

Permissions only apply to objects that are shared among different parts of the code. Local objects do not require access permissions since they are guaranteed to execute in the same thread without the need for synchronization.

```
fib: (n: int) int:
    if n < 2:
        return n

    a, b : int@
    finish:
        @ [+a, =n]: a = fib(n - 1)
        @ [+b, =n]: b = fib(n - 2)

    return a + b
```

Program 1. Parallel computation of the nth Fibonacci number using the `finish` block for synchronization. `int@` defines a shared object of base type `int`.

Objects can have three different permissions on a method of code block: If no special annotation is added, the default permission is *Read permission*, which allows function to access a certain object, but an attempt to modify it will result in a compile-time error. If the programmer wants the shared object to be modified, then a *Full permission* is required and the variable should be prepended with a + sign. Finally, if only the reference is needed, without any read or write, a *Null permission* can be annotated by using the - sign. The main usage for this permission is to bind a reference to the object to the local context.

Using the same syntax as C++ a variable can be captured by copy or by reference using the = and & prefixes respectively.

Since it is frequent for sub-tasks to require access to the same objects, those operations must be executed inside a special *finish* block. When the execution reaches the *finish* special block, it releases all shared object, so that they can be used by the subtasks. This approach allows for a consistent view of the objects. Inside a finish block tasks can only require a subset of the parent's permission set, which prevents deadlocks between parent and child tasks.

Tasks have further restrictions in order to guarantee the corrected of concurrent programs: Tasks may not have infinite loops or blocking operations, as this could lead to live-locks. Instead, eve programs use a event-based non-blocking asynchronous API to interact with the Operating System.

The event-based callback system is another of the core features in eve. Any type in the language can enumerate the set of events if can trigger. Events are named types and they can contain objects of any type. Objects that can emit events can be used with the *on* construct to define a event callback. Program 2 shows an implementation of a simple socket-based chat showing the use of the *on* keyword to define callbacks and the @ keyword for parallel execution of tasks. When the socket object receives data, the `on client data` callback is executed, for instance. While the buffer reading is done in the current task, the writes to each client buffer is done in parallel tasks.

The execution model is based on the same task-oriented work-stealing scheduler present in Cilk[6] and many other frameworks. This approach has been

```
import io.socket.*
import util.timeout

main: () void:
    clients: set<socket@>@

    tcp_socket.listen(8080):
        connection = [+clients] (c: connection&) bool:
            client: socket@ = c()
            clients.insert(client)

            on client data [clients]:
                message : vector<char>@ = client.read_buffer()
                @ for (c: socket@ in clients) [message, +c]:
                    c.write_buffer(message)

            on client close [+clients]:
                clients.remove(client)

            return true

        error = [+stderr] (e: error&) bool:
            stderr.write("Failed to start server: %s", error)
            return true
```

Program 2. A TCP broadcast server that accepts connections on port 8080

proved to support several CPU-bounded operations with a good occupation of multiple processors. A fixed number of POSIX threads are created, each with its own queue. Worker threads process the tasks in their queue and, when the queue is empty, they steal tasks from other queues.

Whenever a new task is being scheduled, the required permissions are verified that they are available. If they are not, the task is moved to the end of the queue, for a later execution. Since this adds an unwanted overhead, tasks should require as few permissions as possible.

New tasks can also be scheduled by the kernel, when a new kernel event is generated. These tasks will have to be executed in the right order and they cannot conflict on the shared objects that they required. In order to execute in the right order, the first callback should execute completely. If there are some operations pending because of other IO operations (such as writes), the remaining callbacks for the first event will only be called when the callback for this new event is completed.

3 Implementation

The implementation of the Eve language is divided in two main components: the compiler and the runtime. The compiler follows a traditional approach, with the code-generator phase emitting C++ code instead of machine code, thus being, in fact, a transpiler. Further compilation with GCC is performed to obtain binary files. The generated code makes heavy use of the Eve runtime to obtain parallelism and to enforce proper synchronization of data.

The Eve runtime architecture (in Figure 1) has a task management core, which is responsible for task handling. This includes creating and managing the worker POSIX threads, the management of tasks, load balancing of tasks using a work-stealing approach and also to guarantee proper access to shared objects. Additionally, the core of the runtime is also responsible for wrapping the *epoll* system calls, enabling the transition from kernel callbacks to events in Eve. The Libraries package exposes common system tasks, such as socket operations, using event handling for callback registration.

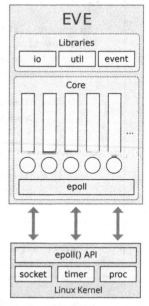

Fig. 1. Architecture of the Eve runtime, and its connection with the Linux kernel using the **epoll** interface

The work-stealing approach was heavily based on the THE algorithm[7] from Cilk[6], with the suspend-steal method[8] for avoiding overheads of double stealing. Since the runtime integrates tightly with epool, workers call epoll_wait() instead of sleeping when it has no available tasks for running.

While events in Eve are instances of any class, event emitters have to extend the **emitter<T>** class, indicating that it can emit events of type T. Each instance of the class stores callbacks for this event on this object. This allows for a distributed callback table, effectively avoiding unnecessary contention with global table locks.

4   Evaluation

In this section we compare the performance of the Eve platform with existing popular frameworks for high-performance IO and parallel programming. The evaluation focused on two programs: Echo Server, representative of IO-intensive applications; and Atomic Counter, representative of concurrent programs with synchronization.

In terms of Lines of Code, one heuristic frequently used to compare complexity of programming expression, programs written in Eve are smaller than other low-level frameworks such as libev, TBB or Fork/Join. It also performs fairly well against higher-level frameworks such as gevent and REV despite achieving much better performance.

Each execution was repeated 30 times from which the average values and respective standard deviations are shown. Additionally, a first execution was

Table 1. Hardware specification of benchmark hosts

	Ingrid	Astrid
Motherboard	Dell Inc. 0CRH6C	SuperMicro X9DAi
Processor	2x Intel(R) Xeon(R) X5660 2.80GHz, 24 hardware threads	2x Intel(R) Xeon(R) E5-2650 2.00GHz, 32 hardware threads
Memory	24 GB DDR3 1333 MHz	32 GB DDR3 1600 MHz
Connectivity	Broadcom Corporation NetXtreme BCM5761 Gigabit Ethernet PCIe	Intel Corporation I350 Gigabit Network Connection

performed before the 30 repetitions to avoid interference of the JIT compilation and caching mechanisms. The information of the two machines used is presented in Table 1. Single host benchmarks were executed on *Astrid*. For communication benchmarks, *Astrid* was used for the server while *Ingrid* was used for the client. The two hosts were directly connected using a ethernet cable, to avoid external interference.

The following versions were used: GCC 4.7.2; Erlang R15B01 (-S16); Go 1.0.2; GHC 7.4.2; node.js 0.6.19; Ruby 1.9.3p194; Python 2.7.3; Java OpenJDK 23.7-b01; libev 1.4-2; Intel TBB 4.0+r233-1; gevent 0.13.7; REV 0.3.2.

4.1 Echo Server

Facilitating the developing high-performance web applications is one of the goals of Eve. This benchmark compares Eve to other languages and frameworks used for this purpose. The test consists of creating a server that accepts TCP connections and re-emits the received data until the socket is closed. Although very simple, this test enables the comparison of key features of web servers. The first measured attribute is the request throughput. This indicates the number of requests per second the server can handle. The second measured attribute is latency. Low latency times are critical for soft real-time applications. Additionally, even for other applications, latency higher than 100ms is noticeable and has been linked to lower user dissatisfaction, higher bounce rates and overall lower revenue [9].

For this benchmark, the following solutions were tested: `eve`, `erlang`, `haskell`, `go` and `Node.js` are implementations of an echo server using the respective languages, `rev` is an implementation using the Ruby Event Machine platform, `gevent` and `libev` make use of the homonymous libraries (for python and C++ respectively), and finally `cluster` is a Node.js application that uses the cluster library for parallelism. The source code for each application was selected from an existing benchmark, publicly available at `https://github.com/methane/echoserver`. However, this benchmark suite does contain the cluster implementation. Additionally, the client software used the thread-per-connection model which delivered low performance. A new implementation based on this code was created using the Eve runtime. For each test, 150 concurrent connections were created, each sending 10000 sixteen byte messages.

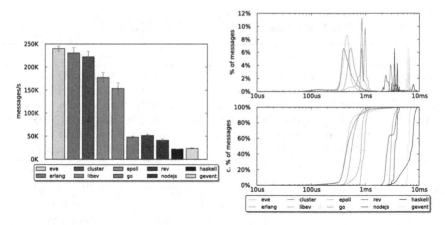

Fig. 2. Request throughput of the echo servers on the left, and reply latency on the right

Figure 2 indicate the performance obtained using these solutions. The `gevent` implementation is the slowest of all alternatives. This is most likely because the entire framework is executed by the python interpreter which is inherently slower than a native implementation. This is also true for `Node.js` and `rev`, although not to the same extent (the event loop is implemented in native code). Additionally, `gevent` uses the *libevent* library while `Node.js` uses *libuv*and `rev` uses a custom implementation. According to [10], *libev* outperforms *libevent/libevent2* which also reinforces the poor performance of `gevent`. The `epoll` implementation makes direct access to the `epoll()` system call using C++ while `libev` uses the wrapper library around `epoll()` on UNIX systems. As expected, their performance is much better than the already mentioned solutions. In fact, `libev` alone is 3.88 times faster than `Node.js`. However, in our case, the `epoll` implementation is slightly worse than `libev`. This is because the benchmarked `epoll` code is poorly optimized, making use of unnecessary memory allocations that are not present in `libev`.

All the remaining solutions make use of multi-threaded runtime environments and were expected to outperform the single-threaded implementations. This is not true for `haskell` and `go`. Regarding the first case, the `haskell` runtime has known IO scalability issues. According to [11] this will be fixed in GHC version 7.8.1, which has not yet been released. The reason behind `go`'s poor performance is more obscure since documentation of its runtime architecture is not available. Both the `erlang` runtime and `cluster` implementation show good performance. Nonetheless, the `eve` framework surpasses both with a 35.5% increase in throughput on localhost, and a more modest 3% increase compared to `erlang` and 7% increase compared to `cluster` on different hosts. One interpretation of these values is that the Eve runtime is more optimized and/or requires less operations. In fact, the `erlang` language was designed for real-time systems and each actor is scheduled using a preemptive fair algorithm. Even if no preemption occurs, this algorithm is more expensive than the execution of eve tasks. Regardless, even though the Eve runtime provides less guarantees on the response time, the obtained latency and jitter are comparable if not better than `erlang`'s.

Considering the `libev` implementation as a baseline for a single-threaded runtime, one would expect the performance of parallel implementations to achieve better speedups. Two reasons were found that can explain this fact. The first is the very nature of the problem. Unlike CPU intensive tests, the echo server test is IO intensive. In particular, `read/write()` operations require large memory bandwidth, which unfortunately does not scale with added worker threads. To mitigate this bottleneck zero-copy operations could be implemented [12]. The second has to deal with normal parallel slowdown causes. Problems such as cache misses aggravate the memory bandwidth bottleneck and are more common in parallel architectures due to inter-process invalidation [13]. Additionally, synchronization is required to maintain a coherent application state. This synchronization is employed by the Eve runtime (using spinlocks, monitors and atomic operations), but also by the Linux kernel since spinlocks and mutexes are used in epoll functions to prevent race-conditions. Even in the absence of concurrent accesses, these primitives incur in additional overhead that is not present in single threaded architectures. Additionally, this overhead may increase when used simultaneously by more threads.

4.2 Atomic Counter

The echo test described in the previous section exemplifies an embarrassingly parallel problem. There is no shared state between clients, which allows them to be handled separately without synchronization. The atomic counter test is a modification to this example, where shared state is maintained. In particular, a single variable `counter` is accessed by all clients. Two types of operations are permitted: *read* which allows each client to retrieve the value stored in `counter` and *increment* which atomically reads and increases stored value by one and

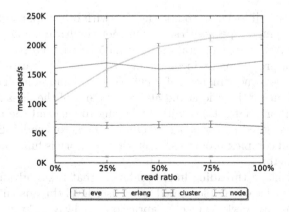

Fig. 3. Throughput of the atomic counter servers subject to the percentage of read operations

returns the new value. These operations are transmitted through the network using a single byte 00 and 01 respectively. Because both operations require a response packet, this application has similar IO patterns to the echo server, allowing the previous results to estimate an upper limit on performance.

Ideally, read operations can execute in parallel but each increment operation must be executed in mutual exclusion. The Eve implementation makes use of the language's access permissions to achieve this semantics. Erlang however, does not have this feature. For this reason, the counter is maintained by a single actor, using message passing for synchronization. This solution sequentializes all accesses, including read operations. The remaining actions are still executed in parallel (e.g.: IO, parsing). With Node.js cluster library, each worker executes in a new process. For this reason, shared memory solutions are not possible. For testing purposes we decided to approach this limitation with a commonly used alternative: in-memory databases. In particular we selected mongodb which supports the required atomic operations. Figure 3 shows the throughput obtained for each server. The erlang implementation suffers from performance loss, averaging at 74%. The large standard deviation observed for this test is very high, ranging from 20.99% to 27.04%.

The proportion of read operations are key to the performance of the Eve runtime. On one end, with 100% read operations the counter value is constant and complete parallelization is possible. The performance obtained for this case is around 90% of the expected value, indicating that the overhead of additional synchronization is low. For this ratio, Eve outperforms the erlang by 25%. On the other end, with 0% read operations, each action must wait for its predecessor to relinquish access to the shared variable. In this case, the performance drops to 43.5%, being slower than erlang by 35%. The other implementations do not suffer significantly from this ratio: erlang's implementation sequentializes every operation and mongodb uses atomic operations instead.

5   Related Work

In this section we will focus on comparing Eve with other approaches that combine the event oriented aspect with shared memory multithreading. As previously mentioned, the Actor implementation in Scala[5]. Scala actors have two possible behaviors for processing an incoming message, one with threading semantics and other with the same semantics of event-based programming. The second approach is based on continuations and allows for parts of the message processing to be scheduled for a later time, without having to suspend the thread. While this approach has good performance results on the actor model, Eve allows for more flexible and complex programs, given that memory is fully shared, and not partitioned by actor.

Capriccio[14] has a threading implementation that takes advantage of asynchronous IO. Capriccio is implemented using user-level threads on top of coroutines. In terms of performance, Capriccio is always slower than epoll, something that does not occur in our micro-benchmarks. Eve is a full programming language, while Capriccio is a library that implements the POSIX threading

API, which allows for usage in existing applications without much work. On the other hand, the language features of Eve allow for more information regarding shared objects, automatically synchronizing accesses, something not possible in Capriccio.

Events and Threads have also been combined in GHC[15]. The main difference to Capriccio is that there was an explicit asynchronous IO API with event handlers, like in Eve. However, the threading API, including synchronization using mutexes, is explicit unlike in Eve. Furthermore, the GHC makes use of Software Transactional Memory, while Eve does not. Another work on GHC[16] has also improved the performance of asynchronous IO on multithreaded environments by improving the data structures on which the event handlers are stored, but in multicore environments, each event source is attached to a single thread.

Libasync-smp[17] allows event handlers to be executed in parallel, as long as they do not share any mutable state. This is done by assigning a tag ("color") to events according to the shared state they use in their computations. Thus, events of different colors can be executed in parallel without any extra synchronization. This approach is more similar to Eve, but less expressive as Eve requires information regarding the variables and automatically detects the events that can execute in parallel. In Libasync-smp programmers must express that using colors, and fine-grained synchronization using shared variables is not supported. Instead all events that shared memory, even if only in a small part of the handler, execute serially.

Mely[18] uses the same API as Libasync-smp, but uses workstealing to lower scheduling overheads to improve performance with short-running events. The workers steal colors instead of tasks, in order to maintain the serial execution inside each color. Although this is close to the implementation of Eve, the same drawbacks of using colored events instead of annotating variables applies to Mely.

Finally, Eve can be compared to Æminium[19] in the sense that Æminium also uses access permissions on variables to automatically manage synchronization between different running tasks. While Æminium automatically parallelizes the whole code based on the access permissions, Eve uses programmer annotations to mark parallelization points in the code. However Æminium is only concerned with CPU-bounded parallelism, without any event-oriented API.

Node.Scala[20] also shares a similar approach to Eve. Programmers write Scala applications using a single-threaded event-loop approach, with the same API as in Node.js. Event handlers can then be executed in parallel whether or not they are marked as exclusive or not. Compared to Node.Scala, Eve can parallelize more than just event callbacks, featuring a full work-stealing scheduler, more suitable for CPU-intensive tasks, while Node.Scala is optimized only for IO processing.

6   Conclusions and Future Work

Event-driven architectures have been proved to work well for network-based applications, but it has been hard to integrate asynchronous IO APIs in shared-memory multithreaded programming. This difficulty is two-folded. The expressiveness of using multithreaded programming is not directly compatible with the traditional callback-based single-threaded event-loop approach. Performance is other field in which combining these two different programming styles is not trivial, as event-loops are mostly bound to a single thread and require extra synchronization, which adds an overhead.

We propose Eve as a parallel event-oriented language, in which programmers use a event-oriented programming style and special syntax for creating new parallel tasks, and for access permissions on variables. This small extra annotations on the code allow for parallel execution of different parts of the code, as well as a guarantee of a safe parallel event callbacks execution.

Our benchmarks have shown Eve to have a similar performance as Intel TBB and Java ForkJoin frameworks in CPU-bounded programs. Additional, Eve outperformed other languages in IO-bounded programs by making a more efficient use of threads in event-based programming. A Localhost share-nothing application had a 35.5% improvement over the second best solution, and server-only execution had a 7% increase. Another IO application with some 50% of the requests requiring synchronization was 23% faster than the next best solution.

For future work, it would be important to improve the performance of epoll in a multithread environment. The epoll set is currently shared by all workers, causing synchronization to happen at the kernel level. It would be interesting to have a epoll set per worker, in order to minimize contention, with an extra global set for load-balancing.

Acknowledgments. This work was partially supported by the Portuguese Research Agency FCT, through CISUC (R&D Unit 326/97), the CMU|Portugal program (R&D Project Aeminium CMU-PT/SE/0038/2008), the iCIS project (CENTRO-07-ST24-FEDER-002003), co-financed by QREN, in the scope of the Mais Centro Program and European Union's FEDER and by the COST framework, under Actions IC0804 and IC0906. The first author was also supported by the Portuguese National Foundation for Science and Technology (FCT) through a Doctoral Grant (SFRH/BD/84448/2012).

References

1. Dabek, F., Zeldovich, N., Kaashoek, F., Mazieres, D., Morris, R.: Event-driven programming for robust software. In: Proceedings of the 10th Workshop on ACM SIGOPS European Workshop, pp. 186–189. ACM (2002)
2. Krohn, M.N., Kohler, E., Kaashoek, M.F.: Events can make sense. In: USENIX Annual Technical Conference, pp. 87–100 (2007)
3. Ousterhout, J.: Why threads are a bad idea (for most purposes). Presentation given at the 1996 Usenix Annual Technical Conference, vol. 5 (1996)
4. von Behren, J.R., Condit, J., Brewer, E.A.: Why events are a bad idea (for high-concurrency servers). In: HotOS, pp. 19–24 (2003)
5. Haller, P., Odersky, M.: Scala actors: Unifying thread-based and event-based programming. Theoretical Computer Science 410(2), 202–220 (2009)

6. Blumofe, R.D., Joerg, C.F., Kuszmaul, B.C., Leiserson, C.E., Randall, K.H., Zhou, Y.: Cilk: An efficient multithreaded runtime system, vol. 30. ACM (1995)
7. Frigo, M., Leiserson, C.E., Randall, K.H.: The implementation of the cilk-5 multithreaded language. SIGPLAN Not. 33(5), 212–223 (1998)
8. Kumar, V., Frampton, D., Blackburn, S.M., Grove, D., Tardieu, O.: Work-stealing without the baggage. SIGPLAN Not. 47(10), 297–314 (2012)
9. Hamilton, J.: The cost of latency (2009),
   http://perspectives.mvdirona.com/2009/10/31/TheCostOfLatency.asp
10. Lehmann, M.A.: Benchmarking libevent against libev (2011),
    http://libev.schmorp.de/bench.html/ (online; accessed August 31, 2013)
11. Voellmy, A., Wang, J., Hudak, P., Yamamoto, K.: Mio: A high-performance multicore io manager for ghc
12. Thadani, M.N., Khalidi, Y.A.: An efficient zero-copy I/O framework for UNIX. Citeseer (1995)
13. Eggers, S.J., Katz, R.H.: The effect of sharing on the cache and bus performance of parallel programs. SIGARCH Comput. Archit. News 17(2), 257–270 (1989)
14. Von Behren, R., Condit, J., Zhou, F., Necula, G.C., Brewer, E.: Capriccio: scalable threads for internet services. ACM SIGOPS Operating Systems Review 37(5), 268–281 (2003)
15. Li, P., Zdancewic, S.: Combining events and threads for scalable network services implementation and evaluation of monadic, application-level concurrency primitives. ACM SIGPLAN Notices 42(6), 189–199 (2007)
16. O'Sullivan, B., Tibell, J.: Scalable i/o event handling for ghc. ACM Sigplan Notices 45, 103–108 (2010)
17. Zeldovich, N., Yip, A., Dabek, F., Morris, R., Mazieres, D., Kaashoek, M.F.: Multiprocessor support for event-driven programs. In: USENIX Annual Technical Conference, General Track, pp. 239–252 (2003)
18. Gaud, F., Geneves, S., Lachaize, R., Lepers, B., Mottet, F., Muller, G., Quéma, V.: Efficient workstealing for multicore event-driven systems. In: 2010 IEEE 30th International Conference on Distributed Computing Systems (ICDCS), pp. 516–525. IEEE (2010)
19. Stork, S., Marques, P., Aldrich, J.: Concurrency by default: using permissions to express dataflow in stateful programs. In: Proceedings of the 24th ACM SIGPLAN Conference Companion on Object Oriented Programming Systems Languages and Applications, pp. 933–940. ACM (2009)
20. Bonetta, D., Ansaloni, D., Peternier, A., Pautasso, C., Binder, W.: Node.Scala: Implicit parallel programming for high-performance web services. In: Kaklamanis, C., Papatheodorou, T., Spirakis, P.G. (eds.) Euro-Par 2012. LNCS, vol. 7484, pp. 626–637. Springer, Heidelberg (2012)

Dependency-Based Automatic Parallelization of Java Applications

João Rafael, Ivo Correia, Alcides Fonseca, and Bruno Cabral

University of Coimbra, Portugal
{jprafael,icorreia}@student.dei.uc.pt, {amaf,bcabral}@dei.uc.pt

Abstract. There are billions of lines of sequential code inside nowadays software which do not benefit from the parallelism available in modern multicore architectures. Transforming legacy sequential code into a parallel version of the same programs is a complex and cumbersome task. Trying to perform such transformation automatically and without the intervention of a developer has been a striking research objective for a long time. This work proposes an elegant way of achieving such a goal. By targeting a task-based runtime which manages execution using a task dependency graph, we developed a translator for sequential JAVA code which generates a highly parallel version of the same program. The translation process interprets the AST nodes for signatures such as read-write access, execution-flow modifications, among others and generates a set of dependencies between executable tasks. This process has been applied to well known problems, such as the recursive Fibonacci and FFT algorithms, resulting in versions capable of maximizing resource usage. For the case of two CPU bounded applications we were able to obtain 10.97x and 9.0x speedup on a 12 core machine.

Keywords: Automatic programming, automatic parallelization, task-based runtime, symbolic analysis, recursive procedures.

1 Introduction

Developing software capable of extracting the most out of a multicore machine usually requires the usage of threads or other language provided constructs for introducing parallelism [1,2]. This process is often cumbersome and error prone, often leading to the occurrence of problems such as deadlocks and race conditions. Furthermore, as the code base increases it becomes increasingly harder to detect interferences between executing threads. Thus, one can understand why sequential legacy applications are still the most common kind and, in some cases, preferred as they provide a more reliable execution.

Automatic parallelization of existing software has been a prominent research subject [3]. Most available research focuses on the analysis and transformation of loops as the main source of parallelism [4,5]. Other models have also been studied, such as the parallelization of recursive methods [6], and of sub-expressions in functional languages.

L. Lopes et al. (Eds.): Euro-Par 2014 Workshops, Part II, LNCS 8806, pp. 182–193, 2014.
© Springer International Publishing Switzerland 2014

Our contribution is both a framework and a tool for performing the automatic parallelization of sequential JAVA code. Our solution extracts instruction *signatures* (read from memory, write to memory, control flow, etc.) from the application's AST and infers *data dependencies* between instructions. Using this information we create a set of tasks containing the same operations as the original version. The execution of these tasks is conducted by the Æminium Runtime which schedules the workload to all available cores using a work-stealing algorithm [7]. This approach supports a different number of processor cores by adjusting the number of worker threads and generated tasks, as long as there is enough latent parallelism in the program. With a simple runtime optimization, our experiments show a 9.0 speedup on a 12-core machine for the naive recursive Fibonacci implementation.

The remainder of this paper is organized as follows: in Section 2 we discuss the related work. Section 3 specifies the methodology used by the Æminium compiler throughout the entire process, from signature analysis to code generation. In Section 4 we conduct benchmarking tests and analyze the results. Finally, in Section 5 we present a summary of this paper's contributions and discuss future work.

2   Related Work

Extracting performance from a multicore processor requires the development of tailored, concurrent applications. A concurrent application, is composed by a collection of execution paths that may run in parallel. The definition of such paths can be done explicitly by the programmer with the aid of language supported constructs and libraries. An example of this approach is Cilk [8]. In the Cilk language, the programmer can introduce a division on the current execution path through the use of the *spawn* keyword. The opposite is achieved with the *sync* statement. When this statement is reached, the processor is forced to wait for all previously spawned tasks. A similar approach is used by OpenMP [9] where the programmer annotates a C/C++ program using pre-compiler directives to identify code apt for parallelism. Parallelism can also be hidden from the programmer. This is the case of paralleled libraries such as ArBB [8]. These libraries provide a less bug-prone design by offering a black-box implementation, where the programmer doesn't need to ponder concurrency issues but, still has no control over the amount of threads spawned for each library invocation.

For existing sequential program, these solutions require at least a partial modification of the application's source code. This may impose high rework costs, specially in the case of large applications, and may inadvertently result in the introduction of new bugs.

Automatic parallelization is an optimization technique commonly performed by compilers which target multicore architectures. By translating the original single threaded source code into a multi-threaded version of the same program, these compilers optimize resource usage and achieve lower execution times. Like all compiler optimizations, the semantics of the original source code must be preserved. As such, compilers must ensure the correct execution order between operations on multiple threads, taking into account their precedence in the original program.

One of the primary targets for automatic parallelization are loops. Numerical and scientific applications often contain loops consisting mostly of arithmetic operations. These loops provide a good source of parallelism due to the lack of complex control structures and can be parallelized with techniques such as *doall*, *doacross* and *dopipe* [10]. When dependencies between iterations are found the compiler may attempt to remove them by applying transformations such as variable privatization, loop distribution, skewing and reversal. These modifications are extensively described in [4].

Many algorithms however, are best implemented using a recursive definition as this is often the nature of the problem itself. The parallel resolution of each of the sub-problems has also been analyzed. In [11] this method is applied to the functional language LISP by the introduction of the **letpar** construct. This model can be used with success because the semantics of functional programming imply that there is no interference between sub-expressions. For non-functional languages, a technique known as thread-level speculation executes the operations optimistically assuming no interference. If such speculation is wrong, specialized hardware is used to rollback the faulty threads into a previous checkpoint [12]. In [13] recursion-based parallelism is applied to the JAVA language. In order to avoid interference between sub-expressions, a static analysis of read and write signatures is performed and the resulting data stored. At runtime, this information is used to check which methods can be executed in parallel by replacing the parameters with the actual variables in the stored method signatures. However, this runtime verification inadvertently introduces overhead. Our approach, on the other hand, does not resort to runtime support for dealing with this problem. By adding two new signatures, **merge** and **control**, we are able to solve this problem without a runtime penalty.

3   Methodology

In order to extract parallelism from sequential programs, our framework decomposes a program into tasks to be scheduled at runtime using a work-stealing algorithm [7]. The entire process is depicted in figure 1. The first stage of the compilation process is the generation of the application's AST. This task is accomplished using Eclipse's JDT Core component which provides an API to read, manipulate and rewrite JAVA code. Each AST node is augmented with semantic information in the form of *signatures*. Signatures are a low-level description of what an instruction does, such as a read from a variable or a jump in the flow of the application. By transversing the AST in the same order as it would be executed, *data dependencies* and *control dependencies* are extracted and stored. Data dependencies identify mandatory precedence of operations due to concurrent access of the same variables whereas control dependencies indicate that the first operation designates whether or not the second executes. After this analysis,

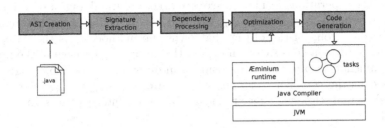

Fig. 1. Parallelization process used in the Æminium framework. Filled stages identify the source-to-source compilation described in this paper.

an optional phase of optimization takes place where redundant dependencies are removed and nodes are assigned into tasks. This optimization is repeated until no improvement is observed or a predefined threshold is achieved. Finally, this information is used to produce JAVA code for each task respecting the data and control dependencies in the program.

3.1   Signature Extraction

The analysis of the source program starts with the extraction of *signatures* for each node in the AST. Formally, signatures can be defined as predicates $S : \mathbb{A} \times \mathbb{D}^+ \to \{true, false\}$, where $\mathbb{A}$ is a set of AST nodes and $\mathbb{D}^+$ is a set of ordered datagroup tuples. A datagroup is a hierarchical abstraction of memory sections whose purpose is to facilitate static analysis of the application's memory (i.e.: function scopes, variables). A single datagroup, $\phi \in \mathbb{D}$, encompasses the entire application. This datagroup is broken down by classes, methods, fields, scopes, statements, expressions and variables forming sub-datagroups $\tau := (\phi, \varphi_0, \cdots, \varphi_n)$. As an example, a local variable v inside a method m of a class c is identified by $\tau_{var} := (\phi, \varphi_c, \varphi_m, \varphi_{var})$. An additional datagroup $\psi \in \mathbb{D}$ describes all memory sections unknown to the code submitted for analysis (i.e.: external libraries or native calls). Furthermore, two special datagroups τ_{this} and τ_{ret} are used as placeholders and are, in later stages, replaced by the actual datagroups that represent the object identified by the this keyword and the object returned by the containing method. A current limitation of the compiler, which we are currently working on, is the lack of array subdivision. As such, an entire array and each of its inner values are only modeled as a single datagroup.

Signatures are grouped into five categories. The $\mathbf{read}(\alpha, \tau)$ predicate indicates that operations in the sub-tree with root α can read memory belonging to datagroup τ. Likewise, $\mathbf{write}(\alpha, \tau)$ expresses that operations in the same sub-tree can write to datagroup τ. A more complex signature is $\mathbf{merge}(\alpha, \tau_a, \tau_b)$. This signature implies that after operations in α, τ_a is accessible through τ_b. In other words, τ_b contains a reference to τ_a (i.e.: τ_b is an alias for τ_a), and an operation to one of these datagroups might access or modify the other. The fourth predicate, $\mathbf{control}(\alpha, \tau)$, denotes the possibility of operations in α to alter the execution flow of other operations inside the scope marked by the datagroup τ. The last predicate $\textbf{call}_m(\alpha, \tau_o, \tau_r, \tau_{p_0}, \cdots, \tau_{p_n})$ is used as a placeholder for method calls; τ_o is the datagroup of the object that owns the method, τ_r is the datagroup where the return value is saved and τ_{p_x} is the datagroup for each of the invocation arguments. In program 1 the reader can observe an example of signatures extracted by the compiler. Also note that a $\textbf{merge}(\alpha_{ret_1}, \tau_n, \tau_{ret})$ signature is detected as well. However, since $\textbf{n}$ and $\textbf{ret}$ are both integers this signature can be omitted.

```
int f(int n) {
    if (n < 2) { // read(α_cond, τ_n)
        return n; // write(α_ret_1, τ_ret), control(α_ret_1, τ_f)
    }
    return f(n - 1) + f(n - 2); // call_f(α_inv_1, ∅, τ_inv_1, τ_p0)
}
```

Program 1. The Fibonacci function with a excerpt of the extracted signatures indicated in comments. *inv* stands for function invocation, *ret* for return value, f for the current function f and *p0* is the first argument of the invocation.

Signature extraction is executed as a 2-pass mechanism. In the first pass, signatures for each node are collected and stored. In the second pass, the transitive closure is computed by iteratively adding each sub-node signature set with the one from its parent. In this step, $\textbf{call}_m$ signatures are replaced with the full signature set of the corresponding method. The set is trimmed down by ignoring irrelevant signatures such as modifications to local variables, and modified so that the signatures have meaning in the new context: (1) formal parameter datagroups are replaced by the argument datagroups τ_{p_x} (2) the τ_{this} datagroup is replaced by τ_o and (3) the τ_{ret} datagroup is replaced by τ_r. During this same step, $\textbf{merge}$ signatures are also removed in a pessimistic manner by adding all the $\textbf{read}$ and $\textbf{write}$ signatures as required to preserve the same semantics.

Regarding external functions, the compiler assumes they read and write to the ψ datagroup (ensuring sequential execution). For a more realistic (and better performing) analysis, the programmer can explicitly indicate the signature set for these functions in a configuration file (e.g.: to indicate that $\texttt{Math.cos(x)}$ only reads from its first parameter τ_{p_0} and writes to τ_{ret}).

3.2   Dependency Processing

In a sequential program, operation ordering is used to ensure the desired behavior. Line ordering, operator precedence, and language specific constructs (i.e.: conditional branches, loops, etc.) define an execution order σ_t on the set of AST nodes. Our compiler starts by assigning each executable node to a separate æminium task. As such, the same total order can be applied to the set of tasks. Dependencies between tasks are used to define a partial order σ_p, obtained by an arbitrary relaxation of σ_t. The operator $\alpha \prec_x \beta$ is used to indicate precedence

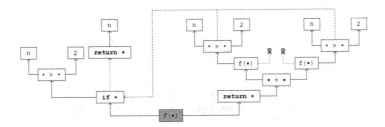

Fig. 2. Tasks generated for program 1 without optimization. Dotted arrows identify child scheduling. Solid arrows are used to represent strong dependencies while dashed arrows indicate weak dependencies. Filled tasks is the function root task

of α over β on the σ_x order. Therefor, when σ_x is the partial order of tasks σ_p, then $\alpha \prec_p \beta$ indicates the existence of a dependency from task β to task α. For the dependency set to be correct, any possible scheduling that satisfies σ_p has to have the exact same semantics has the one obtained with σ_t. The following rules are used to ensure this property:

1. A task that may read from a datagroup must wait for the termination of the last task that writes to it;

$$\frac{\alpha \prec_t \beta, \quad \forall \alpha, \beta \in \mathbb{A} \quad \mathbf{write}(\alpha, \tau), \mathbf{read}(\beta, \tau)}{\therefore \alpha \prec_p \beta}$$

2. A task that may write to a datagroup must wait for the conclusion of all tasks that read from it since the last write;

$$\frac{\alpha \prec_t \beta \prec_t \gamma, \quad \forall \alpha, \beta, \gamma \in \mathbb{A} \quad \mathbf{write}(\alpha, \tau), \mathbf{read}(\beta, \tau), \mathbf{write}(\gamma, \tau)}{\therefore \beta \prec_p \gamma}$$

If two tasks may write to the same datagroup and there is no intermediary task that reads from it, then the latter task must wait for the former to complete; [1]

$$\frac{\alpha \prec_t \beta, \quad \forall \alpha, \beta \in \mathbb{A} \quad \mathbf{write}(\alpha, \tau), \mathbf{write}(\beta, \tau)}{\therefore \alpha \prec_p \beta}$$

3. After a datagroup merge, the three previous restrictions must be ensured across all datagroups;

$$\frac{\alpha \prec_t \beta \prec_t \gamma, \quad \forall \alpha, \beta, \gamma \in \mathbb{A} \quad \mathbf{write}(\alpha, \tau_a), \mathbf{merge}(\beta, \tau_a, \tau_b), \mathbf{read}(\gamma, \tau_b)}{\therefore \alpha \prec_p \gamma}$$

---

[1] This rule applies when operations require both read and write access (such as the increment operator), or when tasks span more than a single operation.

$$\frac{\alpha \prec_t \beta \prec_t \gamma, \quad \forall \alpha, \beta, \gamma \in \mathbb{A}}{\therefore \alpha \prec_p \gamma} \mathbf{read}(\alpha, \tau_a), \mathbf{merge}(\beta, \tau_a, \tau_b), \mathbf{write}(\gamma, \tau_b)$$

$$\frac{\alpha \prec_t \beta \prec_t \gamma, \quad \forall \alpha, \beta, \gamma \in \mathbb{A}}{\therefore \alpha \prec_p \gamma} \mathbf{write}(\alpha, \tau_a), \mathbf{merge}(\beta, \tau_a, \tau_b), \mathbf{write}(\gamma, \tau_b)$$

4. Control signatures enforce dependencies from all the tasks of the scope whose execution path can be altered.

$$\frac{\alpha \prec_t \beta, \quad \forall \alpha \in \mathbb{A}, \beta \in \tau_{scope} \qquad \mathbf{control}(\alpha, \tau_{scope}),}{\cdot \quad \alpha \prec_{\gamma_l} \beta}$$

The set of dependencies is generated by transversing the AST tree using order σ_t and processing the signatures obtained in Section 3.1. A lookup table is used to store the set of tasks that access each datagroup. Furthermore, the information regarding which datagroups are merged is also stored. For each task, all of its signatures are parsed and dependencies are created to ensure properties 1 to 4. These data structures are updated dynamically to reflect the changes introduced. If a conditional jump is encountered, duplicates of the structures are created and each branch is analyzed independently. When the execution paths converge, both data structures are merged: 1) disparities between tasks are identified and replaced with the task that encloses the divergent paths. 2) datagroup merge sets are created by the pair-wise reunion of sets from both branches.

In Figure 2 we can observe the set of tasks generated from the AST for Program 1. Dotted arrows identify the optional *child* scheduling that occurs when the parent task is executing. Dashed arrows indicate a *weak dependency* relationship meaning the source task must wait for completion of the target task. Solid arrows denote a *strong dependency*, one where in addition to the property of weak dependency also signifies that the source task must create and schedule the target task before its execution.

3.3   Optimization

Optimization is an optional step present in most compilers. The Æminium java to java compiler, in its current shape, is capable of performing minor modifications to the generated code in order to minimize runtime overhead. This overhead is closely related to task granularity and the number of dependencies generated. As such, the optimization step focuses on these two properties. Nevertheless, on the post-compilation of the generated code, all the expected optimizations performed by the native JAVA compiler still occur.

This step solves the optimization problem using an iterative approach by finding small patterns that can be locally improved. The transformations described in the following sections are applied until no pattern is matched or a maximum number of optimizations is reached.

Redundant Dependency Removal. The algorithm for identifying task dependencies performs an exhaustive identification of all the data and control dependencies between tasks. And, although these dependencies are fundamental for guaranteeing the correct execution of the parallel program, they are often redundant. The omission of such dependencies from the final code will not help to increase parallelism but will lower the runtime overhead. We identify two patterns of redundancy. The first instance follows directly from the transitivity relation of dependencies: given three tasks α, β and γ, if $\alpha \prec_p \beta$ and $\beta \prec_p \gamma$ then $\alpha \prec_p \gamma$. If the former is present it can be omitted from the dependencies set. The second instance takes into account the definition of child tasks. If $\alpha \prec_p \beta$, $\alpha \prec_p \gamma$ and, simultaneously, β is a child task of γ, then the former dependency can be omitted. This is possible because the runtime only moves a task to the COMPLETED state when it and all it's children tasks have finished.

Task Aggregation. The first pass is to create one task per each node of the AST. However, the execution of a parallel program with one task for each AST node is several times slower than the sequential program, which makes task aggregation mandatory. By coarsening the tasks, we are able to lower the scheduling overhead and the memory usage. This optimization step attempts to reduce the number of generated tasks by merging the code of several tasks together in one task. The **aggregate**(α, β) operation has the following semantics: given two tasks $\alpha, \beta \in \mathbb{A}$, such that α is a strong dependency of β, we merge α into β by transferring all the dependencies of α into β, and placing the instructions of α before the instructions of β or a place of equal execution semantics (such as the right-hand side of an assignment expression).

Given that the code inside each task executes sequentially, by over-aggregating tasks the parallelism of the program is reduced. As such, we identify two types of task aggregation. *Soft aggregation* reduces tasks without hindering parallelism: if task β depends on α, and there is no other task γ that also depends on α, then α can be merged into β without loss of parallelism.

$$soft \triangleq \alpha \prec_p \beta \land \nexists \alpha \prec_p \gamma \Rightarrow \textbf{aggregate}(\alpha, \beta) \quad \alpha, \beta, \gamma \in \mathbb{A}$$

Hard aggregation on the other hand attempts to merge tasks even in other scenarios, such as lightweight arithmetic operations. Currently the optimizer aggregates all expressions with the exception of method invocations (including constructor calls). Also, statements where execution must be sequential (e.g.: the **then** block of an **if** statement) and their aggregation does not violate dependency constraints are also aggregated. Optionally full sequentialization of cycles can also take place. Using this feature disables parallelization of loops, but generates a lower runtime memory footprint.

3.4   Code Generation

The Æminium runtime executes and handles dependencies between Task's. These objects contain information about their state, and their dependencies. The actual code executed by each task exists in a execute() method of a class that implements the Body interface. This factorization allows for reuse of the same body object for multiple tasks. Bodies are constructed with a single parameter: a reference to the parent body if it exists and null otherwise. This allows access to fields of upper tasks where local variables and method parameters will be stored. Inside the constructor of the body, its task is created by calling the Aeminium.createTask() function which receives the body as it first parameter. The second parameter defines a *hints* object used by the runtime to optimize scheduling. This functionality is not used by the compiler and the default value of NO_HINTS is used. Strong dependencies of the task are instantiated in the constructor of the task body. This operation must take place after the creation of the task object (since it must be available as the parent task when scheduling those dependencies), and before the schedule of the task itself (since those tasks will be used inside the task dependency list).

Methods. In real-life applications, the same method is invoked many times in different places. This makes the already mentioned approach of accessing parent's fields unsatisfactory for translating method tasks as it would require replicating the same method based on it where it is invoked. Instead, in addition to the parent object, these tasks receive the invocation arguments as arguments to the constructor of the task body. However, this requires those values to be known when the task is created. Therefore, its instantiation must take place inside the execute() method of corresponding method invocation expressions, where the tasks that compute each argument have already completed. Nonetheless, method invocation expressions, as well as all other expressions, must save their value in a special field ret before they reach the COMPLETED state. In order to do so, the return task of the invoked method places the value in ret upon its own execution. Furthermore, as a consequence of having all values computed prior to the construction of a method task, it is possible to conduct a runtime optimization. By checking if enough parallelism is already achieved – by checking if enough tasks are queued and all threads are currently working – it is possible to invoke the sequential (original) method. This optimization allows us to almost entirely remove the overhead of the runtime once enough parallelism has been reached.

Loops. Loop statements such as while, for, and do...while allow for multiple iterations to execute the same lines of code. However, the actual instructions may vary from iteration to iteration. Furthermore, the instructions on the first iteration must wait for instructions prior to the loop (e.g. a variable declaration) while subsequent instructions only need to wait for one on the previous iteration (last modification). To allow this duality of dependencies two trees of tasks are created for each loop. The former contains dependencies belonging to the first iteration while the latter includes dependencies associated with the following iterations. The parent task of this second tree contains a previous field that points to the preceding instance, and inside the execute() method creates another instance of itself. Sub-tasks make use of this field to reference tasks of the previous iteration for their dependency list.

4   Evaluation

To validate our approach we compiled three sample applications using the
Æminium compiler and executed the resulting tasks in a machine with the following specification: 2 Intel®Xeon®Processor X5660 (6 cores each, with hyper-
threading, forming a total of 24 threads) and 24 GB of RAM. The applications
include the recursive implementation of the Fibonnaci program already mentioned in Section 3, an application to numerically approximate the integral of
a function given an interval, and finally a simple implementation of the Fast
Fourier Transform (FFT) on an array of 2^{22} random complex numbers. The
FFT application requires the generation of an array of `Complex` objects. This
step is not considered for the benchmark time as it requires sequential invocations to `Random.nextDouble()`. Also, in order to minimize runtime overhead of
cycle scheduling the option to sequentialize loops (as described in 3.3) was used.
Each experiment was repeated 30 times. The results are depicted in Table 1 and
Figure 3.

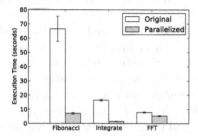

Fig. 3. Execution time before and
after parallelization

Fig. 4. Scalability benchmark for
the three tests

Table 1. Measured average execution time (standard deviations) and speedups for the
three benchmarks

Application	Sequential	Parallel	Speedup
Fibonacci	55.56 (8.90) s	6.17 (v0.59) s	09.00
Integrate	16.46 (0.56) s	1.50 (0.19) s	10.97
FFT	07.80 (0.40) s	5.33 (0.40) s	01.46

The first benchmark computes the 50th Fibonacci number. The sequential
execution of this problem took on average 55.56 seconds to complete, while the
parallel version only took 6.17 seconds. Although it consists of a 9.00x increase
in performance ($p = 0.973$), it is well bellow the possible 12x (linear) speedup.
The scalability test shown in Figure 4 indicates the cores/speedup relation. The
dashed line is the desired linear speedup. The dotted lines identify the the least-
squares method fitted to the Amdahl's law [14] with the exception of the third
benchmark where an adjustment for linear ovearhead h was added.

The second benchmark computes the integral of the function $f(x) = x^3 + x$ in the interval $[-2101.0, 200.0]$ up to 10^{-14} precision. The behaviour of this test is similar to the previous, but with a slightly higher $p = 0.978$. The FFT benchmark shows the lowest speedup among the three executed benchmarks ($p_{amdahl} = 0.311$ or $p = 0.972, h = 0.746,$). It is also the one with highest memory usage. This suggests that memory bandwidth is the primary bottleneck of this particular implementation. In fact, this is the case for naïve FFT implementations as indicated in [15]. As a consequence, for larger arrays the speedup decreases as cache hits become less and less frequent due to false sharing.

5   Conclusion and Future Work

By targeting a task-based runtime, our framework is capable of automatically parallelizing a subset of existing java code. This solution provides respectable performance gains without human intervention. The compiler is able to detect parallelism available in loops, recursive method calls, statements and even expressions. The benchmarks executed show near-linear speedup for a selected set of CPU bounded applications.

Future work for this project includes testing the approach on a large suite of Java programs. In order to do that, the full set of Java instructions needs to be supported. This includes exception handling, reflection instructions (such as `instanceof`), class inheritance, interfaces, etc. The results on a large codebase would allows for a thorough analysis of the performance and optimizations required. One of the potential optimizations if the usage of a cost analysis approach to efficiently conduct hard aggregation of small tasks. This analysis should also take into account task reordering to further merge task chains. The current implementation of loop tasks introduces too much overhead to be of practical use, so the creation of tasks that work in blocks or strides should provide a better performing model.

Acknowledgments. This work would not have been possible without the contributions to the Aeminium language and runtime from Sven Stork, Paulo Marques and Jonathan Aldrich. This work was partially supported by the Portuguese Research Agency FCT, through CISUC (R&D Unit 326/97), the CMU|Portugal program (R&D Project Aeminium CMU-PT/SE/0038/2008), the iCIS project (CENTRO-07-ST24-FEDER-002003), co-financed by QREN, in the scope of the Mais Centro Program and European Unions FEDER and by the COST framework, under Actions IC0804 and IC0906. The third author was also supported by the Portuguese National Foundation for Science and Technology (FCT) through a Doctoral Grant (SFRH/BD/84448/2012).

References

1. Arnold, K., Gosling, J., Holmes, D.: The Java programming language. Addison Wesley Professional (2005)
2. van Biema, M.: A survey of parallel programming constructs. Columbia University Computer Science Technical Reports. Department of Computer Science, Columbia University (1999)
3. Banerjee, U., Eigenmann, R., Nicolau, A., Padua, D.: Automatic program parallelization. Proceedings of the IEEE 81(2), 211–243 (1993)
4. Banerjee, U.: Loop Transformations for Restructuring Compilers: The Foundations. Springer (1993)
5. Feautrier, P.: Automatic parallelization in the polytope model. In: Perrin, G.-R., Darte, A. (eds.) The Data Parallel Programming Model. LNCS, vol. 1132, pp. 79–103. Springer, Heidelberg (1996)
6. Bik, A.J., Gannon, D.B.: Automatically exploiting implicit parallelism in java. Concurrency - Practice and Experience 9(6), 579–619 (1997)
7. Blumofe, R.D., Leiserson, C.E.: Scheduling multithreaded computations by work stealing. J. ACM 46(5), 720–748 (1999)
8. Randall, K.: Cilk: Efficient multithreaded computing. Technical report, Cambridge, MA, USA (1998)
9. Dagum, L., Menon, R.: Openmp: an industry standard api for shared-memory programming. IEEE Computational Science Engineering 5(1), 46–55 (1998)
10. Ottoni, G., Rangan, R., Stoler, A., August, D.I.: Automatic thread extraction with decoupled software pipelining. In: Proceedings of the 38th Annual IEEE/ACM International Symposium on Microarchitecture, MICRO-38, 12 p. (November 2005)
11. Hogen, G., Kindler, A., Loogen, R.: Automatic parallelization of lazy functional programs. In: Krieg-Brückner, B. (ed.) ESOP 1992. LNCS, vol. 582, pp. 254–268. Springer, Heidelberg (1992)
12. Bhowmik, A., Franklin, M.: A general compiler framework for speculative multi-threading. In: Proceedings of the Fourteenth Annual ACM Symposium on Parallel Algorithms and Architectures, SPAA 2002, pp. 99–108. ACM, New York (2002)
13. Chan, B., Abdelrahman, T.S.: Run-time support for the automatic parallelization of java programs. J. Supercomput. 28(1), 91–117 (2004)
14. Amdahl, G.M.: Validity of the single processor approach to achieving large scale computing capabilities. In: Proceedings of the Spring Joint Computer Conference, AFIPS 1967, April 18-20, pp. 483–485. ACM, New York (1967)
15. da Silva, C.P., Cupertino, L.F., Chevitarese, D., Pacheco, M.A.C., Bentes, C.: Exploring data streaming to improve 3d fft implementation on multiple gpus. In: 2010 22nd International Symposium on Computer Architecture and High Performance Computing Workshops (SBAC-PADW), pp. 13–18. IEEE (2010)

A Scalable Parallel Approach
for Subgraph Census Computation

David Aparicio, Pedro Paredes, and Pedro Ribeiro

CRACS & INESC-TEC, Faculdade de Ciencias, Universidade do Porto
R. Campo Alegre, 1021/1055, 4169-007 Porto, Portugal
{daparicio,pparedes,pribeiro}@dcc.fc.up.pt

Abstract. Counting the occurrences of small subgraphs in large networks is a fundamental graph mining metric with several possible applications. Computing frequencies of these subgraphs is also known as
the subgraph census problem, which is a computationally hard task. In
this paper we provide a parallel multicore algorithm for this purpose. At
its core we use FaSE, an efficient network-centric sequential subgraph
census algorithm, which is able to substantially decrease the number of
isomorphism tests needed when compared to past approaches. We use
one thread per core and employ a dynamic load balancing scheme capable of dealing with the highly unbalanced search tree induced by FaSE
and effectively redistributing work during execution. We assessed the
scalability of our algorithm on a varied set of representative networks
and achieved near linear speedup up to 32 cores while obtaining a high
efficiency for the total 64 cores of our machine.

Keywords: Graph Mining, Subgraph Census, Parallelism, Multicores.

1 Introduction

Graphs are a flexible and powerful abstraction of many real-life systems. An
essential graph mining primitive is to compute the frequency of small subgraphs
in large networks. This is known as the *subgraph census* problem, and lies at the
core of several graph mining methodologies, such as network motifs discovery [6]
or graphlet based metrics [8]. Counting subgraphs is, however, a *computationally hard* task, closely related to *subgraph isomorphism*, a classical NP-Complete
problem . This implies that the execution time grows exponentially with the size
of the network or the subgraphs being analyzed. Speeding up this computation
would have a significant and broad impact, making new size limits computationally feasible, hence leading to a new insight on the networks.

Subgraph census algorithms generally follow one of three different paradigms;
network-centric algorithms, such as ESU [16], compute the frequency of all subgraphs with a certain number of nodes and then verify the type of each subgraph.
By contrast, *subgraph-centric* algorithms, such as the one by Grochow and Kellis [3], compute the frequency of only one individual subgraph type at a time.
Set-centric approaches, such as g-tries as used in [9], are conceptually in the

L. Lopes et al. (Eds.): Euro-Par 2014 Workshops, Part II, LNCS 8806, pp. 194–205, 2014.

middle and allow the user to compute the frequency of a customized set of subgraphs that can be larger than a single subgraph but at the same time smaller than all possible subgraphs of a certain size.

Here we are mainly concerned with the network-centric approach. In particular, we focus on the FaSE algorithm which is one of the most efficient sequential alternatives for this conceptual approach to subgraph census [7]. The main contribution of this paper is a scalable parallel version of FaSE geared towards multicore architectures, which are nowadays ubiquitous, even on personal computers, making them an ideal target for end users. Using an efficient dynamic load balancing scheme our parallel algorithm is able to redistribute the work contained in the highly unbalanced search tree produced by FaSE. We tested our approach on a series of representative networks, obtaining very promising results, with an almost linear speedup up to 32 cores and high efficiency for 64 cores. Sequential FaSE was already one or two orders of magnitude faster than state-of-the-art algorithms and so our parallel version constitutes, to the best of our knowledge, the fastest multicore network-centric algorithm.

The remainder of this paper is organized as follows. Section 2 formalizes the problem and describes related work. Section 3 gives an overview of the sequential FaSE algorithm. Section 4 details our parallel approach, while section 5 shows our experimental results. Finally, section 6 sums up the presented work and gives some possible directions for future research.

2   The Subgraph Census Problem

This section details more formally the problem tackled in this paper.

Definition 1 (Subgraph Census Problem). *Given an integer k and a graph G, determine the frequency of all connected induced subgraphs of size k in G. Two occurrences of a subgraph are considered different if they have at least one node that they do not share.*

As previously stated, this metric plays a central role in several graph mining methodologies. For instance, a network motif is defined as a statistically *overrepresented subgraph*, that is, a subgraph that appears more times than what would be expected [6]. In practice, this means that the census must be computed both on the original network and on an ensemble of randomized networks [10].

2.1   Related Work

There are several existing sequential algorithms for the subgraph and classical examples are ESU [16] and Kavosh [4]. They are conceptually similar, both being network-centric and enumerating all possible subsets of k connected nodes, relying on a third-party algorithm (nauty[1]) to identify the associated subgraph

---

[1] http://cs.anu.edu.au/~bdm/nauty/

type. This means that each subgraph occurrence implies an individual isomorphism test. NetMODE augments this approach by considering very small subgraph sizes and either caching isomorphism tests or building fast specialized heuristics for a particular subgraph size. QuateXelero [5] and our own work with FaSE [7] are two very recent algorithms which offer a different improvement by avoiding the need to do one isomorphism test per occurrence. To that end, they both encapsulate the topology of the subgraphs being enumerated on an auxiliary data-structure (a quaternary tree in the case of QuateXelero, and a g-trie in the case of FaSE). Other algorithms are either subgraph-centric, such as the work by Grochow and Kellis [3] or set-centric, such as gtrieScanner [9]. Here we concentrate on the network-centric approach and use FaSE as the basis for our parallel algorithm.

Regarding parallel approaches, there are less alternatives. We provided a distributed memory approach for both FSU [12] and g-tries [11], using MPI. This work stands out because it is aimed at shared memory environments with multiple cores. A shared memory parallelization of the set-centric g-trie methodology was also presented in [2]. This work diverges in its base sequential algorithm and uses a different conceptual approach. Another parallel algorithm is given by Wang et al [15]; however, they employ a static pre-division of work and provide very limited experimental results while our approach dynamically balances load by redistributing work during the computation and perform a more detailed scalability analysis. Afrati et al. [1] provide a parallel map-reduce subgraph-centric approach, from which we differ in both the target platform and the algorithmic methodology. For more specific subgraph types there are other parallel alternatives such as Fascia [14] (a multicore subgraph-centric method for approximate count of non-induced tree-like subgraphs) or Sahad [17] (a Hadoop subgraph-centric method for tree subgraphs), but here we aim towards generality and all possible subgraph types.

3   Sequential FaSE Algorithm

As previously said, FaSE follows a network-centric paradigm. However, contrarily to what previous approaches did, FaSE does not withhold the isomorphism tests until the end of the enumeration. Instead, it partitions the subgraphs into intermediate classes during the enumeration process. The only requisite is that if two subgraphs pertain to the same intermediate class they are isomorphic. Thus, a single isomorphism test per intermediate class is needed, contrasting to previous methods that required one per enumerated subgraph. This results in a major speedup when comparing with past approaches, since the number of intermediate classes will be much smaller than the number of subgraph occurrences, which is corroborated by the experimental results.

In practice the algorithm uses two main concepts: an enumeration process and a tree that stores the information of both the intermediate classes and the subgraphs being enumerated. The enumeration process simply iterates through each subgraph occurrence and can be performed using any existing methods, provided it works by incrementally growing a set of connected vertices that partially represents the current subgraph. Furthermore, a tree is used to encapsulate the topological features of the enumerating subgraphs. It does so by generating a new label, using a generic operation called *LS-Labeling*, which represents the information introduced by each newly added vertex and uses it to describe an edge in a tree. This effectively partitions the set of subgraphs into the mentioned intermediate classes. This entire process is summarized in Algorithm 1.

Algorithm 1. The FaSE Algorithm

Input: A graph G, a g-trie T and a subgraph size k
Result: Frequencies of all k-subgraphs of G

1: **procedure** FASE(G, T, k)
2:     $T \leftarrow \emptyset$
3:     **for all** vertex v of G **do**
4:         ENUMERATE$(\{v\}, \{u \in N(v) : u > v\}, T.root)$
5:     **for all** l in $T.leaves()$ **do**
6:         $frequency[$CANONICALLABEL$(l.Graph)]$ += $l.count$

7: **procedure** ENUMERATE$(V_s, V_{ext}, current)$
8:     **if** $|V_s| = k$ **then**
9:         $current.count$++
10:     **else**
11:         **for all** vertex v in V_{ext} **do**
12:             $V'_{ext} \leftarrow V_{ext} \cup \{u \in N_{exc}(v, V_s) : u > V_s[0]\}$
13:             $V'_s \leftarrow V_s \cup \{v\}$
14:             $current' \leftarrow current.Child(LSLabel(V_s))$
15:             ENUMERATE$(V'_s, V'_{ext}, current')$

3.1 Enumeration

As mentioned above, the enumeration process can be done by any algorithm that grows a set of connected vertices. The reason to enforce so is to allow the creation of a label describing the addition of the vertex and hence partition the subgraphs set. The previously mentioned ESU [16] and Kavosh [4] algorithms fit this constraint and since they present similar execution time, both would be a good choice to integrate into FaSE. In our implementation we opted to use ESU, which we will now describe in more detail.

It essentially works by enumerating all size k subgraphs only once. It does so by keeping two ordered sets of vertices: V_s and V_{ext}. The former represents the partial subgraph that is currently being enumerated as a set of connected vertices. The latter represents the set of vertices that can be added to V_s as a valid extension. To begin, it takes each vertex v in the network sets $V_s = \{v\}$ and $V_{ext} = N(v)$, where $N(v)$ are the neighbors of v (lines 3 and 4). Then, one element u of V_{ext} is removed at a time, and a recursive call is made adding u to V_s and each element in $N_{exc}(u, V_s)$ with label greater than $V_s[0]$ to V_{ext} (lines 12 and 13). $N_{exc}(u, V_s)$ are the exclusive neighbors, that is they are the neighbors of

u that are not neighbors of V_s. This, along with the condition $u > V_s[0]$, ensure that there is no subgraph enumerated twice. When the size of V_s reaches k it means that V_s constitutes a new occurrence of a size k subgraph (line 8).

3.2   Using a Tree to Encapsulate Isomorphism Information

The enumeration step is wrapped by a data structure that stores information of the subgraphs being enumerated in order to divide them into intermediate classes. The conditions set on the behavior of the enumeration algorithm allow for the use of a tree, as previously described. This tree, which is called a g-trie, represents a different intermediate class in each node. When adding a new vertex to the current subgraph, a new label is generated describing its relation to the previously added vertices. This label will govern the edges in the tree, that is, each edge is represented by a label generated by a vertex addition.

Label generation in each step is done by using a generic process called *LS-Labeling* which deterministically partitions the different subgraphs into iso-morphic classes. Additionally, it is required that it runs in polynomial time, as otherwise it would be pointless to use the actual tree since we could simply use the labeling as the isomorphism test. Thus there is a trade off between time spent in creating the label and time spent enumerating and running isomorphism tests on subgraphs. In this paper we use an *adjacency list labeling*, which generates a label corresponding to an ordered list of at most $k-1$ integers where each value i $(0 < i < k)$ is present if there is a connection from the new vertex to the i-th added vertex. More details on this can be found in the original FaSE paper [7].

Figure 1 summarizes the FaSE algorithm. The tree on the left represents the implicit recursion tree ESU creates. Note that it is naturally skewed towards the left. This is an important fact that justifies why, as we will see later, we need to redistribute work in the parallel version of the algorithm. The induced g-trie on the right is a visual representation of the actual g-trie that FaSE creates.

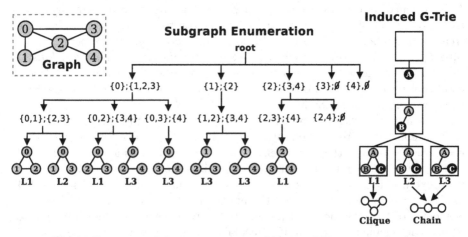

Fig. 1. Summary of the enumeration and encapsulation steps of FaSE

4   Parallel FaSE Algorithm

A main characteristic of our sequential algorithm is that it generates independent branches. Each V_s and V_{ext} pair can thus be regarded as a *work unit* and, along with the position in the g-trie, are sufficient to resume computation. At the start, V_s corresponds to each single node in the network and V_{ext} to its neighbors with higher index. As we have seen before, this distribution is intrinsically unbalanced since it places bigger restrictions on higher indexed nodes. Furthermore, in the subgraph census problem, a few vertices, such as hubs, may have most of the computing time while others are much lighter in comparison. In our work we developed a strategy to efficiently distribute these work units among the computing resources.

We decided to use one central g-trie, as opposed to one g-trie per thread. While this option leads to contention when accessing the g-trie, it saves memory and removes the redundant work caused by multiple threads creating their own g-trie, with most connections being common for every thread. A major factor for the efficiency of the sequential algorithm is that it does not create a queue of work units, and instead implicitly stores them in the recursive stack. To achieve the best efficiency we kept this characteristic in our parallel approach.

Our target platforms are multicore architectures, given their ubiquity and ease of access for end users. Our implementation was done using Pthreads, which are supported by all major operating systems.

4.1   Overall View

The algorithm starts by dividing the vertices evenly between the threads, with one thread per core. All threads do the enumeration process separately, using their respective V_s and V_{ext}. If a thread arrives at a new type of node it updates the g-trie. All threads see this change and do not need to update the g-trie if the node is found again. When a thread P finishes its initially assigned work units it sends a work request to an active thread Q. Thread Q stops its computation, builds a work tree corresponding to its current state, gives half of the work to P and informs it that it can resume work. Both threads execute their respective portion starting at the bottom of the work tree so that only one V_s is needed for a given point of sharing, exploiting graph sub-topology between g-trie's ancestor and descendant nodes. After the enumeration phase is completed, the resulting leafs are split between the threads and isomorphism tests are performed to assert to which subgraph type each leaf corresponds to. In the end, the subgraph frequencies computed by all threads are aggregated.

4.2   Parallel Subgraph Frequency Counting

Algorithm 2 details our parallel FaSE algorithm. The graph G, the g-trie T and the subgraph size k are global variables, while *current* is a pointer to the g-trie location and is local for each thread. Computation starts with an initially empty g-trie (line 2) and work queues (line 3) for every thread. The condition in

---

Algorithm 2. The Parallel FaSE Algorithm

Input: A graph G, a G-Trie T and a subgraph size k
Result: Frequencies of all k-subgraphs of G

1: **procedure** PARALLELFASE(G, T, k)
2:    $T \leftarrow \emptyset$
3:    $W \leftarrow \emptyset$
4:    $i, j \leftarrow thread_{id}$
5:    **while** $i \leq |V(G)|$ **do**
6:        $v \leftarrow V(G)_i$
7:        **if** WORKREQUEST(P) **then**
8:            W.ADDWORK()
9:            $(W_Q, W_P) \leftarrow$ SPLITWORK(W)
10:           GIVEWORK(W_P, P)
11:           RESUMEWORK(W_Q)
12:        ENUMERATE$(\{v\}, \{u \in N(v) . u \succ v\}, T.root)$
13:        $i \leftarrow i + num_{threads}$
14:    **while** $j \leq |T.leaves()|$ **do**
15:        $l \leftarrow T.leaves()_j$
16:        $frequency[$CANONICALLABEL$(l.Graph)]$ += $l.count$
17:        $j \leftarrow j + num_{threads}$

---

line 12 of Algorithm 1, $u > V_s[0]$, makes vertices with a smaller index probably computationally heavier than higher indexed vertices. For that reason, network vertices are split in a round-robin fashion, giving all threads $|V(G)|/num_{threads}$ top vertices to initially explore (lines 4 to 6 and 13). This division is not necessarily balanced but finding the best possible division is as computationally heavy as the census itself. If a thread does not receive a work request it does the enumeration process starting at each of its assigned vertices (line 12). The **enumerate()** procedure is very similar to the sequential version but with V_s and V_{ext} now being thread local and the *count* variable becoming an array indexing threads, i.e. $count[thread_{id}]$, in each leaf. Another relevant difference is that, when a new node in the g-trie needs to be created, its parent node has to be locked before creation. This is done to ensure that the same node is not created by multiple threads. Regarding work distribution, when a thread Q receives a work request from P, it needs to stop its computation, add the remaining work to W (line 8), split the work (line 9), give half of it to P (line 10) and resume its computation (line 11). After the enumeration phase is finished, the leafs are also distributed among the threads and isomorphism tests are performed to verify the appropriate canonical type of each occurrence in parallel (lines 14 to 17).

4.3   Work Request

When a thread P has completed its assigned work it asks a random thread Q for work. Random polling has been established as an efficient heuristic for dynamic load balancing [13] and, furthermore, in our case predicting exactly how much computation each active thread still has in its work tree can not be done without a serious overhead. If Q sends some unprocessed work, then P computes the work it was given. If Q did not have work to share, P tries asking another random thread. When all threads are trying to get work and no more work units are left to be computed, the enumeration phase ends.

4.4   Work Sharing

When a thread is computing and receives a work request, the execution is halted and work sharing is performed. In Figure 2 we show a work tree of a thread Q and its division with thread P. The work tree is built by the recursive calls to addWork(). The squares represent V_{used} and the current position in the g-trie. We only need the V_s of the deepest level since the parent g-trie nodes share the same vertices. The dotted nodes are work-units still to be explored. Note that these nodes are not stored in the g-trie, and they will be explored by the threads after sharing is performed and are presented only to give a more accurate view of the complete work tree generated by FaSE.

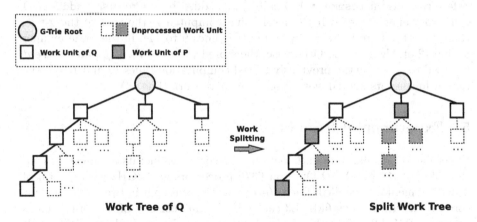

Fig. 2. The constructed work tree of a thread Q and its division when a work request is received from thread P

During work division, each thread is given a g-trie level, constituted by V_s, V_{used} and the current g-trie position. In the given example, Q gets level 3 and 1 while P receives 2 and 4. The topmost level is fully split since that corresponds to the initial division from lines 4 to 6 of Algorithm 2.

4.5   Work Resuming

When work is shared the threads need a mechanism to resume their computation and that process is illustrates in Algorithm 3. The work levels are ordered from top to bottom (lines 2 and 3) so that only one V_s is necessary. If a work request is received, the general process of work sharing is performed (lines 4 to 8). No call to addWork() is necessary since the work was either added previously to W

Algorithm 3. Algorithm for resuming work after sharing is performed

---

1: **procedure** RESUMEWORK(W)
2:     ORDERBYLOWEST(W)
3:     **for all** level L of W **do**
4:         **if** WORKREQUEST(P) **then**
5:             $(W_Q, W_P) \leftarrow$ SPLITWORK(W)
6:             GIVEWORK(W_P, P)
7:             RESUMEWORK(W_Q)
8:             **return**
9:         **if** $L.depth = 0$ **then**
10:            **for all** vertex v of $L.V_{ext}$ **do**
11:                ENUMERATE($\{v\}, \{u \in N(v) : u > v\}, T.root$)
12:        **else**
13:            ENUMERATE($L.V_s, L.V_{ext}, L.current$)
14:    ASKFORWORK()

---

before the current `resumeWork()` call or was added by the recursive `addWork()` calls from `enumerate()`. If the level being computed is the root of the g-trie, the top vertices are individually computed (lines 9 to 11), in the same manner as line 12 of Algorithm 2. Otherwise, the stored values of V_s, V_{used} and *current* are used to continue the previously halted computation (lines 12 and 13). If the thread finishes its alloted work it asks for more work (line 14).

5   Experimental Results

Experimental results were gathered on a 64-core machine; its architecture consists of four 16-core AMD Opteron 6376 processors at 2.3GHz with a total of 252GB of memory installed. Each 16-core processor is split in two banks of eight cores, each with its own 6MB L3 cache. Each bank consists of sets of two cores sharing a 2MB L2 and a 64KB L1 instruction cache. Every single core has a dedicated 16KB L1 data cache. The turbo boost functionality was disabled because that would lead to inconsistent results by having executions with less cores running at an increased clock rate. All code was developed in C++11 and compiled using gcc 4.8.2.

We used over a dozen real-world networks and present here the results for a representative subset of them. In Table 1 a general view of the content and dimension of the chosen seven networks is shown. To showcase the general scalability of our algorithm, networks that vary in their field of application, their use of edge direction and their dimension were chosen. To decide what k to use, we simply opted for choosing one that gave a sufficiently large sequential time for parallelism to be meaningful but not so large that it would take more than a few hours to complete the computation.

Table 1. The set of seven different representative real networks used for our parallel performance testing

Network	$|V(G)|$	$|E(G)|$	$\frac{|E(G)|}{|V(G)|}$	Directed	Description	Source
jazz	198	2,742	13.85	No	Collaborations of jazz musicians	[1]
polblogs	1,491	19,022	12.76	Yes	Hyperlinks of politics weblogs	[2]
netsc	1,589	2,742	1.73	No	Network experiments co-authorship	[2]
facebook	4,039	88,234	21.85	No	Facebook friend circles	[3]
company	8,497	6,724	0.79	Yes	Media companies ownership	[4]
astroph	18,772	198,050	10.55	No	Astrophysics papers collaborations	[3]
enron	36,692	367,662	10.02	Yes	Email network	[3]

Table 2. General execution information and results

Network	Subgraph size	#Leafs found	#Subgraph types found	Sequential time (s)	#Threads: speedup			
					8	16	32	64
jazz	6	3,113	112	295.95	6.75	14.86	29.92	49.74
polblogs	6	409,845	9,360	1,722.55	7.85	15.56	30.04	47.48
netsc	9	445,410	14,151	295.12	7.83	15.05	23.82	26.54
facebook	5	125	19	3,598.41	7.67	15.34	31.00	51.81
company	6	1,379	310	739.12	7.94	15.81	31.02	48.53
astroph	4	17	6	179.47	6.62	13.60	24.69	30.42
enron	4	17	6	1,370.46	7.70	13.32	25.44	35.85

To have the parallel version with one thread performing similarly to the sequential algorithm, work queues were not artificially created. This choice lead to a very small overhead (less than 5% for all tested cases) and, henceforth, parallel execution with one thread will be referred to as the *sequential time*.

Our algorithm's performance was evaluated up to 64 cores and results are presented in Table 2. In that table, the size of the subgraphs being queried, along with the number of g-trie leafs (the intermediate classes) and the actual number of different subgraph types are shown. The sequential time and the obtained speedups for 8, 16, 32 and 64 cores are also shown.

The results are promising and close to linear speedup up to 32 cores for every case. Due to the machine's architecture we did not achieve linear speedups for 64 cores but still managed to obtain a high efficiency for 4 of the 7 cases. Note that our algorithm performs worse in networks where many leafs need to be created. This problems arises because an unique g-trie is used and must be protected when a new node, leaf or label is inserted. Cases were found where speedups were severely limited by this factor. On the other hand, using one

---

[2] Arenas: http://deim.urv.cat/~aarenas/data/welcome.htm

[3] Mark Newman: http://www-personal.umich.edu/~mejn/netdata/

[4] SNAP: http://snap.stanford.edu/data/

[5] Pajek: http://vlado.fmf.uni-lj.si/pub/networks/data/

g-trie per thread would lead to much redundant work that would deteriorate our algorithm's performance. Memory also becomes a concern when many threads are used because each leaf has an array to store the frequencies. This limits the size of the subgraphs and networks that can be run. Another problem related to storing the frequencies in the g-trie is that it can sometimes lead to false sharing since many threads could be updating the array at the same time. A better option would be to instead have each thread keep an array of the frequencies for each leaf but, since the g-trie is created during runtime, the total number of leafs is not known and setting a unique *id* for each one would require resorting to locks. Finally, it was observed that memory allocations became heavier when more threads were used. Something that could be further explored is an efficient pre-alocation of memory, where the threads would retrieve it when needed. Furthermore, an adjacency matrix was used to represent the input network that, while giving the best possible algorithmic complexity for verifying node connections, imposes a quadratic memory representation. Different memory allocators, like `jemalloc` and `tcmalloc`, were tried but found no significant performance improvement.

By comparison, we have previous work parallelizing a set-centric approach with g-tries for multicore architectures [2] and obtained almost linear speedup for every case we tested. Besides using a conceptually different base algorithm (here we follow a network-centric algorithm). The main difference between the two approaches is that, in [2], the g-trie was pre-created before subgraph counting, removing the need to have locks when modifying the g-trie and making it possible to have subgraph frequencies outside of the g-trie, thus eliminating false sharing.

6   Conclusion

In this paper we presented a scalable parallel algorithm for the subgraph census problem. At the core or our method lies the `FaSE` algorithm, an efficient network-centric sequential approach which is able to drastically reduce the number of isomorphism tests needed when comparing to previous approaches such as `ESU` or `Kavosh`. `FaSE` induces a highly unbalanced search tree with independent branches and we devised a dynamic load balancing scheme capable of an efficient redistribution of work during execution time. We tested our algorithm on a set of representative networks and we achieved an almost linear speedup up to 32 cores and a high efficiency for the total 64 cores of our machine. To the best of our knowledge, this constitutes the fastest available method for a network-centric approach, allowing users to expand the limits of subgraph census applicability, not only on more dedicated computing resources, but also on their personal multicore machines.

In the near future it is our intention to explore a hybrid methodology capable of mixing both shared and distributed memory approaches. We also intend to carefully examine the possibility of using GPUs for computing a subgraph census. Finally, on a more practical angle, we will use our method to analyze several data sets, searching for new subgraph patterns that can lead to novel insight into the structure of these real-life networks.

Acknowledgments. David Aparicio is funded by an FCT Scolarship Grant from the project Sibila (NORTE-07-0124-FEDER-000059) financed by Fundo Europeu do Desenvolvimento Regional (FEDER). Pedro Ribeiro is funded by an FCT Research Grant (SFRH/BPD/81695/2011).

References

1. Afrati, F.N., Fotakis, D., Ullman, J.D.: Enumerating subgraph instances using map-reduce. In: IEEE 29th International Conference on Data Engineering (ICDE), pp. 62–73. IEEE CS, Los Alamitos (2013)
2. Aparicio, D., Ribeiro, P., Silva, F.: Parallel subgraph counting for multicore architectures. In: IEEE International Symposium on Parallel and Distributed Processing with Applications. IEEE CS (August 2014)
3. Grochow, J., Kellis, M.: Network motif discovery using subgraph enumeration and symmetry-breaking. Research in Computational Molecular Biology, 92–106 (2007)
4. Kashani, Z., Ahrabian, H., Elahi, E., Nowzari-Dalini, A., Ansari, E., Asadi, S., Mohammadi, S., Schreiber, F., Masoudi-Nejad, A.: Kavosh: a new algorithm for finding network motifs. BMC Bioinformatics 10(1), 318 (2009)
5. Khakabimamaghani, S., Sharafuddin, I., Dichter, N., Koch, I., Masoudi-Nejad, A.: Quatexelero: An accelerated exact network motif detection algorithm. PLoS One 8(7), e68073 (2013)
6. Milo, R., Shen-Orr, S., Itzkovitz, S., Kashtan, N., Chklovskii, D., Alon, U.: Network Motifs: Simple Building Blocks of Complex Networks. Science 298(5594) (2002)
7. Paredes, P., Ribeiro, P.: Towards a faster network-centric subgraph census. In: Proceedings of the 2013 IEEE/ACM International Conference on Advances in Social Networks Analysis and Mining, pp. 264–271. ACM, NY (2013)
8. Pržulj, N.: Biological network comparison using graphlet degree distribution. Bioinformatics 26(6), 853–854 (2010)
9. Ribeiro, P., Silva, F.: G-tries: a data structure for storing and finding subgraphs. Data Mining and Knowledge Discovery 28, 337–377 (2014)
10. Ribeiro, P., Silva, F., Kaiser, M.: Strategies for network motifs discovery. In: IEEE International Conference on e-Science, pp. 80–87. e-Science (2009)
11. Ribeiro, P., Silva, F., Lopes, L.: Efficient parallel subgraph counting using g-tries. In: IEEE International Conference on Cluster Computing (Cluster), pp. 1559–1566. IEEE CS (September 2010)
12. Ribeiro, P., Silva, F., Lopes, L.: Parallel discovery of network motifs. Journal of Parallel and Distributed Computing 72, 144–154 (2012)
13. Sanders, P.: Asynchronous random polling dynamic load balancing. In: Aggarwal, A.K., Pandu Rangan, C. (eds.) ISAAC 1999. LNCS, vol. 1741, pp. 37–48. Springer, Heidelberg (1999)
14. Slota, G.M., Madduri, K.: Fast approximate subgraph counting and enumeration. In: 42nd International Conference on Parallel Processing, pp. 210–219 (2013)
15. Wang, T., Touchman, J.W., Zhang, W., Suh, E.B., Xue, G.: A parallel algorithm for extracting transcription regulatory network motifs. In: IEEE International Symposium on Bioinformatics and Bioengineering, pp. 193–200 (2005)
16. Wernicke, S.: Efficient detection of network motifs. IEEE/ACM Transactions on Computational Biology and Bioinformatics, 347–359 (2006)
17. Zhao, Z., Wang, G., Butt, A.R., Khan, M., Kumar, V.A., Marathe, M.V.: Sahad: Subgraph analysis in massive networks using hadoop. In: International Parallel and Distributed Processing Symposium, pp. 390–401 (2012)

Lace: Non-blocking Split Deque
for Work-Stealing

Tom van Dijk* and Jaco C. van de Pol

Formal Methods and Tools, Dept. of EEMCS, University of Twente
P.O.-box 217, 7500 AE Enschede, The Netherlands
{t.vandijk,vdpol}@cs.utwente.nl

Abstract. Work-stealing is an efficient method to implement load balancing in fine-grained task parallelism. Typically, concurrent deques are used for this purpose. A disadvantage of many concurrent deques is that they require expensive memory fences for local deque operations.

In this paper, we propose a new non-blocking work-stealing deque based on the split task queue. Our design uses a dynamic split point between the shared and the private portions of the deque, and only requires memory fences when shrinking the shared portion.

We present Lace, an implementation of work-stealing based on this deque, with an interface similar to the work-stealing library Wool, and an evaluation of Lace based on several common benchmarks. We also implement a recent approach using private deques in Lace. We show that the split deque and the private deque in Lace have similar low overhead and high scalability as Wool.

Keywords: work-stealing, task-based parallelism, dynamic load balancing, lock-free algorithm, non-blocking deque.

1 Introduction

1.1 Task-Based Parallelism

In recent years, the importance of using parallelism to improve the performance of software has become self-evident, especially given the availability of multicore shared-memory systems and the physical limits of processor speeds. Frameworks like Cilk [3,9] and Wool [7,8] allow writing parallel programs in a style similar to sequential programs [1].

In task-based parallelism, a computation is divided into small tasks. Each task only depends on the results of its own immediate subtasks for its execution. Multiple independent subtasks can be executed in parallel. Especially recursive algorithms are easily parallelized.

Cilk, Wool, and similar task-based parallel frameworks use keywords **spawn** and **sync** to expose parallelism. The **spawn** keyword creates a new task. The **sync** keyword matches with the last unmatched **spawn**, i.e., operating as if spawned tasks are stored on a stack. It waits until that task is completed and

---

* The first author is supported by the NWO project MaDriD, grant nr. 612.001.101.

L. Lopes et al. (Eds.): Euro-Par 2014 Workshops, Part II, LNCS 8806, pp. 206–217, 2014.
© Springer International Publishing Switzerland 2014

```
 1 def spawn(task):               11 def steal_work(victim):
 2   self.tasks.push(task)         12   t = victim.tasks.steal()
                                   13   if t != None:
 3 def sync():                     14     t.thief = self
 4   status, t = self.tasks.pop()  15     t.result = t.execute()
 5   if status = STOLEN:           16     t.done = True
 6     while not t.done:
 7       steal_work(t.thief)       17 thread worker(id, roottask):
 8     self.tasks.pop_stolen()     18   if id = 0: roottask.execute()
 9     return t.result             19   else: forever:
10   else: return t.execute()      20     steal_work(random_victim())
```

Fig. 1. Simplified algorithm of work-stealing using leapfrogging when waiting for a stolen task to finish, i.e., steal from the thief. Note that stolen tasks are not removed from the task pool until completed.

retrieves the result. Every **spawn** during the execution of the program must have a matching **sync**. In this paper, we follow the semantics of Wool. In the original work-stealing papers, **sync** waits for all locally spawned subtasks, rather than the last unmatched subtask.

1.2 Work-Stealing

Work-stealing is a technique that efficiently implements load-balancing for task-based parallelism. It has been proven to be optimal for a large class of problems and has tight memory and communication bounds [4]. In work-stealing, tasks are executed by a fixed number of workers. Each worker owns a task pool into which it inserts spawned tasks. Idle workers steal tasks from random victims.

See Figure 1 for a simplified work-stealing algorithm. Workers start executing in **worker**. One worker executes the first task. The other workers steal from random victims. The task pool **tasks** acts like a stack with methods **push** and **pop**, and provides **steal** for potential thieves. Tasks are typically stolen from the bottom of the stack, since these tasks often have more subtasks. This reduces the amount of total steals necessary and thus the overhead from stealing.

When synchronizing with a stolen task, the victim steals from the thief until the stolen task is completed. By stealing back from the thief, a worker executes subtasks of the stolen task. This technique is called leapfrogging [16]. When stealing from random workers instead, the size of the task pool of each worker could grow beyond the size needed for complete sequential execution [8]. Using leapfrogging rather than stealing from random workers thus limits the space requirements of the task pools to those of sequential execution.

1.3 Work-Stealing Deques

Task pools are commonly implemented using double-ended queues (deques) specialized for work-stealing. The first provably efficient work-stealing scheduler for fully strict computations was presented in 1994 [4] and its implementation in

Cilk in 1996 [3]. One improvement of the original Cilk algorithm is the THE protocol in Cilk-5 [9], which eliminates acquiring the lock in push and in most executions of pop, but every steal still requires locking.

The first non-blocking work-stealing deque is the ABP algorithm, which uses a fixed-size array that might overflow [2]. Two unbounded non-blocking deques were proposed, the deque by Hendler et al. based on linked lists of small arrays [10], and the Chase-Lev deque that uses dynamic circular arrays [5].

In weak memory models that allow reordering loads before stores, most deques that allow any spawned task to be stolen require a memory fence in every pop operation. Memory fences are expensive. For example, the THE protocol spends half of its execution time in the memory fence [9].

Several approaches alleviate this problem. The split task queue by Dinan et al. [6], designed for clusters of multiprocessor computers, allows lock-free local access to a private portion of the queue and can transfer work between the public and private portions of the queue without copying tasks. Thieves synchronize using a lock and the local process only needs to take the lock when transferring work from the public portion to the private portion of the queue. Michael et al. propose relaxed semantics for work-stealing: inserted tasks are executed *at least* once instead of *exactly* once, to avoid requiring memory fences and atomic instructions [12]. In the work scheduler Wool [7], originally only the first N tasks in the deque can be stolen, where N is determined by a parameter at startup. Only executing pop on stealable tasks requires a memory fence. In a later version, the number of stealable tasks is dynamically updated [8].

In some work-stealing algorithms, shared deques are replaced by private deques, and work is explicitly communicated using a message-passing approach. Recently, Acar et al. proposed two algorithms for work-stealing using private deques [1]. See further [1] for an overview of other work with private deques.

Tasks are often stored as pointers that are removed from the deque when the task is stolen [9,2,10,5]. To virtually eliminate the overhead of task creation for tasks that are never stolen, Faxén proposed a direct task stack, storing tasks instead of pointers in the work queue, implemented in Wool [7,8]. Rather than synchronizing with thieves on the metadata of the queue (e.g. variables top and bot in the ABP algorithm), Wool synchronizes on the individual task descriptors, using locks when synchronizing with potential thieves, similar to the THE protocol. Sundell and Tsigas presented a lock-free version of Wool [15,8], which still synchronizes on the individual task descriptors.

1.4   Contributions

Acar et al. write that concurrent deques suffer from two limitations: 1) local deque operations (mainly pop) require expensive memory fences in modern weak-memory architectures; 2) they can be very difficult to extend to support various optimizations, especially steal-multiple extensions [1]. They lift both limitations using private deques. Wool reduces the first limitation for concurrent deques by using a dynamic number of stealable tasks, but is difficult to extend for steal-multiple strategies, since tasks must be stolen individually.

We present a work-stealing algorithm that eliminates these limitations using concurrent deques, by combining a non-blocking variant of the split task queue [6] with direct task stealing from Wool [7,8]. This algorithm splits the deque into a shared portion and a private portion. The split point between these portions is modified in a non-blocking manner.

We present an implementation of this algorithm in a C library called Lace[1], which has the same interface as Wool. We evaluate the performance of Lace using several benchmarks, including standard Cilk benchmarks and the UTS benchmark [13]. We compare our algorithm with Wool and with an implementation of the receiver-initiated private deque algorithm [1] in the Lace framework. Our experiments show that our algorithm is competitive with both Wool and the private deque algorithm, while lifting both limitations described in [1]. Compared to the private deque algorithm, our algorithm allows stealing of all tasks in the shared deque without cooperation of the owner, while the private deque algorithm requires cooperation of the owner for every steal transaction.

2 Preliminaries

We assume a shared memory system with the x86 memory model. The x86 memory model is not sequentially consistent, but allows reordering loads before stores. Memory writes are buffered before reaching the memory, hence reads can occur before preceding memory writes are globally visible. Memory fences flush the write buffer before reading from memory. Apart from memory fences, we use the atomic memory operation compare_and_swap (cas) to ensure safety. The cas operation atomically compares a value in memory to an expected value and modifies it only if the values match. We use cas to ensure that exactly one worker performs a transition.

We assume that the system consists of one or more processor chips and one or more memory chips, connected using an interconnection network, for example in Non-Uniform Memory Access (NUMA) shared-memory systems. We also assume that data on this interconnection network is transferred in blocks called cachelines, which are typically 64 bytes long.

3 Algorithm

3.1 Design Considerations

To obtain a low execution time when performing work-stealing with all available workers, we aim at low overhead compared to purely sequential programs and good scalability with increasing worker count. Memory fences and cas operations increase the overhead compared to purely sequential programs. Some memory fences are unavoidable, since thieves may steal a task while the owner is retrieving it. By splitting the deque into a shared deque and a private deque (see Figure 2),

---

[1] Lace is available at http://fmt.ewi.utwente.nl/tools/lace/

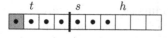

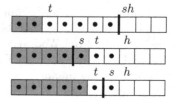

Fig. 2. The split deque, with tail t, split point s and head h. A task at position x is **stolen** if $x < t$. It is **shared** if $x < s$, and **private** otherwise. Of the 7 tasks in this example, 4 are **shared** and 1 is **stolen**.

Fig. 3. The owner shrinks the shared portion of the deque, but thieves may have stolen tasks beyond the new split point. The owner detects this and updates the split point to its final position.

we only need a memory fence when shrinking the shared deque, to detect the scenario of Figure 3. Also, `cas` operations are only needed to coordinate stealing.

The deque is described using variables `tail`, `split` and `head`, which are indices in the task array. To steal work, thieves only require knowledge of `tail` and `split`, and only need to modify `tail`. The owner uses `head` and `o_split` (a private copy of `split`) to operate on the private deque. The owner only accesses `tail` and `split` when changing the split point.

Thieves are not allowed to change the split point, since this would force a memory fence on every execution of `pop`. Instead, thieves set a shared flag `splitreq` on a dedicated cacheline when there are no more unstolen shared tasks. Since `splitreq` is checked at every execution of `pop` and `push`, it should always be in the processor cache of the owner, and no traffic on the interconnect network is expected until the flag is set. There is no other communication between the owner and the thieves, except when tasks are stolen soon after their creation, or when the owner is waiting for an unfinished stolen task.

If the owner determines that all tasks have been stolen, it sets a flag `allstolen` (and a private copy `o_allstolen`). Thieves check `allstolen` first before attempting to steal tasks, which results in a small performance gain. When the owner already knows that all tasks are stolen, it does not need to shrink the shared deque until new tasks are added.

Similar to the direct task stack in Wool, the deque contains fixed-size task descriptors, rather than pointers to task descriptors stored elsewhere. Stolen tasks remain in the deque. The result of a stolen task is written to the task descriptor. This reduces the task-creation overhead of making work available for stealing, which is important since most tasks are never stolen. Another advantage is that the cachelines accessed by a thief are limited to those containing the task descriptor and the variables `tail`, `split` and (rarely) `splitreq`, while in designs that use pointers, there is at least one additional accessed cacheline. If task descriptors are properly aligned and fit into one cacheline, then thieves only access two cachelines per successful steal. Also, in a pointer-based design, there are many pointers per cacheline, which can increase contention on that cacheline.

```
 1 def steal():                    31 def pop_stolen():
 2   if allstolen: return None     32   head = head-1
 3   (t,s) = (tail,split)          33   if ! o_allstolen:
 4   if t < s:                     34     allstolen = 1
 5     if cas((tail,split),        35     o_allstolen = 1
             (t,s), (t+1,s)):
 6       return Task(t)            36 def grow_shared():
 7     else: return None           37   new_s = (o_split+head+1)/2
 8   if ! splitreq: splitreq=1     38   split = new_s
 9   return None                   39   o_split = new_s
                                   40   splitreq = 0
10 def push(data):
11   if head == size: return FULL  41 def shrink_shared():
12   write task data at head       42   (t,s) = (tail,split)
13   head = head + 1               43   if t != s:
14   if o_allstolen:               44     new_s = (t+s)/2
15     (tail,split) = (head-1,head)45     split = new_s
16     allstolen = 0               46     o_split = new_s
17     if splitreq: splitreq=0     47     MFENCE
18     o_split = head              48     t = tail # read again
19     o_allstolen = 0             49     if t != s:
20   elif splitreq: grow_shared()  50       if t > new_s:
                                   51         new_s = (t+s)/2
21 def pop():                      52         split = new_s
22   if head = 0: return EMPTY,-   53         o_split = new_s
23   if o_allstolen:               54       return False
24     return STOLEN, Task(head-1) 55   allstolen = 1
25   if o_split = head:            56   o_allstolen = 1
26     if shrink_shared():         57   return True
27       return STOLEN, Task(head-1)
28   head = head-1
29   if splitreq: grow_shared()
30   return WORK, Task(head)
```

Fig. 4. Algorithm of the non-blocking split deque. Thieves have access to the cacheline with `tail`, `split` and `allstolen` and to the cacheline with `splitreq`. The owner also has access to the cacheline with `head`, `o_split` and `o_allstolen`.

3.2 Algorithms

See Figure 4 for the deque algorithms. Note that if `allstolen` is not set, then `tail` $\leq$ `split` $\leq$ `head`. If `allstolen` is set, then `tail` $\geq$ `split` and `tail` $\geq$ `head`.

The **steal** operation tries to steal a task by increasing `tail`, using `cas` on the (consecutive) variables `tail` and `split`. The `cas` operation fails when other thieves have changed `tail`, or when the owner has changed `split`. If there is no available work, then `splitreq` is set. It is important that `splitreq` is only written to if it must be changed, to avoid unnecessary communication.

Method **push** adds a new task to the deque and increases `head`. If this is the first new task (i.e., `allstolen` is set), then `tail` and `split` are set to reflect that the new task is shared and that it is the next task to be stolen. All tasks before the new task remain stolen tasks. Note that `tail` and `split` must be updated simultaneously. If thieves have set `splitreq`, then `push` calls `grow_shared` to move the split point.

Method `pop` determines whether the last task is stolen. This is the case when `allstolen` is set, or when all tasks are shared (i.e., `o_split = head`) and the method `shrink_shared` reports that all tasks are stolen. If the last task is stolen, then it remains on the deque. If the last task is not stolen, then `head` is decreased, and if `splitreq` is set, `pop` calls `grow_shared`.

If the last task is stolen, then `pop_stolen` is called after the stolen task is completed (see Figure 1). Leapfrogging may have changed the state of the deque, therefore `allstolen` is set again, since the remaining tasks are still stolen.

In `grow_shared`, the new value of the split point is the ceiling of the average of `split` and `head`. Since `grow_shared` is only called if not `allstolen`, i.e., `split ≤ head`, the shared deque will always grow and therefore atomic operations or memory fences are not necessary.

Method `shrink_shared` moves the split point to decrease the size of the shared deque. It then detects whether thieves have stolen tasks beyond the new split point, and if so, it moves the split point again. If all tasks were stolen, then `shrink_shared` sets `allstolen` and returns `True`. It returns `False` otherwise. Since `shrink_shared` is called by the owner only if `split = head`, line 43 really checks whether `tail = head`, i.e., whether all tasks are stolen. If not, then the split point is moved between `tail` and `split`. The memory fence ensures that the new split point is globally visible before reading `tail`. Once the new split point is globally visible, no tasks can be stolen beyond the new split point. Therefore, we only need to check once whether more tasks are stolen. If at that point all remaining tasks are stolen, then `allstolen` is set and `shrink_shared` returns `True`. If not, then if only some tasks are stolen beyond the new split point, the split point is moved again. Finally, `shrink_shared` returns `False`.

3.3 Extensions

There are several possible extensions to the work-stealing deque.

Resizing. Our work-stealing deque uses a fixed-size array. Given that virtual memory is several orders of magnitude larger than real memory and the ability of modern operating systems to allocate only used pages, we can avoid overflows by allocating an amount of virtual memory much higher than required. The deque could be extended for resizing, for example using linked lists of arrays, but we feel this is unnecessary in practice.

Steal-multiple strategies. One extension to work-stealing is the policy to steal more than one task at the same time, e.g., stealing half the tasks in the deque, which has been argued to be beneficial in the context of irregular graph applications [11,6]. This is easily implemented by modifying line 5 to steal multiple tasks, and executing the stolen tasks in reverse order (last one first). However, in experiments on a single NUMA machine, this did not improve performance.

Other memory models. The algorithm in Figure 4 is designed for the x86 TSO memory model, which only allows reordering loads before stores. Weaker memory models may for example allow reordering stores. Assuming that reordering only takes place on independent operations, we believe no additional memory fences are required in Figure 4 to ensure correctness. Memory fences are however required in Figure 1 to ensure that `result` is set before `done`.

4 Evaluation

We implemented Lace, a C library that provides a work-stealing framework similar to Wool and Cilk. The library creates one POSIX thread (*pthread*) for each available core. Our implementation is NUMA-aware, i.e., all pthreads are pinned to a NUMA domain and their program stack and the deque structures for each worker are allocated on the same NUMA domain as the worker.

We evaluate Lace using several benchmarks compared to the work-stealing framework Wool [8] using the classic leapfrogging strategy. This version of Wool has a dynamic split point and does not use locking. We compare the performance of Lace and Wool, for two reasons. Our implementation resembles the implementation of Wool, making a comparison easier. Also, [8] and [14] show that Wool is efficient compared to Cilk++, OpenMP and the Intel TBB framework, with a slight advantage for Wool. We also compare our algorithm to the receiver-initiated version of the private deque of Acar et al. [1], using the alternative `acquire` function, which we implemented in the Lace framework.

4.1 Benchmarks

For all benchmarks, we use the smallest possible granularity and do not use sequential cut-off points, since we are interested in measuring the overhead of the work-stealing algorithm. Using a larger granularity and sequential cut-off points may result in better scalability for some benchmarks.

Fibonacci. For a positive integer N, calculate the Fibonacci number by calculating the Fibonacci numbers $N - 1$ and $N - 2$ recursively and add the results. This benchmark generates a skewed task tree and is commonly used to benchmark work-stealing algorithms, since the actual work per task is minimal. Number of tasks: 20,365,011,073 (`fib` 50).

Queens. For a positive integer N, calculate the number of solutions for placing N queens on a $N \times N$ chessboard so that no two queens attack each other. Each task at depth i spawns up to N new tasks, one for every correct board after placing a queen on row i. Number of tasks: 171,129,071 (`queens` 15).

Unbalanced Tree Search. This benchmark is designed by Olivier et al. to evaluate the performance for parallel applications requiring dynamic load balancing. The algorithm uses the SHA-1 algorithm to generate geometric and binomial trees. The generated binomial trees (T3L) have unpredictable subtree sizes and depths and are optimal adversaries for load balancing strategies [13]. The geometric tree (T2L) appears to be easy to balance in practice. Number of tasks: 96,793,509 (`uts` T2L) and 111,345,630 (`uts` T3L).

Rectangular matrix multiplication. Given N, compute the product of two random rectangular $N \times N$ matrices A and B. We use the `matmul` algorithm from the Cilk benchmark set. Number of tasks: 3,595,117 (`matmul` 4096).

Benchmark	Lace		Speedup		Benchmark	Wool		Speedup	
	T_1	T_{48}	T_S/T_{48}	T_1/T_{48}		T_1	T_{48}	T_S/T_{48}	T_1/T_{48}
fib 50	144	4.13	34.5	34.9	fib 50	185	4.38	34.1	42.2
uts T2L	86.0	1.81	46.1	47.4	uts T2L	85.1	2.00	42.5	42.5
uts T3L	44.2	2.23	18.7	19.9	uts T3L	44.3	2.12	19.4	20.9
queens 15	602	12.63	42.2	47.7	queens 15	539	11.23	47.5	48.0
matmul 4096	781	16.46	47.0	47.5	matmul 4096	780	16.40	47.2	47.5
	Private deque					T_S		Sequential	
fib 50	208	5.22	23.2	39.8	fib 50	149.2	-	-	-
uts T2L	86.1	1.83	45.7	47.0	uts T2L	84.5	-	-	-
uts T3L	44.8	2.55	17.3	17.5	uts T3L	43.11	-	-	-
queens 15	541	11.34	43.3	47.7	queens 15	533	-	-	-
matmul 4096	774	16.34	47.3	47.4	matmul 4096	773	-	-	-

Fig. 5. Averages of running times (seconds) for all benchmarks. Speedups are calculated relative to both the time of the sequential version (T_S) and the parallel version with one worker (T_1). Each T_{48} data point is the average of 50 measurements. Each T_1/T_S data point is the average of 20 measurements.

4.2 Results

Our test machine has four twelve-core AMD Opteron 6168 processors. The system has 128 GB of RAM and runs Scientific Linux 6.0 with kernel version 2.6.32. We considered using less than 48 cores to reduce the effects of operating system interference, but we did not see significant effects in practice. We compiled the benchmarks using gcc 4.7.2 with flag -O3.

See Figure 5 for the results of the benchmark set. Each T_{48} data point is the average of 50 measurements. Each T_1 and T_S data point is the average of 20 measurements. This resulted in measurements with three significant digits. In general, Figure 5 shows similar performance for all three algorithms. The three benchmarks uts T2L, queens and matmul are trivial to parallelize and have no extra overhead with 48 workers, i.e., $T_1/T_{48} \approx 48$.

Comparing T_S and T_1 for all benchmarks, we see that the overhead of work-stealing is small for all three work-stealing algorithms, with the exception of the fib benchmark. For benchmark fib with our algorithm, $T_1 < T_S$, which appears to be related to compiler optimizations. During implementation, we observed that variation in T_1 is often related to code generation by the compiler. In some cases, removing unused variables and other minor changes even increased T_1 by up to 20%. It is therefore difficult to draw strong conclusions regarding the overhead of the algorithms, except that it is small compared to the sequential program.

We measured the runtimes of fib and uts T3L using 4, 8, 16, 24, 32 and 40 workers to obtain the speedup graph in Figure 6. This graph suggests that the fib benchmark scales well and that similar results may be obtained using a higher number of processors in the future. The scalability of the uts T3L benchmark appears to be limited after 16 workers. We discuss this benchmark below.

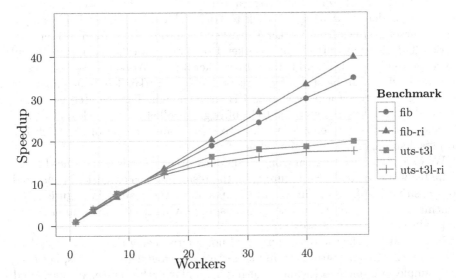

Fig. 6. Absolute speedup graph (T_1/T_N) of the `fib` and `uts` T3L benchmarks using Lace with our algorithm and Lace with the private deque receiver initiated (`-ri`) algorithm. Each data point is based on the average of 20 measurements.

Benchm.	#steals	#leaps	#grows	#shrinks
fib 50	865	50,569	70,789	97,750
uts T2L	4,554	82,440	72,222	57,701
uts T3L	158,566	4,443,432	2,173,006	846,509
queens 15	1,964	6,053	5,694	6,618
matmul 4096	2,492	12,456	13,081	9,911

Fig. 7. The average total number of steals, leaps, grows and shrinks over 7 runs with 48 workers

Algo.	T_1	T_{48}	T_1/T_{48}
Lace	44.26	1.154	38.3
Private	44.83	1.240	36.2
Wool	44.27	1.172	37.8

Fig. 8. Averages of runtimes (seconds) of `uts` T3L with transitive leapfrogging (Wool) or random stealing (Lace/Private)

We also measured the average number of steals during a parallel run with 48 workers. See Figure 7. We make a distinction between normal stealing when a worker is idle, and leapfrogging when a worker is stalled because of unfinished stolen work. We also measured the amount of split point changes by `grow_shared` and `shrink_shared`. The number of 'grows' indicates how often thieves set `splitreq`. The number of 'shrinks' is equal to the number of memory fences. In the `uts` T3L benchmark, the high number of leaps and split point changes may indicate that the stolen subtrees were relatively small.

4.3   Extending Leapfrogging

Benchmark `uts` T3L appears to be a good adversary for all three algorithms. This is partially related to the leapfrogging strategy, which forces workers that wait for the result of stolen tasks to steal from the thief. This strategy can result in chains of thieves waiting for work to trickle down the chain. For example, when worker 2 steals from worker 1, worker 1 will only steal from worker 2. If worker 3 steals from worker 2 and worker 4 steals from worker 3, new tasks will be generated by worker 4 and stolen by worker 3 first. Worker 3 then generates new work which can be stolen by workers 2 and 4. Worker 1 only acquires new work if the subtree stolen by worker 4 is large enough. The updated version of Wool [8] implements an extension to leapfrogging, called transitive leapfrogging[2]. Transitive leapfrogging enables workers to steal from the thief of the thief, i.e., still steal subtasks of the original stolen task.

We extended Lace to steal from a random worker whenever the thief has no available work to steal. See Figure 8 for the results of this extension, compared to transitive leapfrogging in Wool. Compared to the results in Figure 5, all benchmarks now have reasonable speedups, improving from a speedup of 20x to a speedup of 36x with 48 workers.

Our extension has the disadvantage of not guaranteeing the upper bound on the stack size that leapfrogging and transitive leapfrogging does. It is, however, very simple to implement, while resulting in similar performance. We measured the peak stack depth with the uts T3L benchmark for all 48 workers. We observed an increase from a peak stack depth of 6500-12500 tasks with normal leapfrogging to 17000-21000 tasks with the random stealing extension. Since every task descriptor for uts T3L is 64 bytes large (including padding), this strategy required at most 1 extra megabyte per worker for uts T3L. We also observed that the number of 'grows' decreased by 50%.

5   Conclusion

In this paper, we presented a new non-blocking split deque for work-stealing. Our design has the advantage that it does not require memory fences for local deque operations, except when reclaiming tasks from the shared portion of the deque. Furthermore, we implemented this deque in a C library called Lace, which has an interface similar to Wool. This framework has the advantage of a small source code footprint. We also implemented the receiver-initiated version of the private deque algorithm described by Acar et al. in Lace.

Our experiments show that our algorithm is competitive with Wool and with the private deque algorithm. We gain near optimal speedup for several benchmarks, with very limited overhead compared to the sequential program. Extending leapfrogging with random stealing greatly improves scalability for the uts T3L benchmark.

Several open questions remain. When growing the shared deque, the new split point is the average of split and head, and when shrinking the shared deque, the new split point is the average of tail and head. It is unknown whether more optimal strategies exist. A limitation of our approach is that tasks can only be

---

[2] This feature is documented in the distribution of Wool version 0.1.5alpha, which is currently available at http://www.sics.se/~kff/wool/

stolen at the tail of the deque. This limits work-stealing strategies. Designs that allow stealing any task may be useful for some applications. Our benchmarks all consist of uniformly small tasks. Benchmarking on larger or irregular sized tasks may be disadvantageous for the private deque algorithm, since it requires owner cooperation on every steal. Finally, we performed our experiments on a single NUMA machine. On such machines, communication costs are low compared to distributed systems. It may be interesting to compare the work-stealing algorithms on a cluster of computers using a shared-memory abstraction. Especially steal-multiple strategies may be more beneficial when communication is more expensive.

References

1. Acar, U.A., Charguéraud, A., Rainey, M.: Scheduling parallel programs by work stealing with private deques. In: PPOPP, pp. 219–228. ACM (2013)
2. Arora, N.S., Blumofe, R.D., Plaxton, C.G.: Thread Scheduling for Multiprogrammed Multiprocessors. Theory Comput. Syst. 34(2), 115–144 (2001)
3. Blumofe, R.D., Joerg, C.F., Kuszmaul, B.C., Leiserson, C.E., Randall, K.H., Zhou, Y.: Cilk: An Efficient Multithreaded Runtime System. J. Parallel Distrib. Comput. 37(1), 55–69 (1996)
4. Blumofe, R.D., Leiserson, C.E.: Scheduling Multithreaded Computations by Work Stealing. In: FOCS, pp. 356–368. IEEE Computer Society (1994)
5. Chase, D., Lev, Y.: Dynamic circular work-stealing deque. In: SPAA, pp. 21–28. ACM (2005)
6. Dinan, J., Larkins, D.B., Sadayappan, P., Krishnamoorthy, S., Nieplocha, J.: Scalable work stealing. In: SC. ACM (2009)
7. Faxén, K.F.: Wool-A work stealing library. SIGARCH Computer Architecture News 36(5), 93–100 (2008)
8. Faxén, K.F.: Efficient Work Stealing for Fine Grained Parallelism. In: ICPP, pp. 313–322. IEEE Computer Society (2010)
9. Frigo, M., Leiserson, C.E., Randall, K.H.: The Implementation of the Cilk-5 Multithreaded Language. In: PLDI, pp. 212–223. ACM (1998)
10. Hendler, D., Lev, Y., Moir, M., Shavit, N.: A dynamic-sized nonblocking work stealing deque. Distributed Computing 18(3), 189–207 (2006)
11. Hendler, D., Shavit, N.: Non-blocking steal-half work queues. In: PODC, pp. 280–289. ACM (2002)
12. Michael, M.M., Vechev, M.T., Saraswat, V.A.: Idempotent work stealing. In: PPOPP, pp. 45–54. ACM (2009)
13. Olivier, S., Huan, J., Liu, J., Prins, J., Dinan, J., Sadayappan, P., Tseng, C.W.: UTS: An Unbalanced Tree Search Benchmark. In: Almási, G.S., Caşcaval, C., Wu, P. (eds.) KSEM 2006. LNCS, vol. 4382, pp. 235–250. Springer, Heidelberg (2007)
14. Podobas, A., Brorsson, M.: A comparison of some recent task-based parallel programming models. In: Programmability Issues for Multi-Core Computers (MULTIPROG 2010), Pisa (January 2010)
15. Sundell, H., Tsigas, P.: Brushing the Locks out of the Fur: A Lock-Free Work Stealing Library Based on Wool. In: The Second Swedish Workshop on Multi-Core Computing MCC 2009. University of Borås. School of Business and Informatics (2009)
16. Wagner, D.B., Calder, B.: Leapfrogging: A portable technique for implementing efficient futures. In: PPOPP, pp. 208–217. ACM (1993)

Evaluating Execution Time Predictability of Task-Based Programs on Multi-Core Processors

Thomas Grass[1,2], Alejandro Rico[2], Marc Casas[2],
Miquel Moreto[1,2], and Alex Ramirez[1,2]

[1] Universitat Politècnica de Catalunya, 08034, Barcelona, Spain
[2] Barcelona Supercomputing Center, 08034, Barcelona, Spain

Abstract. Task-based programming models are becoming increasingly important, as they can reduce the synchronization costs of parallel programs on multi-cores. Instances of the same task type in task-based programs consist of the same code, which leads us to the hypothesis that their performance should be regular and thus their execution time should be predictable. We evaluate this hypothesis for a set of 12 task-based programs on 4 different machines: a high-end Intel SandyBridge, an IBM POWER7, an ARM Cortex-A9 and an ARM Cortex-A15. We show, that predicting execution time assuming performance regularity can lead to errors of up to 92%. We identify and analyze three sources of execution time impredictability: input dependence, multiple behaviors per task type and resource sharing. We present two models based on linear interpolation and clustering, reducing the prediction error to less than 12% for input dependent task types and to less than 2% for task types with multiple classes of behavior. All in all, this work invalidates the assumption that performance is always regular across instances of the same task type and quantifies its variability on a wide range of benchmarks and multi-core systems.

Keywords: Execution Time Predictability, Task-Based Programming Models, Multi-Core.

1 Introduction

Multi-core systems are integrating an increasing number of processor cores on a single chip. This makes it difficult for programmers to exploit the available on-chip thread-level parallelism.

Task-based programming models allow the programmer to specify program parts called *tasks*. Tasks may execute concurrently and are typically instantiated many times during execution. A runtime environment dynamically maps task instances to threads. The intuitive program partitioning improves programmability. At the same time, dynamic task scheduling reduces the inherent synchronization costs of other shared memory programming models thanks to a better load balancing [1].

The fact that all instances of the same task type consist of the same static code suggests that they should exhibit similar performance and execution time and,

L. Lopes et al. (Eds.): Euro-Par 2014 Workshops, Part II, LNCS 8806, pp. 218–229, 2014.

therefore, execution time should be predictable. In this paper, we investigate the execution time predictability of task-based programs based on performance regularity. We carry out an analysis on four different state-of-the-art multi-core machines, two based on ARM Cortex-A9 MPCore and Cortex-A15 MPCore mobile CPUs, and the other two based on high-end Intel Sandy Bridge and IBM POWER7 CPUs. This allows us to investigate if performance regularity depends on the architecture. We expect performance variability to increase when increasing the number of execution threads competing for shared resources. Therefore, we analyze performance variability on a per-task-instance basis for thread counts ranging from one to the number of cores on each machine. We reach similar conclusions for the different machines, but find that architectures with more aggressive performance optimizations show a higher performance variability.

We identify three sources of variability across instances of the same task type: input dependence, multiple classes of behavior and contention on accessing shared resources. For programs suffering from resource contention, we investigate how sharing decreases performance and increases performance variability. We also present a model based on linear interpolation to predict execution time of input dependent task types. Furthermore, we use a clustering algorithm to identify different behaviors in the same task type. Using our interpolation model and clustering algorithm, we dramatically increase the accuracy of execution time prediction. Prediction errors over 80% are reduced to less than 12% for input dependent cases and less than 2% on the presence of multiple behaviors.

The contributions of this paper are the following:

- An analysis of performance variability across instances of the same task type in task-based programs running on multi-core systems. This analysis shows the variability on an instance by instance basis.
- A classification of sources of execution time variability on instances of the same task type.
- A low-complexity model based on linear interpolation for predicting the execution time of a task instance as a function of its instruction count.
- The use of a clustering algorithm to identify different classes of behavior in the same task type. In our example, we successfully classify task instances into clusters that exhibit, each of them, regular performance.

2   Related Work

To the best of our knowledge, this is the first analysis of execution time predictability on task-based programs. However, there are other performance analyses of task-based programs focusing on other aspects.

Duran et al. [4] present a benchmark suite consisting of task-based OpenMP programs. They give examples for different kinds of performance analyses of these benchmarks. They evaluate total execution time as a function of various parameters such as processor count and task creation cut-off parameters. Other works [14,15] investigate task granularity and task creation cost as performance-limiting factors in task-based programs. However, these works neither analyze performance on a per-task-instance basis nor task execution time predictability.

There are other works that use analytical models to predict execution time [8,10,6]. These works use mathematical models to compute the delays of certain events during execution. Most past works compute delays for events at the instruction-level, such as instruction issue and commit, branch mispredictions and cache misses. Our model works at a coarser granularity by computing the delay of whole individual tasks.

Performance predictability of parallel applications on large HPC systems has been explored from many perspectives. Some approaches combine the efficiency of analytical models with the accuracy of simulation to generate accurate and fast performance predictions [16]. Other approaches [9] explore performance predictability by developing application-specific performance models, which are formulated from an analysis of the code, inspection of key data structures, and analysis of traces gathered at runtime. While this methodology provides fast and accurate predictions, it is application specific and it requires a deep understanding of the scientific codes. These works target MPI applications while the work in this paper focuses on shared memory task-based programs.

3   Execution Time Predictability of Task-Based Programs

Many parallel implementations of numerical algorithms decompose the problem domain into sub-domains called *blocks* or *tiles*. In task-based programming models the programmer specifies parts of a program as work units called *tasks*, each one to perform a different operation. A task is usually instantiated many times, each instance performing the common operation of the task on a separate block or tile. Task instances can be scheduled to threads whenever they have their dependencies satisfied. Typically, a thread executes many task instances before reaching a synchronization point.

The fact that instances of the same task type consist of the same code leads us to the assumption that they consist of similar numbers of instructions, exhibit similar performance and therefore their execution time is predictable. However, this assumption turns out to be wrong in some cases. Fig. 1 shows the total execution time prediction error for a set of task based programs, assuming the time of the first or the second executed instance for all instances of a task type. The error is calculated according to Eqn. 1, with T the set of task instances of the same task type, C_{Sample} the cycle count of the sample task instance and C_i the cycle count of task instance i. We only investigate time spent in task execution and ignore operating system and runtime system overheads.

$$Err = \left(1 - \left|\frac{\sum_{i \in T} C_{Sample}}{\sum_{i \in T} C_i}\right|\right) \cdot 100\% \tag{1}$$

Before conducting our detailed analysis, we envision three potential sources of performance variability that potentially degrade performance predictability:

- *Input dependence*: The behavior of a task instance is input dependent. An example is sparse algorithms in which task instances perform different amounts of computation or exhibit different memory access patterns.

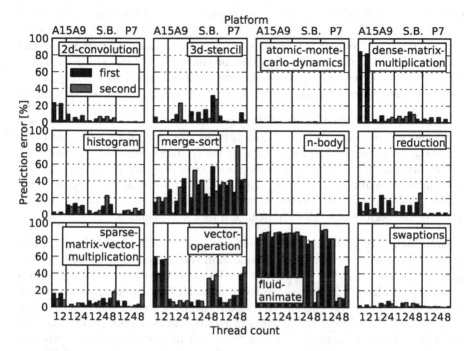

Fig. 1. Percent error when assuming the execution time of the first / second executed task instance for all task instances to predict total execution time. Results shown for four different machines (see Tab. 2) and different thread counts.

- *Several types of behavior per task type*: Task instances of the same type perform one out of several possible types of computation. An example is recursive algorithms in which some task instances create more child tasks, while others perform the actual computation when the recursion terminates.
- *Shared resources contention*: Multiple threads interfere with each other when accessing shared resources. Different instances of the same task type may suffer from different degrees of interference caused by other threads running in the system and accessing shared resources. This includes shared caches, interconnect structures and memory bandwidth.

4 Experimental Setup

In this section we present the experimental setup used for the performance analysis in this paper. First, we give a brief overview of OmpSs [5], the task-based programming model used for our analysis. Afterwards, we explain how we measure the performance of OmpSs programs on a per-task basis. We present the investigated benchmarks and explain how we configured them to obtain meaningful results. Finally, we present the platforms on which we run our experiments.

Programming Model: OmpSs is an extension of OpenMP 3.0. It consists of the Mercurium compiler and the NANOS++ runtime environment. In addition to the features of OpenMP 3.0, it allows to annotate tasks with data inputs and outputs. The NANOS++ runtime system automatically manages inter-task data dependencies and schedules and synchronizes task instances accordingly. These OmpSs features were included in the recent OpenMP 4.0 specification.

Measuring the Performance of Tasks: We measure cycle count, instruction count and numbers of L1 (data), L2 (data) and L3 cache misses using hardware performance counters. We modify Mercurium to insert calls to a low-overhead instrumentation library at the beginning and the end of each task instance. This instrumentation library is an interface to the PAPI library [3]. Since NANOS++ can suspend a task instance before it completes, we also instrument NANOS++ to pause the performance measurement if a task is suspended.

Benchmarks: In this paper we investigate a set of 12 parallel benchmarks. They are task-based programs implemented in the OmpSs programming model. The benchmarks and their key characteristics are listed in Tab. 1. They cover a wide range of algorithms that are widely used in HPC scientific applications and include programs with different compute-to-memory ratios, different memory access patterns and different amounts of parallelism and synchronization. The first ten benchmarks have been successfully used in previous works to evaluate HPC clusters [12,13], while *fluidanimate* and *swaptions* are part of the PARSEC benchmark suite [2]. As we conduct this work, these are the only benchmarks of the PARSEC suite for which there is an OmpSs implementation available. We perform ten executions of each benchmark for each configuration and choose the fastest one for our evaluation to minimize OS noise.

Application Tuning: We classified the benchmarks according to whether they are compute-intensive or not. Because the working sets of all concurrently executing task instances fit into the last level cache, we considered the following benchmarks as compute-intensive: *2d-convolution*, *3d-stencil*, *atomic-monte-carlo-dynamics*, *merge-sort*, *dense-matrix-multiplication*, *fluidanimate* and *swaptions*.

We optimized compute-intensive benchmarks by adjusting the task working set to fit into the on-chip last-level cache. This is one of the most straightforward optimizations applied by programmers in blocked numerical algorithms. The most cache constrained configuration is the Cortex-A9 running with four threads. Therefore, we adjusted the task working set to fit a fourth of the last-level cache in the Cortex-A9 chip. We use the same configuration for all platforms to have the same basis for comparison.

For the remaining benchmarks, we configured the task working set for the resulting task instances to be at least 100 000 instructions long. By doing so, we ensure that the time spent in task execution is significantly larger than the time spent in performance measurement code. The number of task instances per

Table 1. Investigated benchmarks

Benchmark	Properties
2d-convolution	Strided accesses
3d-stencil	Strided accesses
atomic-monte-carlo-dynamics	Embarrassingly parallel
dense-matrix-multiplication	High data reuse, compute bound
histogram	Atomic operations
merge-sort	Recursion, many synchronizations
n-body	Irregular memory accesses
reduction	Parallelism decreases over time
sparse-matrix-vector-multiplication	Load imbalance, memory bound
vector-operation	Regular, memory bound
fluidanimate	Variable task instance size
swaptions	Regular, computation bound

Table 2. Investigated machines

Micro-arch.	Cores	L1 size	L2 size	L3 size	Memory
ARM Cortex-A15 MPCore	2	32KB+32KB per core	1MB shared	n/a	2GB 32-bit DDR3L-1600
ARM Cortex-A9 MPCore	4	32KB+32KB per core	1MB shared	n/a	2GB 32-bit DDR3L-1500[1]
Intel Sandy Bridge	8	32KB+32KB per core	256KB per core	20MB shared	32GB 64-bit DDR3-1600
IBM POWER7	8	32KB+32KB per core	256KB per core	32MB shared	64GB 64-bit DDR3-1600

application is adjusted to a large enough number so there is enough parallelism to use all threads at all times.

Investigated Platforms: Tab. 2 gives an overview of the characteristics of the four machines used for the evaluation in this paper. The first two platforms are based on low-power mobile systems-on-a-chip, while the other two are high-end machines used in HPC environments. This selection of machines covers three of the most important ISAs nowadays: x86-64, POWER ISA, and ARMv7. Even

---

[1] DDR3L-1600 connected to a 750MHz interface.

though ARM microprocessors are not used in HPC environments yet, there is an increasing interest in integrating ARM chips in future server and HPC machines [7,13]. Besides, these four machines cover a wide range of performance levels as well as different ISAs, CPU, cache and memory technologies.

5   Evaluation

The results of the experiments conducted in the scope of this paper show that, despite the obvious intuition, performance can be irregular across the instances of the same task type. This directly affects execution time prediction (shown in Fig. 1). In this section, we first show the results of our performance analysis on a per-task-instance basis. Afterwards, we present a case of input dependent task behavior and present a model to estimate the execution time of a task instance as a function of its instruction count. We also show a case of multiple classes of behavior within a single task type. We use a clustering technique to distinguish different classes of behavior and improve execution time predictability. Finally, we explain how resource sharing affects performance regularity and analyze contention on different resources in the memory hierarchy.

5.1   Per-Task-Instance Performance Analysis

Fig. 2 shows boxplots of the measured instructions per cycle (IPC) per task type. Each chart corresponds to one task type and shows the measured results on four different platforms. Only one thread per core is executed in each experiment, which limits the configurations to two threads (Cortex-A15), four threads (Cortex-A9), and eight threads (Intel Sandy Bridge and IBM POWER7). The solid box contains the interquartile range of the measured IPC values of all instances of the respective task type, i.e., 50% of the observations are within this range. The horizontal line within the box indicates the median. The whiskers extend from the 5th to the 95th percentile. The lower and upper 5% of the measured IPC values are treated as outliers.

Most of the investigated benchmarks only have one task type, whereas *merge-sort*, *n-body* and *reduction* have two and *fluidanimate* has eight. The different task types of *fluidanimate* show similar performance variability. Therefore, we limit our evaluations to the task type ComputeForcesMT which accounts for 40% of *fluidanimate*'s total instruction count.

In our results we observe two general classes of behavior. The first class consists of benchmarks for which IPC does not significantly degrade when increasing the number of execution threads. This behaviour is exposed by the benchmarks *2d-convolution*, *atomic-monte-carlo-dynamics*, *merge-sort* (both tasks), *n-body* (both tasks), *reduction* (both tasks), *fluidanimate* (all task types) and *swaptions*. We make the important observation that *2-d convolution*, *atomic-monte-carlo-dynamics* and *n-body* (task type 1) present a nearly constant IPC with very low variability. This behavior is persistent across the different platforms.

The second class of behavior consists of the benchmarks for which IPC degrades when increasing the number of execution threads. This phenomenon is

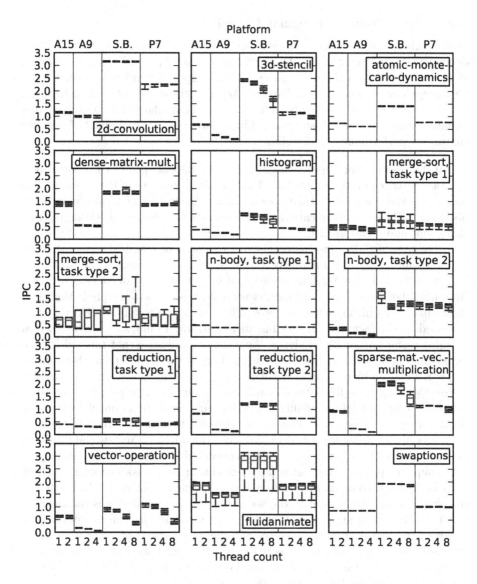

Fig. 2. IPC variation per task type on four different platforms (ARM Cortex-A9 and A15, Intel Sandy Bridge and IBM POWER7)

known as work time inflation [11]. In our benchmark suite, this behavior is exposed by the benchmarks *3d-stencil*, *histogram*, *sparse-matrix-vector-multiplication* and *vector-operation*. For these benchmarks, we also observe an increasing performance variability. Note that the variability shown in Fig. 2 directly relates to the prediction error shown in Fig. 1.

5.2   Predictability of Irregular Behavior

In this subsection we identify three sources of irregular behavior, namely input dependence, multiple classes of behavior per task type and resource sharing. We predict execution time of task types with input dependent behavior using an interpolation-based model. For task types with several classes of behavior we use a clustering algorithm to detect clusters of similar behavior and predict execution time on a per-cluster basis. Finally, we analyze the impact of resource sharing on performance predictability.

Input Dependence: Input dependence is the dependence of the control flow of a task instance on the input data. Fig. 3 shows heatmaps of the programs *fluidanimate* and *merge-sort*. Heatmaps are a representation of a two-dimensional histogram. The colours indicate how many task instances have a certain instruction count and a certain IPC.

In the case of *fluidanimate*, the instruction count of task instances varies between 1 million and 70 million instructions, while IPC tends to be higher for higher instruction counts. This results in different numbers of execution cycles. Assuming the same cycle count for all task instances leads to the prediction error shown in Fig. 1 which reaches over 80%. The instruction count and IPC variation is caused by the fact that all task instances perform an index computation that is highly inefficient for high indexes. We want to emphasize that this index computation is part of the default implementation of the *fluidanimate* benchmark and is not caused by porting the benchmark to the OmpSs programming model.

For the programs *fluidanimate* and *merge-sort* (task type 1) we apply a sampling-based model to predict execution time as a function of instruction count for all task instances. This model assumes that the instruction count of each task instance is known apriori and works as follows. First, we add instruction count and execution time of the first executed task instance to the (empty) set of support points. Afterwards, for each encountered task instance we check if its instruction count is less than 90% of the smallest or more than 110% of the largest instruction count in the set of support points. If this is the case, we add it to the set of support points. Otherwise, we predict the execution time by linear interpolation within the set of support points or by constant extrapolation in the range outside the support points. Fig. 4 shows that the error of the total execution time prediction based on this model stays below 12% for all configurations on the Intel Sandy Bridge machine.

Multiple Behaviors Per Task Type: For *merge-sort* (task type 2) we observe two clusters in the heatmap plot, indicating two different behaviors. Strictly speaking, this is also a case of input dependence. However, the difference to the type of input dependence covered in the previous section is that there are multiple classes of behavior. This is caused by the recursive implementation of the merge sort algorithm. A task instance either creates two child instances, resulting in the cluster on the left, or it performs a sorting operation, resulting in the cluster on the right. Predicting execution time based on the assumption of regular execution time and IPC leads to the error shown in Fig. 1.

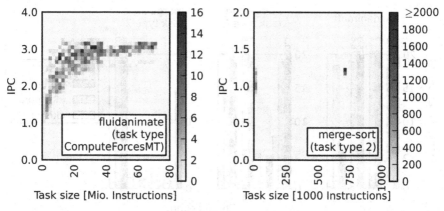

Fig. 3. Instruction count vs. IPC histogram of benchmarks *fluidanimate* (task type ComputeForcesMT) and *merge-sort* (task type 2)

For the aforementioned case, we perform a k-means clustering of all task instances into two clusters, according to their instruction count. For each cluster, we determine the centroid and chose the task instance closest to the centroid as a representative of the respective cluster. Finally, we estimate the total execution time of each cluster by multiplying the execution time of the representative by the number of task instances in the cluster. Fig. 4 shows that the error of the total execution time prediction based on this method is smaller than 2% for all configurations on the Intel Sandy Bridge machine.

Resource Sharing: The third source of irregular behavior we identified is resource sharing. In the following, we present four examples of resource sharing. These examples have in common that contention on shared resources affects the performance of task instances of the same task type to a different extent. This increases performance variability and thus decreases performance predictability. Fig. 5 shows boxplots of L2 data cache and L3 cache misses per 1000 executed instructions (misses per kilo-instruction, MPKI) of the benchmarks for which we observed a decrease of IPC for increasing thread counts. The measured number of L3 cache misses includes misses caused by L2 data cache misses due to the limitations of the available hardware performance counters.

For *3d-stencil* we observe an increase of L2 MPKI when increasing the number of threads. However, L3 MPKI stays nearly constantly low. Our theory is that the increased L2 MPKI is caused by invalidations of data residing in the private L2 caches by other threads.

The *histogram* benchmark shows not only an increase of L2 MPKI for increasing thread counts, but also an increase in L2 MPKI variability. For increasing thread counts there might be several threads competing to execute an atomic operation, resulting in higher contention. Furthermore, the execution of the atomic operation itself can invalidate data in other threads' private caches.

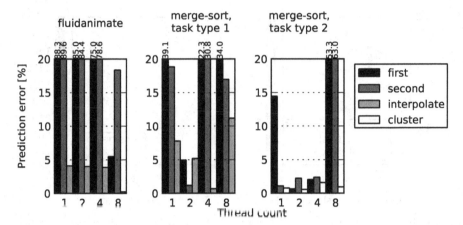

Fig. 4. Execution time prediction error using interpolation model (*fluidanimate* and *merge-sort*, task type 1) and clustering (*merge-sort*, task type 2)

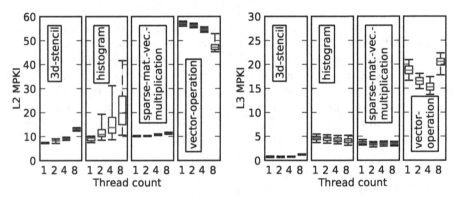

Fig. 5. L2 data and L3 cache misses per 1000 instructions (MPKI) for *3d-stencil*, *histogram*, *sparse-matrix-vector-multiplication* and *vector-operation*, executed on Intel Sandy Bridge with 1, 2, 4 and 8 threads

In case of *sparse-matrix-vector-multiplication*, L2 MPKI and L3 MPKI are nearly constant for increasing thread counts. Since the benchmark does not use shared data, the decrease in IPC has to occur due to the limited capacity of shared resources, e.g. memory bandwidth or cache bandwidth.

For *vector-operation* we observe a decrease of L2 MPKI when increasing the number of execution threads. As memory bandwidth saturates for increasing thread counts, threads progress at a slower rate and thus cause less demand misses in the L2 cache.

6   Conclusions and Future Work

The analysis in this paper shows that the naive assumption of regular performance within a task type is not always valid. However, we show that accurate performance predictions can be derived from detailed performance information of a relatively small number of task instances.

We present techniques to improve prediction accuracy for task types with irregular performance. These techniques are based on linear interpolation and clustering. The prediction error is reduced from over 80% to less than 12% for input dependent cases and less than 2% when having multiple classes of behavior. Further research is needed to improve execution time predictability of task-based programs experiencing contention on shared resources.

We envision a potential application of the insights in this paper in the fields of multi-core architecture simulation and dynamic task scheduling on multi-cores. If the performance of a task type is predictable it is only necessary to simulate a subset of all task instances, and smart scheduling techniques can be applied with apriori-knowledge of the execution time of a task instance.

References

1. Amarasinghe, S., et al.: ASCR programming challenged for exascale computing. Report of the 2011 Workshop on Exascale Programming Challenges (2011)
2. Bienia, C., et al.: Benchmarking Modern Multiprocessors. PhD thesis, Princeton University (January 2011)
3. Browne, S., et al.: A portable programming interface for performance evaluation on modern processors. Journal of High Performance Computing Applications 14(3), 189–204 (2000)
4. Duran, A., et al.: Barcelona openmp tasks suite: A set of benchmarks targeting the exploitation of task parallelism in openmp. In: ICPP 2009, pp. 124–131 (2009)
5. Duran, A., et al.: OmpSs: a proposal for programming heterogeneous multi-core architectures. Parallel Processing Letters 21(02), 173–193 (2011)
6. Genbrugge, D., et al.: Interval Simulation: Raising the Level of Abstraction in Architectural Simulation. In: HPCA 2010, pp. 1–12 (2010)
7. Halfhill, T.R.: ARM's 64-Bit Makeover. Microprocessor Report (December 24, 2012)
8. Karkhanis, T.S., et al.: A first-order superscalar processor model. In: ISCA, Washington, DC, USA, p. 338 (2004)
9. Kerbyson, D.J., et al.: Predictive Performance and Scalability Modeling of a Large-scale Application. In: Supercomputing 2001, p. 37 (2001)
10. Nussbaum, S., et al.: Modeling superscalar processors via statistical simulation. In: PACT, pp. 15–24 (2001)
11. Olivier, S.L., et al.: Characterizing and mitigating work time inflation in task parallel programs. In: 2012 International Conference for High Performance Computing, Networking, Storage and Analysis (SC), pp. 1–12. IEEE (2012)
12. Rajovic, N., et al.: Experiences with Mobile Processors for Energy Efficient HPC. In: DATE 2013, pp. 464–468 (2013)
13. Rajovic, N., et al.: Supercomputing with Commodity CPUs: Are Mobile SoCs Ready for HPC? In: SC 2013 (2013)
14. Rico, A., et al.: Available Task-level Parallelism on the Cell BE. Scientific Programming 17(1-2), 59–76 (2009)
15. Schmidl, D., Philippen, P., Lorenz, D., Rössel, C., Geimer, M., an Mey, D., Mohr, B., Wolf, F.: Performance analysis techniques for task-based openMP applications. In: Chapman, B.M., Massaioli, F., Müller, M.S., Rorro, M. (eds.) IWOMP 2012. LNCS, vol. 7312, pp. 196–209. Springer, Heidelberg (2012)
16. Snavely, A., et al.: A Framework for Performance Modeling and Prediction. In: Supercomputing 2002, pp. 1–17 (2002)

SchedMon: A Performance and Energy Monitoring Tool for Modern Multi-cores

Luís Taniça, Aleksandar Ilic, Pedro Tomás, and Leonel Sousa

INESC-ID/IST, Universidade de Lisboa, Lisbon, Portugal
{Luis.Tanica,Aleksandar.Ilic,Pedro.Tomas,Leonel.Sousa}@inesc-id.pt

Abstract. Accurate characterization of modern systems and applications requires run-time and simultaneous assessment of several execution-related parameters. Although hardware monitoring facilities in modern multi cores allow low-level profiling, it is not always easy to convert the acquired data into insightful information. For this, a low-overhead monitoring tool (SchedMon) is proposed herein, which relies on hardware facilities and interacts with the operating system scheduler to capture the run-time behavior of single and multi-threaded applications, even in presence of nested parallelism. By tracking the attainable performance, power and energy consumption of monitored applications, SchedMon also allows their insightful characterization with the Cache-aware Roofline model. In addition, the proposed tool provides application monitoring, either in their entirety or at the level of the function calls, without requiring any changes to the original source code. Experimental results show that SchedMon introduces negligible execution overheads, while capturing the interference of several co-scheduled SPEC2006 applications.

Keywords: Power and performance monitoring, application characterization, power and performance counters.

1 Introduction

Modern computing systems are complex heterogeneous platforms capable of sustaining high computing power. However, taking advantage of such complex systems requires accurate real-time monitoring tools to characterize the execution of running application. As such, these tools allow identifying possible application and architecture performance bottlenecks for real-case scenarios, thus giving both the programmer and the computer architect hints on potential optimization targets. While many profiling tools are developed in the last years, *e.g.*, PAPI [4] and OProfile [5], it is not always easy to convert the acquired data into insightful information. This is particularly true for modern processors, which comprise very complex architectures, including deep memory hierarchy organizations, and for which several architectural events must be simultaneously analyzed.

Taking into account the complexity of modern processor architectures and the effects of having different applications running concurrently in multiple cores, the Cache-aware Roofline Model (CARM) [7] was proposed, which unveils architectural details that are fundamental in nowadays application and architectural

L. Lopes et al. (Eds.): Euro-Par 2014 Workshops, Part II, LNCS 8806, pp. 230–241, 2014.

optimization. The CARM [7] is a single-plot model that shows the practical limitations and performance upper-bound of modern multi-core general-purpose architectures. It models the attainable performance of a computer architecture by relating the peak floating-point performance (Flops/s), the operational intensity (Flops/byte), and the peak memory bandwidth for each cache level in the memory hierarchy (Bytes/s). Hence, the CARM considers data traffic across both on-chip and off-chip memory domains, as it is perceived by the core.

In this paper, a new application-oriented performance and energy monitoring tool (SchedMon) is proposed[1] that provides full control over the underlying hardware interfaces and translates their full functionality into an intuitive command-line interface. SchedMon allows not only to obtain the hardware event counts of the target application, but also to perform run-time sampling of the application execution either in its entirety or at the level of the function calls. As a result, it allows a finer granularity evaluation of the benchmarking application without requiring any changes to the original source code. In addition, SchedMon is not limited to single-threaded applications, as it allows per-thread monitoring of nested child threads and the complete scheduling path reconstruction of a multi-threaded application execution. Experimental results demonstrate that the proposed SchedMon is a highly accurate low overhead monitoring tool that also allows identifying the interference between multiple running applications.

2   Related Work

Most modern processors contain Performance Monitoring Units (PMUs) that can be configured to count micro-architectural events such as clock cycles, retired instructions, branch miss-predictions and cache misses. To count these events, a small set of Model-Specific Registers (MSRs) is provided, which limits the total number of events that can be simultaneously measured (*e.g.*, 4 on Intel Ivy Bridge and AMD Athlon, and 6 on ARM Cortex-A8).

Recent architectures also provide a set of specific MSRs that allow extracting power consumption information at runtime (*e.g.*, Running Average Power Limit (RAPL) on Intel [8] and "Current Power in Watts" MSR on AMD [2]). However, special permissions might be required in order to access these MSRs.

There are several options in the literature that provide access to performance and/or energy hardware counters, *e.g.*, perfctr [11] and perfmon2 [9] (deprecated from kernel 2.6.32) and perf_events [13], which are low-level interfaces. Perf_events is built around file descriptors, and it can be configured by using a single system call. Furthermore, from Linux kernel 3.14, it includes a RAPL interface. Nevertheless, both energy and performance MSRs can be assessed and configured through the Linux MSR driver.

Since the previous described interfaces are not always trivial for the common user, there are also several other tools that target flexibility and easy configuration. This is the case of PAPI [4], OProfile [5], perf [1], SpyMon [3] and LIKWID [12], among others. Some of these tools make use of the perf_events

---

[1] The proposed tool is available at http://sips.inesc-id.pt/tools/schedmon/

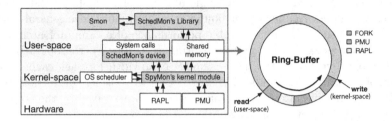

Fig. 1. SchedMon's components interaction and disposition in the OS privilege layers

interface in order to obtain its functionality (PAPI, OProfile and perf), while LIKWID uses the Linux MSR interface directly.

3   Scheduler-Based Monitoring Tool: SchedMon

The herein proposed SchedMon monitoring tool targets the profiling of complex applications with nested multi-threading, either in its entirety or at the level of user-specified functions. Accuracy of the measurements are achieved by interfacing with the Operating System (OS) scheduler such as to guarantee monitoring isolation from external threads. To fulfill the target objectives while imposing minimum overheads to the running applications, it encapsulates its full functionality in two specifically developed components, namely: *i*) a Linux kernel module, or driver, which implements the SchedMon core functionalities; and *ii*) a user-space tool (smon), which extracts the whole functionality of the underlying driver and translates it into a simple and intuitive user interface.

Figure 1 illustrates the disposition of the SchedMon's components in the OS privilege layers, as well as their interaction mechanisms. The communication between the user-space and the driver is made by means of memory mapping and I/O specific system-calls (mmap and ioctl) to the SchedMon's device. The SchedMon's device represents a specially created file in /dev directory, which triggers specific driver functions upon receiving the requests from the user-space. The set of user-space requests is integrated in the SchedMon's library to ease the access to the driver functionality from the smon user-space tool.

An additional communication mechanism between the main SchedMon's components is provided via a memory-mapped Ring-Buffer. The Ring-Buffer represents a shared memory medium between the user- and kernel-space, and it holds the requested monitoring information (samples). The monitoring samples are obtained by the Linux kernel module, which is responsible for the direct interaction with the hardware monitoring facilities. For example, the monitoring samples may refer to the performance and power/energy consumption information, which is obtained from the PMU and RAPL facilities, respectively. In addition, a set of software events is also provided as monitoring samples, e.g., task scheduling or fork events, which are obtained by direct interaction with the OS scheduler.

By coupling the functionality of the driver and `smon` tool, `SchedMon` also integrates novel approaches for performance analysis based on CARM and function call tracing, easing application performance evaluation and bottleneck detection.

3.1 SchedMon's Linux Driver

As previously referred, `SchedMon`'s driver integrates the main functionality of the tool. It is specifically designed to provide a finer control over the tool execution, as well as to reduce the amount of monitoring overheads.

Depending on the user-space request, different system call types trigger different operation modes in the `SchedMon`'s driver, namely:

- `ioctl` for setting event configurations and registering monitoring tasks;
- `mmap` for initializing the shared memory `Ring-Buffer`;
- `poll` to implement the synchronization mechanisms that coordinate the read and write operations over the allocated `Ring-Buffer`.

By relying on these calls, the full control and configuration of `SchedMon`'s driver can be attained from the user-space. In brief, these mechanisms allow exploiting the full functionality of the driver, including: *i*) profiling configuration (events, event-sets and profiling environment); *ii*) profiling of multi-threaded applications; *iii*) OS scheduling event detection; and *iv*) handling of different sample types, sampling methods and event multiplexing.

In particular, `SchedMon` keeps all the profiling configurations (events, event-sets and environment) inside the driver. As presented in Fig. 2, there are three main structures for registering the performance configurations, namely:

- `event` - holds configuration of an architecture-specific Performance Monitoring Event (PME), e.g., Intel's event-specific `PERFEVTSEL` configuration [8];
- `event-set` - a set of PMEs to be configured in the PMU, including selected Performance Fixed Counters (PFCs) [8];
- `environment` - contains all the profiling configurations for a specific execution monitoring, *e.g.*, required event-sets and sampling interval duration.

This hierarchal organization of profiling configuration allows not only reusing the same event configurations across different event-sets, but also reusing the same event-sets across distinct runs.

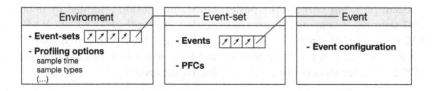

Fig. 2. `SchedMon` main structures for profiling configuration

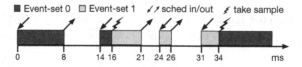

Fig. 3. Sampling process example for a sampling time interval of 20*ms* and 2 event-sets

When profiling multi-threaded applications, SchedMon differentiates two types of tasks: leaders and children. In detail, each application specified to the SchedMon from the user-space is appointed as a leader. In case of multi-threaded applications, each additional task descending from the leader is automatically registered into the driver (as a child) by inheriting the leader's environment. It is worth emphasizing that SchedMon does not only allow monitoring of the tasks that directly descend from the leader, but also monitoring of all the tasks that descend from the children, recursively.

The SchedMon driver also implements OS scheduling event detection in order to attain the full control over the execution of monitored tasks and to provide accurate monitoring information. For example, SchedMon provides a per-task monitoring isolation by detecting the exact intervals when the task is "scheduled in" or "scheduled out" to/from a specific Logical Processor Core (LPC). This also allows performing counter readings with low-overheads and without interrupting the task execution, i.e., in the interval after the current task is "scheduled out" and before the next task is "scheduled in". The overall scheduling event detection functionality relies on the following Linux tracepoints:

- sched_switch() is used to detect when a monitored task is scheduled in or out, in which case it performs the PMU context switch, by saving and restoring the PMU configuration and counts depending on the detected task;
- sched_process_exec() is used to initiate application monitoring exactly from the beginning of its execution;
- sched_process_fork() is used for detection of forked tasks (children) when profiling simple or nested multi-threaded applications;
- sched_migrate_task() is used to track migration of threads across LPCs;
- sched_process_exit() is used to detect the termination of monitored tasks.

Different sample types can be selected via the environment structure during the registration of a target task. SchedMon driver provides five sample types:

- PMU samples that contain the performance information (enabled by default);
- EPC samples for energy/power consumption information (e.g., via RAPL);
- MIG samples that provide migration information for a monitored task;
- FORK samples with the information about the generated children tasks;
- SCHED samples that contain context switch information.

In order to extract the profiling information at regular time intervals, the SchedMon driver also implements the sampling functionality. To obtain accurate samples that correspond to well defined application run-time intervals, SchedMon combines context switch detection with high-resolution timers (*i.e.*, samples are taken according to the run-time of the target task, which might not correspond to the wall-time). If more than one event-set is provided, SchedMon divides the sampling interval by the number of required event-sets. It then switches the event-sets in a round-robin fashion, thus allowing to virtually extend the limited number of available counters (event multiplexing). The final sample is obtained by scaling the counts from different event-sets based on the total number of retired instructions. To illustrate this process, Fig. 3 presents a real-case scenario with a 20ms sampling interval and two configured event-sets. As it can be seen, each event-set is assigned with a 10ms run-time sampling interval. Hence, the Event-set 0 counts are obtained at 16ms wall-time, since it refers to 10ms of task run-time (the task was scheduled out between 8ms and 14ms). Then, the PMU is configured for the Event-set 1 and the final sample is obtained at 34ms. When profiling multi-threaded applications, multiplexing is applied to each thread individually, thus providing samples per thread.

3.2   Smon: User-Space Tool

The SchedMon's user-space component, smon, is integrated in the tool in order to facilitate the access and handling of the underlying driver. The main functionalities of smon include: *i*) the creation of events; *ii*) the definition of event-sets; and *iii*) advanced application profiling and analysis, e.g., with CARM.

The herein proposed tool also integrates function call tracing, which refers to the process of performance monitoring at the level of a specific function within the monitored application. Smon implements this functionality by recurring to the ptrace() system call and by injecting a trap instruction at the entering and returning points of the target task function call (depicted as "CC" in Fig. 4). Smon is also able to detect whenever a new process is forked or switches its execution image, thus allowing call tracing for multi-threaded applications or even when different tasks execute distinct binaries.

In order to translate the SchedMon's full functionality to the end-user in a simple and intuitive way, Smon provides a command-line interface that is composed by the following 4 main commands:

- smon-event for inserting new PME configurations into the tool;
- smon-evset for defining new event-sets from already defined events;

```
00000000040057c <hello>:
  40057c: 55          CC      push    %rbp
  40057d: 48 89 e5            mov     %rsp,%rbp
  400580: bf a4 06 40 00      mov     $0x4006a4,%edi
  400585: e8 c6 fe ff ff      callq   400450 <puts@plt>
  40058a: 5d                  pop     %rbp
  40058b: c3          CC      retq
```

Fig. 4. Function call tracing instrumentation process

- smon-profile for profiling a specified application, where several additional parameters can be configured, such as sampling time interval, the required sample types, the shared-memory size and the event-sets;
- smon-carm for performance evaluation of the target application according to the CARM, with predefined event-set configurations and multiplexing.

4   Evaluation Results

To evaluate the proposed tool, we performed a set of experiments in a system with a quad-core Intel i7 3770K processor (Ivy Bridge), containing 8 LPCs in hyper-threading mode and a memory organization comprising 3 cache levels, i.e., L1 (32kB), L2 (256kB) and L3 (8MB). The L1 and L2 cache levels are shared among the LPCs within the same core, while the last level cache (L3) is shared among all the cores. The system contains a two-channel DDR3 DRAM memory, operating at 2×933MHz. During the experimental evaluation, the processor clock was set at a fixed frequency of 3.5GHz. Application characterization within the SchedMon tool is performed by relying on the built-in hardware monitoring facilities, i.e., 3 PFCs and 4 general-purpose counters for performance monitoring, and a RAPL interface for energy consumption monitoring [8]. It is important to refer that, in the following experiments, changing the sampling time intervals do not significantly affect the performance behavior.

4.1   Performance Analysis: Application Interference

To evaluate the capability of the proposed tool to capture the interference when several real-world applications are simultaneously co-scheduled, we conducted the experimental evaluation by relying on four distinct SPEC CPU2006 benchmarks, namely: milc, namd, GemsFDTD and tonto [6].

Figure 5 presents the experimentally obtained performance (in Gflops/s) in different time intervals, when the tested benchmarks are executed without any interference of the other applications (see Fig. 5(a), 5(c), 5(e) and 5(g)) and when all four applications are simultaneously co-scheduled (see Fig. 5(b), 5(d), 5(f) and 5(h)). As shown in Fig. 5, during the execution, each benchmark process was pinned to a specific LPC, i.e., milc to core 0, namd to core 1, GemsFDTD to core 2, and tonto to core 3. For each run, the sampling interval was set to 20ms.

By analyzing Fig. 5, several important observations can be extracted. First, due to a shared resource contention, all tested applications achieve lower performance when simultaneously co-scheduled. This can be especially observed for milc benchmark, which performance degradation is higher than 20% when compared to the solo execution (see Fig. 5(a) vs. 5(b)). Second, it can also be observed that the duration of each benchmark is extended when its execution is interfered by other applications. For example, the overall execution time of milc benchmark is increased for about 34% over the solo execution.

Another interesting observation can be made regarding the execution footprint of a single tested application, i.e., the shape of the plot. In detail, SchedMon allows

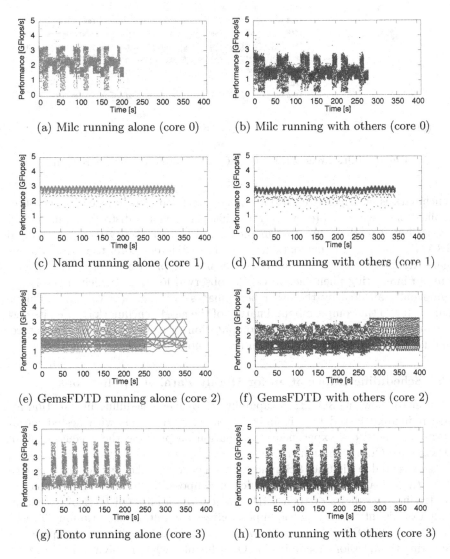

(a) Milc running alone (core 0)

(b) Milc running with others (core 0)

(c) Namd running alone (core 1)

(d) Namd running with others (core 1)

(e) GemsFDTD running alone (core 2)

(f) GemsFDTD with others (core 2)

(g) Tonto running alone (core 3)

(h) Tonto running with others (core 3)

Fig. 5. Performance analysis of SPEC CPU2006 benchmarks (20ms sampling interval)

detecting different performance phases of the application, which correspond to different parts of the execution. For instance, when running the `milc` benchmark alone (see Fig. 5(a)), at least three distinct execution phases can be identified, where each of them occurs at regular time intervals and delivers different attainable performance. This can also be observed for `tonto` benchmark in Fig. 5(g), which has at least two distinct execution phases.

Moreover, as shown in Fig. 5, co-scheduling several applications also affects the shape of their execution footprint. For example, the shape of the `GemsFDTD`

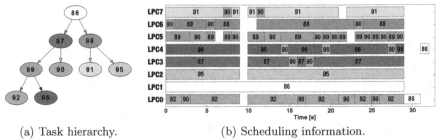

(a) Task hierarchy.   (b) Scheduling information.

Fig. 6. Multi-thread FDTD OpenCL application full reconstruction

benchmark is clearly distorted due to the interference introduced by the other applications (see Fig. 5(e) vs. 5(f)). This performance distortion can mainly be attributed to the contention in the shared memory subsystem (i.e., L3 and DRAM), since each benchmark was run in a different core, thus they do not share the in-core computational resources nor the private set of caches. Therefore, an interesting phenomenon can be observed for namd, which shape is not significantly affected by the other benchmarks (see Fig. 5(c) vs. 5(d)). This is mainly due to the compute-bound nature of the namd benchmark [3], i.e., its performance is mainly limited by the computation capabilities of the architecture, and does not significantly depend on the memory subsystem capabilities.

4.2   Scheduling Information for Highly Parallel Applications

In order to show the SchedMon capability to deliver scheduling information for each individual forked task in multi-threaded applications with nested parallelism, we based our experimental evaluation on profiling the execution of an FDTD OpenCL application [10].

As presented in Fig.6(a), SchedMon allows generating the task dependency tree of the target parallel application, which is composed by 9 tasks (enumerated by the trailing two digits of their PID). Hence, the additional level of execution complexity is introduced by the impossibility of simultaneously running 9 tasks on 8 available LPCs. As it is shown in Fig. 6(b), SchedMon was capable of capturing the decisions made by the OS scheduler when resolving this issue. In detail, the OS scheduler interleaves the execution of different tasks by assigning a certain portion of their computational load to different LPCs. Hence, in order to provide load balancing, it constantly migrates the task 90 to different LPCs, e.g., from LPC5 to LPC6 at around 5ms. As it can be observed, SchedMon provides detailed scheduling information of highly parallel applications on a per-thread basis, even for tasks that do not descend directly from the main thread.

4.3   Application Profiling at the Level of Function Calls

As previously referred, real-world applications may contain several distinct execution phases with different requirements and performance levels (see milc

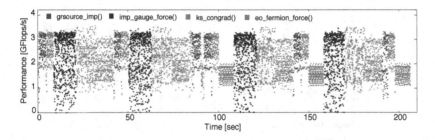

Fig. 7. Milc performance colored according to the function call tracing profile

benchmark in Fig. 5(a)). In order to ease the detection of bottlenecks and to provide an in-depth analysis, SchedMon allows application profiling at the level of individual function calls without instrumenting the source code.

Figure 7 depicts the performance analysis of milc benchmark. Different colors of experimentally obtained performance samples refer to different high-level function calls. As it can be observed, each previously referred distinct performance phase in milc benchmark corresponds to a different high-level function. Hence, this allows not only evaluating different execution parts of a given application, but also locating possible performance bottlenecks within the application.

4.4 CARM and Power Evaluation

In order to detect the possible architectural bottlenecks, SchedMon integrates the insightful performance analysis based on the CARM. Figure 8(a) presents the CARM evaluation for tonto, with the samples colored according to the traced high-level function calls. As it can be observed, tonto contains two distinct execution phases that attain different performance levels, namely: *i*) a memory bound region, corresponding to the make_fock_matrix() function; and *ii*) a higher performance region corresponding to the make_constraint_data() and add_constraint() functions. From the CARM perspective, the latter presents a compute bound behavior for DLB(ADD,MUL) and SSE(ADD,MUL) rooflines.

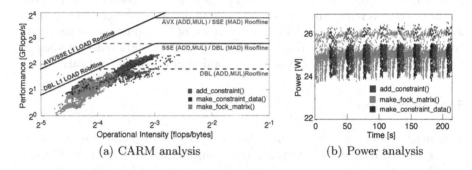

(a) CARM analysis   (b) Power analysis

Fig. 8. Evaluation of the SPEC CPU2006 benchmark tonto (sample time of 50*ms*)

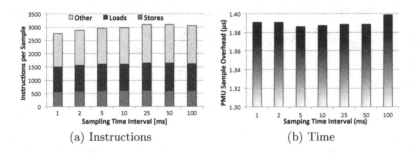

Fig. 9. Overhead of taking a PMU sample for different sampling intervals

Figure 8(b) presents the experimentally measured power consumption for different phases of tonto execution. As it can be observed, different high-level functions also yield different power consumption levels, e.g., make_constraint_data and add_constraint present slightly higher consumption than make_fock_matrix.

4.5   Overhead Discussion

Finally, to assess the overheads imposed by SchedMon, two different tests were performed, namely: *i*) the tool was executed with a dummy (empty) application to obtain the total number of instructions for taking a PMU sample (see Fig. 9(a)); and *ii*) the driver was instrumented to obtain the time required to take a PMU sample (see Fig. 9(b)). In both tests, the tool was configured to monitor 7 events (3 PFC and 4 general-purpose) across different sampling intervals.

As it can be observed in Fig.9(a), SchedMon presents a median overhead of around 3000 instructions for taking a PMU sample, which remains constant across different sampling intervals. It can also be observed in Fig. 9(b) that the time for taking a PMU sample is constant for different sampling intervals ($\approx$1.39us). As such, for a sampling time interval of 25ms, an overhead of less than 0.006% is expected, which represents a negligible value to the overall execution.

It is worth emphasizing that the comparison of introduced overheads among the proposed SchedMon and different state-of-the-art monitoring tools is not provided, due to the impossibility of conducting the evaluation on a completely fair basis. This is mainly due to different functional principles of different tools, which generally require internal instrumentation of individual tool components. For example, since most of the available tools use the perf_events interface, it would be required to patch the kernel to obtain fair overheads comparison.

5   Conclusion

This paper proposes a new monitoring tool (SchedMon), which provides the means for tracking and monitoring the complete behavior of nested multi-threaded applications, either in their entirety or at the level of the function calls, without requiring any changes to the original source code. The proposed monitoring tool provides highly accurate measurements with a low overhead by interacting with the OS scheduler. To unveil optimization opportunities in nowadays applications, the proposed SchedMon tool not only allows tracking each of the child threads and plotting its execution on the Cache-aware Roofline Model (CARM), as it also provides the means to measure the processor power and energy consumption. SchedMon's functionality can also be used to identify the interference between multiple running applications.

Acknowledgment. This work was supported by national funds through FCT (Fundação para a Ciência e a Tecnologia), under projects PEst-OE/EEI/LA0021/2013 and PTDC/EEI-ELC/3152/2012.

References

1. Perf Wiki tutorial on perf, https://perf.wiki.kernel.org/index.php (accessed: June 25, 2013)
2. AMD. Architecture programmer's manual. Volume 2: System Programming (2013)
3. Antão, D., Taniça, L., Ilic, A., Pratas, F., Tomás, P., Sousa, L.: Monitoring performance and power for application characterization with the cache-aware roofline model. In: Wyrzykowski, R., Dongarra, J., Karczewski, K., Waśniewski, J. (eds.) PPAM 2013, Part I. LNCS, vol. 8384, pp. 747–760. Springer, Heidelberg (2014)
4. Browne, S., Dongarra, J., Garner, N., Ho, G., Mucci, P.: A portable programming interface for performance evaluation on modern processors. International Journal of High Performance Computing Applications 14(3), 189–204 (2000)
5. Cohen, W.: Tuning programs with OProfile. Wide Open Magazine 1, 53–62 (2004)
6. Henning, J.L.: SPEC CPU2006 benchmark descriptions. ACM SIGARCH Computer Architecture News 34(4), 1–17 (2006)
7. Ilic, A., Pratas, F., Sousa, L.: Cache-aware Roofline model: Upgrading the loft. Computer Architecture Letters PP(99), 1–1 (2013)
8. Intel. Intel 64 and ia-32 architectures software developer's manual. Volume 3: System Programming Guide (2013)
9. Jarp, S., Jurga, R., Nowak, A.: Perfmon2: A leap forward in performance monitoring. Journal of Physics: Conference Series 119, 042017 (2008)
10. Kuan, L., Tomas, P., Sousa, L.: A comparison of computing architectures and parallelization frameworks based on a two-dimensional FDTD. In: Proceedings of the International Conference on High Performance Computing and Simulation, HPCS 2013, pp. 339–346. IEEE (2013)
11. Pettersson, M.: Perfctr: Linux performance monitoring counters driver (2009)
12. Treibig, J., Hager, G., Wellein, G.: Likwid: A lightweight performance-oriented tool suite for x86 multicore environments. In: Proceedings of the International Conference on Parallel Processing Workshops, ICPPW 2010, pp. 207–216. IEEE (2010)
13. Weaver, V.M.: Linux perf_event features and overhead. In: Proceedings of the International Workshop on Performance Analysis of Workload Optimized Systems, FastPath 2013, p. 80 (2013)

Exploiting Hidden Non-uniformity of Uniform Memory Access on Manycore CPUs

Balazs Gerofi[1], Masamichi Takagi[2], and Yutaka Ishikawa[1]

[1] Graduate School of Information Science and Technology,
The University of Tokyo, Tokyo, Japan
bgerofi@il.is.s.u-tokyo.ac.jp, ishikawa@is.s.u-tokyo.ac.jp
[2] RIKEN Advanced Institute for Computational Science, Kobe, Japan
masamichi.takagi@riken.jp

Abstract. As the rate of CPU clock improvement has stalled for the last decade, increased use of parallelism in the form of multi- and many-core processors has been chased to improve overall performance. Current high-end manycore CPUs already accommodate up to hundreds of processing cores. At the same time, these architectures come with complex on-chip networks for inter-core communication and multiple memory controllers for accessing off-chip RAM modules. Intel's latest Many Integrated Cores (MIC) chip, also called the Xeon Phi, boasts up to 60 CPU cores (each with 4-ways SMT) combined with eight memory controllers. Although the chip provides Uniform Memory Access (UMA), we find that there are substantial (as high as 60%) differences in access latencies for different memory blocks depending on which CPU core issues the request, resembling Non-Uniform Memory Access (NUMA) architectures.

Exploiting the aforementioned differences, in this paper, we propose a memory block latency-aware memory allocator, which assigns memory addresses to the requesting CPU cores in a fashion that it minimizes access latencies. We then show that applying our mechanism to the A-star graph search algorithm can yield performance improvements up to 28%, without any need for modifications to the algorithm itself.

1 Introduction

Although Moore's Law continues to drive the number of transistors per square mm, the recent stop of frequency and Dennard scaling caused an architectural shift in processor design towards multi- and many-core CPUs. Multicore processors usually implement a handful of complex cores that are optimized for fast single-thread performance, while manycore units come with a large number of simpler and slower but much more power-efficient cores that are optimized for throughput-oriented parallel workloads [1].

There have been manycore chips already built with 48 [2], 64 [3], 72 [4] cores and even an experimental processor with 1000 cores [5] has been announced. The Intel® Xeon Phi™ product family, also referred to as Many Integrated Cores (MIC), is Intel's latest manycore CPU providing sixty x86 cores [6].

L. Lopes et al. (Eds.): Euro-Par 2014 Workshops, Part II, LNCS 8806, pp. 242–253, 2014.
© Springer International Publishing Switzerland 2014

Although manycore CPUs tend to come with complex networks-on-chip (NOC) and with multiple memory controllers [7], with respect to memory access there are mainly two approaches. Uniform memory access (UMA) architectures provide uniform access latencies for the entire physical memory regardless which CPU core is generating the request, while on the other hand, non-uniform memory access (NUMA) architectures allow explicit differences in terms of memory access latencies depending on the physical address and the CPU core that is accessing it [8]. Despite the fact that the large number of CPU cores and complex on-chip networks make it increasingly difficult to keep access latencies uniform, most of the existing manycore processor do follow the UMA approach for the sake of easy programmability.

The Xeon Phi also provides uniform memory access officially. However, we find that memory access latencies differ significantly depending on which CPU core accesses a given physical address. Access latencies to the same memory block can vary by up to 60% when issuing requests from different CPU cores, resembling NUMA architectures. Notice, that the above mentioned latency differences are at the memory level, unlike for caches in NUCA architectures [9].

Applications which access small data structures in a relatively random fashion, such as those operating on Recursive Data Structures (RDS) may experience significant performance degradation simply by accessing memory blocks that are located *far* from the CPU core that generates the request. RDSs include linked lists, trees, graphs, etc., where individual nodes are dynamically allocated from the heap, and nodes are linked together through pointers to form the overall structure [10]. For example, the A* (A-star) algorithm [11], a widely used graph search heuristic in artificial intelligence, exhibits exactly such characteristics.

Inspired by the above described observation, in this paper, we propose a memory allocator that is memory block latency-aware, i.e., it allocates memory to particular CPU cores in a fashion that it minimizes access latencies. In summary, we make the following contributions:

- We point out that *hidden non-uniformity* in otherwise uniform memory access architectures *can be significant on manycore CPUs.*
- We propose *a memory allocator*, which is optimized for allocating small data structures in a *memory block latency-aware* fashion and it lays out memory in a way that access latencies for the requesting CPU cores are minimized.
- We show that applying our allocator can yield up to 28% performance improvements for the A-star graph search algorithm solving a 16-tile puzzle, without any need for modifications to the application itself.

The rest of this paper is organized as follows. We begin with providing a detailed overview of the Xeon Phi along with measurements on memory block latencies as seen from different CPU cores in Section 2. Section 3 discusses our target application, the A-star algorithm and Section 4 describes the proposed memory allocator. Experimental evaluation is given in Section 5. Section 6 provides further discussion, Section 7 surveys related work, and finally, Section 8 presents future plans and concludes the paper.

2   Background and Motivation

In this Section we provide an overview of the Xeon Phi processor focusing in particular on components that contribute to memory access latency. The architectural overview of the Intel Xeon Phi processor is shown in Figure 1. The chip we used in this paper comes on a PCI Express card, with 60 CPU cores, where each core supports four hyperthreads (i.e., 4-way symmetric multithreading).

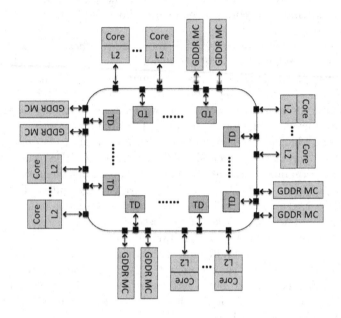

Fig. 1. Architectural overview of the Intel Xeon Phi manycore CPU. *The chip consists of 60 CPU cores, each core with 4-way symmetric multithreading and a 512kB private slice of the unified L2 cache. There are 8 GDDR memory controllers and 64 cache tag directories, which are all connected with a bidirectional ring.*

Each processor core runs on up to 1.2GHz and besides the relatively low clock frequency (compared to standard multi-core Xeon chips), cores on the Xeon Phi have no support for out-of-order execution [6]. All CPU cores have their own 32kB L1 caches (both data and instruction) and a 512kB private slice of the unified L2 cache. Both the L1 and L2 caches use the standard MESI protocol [12] for maintaining the shared state among cores. To address potential performance limitations resulting from the lack of an O (Owner) state found in the MOESI protocol [13], the Intel Xeon Phi processor coherence system uses a distributed tag directory (DTD) of ownership similar to that implemented in many multiprocessor systems [14].

The card is equipped with 8 Gigabytes of GDDR5 memory for which there are eight GDDR5 memory controllers encompassed in the chip and all components are connected via a bi-directional ring. Intel does not provide detailed information on how memory blocks are assigned to DTDs and memory controllers, but assumably a hash function based on the address of the line is used [15]. There is also no support for modifying the mapping.

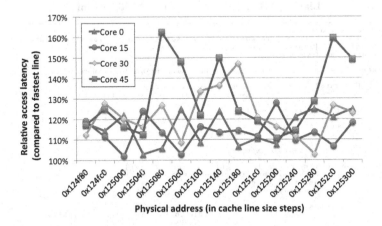

Fig. 2. Differences in memory access latency on subsequent memory blocks seen from four CPU cores. *Data is ensured to be in RAM by invalidating both L1 and L2 caches before each access and prefetching is disabled.*

When a core encounters a cache miss, it requests the line from the corresponding DTD and eventually, from the corresponding memory controller. Considering the distances between CPU cores, DTDs, and memory controllers, one can expect that access latencies to the same memory block likely vary across different CPU cores.

We have developed a simple benchmark tool that measures differences in memory latencies depending on which CPU core accesses a particular memory block. Note that data is always ensured to be in RAM by invalidating both L1 and L2 caches before each access as well as disabling the compiler generated prefetch instructions. Figure 2 reveals our findings for a couple of subsequent memory blocks as seen from four different CPU cores. The X axis shows the physical address of the given memory block, while Y axis represents the relative access latency compared to the fastest access (lower is better). As shown, there are significant differences among the values. For example, accessing the physical address 0x125080 from CPU core 45 is approximately 60% slower than from core 0. Such differences can easily show up in application performance, especially when taking into account that the Xeon Phi cores can do only in-order execution.

3   The A* Algorithm

This Section gives an overview of the A* (A-star) algorithm [11] emphasizing attributes that can be exploited by a memory block latency-aware memory allocator for improving overall performance.

Listing 1.1. Pseudo code of the A* algorithm

```
1   function A*(start , goal )
2       closedset := the empty set      // The set of nodes already evaluated.
3       openset := {start}      // The set of tentative nodes to be evaluated.
4       start.came_from := NULL
5
6       start.g_score := 0      // Cost from start along best known path.
7
8       // Estimated total cost from start to goal.
9       start.f_score := start.g_score + heuristic_cost_estimate(start , goal)
10
11      while openset is not empty
12          current := the node in openset having the lowest f_score value
13          if current = goal
14              return reconstruct_path(goal)
15
16          remove current from openset
17          add current to closedset
18          for each neighbor in neighbor_nodes(current)
19              // Find neighbor in closedset
20              if neighbor in closedset
21                  continue
22
23              tentative_g_score := current.g_score +
24                                   dist_between(current , neighbor)
25
26              if neighbor not in openset or
27                  tentative_g_score < neighbor.g_score
28                  neighbor.came_from := current
29                  neighbor.g_score := tentative_g_score
30
31                  neighbor.f_score := neighbor.g_score +
32                                      heuristic_cost_estimate(neighbor , goal)
33
34                  if neighbor not in openset
35                      add neighbor to openset
36
37          return failure
38
39  function reconstruct_path(current_node)
40      if current_node.came_from
41          p := reconstruct_path(current_node.came_from)
42          return (p + current_node)
43      else
44          return current_node
```

A* is an informed best-first graph search algorithm which aims at finding the lowest cost path from a given start to a goal node. During the search, both the cost from the start node to current node and the estimated cost from the current node to a goal state are minimized [16]. The pseudo code of the A* algorithm is shown in Listing 1.1. The A* algorithm uses two sets of nodes for housekeeping, the so-called *open-set* holds nodes to which the search can continue in subsequent steps, while the *closed-set* stores nodes that have been already evaluated.

Depending on the problem being solved, these sets can grow considerably large while at the same time lookup operations from these sets are required in each iteration of the algorithm (see line 20 and 26 of the pseudo code). In order to attain good lookup performance hash tables are normally utilized, however, as a result memory accesses come with very low data locality, i.e., following a nearly random access pattern. Moreover, problem state (i.e., a node of the graph) can be often represented with relatively small data structures, fitting easily into the size of one cache line. As we will show later through quantitative evaluation, the above mentioned characteristics of the A* algorithm suit well the assumptions we described earlier in Section 1.

With respect to utilizing multiple CPU cores, since we are focusing on the effect of hidden non-uniformity of memory accesses, we simply use different goal states on different CPU cores. This keeps the parallel code simple, because open and closed sets are separated per core, and it also eliminates the possibility of false sharing. Note that there are several studies on how to parallelize efficiently the A* algorithm when searching a shared global state [17], [18], [19] and further investigating this issue is outside the scope of this paper.

4   Memory Block Latency-Aware Memory Allocator

We now describe the design and implementation of the memory block latency-aware memory allocator.

As mentioned earlier we developed a simple tool that measures access latencies to a particular memory block from different CPU cores. We used this tool to build a latency data base, in which for each memory block (i.e., the physical memory address of the block) access latencies for all CPU cores are stored. The basic idea is that when memory is requested by the application the runtime system pre-allocates a large chunk of memory and queries the physical addresses of the corresponding pages from the acquired mapping. For the purpose of obtaining the physical translation of an arbitrary virtual address, we introduced a new system call (see below for details on the kernel we used). Once the physical addresses are known, the latency data base is consulted to determine which memory blocks have low latency access from CPU cores used by the application and the runtime places the addresses onto the corresponding per-core allocator lists. Although we are explicitly targeting small memory requests in this paper, it is worth mentioning that larger allocations can be still satisfied simply by falling back to the regular glibc memory allocator. For further discussion on larger allocation sizes as well as on the memory efficiency of the proposed system refer to Section 6.

The architecture of the memory block latency-aware allocator is shown in Figure 3. The colored addresses on the left of the Figure represent memory blocks which can be accessed with low latency by the CPU core designated by the same color. The per-core lists hold these addresses (denoted by the black squares) for each application core and memory allocation requests are directly satisfied from these lists.

With regards to implementation details, the RIKEN Advanced Institute of Computational Science and the Information Technology Center at the University of Tokyo have been designing and developing a new scalable system software stack for a new heterogeneous supercomputer. Part of this project is an operating system kernel targeting manycore processors [20]. Our OS kernel is binary compatible with Linux and supports all system calls so that applications using pthreads can be executed without modifications.

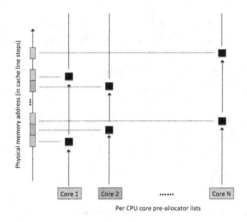

Fig. 3. Memory block latency-aware per-core allocator lists. *The colored rect angles on the left indicate low latency memory blocks when accessed from a CPU core denoted by the same color.*

We have implemented the proposed allocator on top of our custom OS kernel in the form of a library interposed between the application and glibc. We note that as a proof of concept our prototype implementation distributes memory blocks during initialization (i.e., memory pre-allocation) phase of the application, but utilizing dedicated allocator threads the technique can be easily adapted to an actual runtime solution. As for the memory block latency data base, it is simply a collection of files which we store on local SSDs for fast access. It is also worth mentioning that our custom kernel does not migrate application threads among CPU cores, i.e., threads are pinned to the same core throughout the whole execution of an application. This is with particular importance, since memory addresses returned by the allocator yield low latency access only for the core which performs the allocation and moving a thread to another core would defeat the very purpose of the policy. Besides the custom system call for obtaining physical address for a user mapping, we also provide a special call that returns the APIC CPU core ID so that threads can easily determine where they execute.

5   Evaluation

5.1   Experimental Setup

Throughout our experiments the host machine was an Intel® Xeon® CPU E5-2670. For the manycore processor we used the *Knights Corner* Xeon Phi 5110P card, which is connected to the host machine via the PCI Express bus. As mentioned earlier, it provides 8GB of RAM and a single chip with 60 x86 cores running on up to 1.2GHz, each processor core supporting a multithreading depth of four. The chip includes coherent L1 and L2 caches and the inter-processor network is a bidirectional ring [6].

5.2   Results

We used the A* algorithm solving the 16 tile puzzle problem to evaluate our proposal, but it is worth noting that our approach could be generally applied to a wide range of Recursive Data Structures (RDSs). RDS includes familiar objects such as linked lists, trees, graphs, etc., where individual nodes are dynamically allocated from the heap, and nodes are linked together through pointers to form the overall structure [10].

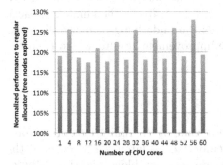
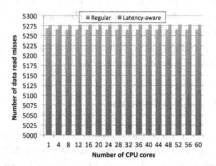

(a) Relative performance to regular allocator.

(b) Average number of memory read accesses that miss the internal cache per A* iteration. *(On CPU core 0.)*

Fig. 4. Performance of memory block latency-aware allocator compared to regular pre-allocation on the A* algorithm solving a 16 tile puzzle.

Specifically, we used a publicly available A* code [21] as reference implementation. The state space of the 16 tile puzzle is large enough so that the search graph does not fit into the L2 cache of the Xeon Phi, and thus making the lookup operations generate actual memory accesses.

We used two configurations of the application. First, we ran with regular memory pre-allocator, i.e., memory is simply divided among the threads. We then modified the allocation routine to call into our library and use the memory block latency-aware allocation. We measured the number of graph nodes the algorithm explores in unit time and report the normalized improvement of the memory block aware allocator compared to the regular solution. Results are indicated by Figure 4a, where each measurement was repeated five times and the chart shows the average values.

As seen, performance improvement scales from 17% to 28% and varies depending on the number of CPU cores utilized in the application. Initially we expected there would be a gradual increase in performance improvement with the growing number of cores, assuming that the on-chip traffic is better balanced among the CPU cores and the memory controllers, an observation which had been also pointed out for NUMA architectures previously [22]. Surprisingly, however, there seem to be no direct relation between the performance improvement and the number of cores involved in the execution. As the Figure shows, utilizing 12 and 20 cores yields the lowest improvement. Besides the random nature of the regular allocator in terms of memory block latencies, we believe the distributed tag directory based cache coherence may also contribute to this effect. Intel doesn't provide any details about the characteristics of the on-chip network and thus it is hard to assess whether traffic congestion occurs due to communication between cores and the tag directories or the memory controllers. Nevertheless, we do observe the highest improvement for 56 CPU cores.

We also measured the number of read accesses that missed the internal data cache on CPU core 0, where the same goal state was used across all runs to ensure fair comparison. Results are shown in Figure 4b. As the number of cache misses is approximately the same regardless the underlying memory allocator, we believe that the observed performance improvement results indeed from the lower latency memory accesses.

6   Discussion

This Section provides a short discussion on some of the limitations of our proposed approach. First, since we exploit memory access latency differences at the memory block level, allocations larger than a memory block size (i.e., 64bytes on x86 64bit) cannot be laid out in a continuous fashion on to low latency memory blocks. At present, we simply return a regular allocation, however, splitting structures in a clever way could also help to overcome this limitation [23]. Second, the smaller the number of cores utilized by the application, the lower the ratio of low latency memory blocks becomes corresponding to the participating cores. Consequently, our allocator provides the best memory usage efficiency when the entire chip is utilized.

Third, we also need to note that our technique favors applications, where the per-core data sets are distinct. Communication between the cores of course is inevitable, and if necessary data from one core's low latency line could be copied over to another one's, such as it would be required for the EM3D application [10]. Forth, one might argue that spreading memory allocations over low latency memory blocks will increase the price of TLB misses. In our experiments we used large pages for memory mappings and both in case of regular and low latency allocators, the per-core memory used could be covered by the L2 TLB entries.

Despite the above mentioned restrictions, we emphasize that our intention is to demonstrate that it is possible to take advantage of hidden memory latency differences in current many-core CPUs.

7   Related Work

As we mentioned earlier, the hidden non-uniformity of the UMA property officially provided by the Xeon Phi closely resembles non-uniform memory access (NUMA) architectures.

A large body of management policies for memory and thread placement in NUMA architectures have been previously proposed. Bolosky et al investigated page replacement policies so that data are placed close to the process that is using them [24]. LaRowe et al. built an analytic model of the memory system performance of a local/remote NUMA architecture and investigated heuristics when pages should be moved or remotely referenced [25]. Verghese et al. studied the performance improvements provided by OS supported dynamic page migration and replication in NUMA environments where remote access latencies were significantly higher than those to local memory [26]. Avdic et al. demonstrated the correlation of memory access latency with difference between cores and memory controllers through parallel sorting on the Intel SCC [27]. Although the goal of the above mentioned studies is similar in nature to ours, i.e., to optimize for access locality, they explicitly deal with NUMA system where the granularity of access inequality is at least page size. On the contrary, we exploit hidden non-uniformities at the memory block level.

Some recent studies approach memory management issues from the aspect of resource contention. Knauerhase et al. argued that the OS can use data obtained from dynamic runtime observation of task behavior to ameliorate performance variability and more effectively exploit multicore processor resources, such as the memory hierarchy [28]. Another recent work points out that performance degradation in current NUMA systems doesn't mainly derive from the cost of remote accesses. Instead, congestion on memory controllers and interconnects caused by memory traffic from data-intensive applications hurts performance much more [22]. As the Xeon Phi's on-chip network connects a large number of various components, network congestion during communication among CPU cores, cache tag directories and memory controllers likely constitute to performance degradation of memory intensive applications. We believe that part of the merit of assigning low latency memory blocks to CPU cores is the alleviation of on-chip traffic congestion.

8   Conclusion and Future Work

Many-core CPUs come with an increasing number of components, such as CPU cores, memory controllers, cache tag directories, etc., and the on-chip networks connecting these components are becoming more and more complex. Nevertheless, uniform memory access is still the most frequently provided memory model due to its ease of programmability.

In this paper, we have pointed out that many-core CPUs, such as Intel's Xeon Phi, can exhibit substantial hidden non-uniformity in memory access latencies among CPU cores accessing the same memory block. To the best of our knowledge, this is the first time such differences have been shown for a UMA architecture. We have proposed a latency-aware memory allocator and demonstrated its superior performance on the A* search algorithm. Most importantly, we encourage chip manufacturers not to hide such differences or at least to provide the system with the ability to reconfigure mappings so that NUMA properties could be explicitly leveraged at the software level.

In the future, we intend to look at further possible usage scenarios accelerating applications relying on recursive data structures, such as the EM3D or Barnes-Hut's N-body problem [10] and Monte-Carlo based tree search algorithms.

Acknowledgment. This work has been partially supported by the CREST project of the Japan Science and Technology Agency (JST) and by the National Project of MEXT called Feasibility Study on Advanced and Efficient Latency Core Architecture.

References

1. Saha, B., Zhou, X., Chen, H., Gao, Y., Yan, S., Rajagopalan, M., Fang, J., Zhang, P., Ronen, R., Mendelson, A.: Programming model for a heterogeneous x86 platform. In: Proceedings of the 2009 ACM SIGPLAN Conference on Programming Language Design and implementation, PLDI 2009, pp. 431–440. ACM, New York (2009)

2. Intel Corporation: Single-Chip Cloud Computer (2010),
   https://www-ssl.intel.com/content/www/us/en/
   research/intel-labs-single-chip-cloud-computer.html

3. Adapteva: Epiphany-IV 64-core 28nm Microprocessor, E64G401 (2014),
   http://www.adapteva.com/epiphanyiv

4. Tilera: TILE-Gx8072 Processor Product Brief (2014),
   http://www.tilera.com/sites/default/files/
   images/products/TILE-Gx8072_PB041-03_WEB.pdf

5. The University of Glasgow: Scientists squeeze more than 1,000 cores on to computer chip (2010),
   http://www.gla.ac.uk/news/archiveofnews/
   2010/december/headline_183814_en.html

6. Intel Corporation: Intel Xeon Phi Coprocessor System Software Developers Guide (2013),
   https://www-ssl.intel.com/content/www/us/en/processors/
   xeon/xeon-phi-coprocessor-system-software-developers-guide.html

7. Nychis, G.P., Fallin, C., Moscibroda, T., Mutlu, O., Seshan, S.: On-chip Networks from a Networking Perspective: Congestion and Scalability in Many-core Interconnects. In: SIGCOMM 2012, pp. 407–418. ACM, New York (2012)

8. Lameter, C.: NUMA (Non-Uniform Memory Access): An Overview. ACM Queue 11(7), 40 (2013)

9. Kim, C., Burger, D., Keckler, S.: Nonuniform cache architectures for wire-delay dominated on-chip caches. IEEE Micro 23(6), 99–107 (2003)

10. Luk, C.K., Mowry, T.C.: Compiler-based prefetching for recursive data structures. In: ASPLOS VII, pp. 222–233. ACM, New York (1996)

11. Hart, P., Nilsson, N., Raphael, B.: A Formal Basis for the Heuristic Determination of Minimum Cost Paths. IEEE Transactions on Systems Science and Cybernetics 4(2), 100–107 (1968)

12. Ivanov, L., Nunna, R.: Modeling and Verification of Cache Coherence Protocols. In: The 2001 IEEE International Symposium on Circuits and Systems, ISCAS 2001, vol. 5, pp. 129–132 (2001)

13. Hackenberg, D., Molka, D., Nagel, W.E.: Comparing Cache Architectures and Coherency Protocols on x86-64 Multicore SMP Systems. In: Proceedings of the 42nd Annual IEEE/ACM International Symposium on Microarchitecture, MICRO 42, pp. 413–422. ACM, New York (2009)
14. Hennessy, J.L., Patterson, D.A.: Computer Architecture - A Quantitative Approach, 5th edn. Morgan Kaufmann (2012)
15. Ramos, S., Hoefler, T.: Modeling Communication in Cache-coherent SMP Systems: A Case-study with Xeon Phi. In: HPDC 2013, pp. 97–108. ACM, New York (2013)
16. Russell, S., Norvig, P.: Artificial Intelligence: A Modern Approach, 3rd edn. Prentice Hall Press, Upper Saddle River (2009)
17. Dutt, S., Mahapatra, N.: Parallel A* algorithms and their performance on hypercube multiprocessors. In: Proceedings of Seventh International Parallel Processing Symposium, pp. 797–803 (April 1993)
18. Burns, E., Lemons, S., Zhou, R., Ruml, W.: Best-first Heuristic Search for Multicore Machines. In: Proceedings of the 21st International Jont Conference on Artifical Intelligence, IJCAI 2009, pp. 449–455. Morgan Kaufmann Publishers, San Francisco (2009)
19. Rios, L.H.O., Chaimowicz, L.: A Survey and Classification of A* Based Best-First Heuristic Search Algorithms. In: da Rocha Costa, A.C., Vicari, R.M., Tonidandel, F. (eds.) SBIA 2010. LNCS, vol. 6404, pp. 253–262. Springer, Heidelberg (2010)
20. Gerofi, B., Shimada, A., Hori, A., Ishikawa, Y.: Partially Separated Page Tables for Efficient Operating System Assisted Hierarchical Memory Management on Heterogeneous Architectures. In: CCGrid 2013 (May 2013)
21. Heyes-Jones, J.: A* Algorithm Tutorial (2013),
http://heyes-jones.com/astar.php
22. Dashti, M., Fedorova, A., Funston, J., Gaud, F., Lachaize, R., Lepers, B., Quema, V., Roth, M.: Traffic Management: A Holistic Approach to Memory Placement on NUMA Systems. In: ASPLOS 2013, pp. 381–394. ACM, New York (2013)
23. Chilimbi, T.M., Davidson, B., Larus, J.R.: Cache-conscious Structure Definition. In: PLDI 1999, pp. 13–24. ACM, New York (1999)
24. Bolosky, W., Fitzgerald, R., Scott, M.: Simple but Effective Techniques for NUMA Memory Management. In: SOSP 1989, pp. 19–31. ACM, New York (1989)
25. LaRowe, J. R.P., Ellis, C.S., Holliday, M.A.: Evaluation of NUMA Memory Management Through Modeling and Measurements. IEEE Trans. Parallel Distrib. Syst. 3(6), 686–701 (1992)
26. Verghese, B., Devine, S., Gupta, A., Rosenblum, M.: Operating system support for improving data locality on cc-numa compute servers. In: ASPLOS VII, pp. 279–289. ACM, New York (1996)
27. Avdic, K., Melot, N., Keller, J., Kessler, C.: Parallel sorting on Intel Single-Chip Cloud Computer. In: Proceedings of the 2nd Workshop on Applications for Multi and Many Core Processors (2011)
28. Knauerhase, R., Brett, P., Hohlt, B., Li, T., Hahn, S.: Using os observations to improve performance in multicore systems. IEEE Micro 28(3), 54–66 (2008)

Characterization of a List-Based Directory Cache Coherence Protocol for Manycore CMPs*

Ricardo Fernández-Pascual, Alberto Ros, and Manuel E. Acacio

Dept. de Ingeniería y Tecnología de Computadores, Universidad de Murcia, Spain
{rfernandez,aros,meacacio}@um.es

Abstract. The development of efficient and scalable cache coherence protocols is a key aspect in the design of manycore chip multiprocessors. In this work, we review a kind of cache coherence protocols that, despite having been already implemented in the 90s for building large-scale commodity multiprocessors, have not been seriously considered in the current context of chip multiprocessors. In particular, we evaluate a directory-based cache coherence protocol that employs distributed simply-linked lists to encode the information about the sharers of the memory blocks. We compare this organization with two protocols that use centralized sharing codes, each one having different directory memory overhead: one of them implementing a non-scalable bit-vector sharing code and the other one implementing a more scalable limited-pointer scheme with a single pointer. Simulation results show that for large-scale chip multiprocessors, the protocol based on distributed linked lists obtains worse performance than the centralized approaches. This is due, principally, to an increase in the contention at the directory controller as a consequence of being blocked for longer time while updating the distributed sharing information.

1   Introduction

As the number of cores implemented in chip multiprocessors (CMPs) increases following Moore's law, design decisions about communication and synchronization mechanisms among cores become a key aspect for the performance of the multicore. If the current trend continues, multicore architectures with tens of cores (i.e., manycores) will employ a sharing memory model that will rely on a cache coherence protocol implemented in hardware to maintain the coherence of the data stored in the private caches [9]. This way, communication and synchronization (usually implemented through normal load and store instructions to shared addresses) require an efficient cache coherence protocol to achieve good performance levels.

The design of efficient cache coherence protocols for systems with a large number of cores has been already studied for traditional multiprocessors. In

---

* This work has been supported by the Spanish MINECO, as well as European Commission FEDER funds, under grant "TIN2012-38341-C04-03".

L. Lopes et al. (Eds.): Euro-Par 2014 Workshops, Part II, LNCS 8806, pp. 254–265, 2014.

that context, the most scalable protocols —those which kept sharing information in a directory distributed among nodes— were classified in two categories [5]: *memory-based* schemes and *cache-based* schemes. Memory-based schemes store the sharing information about all the cached copies of each block in a single place, which is the home node of that block. In traditional multiprocessors, the home node was associated with the main memory, and that is why they were called memory-based schemes. On the other hand, in cache-based schemes not all the sharing information about a single block is stored in the home node. Instead, it is distributed among the caches holding copies of the block while the home node only contains a pointer to one of the sharers. Usually, one or two pointers are stored along with each copy of the block, forming a distributed linked list of sharers.

Nowadays, current cache coherence proposals for manycore architectures assume centralized directory schemes. In the context of multicore architectures, the name of *memory-based* is not very suitable because the home node is now associated with the last level cache (LLC) in the chip, which is the L2 cache in this work. Hence, we will use the term *centralized sharing code*. On the other hand, although distributed schemes where employed in several commodity multiprocessors in the 90s ([6,3,7,12]), they have not been analyzed in the context of multicore architectures. The main advantage of these schemes, which we will call *distributed sharing code* schemes, is that they have lower directory memory overhead than the centralized sharing code ones with the same precision [5]. However, they show several disadvantages, such as higher cache miss latency, some modifications that must be introduced in the private caches, and the increased complexity for managing cache evictions.

In this work, we evaluate the performance of a distributed sharing code scheme in the context of CMPs. Particularly, we implement the simplest version of this scheme which is based on the use of simply-linked lists, which we will call *List*. We compare the performance of the implemented sharing code with two centralized organizations. The first one employs a non-scalable bit-vector (full-map) sharing code. This configuration will be our baseline (called *Base*). The second one is a limited pointer scheme that uses a single pointer. We call this configuration *1-pointer*. The three protocols use the MESI states and behave as similarly as possible in all other aspects. Simulation results show that the three configurations obtain similar performance for 16-core CMPs. However, for 64-core CMPs, the distributed sharing code *List* obtains worse performance. We found that the reason for this performance degradation is the increased contention that the *List* protocol introduces at the level of the directory controller. This due to excessive locking time for updating the list of sharers upon cache misses and evictions.

2   A Coherence Protocol Based on Simply-Linked Lists

The main difference between the protocol considered and evaluated in this work (called *List*) and a traditional directory-based MESI cache coherence protocol is that the former stores directory information in a distributed way. Particularly, the home node in the *List* protocol stores the identity of one of the sharers of the memory block. This is done by means of a pointer field stored in the L2 entry of each memory block (in the tags' portion of the L2 cache). The set of sharers is represented using a simply-linked list, which is constructed through pointers in each of the L1 cache entries. This way, each of the sharers can store the identity of the next sharer in the list or the null pointer if it is the last element in the list (the null pointer is represented by codifying the identity of the sharer itself, i.e., the end of the list points to itself). Therefore, directory information in this protocol is distributed between the home node and the set of sharers of every memory block. As it will be shown, the fact that most of the directory storage is moved to the L1 caches (which are much smaller than the L2 cache) brings important advantages like reduced requirements of the directory structure in terms of memory overhead (and thus, energy consumption) and improved scalability. As an example, assuming n 6 core CMP configuration, Figure 1 illustrates how directory information is stored when cores 1, 3 and 5 hold read-only copies of a memory block B, for which node 0 is the home node.

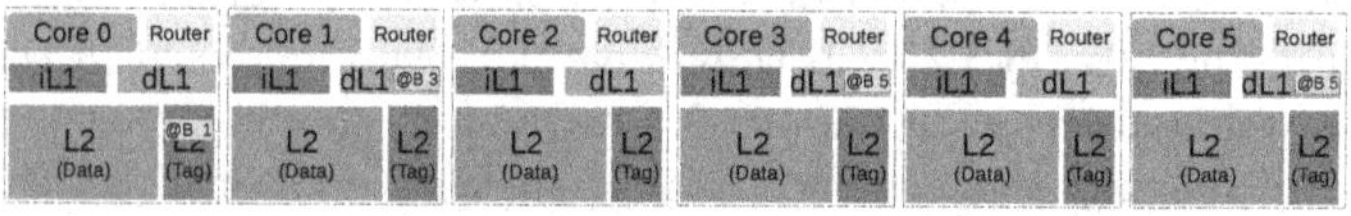

Fig. 1. Example of a simply-linked list for memory block B when cores 1, 3 and 5 are the sharers. Node 0 is the home for block B

Since directory information is stored in a distributed way in the *List* protocol, several messages are required between the sharers and the home node to update this information. Some of these messages would not be needed in a traditional directory protocol. List updates in the *List* protocol are always initiated from the home node, which remains blocked (i.e., other requests for this memory block are not attended) until the modification of the list structure has been completed. This way, we guarantee that two or more update operations cannot take place simultaneously.

2.1 How Read Misses Are Managed

The procedure to resolve read misses for uncached data (i.e., when the memory block is not held by any of the private caches) is almost identical in both the protocol with a distributed sharing code considered in this work (*List*) and a traditional directory protocol with a centralized sharing code (such as *Base*): once the request (read miss) reaches the corresponding home L2 bank, it sends back a message with the memory block to the requester, which subsequently responds with the *Unblock* message to the directory. The home L2 bank uses the pointer available in the tags' part of the L2 cache to store the identity of the only sharer up to the moment.

When the home L2 bank does not maintain a copy of the requested memory block, the directory controller will send a request to memory and once data is received, it will be stored in the L2 cache and a copy of the memory block will be sent to the requester. In this case, the memory block will be put in the E (Exclusive) state in the private cache that suffered the miss.

The main difference between the *List* and *Base* protocols with respect to read misses is observed when one or more copies of the memory block already exist. In this case, the home L2 bank in *List* stores the identity of just one of the sharers. This information is sent to the requester along with the corresponding memory block. Then, the requester stores the memory block in its L1 cache and sets up the pointer field in the corresponding entry of this cache level to the identifier included in the response message (its *next sharer*). After this, it sends an *Unblock* message to the home L2 bank, which overwrites the pointer field with the identity of the requester. This way, the list structure keeps the identity of the sharers of a particular memory block in reverse order to how read misses were processed by the home L2 cache bank.

If, on the contrary, the memory block is found in the M (Modified) state in the home L2 cache bank (it has been previously modified in one of the L1 caches), the read miss is forwarded by the directory controller to the only L1 cache that holds a valid copy of it (the one that modified it). Upon receiving the forwarded request, the corresponding L1 cache responds directly to the requester with a message containing the memory block and its own identity. Then, the requester proceeds just like in the previous case.

As it can be observed, updates of the list structure used to keep the identity of all the sharers of every memory block do not need to introduce any new messages in the *List* protocol with respect to *Base*. This is because response messages are used to transport all the information (one identifier in this case) required to maintain the list structure.

2.2 How Write Misses Are Managed

Write misses are resolved by invalidating all the copies of the memory block held by the L1 caches. The corresponding directory controller at the home L2 cache bank starts the invalidation process in parallel with sending the response message with data back to the requester.

On a write miss, in a traditional directory protocol with a centralized sharing code (such as *Base*), the directory controller at the corresponding home L2 cache bank sends one invalidation message to each one of the sharers. In this case, all the information about the sharers is completely stored at the home L2 cache bank, and therefore, invalidation messages can be sent in parallel (although if the interconnection network does not provide multicast support they would be created and dispatched by the directory controller sequentially). On the contrary, the invalidation procedure in a directory protocol with a distributed sharing code (such as *List*) must be done serially. In this case, the home L2 cache bank only knows the identity of one of the sharers, which in turn knows the identity of the next one, and so on. This way, invalidation messages must be created and sent one after another, as the list structure is traversed. Once the last sharer is reached, a single acknowledgement message is sent to the requester as a notification that all the copies in the L1 caches have been deleted. As it can be noted, the latency of write misses is therefore increased, especially for widely shared memory blocks. But this also brings one advantage: whereas in the *Base* protocol all invalidation messages entail the corresponding acknowledgement response, in the *List* protocol just one acknowledgement is required. This obviously reduces network traffic when the number of sharers is large.

The memory block on a write miss is sent just like in the case of a read miss, taking into account whether the block is in M state or not.

For both the *Base* and *List* protocols, the requester sends the *Unblock* message to the home L2 cache bank only when the invalidation procedure has finished (it has collected all the acknowledgements to the invalidation messages sent by the directory controller in the case of the *Base* protocol, or the only acknowledgement response that is needed in the *List* one) as well as the response with data has arrived. As in the case of read misses, upon receiving the *Unblock* message the directory controller takes note of the new holder of the memory block using the pointer available at the L2 cache.

This way, the number of messages required in the *List* protocol to resolve write misses is lower or equal than what is needed in the *Base* protocol. The counterpart is that invalidation messages in *List* proceed serially, which presumably can increase write miss latency.

2.3   How Replacements Are Managed

Replacements of memory blocks in M state (i.e., blocks that have been modified by the local core) proceed exactly the same way in both *List* and *Base* protocols. In these cases, the private L1 cache sends a request to the corresponding home L2 bank asking for permission, and upon receiving authorization from the L2 cache, the L1 cache sends the modified memory block, which is kept at the L2 cache. By requiring the L1 cache to ask for authorization before sending the replaced data to L2, the protocol avoids some race conditions that complicate its design (and that, if not correctly addressed, would lead to deadlocks).

However, the main difference between the *List* and *Base* protocols has to do with the management of replacements of clean data (memory blocks that have not been modified locally, and thus, for which the L2 cache has a valid copy). Whereas in the *Base* protocol replacements of this kind are silent (the replaced line is simply discarded and no message has to be sent to the L2 cache), the *List* protocol requires involving the home L2 cache bank and other nodes in the replacement process. This is needed to ensure that the list structure is correctly maintained after a replacement has taken place. Although not sending replacement hints for clean data in the *Base* protocol can lead to the appearance of some unnecessary invalidations, previous works have demonstrated that this is preferable to the waste of bandwidth and increase in the occupancy of cache and directory controllers that otherwise would be suffered. This is especially true when the number of cores is large.

As with replacements of modified data, before a clean memory block can be replaced in the *List* protocol, a replacement request must be sent to the corresponding home L2 cache. When the L2 receives it and it is ready to handle it, it sends a message authorizing the replacement. This message is answered with another that carries the value of the pointer field kept at the L1 cache which stores the identity of the following L1 cache in the list of sharers. If the identity of the replacing node coincides with the sharer stored at the L2 cache, then the value of the pointer at the L2 cache is changed to the identity of the node included in the replacement request, and an acknowledgement message is immediately sent back to the L1 cache that initiated the replacement. Upon reception of this message, the L1 cache can discard the memory block and the replacement operation is completed. Otherwise, the L2 cache forwards the replacement request to the sharer codified in its pointer field. The message keeps propagating through the list of sharers until the node that precedes the replacing node in the list is reached. At this point, the pointer in the preceding node is updated with the information included in the message (the identity of the node following the replacing node) and an acknowledgement is sent to the replacing L1 cache. Finally, the replacing node sends an acknowledgement to the L2 and the operation completes.

As we will show next, the fact that replacements for clean data in the *List* protocol cannot be done silently significantly increases the number of messages on the interconnection network (bandwidth requirements) and, what is more important, the occupancy of the directory controllers at the L2 cache. It is important to note that although write buffers are used at the L1 caches to prevent delaying unnecessarily the cache miss that caused the replacement, the fact that the directory controller "blocks" the memory block being replaced results in longer latencies for subsequent misses to the replaced address.

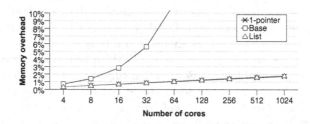

Fig. 2. Memory overhead of the evaluated protocols

3   Directory Memory Overhead Analysis

One of the reasons why directory protocols based on a distributed sharing code were popular two decades ago was their good scalability in terms of the amount of memory required to store sharing information. In the end, this results into lower area requirements and, what is more important nowadays, better scalability in terms of static power consumption. Whereas the amount of bits required per directory entry with a bit-vector sharing code (as the one used in the *Base* protocol) grows linearly with the number of processor cores (one bit per core), for a protocol like *List* the experienced growth is logarithmic. Additionally, the *List* protocol needs one extra pointer in every entry of each L1 cache, but this is not a problem since the number of entries in the L1 caches is much smaller that in the L2 cache banks.

Figure 2 compares the directory protocols considered in this work in terms of the memory overhead each one of them introduce. Particularly, we measure the percentage of memory added by each protocol with respect to the total amount of bits dedicated to the L1 and L2 caches. As we can see, the scalability of the *Base* protocol is restricted to configurations with a small number of cores (as expected). Replacing the bit vector used in each of the L2 cache entries of *Base* with a limited pointer sharing code with one pointer (*1-pointer*) ensures scalability. In this case, the number of bits per entry grows as $\log_2 N$, being N the total number of cores[1]. Finally, the scalability of the *List* protocol is very close to that of *1-pointer*. L1 caches are small, and therefore, the memory overhead that the pointers add at this cache level does not make any noticeable difference.

4   Evaluation Environment

We have done the evaluation of the cache coherence protocols mentioned in this work using the PIN [8] and GEMS 2.1 [10] simulators, which have been connected in a similar way as proposed in [11]. PIN obtains every data access performed by the applications while GEMS models the memory hierarchy and calculates the memory access latency for each processor request. We model the interconnection network with the Garnet [1] simulator. The simulated architecture corresponds to a single chip multiprocessor (*tiled*-CMP) with either 16 or 64 cores. The most relevant simulation parameters are shown in Table 1.

For this work, we have implemented in GEMS a traditional directory-based cache coherence protocol (called *Base*) using full-map sharing vectors, another protocol (called *1-pointer*) that uses a single pointer to the owner as sharing information similarly to AMD's *MagnyCours* [4], and a protocol (which we have called *List*) that uses a distributed sharing code implemented by means of linked lists, described in Section 2. In all the protocols, the L2 cache is strictly inclusive with respect to the L1. Hence, the sharing code can be stored along with the L2 cache tags.

We have used all the applications from the SPLASH-2 benchmark suite with the recommended sizes [13]. We have accounted for the variability of parallel applications as discussed in [2]. To do so, we have performed a number of simulations for each application and configuration inserting random variations in

---

[1] We also consider the *overflow* bit required in each entry to know when two or more sharers are present, and therefore, coherence messages have to be broadcasted.

Table 1. System parameters

Memory parameters	
Block size	64 bytes
L1 cache (data & instr.)	32 KiB, 4 ways
L1 access latency	1 cycle
L2 cache (shared)	512 KiB/tile, 16 ways
L2 access latency	12 cycle
Cache organization	Inclusive
Directory information	Included in L2
Memory access time	160 cycles
Network parameters	
Topology	2-D mesh (4×4 or 8×8)
Routing method	X-Y determinist
Message size	5 flits (data), 1 flit (control)
Link time	1 cycle
Bandwidth	1 flit per cycle

each main memory access. All results in this work correspond to the parallel part of the applications.

5   Evaluation Results

In this section we explain the results of the experiments. We analyze the miss latency and how it is distributed, the network traffic and the execution time of the applications with each protocol, both for 16- and 64-core configurations.

5.1   L1 Miss Latency

Cache miss latency is a key aspect of the performance of a multiprocessor, and the sharing code used by the coherence protocol can affect it significantly. Figure 3 shows the normalized latency of L1 cache misses for configurations with 16 and 64 cores. This latency has been divided in four parts: the time to arrive to L2 (*Reach_L2*), the time spent waiting until the L2 can attend the miss (*At_L2*), the time spent waiting to receive the data from main memory (*Main_memory*) and the time after the L2 sends the data or forwards the request until the requester receives the memory block (*To_L1*). The *Main_memory* time will be 0 for most misses because the data can be found on chip most times, but it is still a significant part of the average miss latency.

We can see that, for 16 cores (Figure 3(a)), miss latency is not much affected by the sharing code employed. There is only a small increase in the *To_L1* time for *1-pointer* and a slightly higher increase for *List*. In both cases, this is due to an increase in the latency of write misses. This increase happens for different reasons in each case. In `1-pointer` it is due to the higher number of messages required to invalidate the sharers (a broadcast each time), while in *List* it is due to serial nature of the invalidation process, as explained in Section 2.

When we look at the results for 64 cores (Figure 3(b)), we see a higher increase in the *To_L1* latency due to the higher number of cores that need to receive invalidation messages. However, the most worrying aspect of the results is the

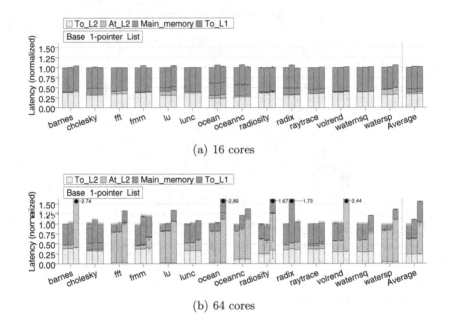

(a) 16 cores

(b) 64 cores

Fig. 3. L1 cache miss latencies

sharp increase in many benchmarks of the time spent waiting for the L2 cache to attend the miss (*At_L2*). We see that, even when using the *Base* protocol, some applications start to suffer the effects of L2 contention when going from 16 to 64 processors, but the *List* protocol exacerbates this effect. This happens because the time needed to update the sharing list grows quicker than for the protocols with centralized sharing information due to its sequential nature in the case of *List*. Moreover, to avoid inconsistencies in the list, the update process happens in mutual exclusion (i.e., only one update action can be done at the same time to the same list), which forces the L2 cache to remain blocked and unable to answer to other requests to the same memory block. For this reason, contention will increase with the number of cores that access the line. The sharing list needs to be updated also in case of a replacement of a shared line, as explained in Section 2, which further increases L2 contention.

5.2   Network Traffic

Figure 4 shows the normalized traffic that travels through the network measured in flits for configurations of 16 and 64 cores. This traffic has been divided in the following categories: data messages due to cache misses (*Data*), data messages due to replacements (*WBData*), control messages due to cache misses (*Control*), control messages due to replacements of private data (*WBControl*) and control messages due to replacements of shared data (*WBSharedControl*).

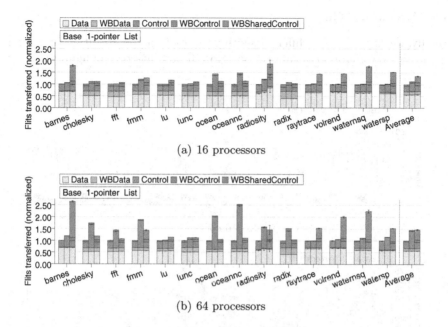

(a) 16 processors

(b) 64 processors

Fig. 4. Interconnection network traffic

As can be seen in the results for the 16-core configuration (Figure 4(a)), the sharing code used by *1-pointer* increases the traffic due to control messages because this protocol needs to perform a broadcast of the invalidation message whenever there is more than one sharer. On the other hand, *List* has the same amount of traffic due to control messages for misses than *Base* (although the messages are processed sequentially instead of in parallel), but it increases significantly the traffic due to replacements, especially in the case of the replacements of shared data which can be done silently in the case of the other two protocols. The replacement process, which updates the sharing list sequentially, contributes to the increase of the L2 contention.

For the 64-core case (Figure 4(b)), the traffic of *1-pointer* overcomes, on average, that of *List* because the cost of the broadcast communication required by the invalidations grows quickly with the number of cores. This demonstrates that although *1-pointer* is as scalable as *List* in terms of storage overhead, it is much less scalable in terms of traffic, and consequently in the energy consumption of the interconnection network. This makes the *1-pointer* protocol unsuitable for a larger number of cores.

Finally, we also see that the traffic due to replacements of shared data increases a great deal for 64 cores in the case of the *List* protocol, especially for some benchmarks. This further shows that replacements handling is one key weak point of the sharing code used by this protocol.

5.3   Execution Time

Finally, we show how the different sharing codes affect the execution time of the applications in Figure 5, as always both for 16- and 64-core configurations.

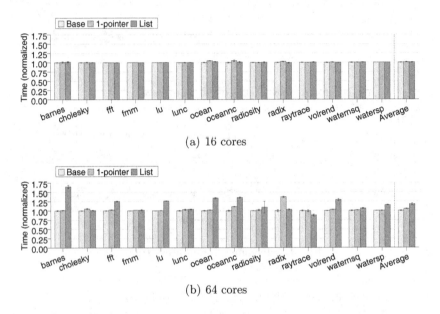

(a) 16 cores

(b) 64 cores

Fig. 5. Execution time

The 16-core configuration (Figure 5(a)) is almost unaffected by the sharing code in terms of execution time. However, in the case of 64 cores (Figura 5(b)) some applications suffer a significant increase in the execution time especially for the *List* protocol. This increase can be observed most clearly in *barnes*, *fft, lu, ocean, oceannc* and *volrend*. If we look back to the miss latency results (Figure 3(b)), we can see that these are precisely the applications whose waiting time at L2 cache increases the most.

6   Conclusions

In this work we have evaluated the behavior of a cache coherence protocol with distributed sharing information based on simply linked lists in the context of a multicore architecture. We have seen that protocols of this kind scale well from the point of view of the amount of memory required for storing sharing information. However, in terms of execution time, although it works as well as the alternatives based on centralized sharing information for a small number of cores, it does not scale well with the number of cores. We have shown that this is, for the most part, due to a higher contention at the directory controllers (at the

L2 cache banks in our case) which stay blocked for much longer and delaying other misses to the same memory block. We have identified the handling of replacements as the main contributor to this problem. Replacements work worse than in the other protocols because the L2 cache controller stays blocked longer and because shared replacements cannot be done silently.

Despite the results obtained until now, we think that this kind of protocols based on distributed sharing information present interesting possibilities which are worth exploring in the context of manycore architectures with a large number of cores. In this way, as future work we plan to reduce the L2 cache busy time by means of improved replacement strategies.

References

1. Agarwal, N., Krishna, T., Peh, L.S., Jha, N.K.: GARNET: A detailed on-chip network model inside a full-system simulator. In: IEEE Int'l Symp. on Performance Analysis of Systems and Software (ISPASS), pp. 33–42 (April 2009)
2. Alameldeen, A.R., Wood, D.A.: Variability in architectural simulations of multi-threaded workloads. In: 9th Int'l Symp. on High-Performance Computer Architecture (HPCA), pp. 7–18 (February 2003)
3. Clark, R., Alnes, K.: An SCI chipset and adapter. In: HotInterconnects Symp. IV, pp. 221–235 (August 1996)
4. Conway, P., Kalyanasundharam, N., Donley, G., Lepak, K., Hughes, B.: Blade computing with the AMD Opteron^{TM} processor ("Magny Cours"). In: 21st HotChips Symp. (August 2009)
5. Culler, D.E., Singh, J.P., Gupta, A.: Parallel Computer Architecture: A Hardware/Software Approach. Morgan Kaufmann Publishers, Inc. (1999)
6. Gustavson, D.B.: The scalable coherent interface and related standards proyects. IEEE Micro 12(1), 10–22 (1992)
7. Lovett, T., Clapp, R.: STiNG: A cc-NUMA computer system for the commercial marketplace. In: 23rd Int'l Symp. on Computer Architecture (ISCA), pp. 308–317 (June 1996)
8. Luk, C.K., Cohn, R., Muth, R., Patil, H., Klauser, A., Lowney, G., Wallace, S., Reddi, V.J., Hazelwood, K.: Pin: Building customized program analysis tools with dynamic instrumentation. In: 2005 ACM SIGPLAN Conf. on Programming Language Design and Implementation (PLDI), pp. 190–200 (June 2005)
9. Martin, M.M.K., Hill, M.D., Sorin, D.: Why on-chip cache coherence is here to stay. Communications of the ACM 55(7), 78–89 (2012)
10. Martin, M.M., Sorin, D.J., Beckmann, B.M., Marty, M.R., Xu, M., Alameldeen, A.R., Moore, K.E., Hill, M.D., Wood, D.A.: Multifacet's general execution-driven multiprocessor simulator (GEMS) toolset. Computer Architecture News 33(4), 92–99 (2005)
11. Monchiero, M., Ahn, J.H., Falcón, A., Ortega, D., Faraboschi, P.: How to simulate 1000 cores. Computer Architecture News 37(2), 10–19 (2009)
12. Thekkath, R., Singh, A.P., Singh, J.P., John, S., Hennessy, J.L.: An evaluation of a commercial cc-NUMA architecture: The CONVEX Exemplar SPP1200. In: 11th Int'l Parallel Processing Symp. (IPPS), pp. 8–17 (April 1997)
13. Woo, S.C., Ohara, M., Torrie, E., Singh, J.P., Gupta, A.: The SPLASH-2 programs: Characterization and methodological considerations. In: 22nd Int'l Symp. on Computer Architecture (ISCA), pp. 24–36 (June 1995)

Coarse/Fine-grained Approaches for Pipelining Computing Stages in FPGA-Based Multicore Architectures*

Ali Azarian and João M.P. Cardoso

Faculty of Engineering, University of Porto and INESC-TEC, Porto, Portugal
azarian@fe.up.pt, jmpc@acm.org

Abstract. In recent years, there has been increasing interest on using task-level pipelining to accelerate the overall execution of applications mainly consisting of producer/consumer tasks. This paper presents coarse/fine-grained data flow synchronization approaches to achieve pipelining execution of the producer/consumer tasks in FPGA-based multicore architectures. Our approaches are able to speedup the overall execution of successive, data-dependent tasks, by using multiple cores and specific customization features provided by FPGAs. An important component of our approach is the use of customized inter-stage buffer schemes to communicate data and to synchronize the cores associated to the producer/consumer tasks. The experimental results show the feasibility of the approach when dealing with producer/consumer tasks with out-of-order communication and reveal noticeable performance improvements for a number of benchmarks over a single core implementation and not using task-level pipelining.

Keywords: Multicore Architectures, Task-level Pipelining, FPGA, Producer/Consumer, Data synchronization.

1 Introduction

Techniques to speed up processing are becoming more and more important. Task-level pipelining is an important technique for multicore based systems, especially when dealing with applications consisting of producer/consumer *(P/C)* tasks (see, e.g., [1]). It may provide additional speedups over the ones achieved when exploring other forms of parallelism. In the presence of multicore based systems, task-level pipelining can be achieved by mapping each task to a distinct core and by synchronizing their execution according to data availability. Task-level pipelining can accelerate the overall execution of the applications consisting mainly of the P/C tasks by partially overlap the execution of data-dependent tasks (herein: Computing Stages).

* This work was partially supported by Fundação para a Ciência e Tecnologia (FCT) under PhD grant SFRH/BD/80481/2011.

L. Lopes et al. (Eds.): Euro-Par 2014 Workshops, Part II, LNCS 8806, pp. 266–278, 2014.

Many applications, such as image/video processing, are structured as a sequences of data-dependent computing stages, use the P/C pair communication paradigm, and are thus amenable to pipelining execution [2,3]. Using task-level pipelining, a consumer computing stage (e.g., identifying a loop or a set of nested loops) may start execution before the end of the producer computing stage, based on data availability. Performance gains can be achieved as the consumer can process data as soon as it becomes available.

There are two types of data synchronization granularity between the producer and the consumer: *Fine-grained* (referred herein as *FG*) and *Coarse-grained* (referred herein as *CG*). In fine-grained schemes, each data element is used to synchronize computing stages. In coarse-grained data synchronization schemes, instead of each data element, chunks of elements or an entire array of elements (e.g., an image) is considered to synchronize computing stages.

In our previous work [4], we presented an approach for fine-grained task-level pipelining in the context of FPGA-based multicore architectures. In this paper, we explore different coarse/fine-grained data synchronization schemes implemented in customized multicore architectures for pipelining out-of-order computing stages. We evaluate our approaches with FPGA implementations and measurements with a set of out-of-order benchmarks (image processing kernels) running on an FPGA board. We compare the execution speedup obtained by our fine- and coarse-grained approaches to task-level pipelining over the execution of the benchmarks in a single core and without using task-level pipelining. The results reveal the effectiveness of coarse/fine-grained techniques regarding execution speedups and inter-stage buffer requirements for out-of-order benchmarks. The experiments also analyze the impact of increasing the size of the local memory used in the inter-stage buffer.

The remainder of this paper is organized as follows. Section 2 presents our fine-grained data synchronization approaches for pipelining computing stages. In Section 3, we present our coarse-grained data synchronization approaches. Section 4 presents the experimental results. Section 5 describes the previous related work in task-level pipelining. Finally, Section 6 concludes this paper.

2 Fine-grained Approaches (FG)

In the context of data communication and synchronization between cores, there are several approaches to overlap some of the execution steps of computing stages (see, e.g., [2,5]). In these approaches, functions or loops waiting for data may start computing as soon as the required data items are produced in a previous function or by a certain iteration of a previous loop. Decreasing the overall program execution time is achieved by mapping each stage to a distinct core (processor) and by overlapping the execution of computing stages. For task-level pipelining, the applications are split into sequences of tasks (computing stages) that represent P/C pairs. To perform fine-grained communication, in the simple case of a sequence of two data-dependent computing stages (one as a producer and the other as a consumer), FIFOs can be used to communicate data between the stages. FIFO channels with blocking reads/writes are sufficient to synchronize data communications [6,5]. The use of FIFO channels is strictly dependent on the order imposed by the communication pattern between P/C pairs. Although FIFO channels are an effective solution for in-order P/C pairs, they may not be efficient or practicable for out-of-order P/C pairs. Thus, it is necessary to use other data communication mechanisms [4,7].

In our previous work, we presented a fine-grained data communication approach by considering an inter-stage buffer (*ISB*) between P/C pairs [4]. To consider frequent communication of data between P/C pairs in these systems, we assume in this paper that the producer and the consumer computing stages process N arrays. The baseline architecture consists of experiments using a single core with two data-dependent computing stages executing sequentially. The execution time of this scheme provides a criterion to compare the performance impact of different proposed coarse/fine-grained data synchronization and communication approaches using task-level pipelining. Although our fine-grained schemes can deal with a variable number of images, we assume $N = 50$ images.

2.1 FG Scheme Using Standard FIFO

In order to pipeline computing stages, the producer and the consumer can be implemented as shown in Figure 1. In this scheme, computing stages are split into two cores: one core as a producer and the other core as a consumer. The communication component between P/C pairs can be a simple FIFO. Reads and writes from/to the FIFO are blocking. When the FIFO is full, the producer waits to write into the FIFO. Similarly, when the FIFO is empty, the consumer waits until a data element is written to the FIFO. The producer sends data elements (e.g., d_0, d_1) into the FIFO and the consumer reads data from the FIFO as soon as it is available. The communication over FIFO channels requires that the consumer reads FIFO data by the same order producer writes FIFO data, otherwise the system enters in a deadlock status.

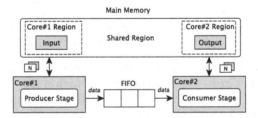

Fig. 1. Fine-grained data synchronization scheme using a FIFO

2.2 FG Scheme with ISB (Inter-Stage Buffer)

We have been exploring an alternative inter-stage scheme to provide task-level pipelining between P/C pairs and to overcome the limitations related to inter-stage communications based on FIFOs. Instead of a FIFO, we use an ISB between

P/C pairs. As illustrated in Figure 2, for each data element being communicated between the producer and the consumer, there is an empty/full flag. The empty/full tagged memories have been used in [8], in the context of shared memory multi-threaded/multi-processor architectures. Our ISB provides an extension to the empty/full tag memory model that considers a cache-based approach.

In our scheme (see Fig.2), the producer is connected to the ISB using one channel responsible for communication between the producer and the ISB. The consumer is connected to the ISB by using two channels: *sending (requesting index)* and *receiving (reading data)*. Our current approach uses blocking write over the sending channel of the ISB and blocking read from the ISB over the receiving channel. The consumer gets data from the ISB using the receiving channel. The sending channel transmits the requests to the ISB concurrently. In the architectures we use, the producer and the consumer are both connected to an external shared memory[1]. The ISB gets the requested index from the consumer side and checks the status of the respective flag addressed by the hash function and verifies if the index matches. If the requested element is present (i.e., if the respective flag bit is full and the index matches) in the ISB local buffer, it is sent to the consumer and respective flag is set to empty. If consumer requests an index which is not available in the local memory, the ISB checks if it is available in main memory.

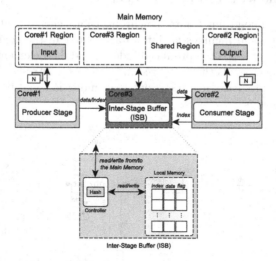

Fig. 2. Fine-grained data synchronization scheme using an Inter-Stage Buffer (ISB) between P/C pairs

For each produced array element, the producer sends its index and value to the ISB (e.g., i as an index and $A[i]$ as a value). The ISB receives the index from

---

[1] Note that the techniques presented in this paper can be also used in architectures with distributed memories. The use of distributed memories possibly will increase the performance impact of using task-level pipelining.

producer side and maps the index into the local memory using a simple hash function (e.g., using a number of least significant bits of the binary representation of the index). The index and value produced are then stored in the ISB local memory location defined by the address given by the hash function. Related to the value stored in the ISB, there is a flag that indicates if a data element was produced and thus can be consumed by the consumer. Although reading/writing from/to local (on-chip) memory of the ISB is fast, the limitation of the size of local memory may be a bottleneck to store all produced data in out-of-order P/C pair cases. We may have a deadlock situation as the producer may stop to produce data if the ISB local memory is full. To avoid deadlock situations, we would need to determine before system deployment the minimum size of the local memory needed. Such approach was proposed by [3] in the context of task-level pipelining of application-specific architectures, where the buffer size was determined using RTL simulation. Thus, to circumvent this problem, we use the main memory if the flag bit in the local memory is full. In this case, the ISB stores the flag and the data value in the main memory without using the hash function. If both flag bits of the local and main memory are empty, the consumer waits until the requested index (and related data element) is produced and is stored in local or in main memory.

2.3   FG Scheme with ISB in Consumer

Figure 3 shows a fine-grained data synchronization scheme that uses a FIFO between P/C pairs and includes an inter-stage buffer in the consumer. In this scheme, the producer sends the produced indexes and data elements through the FIFO. The consumer sends the requested index to the controller. The controller reads the FIFO and checks if the current read index is equal to the requested index of the consumer.

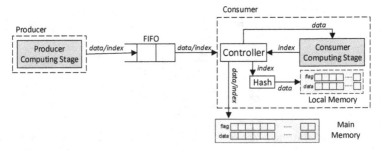

Fig. 3. Fine-grained data synchronization scheme using a FIFO between P/C pairs and considering the inter-stage buffer in the consumer

If the indexes are equal, the controller reads data from the FIFO and sends it to the consumer directly. If the read index from the FIFO is different from the requested index, the controller maps the index into the local memory of the consumer. The local memory structure is based on the empty/full flag bit synchronization model. If the read index cannot be stored in local memory, the controller stores the index and data in external memory. In a similar way, if the requested index of consumer is not equal to the read index from the FIFO and the consumer cannot load the requested index from the local memory or from external memory, the controller stops reading the next requested index from the consumer until the requested index is available in local or in external memory.

3 Coarse-grained Approaches (CG)

We present two different types of coarse-grained multicore architectures using FIFOs between the producer/consumer pairs and a shared main memory.

3.1 CG Scheme with One FIFO

In this scheme, the FIFO contains the *id* of producing arrays (e.g., an image). The producer stores the produced arrays in an external memory and puts the *id* (e.g., base address of an image in external memory) in the FIFO (see, Figure 4 (a)). The consumer gets the *id* from the FIFO and reads the array directly from the external memory using the base address of the array. Reading/writing from/to the FIFO are blocking. If the FIFO is full, the producer stops producing. Similarly, if the FIFO is empty, the consumer waits until the producer puts an *id* into the FIFO. The producer computes the *id* for each array (e.g., image) and store data in external memory based on the base address of each array. In the consumer side, the *id* read from the FIFO and the array data elements are loaded from the external memory. In this scheme, the number of temporary arrays (herein referred as M) stored in external memory is an important property. If $M = 1$, it means that the producer waits for the consumer to consume the entire previously generated array before generating another array. As soon as the *id* of the array is available, the consumer can read the array from external memory. Similarly, the producer is waiting for the confirmation *id* that indicates the consumption of the array. Thus, when $M = 1$, the producer and consumer run without task-level pipelining (e.g., sequentially) over the single core. Therefore, task-level pipelining is achieved when the minimum number of temporary arrays is $M > 1$.

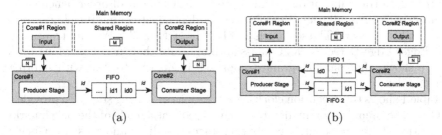

(a)   (b)

Fig. 4. Coarse-grained data synchronization block diagram using: (a) a single FIFO; (b) two FIFOs

3.2   CG Scheme with Two FIFOs

In this scheme, *FIFO 1* (write from the consumer side/read from the producer side) and *FIFO 2* (write from the producer side/read from the consumer side) are located between P/C pairs (see Figure 4(b)). In this scheme, FIFO 2 stores the *id* of producing arrays. Similarly, FIFO 1 stores the *id* of consuming arrays. When the consumer puts the consumed array's *id* into FIFO 1, the producer can reuse the memory by storing the new produced array in the location related to the *id* from FIFO 1. It means that the number of temporary stored arrays in external memory (referred herein as M) is less or equal than the number of arrays being computed (N). However, in a previous scheme (using one FIFO) the number of temporary stored arrays in external memory was equal to the number of arrays. Therefore, the producer can store the new array in external memory as soon as it is free. In a similar way, the consumer reads the id from FIFO 2, consumes the array and sends the id to the producer using FIFO 1.

4   Experimental Results

For evaluating our task-level pipelining approaches, we used a Genesys Virtex-5 XC5LX50T FPGA Development Board [9]. Figure 5 shows the target architecture which was implemented using Xilinx EDK 12.3 tools. We used Xilinx MicroBlaze processors (MB) [10] as cores. Each MicroBlaze is connected to on-chip local memory (BRAMs). The MicroBlaze processors use Xilinx Fast Simplex Link (FSL) to communicate directly with each other. All MicroBlaze processors are connected to the shared DDR RAM memory through the PLB. In Figure 5(a) (two cores architecture), MicroBlaze 1 and MicroBlaze 2 are responsible to execute the codes for the producer and consumer, respectively. In Figure 5(b) (three cores architecture), we use an additional MicroBlaze (MicroBlaze 3) to implement the ISB schemes. Although these architectures may not be the fastest solutions, they provide the flexibility and ease of programmability required to explore and evaluate different fine and coarse-grained data communication and synchronization schemes.

Table 1 presents a set of image processing benchmarks used in our experiments. By considering that most image/video processing benchmarks have out-of-order data communication patterns, we use a set of out-of-order benchmarks in our experiments, all consisting of two data-dependent computing stages (producer and consumer). The set consists of Fast DCT (FDCT), Wavelet transform, FIR-Edge, Edge-Detection and Gaussian blur. Note that in our previous work [4], we shown that our fine-grained approach is efficient to deal with in-order benchmarks.

Table 1 shows the execution clock cycles of each computing stage. To provide a P/C data communication model, the original sequential code of the benchmarks is partitioned into the separate computing stages (producer and consumer), being each stage a sequence of loops or nested loops. We organize our results into two categories, fine-grained and coarse-grained results.

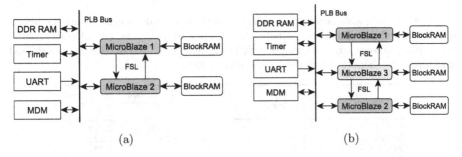

Fig. 5. Target architectures with: (a) two MicroBlazes; (b) three MicroBlazes

Table 1. Benchmarks used in the experiments

Benchmarks	Pattern	Stages	Clock Cycles		
			S1	S2	Overall
Fast DCT (FDCT)	out-of-order	two ($S1$ and $S2$)	27,450,111	27,816,150	55,266,261
Wavelet Transform	out-of-order	two ($S1$ and $S2$)	69,660,426	67,260,579	136,921,005
FIR-Edge	out-of-order	two ($S1$ and $S2$)	27,546,828	20,245,503	47,792,331
Edge-Detection	out-of-order	two ($S1$ and $S2$)	7,891,875	7,152,558	15,044,433
Gaussian blur	out-of-order	two ($S1$ and $S2$)	1,544,962	263,459	1,808,421

4.1 Fine-grained Results

Table 2 shows the speedups obtained by considering fine-grained data synchronization schemes with task-level pipelining vs. a single core architecture. For comparisons, we use the highly optimistic theoretical speedup bounds (herein: Upperbound A) for each application as calculated with Equation 1. This upper bound reflects how the execution times of tasks are balanced (maximum of Upperbound is 2 and corresponds to the execution time equally split over the two tasks and optimistic overlapping of execution of the tasks). In order to have an idea about the possible upperbound (also optimistic) when data are communicated between the two tasks (stages) using local buffers, we include Upperbound B speedups. These were obtained calculating the execution time of each stage considering the unrealistic scenario of inter-stage communicated data being fully stored/loaded to/from internal FIFOs (as if data communication could be in-order) instead of randomly stored/loaded in/from memory (local or external).

$$Theoretical\ Speedupbound = (T_{Stage1} + T_{Stage2})\ /\ Max(T_{Stage1}, T_{Stage2})\quad (1)$$

From Table 2, the highest speedup for all benchmarks in fine-grained data synchronization model is obtained when using the ISB between P/C pairs. Although including the ISB into the consumer may reduce the FPGA resources required, it may not provide the same performance for out-of-order benchmarks compared with the scheme using a separate ISB. The results with a separate ISB illustrate speedups from 1.14× to 1.57×. For FIR-Edge and Gaussian blur benchmarks, the measured speedups are fairly close to the theoretical speedup

Table 2. Speedups obtained by considering fine-grained data synchronization schemes with task-level pipelining vs. a single core baseline architecture, considering $N = 50$ arrays being computed, also compared with the theoretical and maximum upperbound speedups. The default size of the local buffer is 1024.

Benchmark	Inter-Stage Buffer (ISB)	ISB in Consumer	Theoretical Upperbound	
			A	B
FDCT	1.38×	1.37×	1.99×	2.42×
Wavelet	1.46×	1.27×	1.97×	2.22×
FIR-Edge	1.57×	1.21×	1.72×	1.73×
Edge-Detection	1.39×	1.21×	1.91×	1.94×
Gaussian blur	1.14×	0.55×	1.17×	1.28×

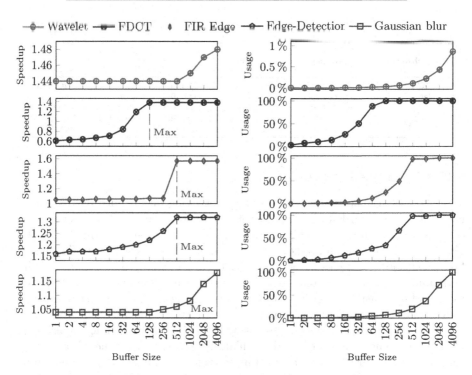

Fig. 6. The impact of increasing the ISB buffer size on speedup (on left) and the percentage of data communicated between stages using the local buffer (Usage) results (on right)

bounds of 1.72× (FIR-Edge) and 1.16× (Gaussian blur). In the case of FDCT, Wavelet and Edge-Detection benchmarks, although the speedup is considerable, we have an small gap between the theoretical speedup and the real FPGA-based achieved speedup (e.g., 1.38× to 1.99× for FDCT).

In the case of the ISB in consumer, the performance resultant when using task-level pipelining is lower. For example, in the case of Gaussian blur benchmark, the achieved performance is even lower than sequential execution of the benchmark (0.55×).

We evaluated the impact of increasing the size of the local buffer (up to 4096 considering the limitation of BRAMs on our FPGA board) on the local memory usage and on the speedup (see Figure 6). The highest speedup for all benchmarks is obtained when the usage of local memory is at maximum. For example, in FDCT, we obtained the maximum usage of local memory (100%) by considering the size of local buffer to 128. Similarly, in Edge-detection and Gaussian blur benchmarks, the maximum usage of local memory was obtained when the size of local buffer is greater than 512, 2048 for FIR-Edge and 4096 for Gaussian blur. The communication pattern in the wavelet transform benchmark allowed only the 0.86% usage of local memory when considering a local buffer with size 4096.

4.2   Coarse-grained Results

Figure 7 shows the achieved speedups in the coarse-grained data synchronization scheme using one FIFO (CG One FIFO) and two FIFOs (CG Two FIFOs) between P/C pairs. In these experiments, we considered a number of arrays (N) being computed. For instance, in CG Scheme with one FIFO, the number of temporary arrays (M) is equal to the number of arrays being produced/consumed. As expected, If $N = 1$ and $M = 1$, the producer waits for the availability of temporary array in external memory, thus, the producer and consumer execute sequentially and therefore, none speedups are achieved. When the number of temporary arrays in external memory is $M > 1$, the producer can process the next array while the consumer core is consuming (processing) the previous array. As shown in Figure 7(a), the results show that increasing the number of arrays being computed (N) and allowing two temporary arrays being stored ($M = 2$) in external memory significantly increases the performance. The performance

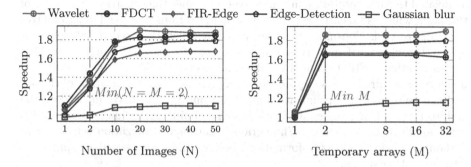

Fig. 7. Speedups achieved by considering coarse-grained data synchronization schemes using: (a) one FIFO; (b) two FIFOs for $N = 50$

significantly increases for values of N between 2 and 20 and stays almost the same for $N > 20$.

Figure 7(b) shows the results when using two FIFOs between P/C pairs. In this scheme, the number of temporary arrays is $1 < M \leq N$. Based on the limitation of available memory on our experimental board, we consider the range of 1 to 32 for temporary arrays (M) and $N = 50$. The results show that the performance with the number of temporary arrays $M = 2$ is very close to the one obtained when increasing the value of M. This is somehow expected as the existence of only one core for the producer and one core for the consumer only allows two temporary arrays being processed (one produced and one consumed). The producing of additional arrays while the consumer is still consuming the previous one, or the consuming of another array while the producer is still being producing the next one, seems as expected to have a small impact on performance.

5   Related Work

In the context of data synchronization, there are several approaches to overlap some of the execution steps of computing stages (see, e.g., [11], [7],[6] and [5]). In these approaches, task-level pipelining model can be easily provided by using a FIFO channel between producer/consumer tasks. Each FIFO stage stores an array element or a set of array elements. Array elements in each FIFO stage can be consumed by a different order than the one they have been produced. The FIFO approach is sufficient when the order of consuming data is the same as the order of producing the data. However, the FIFO may not be efficient when the order of producing and consuming data is not the same. In the presence of in-order P/C pairs, several attempts have been made to resolve the data communication for out-of-order tasks in compile time. For instance, Turjan et al. [7],[6],[12] address a task-level pipelining model maintaining the simple solution based on the FIFO between P/C tasks and using a reordering mechanism to deal with out-of-order tasks. In their approach, the order of the producer and consumer is determined by using a *rank* and *read* functions. The rank function is associated to each iteration point and gives a number that expresses the order of this point which is executed relatively to other iterations. The read function gives the order of each Consumer iteration point in which the needed data element arrives through the FIFO. Based on the order of each P/C pair, a controller checks whether a FIFO channel is sufficient for every P/C pair or an additional memory is required. These approaches may not be feasible for all applications and can be seen as an optimization phase for our approach. We focused on the architectural schemes to enable task-level pipelining given in-order or out-of-order applications with coarse/fine-grained data synchronization schemes and without requiring code transformations besides the ones needed to split code into computing stages.

6 Conclusions

We presented fine- and coarse-grained approaches for task-level pipelining in the context of FPGA-based multicore architectures. Our approaches are able to provide task-level pipelining for out-of-order computing stages in runtime. We analyzed and compared different implementations of fine- and coarse-grained data synchronization schemes for a set of out-of-order producer/consumer benchmarks.

All solutions proposed in this paper were implemented using an FPGA board. The results with an Inter-Stage Buffer (ISB) between producer/consumer cores show speedups from 1.14× to 1.57× for the benchmarks used when using our multicore-based task-level pipelining approaches over the sequential execution of computing stages in a single core. The results also show that an ISB consisting of local (on-chip) memory is an efficient solution for out-of-order data communication between the producer and the consumer. In addition, the results show that small sizes of local memory in the ISB are sufficient to achieve high percentages of inter-stage data communication using local memory and to achieve close to maximum speedups. In the case of the task level pipelining using the coarse-grained data synchronization model, the results show that a number of temporary arrays in external memory equal to 2 is sufficient to achieve significant performance improvements.

Ongoing work is focused on experiments with additional benchmarks, different hash functions, and the impact of application dependent inter-stage communication schemes. Future work will address other schemes for the inter-stage buffer and additional optimizations.

References

1. Kim, D., Kim, K., Kim, J., Lee, S., Yoo, H.: Memory-centric network-on-chip for power efficient execution of task-level pipeline on a multi-core processor. IET Computers & Digital Techniques 3(5), 513–524 (2009)
2. Ziegler, H., So, B., Hall, M., Diniz, P.: Coarse-grain pipelining on multiple FPGA architectures. In: Proc. 10th IEEE Symposium on Field-Programmable Custom Computing Machines, FCCM 2002, pp. 77–86 (2002)
3. Rodrigues, R., Cardoso, J.M.P., Diniz, P.C.: A data-driven approach for pipelining sequences of data-dependent loops. In: Proc. 15th IEEE Symposium on Field-Programmable Custom Computing Machines, FCCM 2007, pp. 219–228 (2007)
4. Azarian, A., Cardoso, J.M.P., Werner, S., Becker, J.: An FPGA-based multi-core approach for pipelining computing stages. In: Proc. 28th ACM Symposium on Applied Computing. SAC 2013, pp. 1533–1540. ACM (2013)
5. Ziegler, H., Hall, M., Diniz, P.: Compiler-generated communication for pipelined fpga applications. In: Proc. 40th Design Automation Conf., pp. 610–615 (2003)
6. Turjan, A., Kienhuis, B., Deprettere, E.: A technique to determine inter-process communication in the polyhedral model. In: Proc. 10th Int'l Workshop on Compilers for Parallel Computers (CPC 2003), pp. 1–9 (2003)
7. Turjan, A., Kienhuis, B., Deprettere, E.: Solving out-of-order communication in kahn process networks. Journal of VLSI Signal Processing Systems for Signal, Image, and Video Technology 40(1), 7–18 (2005)

8. Smith, B.J.: Architecture and applications of the hep multiprocessor computer system. Real-Time Signal Processing IV 298, 241–248 (1982)
9. Digilent, Inc.: Genesys Board Reference Manual (September 2013)
10. Xilinx, Inc.: MicroBlaze Processor Reference Guide v12.3 (2010)
11. Byrd, G., Flynn, M.: Producer-consumer communication in distributed shared memory multiprocessors. Proc. of the IEEE 87(3), 456–466 (1999)
12. Turjan, A., Kienhuis, B., Deprettere, E.: Realizations of the extended linearization model. In: Domain-Specific Processors: Systems, Architectures, Modeling, and Simulation, pp. 171–191. CRC Press (2003)

Improving Energy and Performance with Spintronics Caches in Multicore Systems

William Tuohy[1], Cong Ma[2], Pushkar Nandkar[2],
Nishant Borse[2], and David J. Lilja[2]

[1] Department of Computer Science and Engineering, University of Minnesota - Twin Cities, Minneapolis MN 55455, USA
[2] Department of Electrical and Computer Engineering
University of Minnesota - Twin Cities, Minneapolis MN 55455, USA

Abstract. Spintronic memory (STT-MRAM) is an attractive alternative technology to CMOS since it offers higher density and virtually no leakage current. Spintronic memory continues to require higher write energy, however, presenting a challenge to memory hierarchy design when energy consumption is a concern. Various techniques for reducing write energy have been studied in the past for a single processor, typically focusing on the last-level caches while keeping the first level caches in CMOS to avoid the write latency. In this work, use of STT-MRAM for the first level caches of a multicore processor is motivated by showing that the impact on throughput due to increased write latency is offset in many cases by increased cache size due to higher density. The Parsec benchmark suite is run on a modern multicore platform simulator, comparing performance and energy consumption of the spintronic cache system to a CMOS design. A small, fully-associative level-0 cache is then introduced (on the order of 8-64 cache lines), and shown to effectively hide the STT-MRAM write latency. Performance degradation due to write latency is restored or slightly improved, while cache energy consumption is reduced by 30-50% for 12 of the 13 benchmarks.

1 Introduction

As CMOS technology starts to face serious scaling and power consumption issues, the current SRAM designs become unable to meet the demand of big, fast and low power on-chip cache for multi-core implementations. A new technology, Spin-Transfer Torque-Magnetic RAM (STT-MRAM), one of the novel non-volatile memory family, has drawn substantial attention in recent years. STT-MRAM offers higher density than traditional SRAM cache, and its non-volatility facilitates low leakage power [13]. Also, STT-MRAM is one of few candidates that has almost the same read latency as current SRAM technology. With this higher cell density and low leakage power, STT-MRAM is generally considered as a viable potential alternative to SRAM in future on-chip caches.

STT-MRAM technology suffers from high dynamic energy consumption, however, due to high write current and longer write latency [16]. As others have shown, leakage power at the large last-level caches is the dominant energy consumer in CMOS cache hierarchies [1,9]. This work will consider a cache hierarchy

L. Lopes et al. (Eds.): Euro-Par 2014 Workshops, Part II, LNCS 8806, pp. 279–290, 2014.

with STT-MRAM last-level cache and CMOS first-level cache as the baseline configuration, and study the impact of converting the first-level cache to STT-MRAM as well. The impact on performance and energy over a range of write latencies is analyzed in detail. As would be expected, STT-MRAM reduces leakage power of the first-level cache, but increases energy consumed by processor writes significantly.

The write latency of STT-MRAM has the effect of reducing the available bandwidth into the cache, since this latency cannot be hidden with pipelining or other techniques. To address this fundamental limit, a small fully-associative level-0 (L0) cache was placed in front of the main L1 cache, similar to that proposed in [10]. This structure can be very small, yet have several benefits. By acting as a write-back cache, it absorbs processor writes at full bandwidth, and aggregates them into cache-line size writes to the STT L1 cache in the form of write backs. This technique improves bandwidth into the L1 cache, and can save energy if most of the processor writes can be absorbed there. Simulations show that performance lost due to high write latency can be recovered, while total cache energy consumption is reduced by 30% to 50% for 12 of the 13 benchmarks analyzed.

The contributions of this work include:

1. A detailed performance and energy-consumption study comparing a CMOS to a STT-MRAM first-level cache
2. An analysis of how well a small, fully-associative level-0 cache can overcome the performance degradation caused by long write latency of STT-MRAM
3. An energy comparison of dynamic energy consumed by the caches with and without the added level-0 cache

2   Experimental Methodology

Architectural simulations were performed with the gem5 simulator [4] running the Parsec benchmark suite [3]. A sampling technique similar to that described in SMARTS [22] was used to reduce simulation time while maintaining accuracy. All data is reported just for the parallel region-of-interest (ROI) using checkpoints compiled into the source by [5]. A four-processor system was simulated using a four-wide out-of-order execution model running at 2GHz. The first level cache is private to each CPU, while the last-level cache is shared. Cache coherence is enforced using the MESI protocol with inclusion. The sampled simulation data was verified by running complete simulations of the benchmark on selected configurations, and were found to be quite accurate. Table 1 lists the values of system parameters simulated for each benchmark. Every combination of these parameters was simulated. Cache read latency was assumed to be the same for CMOS and STT-MRAM technologies for the sizes utilized. The Parsec medium data set was used for full simulation runs due to runtime, so the sample runs use that data set as well.

To increase simulation throughput further, multiple simulations were run in parallel on non-overlapping regions of the program. Multiple checkpoints for

Table 1. Simulated Cache Configurations

Parameter	Values
L1 DCache Size	64K CMOS, 128K & 256K STT
STT L1 Write Latency	3ns, 5ns, 8ns
Cache Read Latency	L0 1 cycle, L1 3 cycles, L2 7 cycles (accessed sequentially)
L0 DCache Arrangement	baseline none; 512B, 1K, 4K fully-associative, private
L1 DCache Arrangement	2-way associative, private per CPU
L2 Cache Arrangement	4MB STT, 6ns write, 8-way associative, shared
Coherence Protocol	MESI with inclusion

each benchmark were created at 50 million cycle intervals using the simple atomic CPU model, starting at the ROI. The number of checkpoints created ranged from four for *canneal* to eighty-seven for *freqmine*. From each of these checkpoints, simulations were run in parallel, using GNU Parallel [19] to run thousands of small simulations in a relatively short period of time. Twenty-five samples were gathered from each checkpoint for every configuration simulated. The simulator was modified to allow switching between the simpler timing model CPU and the detailed out-of-order CPU model at different intervals. The simpler timing CPU was used to run the simulation forward for 900K cycles between periods of detailed simulation, keeping the caches and other dynamic structures active. The detailed out-of-order model was then switched in and run for 500K cycles, with the simulation statistics reset at each switchover. Performance impact was measured by comparing the instructions-per-cycle (IPC) of the benchmarks for the different configurations of cache size and write latency. The IPC of each benchmark was computed from the sampled set of IPCs of each interval simulated. Confidence intervals for 95% confidence were computed as well, using the techniques from [14]. In most cases the confidence intervals were very small so they do not change interpretation of the data.

Performance data and event counts relevant to dynamic cache energy consumption were gathered from the simulation statistics. Cacti [7] was modified to model the increased density of STT-MRAM devices, as well as the different leakage power and access transistor sizes required for different access times. A 32nm high-performance process was modeled by changing to bit-cell size from 146 F^2 to 40 F^2 with no leakage. Cacti is now able to model the fully associative caches used in this study. Parallel tag and data access was modeled for the L0 and L1 caches, while serial tag lookup was modeled for the L2. Conservative models were used for all values: L0 and L1 word write energy uses the line access value, since most of the energy is consumed in the peripheral circuitry rather than bit-cell access; array line loading still assumes a 6T cell array, in addition to the larger access transistor for STT. Access energy values include both tag and data array access, and leakage values include tag arrays and the different amounts of circuitry for the different cache sizes and arrangements. For STT-MRAM arrays, a per-bit energy of 300 fJ was added to the Cacti access energy for write operations, 64b for word writes and 512b for cache lines. Table 2 lists

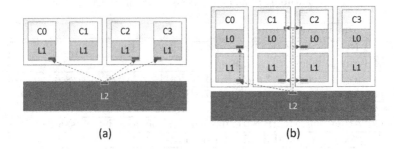

Fig. 1. The two-level hierarchy (a) evaluated in Sec. 3, with CMOS and STT-MRAM as the L1. Then a small fully-associative L0 is added (b) and evaluated in Sec. 4.

Table 2. Energy consumption parameters for the various cache structures

Structure	CMOS L1	STT L1		STT L2	CMOS Level-0		
size	64kB	128kB	256kB	4MB 8-way	512B	1kB	4kB
read (nJ)	0.032	0.033	0.062	0.385	0.0165	0.0165	0.0168
lineWrite(nJ)	0.055	0.220	0.230	0.290	0.0165	0.017	0.0203
wordWrite(nJ)	0.055	0.086	0.096	-	0.0165	0.017	0.0203
leakage(mW)	25	10.0	11.7	92	4.1	4.26	5.65

the power and energy parameters used to compute energy consumption from simulation activity.

3   Converting First Level from CMOS to STT-MRAM

Use of STT-MRAM at different levels of cache creates opposing performance effects. The increased write latency can degrade performance when this latency is exposed, while the larger caches enabled by higher density may increase performance for some programs. It has been seen that the increased latency at the L2 cache does not typically have much impact on performance due to a lower demand on the bandwidth [13]. The cache hierarchies evaluated in this paper are shown in Fig. 1. The configuration names and cache sizes listed in Table 3 are used in the figures and graphs that follow.

3.1   Performance Impact With L1 STT-MRAM

Typical sizes for L1 and L2 in CMOS are assumed to be 64kB for the L1 data cache, and 1MB for a shared L2 unified cache. For the STT-MRAM L2, a density increase of 4× is assumed, so a cache of 4MB would fit in roughly the same chip area and therefore have similar read latency, since read latency is a strong

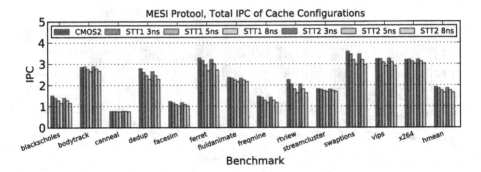

Fig. 2. Total IPC for Parsec benchmarks on a 4-CPU CMP, comparing CMOS2 (left-most bar) to STT1 and STT2 with varying write latency. Harmonic mean of IPC across all benchmarks is also shown, 1.9 for CMOS2. Mean IPC for STT1 is lower by 3% for 3ns write, 9% for 5ns, and 14% for 8ns writes. STT2 is virtually identical to STT1.

function of the length of wires and array size. For the L1 cache, while STT-MRAM density is still high, the actual cache design may be limited by the access transistor size rather than the magnetic tunnel junction device, so we model both 2× and 4× increase in L1 size. Since prior work [2] has shown little or no benefit from typical L3 cache sizes for the Parsec benchmarks, and because use of a third cache level would add more dynamic and static energy, we begin our analysis with a two-level cache hierarchy.

Figure 2 compares performance of CMOS2 to STT2 and STT1, with STT-MRAM write latencies ranging from 3ns to 8ns across all the Parsec benchmarks. The data is the sum of the individual core IPCs for a 4-CPU CMP, showing total system throughput. The best case was no slowdown, while the worst was about -27% for *rtview* at 8ns write latency. Eight of the thirteen benchmarks see less than about 5% slowdown at the 3ns STT-MRAM technology point. Recent work has shown experimental results achieving writes in the 1ns range [24,25], so it may not be overly optimistic to presume that STT-MRAM write latency in this range may become standard. At this design point, the worst slowdown among all benchmarks is less than 10%. There also appears to be little difference in performance between the two STT-MRAM L1 cache sizes considered, indicating that the larger L1 of STT2 does not provide significant improvement. Chip area may be better allocated to other features to improve throughput.

Table 3. Two-Level Hierarchy Configuration Names

Baseline Configuration Names	L1 Cache	L2 Cache
CMOS2	CMOS 64K	STT 4MB
STT1	STT 128K	STT 4MB
STT2	STT 256K	STT 4MB

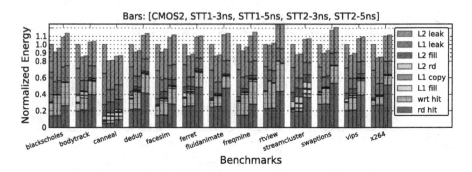

Fig. 3. Breakdown of energy consumption in the 2-level hierarchy, normalized to CMOS2

3.2 Energy Consumption With L1 STT-MRAM

Figure 3 shows the energy consumption of STT1 and STT2 cache configurations, normalized to CMOS2 (the leftmost bar of each benchmark). Though significantly reduced by implementing the L2 cache as STT-MRAM instead of CMOS, L2 leakage is still a large contributor to total cache energy consumption. L1 leakage (2nd segment from top) is also a large percentage of the total in the CMOS2 configuration. The STT1 configuration shows a drop in total energy compared to CMOS2, while the STT2 configuration causes an increase in total energy on most benchmarks due to higher dynamic read energy caused by the heavier loading of the internal array. Since performance was not improved with the larger L1 cache of STT2, L1 capacity does not appear to be the best use of chip area for these workloads. Dynamic energy of processor read and write hits to the L1 cache are the next significant cause of energy consumption in most benchmarks. The large amount of dynamic write hit energy indicates a significant amount of program data stores, which are likely the main cause of the performance drops seen in Figure 2. A technique to improve performance of writes to a high-latency structure, while reducing total energy consumption, would benefit the system in this case. One method to reduce both dynamic and static energy consumed by read and write operations is to use smaller structures, which also allow for faster access time. A fully-associative structure as small as 8 cache lines was added to the system to address these issues, with significant improvement observed.

4   Addition of Fully-Associative Level-0 Cache

The performance impact of STT-MRAM cache is due to reduced bandwidth into the cache stalling the processor. The portion of energy consumption due to processor writes that hit the L1 cache is a function of the number of writes in the program and the cache performance. To address both of these issues, the addition of a small fully-associative structure in front of the STT-MRAM cache

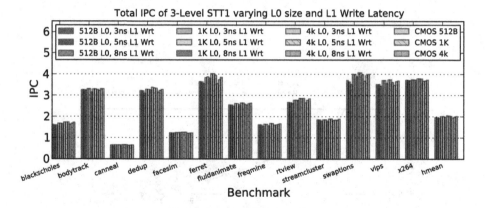

Fig. 4. Total IPC of benchmarks with L0 cache of various sizes, shown for the range of STT write latency from 3-8ns. The IPC drop seen in the two-level hierarchy with increasing write latency is not seen at the 3ns and 5ns configurations. The 8ns writes show a slight drop in some cases. The mean IPCs show no drop with added write latency.

is evaluated, similar to the scheme in [10]. This hierarchy is shown in Fig. 1b. A small structure can be fast enough to keep up with the processor when writes hit, and low enough energy to not offset the gains from implementing the larger L1 cache with STT-MRAM. By acting as a regular write-back cache, effective bandwidth to the L1 cache is increased by converting single-word writes into cacheline writes. By absorbing a high enough percentage of the processor writes, energy is reduced at the L1 cache since there are fewer write events. While at a much smaller scale, the goals are similar to the write aggregation schemes of mass storage systems [20,6].

Figure 4 shows the performance of the STT1 configuration with the added L0 cache of various sizes, ranging from 512B (8 lines) to 4KB (64 lines). As with the trends seen in Fig. 2, the difference in performance between STT1 and STT2 was negligible, so STT2 graphs are not shown. The drop in IPC with increased write latency is effectively eliminated in this scheme. In some benchmarks there is a small increase in performance with increased L0 size, on the order of 10% for *ferret* and *swaptions*, but most show little or no increase. Also shown, in the rightmost bars of each benchmark, is performance of a CMOS L1 of 64kB and the added L0 cache of the same three sizes to ensure a fair baseline. Performance was identical to or slightly below the STT1 performance for the same L0 size. This indicates that the L0 cache does hide the L1 write latency, while also allowing the larger L1 size to increase performance in some cases.

4.1   Energy Consumption With Level-0 Cache

Including the L0 cache in the hierarchy changes the number of events seen at the different cache levels. If enough high-energy events such as STT-MRAM

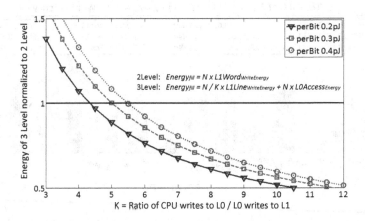

Fig. 5. Model of energy consumption in the L0 and L1 caches combined, as a function of the L1 STT-MRAM bit-cell write energy. Energy in the three-level (L0 + L1) is shown normalized to the two-level configuration (L1 only). The X-axis is the ratio of the number of CPU writes absorbed by the L0 to the number of lines written back from the L0 to the L1. As L1 bit-cell writes use less energy, relatively fewer writes need to be absorbed by the L0 to break even on energy.

writes are eliminated, the total energy consumed in the cache system is reduced. Figure 5 models the change in energy consumption as the effectiveness of the L0 in absorbing CPU writes changes. Portions of the energy equation that are not reduced, such as L0 write energy and leakage, create a lower limit and cause the slope to reduce farther to the right on the X-axis. The values in Table 2 use 0.3 pJ/bit for STT-MRAM write energy calculations.

Figure 6 shows the breakdown of energy consumption with the L0 cache in place. The two leftmost bars of each benchmark show the original CMOS and STT1 data of the two-level system, while the three rightmost bars show the different L0 cache sizes with a 128KB STT-MRAM L1 cache (STT1). While the motivation for use of the L0 cache was to reduce L1 dynamic write energy (the second segments from the bottom in each bar, respectively), L1 dynamic read energy also dropped significantly. The lowest two segments of the CMOS2 and STT1 bars are replaced by the low three segments of the L0 bars, which include L0 dynamic energy and L1 accesses. L0 leakage is also added, the third segment from the top. Examining the data for one benchmark, *blackscholes*, it can be seen that dynamic write energy (2nd segment from the bottom) grew significantly when going from CMOS2 to STT1. When the L0 was added, dynamic write energy was reduced to about the same magnitude as CMOS2 for the 512B case, and even further for the 1kB L0 case. The effectiveness in absorbing writes, K in Fig. 5, increased with the larger L0.

The size of the L0 does not change the total dynamic energy significantly for about half of the benchmarks. For others, such as *blackscholes, dedup,* and *freqmine,* a larger L0 further reduces L1 energy by reducing the L0 miss rate, as

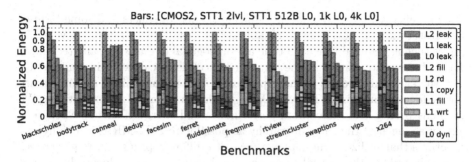

Fig. 6. Energy breakdown normalized to CMOS2 (two-level), showing CMOS2 and STT1 two-level, followed by STT1 with the three L0 cache sizes added. The lowest segments show L1 read for the two-level and L0 total dynamic energy for the 3-level; the 2nd segments show L1 write hits for the two-level and L1 line fills for the 3-level, one motivation for the L0 cache. Dynamic read energy is reduced significantly as well as write energy, indicating that the L0 is quite effective.

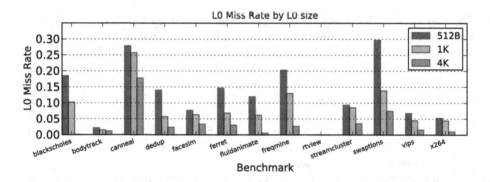

Fig. 7. Miss rate at the L0 cache for each benchmark as L0 size is increased. Bars for *blackscholes* at 4k and *rtview* are too small to show up at this scale.

shown in Fig. 7. Since the L0 modeled here is so small, it does not seem likely that the benchmark dataset size would make much difference in these results, but this should be verified with further simulation. Total energy consumption is reduced in the range of 30-50% from CMOS2 levels. For STT1 the gains are similar except for the *canneal* benchmark, which has poor locality and is more sensitive to memory latency than any other system parameter.

5   Related Work

To address the write power and latency problems, researchers have proposed several techniques: decreasing the retention time [16,17,9], modifying the cache hierarchy to use a mix of structures with different properties [13,23,11,17,21,8], implementing policies to limit write operations to high-power structures [15,26,12,18,1]. Decreasing the retention time trades reliability for area and energy on a device level, requiring the use of timers and some form of data restoration or movement to reliable structures. Device or circuit-level techniques such as reduced retention time are orthogonal to our work; any technique that reduces write energy at the array or bit-cell level can work in conjunction with the cache hierarchies we have proposed. The various mixed structures are mostly focused on using STT-MRAM at the larger L2 and LLC structures. We are focused on getting maximum performance and energy efficiency when converting as much of the cache hierarchy as possible to STT-MRAM. The hybrid structures that utilize cache sets or ways with different properties require other hardware such as timers and predictors to decide where to allocate lines, and when to move lines from more volatile to less volatile areas. This extra data movement is overhead for energy consumption. Our scheme does not require any new hardware other than normal cache controllers and replacement logic.

6   Conclusions

The impact on performance and energy consumption of STT-MRAM use as first-level cache in a modern chip-multiprocessor has been evaluated, first with a standard two-level hierarchy and then with the addition of a small fully-associative structure. Performance with the STT-MRAM first-level cache was degraded in most benchmarks, and continued to degrade further as write latency was increased. Energy consumption of this configuration varied from a best-case of 20% reduction to worst-case of over 15% increase, since the various components such as leakage and write events changed significantly. Processor writes that hit the L1 cache became a high consumer of energy, more so than cache line fills and other events, in most benchmarks.

To address the performance penalty and potentially reduce energy consumption further, a small fully-associative structure was added to the system to act as a level-0 cache. When used as a standard write-back cache with no other additional hardware, a structure as small as eight cache lines was shown to be completely effective at eliminating the performance penalty, and in some cases enabled even higher performance to be realized by the larger STT-MRAM L1 cache. The total energy consumption of the cache hierarchy was reduced in the range of 30-50% for every benchmark except *canneal*, showing that STT-MRAM can be effectively used at the lower levels of the cache hierarchy when augmented with this small, fast structure to hide the write latency. The resulting system has no performance loss due to slow write operations, and in some cases speedups were observed, in addition to significant energy savings.

References

1. Ahn, J., Yoo, S., Choi, K.: Dasca: Dead write prediction assisted stt-ram cache architecture. In: 2014 IEEE 20th International Symposium on High Performance Computer Architecture, HPCA 2014 (February 2014)

2. Bhadauria, M., Weaver, V.M., McKee, S.A.: Understanding PARSEC performance on contemporary CMPs. In: IEEE International Symposium on Workload Characterization, IISWC 2009, pp. 98–107 (2009)

3. Bienia, C.: Benchmarking Modern Multiprocessors. Ph.D. thesis, Princeton University (January 2011)

4. Binkert, N., Beckmann, B., Black, G., Reinhardt, S.K., Saidi, A., Basu, A., Hestness, J., Hower, D.R., Krishna, T., Sardashti, S., Sen, R., Sewell, K., Shoaib, M., Vaish, N., Hill, M.D., Wood, D.A.: The gem5 simulator. SIGARCH Comput. Archit. News 39(2), 1–7 (2011), http://doi.acm.org/10.1145/2024716.2024718

5. Gebhart, M., Hestness, J., Fatehi, E., Gratz, P., Keckler, S.W.: Running parsec 2.1 on m5. Tech. rep., The University of Texas at Austin, Department of Computer Science (October 2009)

6. Gill, B.S., Modha, D.S.: Wow: Wise ordering for writes - combining spatial and temporal locality in non-volatile caches. In: Proceedings of the 4th Conference on USENIX Conference on File and Storage Technologies, FAST 2005, vol. 4, p. 10. USENIX Association, Berkeley (2005)

7. Hewlett-Packard Development Company, L.: Cacti 6.5 (2009), http://www.hpl.hp.com/research/cacti/

8. Jadidi, A., Arjomand, M., Sarbazi-Azad, H.: High-endurance and performance-efficient design of hybrid cache architectures through adaptive line replacement. In: ISLPED 2011: Proceedings of the 17th IEEE/ACM International Symposium on Low-Power Electronics and Design. IEEE Press (August 2011)

9. Jog, A., Mishra, A.K., Xu, C., Xie, Y., Narayanan, V., Iyer, R.K., Das, C.R.: Cache revive: Architecting volatile STT-RAM caches for enhanced performance in CMPs. In: DAC 2012: Proceedings of the 49th Annual Design Automation Conference, pp. 243–252 (2012)

10. Jouppi, N.P.: Improving direct-mapped cache performance by the addition of a small fully-associative cache and prefetch buffers. ACM SIGARCH Computer Architecture News 18, 364–373 (1990)

11. Kim, Y., Gupta, S.K., Park, S.P., Panagopoulos, G., Roy, K.: Write-optimized reliable design of STT MRAM. In: ISLPED 2012: Proceedings of the 2012 ACM/IEEE international symposium on Low Power Electronics and Design. ACM Request Permissions (July 2012)

12. Kwon, K.W., Choday, S.H., Kim, Y., Roy, K.: AWARE (Asymmetric Write Architecture With REdundant Blocks): A High Write Speed STT-MRAM Cache Architecture. IEEE Transactions on Very Large Scale Integration (VLSI) Systems 22(4), 712–720

13. Park, S.P., Gupta, S., Mojumder, N., Raghunathan, A., Roy, K.: Future cache design using STT MRAMs for improved energy efficiency: devices, circuits and architecture. In: DAC 2012: Proceedings of the 49th Annual Design Automation Conference. ACM Request Permissions (June 2012)

14. Patil, S., Lilja, D.J.: Using resampling techniques to compute confidence intervals for the harmonic mean of rate-based performance metrics. Computer Architecture Letters 9(1), 1–4 (2010)

15. Rasquinha, M., Choudhary, D., Chatterjee, S., Mukhopadhyay, S., Yalamanchili, S.: An energy efficient cache design using spin torque transfer (STT) RAM. In: ISLPED 2010: Proceedings of the 16th ACM/IEEE International Symposium on Low Power Electronics and Design. ACM Request Permissions (August 2010)

16. Smullen, C.W.I., Mohan, V., Nigam, A., Gurumurthi, S., Stan, M.R.J.: Relaxing Non-Volatility for Fast and Energy-Efficient STT-RAM Caches. In: 2011 IEEE 17th International Symposium on High Performance Computer Architecture (HPCA), pp. 50–61 (2011)
17. Sun, Z., Bi, X., Li, H.H., Wong, W.F., Ong, Z.L., Zhu, X., Wu, W.: Multi retention level STT-RAM cache designs with a dynamic refresh scheme. In: MICRO-44 2011: Proceedings of the 44th Annual IEEE/ACM International Symposium on Microarchitecture. ACM Request Permissions (December 2011)
18. Sun, Z., Li, H., Wu, W.: A dual-mode architecture for fast-switching STT-RAM. In: ISLPED 2012: Proceedings of the 2012 ACM/IEEE International Symposium on Low Power Electronics and Design. ACM Request Permissions (July 2012)
19. Tange, O.: Gnu parallel - the command-line power tool. ;Login: The USENIX Magazine 36(1), 42–47 (2011), http://www.gnu.org/s/parallel
20. Varma, A., Jacobson, Q.: Destage algorithms for disk arrays with non-volatile caches. In: Proceedings of the 22nd Annual International Symposium on Computer Architecture, pp. 83–95 (June 1995)
21. Wu, X., Li, J., Zhang, L., Speight, E., Xie, Y.: Power and performance of read-write aware hybrid caches with non-volatile memories. In: Design, Automation Test in Europe Conference Exhibition, DATE 2009, pp. 737–742 (April 2009)
22. Wunderlich, R.E., Wenisch, T.F., Falsafi, B., Hoe, J.C.: SMARTS: accelerating microarchitecture simulation via rigorous statistical sampling. In: ISCA 2003: Proceedings of the 30th Annual International Symposium on Computer Architecture. ACM (June 2003)
23. Xu, W., Sun, H., Wang, X., Chen, Y., Zhang, T.: Design of last-level on-chip cache using spin-torque transfer ram (stt ram). IEEE Transactions on Very Large Scale Integration (VLSI) Systems 19(3), 483–493 (2011)
24. Yoda, H., Fujita, S., Shimomura, N., Kitagawa, E., Abe, K., Nomura, K., Noguchi, H., Ito, J.: Progress of STT-MRAM technology and the effect on normally-off computing systems. In: 2012 IEEE International Electron Devices Meeting (IEDM), pp. 11.3.1–11.3.4 (2012)
25. Zhao, H., Glass, B., Amiri, P.K., Lyle, A., Zhang, Y., Chen, Y.J., Rowlands, G., Upadhyaya, P., Zeng, Z., Katine, J.A., Langer, J., Galatsis, K., Jiang, H., Wang, K.L., Krivorotov, I.N., Wang, J.P.: Sub-200 ps spin transfer torque switching in in-plane magnetic tunnel junctions with interface perpendicular anisotropy. Journal of Physics D: Applied Physics 45(2), 025001 (2011)
26. Zhou, P., Zhao, B., Yang, J., Zhang, Y.: Energy reduction for STT-RAM using early write termination. In: ICCAD 2009: Proceedings of the 2009 International Conference on Computer-Aided Design. ACM Request Permissions (November 2009)

Performance Measurement for the OpenMP 4.0 Offloading Model

Robert Dietrich[1], Felix Schmitt[1], Alexander Grund[1], and Dirk Schmidl[2]

[1] Center for Information Services and High Performance Computing,
Technische Universität Dresden, 01062 Dresden, Germany
{robert.dietrich,felix.schmitt}@tu-dresden.de,
alexander.grund@mailbox.tu-dresden.de
[2] IT Center, RWTH Aachen University, 52056 Aachen, Germany
schmidl@itc.rwth-aachen.de

Abstract. OpenMP is one of the most widely used standards for enabling thread-level parallelism in high performance computing codes. The recently released version 4.0 of the specification introduces directives that enable application developers to offload portions of the computation to massively-parallel target devices. However, to efficiently utilize these devices, sophisticated performance analysis tools are required. The emerging OpenMP Tools Interface (OMPT) aids the development of portable tools, but currently lacks the support for OpenMP 4.0 target directives. This paper presents a novel approach to measure the performance of applications utilizing OpenMP offloading. It introduces *libmpti*, an OMPT-based measurement library for Intel MIC target devices. For host-side analysis we extended the OPARI2 instrumenter and prototypically integrated the complete approach into the state-of-the-art tool infrastructure Score-P. We demonstrate the effectiveness of the presented method and implementation with a Conjugate-Gradient (CG) kernel on an Intel Xeon Phi coprocessor. Finally, we visualize the obtained performance data with Vampir.

Keywords: performance analysis, offloading, OpenMP 4.0, Intel MIC, Score-P.

1 Introduction

The directive-based programming model OpenMP is a popular way to develop multi-threaded applications. Version 4.0 [9] of the specification introduces directives for computation offloading; thus, taking the availability of accelerator hardware in recent computing systems and processors into account. Although OpenMP 4.0 provides an interface for programming of heterogeneous hardware, it does not ensure that the available resources are efficiently exploited, e.g. load-balancing is getting more tedious. To identify and resolve new potential inefficiencies performance tools are challenged to support the offloading directives.

For the simple reason that OpenMP does not provide a standardized performance monitoring interface yet, several individual analysis approaches have emerged. Depending on the approach they come with inherent limitations and advantages. Although it is not yet part of the specification, the OpenMP Architecture Review Board released

L. Lopes et al. (Eds.): Euro-Par 2014 Workshops, Part II, LNCS 8806, pp. 291–301, 2014.

the OpenMP Tools Interface (OMPT) as a technical report [2]. OMPT specifies an application programming interface (API) that enables tool builders to develop portable libraries for performance monitoring. First implementations of OMPT are available for open-source OpenMP runtimes. However, OMPT is built on version 3.1 of the OpenMP specification and lacks support for offloading directives.

This work presents a portable method to measure the performance of OpenMP 4.0 computation offloading. We further contribute with a prototypic implementation into the measurement infrastructure Score-P. With regard to the OpenMP standard we build our approach upon OMPT. As it is already a part of the Score-P infrastructure we use the source-to-source instrumenter OPARI2 to implement features that are missing in OMPT. We evaluate the proposed methods with an OMPT implementation in the open-source version of the Intel OpenMP runtime [1] on the Intel Many Integrated Core (MIC) architecture using a Conjugate-Gradient kernel.

The remainder of this paper is organized as follows: Section 2 presents related work in the area of OpenMP performance analysis. In section 3 we depict the two OpenMP instrumentation approaches this work is based on. Our contribution is discussed in section 4 and the integration into the Score-P infrastructure in section 5. We demonstrate the practicality of the proposed method by applying it to a use case in section 6. Finally, we conclude this paper and outline future work in section 7.

2   Related Work

Score-P [6] is a unified performance measurement infrastructure for several tools like Vampir [4] and Scalasca [3]. It supports different programming models such as MPI, OpenMP and CUDA and it allows to generate profiles in CUBE format as well as traces in OTF2 format. Considering OpenMP measurement, Score-P uses OPARI2 to instrument application code and implements the POMP2 interface.

Scalasca [3] is a scalable performance analysis toolset which can handle Score-P generated profiles and traces. It supports the analysis of hybrid MPI+OpenMP applications on the Intel Xeon Phi coprocessor using Intel's symmetric execution model for MIC [10], i.e. MPI communication is used between host and coprocessor. Our work is different as we focus on the asymmetric offloading model based on OpenMP 4.0. Nevertheless, our approach can be used for hybrid MPI+OpenMP programs on multiple hosts and coprocessors.

Vampir [4] is a scalable visualization tool for OTF and OTF2 trace files. It consists of a client front end and a parallel server back end. Information is visualized in various displays, including an event timeline, function and message statistics and call stacks. The integration of our measurement approach into Score-P allows us to use Vampir to display performance data for offloaded regions.

HPCToolkit [5] is a set of sampling-based tools for measuring, evaluating and visualizing performance data for MPI, OpenMP and CUDA applications. Considering OpenMP, HPCToolkit uses the OMPT interface to query state information for OpenMP threads. States can include for example if a thread is currently executing a parallel region, it is idle or waiting on another. As OMPT currently does not provide support for OpenMP target devices HPCToolkit cannot gather respective state information.

The CUDA Profiling Tools Interface (CUPTI) [8] is a proprietary tools interface by NVIDIA for their CUDA architecture, which is used by many tools like e.g. Vampir-Trace and Score-P. It provides an API that allows tools to register for event callbacks, measure performance counters, metrics and activity records. Since the CUPTI library resides in the host address space, the tool is not required to transfer performance information from the target device explicitly.

3   OpenMP Instrumentation

The OpenMP specification does not define a performance monitoring interface yet, but a technical report (TR) which covers such an interface has been released by the OpenMP Architecture Review Board. As upcoming OpenMP specifications will eventually include this TR we base our work on it. However, OpenMP 4.0 offloading directives are neither defined in the current proposal nor is their implementation available in publicly accessible OpenMP runtimes. To instrument OpenMP offloading anyway we prototypically extended the instrumenter OPARI2.

3.1   OMPT

OMPT [2] addresses two strategies for performance data collection: asynchronous sampling and event-based monitoring. For tools that employ asynchronous sampling OMPT provides routines to query information about the state of each OpenMP thread. States are classified to be either mandatory, optional or flexible. In contrast to mandatory states, an OpenMP implementation does not need to maintain optional states. Aside from that it has some freedom when reporting a transition to a flexible state.

Event-based tools, like e.g. Score-P, can register function callbacks for particular events that are triggered by the OpenMP runtime system. OMPT provides begin and end events for most OpenMP constructs. However, the set of mandatory events is small and allows tools to collect only basic information about the runtime behavior of OpenMP programs. To gather more performance-critical information tools have to register for optional events that might not be available for a given OpenMP runtime system.

OMPT is intended to be implemented by a compiler, an OpenMP runtime system or a mixture of both. Therefore the interface defines function pointer addresses for outlined functions of parallel regions and tasks as the only meta information on constructs. The function pointers can be used to distinguish OpenMP constructs of the same type, respectively identify regions of the same construct and to obtain source-code information if available.

3.2   OPARI2

OPARI2 is the current version of the source-to-source instrumentation tool OPARI (OpenMP Pragma and Region Instrumenter) [7], which inserts calls to the POMP2 monitoring interface at OpenMP pragmas and library calls. Similar to the events defined in the OMPT interface the POMP2 event model provides events for the begin and the end of an OpenMP construct, enabling tools to gather performance information for OpenMP programs.

As the OPARI2 instrumentation modifies the source code directly it is independent of a specific OpenMP implementation but requires recompilation of the application. Additionally, OPARI2 creates *POMP2 region handles* for OpenMP constructs, e.g. *parallel regions* and *tasks*, which include source information such as the file and line number of the construct. Tools can utilize these handles to correlate performance information directly with the source code, thereby aiding developers to easily identify performance-critical code.

4   Measuring the OpenMP 4.0 Offloading Model

The OpenMP 4.0 specification introduces several new directives. This work focuses on the measurement of the offloading model. We use the terms *host device* and *target device* according to the specification. The *host device* is the system *from which* code within an OpenMP *target* construct is Since applications are started from the *host device*, this is furthermore where the measurement environment executes. A *target device* describes an accelerator or coprocessor *to which* the mentioned *target* region is offloaded. Regularly, *host device* and *target device* do not share a common address space, which must be taken into account when designing adequate tool support.

4.1   OpenMP 4.0 Target Directives

OpenMP 4.0 introduces the target directives to enable computation offloading. Encountering a *target* construct implicitly creates a device data environment and the subsequent statement, loop or structured block is executed on the target device. The *target data* construct explicitly creates a device data environment which can be used to avoid implicit data transfers between host and target device for enclosed target regions.

When a *map* clause is present for a *target* or *target data* construct and the data have not been mapped in a surrounding data environment before, they are mapped explicitly, according to the specified variables and map-types, at the beginning and end of the block. Map-types are *alloc, to, from*, and *tofrom*. Depending on the hardware configuration and the OpenMP runtime implementation, the mapping invokes a data transfer. Variables not declared but referenced in a *target* construct are treated as if they appeared in a *map* clause with a map-type *tofrom*, thus, they are implicitly transferred to and from the target device. The *target update* construct is a stand-alone directive and makes data on the host and target device consistent, according to the variables specified in the *motion-clause*. Motion-clauses are *to* and *from* and update data on the target or on the host, respectively. If a *device* clause is present in a target directive, it specifies the target device. Otherwise the default device is used. When an *if* clause is present and its expression evaluates to false the target directive does not take effect, as data are not mapped nor is the execution offloaded to the target device.

There are other new directives in OpenMP 4.0 that might influence the execution efficiency, such as e.g. the *teams*, the *distribute* and the *simd* directive. However, we do not observe them in terms of performance measurement within the scope of this paper.

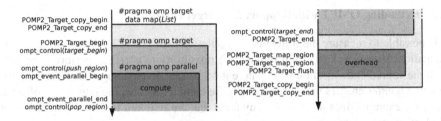

Fig. 1. Execution sequence of measurement routines for an OpenMP parallel region enclosed in a target region. A separate device data region has been added to measure the explicit mapping of variables. OpenMP constructs are instrumented with POMP2 and OMPT calls.

4.2 Measurement Approach

The measurement of OpenMP target regions and other enclosed regions can be achieved with a combination of OPARI2 instrumentation and OMPT callbacks. Figure 1 shows the execution sequence of measurement routines for a simple program with a *parallel* construct enclosed by a *target* construct. To record the runtime of a *target* region, timing routines are added before the directive and after the associated code (statement, loop or structured block). For *target data* regions a time stamp is recorded before the respective begin directive and at the beginning of the associated code as well as at the end of the associated code and after the *target data* region. As *target data* regions are executed on the host device, the deployed measurement environment can directly record the resulting data transfer times. If data transfers are only asynchronously invoked (e.g. for GPGPUs), this approach does not measure the effective mapping. However, these types of data transfers can be measured by other means (e.g. libcupti for CUDA devices).

Measuring data transfers for a *target* construct with a *map* clause is a bit more tedious. To obtain the transfer time for explicit data transfers specified in the *map* clause, we move the respective clause to a newly generated *target data* construct enclosing the original *target* construct. However, there might occur implicit data transfers that are invoked simply by referencing variables that are not declared for the target device. This implicit data mapping can be recorded as part of the *target* region overhead, which is measured by calling a timing routine before the execution of the respective directive and at the beginning of the associated code as well as at the end of the associated code and after the *target* region.

To record the execution of OpenMP constructs that are enclosed in a *target* region we register callbacks for OMPT events. We record events on the master thread of a thread team executing a parallel region and each explicit task. Additionally, we measure some optional events when available, such as barriers. Source-code correlation for these events is added by inserting *ompt_control* calls passing a region handle that is later mapped to the corresponding statically created POMP2 region handle. After the target region finishes execution, the target device buffer is flushed (*POMP2_Target_flush*). This introduces most of the measurement overhead, but only at synchronous points in the program execution. Furthermore, we insert synchronization points before and after a target region that are necessary to convert the target device time stamps to host device time stamps.

4.3   Extending OMPT with Support for Target Directives

It is possible to measure the offloaded computation using OMPT without prior instrumentation. However, this would remove the possibility to correlate performance data with the source-code location from where it originates. Even though OMPT's *outlined function pointer* enables the tool to identify the calling function, the Intel MIC software stack for example does not provide any tools that are required to evaluate a backtrace to identify source file and line for a memory address.

Without instrumentation, performance tools that use OMPT must be able to register callbacks for *synchronization points* at which performance data can safely be collected from the target device. Such synchronization points could be the begin and end of a target region. Similar callbacks would be beneficial to measure the data transfers induced by *target update* directives. Note that none of these are yet available but they are likely to be added to a future version of OMPT. Within the callback, the host tool could notify the target device to flush its buffers and transfer the collected records to the host.

5   Integration into Score-P and OPARI2

5.1   Measurement Control Flow

We integrated our approach into the measurement infrastructure Score-P since it already supports OpenMP performance analysis using OPARI2. When the Score-P compiler wrapper detects OpenMP code, it invokes the OPARI2 instrumenter which has been extended to enable the instrumentation of new OpenMP 4.0 directives. At application start a small measurement library called *libmpti* that implements the OMPT interface is preloaded on the target device. This library is responsible for capturing performance-related events on the target device using OMPT. Once control is returned to the host device after the *target* region has been executed, performance records are transferred from the target to the host device by Score-P. The complete control flow is illustrated in figure 2.

5.2   Extensions to the POMP2 Interface

To properly support the measurement of OpenMP 4.0 *target* constructs, we added six functions to the POMP2 interface (cf. figure 1). *POMP2_Target_begin/end* are inserted before and after the *target* construct in order to perform host/target time synchronization and setup appropriate data structures. Several calls to *POMP2_Target_map_region* are inserted after the *target* construct to map runtime identifiers for OpenMP constructs, which are integral numbers, to their corresponding POMP2 region handles. The latter contain source code information but cannot be used directly on the target device because the OMPT interface allows to pass only values of type *uint64_t* to *ompt_control*. *POMP2_Target_flush* is called directly before *POMP2_Target_end* and initiates the transfer of target device records from *libmpti* to Score-P on the host device. Finally, *POMP2_Target_copy_begin/end* calls are added by OPARI2 around both begin and end of a *target data* directive to measure the execution time of data transfers.

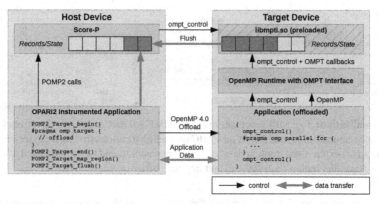

Fig. 2.   Control and Data Flow: Host OpenMP activities are captured by Score-P using the POMP2 interface. Performance records for offloaded application parts are measured using *libmpti*, which implements OMPT on the target device, and transferred to the host during *POMP2_Target_flush*. OpenMP constructs enclosed in a *target* construct are instrumented with *ompt_control* calls to track their execution. The hatched area is the only platform-dependent part.

5.3   MIC Performance Tools Interface

The **MIC P**erformance **T**ools **I**nterface (*libmpti*) is a small library which implements the OMPT interface for the Intel MIC architecture and is compiled as native MIC code (i.e. using the *-mmic* compiler argument). Since the OMPT-instrumented open-source version of the Intel OpenMP runtime cannot be compiled as a fat binary for the host and the MIC, the library cannot be linked against the created executable directly. Instead, *libmpti* is preloaded at application start using Unix' *LD_PRELOAD* mechanism. With regard to Score-P, *libmpti* is not used directly in offloaded measurement code but only by means of the portable OMPT control mechanism.

Registering for OMPT events, the library can record execution times for parallel regions and explicit tasks on the target device. Per-thread data is available via OMPT but not recorded as this would incur significant runtime overhead. Furthermore, *libmpti* tracks the current state of each thread executing on the target device. This state includes only a stack of identifiers designating the currently executed construct. A region identifier is pushed on this stack using *ompt_control* calls inserted via OPARI2 instrumentation directly before an OpenMP *parallel* or *task* construct. Similarly, the current identifier is popped from the stack after the respective construct has been left. This allows *libmpti* to correlate generic region identifiers with target device records. When Score-P receives those records from *libmpti*, it can map them to POMP2 region handles which include information such as the source file and line number on the host device.

5.4   Visualization

Integration of our offloading measurement approach into Score-P allows developers to take advantage of its OTF2 trace output. Resulting traces can be readily visualized in the Vampir trace viewer. For offloading records created using *libmpti*, Score-P can internally utilize the same mechanisms and data structures as for traditional OpenMP performance data, resulting in a homogeneous Vampir experience for the user.

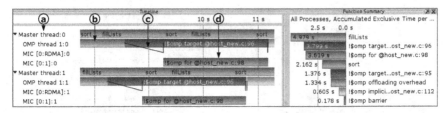

Fig. 3. Visualization: Two MPI processes using OpenMP 4.0 *task* and *target* directives for heterogeneous computation: (a) naming of new MIC offloading locations (b) target device initialization overhead (c) explicit and implicit data transfers between host and target visualized as RDMA messages (d) parallel region (*parallel for*) and implicit barrier on target device

Vampir allows to display hierarchies of processes and threads (*locations*) to present OpenMP threads as children of the spawning process. Therefore, we create new child locations for offloaded OpenMP, too. We add a new target location for each explicit task and each master thread in a thread team executing a parallel region. This also includes measurement and visualization of nested parallelism. As a result, we create similar experience to the visualization of CUDA kernels with dynamic parallelism. As threads on an OpenMP target device are similar to locations (*streams*) on different CUDA devices, we furthermore create a resembling naming for those executing on the MIC architecture (see Figure 3 (a)).

Differences between the visualization of traditional and offloaded OpenMP code are primarily in data transfers. OpenMP 4.0 uses both implicit and explicit data transfers between host and target. In the case of Intel's Xeon Phi coprocessor device, the connection is realized using the PCI-Express interface and data transfers over this interface can suffer from both latency and bandwidth restrictions. Hence, developers must be able to identify OpenMP constructs that result in poor application performance due to such transfers.

For data transfers, one RDMA location per target device is added. On this location, we use the same visualization for both explicit and implicit transfers (see Figure 3 (c)). All transfers are marked as RDMA messages from the spawning host thread to the target's RDMA location. Note that for implicit transfers, this also includes the launch overhead for the target region as the two cannot be distinguished using OpenMP means.

6 Experiments on Intel Xeon Phi

We use an implementation of the sparse Conjugate-Gradient (CG) method to evaluate our measurement approach. The algorithm consists of a matrix-vector multiplication and some vector operations which have been offloaded to the target device. Additionally, a *target data* construct was added to keep all vectors and the matrix on the target until the computation has finished.

Figure 4 compares the visualization of the performance data with the same kernel parallelized using OpenMP on an Intel Xeon Phi coprocessor and OpenACC on a NVIDIA C2050 Fermi GPU. In both cases the target is shown as a separate location in the timeline view where offloaded kernels are illustrated as activities on the target location. This makes it easy for programmers already familiar with OpenACC and Vampir

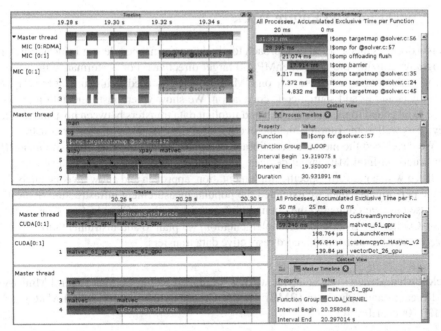

Fig. 4. Performance results for the CG method visualized in Vampir for OpenMP 4.0 (top screenshot) and OpenACC (bottom screenshot). Both show a timeline view (top-left), call stack views for the target/device (middle-left) and the host (bottom-left), a function summary (top-right) and the context view (bottom-right).

to navigate through the OpenMP target device activities. An advantage of *libmpti* is that more detailed information is collected for the target device. As shown in the process timelines in figure 4 (top), the call stack presents information on different OpenMP regions, e.g. synchronization in barriers on the target and their nesting.

To investigate the measurement overhead on our test system, which is equipped with two Intel Knights Corner devices with B0 stepping, 61 cores at 1090 MHz and 8 GB GDDR5 at 5.5 GT/s, we compare the instrumented with the original code version. We repeated each test 50 times and used 120 threads on the coprocessor. The average time for the computational part of the solver was 5.21 sec in the original case and 5.82 sec including performance measurement. The overhead for the measurements was about 12 %, which mainly stems from flushing the target device buffer at a synchronous point in the program execution. It depends only on a fixed offloading latency and the number of target device records to be transferred.

Intel allows to gather basic performance information for the offloaded regions by setting the environment variable *OFFLOAD_REPORT*. This results in a text report with information about all regions. For our CG solver the report contained 600 entries, 598 compute regions and one entry for the enter and exit of the data region. In the trace we also observed 598 compute regions on the target device and the data region was shown as a separate region in the call stack of the master process. The accumulated time of all regions in the measured trace was 5.82 sec which exactly matches the average compute time for the kernel in the instrumented case.

7   Conclusion and Future Work

This work presents a portable approach to obtain performance relevant information on programs utilizing the new OpenMP 4.0 target directives. For performance measurement on the target device we rely on OMPT. OPARI2 is used to instrument the *target* constructs and to add source-code correlation. We show where instrumentation hooks have to be added to measure explicit and implicit data transfers between host and target device as well as the runtime and the overhead for the execution of a *target* construct.

We developed the measurement library *libmpti* to record the execution of OpenMP constructs on Intel MIC target devices. For another target device, *libmpti* needs to be replaced with a platform-specific implementation. approach and allow a visual analysis of the performance data we extended the popular measurement infrastructure Score-P. In a use case we compared the obtained information with an OpenACC version of the same CG kernel. To extend our implementation, we plan to add instrumentation of the *target update* directive and record respective data transfers.

Acknowledgements. Parts of this work were funded by the German Federal Ministry of Research and Education (BMBF) under Grant Numbers 01IH11006(LMAC) and 01IH13008(ELP).

References

1. Mellor-Crummey, J., et al.: OMPT support branch of the open source Intel OpenMP runtime library (December 2013),
   http://intel-openmp-rtl.googlecode.com/
   svn/branches/ompt-support
2. Eichenberger, A., Mellor-Crummey, J., Schulz, M., Copty, N., Cownie, J., Dietrich, R., Liu, X., Loh, E., Lorenz, D.: OpenMP Technical Report 2 on the OMPT Interface (March 2014)
3. Geimer, M., Wolf, F., Wylie, B.J.N., Erika Abraham, D.B., Mohr, B.: The Scalasca performance toolset architecture. Concurrency and Computation: Practice and Experience 22(6), 702–719 (2010)
4. Knüpfer, A., Brunst, H., Doleschal, J., Jurenz, M., Lieber, M., Mickler, H., Müller, M.S., Nagel, W.E.: The Vampir Performance Analysis Tool-Set. In: Resch, M., Keller, R., Himmler, V., Krammer, B., Schulz, A. (eds.) "Tools for High Performance Computing", Proceedings of the 2nd International Workshop on Parallel Tools for High Performance Computing. Springer, Stuttgart (2008)
5. Liu, X., Mellor-Crummey, J., Fagan, M.: A new approach for performance analysis of OpenMP programs. In: Proceedings of the 27th International ACM Conference on International Conference on Supercomputing, pp. 69–80. ACM (2013)
6. Mey, D., Biersdorf, S., Bischof, C., Diethelm, K., Eschweiler, D., Gerndt, M., Knüpfer, A., Lorenz, D., Malony, A., Nagel, W.E., Oleynik, Y., Rössel, C., Saviankou, P., Schmidl, D., Shende, S., Wagner, M., Wesarg, B., Wolf, F.: Score-P: A Unified Performance Measurement System for Petascale Applications. In: Bischof, C., Hegering, H.G., Nagel, W.E., Wittum, G. (eds.) Competence in High Performance Computing 2010, pp. 85–97. Springer (2012)
7. Mohr, B., Malony, A.D., Shende, S., Wolf, F.: Design and Prototype of a Performance Tool Interface for OpenMP. The Journal of Supercomputing 23(1), 105–128 (2002)

8. NVIDIA: CUDA Toolkit Documentation — CUPTI (July 2013),
   http://docs.nvidia.com/cuda/cupti/index.html
9. OpenMP Architecture Review Board: OpenMP application program interface version 4.0
   (July 2013), http://www.openmp.org/mp-documents/OpenMP4.0.0.pdf
10. Wylie, B.J., Frings, W.: Scalasca support for MPI+OpenMP parallel applications on large-
    scale HPC systems based on Intel Xeon Phi. In: Proceedings of the Conference on Extreme
    Science and Engineering Discovery Environment: Gateway to Discovery, p. 37. ACM (2013)

Bypassing the Conventional Software Stack Using Adaptable Runtime Systems

Simon Andreas Frimann Lund, Mads R. B. Kristensen,
Brian Vinter, and Dimitrios Katsaros

Niels Bohr Institute, University of Copenhagen, Denmark
{safl,madsbk,vinter}@nbi.dk
Computer Science Department, University of Copenhagen, Denmark
rth738@alumni.ku.dk

Abstract. High-level languages such as Python offer convenient language constructs and abstractions for readability and productivity. Such features and Python's ability to serve as a steering language as well as a self-contained language for scientific computations has made Python a viable choice for high-performance computing. However, the Python interpreter's reliance on shared objects and dynamic loading causes scalability issues that at large-scale consumes hours of wall-clock time just for loading the interpreter.

The work in this paper explores an approach to bypass the conventional software stack, by replacing the Python interpreter on compute nodes with an adaptable runtime system capable of executing the compute intensive portions of a Python program. Allowing for a single instance of the Python interpreter, interpreting the users' program and additionally moving program interpretation off the compute nodes. Thereby avoiding the scalability issue of the interpreter as well as providing a means of running Python programs on restrictive compute notes which are otherwise unable to run Python.

The approach is experimentally evaluated through a prototype implementation of an extension to the Bohrium runtime system. The evaluation shows promising results as well as identifying issues for future work to address.

Keywords: Scalability, Python, import problem, dynamic loading.

1 Introduction

Python is a high-level, general-purpose, interpreted language. Python advocates high-level abstractions and convenient language constructs for readability and productivity. The reference implementation of the Python interpreter, CPython, provides rich means for extending Python with modules implemented in lower-level languages such as C and C++. Lower-level implementations can be written from scratch and conveniently map to Python data-structures through Cython[4], function wrappers to existing libraries through SWIG[3,2], or using the Python ctypes[1] interface.

---

[1] http://docs.python.org/2/library/ctypes.html

L. Lopes et al. (Eds.): Euro-Par 2014 Workshops, Part II, LNCS 8806, pp. 302–313, 2014.
© Springer International Publishing Switzerland 2014

The features of the language itself and its extensibility make it attractive as a steering language for scientific computing, which the existence of Python at high-performance compute sites confirms. Furthermore, there exists a broad range of Python wrappers to existing scientific libraries and solvers[11,20,13,8,9].

Python transcends its utilization as a steering language. SciPy[2] and its accompanying software stack[17,18,12] provides a powerful environment for developing scientific applications. The fundamental building block of SciPy is the multidimensional arrays provided by NumPy[17]. NumPy expands Python by providing a means of doing array-oriented programming using array-notation with slicing and whole-array operations. The array-abstractions offered by NumPy provides the basis for a wealth of existing[6] and emerging[19,21,14] approaches that increases the applicability of Python in an HPC environment. Even though advances are made within these areas, a problem commonly referred to as the the *import problem*[1,15,22] still persists at large-scale compute sites. The problem evolves around dynamic loading of CPython itself, built-in modules, and third party modules. Recent numbers reported on Hopper[22] state linear scale with the number of cores, which amount to a startup time of 400 seconds on 1024 cores and one hour for 8000 cores.

The approach in this paper explores a simple idea to avoid such expensive startup costs: execute one instance of the Python interpreter regardless of the cluster size. Furthermore, we allow the Python interpreter to run on an external machine that might not be part of the cluster. The machine can be any one of; the user's own laptop/workstation, a frontend/compile node, or a compute node, e.g. any machine that is accessible from the compute-site.

A positive complementary effect, as well as a goal in itself, is that the Python interpreter and the associated software stack need not be available on the compute nodes.

The work in this paper experimentally evaluates the feasibility of bypassing the conventional software stack, by replacing the Python interpreter on the compute nodes with an adaptable runtime system capable of executing the computationally heavy part of the users' program. The approach facilitates the use of Python at restrictive compute-sites and thereby broadens application of Python in HPC.

2   Related Work

The work within this paper describes, to the authors knowledge, a novel approach for handling the Python *import problem*. This section describes other approaches to meeting the same end.

Python itself support a means for doing a user-level override of the import mechanism[3] and work from within the Python community has improved upon the import system from version 2.6 to 2.7 and 3.0. In spite of these efforts, the problem persists.

---

[2] http://www.scipy.org/stackspec.html

[3] http://legacy.python.org/dev/peps/pep-0302/

One aspect of the *import problem* is the excessive stress on the IO-system caused by the object-loader traversing the filesystem looking for Python modules. Path caching through collective operations is one approach to lowering overhead. The mpi4py[7] project implements multiple techniques to path caching where a single node traverses the file-system and broadcasts the information to the remaining $N-1$ nodes. The results of this approach show significant improvements to startup times from hours to minutes but relies on the *mpi4py* library and requires maintenance of the Python software-stack on the compute-nodes.

Scalable Python[4], first described in[9], addresses the problem at a lower level. Scalable Python, a modification of CPython, seeks to address the *import problem* by implementing a parallel IO layer utilized by all Python import statements. By doing so only a single process, in contrast to N processes, perform IO. The result of the IO operation is broadcast to the remaining $N - 1$ nodes via MPI. The results reported in[9] show significant improvements towards the time consumed by Python import statements at the expense of maintaining a custom CPython implementation.

Relying on dynamically loaded shared objects is a general challenge for large-scale compute-sites with a shared filesystem. SPINDLE[10] provides a generic approach to the problem through an extension to the GNU Loader.

The above described approaches apply different techniques for improving performance of dynamic loading. A different strategy which in this respect is thematically closer to the work within this paper is to reduce the use of dynamic loading. The work in[15] investigate such strategy by replacing as much dynamic loading with statically compiled libraries. Such technique in a Python context can by applied through the use of Python freeze[5] and additional tools[6] exists to support it.

3   The Approach

The previous sections describe and identify the CPython import system as the culprit guilty of limiting the use of Python / NumPy at large-scale compute sites. Dynamic loading and excessive path searching are accomplices to the havoc raised. The crime committed is labelled as the Python *import problem*.

Related work let the culprit run free and implement techniques to handling the havoc raised. The work within this paper focuses on restricting the culprit and thereby preventively avoiding the problem.

The idea is to run a single instance of the Python interpreter, thereby keeping the overhead constant and manageable. The remaining instances of the interpreter are replaced with a runtime system capable of efficiently executing the portion of the Python / NumPy program responsible for communication and computation. Leaving the task of interpreting the Python / NumPy program,

---

[4] https://gitorious.org/scalable-python

[5] https://wiki.python.org/moin/Freeze

[6] https://github.com/bfroehle/slither

conditionals, and general program flow up to the interpreter. The computation-ally heavy parts are delegated to execution on the compute nodes through the runtime system.

3.1 Runtime System

The runtime used in this work is part of the Bohrium[19] project[7]. The Bohrium runtime system (BRS) provides a backend for mapping array operations onto a number of different hardware targets, from multi-core systems to clusters and GPU enabled systems. It is implemented as a virtual machine capable of making runtime decisions instead of a statically compiled library. Any programming language can use BRS in principle; in this paper though, we will use the Python / NumPy support exclusively.

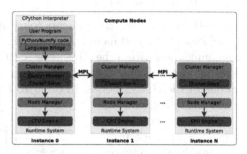

Fig. 1. Illustration of communication between the runtime system components *without* the use of the proxy component

The fundamental building block of BRS is the representation of programs in the form of *vector bytecode*. A vector bytecode is a representation of an operation acting upon an array. This can be one of the standard built-in operations such as element-wise addition of arrays, function promotion of trigonometric functions over all elements of an array, or in functional terms: map, zip, scan and reduction, or an operation defined by third party.

BRS is implemented using a layered architecture featuring a set of interchangeable *components*. Three different types of components exist: *filters*, *managers*, and *engines*. Figure 1 illustrates a configuration of the runtime system configured for execution in a cluster of homogenous nodes. The arrows represent vector bytecode sent through the runtime system in a top-down fashion, possibly altering it on its way.

Each component exposes the same C-interface for initialization, shutdown, and execution thus basic component interaction consists of regular function calls. The component interface ensures isolation between the language bridge that runs the CPython interpreter and the rest of Bohrium. Thus, BRS only runs a single instance of the CPython interpreter no matter the underlying architecture – distributed or otherwise.

Above the runtime, a language bridge is responsible for mapping language constructs to vector bytecode and passing it to the runtime system via the C-interface.

Managers manage a specific memory address space within the runtime system and decide where to execute the vector bytecode. In figure 1 a node manager manages the local address space (one compute-node) and a cluster-manager

---

[7] http://www.bh107.org

which handles data distribution and inter-node communication through MPI. At
the bottom of the runtime system, we have the execution engines, which are responsible for providing efficient mapping of array operations down to a specific
processing unit such as a CPU or a GPU.

3.2 Proxy Manager

Currently, all Bohrium components communicate using local function calls, which
translates into shared memory communication. Figure 1 illustrates the means of
communication within the BRS prior to the addition of the proxy component. As
a result, the language bridge, which runs a CPython interpreter, must execute
on one of the cluster-nodes. In order to circumvent this problem, we introduce
a new *proxy* component.

This new component
acts as a network proxy
that enables Bohrium com-
ponents to exchange vec-
tor bytecode across a network. Figure 2 illustrates
the means for communi-
cation which the Proxy
component provides. By
using this functionality,
separation can be achieved

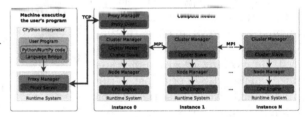

Fig. 2. Illustration of communication between the runtime system components *with* the use of the proxy component

between the implementation of any application using Bohrium and the actual
hardware on which it runs. This is an important property when considering
cases of supercomputers or clusters, which define specific characteristics for the
execution of tasks on them.

The proxy component is composed of two parts – a server and a client. The
server exposes the component interface (init, execute, and shutdown) to its parent component in the hierarchy whereas the client uses its child component
interface. When the parent component calls execute with a list of vector bytecodes, the server serialize and sends the vector bytecodes to the client, which
in turn uses its child component interface to push the vector bytecodes further
down the Bohrium hierarchy. Besides the serialized list of vector bytecodes, the
proxy component needs to communicate array-data in two cases.

When the CPython interpreter introduces existing NumPy arrays and Python
scalars to a Bohrium execution. Typically, this happens when the user application loads arrays and scalars initially. When the CPython interpreter access the
result of a Bohrium execution directly. Typically, this happens when the user
application evaluates a loop-condition based on some array and scalar data.

Both the server and the client maintain a record of array-data locations thus
avoiding unnecessary array-data transfers. Only when the array-data is involved
in a calculation at the client-side will the server send the array-data. Similarly,
only when the CPython interpreter request the array-data will the client send
the array-data to the server.

In practice, when the client sends array-data to the server it is because the CPython interpreter needs to evaluate a scalar value before continuing. In this case, the performance is very latency sensitive since the CPython interpreter is blocking on the scalar value. Therefore, it is crucial to disable Nagle's TCP/IP algorithm[16] in order achieve good performance. Additionally, the size of the vector bytecode lists is significantly greater than the TCP packet header thus limiting the possible advantage of Nagle's TCP/IP algorithm. Therefore, when the proxy component initiates the TCP connection between server and client it sets the `TCP_NODELAY` socket option.

4   Evaluation

The basic idea of the approach is to have a single instance of CPython interpreting the user's program, such as figure 2 illustrates. With a single isolated instance of the interpreter the *import problem* is solved by design. The second goal of the approach is to facilitate execution of a Python program in a restricted environment where the Python software stack is not available on the compute nodes.

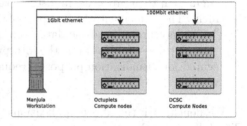

Fig. 3. Octuplets and DCSC two physically and administratively disjoint clusters of eight and sixteen nodes. Octuplets is a small-scale research-cluster managed by the eScience group at the Niels Bohr Institute. DCSC is a larger compute-site for scientific computation in Denmark. Gbit ethernet facilitate the connection between Manjula and the octuplet cluster and 100Mbit ethernet between Manjula and DCSC.

The potential *Achilles heel* of the approach is in its singularity, with a single *remote* instance of the interpreter network latency and bandwidth limitations potentially limit application of the approach.

Network latency can stall execution of programs when the round-trip-time of transmitting vector bytecode from the interpreter-machine to the compute node exceeds the time spent computing on previously received vector bytecode. Bandwidth becomes a limiting factor when the interpreted program needs large amounts of data for evaluation to proceed interpretation and transmission of vector bytecode. The listing below contains descriptions of the applications used as well as their need for communication between interpreter and runtime. The sourcecode is available for closer inspection in the Bohrium repository[8].

Black Scholes implements a financial pricing model using a partial differential equation, calculating price variations over time[5]. At each time-step the interpreter reads out a scalar value from the runtime representing the computed price at that time.

---

[8] http://bitbucket.org/bohrium/bohrium

Heat Equation simulates the heat transfer on a surface represented by a two-dimensional grid, implemented using jacobi-iteration with numerical convergence. The interpreter requires a scalar value from the runtime at each time-step to evaluate whether or not simulation should continue. Additionally when executed with visualization the entire grid is required.

N-Body simulates interaction of bodies according to the laws of Newtonian physics. We use a straightforward algorithm that computes all body-body interactions, $O(n^2)$, with collisions detection. The interpreter only needs data from the runtime at the end of the simulation to retrieve the final position of the bodies. However, the interpreter will at each time-step, when executed for visualization purposes, request coordinates of the bodies.

Shallow Water simulates a system governed by the Shallow Water equations. The simulation initates by placing a drop of water in a still container. The simulation then proceeds, in discrete time steps, simulating the water movement. The implementation is a port of the MATLAB application by Burkardt [9]. The interpreter needs no data from the runtime to progress the simulation at each time-step. However, the interpreter will at each time-step, when executed for visualization purposes, request the current state of the simulated water.

We benchmark the above applications on two Linux-based clusters (Fig. 3). The following subsections describe the experiments performed and report the performance numbers.

4.1   Proxy Overhead

We begin with figure 4 which show the results of running the four benchmark applications on the octuplet cluster using eight compute nodes and two different configurations:

With Proxy The BRS configured with the proxy component and the interpreter is running on Manjula. This configuration is equivalent to the one illustrated in figure 2.

Without Proxy The BRS configured without the proxy component. The interpreter is running on the first of the eight compute nodes. This setup is equivalent to the one illustrated in figure 1.

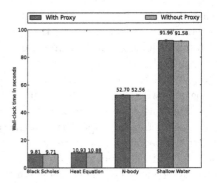

Fig. 4. Elapsed wall-clock time in seconds of the four applications on the octuplet compute nodes with and without the proxy component

We cannot run Python on the DCSC cluster for the simple reason that the software stack is too old to compile Python 2.6 on the DCSC compute nodes.

---

[9] http://people.sc.fsu.edu/~jburkardt/m_src/shallow_water_2d/

Thus, it is not possible to provide comparable results of running with and without the Proxy component.

The purpose of this experiment is to evaluate the overhead of introducing the proxy component in a well-behaved environment. There were no other users of the network, filesystem, or machines. Round-trip-time between Manjula and the first compute node was average at $0.07ms$ during the experiment. The error bars show two standard deviations from the mean. The overhead of adding the proxy component is within the margin of error and thereby unmeasurable.

4.2 Latency Sensitivity

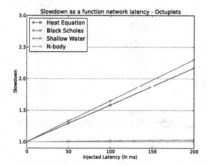 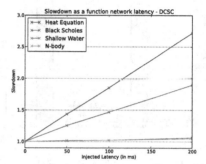

Fig. 5. Slowdown of the four applications as a function of injected latency between Manjula and octuplet compute node

Fig. 6. Slowdown of the four applications as a function of injected latency between Manjula and DCSC compute node.

We continue with figures 5 and 6. The BRS configured with the proxy component, running the interpreter on Manjula. Figure 2 illustrates the setup. The purpose of the experiment is to evaluate the approach' sensitivity to network latency. Latencies of 50, 100, 150, and 200ms are injected between Manjula and the compute node running the proxy client. The figures show slowdown of the applications as a function of the injected latency.

The applications Shallow Water and N-body are nearly unmeasurably affected by the injected latency. The observed behavior is as expected since the interpreter does not need any data to progress interpretation. It is thereby possible to overlap transmission of vector bytecode from the interpreter-machine with computation on the compute nodes.

The injected latency does, however, affect the applications Heat Equation and Black Scholes. The observed behavior is as expected since the interpreter requires a scalar value for determining convergence criteria for Heat Equation and sampling the pricing value for Black Scholes. Network latency affects the results from the DCSC cluster the most, with a worst-case of a 2.8 slowdown. This is due to the elapsed time being lower when using the sixteen DCSC compute nodes. Since less time is spent computing more time is spent waiting and thereby a relatively larger sensitivity to network latency.

4.3   Bandwidth Sensitivity

The last experiment sought to evaluate the sensitivity to high network bandwidth utilization. Figures 7 and 8 show the results of an experiment where the four applications were running with visualization updated at each time-step. The BRS configured with the proxy component; Manjula is running the Python interpreter. Figure 2 illustrates the setup.

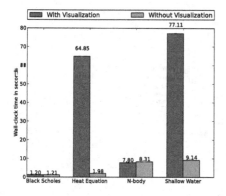 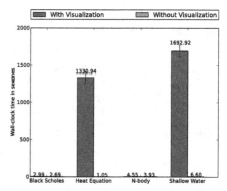

Fig. 7. Elapsed wall-clock time of the four applications with and without visualization on the octuplet compute nodes.

Fig. 8. Elapsed wall-clock time of the four applications with and without visualization on the DCSC compute nodes.

When executing with visualization, the interpreter requires a varying (depending on the application) amount of data to be transmitted from the compute nodes to the interpreter-machine at each time step. Thereby straining the available bandwidth between the interpreter-machine and the compute node running the proxy-client.

Black-Scholes although sensitive to latency due to the need of transmitting the computed price at each time-step, does not require any significant amount of data to be transferred for visualization, neither does the N-Body simulation. However, the two other applications Heat Equation and Shallow Water require transmission of the entire state to visualize dissipation of heat on the plane and the current movement of water. These two applications are sufficient to observe a key concern of the approach.

We observe a slowdown of about ×1260 (Heat Equation) and ×257 (Shallow Water) when running on the DCSC nodes. We observe a slowdown of about ×32.8 (Heat Equation) and ×8.5 (Shallow Water) when running in the octuplet nodes. These results clearly show that network bandwidth becomes a bottleneck, with disastrous consequences in terms of execution time and thus a limiting factor for applying the approach for such use.

The slowdown is much worse when running on the DCSC compute nodes compare to the slowdown on the octuplet nodes. This is due to the interconnect being 100Mbit ethernet to the DCSC in relation to the 1Gbit ethernet connection to the octuplet nodes.

5   Future Work

The evaluation revealed bandwidth bottlenecks when the machine running the interpreter requests data for purposes such as visualization. The setup in the evaluation was synthetic and forced requests of the entire data-set at each time-step without any transformation of the data, it can, therefore, be regarded as a worst-case scenario.

One could argue that the setup is not representative for user behaviour and instead assume that the user would only need a snapshot of data at every $timestep/K$ iteration and with lowered resolution such as every I'th datapoint and thus drastically lowering the bottleneck. However, to address the issue future work will involve compressed encoding of data transmitted as well as suitable downsampling for the visualization purpose.

The primary focus point for future work is now in progress and relates to the effective throughput at each compute-node. The current implementation of the execution engine uses a virtual-machine approach for executing array operations. In this approach the virtual machine delegate execution of each vector bytecode to statically compiled routine. Within this area, a wealth of optimizations are applicable by composing multiple operations on the same data and hereby *fusing* array operations together.

Random-number generators, linear spaces of data, and iotas, when combined with reductions are another common source for optimization of memory uti-lization and locality. Obtaining such optimizations within the runtime require the use of JIT compilation techniques and potentially increase the use dynamic loading of optimized codes. The challenge for this part of future work involves ex-ploration of how to get such optimization without losing the performance gained to runtime and JIT compilation overhead.

6   Conclusions

The work in this paper explores the feasibility of replacing the Python interpreter with an adaptable runtime system, with the purpose of avoiding the CPython scalability issues and providing a means of executing Python programs on restric-tive compute nodes which are otherwise unable to run the Python interpreter.

The proxy component, implemented as an extension to the Bohrium runtime system (BRS), provides the means for the BRS to communicate with a single *re-mote* instance of the Python interpreter. The prototype implementation enabled evaluation of the proposed approach of the paper.

Allowing the interpreter to execute on any machine, possibly users' own work-stations/laptops, leverages a Python user to utilize a cluster of compute nodes or a supercomputer with direct realtime interaction. However, it also introduces concerns with regards to the effect of network latency and available bandwidth, between the machine running the interpreter and the compute node running the proxy client, on program execution. These concerns were the themes for the conducted evaluation.

Results showed that the overhead of adding the proxy component and thereby the ability for the BRS to use a remote interpreter was not measurable in terms of elapsed wall-clock time, as results were within two standard deviations of the measured elapsed wall-clock. The results additionally showed a reasonable tolerance to high network latency, at $50ms$ round-trip-time, slowdown ranged from not being measurable to $\times 1.3 - \times 1.4$. In the extreme case of $200ms$ latency ranged from not being measurable to a slowdown of $\times 1.9 - \times 2.8$.

The primary concern, and focus for future work, presented itself during evaluation of bandwidth requirements. If the Python program requests large amounts of data then the network throughput capability becomes a bottleneck, severely impacting elapsed wall-clock as well as saturating the network link, potentially disrupting other users.

The results show that the approach explored within this paper does provide a possible means to avoid the scalability issues of CPython, allowing direct user interaction and enabling execution of Python programs in restricted environments that are otherwise unable to run interpreted Python programs. The approach is, however, restricted to transmission of data such as vector bytecode, scalars for evaluation of convergence criteria, boolean values, and low-volume data-sets between the interpreter-machine and runtime. This does, however, not restrict processing of large-volume datasets within the runtime on and between the compute nodes.

Acknowledgments. This research has been partially supported by the Danish Strategic Research Council, Program Committee for Strategic Growth Technologies, for the research center 'HIPERFIT: Functional High Performance Computing for Financial Information Technology' (hiperfit.dk) under contract number 10-092299.

References

1. Ahmadia, A.: Solving the import problem: Scalable Dynamic Loading Network File Systems. Technical report, Talk at SciPy conference, Austin, Texas (July 2012), http://pyvideo.org/video/1201/solving-the-import-problem-scalable-dynamic-load
2. Beazley, D.M.: Automated scientific software scripting with SWIG, vol. 19, pp. 599–609. Elsevier (2003)
3. Beazley, D.M., et al.: SWIG: An easy to use tool for integrating scripting languages with C and C++. In: Proceedings of the 4th USENIX Tcl/Tk workshop, pp. 129–139 (1996)
4. Behnel, S., Bradshaw, R., Citro, C., Dalcin, L., Seljebotn, D.S., Smith, K.: Cython: The best of both worlds. Computing in Science & Engineering 13(2), 31–39 (2011)
5. Black, F., Scholes, M.: The pricing of options and corporate liabilities. The Journal of Political Economy, 637–654 (1973)
6. Daily, J., Lewis, R.R.: Using the global arrays toolkit to reimplement numpy for distributed computation. In: Proceedings of the 10th Python in Science Conference (2011)

7. Dalcin, L., Paz, R., Storti, M., Elia, J.D.: MPI for Python: Performance improvements and MPI-2 extensions. Journal of Parallel and Distributed Computing 68(5), 655–662 (2008)
8. Drummond, L.A., Galiano, V., Migallón, V., Penadés, J.: High-level user interfaces for the DOE ACTS collection. In: Kågström, B., Elmroth, E., Dongarra, J., Waśniewski, J. (eds.) PARA 2006. LNCS, vol. 4699, pp. 251–259. Springer, Heidelberg (2007)
9. Enkovaaraa, J., Louhivuoria, M., Jovanovicb, P., Slavnicb, V., Rännarc, M.: Optimizing GPAW. Partnership for Advanced Computing in Europe (September 2012), http://www.prace-ri.eu/IMG/pdf/Optimizing_GPAW.pdf
10. Frings, W., Ahn, D.H., LeGendre, M., Gamblin, T., de Supinski, B.R., Wolf, F.: Massively Parallel Loading. In: Proceedings of the 27th International ACM Conference on International Conference on Supercomputing, ICS 2013, pp. 389–398. ACM, New York (2013)
11. Gawande, K., Webers, C.: PyPETSc User Manual (Revision 1.0). Technical report, NICTA (2009), http://elefant.developer.nicta.com.au/ documentation/userguide/PyPetscManual.pdf
12. Hunter, J.D.: Matplotlib: A 2D Graphics Environment. Computing in Science & Engineering 9(3), 90–95 (2007)
13. Ketcheson, D.I., Mandli, K.T., Ahmadia, A.J., Alghamdi, A., Quezada de Luna, M., Parsani, M., Knepley, M.G., Emmett, M.: PyClaw: Accessible, Extensible, Scalable Tools for Wave Propagation Problems. SIAM Journal on Scientific Computing 34(4), C210–C231 (2012)
14. Kristensen, M.R.B., Vinter, B.: Numerical Python for scalable architectures. In: Proceedings of the Fourth Conference on Partitioned Global Address Space Programming Model, PGAS 2010, pp. 15:1–15:9. ACM, New York (2010)
15. Marion, P., Ahmadia, A., Froehle, B.M.: Import without a filesystem: scientific Python built-in with static linking and frozen modules. Technical report, Talk at SciPy conference, Austin, Texas, July 2012 (2013), https://www.youtube.com/watch?v=EOiEIWMYkwE
16. Nagle, J.: Congestion Control in IP/TCP Internetworks. RFC 896 (January 1984)
17. Oliphant, T.E.: Python for Scientific Computing. Computing in Science & Engineering 9(3), 10–20 (2007)
18. Pérez, F., Granger, B.E.: IPython: A System for Interactive Scientific Computing. Computing in Science & Engineering 9(3), 21–29 (2007)
19. Kristensen, M.R.B., Lund, S.A.F., Blum, T., Skovhede, K., Vinter, B.: Bohrium: a Virtual Machine Approach to Portable Parallelism. In: 2014 IEEE 28th International Parallel and Distributed Processing Symposium Workshops & PhD Forum (IPDPSW). IEEE (2014)
20. Sala, M., Spotz, W., Heroux, M.: PyTrilinos: High-Performance Distributed-Memory Solvers for Python. ACM Transactions on Mathematical Software (TOMS) (March 34, 2008)
21. Smith, K., Spotz, W.F., Ross-Ross, S.: A Python HPC Framework: PyTrilinos, ODIN, and Seamless. In: 2012 SC Companion High Performance Computing, Networking, Storage and Analysis (SCC), pp. 593–599. IEEE (2012)
22. Zhao, Z., Davis, M., Antypas, K., Yao, Y., Lee, R., Butler, T.: Shared Library Performance on Hopper. In: CUG 2012, Greengineering the Future, Stuttgart, Germany (2012)

Comparison of Three Popular Parallel Programming Models on the Intel Xeon Phi

Ashkan Tousimojarad and Wim Vanderbauwhede

School of Computing Science, University of Glasgow, Glasgow, UK
a.tousimojarad.1@research.gla.ac.uk, wim@dcs.gla.ac.uk

Abstract. Systems with large numbers of cores have become common-place. Accordingly, applications are shifting towards increased parallelism. In a general purpose system, applications residing in the system compete for shared resources. Thread and task scheduling in such a multithreaded multiprogramming environment is a significant challenge. In this study, we have chosen the Intel Xeon Phi system as a modern platform to explore how popular parallel programming models, namely OpenMP, Intel Cilk Plus and Intel TBB (Threading Building Blocks) scale on manycore architectures. We have used three benchmarks with different features which exercise different aspects of the system performance. Moreover, a multi-programming scenario is used to compare the behaviours of these models when all three applications reside in the system. Our initial results show that it is to some extent possible to infer multiprogramming performance from single-program cases.

1 Introduction

There are various programming models and runtime libraries that help developers to move from sequential to parallel programming. In this paper, we have chosen three well-known parallel programming approaches to compare their performance on a modern manycore machine. Before going into the details of these models, we would like to introduce the manycore platform chosen for this study:

1.1 Intel Xeon Phi

The Intel Xeon Phi 5110P coprocessor is an SMP (Symmetric Multiprocessor) on-a-chip which is connected to a host Xeon processor via the PCI Express bus interface. The Intel Many Integrated Core (MIC) architecture used by the Intel Xeon Phi coprocessors gives developers the advantage of using standard, existing programming tools and methods. Our Xeon Phi comprises of 60 cores connected by a bidirectional ring interconnect. The Xeon Phi has eight memory controllers supporting 2 GDDR5 memory channels each. The clock speed of the cores is 1.053GHz. According to Jeffers [6], the Xeon Phi provides four hardware threads sharing the same physical core and its cache subsystem in order to hide the latency inherent in in-order execution. As a result, the use of at least two threads per core is almost always beneficial.

L. Lopes et al. (Eds.): Euro-Par 2014 Workshops, Part II, LNCS 8806, pp. 314–325, 2014.

Each core has an associated 512KB L2 cache. Data and instruction L1 caches of 32KB are also integrated on each core. Another important feature of the Xeon Phi is that each core includes a SIMD 512-bit wide VPU (Vector Processing Unit). The VPU can be used to process 16 single-precision or 8 double-precision elements per clock cycle. The third benchmark (Sect. 3.3) utilises the VPUs.

1.2   Parallel Programming Models

In order to have a fair comparison, we have chosen three programming models that are all supported by ICC (Intel C/C++ Compiler).

OpenMP. OpenMP, which is the de-facto standard for shared-memory programming, provides an API using the fork-join model. Threads communicate by sharing variables. OpenMP has been historically used for loop-level and regular parallelism through its compiler directives. Since the release of OpenMP 3.0, it also supports task parallelism. Whenever a thread encounters a `task` construct, a new explicit task is generated. An explicit task may be executed in parallel with other tasks by any thread in the current team, and the execution can be immediate or deferred until later [1].

Intel Cilk Plus. Intel Cilk Plus is an extension to C/C++ based on Cilk++[8]. It provides language constructs for both task and data parallelism. Is has become popular because of its simplicity and higher level of abstraction (compared to frameworks such as OpenMP or Intel TBB). Cilk provides the _cilk_spawn and _cilk_sync keywords to spawn and synchronise tasks; _cilk_for loop is a parallel replacement for sequential loops in C/C++. The tasks are executed within a work-stealing framework. The scheduling policy provides load balance close to the optimal [10].

Intel TBB. Intel Threading Building Blocks (TBB) is another well-known approach for expressing parallelism [9]. Intel TBB is an object-oriented C++ runtime library that contains data structures and algorithms to be used in parallel programs. It abstracts the low-level thread interface. However, conversion of legacy code to TBB requires restructuring certain parts of the program to fit the TBB templates. Each worker thread in TBB has a deque (double-ended queue) of tasks. Newly spawned tasks are put at the back of the deque, and each worker thread takes the tasks from the back of its deque to exploit temporal locality. If there is no task in the local deque, the worker steals tasks from the front of the victims' deques [7].

2   Experimental Setup

All the parallel benchmarks are implemented as C++ programs. They are executed natively on the MIC. For that purpose, the executables are copied to the

Xeon Phi, and we connect to the device from the host using `ssh`. For the OpenMP applications, the `libiomp5.so` library is required. The `libcilkrts.so.5` is needed for Cilk Plus applications and the `libtbb.so.2` library is required for the TBB programs. The path to these libraries should be set before the execution, e.g. export `LD_LIBRARY_PATH=./:$LD_LIBRARY_PATH`. The TBB programs should be compiled with the -ltbb flag. The OpenMP programs need -openmp flag. The Intel compiler `icpc` (ICC) 14.0.2 is used with -O2 -mmic -no-offload flags for compiling the benchmarks for native execution on the Xeon Phi. All speedup ratios are computed against the running time of the sequential code implemented in C++.

3   Single-Programming Benchmarks

Three different benchmarks have been used for the purposes of this study. They are intentionally simple, because we want to be able to reason about the observed differences in performance between the selected models. We first compare the results for each single program.

3.1   Fibonacci

We consider a parallel Fibonacci benchmark as the first testcase. The Fibonacci benchmark has traditionally been used as a basic example of parallel computing. Although it is not an efficient way of computing Fibonacci numbers, the simple recursive pattern can easily be parallelised and is a good example of creating unbalanced tasks, resulting in load imbalance. In order to achieve desirable performance, a suitable cutoff for the recursion is crucial. Otherwise, too many fine-grained tasks would impose an unacceptable overhead to the system. The cutoff limits the tree_depth in the recursive algorithm, which results in generating 2^{tree_depth} tasks.

Figure 1 shows all the results taken from running this benchmark with different programming models. Figure 1(a) shows the speedup chart for the integer number 47 with 2048 unbalanced tasks at the last level of the Fibonacci heap. Cilk Plus and TBB show similar results. Increasing the number of threads causes visible performance degradation for OpenMP. Setting `KMP_AFFINITY=balanced` results in a negligible improvement of the OpenMP performance.

Figure 1(b) shows the importance of a proper cutoff on the performance of this unbalanced problem. Having more tasks (as long as they are not too fine-grained) gives enough opportunities for load balancing.

Total CPU Time

This is a lower-is-better metric that shows the total CPU times consumed in the system from the start until the accomplishment of the job(s). This metric and the detailed breakdown of CPU times are obtained using Intel's VTune Amplifier XE 2013 performance analyser [5]. Figures 1(d) to 1(f) are screenshots taken from the VTune Amplifier when running Fib 47 with cutoff 2048 natively on the

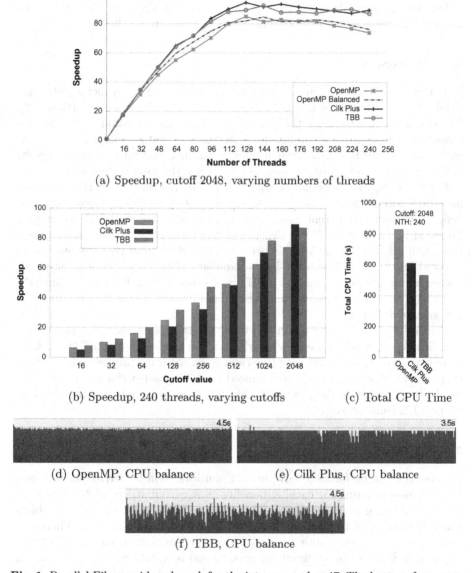

(a) Speedup, cutoff 2048, varying numbers of threads

(b) Speedup, 240 threads, varying cutoffs   (c) Total CPU Time

(d) OpenMP, CPU balance   (e) Cilk Plus, CPU balance

(f) TBB, CPU balance

Fig. 1. Parallel Fibonacci benchmark for the integer number 47. The best performance can be obtained by using Cilk Plus or TBB. Choosing a proper cutoff value is key to good performance. If there are enough tasks in the system, the load balancing techniques become effective and yield better speedup. A detailed breakdown of overall CPU time for the case with 240 threads and cutoff value 2048 is illustrated for each approach in the charts (d) to (f). TBB consumes less CPU time in total while providing good performance, and Cilk Plus has the best performance. The y-axis on the (d) to (f) charts is the time per logical core, from 0 to the maximum number specified in seconds.

Xeon Phi. The x-axis shows the logical cores of the Xeon Phi (240 cores), and the y-axis is the CPU time for each core.[1]

For the Fibonacci benchmark, OpenMP consumes the most CPU time, and its performance is bad, the worst amongst the three approaches.

3.2   MergeSort

This benchmark sorts an array of 80 million integers using a merge sort algorithm. The ith element of the array is initialised with the number $i*((i\%2)+2)$. The cutoff value determines the point after which the operation should be performed sequentially. For example, cutoff 2048 means that chunks of $1/2048$ of the 80M array should be sorted sequentially, in parallel, and afterwards the results will be merged two by two, in parallel to produce the final sorted array.

For the MergeSort benchmark, tasks are not homogeneous, i.e. there are children and parent tasks. The same scenario existed in the previous Fibonacci benchmark, but the parent tasks were integer additions that did not impose overhead to the system. Here, the parent tasks are heavyweight merge operations, and this is what makes this benchmark distinct from the previous one.

As shown in Fig. 2(a) with larger numbers of threads, there is either no noticeable change (in the case of TBB), or a slowdown (in the case of OpenMP and Cilk Plus). Using thread affinity for OpenMP in this case does not make an appreciable difference.

Figures 2(c) to 2(f) are again based on the results obtained by the VTune Amplifier when running the benchmark with 240 threads and cutoff 2048. Since all merges in a branch of the task tree can run on the same core as their children, there would be no need to have balanced load for good performance. In other words, the unbalanced distribution in Fig. 2(f) does not imply a poor behaviour of the TBB runtime system.

3.3   MatMul

This benchmark performs a naive matrix multiplication by a triple nested loop with ikj loop ordering for caching benefits on square matrices of N×N double-precision floating point numbers. This is a completely data parallel problem which fits very well to OpenMP and its `for` worksharing construct. There is a concept similar to the cutoff in the loop parallelism context to control chunking. It specifies the size of chunk for each thread in a data parallel worksharing scenario. If the cutoff value is assumed as the number of chunks, the chunk (grain) size can be specified for the OpenMP `for` as follows: `#pragma omp for schedule(dynamic, N/cutoff)`. The `dynamic` keyword can be replaced by `static` as well. Grain size in the Cilk Plus is similarly specified via a pragma:

---

[1] It should be noted that for all experiments, results from the benchmark's kernel are considered in the figures (a) and (b), while in the other results taken from the VTune Amplifier, all information from the start of the application, including its initial phase and the CPU time consumed by the shared libraries is taken into account.

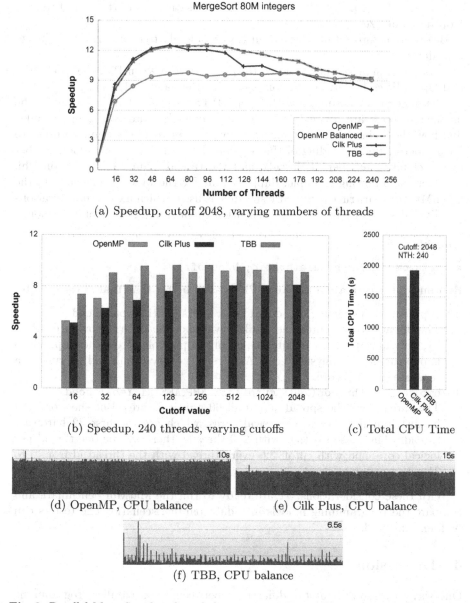

(a) Speedup, cutoff 2048, varying numbers of threads

(b) Speedup, 240 threads, varying cutoffs   (c) Total CPU Time

(d) OpenMP, CPU balance   (e) Cilk Plus, CPU balance

(f) TBB, CPU balance

Fig. 2. Parallel MergeSort benchmark for an array of 80 million integers. This benchmark does not scale well. The best performance, however, can be obtained by using OpenMP or Cilk Plus. For this memory-intensive benchmark, cutoff values greater than 64 are enough to lead to good performance with as many threads as the number of cores. TBB consumes significantly less Total CPU Time. With small number of threads, OpenMP and Cilk Plus yield better performance, but finally (with 240 threads) OpenMP and TBB provide slightly better performance.

`#pragma cilk grainsize = N/cutoff`. Intel TBB has a template function called `parallel_for`, which can be called with `simple_partitioner()` to control the grain size.

Before going into details of the results, we would like to focus on some technical considerations:

In order to achieve automatic vectorization on the Xeon Phi, the Intel TBB and OpenMP codes have to be compiled with the `-ansi-alias` flag.

The `schedule` clause used with OpenMP `for` specifies how iterations of the associated loops are divided (statically/dynamically) into contiguous chunks, and how these chunks are distributed amongst threads of the team. In order to have a better understanding of the relations between the cutoff value (number of the chunks), number of threads, and the thread affinity on the Xeon Phi, consider the following example. Suppose that for the MatMul benchmark, the OpenMP `for` construct with static schedule is used, which means that iterations are divided statically between the execution threads in a round-robin fashion:

Example

`#pragma omp for schedule(static, N/cutoff).`

Runtime of the case(a) on the Xeon Phi is $\approx 3 \times$ better than that of the case(b).

a) `omp_set_num_threads(32)`, `cutoff=32`, `KMP_AFFINITY=balanced`
   The threads will be spread across 32 physical cores. With the balanced affinity, they have to be distributed as evenly as possible across the chip, which is one thread per physical core. As a result, every chunk will be run on a separate physical core.
b) `omp_set_num_threads(240)`, `cutoff=32`, `KMP_AFFINITY=balanced`
   The threads will be spread across all 60 physical cores. But the work will be distributed between 8 physical cores, which are the first 32 hardware threads. The reason is that with 240 threads, there will be one thread per logical core, and with cutoff 32, every thread with the thread id from 0 to 31 gets a chunk of size $N/32$.

With these considerations, we are ready to run the MatMul benchmark and compare the programming models in a data parallel scenario. The results can be found in Fig 3.

4   Discussion

One way to reason about the differences between these parallel programming models is to compare the amount of the Total CPU Time consumed by their runtime libraries. We have therefore summarised the results as the percentage of time spent on the shared libraries in each case.

Table 1 gives a better understanding of where the CPU times have been consumed. For instance, for the OpenMP runtime library, the wasted CPU time generally falls into two categories: I) A master thread is executing a serial region, and the slave threads are spinning. II) A thread has finished a parallel

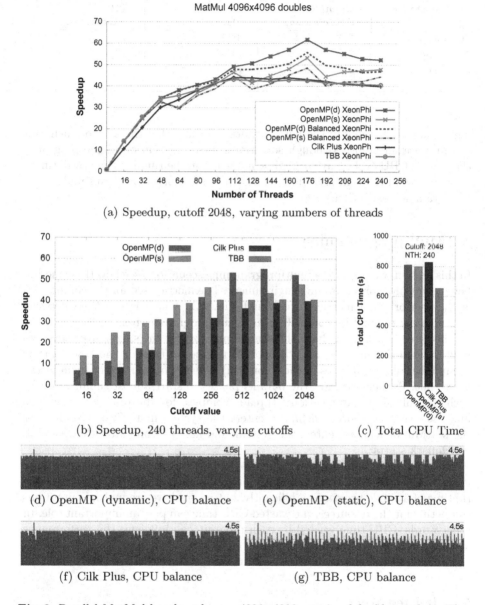

(a) Speedup, cutoff 2048, varying numbers of threads

(b) Speedup, 240 threads, varying cutoffs   (c) Total CPU Time

(d) OpenMP (dynamic), CPU balance   (e) OpenMP (static), CPU balance

(f) Cilk Plus, CPU balance   (g) TBB, CPU balance

Fig. 3. Parallel MatMul benchmark on a 4096×4096 matrix of double numbers. The best results can be obtained by using OpenMP approaches. For the cutoff values greater than 256, OpenMP with dynamic scheduling has the best scaling amongst all. Again the Total CPU Time of TBB is the least amongst all. There is an evident distinction between the distribution of CPU times in the charts (d) and (e) that shows how OpenMP load balancing, when using dynamic scheduling leads to better performance.

Table 1. Percentage of the Total CPU Time consumed by the runtime libraries

Benchmark	OpenMP (`libiomp5.so`)	Cilk Plus (`libcilkrts.so.5`)	TBB (`libtbb.so.2`)
Fibonacci	50%	16%	5%
MergeSort	78%	81%	3%
MatMul	22% *(Dynamic)* 20% *(Static)*	6%	1%

region, and is spinning in the barrier waiting for all other threads to reach that synchronisation point. Although sometimes in solo execution of the programs, these extra CPU cycles have negligible influence on the running time (wall time), we will show in the next section, how they will affect other programs under multiprogrammed execution.

5   Multiprogramming

In this section, we consider a multiprogramming scenario to see how these models behave in a multiprogramming environment. The metric used for the comparison is the user-oriented metric Turnaround Time [3], which is the time between submitting a job and its completion in a multiprogram system.

The three benchmarks have the same input sizes as the single-program cases with the cutoff value 2048 and the default number of threads 240 (the same as the number of logical cores in the Xeon Phi). We do not start all of them at the same time. Rather, we want the parallel phases to start almost simultaneously, such that all of the applications' threads compete for the resources. For that purpose, the MergeSort benchmark enters the system first. Two seconds later the MatMul benchmark enters the system, and half a second after that, the Fib benchmark starts[2].

Based on the single-program results, we expect TBB to perform best because it has the least Total CPU Time in all three benchmarks. It might not affect the runtime of a single program significantly, but when there are multiple programs competing for the resources, the wasted CPU time can play an important role. In other words, CPU time wasted by each program can influence the performance of other programs reside in the system.

The results are shown and discussed in Fig. 4

5.1   Related Work

Saule and Catalyurek [10] have compared the same three programming models on the Intel Xeon Phi. They have focused on the scalability of graph algorithms,

---

[2] The sequential phase of the MergeSort benchmark with the input size 80 million is around 2 seconds, and the initial phase of the MatMul benchmark with the input size 4096×4096 is about half a second.

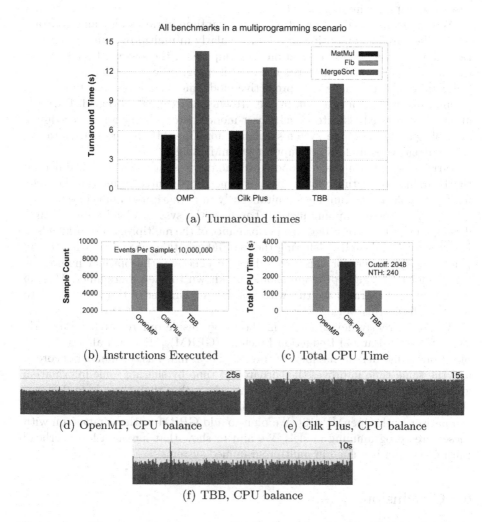

(a) Turnaround times

(b) Instructions Executed

(c) Total CPU Time

(d) OpenMP, CPU balance

(e) Cilk Plus, CPU balance

(f) TBB, CPU balance

Fig. 4. A multiprogramming scenario with the three benchmarks This is what happens when the three benchmarks compete for the resources: (a) shows that the best turnaround times are obtained with TBB. The hardware event, number of Instructions Executed, sampled by the VTune Amplifier in (b), implies a significant difference between TBB and the other two competitors. Results from the Total CPU Time in chart (c) is similar to those in chart (b) and they both show why TBB performs better than OpenMP and Cilk Plus. A detailed breakdown of overall CPU time in the (d) to (f) charts illustrates how OpenMP consumes more CPU time in total, and therefore has the worst performance.

while we have highlighted more differences between these programming models by adding the Total CPU Time as another performance aspect, and targeted the case of multiprogramming as well.

We have shown that the overhead of the runtime libraries play an important role in the parallel computing world, particularly in multiprogrammed systems. Besides the extra energy dissipation they impose on the system, they have noticeable influence on the performance of multiprogram workloads.

Emani et al. in [2] have used predictive modelling techniques to determine an optimal mapping of a program in the presence of external workload. Harris et al. have introduced Callisto [4] as a user-mode shared library for co-scheduling multiple parallel runtime systems (mainly for OpenMP programs). However, their current version does not support OpenMP tasks.

Varistoao ot al [14] have proposed an adaptive space-sharing scheduler for the Barrelfish operating system to overcome the resource contention between multiple applications running simultaneously in a multiprogrammed system.

In [12], a thread mapping method based on the system's load information is developed for OpenMP programs. Performance of the multiprogram workloads in Linux can be improved by sharing the load information and using it for thread placement. However, for this method to be effective, the optimal number of threads for each single program should be known to the programmer. Most of time, though, programs are run with the default number of threads, similar to what we did in this work.

We are currently developing a methodology inside our research framework, called Glasgow Parallel Reduction Machine (GPRM) [11] which allows the applications to use default numbers of threads (i.e. as many as the number of cores), and the same time improves the turnaround time by sharing some information globally. The main focus of GPRM is on tasks rather than threads to decrease the overhead of the runtime system. We have shown its potential, particularly in comparison with OpenMP [13]. We plan to add GPRM to the comparison with these three programming models. We aim to show that having a low-overhead runtime system is crucial in multiprogrammed systems.

6   Conclusion

We have compared some of the performance aspects (in particular speed-up, CPU balance, and the Total CPU Time) of three well-known parallel programming approaches, OpenMP, Cilk and TBB, on the Xeon Phi coprocessor. We used three different parallel benchmarks, Fibonacci, Merge Sort and Matrix Multiplication. Each benchmark has different characteristics which highlight some pros and cons of the studied approaches. Our multiprogramming scenario is to run all three benchmarks together on the system and observe how the different programming models react to this situation.

Based on the results obtained from the single program scenarios, particularly the Total CPU Time, we predicted that the Intel TBB approach would be more suited to a multiprogramming environment, and our experiment confirmed this.

Based on our learnings from these preliminary experiments, we plan to extend the work with more testbenches as well as more programming models.

In addition, since the way Linux deals with multithreaded multiprogramming is sub-optimal, we conclude that there is a need to share additional information on thread placement between the applications present in the system in order to get better performance. We are currently developing this idea inside our novel experimental framework.

References

1. Ayguadé, E., Copty, N., Duran, A., Hoeflinger, J., Lin, Y., Massaioli, F., Teruel, X., Unnikrishnan, P., Zhang, G.: The design of openmp tasks. IEEE Transactions on Parallel and Distributed Systems 20(3), 404–418 (2009)
2. Emani, M.K., Wang, Z., O'Boyle, M.F.: Smart, adaptive mapping of parallelism in the presence of external workload. In: 2013 IEEE/ACM International Symposium on Code Generation and Optimization (CGO), pp. 1–10. IEEE (2013)
3. Eyerman, S., Eeckhout, L.: System-level performance metrics for multiprogram workloads. IEEE Micro 28(3), 42–53 (2008)
4. Harris, T., Maas, M., Marathe, V.J.: Callisto: co-scheduling parallel runtime systems. In: Proceedings of the Ninth European Conference on Computer Systems, p. 24. ACM (2014)
5. Intel: Software development tools: Intel® VTune™ Amplifier XE 2013 (2013), https://software.intel.com/en-us/intel-vtune-amplifier-xe
6. Jeffers, J., Reinders, J.: Intel Xeon Phi Coprocessor High Performance Programming. Newnes (2013)
7. Kim, W., Voss, M.: Multicore desktop programming with intel threading building blocks. IEEE software 28(1), 23–31 (2011)
8. Leiserson, C.E.: The cilk++ concurrency platform. The Journal of Supercomputing 51(3), 244–257 (2010)
9. Reinders, J.: Intel threading building blocks: outfitting C++ for multi-core processor parallelism. O'Reilly Media, Inc. (2007)
10. Saule, E., Catalyurek, U.V.: An early evaluation of the scalability of graph algorithms on the intel mic architecture. In: 2012 IEEE 26th International Parallel and Distributed Processing Symposium Workshops & PhD Forum (IPDPSW), pp. 1629–1639. IEEE (2012)
11. Tousimojarad, A., Vanderbauwhede, W.: The Glasgow Parallel Reduction Machine: Programming shared-memory many-core systems using parallel task composition. EPTCS 137, 79–94 (2013)
12. Tousimojarad, A., Vanderbauwhede, W.: An efficient thread mapping strategy for multiprogramming on manycore processors. In: Parallel Computing: Accelerating Computational Science and Engineering (CSE). Advances in Parallel Computing, vol. 25, pp. 63–71. IOS Press (2014)
13. Tousimojarad, A., Vanderbauwhede, W.: A parallel task-based approach to linear algebra. In: 2014 IEEE 13th International Symposium on Parallel and Distributed Computing (ISPDC), pp. 59–66. IEEE (2014)
14. Varisteas, G., Brorsson, M., Faxen, K.F.: Resource management for task-based parallel programs over a multi-kernel.: Bias: Barrelfish inter-core adaptive scheduling. In: Proceedings of the 2012 Workshop on Runtime Environments, Systems, Layering and Virtualized Environments (RESoLVE 2012), pp. 32–36 (2012)

Exploring the Throughput-Fairness Trade-off on Asymmetric Multicore Systems

Juan Carlos Saez[1], Adrian Pousa[2], Fernando Castro[1],
Daniel Chaver[1], and Manuel Prieto-Matías[1]

[1] Computer Science School, Complutense University, Madrid, Spain
{jcsaezal,fcastror,dani02,mpmatias}@ucm.es
[2] Instituto de Investigacion en Informatica LIDI, UNLP, Argentina
apousa@lidi.info.unlp.edu.ar

Abstract. Symmetric-ISA (instruction set architecture) asymmetric-performance multicore processors (AMPs) were shown to deliver higher performance per watt and area than symmetric CMPs (Chip Multi-Processors). Previous work has shown that this potential of AMP systems can be realizable thanks to the OS scheduler. Existing scheduling schemes that deliver fairness and priority enforcement on AMPs do not cater to the fact that applications in a multiprogram workload may derive different benefit from using fast cores in the system. As a result, they are likely to perform thread-to-core mappings that degrade the system throughput. To address this limitation, we propose Prop-SP, a scheduling algorithm that aims to improve the throughput-fairness trade-off on AMPs. Our evaluation on real hardware, and using scheduler implementations on a general-purpose OS, reveals that Prop-SP delivers a better throughput-fairness trade-off than state-of-the-art schedulers for a wide variety of multi-application workloads.

Keywords: asymmetric multicore, scheduling, operating systems.

1 Introduction

Single-ISA asymmetric CMPs combine several core types with the same instruction-set architecture but different features such as clock frequency or microarchitecture. Previous work has demonstrated that asymmetric designs lead to a more efficient die area usage and a lower power consumption than symmetric CMPs [12]. Notably, combining just two core types simplifies the design and is enough to obtain most benefits from AMPs [13]. Major hardware players appear to be following this trend, as suggested by the recent ARM big.LITTLE processor [2] or the Quick-IA Intel prototype system [5].

Despite their benefits, AMPs pose significant challenges to the system software. One of the main challenges is to efficiently distribute fast-core cycles among the various applications running on the system. This task can be accomplished by the OS scheduler [18,11] or by the VM hypervisor on virtual environments [14]. Most existing proposals have focused on maximizing the system throughput

L. Lopes et al. (Eds.): Euro-Par 2014 Workshops, Part II, LNCS 8806, pp. 326–337, 2014.

[13,21,18,11]. To make this possible the scheduler needs to map to fast cores predominantly application threads that use those cores efficiently since they derive performance improvements (speedup) relative to running on slow cores [13]. Further throughput gains can be achieved by using fast cores to accelerate sequential phases of parallel programs [19,10].

Other important goals such as delivering fairness or priority enforcement on AMPs have drawn less attention from the research community. Previously-proposed OS-level schemes that deliver fairness on AMPs attempt to allocate a *fair* heterogeneous CPU share to the various applications. This can be accomplished by fair-sharing fast cores among applications [3,18] or by factoring in the computational power of the various cores when performing CPU accounting [15]. None of these techniques, however, exploit the fact that applications in a multiprogram workload may derive different benefit from using the fast cores in the AMP. For this reason, assigning the same heterogeneous CPU share to equal-priority applications does not ensure an *even slowdown across applications due to sharing the AMP* [20]. Moreover, not taking into account the diversity in applications' relative speedups when making scheduling decisions on AMPs may also lead to degrading the system throughput [3,18].

To address these shortcomings, we propose Prop-SP, a novel scheduling algorithm that delivers priority enforcement on AMPs and strives to even out the slowdown experienced by equal-priority applications. Our proposal delivers high system throughput without requiring hardware support nor changes in the applications. We qualitatively and quantitatively compare Prop-SP with state-of-the-art schedulers, such as A-DWRR [15] and CAMP [18]. Our experimental analysis reveals that Prop-SP improves the throughput-fairness trade-off for a broad spectrum of multi-application workloads.

The rest of the paper is organized as follows. Section 2 motivates our work. Section 3 outlines the design of the Prop-SP scheduler. Section 4 showcases our experimental results. Section 5 discusses related work and Section 6 concludes.

2   Motivation

We now present an analytical study regarding the system throughput and fairness delivered by previously proposed scheduling algorithms for AMPs. Our analysis demonstrates that existing schedulers that seek to optimize one metric degrade the other significantly, thus achieving unacceptable tradeoffs.

To assess *system throughput* we avoided metrics depending on *instructions per cycle* (IPC) or *instructions per second* (IPS) since they can be misleading to evaluate the performance of multithreaded programs [1]. As such, we opted to use a metric depending on *completion time* instead. In particular, we found that the *Aggregate Speedup* captures differences in throughput caused by diverse asymmetry-aware schedulers considerably better than other metrics proposed for CMPs, such as STP [7]. The *Aggregate Speedup* is defined as follows:

$$Aggregate\ Speedup = \sum_{i=1}^{n} \left(\frac{CT_{slow,i}}{CT_{sched,i}} - 1 \right) \tag{1}$$

Table 1. Synthetic workloads

Workload	SF_1	SF_2	SF_3	SF_4
W1	3.4	3.4	1.2	1.2
W2	3.4	3.4	2.3	2.3
W3	2.3	2.3	1.9	1.9
W4	3.4	3.4	2.7	2.7
W5	3.4	3.4	3.4	3.4
W6	2.5	2.1	1.6	1.2
W7	3.0	2.1	2.1	2.1
W8	3.4	3.0	2.5	2.1
W9	2.9	2.5	2.1	1.2

Table 2. Analytical formulas to approximate the aggregate speedup and unfairness for a workload consisting of n applications running simultaneously under a given thread scheduler.

Metric	Definition
$Agreggate\ Speedup$	$\sum_{i=1}^{n}\left(\frac{1}{\frac{f_i}{SF_i}+(1-f_i)}-1\right)$
$Slowdown_{app}$	$f_{app} + SF_{app} \cdot (1 - f_{app})$
$Unfairness$	$\frac{MAX(Slowdown_1,...,Slowdown_n)}{MIN(Slowdown_1,...,Slowdown_n)}$

where n is the number of applications in the workload, $CT_{slow,i}$ is the completion time of application i when it runs alone in the system and uses slow cores only, and $CT_{sched,i}$ is the completion time of application i under a given scheduler.

Regarding *fairness*, previous works have employed diverse definitions. Some of them define a scheme to be fair if it assigns the same CPU share to equal-priority threads [15]. Others consider a scheme as fair if equal-priority applications suffer the same slowdown due to sharing the system with respect to the situation in which the whole system is available to each application [8,16,6]. The latter definition is more suitable for CMP systems where degradation due to contention on shared resources may occur. Therefore, we opted to use this definition and employ the *unfairness* metric [16,6], which is defined as follows:

$$Unfairness = \frac{MAX(Slowdown_1, ..., Slowdown_n)}{MIN(Slowdown_1, ..., Slowdown_n)} \tag{2}$$

where $Slowdown_i = CT_{sched,i}/CT_{fast,i}$, and $CT_{fast,i}$ is the completion time of application i when running alone in the AMP (with all the fast cores available).

In our analytical study we assessed the effectiveness of different scheduling algorithms when running several synthetic multi-programmed workloads on an AMP system consisting on two fast cores (FC) and two slow cores (SC). All workloads comprise four single-threaded applications each. In this hypothetical scenario, we assume that applications exhibit fast-to-slow performance ratios that range between 1.2 and 3.4, a similar speedup range than that of the SPEC CPU2006 applications running on the Intel Quick-IA asymmetric system, as reported in [5]. Note that for single-threaded programs, the speedup matches the *speedup factor* (SF) of its single runnable thread, defined as $\frac{IPS_{fast}}{IPS_{slow}}$, where IPS_{fast} and IPS_{slow} are the thread's instructions per second ratios achieved on fast and slow cores respectively. Each row in Table 1 shows the speedup factors (SFs) of the four applications in a specific workload (W_i).

We derived a set of analytical formulas (shown in Table 2) to compute the Unfairness and the Aggregate speedup (ASP) of a workload under a given work-conserving[1] scheduler in this scenario. In deriving the formulas we assume that all applications in the workload run continuously for a certain amount of time T. To make the analytical derivation tractable we also assume that each application exhibits a constant SF during the time interval. Throughout the execution the given scheduler allots each application *app* a certain fast-core time fraction, denoted as F_{app}, such that $0 \leq F_{app} \leq 1$, where $F_{app} = 1$ means that the application would be mapped to a fast core the whole time. Equation 3 makes it possible to obtain the fraction of instructions each application completes on a fast core during the time interval – referred to as f_{app}– based on its speedup factor (SF_{app}) and F_{app}. As evident, the formulas to approximate the ASP and Unfairness only depend on SF_{app} and f_{app}. The detailed derivation process for these formulas as well as for Equation 3 can be found in [17].

$$f_{app} = \frac{1}{\frac{1}{SF_{app}} \cdot \left(\frac{1}{F_{app}} - 1\right) + 1} \tag{3}$$

Figure 1 shows the normalized unfairness and aggregate speedup for the analyzed workloads under five asymmetry-aware schedulers. The first one, denoted as HSP (High-SPeedup), assigns all fast cores to the N_{FC} (number of fast cores) threads in the workload that experience the greatest fast-to-slow speedup (for these applications $F_{app}=1$); the remaining threads are mapped to slow cores ($F_{app}=0$). Such a scheduler has been proposed in previous work [13,11]. The second scheduler is an asymmetry-aware round-robin (RR) policy that equally shares fast cores ($F_{app} = \frac{N_{FC}}{n}$) among applications [3,18]. The third scheduler is our proposal, referred to as Prop-SP (Proportional-SPeedup) and explained in detail in Section 3. In the scenario we explored, where workloads consist of equal-priority single-threaded programs, Prop-SP assigns the fast-core share to an application in proportion to its *net speedup* (i.e., $SF_{app} - 1$).

The fourth and fifth schedulers, referred to as Opt-Unfairness and Opt-ASP-Ref, constitute theoretical algorithms. The per-application FC cycle distribution made by Opt-Unfairness ensures the maximum ASP value attainable for the optimal unfairness. Opt-ASP-Ref, on the other hand, achieves the maximum ASP possible ensuring an unfairness value no greater than the one achieved by Prop-SP for a particular workload. We created a simple program which makes use of the analytical formulas in Table 2 to determine per-application fast-core cycle distributions for these theoretical algorithms.

Results from Figure 1 reveal that HSP optimizes the aggregate speedup (the higher ASP, the better) at the expense of obtaining the worst unfairness numbers by far (the higher the unfairness, the worse). As evident, the theoretical Opt-Unfairness scheduler exhibits lower aggregate speedup than HSP in most cases. This fact underscores that, in general, it is not possible to optimize both metrics simultaneously. More importantly, much throughput has to be sacrificed in some cases (up to 20% for W2) to achieve the optimal unfairness. As for the RR scheduler, results highlight that this policy always degrades both fairness and ASP

---

[1] Such a scheduler does not leave idle cores when the total thread count is greater or equal to the number of cores in the platform.

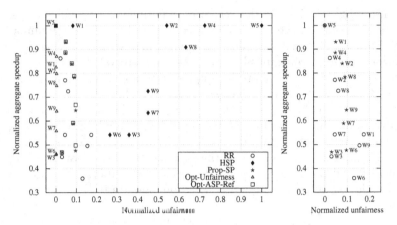

Fig. 1. Aggregate speedup (ASP) and unfairness values for the analyzed workloads under the various schedulers. The closer to the top left corner, the better the ASP-Unfairness tradeoff for the workload in question. Both metrics have been normalized to the (0,1) interval, where 0 represents the minimum value attainable for the metric in the platform and 1 the maximum one. For the sake of clarity, the explicit comparison between RR and Prop-SP has been replicated in a separate figure (right).

compared to Opt-Unfairness, thus providing a suboptimal solution. Notably, RR sacrifices up to 47% of the maximum throughput attainable and in some workloads, such as W1, high throughput reductions are also accompannied by fairness degradation. Finally, the results showcase good properties regarding the Prop-SP scheduler. First, it delivers higher aggregate speedup than Opt-Unfairness and RR across the board. Second, despite the slight fairness degradation, Prop-SP ensures unfairness numbers within 0-10% of the maximum attainable for all workloads (clearly, this is not always the case for HSP and RR). Third, results of the theoretical Opt-ASP-Ref scheduler reveal that Prop-SP delivers ASP numbers very close to the maximum attainable for the provided unfairness.

3   The Prop-SP Scheduler

3.1   The Algorithm

Prop-SP assigns threads to fast and slow cores so as to preserve load balance in the AMP, and periodically migrates threads between fast and slow cores to ensure that they run on fast cores for a specific amount of time. To perform thread-to-core assignments, it relies on two mechanisms: *fast-core credit allocation* and *inter-core swaps*.

Fast-Core Credit Allocation is a mechanism to control the amount of fast-core cycles allotted to the running threads on an AMP. At a high level, fast-core credit allocation works as follows. Each thread has a fast-core credit counter associated with it. When a thread runs on a fast core it consumes credits. Threads that have fast-core credits left (i.e., their credit counter is greater than zero) are preferentially assigned to fast cores by Prop-SP. Every so often, the OS triggers a credit assignment process that allots fast-core credits to applications with runnable threads. The time period elapsed between two consecutive system-wide credit assignments is set dynamically by the scheduler. We will refer to this elapsed period as the *execution period.* Note that we borrowed the idea of associating credits to threads from Xen's Credit Scheduler (CS) [4]. However, credit distribution in Prop-SP is completely different from that of CS.

Prop-SP awards fast-core credits to each application based on its associated *dynamic weight,* which is defined as the product of its net speedup (speedup minus one) and its *static weight.* In this context, the speedup indicates the relative benefit that the application would derive if all fast cores in the AMP were devoted to running threads from this application, with respect to running all threads on slow cores. The speedup is estimated at runtime by Prop-SP without the user intervention (see Section 3.2). The *static weight,* by contrast, is derived directly from the application priority (set by the user).

The credit assignment process entails three steps as detailed in Algorithm 1. After computing dynamic weights (step 1), Prop-SP allots credits to each application based of its dynamic weight in competition with the sum of the dynamic weights of all applications (step 2). Because the actual length of the next execution period is computed afterwards so as to control the migration rate (we will elaborate on this issue later), the credit distribution performed in step 2 is done assuming a fixed-width reference execution period. Once the length of the execution period has been determined, awarded per-application credits are scaled to the actual interval length. Finally, credits awarded to the application are then distributed among its runnable threads (step 3). For sequential programs, per-thread credit-distribution entails increasing the credit counter of the only thread by the amount of credits awarded. For multi-threaded applications, Prop-SP supports two per-thread credit distribution schemes: Even and BusyFCs. Even distributes credits uniformly across runnable threads in the application. BusyFCs goes sequentially through runnable threads and assigns each one the maximum amount of credits it can consume in the next execution period (`cred_per_fc_next_period`) until there are no more credits left to share. We found that the Even scheme is well-suited to coarse-grained parallel applications while BusyFCs turns out beneficial for fine and mid-grained parallel programs. The associated experimental analysis has been omitted due to space constraints.

Inter-Core Swaps is a thread-migration mechanism that ensures that threads with fast-core credits get a chance to use up their credits without disturbing load balance. In order to illustrate how this mechanism works, let us consider an AMP with one fast core and one slow core. Suppose that there are two threads with fast-core credits running on the system, each one mapped to a different core to preserve load balance. Eventually, the thread running on the fast core runs out of fast-core credits. At this point, the scheduler *swaps* both threads between cores to make sure the thread that was running on the slow core gets a chance to consume its fast-core credits while maintaining load balance.

Algorithm 1: Credit Assignment Algorithm

{ • *R is the set of applications with runnable threads.*

• N_{FC} *is the number of fast cores (FCs).*

• CRED_1FC_REF *is the amount of credits consumed on each FC during an execution period used as reference.*

• cred_per_fc_next_period *is the amount of credits consumed on each FC during the next execution period.* }

S:= [ ];   total_weight:=0;   total_credits:=CRED_1FC_REF * N_{FC};

{ **STEP 1** $\Rightarrow$ **Compute apps' dynamic weight and total_weight** }

foreach *app in R* **do**

    speedup$_{app}$:= estimate speedup for *app*;

    dyn_weight$_{app}$:= (speedup$_{app}$ − 1) * static_weight$_{app}$;

    total_weight := total_weight + dyn_weight$_{app}$;

    Insert *app* into S so as to keep S sorted in descending order by dyn_weight$_{app}$;

end

{ **STEP 2** $\Rightarrow$ **Assign credits to apps based on** dyn_weight$_{app}$ }

foreach *app in* S **do**

$$\text{credit}_{app}:=\frac{\text{total\_credits} * \text{dyn\_weight}_{app}}{\text{total\_weight}};$$

end

{ **STEP 3** $\Rightarrow$ **Determine the length of the next execution period and distribute credits among threads** }

Compute cred_per_fc_next_period;

scale_factor:=cred_per_fc_next_period/CRED_1FC_REF;

foreach *app in* S **do**

    credit$_{app}$:=credit$_{app}$ * scale_factor;

    Distribute credit$_{app}$ credits among threads in *app*

end

3.2   Determining the Speedup

At runtime, Prop-SP needs to obtain the relative speedup that an application derives from using all fast cores in the AMP. This value is used by the credit distribution algorithm to compute the application's dynamic weight.

As mentioned in Section 2, the speedup of a single-threaded application matches the SF of its single runnable thread. To determine a thread's SF online, Prop-SP feeds a platform-specific estimation model with values from diverse performance metrics collected over time[2] (such as the IPC or the last-level-cache miss rate). In this work, we leverage the technique proposed in our previous work [19] to aid in the construction of SF estimation models. This technique, which has been proven successful in a AMP prototype system where cores differ in microarchitecture, enables to generate SF models by analyzing offline-

---

[2] In our setting, performance counters are sampled every 200ms, which leads to negligible overhead associated with sampling and SFs estimation.

collected performance counter data from a representative set of single-threaded CPU-bound programs.[3]

To obtain a speedup estimate for a multithreaded application, several factors in addition to the SF must be taken into account [9,19], such as its amount of thread-level parallelism (TLP) or how fast-core credits are distributed among its threads. Prop-SP makes use of the following equations to estimate the application speedup under the BusyFCs and the Even credit-distribution schemes:

$$SP_{BusyFCs} = \frac{SF-1}{(\lfloor \frac{N-1}{N_{FC}} \rfloor +1)^2} + 1 \qquad SP_{Even} = \frac{MIN(N_{FC},N)}{N} \cdot (SF - 1) + 1$$

where N is the number of threads in the application, N_{FC} is the number of fast cores in the AMP and SF is the average speedup factor of the application threads. The detailed derivation process for these formulas can be found in our previous work [19,17].

4   Experimental Evaluation

In our experiments, we analyzed two variants of Prop-SP (static and dynamic), which follow different approaches to determine a thread's SF. The *base* implementation of Prop-SP, referred to as *Prop-SP (dynamic)*, estimates SFs online using hardware counters. *Prop-SP (static)*, on the other hand, asummes a constant SF value for each thread, measured prior to the execution. We compare both versions of Prop-SP against four previously-proposed schemes: RR [3,18], A-DWRR [15], CAMP [19] and HSP (High-SPeedup) [3,11]. In previous work [18], we observed that considering the speedup of the application as a whole rather than the speedup of individual threads when making thread-to-core mappings leads to higher throughput in scenarios where parallel applications are present. As such, for a fairer comparison, we modified HSP to perform thread-to-core assignments taking into account the application-wide speedup rather than per-thread speedup factors.

All the evaluated algorithms have been implemented in the Solaris kernel and tested on real multicore hardware made asymmetric by reducing the processor frequency of a subset of cores in the platform. In particular, we used a multicore server consisting of two AMD Opteron 2435 "Istanbul" hex-core processors (12 cores). Each chip includes a 6MB shared L3 cache shared among cores. Emulated AMP configurations on this system consist of "fast" cores that operate at 2.6GHz and "slow" cores running at 800MHz. To evaluate the different scheduling algorithms, we used two AMP configurations: (1) 2FC-2SC – including two chips with one fast core and one slow core (2) 2FC-10SC – two chips with one fast core and 5 slow cores each.

---

[3] In this work we obtained the SF estimation models by analyzing offline-collected data from a subset of the SPEC CPU 2006 benchmarks. Note that we also experimented with applications different to those employed to generate the models.

Table 3. Multi-application workloads consisting of single- and multithreaded programs

Categories	Benchmarks	Categories	Benchmarks
3STH-1HPH	hmmer, gobmk, h264ref, fma3d_m(9)	4STH	povray, gobmk, bzip2, sjeng
3STH-1HPL	povray, gamess, gobmk, swim_m(9)	3STH-1STM	povray, h264ref, perlbench, astar
2STH-1PSH-1HPM	gamess, bzip2, BLAST(4), wupwise_m(6)	3STH-1STL_A	hmmer, namd, perlbench, soplex
1STH-1STM-1STL-1PSH	gamess, astar, soplex, blackscholes(9)	3STH-1STL_B	hmmer, h264ref, gobmk, milc
1PSH-1PSL	semphy(6), FFTW3D(6)	2STH-2STM_A	povray, bzip2, leslie3d, sphinx3
2PSH-1HPM	BLAST(4), semphy(4), wupwise_m(4)	2STH-2STM_B	gamess, gobmk, xalancbmk, astar
1PSH-1HPL	semphy(6), equake_m(6)	2STH-2STL_A	hmmer, gobmk, lbm, soplex
1HPH-1HPL	fma3d_m(6), equake_m(6)	2STH-2STL_B	povray, h264ref, lbm, omnetpp
1PSH-1HPH	blackscholes(6), fma3d_m(6)	1STH-1STM-2STL	sjeng, leslie3d, lbm, soplex

Our evaluation targets multi-application workloads consisting of HPC bench marks from diverse suites (SPEC CPU 2006 and OMP 2001, PARSEC, NAS Parallel Benchmarks and Minebench). We also experimented with BLAST – a bioinformatics benchmark – and FFTW3D – an HPC benchmark performing the fast Fourier transform. In all experiments, the sum of the number of threads of all applications was set to match the number of cores in the platform, since this is how runtime systems typically configure the number of threads for CPU-bound workloads like the ones we used. We ensure that all applications in the workload are started simultaneously and when an application terminates it is restarted repeatedly until the longest application in the set completes three times. For each application in a workload, CT_{sched} is calculated as the geometric mean of its completion times for the various executions. We measure CT_{fast} for an application by tracking its completion time when running alone in the AMP with its best-performing per-thread credit distribution scheme.

Table 3 shows the analyzed multi-application workloads. The first nine workloads (left) consist of both sequential and parallel applications; the last nine (right) comprise sets of single-threaded programs. In creating the workloads, we categorized applications into three groups with respect to their parallelism: highly parallel (HP), partially sequential (PS) –parallel applications with a sequential component of over 25% of the total execution time– and single-threaded (ST). In order to cater to applications' SFs as well, we further divided the three aforementioned application groups into three subclasses based on their SFs – high (H), medium (M) and low (L). The application categories are shown in the table in the same order as the corresponding benchmarks. For example, in the 1PSH-1HPL category, semphy is the PSH application and equake_m is the HPL one. The number in parentheses next to the name of each multithreaded application indicates the number of threads it runs with.

Figure 2 shows the aggregate speedup and unfairness for the workloads under the various schedulers. Overall, HSP and CAMP, which assign high-speedup applications to fast cores, yield the highest system throughput in most cases but fail to deliver fairness accross the board. RR and A-DWRR, on the other hand, do rather a good job in terms of both fairness and throughput for workloads including single-threaded applications only. However, when multithreaded pro-

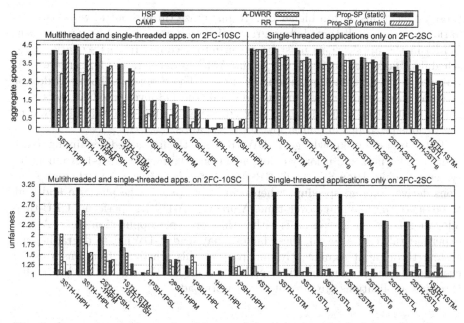

Fig. 2. Aggregate speedup and unfairness of the investigated scheduling algorithms

grams are present in the workload, both schedulers degrade the system through-put significantly. In this scenario, A-DWRR awards higher fast-core share to those applications with a higher thread count. As shown in [18], this may lead to throughput degradation since applications with a high active thread count may experience low benefit from using the scarce fast cores in the platform.

The results reveal that Prop-SP is able to make efficient use of the AMP and improve the throughput-fairness tradeoff for a wider range of workloads. Overall, these benefits are especially pronounced for workloads including multithreaded programs. In this scenario, Prop-SP is able to match the performance of HSP and CAMP for 3STH-1HPH, 1PSH-1PSL and 1PSH-1HPH, while performing in a close range for the remaining application mixes. At the same time, it achieves much lower unfairness numbers than HSP and CAMP across the board and exhibits comparable unfairness to A-DWRR and RR. Moreover, we observe that the inacuracies of the SF estimation model used by Prop-SP (dynamic), do not prevent it from reaping benefits similar to those of the static version.

5 Related Work

A large body of work has advocated the benefits of AMPs over symmetric CMPs [13,12,9]. Despite these benefits, AMP systems pose significant challenges to the system software [15]. OS scheduling is one of the most critical challenges, and this is the focus of our paper.

Most existing asymmetry-aware schedulers strive to optimize the system throughput. Schedulers targeting workloads consisting of single-threaded programs only [13,3,11,21,18] aim to maximize throughput by running on fast cores those applications with a higher SF. To maximize throughput in workload scenarios including multithreaded programs, the amount of thread-level parallelism (TLP) in the applications must be taken into account. In this scenario, some schedulers make use of fast cores in the AMP as accelerators for serial execution phases in parallel applications [18,19,10]. These schemes, however, do not attempt to ensure fairness. In our proposal, the OS-level scheduler acts as a global arbiter that delivers fairness by adjusting the fast-core share allotted to the various programs in multiapplication scenarios.

To the best of our knowledge, A-DWRR [15] is the first scheduler aiming to deliver both fairness and priority enforcement on asymmetric single-ISA multicore systems. Unlike Prop-SP, A-DWRR does not take into account that applications derive different speedups when using fast cores in the platform and that these speedups may vary over time. Moreover, A-DWRR performs CPU-time allocation on a per-thread basis rather than on a per-application basis. As our experimental results reveal, these factors may lead A-DWRR to degrading the system throughput significantly and prevent this scheduler from ensuring an even slowdown for equal-priority applications on AMPs, especially when multithreaded applications are present in the workload.

6   Conclusions

In this paper we proposed Prop-SP, a scheduler that aims to improve the balance between fairness and throughtput on asymmetric multicores. To make this possible, Prop-SP exploits the diversity in the fast-core efficiency of a workload to even out the slowdown experienced by simultaneously running applications (based on their priorities) when sharing the fast cores of an AMP. We implemented Prop-SP in the Solaris kernel and compared it against several state-of-the-art asymmetry-aware schedulers. Our experiments reveal that Prop-SP is able to make efficient use of the AMPs and improve the throughput-fairness tradeoff for a wider range of workloads. The benefits of the Prop-SP policy are especially pronounced for workloads including multithreaded programs.

Key elements for the success of Prop-SP are the credit-based mechanism enabling the scheduler to adjust the fast-core share allotted to the different programs and its reliance on estimation models to approximate application speedup online. As shown in previous work [19], asymmetry-aware schedulers relying on SF estimation models, such as Prop-SP, can be seamlessly extended to different forms of performance asymmetry. Evaluating Prop-SP on cutting-edge AMP prototypes [5] is an interesting avenue for future work.

Acknowledgements. This work has been supported by the Spanish government through the research contract TIN2012-32180 and the HIPEAC[3] European Network of Excellence.

References

1. Alameldeen, A.R., Wood, D.A.: IPC considered harmful for multiprocessor workloads. IEEE Micro 26(4) (2006)
2. ARM: Benefits of the big.LITTLE Architecture (2012)
3. Becchi, M., Crowley, P.: Dynamic Thread Assignment on Heterogeneous Multiprocessor Architectures. In: Proc. of CF 2006, pp. 29–40 (2006)
4. Cherkasova, L., Gupta, D., Vahdat, A.: Comparison of the three CPU schedulers in Xen. SIGMETRICS Perform. Eval. Rev. 35(2), 42–51 (2007)
5. Chitlur, N., et al.: QuickIA: Exploring heterogeneous architectures on real prototypes. In: Proc. of HPCA 2012, pp. 1–8 (2012)
6. Ebrahimi, E., et al.: Fairness via source throttling: a configurable and high-performance fairness substrate for multi-core memory systems. In: ASPLOS 2010 (2010)
7. Eyerman, S., Eeckhout, L.: System-level performance metrics for multiprogram workloads. IEEE Micro 28(3) (2008)
8. Gabor, R., Weiss, S., Mendelson, A.: Fairness and throughput in switch on event multithreading. In: Proc. of MICRO 2006 (2006)
9. Hill, M.D., Marty, M.R.: Amdahl's Law in the Multicore Era. IEEE Computer 41(7), 33–38 (2008)
10. Joao, J.A., et al.: Utility-based acceleration of multithreaded applications on asymmetric CMPs. In: Proc. of ISCA 2013, pp. 154–165 (2013)
11. Koufaty, D., Reddy, D., Hahn, S.: Bias Scheduling in Heterogeneous Multi-core Architectures. In: Proc. of Eurosys 2010 (2010)
12. Kumar, R., et al.: Single-ISA Heterogeneous Multi-Core Architectures: the Potential for Processor Power Reduction. In: Proc. of MICRO, vol. 36 (2003)
13. Kumar, R., et al.: Single-ISA Heterogeneous Multi-Core Architectures for Multi-threaded Workload Performance. In: Proc. of ISCA 2004 (2004)
14. Kwon, Y., et al.: Virtualizing performance asymmetric multi-core systems. In: Proceedings of ISCA 2011 (2011)
15. Li, T., et al.: Operating system support for overlapping-ISA heterogeneous multi-core architectures. In: HPCA 2010, pp. 1–12 (2010)
16. Mutlu, O., Moscibroda, T.: Stall-time fair memory access scheduling for chip multiprocessors. In: Proc. of MICRO 2007 (2007)
17. Pousa, A., et al.: Theoretical study on the performance of an asymmetry-aware round-robin scheduler. TR - 5028A. Dept. of Computer Architecture. UCM (2012), https://artecs.dacya.ucm.es/sites/default/files/dacya-tr5028A.pdf
18. Saez, J.C., et al.: A Comprehensive Scheduler for Asymmetric Multicore Systems. In: Proc. of ACM Eurosys 2010 (2010)
19. Saez, J.C., et al.: Leveraging core specialization via OS scheduling to improve performance on asymmetric multicore systems. ACM TOCS 30(2) (April 2012)
20. Saez, J.C., et al.: Delivering fairness and priority enforcement on asymmetric multicore systems via OS scheduling. In: Proc. of ACM SIGMETRICS (2013)
21. Shelepov, D., et al.: HASS: A Scheduler for Heterogeneous Multicore Systems. ACM SIGOPS OSR 43(2) (2009)

Assembly Operations for Multicore Architectures
Using Task-Based Runtime Systems

Damien Genet[1], Abdou Guermouche[2], and George Bosilca[3]

[1] INRIA, Bordeaux, France
[2] INRIA, LaBRI, Univ. Bordeaux, Bordeaux, France
[3] University of Tennessee, Knoxville, USA

Abstract. Traditionally, numerical simulations based on finite element methods consider the algorithm as being divided in three major steps: the generation of a set of blocks and vectors, the assembly of these blocks in a matrix and a big vector, and the inversion of the matrix. In this paper we tackle the second step, the block assembly, where no parallel algorithm is widely available. Several strategies are proposed to decompose the assembly problem while relying on a scheduling middle-ware to maximize the overlap between stages and increase the parallelism and thus the performance. These strategies are quantified using examples covering two extremes in the field, large number of non-overlapping small blocks for CFD-like problems, and a smaller number of larger blocks with significant overlap which can be met in sparse linear algebra solvers.

1 Introduction

The increasing parallelism and complexity of hardware architectures requires the High Performance Computing (HPC) community to develop more and more complex software. To achieve high levels of optimization and fully benefit of their potential, not only the related codes are heavily tuned for the considered architecture, but the software is often designed as a single entity that aims to simultaneously cope with both the algorithmic and architectural needs. If this approach may indeed lead to extremely high performance, it is at the price of a tremendous development effort, a lesser portability and a poor maintainability.

Alternatively, a more modular approach can be employed. The numerical algorithm is described at a high level, independently of the hardware architecture, as a Directed Acyclic Graph (DAG) of tasks where a vertex represents a task and an edge represents a dependency between tasks. A second layer is in charge of taking the scheduling decisions. Based on these decisions, a runtime system will perform the actual execution of the tasks, maintaining data consistency and ensuring that dependencies are satisfied. The fourth layer consists of the optimized code for the related tasks on the underlying architectures. This approach is starting to give successful results in various domains going from very regular applications [16,3,7] to very irregular ones [14,2,1]. However, building such

L. Lopes et al. (Eds.): Euro-Par 2014 Workshops, Part II, LNCS 8806, pp. 338–350, 2014.

complex applications on top of task-based runtime systems requires algorithmic modifications of some core kernels of the application so that the flexibility offered by the runtime system can be fully exploited. More precisely, these operations need to be expressed as a task graph having enough parallelism to allow the runtime system to overcome all the synchronizations/race conditions which can be met with regular implementations of these kernels.

In this paper, we will focus on a specific operation, namely assembly operation, which can be met in various application fields: *finite elements* (FEM) methods, multifrontal sparse direct solvers, etc. This operation, even if not costly in terms of operations count, is memory-bound and often a performance bottleneck when the number of computational resources increases. Assembly operations can be viewed as scatter/add operations used to process dense contribution blocks to update a global, dense or sparse, matrix. This work is a first step toward a larger context where numerical simulations will be expressed in a task-based paradigm in order to diverge from the traditional fork-join model and relax synchronizations. Our contributions are : 1) A tiled version (which enhances parallelism) of the assembly operation is introduced and implemented on top of two task-based runtime systems. 2) Several *priority based* dynamic scheduling techniques which aim at reducing the makespan of the assembly operation are presented. 3) An experimental study concerning two application fields, namely FEM applications and multifrontal sparse direct solver, is presented.

The remainder of the paper is organized as follows. After a presentation of existing techniques for parallelizing assembly operations, we will introduce our tiled version of the assembly operations and show how it can be expressed in two different task-based paradigms. Finally, we will evaluate our proposed approaches and compare them with state-of-the-art techniques.

2   Related Work

Considering the increasing complexity of modern high performance computing platforms, the need for a portable layer that will insulate the algorithms and their developers from the rapid hardware changes becomes critical. Recently, this portability layer appeared under the denomination of task-based runtime. A lot of initiatives have emerged in the past years to develop efficient runtime systems for modern architectures. As stated above, most of these runtime systems use a task-based paradigm to express concurrency and dependencies by employing a task dependency graph to represent the application to be executed: PaRSEC [8], SMPSs [6], StarPU [5], etc. The main differences between all the approaches are related to whether or not they manage data movements between computational resources, to which extent they focus on task scheduling, and how task dependencies are expressed. These task-based runtime systems aim at performing the actual execution of the tasks, both ensuring that the DAG dependencies are satisfied at execution time and maintaining data consistency. Most of them are designed to allow writing a program independently of the architecture and thus require a strict separation of the different software layers: high-level algorithm, scheduling, runtime system, actual task implementation. Among these frameworks, we will focus in this paper on the StarPU and the PaRSEC runtime systems. The dense linear algebra community has strongly adopted such a modular approach lately [16,3,7] and delivered subsequent production-level solvers. As a result, performance portability is achieved thanks to the hardware abstraction layer introduced by runtime systems. More recently, this approach was considered in more complex/irregular applications : sparse direct solvers [14,2], fast multipole methods [1], etc. The obtained results are promising and illustrate the interest of such a layered approach.

From the numerical simulation point of view, more precisely finite element methods, significant efforts have been made to exploit modern heterogeneous architectures (i.e. multicore systems equipped with accelerators) [13,11]. The main idea is to be able to have efficient implementations of the core kernels needed by the numerical simulation namely assembly operations, linear systems solution, etc, for these architectures. We believe that those efforts are necessary to understand the bottlenecks to obtain a good performance on such heterogeneous architectures. However, we think that the modular approach proposed in this paper, coupled with a fine grain task-based expression of the application will ensure performance portability on any heterogeneous execution platform.

3   Background

3.1   Assembly Operations on Multicore Systems

1: Initialize the matrix A
2: **for each** contribution block c **do**
3:     **for each** entry $c[i][j]$ of c **do**
4:         $A[rmap(c, i), cmap(c, j)] + = c[i][j]$
5:     **end for**
6: **end for**

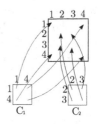

Algorithm 1. Assembly operation

Fig. 1. Assembly operation with 2 contribution blocks

From a general point of view, assembly operations can be viewed as scatter-add operations of each contribution on the matrix following the scheme depicted in Algorithm 1. This operation is commutative and contributions can be treated in any order. For each contribution block, each entry is summed with the corresponding entry of the matrix A. The association between elements of the contribution blocks and entries of A are determined using indirection arrays $rmap$ and $cmap$ which store the correspondence between local indices within the contribution block and global indices within the matrix A. For example, if we consider the assembly operation the contribution block c_1 (which is a 2 by 2 matrix) presented in Figure 1, $rmap(c_1, 1)$ (resp. $cmap(c_1, 1)$) will be equal to 1 while $rmap(c_1, 2)$ (resp. $cmap(c_1, 2)$) will be equal to 4.

Recently, a lot of work has targeted the implementation of efficient assembly operations for finite element methods running on multicore architectures which may be enhanced with accelerators. The main issue with the parallelization of assembly operations comes from the race conditions which occur when two different contribution blocks need to update the same entry of the global matrix. A naive parallelization scheme of the assembly operation is to process the contribution blocks in a sequential way using a parallel implementation of the assembly of a block. This strategy requires the contribution blocks to be large enough to ensure performance.

Moreover, the approach suffers from the lack of scalability: only intra-block parallelism is exploited. More Recently, in [9] Cecka *et al.* introduced a parallelization approach based on a coloring of the contribution blocks where contribution blocks having the same color can be treated in parallel. This property is guaranteed by the fact that blocks having the same color do not contribute to the same entries of the global matrix. This idea has been pushed further by Markall *et al.* in [15] by improving the coloring scheme in a way such that the number of colors used is reduced. Lately, Hanzlikova *et al.* proposed in [12] an approach which extends the work from Cecka by using extra storage to avoid synchronizations needed to prevent race conditions.

3.2 The StarPU Runtime System

As most modern task-based runtime systems, StarPU aims at performing the actual execution of the tasks, both ensuring that the DAG dependencies are satisfied at execution time and maintaining data consistency. The particularity of StarPU is that it was initially designed to write a program independently of the architecture and thus requires a strict separation of the different software layers: high-level algorithm, scheduling, runtime system, actual code of the tasks. We refer to Augonnet *et al.* [5] for the details and present here a simple example containing only the features relevant to this work. Assume we aim at executing the sequence $fun_1(\underline{x}, y)$; $fun_2(\underline{x})$; $fun_1(\underline{z}, w)$, where $fun_{i,i\in\{1,2\}}$ are functions applied on w, x, y, z data; the arguments corresponding to data which are modified by a function are underlined. A task is defined as an instance of a function on a specific set of data. The set of tasks and related data they operate on are declared with the **submit_task** instruction. This is a non blocking call that allows one to add a task to the current DAG and postpone its actual execution to the moment when its dependencies are satisfied. Although the API of a runtime system can be virtually reduced to this single instruction, it may be convenient in certain cases to explicitly define extra dependencies. For that, identification tags can be attached to the tasks at submission time and dependencies are declared between the related tags with the **declare_dependency** instruction. For instance, an extra dependency is defined between the first and the third task in Figure 2 (left). Figure 2 (right) shows the resulting DAG built (and executed) by the runtime. The $id_1 \rightarrow id_2$ dependency is implicitly inferred with respect to the data hazard on x while the $id_1 \rightarrow id_3$ dependency is declared explicitly. Optionally, a priority value can be assigned to each task to guide the runtime system in case multiple tasks are ready for execution at a given moment. In StarPU, the scheduling system is clearly split from the core of the runtime system (data consistency engine and actual task execution). Therefore, not only all built-in scheduling policies can be applied to any high-level algorithm, but new scheduling strategies can be implemented without having to interfere with low-level technical details of the runtime system.

```
submit_task(fun₁, x, y, id=id₁)

submit_task(fun₂, x, id=id₂)

declare_dependency(id₃ ← id₁)

submit_task(fun₁, z, w, id=id₃)
```

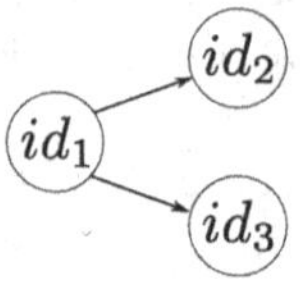

```
1: PING(k) : k = 0 .. N
2: RW A ← (k == 0) ? A(k) : A PONG(k-1)
3:         → A PONG(k)

4: PONG(k) : k = 0 .. N
5: RW A ← A PING(k)
6:         → (k == N) ? A(k) : A PING(k+1)
```

Fig. 2. Basic StarPU-like example (left) and associated DAG (right).

Algorithm 2. Ping-Pong algorithm expressed in the PaRSEC dataflow description

3.3 The PaRSEC Runtime System

As described in [8], PaRSEC is a dataflow programming environment supported by a dynamic runtime, capable of alleviating some of the challenges imposed by the ongoing changes at the hardware level. The underlying runtime is a generic framework for architecture-aware scheduling and management of micro-tasks on distributed many-core heterogeneous architectures. The dynamic runtime is only one side of the necessary abstraction, as it must be able to discover concurrency in the application to feed all computing units. To reach the desired level of flexibility, we support the runtime with a symbolic representation for the algorithm, able to expose more of the available parallelism than traditional programming paradigms. The runtime is capable of freely exploiting this parallelism to increase the opportunities for useful computation, predict future algorithm behaviors and increase the occupancy of the computing units.

Algorithm 2 represents a concise dataflow description of a ping-pong application, where a data A(k) is altered by two tasks, PING and PONG, before being written back into the original location A(k). Line 1 defines the task PING and it's valid execution space, $\forall k \in [0..N]$. Line 2 depicts the input value A for the task PING(k), where if k is 0 the data is read from an array A(), otherwise it is the output A of a previous task PONG(k-1). Line 3 describes the output flow of the tasks PING, where the locally modified data A is transmitted to a task PONG(k). This task PONG(k) can be executed in the context of the same process as PING(k) or remotely, the runtime will automatically infer the communications depending on the location of the source and target tasks. Lines 4 to 6 similarly depict the complementary task PONG.

Each task consists in the addition to the dataflow definition depicted in the above algorithm, several possible implementations of the code to be executed on the data, the so called codelets. Each codelet is targeted toward a specific hardware device (CPU, Xeon Phi, GPU) or a specific language or framework (Open CL). The decision of which of the possible codelets to be executed is controlled by a dynamic scheduling, aware of the state of all local computing resources. Once the scheduling decision is taken, the runtime provides the input data located on the specific resource where the task is to be executed, and upon completion will make the resulting data available for any potential successors. As the task flow definition includes a description of the type of use made by a task for each data (read, write or read/write) the runtime can minimize the data movements while respecting the correct data versioning. Not depicted in this short description are other types of collective communication patterns that can be either described, or automatically inferred from the dataflow description.

4 Taskified Assembly Operation

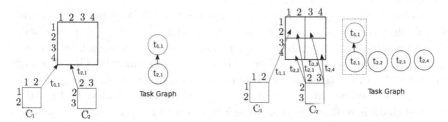

Fig. 3. Naive scheme   **Fig. 4.** Tiled scheme

We introduce in this section a taskified assembly operation where the objective is to enhance parallelism while leaving the management of data constraints and possible race conditions to the underlying runtime system. The main phenomenon which limits the amount of parallelism is the serialization of the assembly of two contribution blocks updating the same block, serialization that prevents possible race conditions. To increase the amount of parallelism, computations must be organized such that conflicting write operations are minimized. A naive approach to express the global assembly operation would be to associate a task to the assembly operation of each contribution block (see Figure 3). In this context, all tasks will be serialized because of the write conflicts on the global matrix. For example, if we consider the assembly operation presented in Figure 3 where this naive scheme is used, the dependency task graph contains 2 tasks (namely $t_{1,1}$ and $t_{2,2}$) which have a write conflict on the global matrix. Note that since the summation operator used during the assembly operation is commutative and associative, the task graph where $t_{1,1}$ is the predecessor of $t_{2,1}$ is also valid. However, for the remaining of this study, we ignore the commutativity of the assembly operation, and will impose a writing order by ordering the tasks generation and declaration. With such an approach, the runtime is now responsible to order the assembly operations with respect to the depicted data dependencies, preventing all conflicts between accesses to the same data.

In order to exhibit more parallelism, one could partition the global matrix into blocks and associate a task to the assembly operation of each contribution block into each tile of the global matrix (see Figure 4). Of course, if a contribution block does not update a tile of the global matrix, the corresponding empty task is not considered. By doing so, the amount of non-conflicting tasks is increased leading to higher degree of parallelism. For example, if we consider now the assembly operation described in Figure 4 where this tile-based scheme is used, we can see that the task graph contains now 5 tasks for which there is only one conflict between $t_{1,1}$ and $t_{2,1}$. When using this scheme, the number of tasks and subsequently the degree of parallelism is strongly linked to blocking factor used for the global matrix. A trade-off needs thus to be found between the needed parallelism and the management overhead induced in the runtime system. The approach to taskify the assembly operation that we propose is a tiled approach where the serialized tasks are sorted according to their computational cost in each chain: the most costly tasks are treated first. The task graph is thus composed by a set of independent chains of tasks. This scheme will be referred to as the *flat assembly operation scheme.*

To overcome the overhead due the management of the large number of tasks, one could decrease the number of tasks for a fixed tile size by merging the chains of the flat assembly scheme into a single tasks. This will produce a fixed number of tasks corresponding to the number of tiles of the global matrix. This approach is similar to [9], in the sense that it builds a set of completely independent tasks preventing all race conditions from occurring. This is illustrated in Figure 4, where the chain is replaced by the dashed box surrounding it. In the rest of the paper, this scheme will be referred to as *no-chain assembly operation scheme.*

4.1   Scheduling Strategies for Taskified Assembly Operations

Taskified assembly operations can are expressed using task dependency graphs composed of independent chains of tasks (an example is given in Figure 4). In this paper, we consider dynamic on-line scheduling strategies which are commonly used in various runtime systems. In order to efficiently assign tasks to the computational resources it is important to take into account the weight of each task in terms of workload and give priority to the largest ones (the larger the contribution the higher its priority is). This strategy is used on the set of ready tasks (i.e. tasks for which the corresponding dependencies are satisfied) and each idle processing unit picks the task with highest priority from the set of ready tasks. By doing so, the processing units are constantly working on the critical path of the execution. Varying the tasks priorities allow for further improvement of the scheduling strategy.

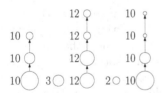

Fig. 5. Fixed priorities

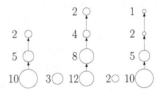

Fig. 6. Adaptive priorities

A first approach to express the critical aspect of a task regarding the length of the chain it belongs to, is to associate a priority related to the cost of the entire chain. This illustrates in Figure 5, where the priorities of the entire chain are constant, and are computed based on the cost of the entire chain. We will refer to this priority scheme as *fixed priority scheme.*

This priority management can be pushed further so that the priorities, not only take into account the absolute length of the critical path but its current length at the moment where the scheduling decision is taken. Thus, the priority of a task is computed based on the remaining workload on the chain it belongs to. This allows the working units to select the tasks that are currently the most critical. Figure 6 depicts the same example as before using this new priority assignment scheme. This time the tasks belonging to a chain have a priority linked to the length of the remaining part of the chain. We will refer to this priority scheme as *adaptive priority scheme.*

One of the major differences between StarPU and PaRSEC is the way the list of ready tasks is managed. In StarPU, the user divides data, precomputes a list of tasks working on those data, and submits, in advance, all the tasks. This sequential submission of tasks creates implicit dependencies between the tasks. In PaRSEC, the dependencies are explicitly specified by the user, and the tasks are dynamically discovered by the runtime based on completed dependencies and the symbolic description of the algorithm. From the scheduling point of view, StarPU gives the opportunity to the user to write his own scheduler while in PaRSEC, a highly optimized scheduler is provided, where priorities are secondary to enforcing a coherent data locality policy.

5 Experimental Results

We evaluate the behavior and performance of our task-based approach on the `riri` platform, composed by 4 Intel E7-4870 processors having 10 cores clocked at 2,40 GHz and having 30 MB of L3 cache. The platform has uniform memory access (UMA) to it's 1 TB of RAM. In all cases the results presented are averages over multiple runs (at least 10), where the outliers have been cleaned. In addition to the results presented here, we also analyzed the standard deviation, but we decided not to report it as is was under the system noise (2%).

We have chosen to illustrate the behavior of our approaches on two different classes of problems. The first class correspond to assembly operations met in finite element methods. We consider in the following study both 2D and 3D finite element continued method applied on structured meshes. The difference between the two cases resides in the connectivity between elements. While on a 2D grid, each element has at most 8 neighbors, in 3D, each hexahedron has 26 neighbors leading to higher overlapping between contribution blocks for the 3D case. The second class correspond to a less structured assembly operations met in a sparse direct method (namely the multifrontal method [10]). The considered configuration has been generated using the MUMPS sparse direct solver [4] using input problems coming from the University of Florida Sparse Matrix Collection [1]. To be more precise, we extracted configurations met during the assembly phases

---

[1] http://www.cise.ufl.edu/research/sparse/matrices

needed by the sparse LU factorization. The contribution blocks for these configurations are very irregular with sizes varying from 0.01% to 99% of father's size.
Thus, we are not analyzing the task-based implementation asymptotically on
large benchmarks, but on real-life cases extracted existing applications. Finally,
two parameters will vary in our experiments, the size of the tile and the number
of computational resources. The bigger the tile size, the lesser parallelism one
will be able to exhibit. Thus, one shall find an acceptable value in sync with the
second parameter, the number of computing resources units available.

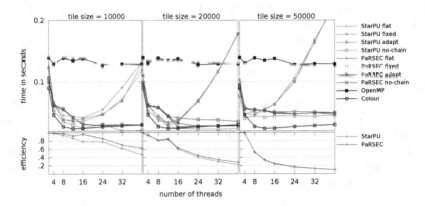

Fig. 7. Comparison of the performance of an assembly operation using a 2D mesh with
2025 blocks of size 121^2 based on the granularity of the operation (as depicted by the
tile size). The matrix has 203k entries and respectively 61, 31, and 13 active tiles (from
left to right).

Figure 7 depicts the performance of the assembly operation when used in
the context of a finite element method application in a 2D mesh case. This
corresponds to a case where the overlapping between contribution blocks is small.
First of all, we can observe that, by increasing the concurrency (leftmost plot),
the taskified assembly operation obtains a very good behavior with all strategies
in PaRSEC. Moreover, we observe that the StarPU implementation has a good
behavior on a small number of processing units but seems less efficient when
the number of resources increases. As shown in the bottom part of the graph
this is mainly due to the overhead induced by the management of the tasks, the
tasks are not compute intensive enough to amortize the overhead of the StarPU
runtime system (which is mainly due to the inference of task dependencies).
Similarly, we can notice that independently from this observation, the *no-chain
assembly operation scheme* behaves well in both runtime systems mainly because
there are no race conditions in this strategy. We can see also, that this strategy
gives performance equivalent to the one obtained with the coloring strategy
described in [9] and outperforms it in certain configurations (typically when
there the global matrix is tiled using fine grain blocks). This illustrates the
interest of our taskified assembly scheme on this simple scenario.

In Figure 8 we investigate the behavior of the taskified assembly operation on the two runtime systems in the context of a finite element method application in a 3D mesh case. This time both the size of the contribution blocks and their overlapping increased in comparison with the 2D case.

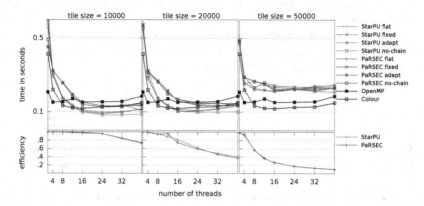

Fig. 8. Comparison of the performance of an assembly operation using a 3D mesh with 512 blocks of size 512^2 based on the granularity of the operation (as depicted by the tile size). The matrix has 185k entries and respectively 121, 44, and 10 active tiles (from left to right).

We can observe that the functioning of our taskified schemes have a good behavior for all tile sizes. Moreover, we can observe that the overhead of the runtime system is negligible compared with the computational cost of the tasks and allow all the strategies to expose a scalable behavior. Concerning the coloring scheme, it is outperformed by all the strategies when the number of computational resources increased. Finally, once again, the *no-chain assembly operation scheme* is the most efficient variant for both runtime systems.

Finally, Figure 9 reports the results gathered in the context of the most irregular and complex case: assembly operations arising in the sparse LU factorization using the multifrontal method. First of all, note that in this case, it is not possible to use the coloring heuristic since the overlapping between contributions blocks may be arbitrarily large (the cost of the coloring heuristic is prohibitive in this case). We can observe that PaRSEC has a good performance with all tiling strategies and all scheduling policies. We can also see that the *adaptive priority* scheduling policy is the one with the most scalable behavior. Finally, we can observe that the overhead induced by the runtime is minimal with PaRSEC. Concerning StarPU, when the granularity of the tiles is small, we measure that the overhead of the runtime system tends to increase with the number of resources leading to a significant performance loss. However, increasing the granularity allows to overcome the runtime overhead and the behavior of StarPU becomes equivalent to the one obtained with PaRSEC. Once again, the *no-chain assembly operation scheme* is the most efficient variant for both runtime systems. Finally, we report also, the behavior of the naive implementation using based on OpenMP where all the global matrix is not tiled and the contribution blocks are treated sequentially using as many threads as provided by the user for each contribution block. We can see, that our taskified assembly scheme is much more stable in terms of behavior and outperforms the OpenMP implementation for most non-trivial cases. Even though our strategies and the OpenMP implementation are extremely close on some experiments, our approach permits to relax synchronizations once integrated into an application, enabling additional overlap between the assembly operations and the rest of the computations and the entire application will benefit. From this perspective, these experimental results illustrate the interest of our taskified scheme.

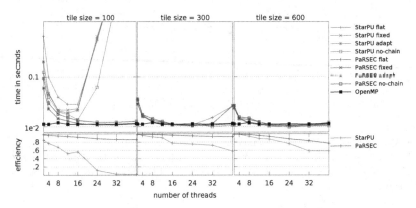

Fig. 9. Comparison of the performance of an assembly operation coming from the MUMPS solver based on the granularity of the operation

6   Conclusion

In this work we evaluated the usability and effectiveness of general-purpose task-based runtime systems for parallelizing the assembly operation, which is a main operation in several application fields. We expressed the assembly operation as tasks with data dependencies between them and provided the resulting task graph to a runtime systems. Several algorithms aiming at enhancing the concurrency while trying to reduce the number of race conditions have been proposed, and they were analyzed under different dynamic constraints: tasks priority and granularity. Overall, the results clearly indicates that for both runtime systems, namely PaRSEC and StarPU, our approach exhibits encouraging performance, especially when the right balance is reached between the task granularity and the overhead of the runtime system.

In the near future, we plan to further extend this work by using accelerators (GPU, Intel Xeon-Phi, etc) to minimize the time-to-solution. This will be done by relying on existing assembly kernels for the different accelerators and leave the data management and scheduling decisions to the runtime systems (the scheduling policies need to be adapted to the heterogeneous context). Moreover, it could be of interest to consider intra-task parallelism which may offer more flexibility to enhance concurrency. In a longer term, this work represents a necessary kernel which will be used to design complex numerical simulation applications on top of modern runtime systems. This will allow the application to run in a more asynchronous way without relying on the classical fork-join paradigm.

Acknowledgments. This work was partially supported by the French ANR through the MN (Solhar ANR-13-MONU-007 project) program, and the US Department of Energy through the DE-FG02-13ER26151.

References

1. Agullo, E., Bramas, B., Coulaud, O., Darve, E., Messner, M., Takahashi, T.: Task-based fmm for multicore architectures. SIAM SISC 36(1) (2014)
2. Agullo, E., Buttari, A., Guermouche, A., Lopez, F.: Multifrontal QR factorization for multicore architectures over runtime systems. In: Euro-Par 2013 Parallel Processing - 19th International Conference, pp. 521–532 (2013)
3. Agullo, E., Demmel, J., Dongarra, J., Hadri, B., Kurzak, J., Langou, J., Ltaief, H., Luszczek, P., Tomov, S.: Numerical linear algebra on emerging architectures: The PLASMA and MAGMA projects. Journal of Physics 180(1) (2009)
4. Amestoy, P.R., Guermouche, A., L'Excellent, J.-Y., Pralet, S.: Hybrid scheduling for the parallel solution of linear systems. Parallel Computing 32(2), 136–156 (2006)
5. Augonnet, C., Thibault, S., Namyst, R., Wacrenier, P.-A.: StarPU: A Unified Platform for Task Scheduling on Heterogeneous Multicore Architectures. Concurrency and Computation: Practice and Experience 23, 187–198 (2011)
6. Badia, R.M., Herrero, J.R., Labarta, J., Pérez, J.M., Quintana-Ortí, E.S., Quintana-Ortí, G.: Parallelizing dense and banded linear algebra libraries using SMPSs. Concurrency and Computation: Practice and Experience 21(18) (2009)
7. Bosilca, G., Bouteiller, A., Danalis, A., Herault, T., Luszczek, P., Dongarra, J.: Dense linear algebra on distributed heterogeneous hardware with a symbolic dag approach. In: Scalable Computing and Communications: Theory and Practice (2013)
8. Bosilca, G., Bouteiller, A., Danalis, A., Faverge, M., Hérault, T., Dongarra, J.J.: PaRSEC: Exploiting heterogeneity to enhance scalability. Computing in Science and Engineering 15(6), 36–45 (2013)
9. Cecka, C., Lew, A.J., Darve, E.: Assembly of finite element methods on graphics processors. Int. J. for Numerical Methods in Engineering 85(5), 640–669 (2011)
10. Duff, I.S., Reid, J.K.: The multifrontal solution of indefinite sparse symmetric linear systems. ACM Transactions on Mathematical Software 9, 302–325 (1983)
11. Fu, Z., Lewis, T.J., Kirby, R.M., Whitaker, R.T.: Architecting the finite element method pipeline for the GPU. Journal of Computational and Applied Mathematics 257, 195–211 (2014)
12. Hanzlikova, N., Rodrigues, E.R.: A novel finite element method assembler for co-processors and accelerators. In: Proceedings of the 3rd Workshop on Irregular Applications: Architectures and Algorithms, ACM, NY (2013)
13. Huthwaite, P.: Accelerated finite element elastodynamic simulations using the GPU. Journal of Computational Physics 257(pt. A), 687–707 (2014)

14. Lacoste, X., Faverge, M., Ramet, P., Thibault, S., Bosilca, G.: Taking advantage of hybrid systems for sparse direct solvers via task-based runtimes. Rapport de recherche RR-8446, INRIA (January 2014)
15. Markall, G.R., Slemmer, A., Ham, D.A., Kelly, P.H.J., Cantwell, C.D., Sherwin, S.J.: Finite element assembly strategies on multi-core and many-core architectures. International Journal for Numerical Methods in Fluids 71(1), 80–97 (2013)
16. Quintana-Ortí, G., Quintana-Ortí, E.S., van de Geijn, R.A., Van Zee, F.G., Chan, E.: Programming matrix algorithms-by-blocks for thread-level parallelism. ACM Trans. Math. Softw. 36(3) (2009)

Shared Memory in the Many-Core Age

Stefan Nürnberger, Gabor Drescher, Randolf Rotta,
Jörg Nolte, and Wolfgang Schröder-Preikschat*

Brandenburg University of Technology Cottbus–Senftenberg, Germany
{snuernbe,rrotta,jon}@informatik.tu-cottbus.de
Friedrich-Alexander University Erlangen-Nuremberg, Germany
{drescher,wosch}@cs.fau.de

Abstract. With the evolution toward fast networks of many-core processors, the design assumptions at the basis of software-level distributed shared memory (DSM) systems change considerably. But efficient DSMs are needed because they can significantly simplify the implementation of complex distributed algorithms. This paper discusses implications of the many-core evolution and derives a set of reusable elementary operations for future software DSMs. These elementary operations will help in exploring and evaluating new memory models and consistency protocols.

1 Introduction

Parallel algorithms are based on distributing computation tasks over multiple execution threads. In shared memory programming models, these threads can access the computation's data directly in a logically shared address space. Most parallel algorithm can be expressed easily with respect to correctness because manual data partitioning and transfers are not necessary, c.f. [10]. Just the inter-task data dependencies require explicit synchronisation.

However, attaining optimal performance with shared memory programming is challenging. In fact, multi- and many-core processors are distributed shared memory (DSM) systems that use message passing internally. They implement the illusion of a shared memory by implicit inter-thread communication. For performance optimisation, it is necessary to understand the distributed structure and the behaviour of the employed consistency protocols, see for example [24].

Message passing could be used directly [19] and would provide explicit control over all communication. But this often requires a considerable effort, which distracts from high-level optimisation. For example, optimising data access locality instead of communication locality and balancing the task decomposition is more effective and easier with shared memory [29]. Furthermore, hardware-based DSMs are efficient on a small scale [21]. On larger scales, software-level DSMs can incorporate algorithm-specific knowledge for higher performance [20,7,4].

* This work was supported by the German Research Foundation (DFG) under grant no. NO 625/7-1 and SCHR 603/10-1, by the Transregional Collaborative Research Centre "InvasIC Computing" (SFB/TR 89, Project C1), and the German Federal Ministry of Education and Research (BMBF) grant no. 01IH13003C.

L. Lopes et al. (Eds.): Euro-Par 2014 Workshops, Part II, LNCS 8806, pp. 351–362, 2014.

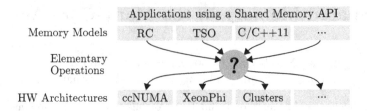

Fig. 1. Elementary operations bridging memory models and hardware

The first software DSMs targeted networks single-threaded computers. With the transition to many-core architectures, the hardware evolved considerably and became more diverse and heterogeneous. Therefore, the many-core age poses a good opportunity to improve upon past DSM research. Examples such as the Quarks DSM for fast networks [8,30] show that rethinking the design of software DSMs is worthwhile. In addition, emerging memory models like in C++11 demand new consistency protocols for software DSMs. A generic infrastructure is needed in order to cope with the many possible combinations of memory models, consistency protocols, and hardware platforms (Fig. 1). This paper presents a set of elementary operations that serve as reusable building blocks for DSMs.

The paper is organised as follows. The design of efficient software-level DSMs depends a lot on the underlying hardware's structure and the interface to the applications on top of the shared memory. Section 2 analyses the implications of the hardware's and software's evolution toward many-core architectures. The section also gives an overview of existing implementation approaches.

Thereafter, Section 3 derives a software architecture of elementary operations from the previous section's analysis. The elementary operations serve as building blocks for DSMs that can be reused in many implementations. They encompass communication mechanisms, memory management operations, and access tracking mechanisms. The final section concludes with a summary and directions of future work.

2   Software DSMs in the Many-Core Age

DSMs provide a shared logical address space across multiple threads, which do not necessarily have global access to all of the memory. The illusion of a shared memory within this address space is created by forwarding access requests and fetching data into local replica. The DSM has to implement mechanisms to detect read and write access, to communicate changes between the replica, and to synchronise concurrent access on behalf of the applications.

Memory models define what applications have to expect about the time and order in which their data changes become visible to other nodes in the worst case. Below these models, consistency protocols define how the DSMs actually achieve a compliant behaviour. Consistency protocols usually provide much stronger guarantees than the memory model they implement. However, programming against a memory model ensures the portability of the applications and leaves space for the hardware-specific optimisation of consistency protocols.

The next subsection summarises existing DSM implementations with focus on core mechanisms. Then, the second subsection discusses the hardware's evolution toward many-core architectures and its impact on DSM implementations. The last subsection discusses related memory models and consistency protocols.

2.1 Common Software DSM Mechanisms

The most distinctive aspect of DSM systems is the handling of data replication. DSMs that always forward access requests to an owner without replication fall into the family of Partitioned Global Address Spaces (PGAS), see for example [11,9,14,32]. They need only little bookkeeping and their implicit communication patterns are still very easy to comprehend. On the downside, repeated access to remote data is inefficient because it is mapped to repeated data transfers. In contrast, replication-based DSMs manage local copies of recently accessed data, see for example [20,7,4]. Similar to hardware-based caches, they try to exploit spatial and temporal locality in the application's data access patterns. While this can speed up the execution of many algorithms, the necessary bookkeeping can induce considerable overhead [30].

DSMs can be split into three categories with respect to the interface they provide to applications: The first category are systems aimed at unmodified legacy shared memory programs, usually implemented as a wrapper around system libraries or included in the operating system [2,16,15,17,20,12,18]. They usually use hardware-support to track the application's memory accesses. Secondly, library-based DSMs provide an explicit programming interface [7,4,30,32,25]. The applications have to call specific functions in order to prepare for data access, commit changes, and request synchronisation. Finally, language-based DSMs provide explicit sharing constructs [11,9,14]. In addition, the compiler can convert shared data access into respective library calls for a library-based DSM. In all three cases, the employed programming languages need a memory model suitable for shared memory programming. Otherwise, the compiler's optimisation can break the consistency by assuming a too weak model [5].

Deeply related to the application interface are mechanisms that detect and track the application's access to shared data. Explicit application programming interfaces export DSM functions to the application. These have to be called tell about read/write accesses and synchronisation requests. In high-level languages like C++, such calls can be hidden quite well behind standard interfaces [32,1]. Language and compiler extensions can be used to convert access to shared variables into respective library calls. An especially interesting approach is abusing transactional memory extensions because these produce detailed read/write logs and library calls for code sections that are marked as transactions.

Another common approach are memory protection traps [25,18]. Within page-based logical address spaces, read/write access rights can be revoked temporarily for individual pages. Any access to such address ranges raises a trap, which is then handled by the consistency protocol. Data modifications in affected pages can be reconstructed by comparing against golden copies. Detecting the destination of individual accesses through separate traps is possible but inefficient. An alternative are virtual machines. These apply binary code transformation and just-in-time compilers to insert DSM library calls where necessary.

Finally, high-level knowledge about memory access patterns can be exploited directly. Some programming models, such as data flow based models, expose coarse grained data dependency information [6]. This is used mainly to order the execution of tasks but can be used also to replicate, update, and invalidate data that is shared by tasks.

2.2   From Single-Core to Many Cores

Early DSM systems like Ivy [20] and Munin [7] targeted networks of single-threaded processors. Apart from expensive high performance computing hardware, the typical inter-processor networks used to be weakly coupled with low bandwidth and very high latency relative to local memory accesses. In comparison to the network, the processors were quite fast and designed for high single-thread performance.

The high latency and processing overhead of the networking hardware penalised high numbers of relatively small messages like they are exchanged by simple consistency protocols [7]. In order to communicate with fewer and larger messages, complex memory models allowed to manually state application-level knowledge and the consistency protocols adapted to observed access patterns. Because of the relatively fast processors, the implied bookkeeping overhead was negligible. Nevertheless, manual message passing seemed to be much more straightforward and easier to optimise [8].

The development of many-core architectures is driven by the need for higher energy and space efficiency [3,27]. In order to increase the compute throughput per watt for parallel computations, inefficient features that just increase the single-thread performance are stripped away from the cores. This leads to small efficient cores, which can be integrated in high number on a single chip. Also, networking hardware is integrated tightly into the processors. On-chip networks like [26] provide high throughput communication between a large number of cores and memory controllers. Likewise low latency processor-interconnects such as QPI, PCIe, and Infiniband are widely used now.

Many-core DSMs have to address three major aspects: *Consistency islands*, *mandatory parallelism*, as well as *diversity and heterogeneity*.

Caches often reduce the communication volume between threads and main memory. The consistency of their replicated data is maintained by cache consistency protocols. These can be efficient even with a large number of threads, but most rely on a fixed upper bound of participating threads [21]. Hence, scaling out many-core processors to larger setups, like in the DEEP project [13], does not extend to global cache consistency. This leads to networks of *consistency islands*. Each island contains many threads that can cooperate through hardware-based cache consistency. The network between islands may provide remote memory access and even atomics to enforce ordering. But remote data replicated in local caches can become inconsistent because no notifications about write accesses are communicated between islands.

In conclusion, software DSMs span multiple consistency islands and the threads inside each island should share their data replica. Otherwise, storing separate replica for each of the many threads would waste memory and cache space. The additional overhead of coordinating the concurrent access to shared replica is hopefully compensated by sharing the costs of replica management between all threads.

Secondly, any bookkeeping overhead of software DSMs is amplified by the slow performance of single threads. For example, remote memory access over Infiniband links can be as fast as $2\mu s$, which corresponds to just 8 cache misses on the Intel Xeon Phi (280ns/miss) [24]. Frequent remote memory accesses might be more efficient than managing local replica. In addition, it is significantly more efficient to use 2MiB instead of 4kiB pages to describe the logical address spaces. Thus, page-based access tracking has to process 512x larger pages.

In consequence, exploiting all types of parallelism in DSM implementations is mandatory to fully utilise the high throughput of whole consistency islands. Just designing simpler protocols like in the Quarks DSM [30] will not be sufficient.

Finally, DSMs have to deal with diversity between and heterogeneity inside many-core platforms, even though they share the same instruction set and data encoding. Depending on the application domain, different design trade offs between network bandwidth, cache size, and micro-architecture features are more efficient. Similarly, mixing cores optimised for single-thread throughput with cores optimised for high parallel throughput is useful for a large class of applications [13]. Hence, abstractions over the platform's structure are needed.

2.3   Memory Models and Consistency Protocols

Memory models define the permitted reordering and elimination of concurrent accesses to shared memory. Applications usually target the memory model of the used programming language or software-level DSM. Compilers and DSMs translate this onto the memory model(s) of the underlying hardware.

The strictest model, called *sequential consistency*, executes all accesses exactly in the order that was expressed by the programmer. However, to improve the performance, modern hardware and compilers employ optimisations that reorder the accesses [22]. For example, the compiler can eliminate any access to memory locations that are considered private by the compiler. Similarly, the hardware does not have to keep modified data in caches consistent with the main memory immediately. This results in a logical reordering of reads and writes from the main memory's point of view. Other common optimisation techniques include store buffers, request queues, out-of-order execution, and speculation techniques such as branch prediction and prefetching.

For single-threaded programs, these optimisations do not result in any observable change of program logic. But surprising effects can arise with multi-threaded programs. Most programming languages do not state their memory model explicitly and the compilers are free to assume a sequential execution of the generated

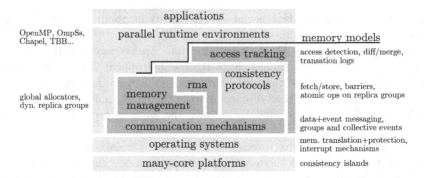

Fig. 2. Architectural overview of memory consistency support for parallel runtimes. The architecture provides basic mechanisms supporting the implementation of a consistency protocol.

instructions. On processors with a *relaxed* memory model, additional synchronisation instructions would be needed to regain the intended behaviour. Newer languages with explicit support for multi-threading, such as C++11, address this issue by defining a memory model based on sequential consistency for data race free programs. There, application programmers have to explicitly resolve data races by applying *atomic operations* instead of normal read/write access.

The compilers, DSM implementations, and low-level system programmers rely on the hardware's memory model. Some architectures provide a formal definition of their model, for example SPARC-TSO. Most architectures, for instance x86, only provide ambiguous descriptions in prose although their models can be specified formally [28]. These models start with very relaxed semantics and provide *memory barriers* to enforce stricter models.

Another common primitive to regain control over concurrent memory access are *atomic operations*. They are especially useful for the implementation of high-level synchronisation primitives and lock-free data structures. These instructions differ between hardware architectures but usually include variants of test-and-set (TAS), compare-and-swap (CAS/DCAS), fetch-and-increment (FAI), and Load Linked/Store Conditional (LL/SC). Depending on the memory model, these operations do not provoke a full memory barrier but only give guarantees for the affected memory addresses and direct data dependencies.

Memory models are a contract between application and system on a semantic level. Below these, consistency protocols represent concrete strategies that achieve compliant effects. Different consistency protocols can realise the same model. Apparently, a consistency protocol for sequential consistency also satisfies more relaxed models and can simply ignore all memory barriers.

3   Elementary Operations for Many-Core DSMs

Future distributed shared memory programming should look more like current shared memory programming on relaxed memory models. The shared memory abstraction needs a flexible definition of its memory consistency model. Relaxations in this model are the key point for performance improvements exploiting implementation freedoms. This is analogous to the memory models provided by hardware. However, the semantics of these models must be defined rigorously [31] in order to be useful and to prove their correctness. There is an ongoing process defining the memory models for shared memory architectures. The semantics of the distributed models must be treated equally.

Most programmers should not need to care about the underlying hardware memory model. Instead, a useful abstraction should let them state the needed guarantees in the form of an explicit memory consistency model. This explicit model is provided by the implementation of a consistency protocol. The implementations of custom protocols benefit from reuse of common functionality. Elementary mechanisms map this functionality to fitting operations on the underlying hardware model. In distributed shared memory, such as clusters of many-cores, this hardware model is most likely heterogeneous, forming consistency islands on which more efficient mappings exist. When consistency related events are restricted to such an island, more efficient implementations of these mechanisms can be used.

Whereas past DSM systems provided the programmer with a distinct programming model, we rather treat DSM as an optimizing feature to existing programming models. The envisioned use case is an augmentation of parallel runtime environments through replication.

In combinations like these, consistency guarantees for programmers must be based on data-race-freedom. Providing fixed guarantees without race freedom requires tight control over the whole stack of programming language, compiler optimizations, and hardware architecture while it significantly inhibits performance optimization. Providing a guatanteed consistency model for data-race-free programs is possible in a compiler-agnostic way.

3.1 Communication Mechanisms

The basic shared memory abstraction provided by a given programming model needs to provide a means by which memory can be managed and accessed. A basic communication mechanism is needed for coordination. It should provide the following features:

Data Transfer as a mechanism to read and write memory contents in a distributed memory system. This will be used by the remote memory functionality and to create and manage replicas of memory locations.

Event Notification as very lightweight mechanism to notify hardware threads of consistency related events like invalidations. Also preemptive notifications are needed to interrupt applications when necessary.

Thread Groups are a basic feature to group the propagation of events. They reflect the overall system topology and are used to bootstrap efficient replication across consistency islands. Groups are dynamic and identify partakers in sharing that need to be involved in consistency related action.

Collective Events must be provided that efficiently disseminate events in a group.

3.2   Memory Management, Replication, and Remote Access

With the global coordination in place, shared memory can be managed. There is no strong requirement on the user-visible interface to this memory, but the runtime is expected to provide some notion of a global address space. The common memory management mechanisms are:

Allocators for globally coordinated memory. They provide the mapping mechanism for named entities of shared memory from which all shared memory operation needs to be bootstrapped. Through this call, a sharing participant is registered and its address space has to be adapted accordingly.

Annotation mechanism to configure the semantics of a shared memory range at runtime. This can be used to provide features like the current ownership declaration from MYO. Many shared-memory systems do not employ this feature since they pertain to exactly one set of semantics.

Replica management is the key aspect of performance improvements in a distributed memory system. Each replica is a locally cached version of the shared-memory location. Caching is the single most important feature in reducing access times to shared memory. Giving guarantees on the actuality of cached data is the concern of consistency model semantics. Operations provided in replica management include creation, update, and invalidation of single replicas and groups. An acknowledgement mechanism must be provided to check for the successful invalidation or update of replicas. Replica management is a background task based on asynchronous messages.

Remote Memory Access used for direct access and modification of a remotely available memory location where replication is not beneficial. Remote memory can be implemented through address space manipulation, mapping areas of remote physical memory on the PCIe bus, or hardware provided RDMA in InfiniBand networks. Whenever such hardware support is not available, the remote memory operations must resort to explicit message passing. Also the GASPI abstraction can be employed as an implementation technique here. However, remote memory operations and their interleaving with local operations on the same memory may have semantics that are hard to describe. Coherence may not be available on some hardware architectures when memory is accessed locally through the processor and concurrently through e.g. an InfiniBand controller. These memory semantics will require additional fences for correct operation. Alternatively, implementations can tunnel local access through the remote access channel, thereby forcing a serialization point with the remote events.

Atomic Operations provide *write atomicity* enforcement, a guarantee that the write operation can be seen either by all other threads, or none. They are a special case of remote memory operations. As far as atomic update operations are concerned, LL/SC should be provided because it can be implemented on asynchronous messages (and is allowed to fail), yet it enables implementation of all other atomic operations (FAI, TAS, CAS, DCAS).

3.3 Access Tracking

Consistency protocols share a couple of additional requirements. These can also be provided as basic mechanisms to ease implementation of new protocols. They concern the connection of application behavior and consistency related events. The proposed mechanisms are:

Access Tracking provides a mechanism to track read and write access to replicas. Depending on the shared memory API and desired memory model semantics this can possibly be made explicit, e.g. using object-oriented programming. In the worst case it must be possible to track every single memory access. Ususally only the first write to a valid replica or read access to an invalid replica needs to be detected. Obvious implementation choices include traps through virtual memory mapping protection mechanisms (i.e. Segmentation Fault handlers), low level virtualization, or compiler instrumentation.

Diff/Merge for memory locations is used in order to weaken exclusive write access, and implement multiple writer protocols. This has been implemented in a variety of distributed shared memory systems to avoid overhead through false sharing. It can also be used to offer lightweight updates of larger sharing units in order to decrease communication bandwidth. The mechanism must offer shadows or transparent copies of affected memory locations (e.g. pages) and an efficient coding for generating, storing and applying a difference mask. This is a prime example for work that should be delegated to helper threads on many-core architectures.

(Versioned) Modification Tracking per replica is needed in a basic form to trigger consistency related actions without explicit calls from the API (see access tracking above). Through additional versioning an implementation of restricted transactional memory can enable lock elision techniques like provided in current off-the-shelf multi-core processors.

The described mechanisms are employed to build the semantics of the desired memory consistency model. Depending on the placement of threads that take part in the sharing of a memory location, the implementation details of the single mechanisms can or rather must vary. If sharing is restricted to a single consistency island, e.g. only among threads of a single accelerator card, some consistency requirements may be provided by hardware directly. As soon as sharing stretches across more than one island, implementations must be adapted to the new situation. Strategic placement of tasks will therefore stay a significant tool for optimized performance in a shared memory system, just like it is with today's ccNUMA architectures.

4 Conclusions and Future Directions

In this paper, the benefits and challenges of distributed shared memory systems were examined with respect to networks of many-core processors. The many-core age provides good opportunities to improve upon past DSM research. For instance, the underlying hardware evolved much from the loose networks of fast single-threaded nodes to the tightly coupled networks of consistency islands with many relatively slow threads. Likewise, the application domains evolved far beyond the first numerical simulation codes. The need for increasingly complex data structures and parallel algorithms pushes toward new parallel languages, programming models, and memory models.

However, implementing efficient DSMs became more challenging. Exploiting effectively, for example, consistency islands and their internal parallelism, raises the effort for basic DSM infrastructure. Fortunately, the memory models and their consistency protocols share many common mechanisms. The paper derived an architecture of elementary operations as building blocks for future DSMs. These help mapping the application's memory model to efficient consistency protocols while reusing common infrastructure.

The *Consistency Kernel* (CoKe) project evaluates the presented elementary operations in detail. This includes efficient hardware abstractions even on hardware without cache coherence like the experimental Intel SCC many-core processor and clusters of Intel Xeon Phi processors. A part of the *OctoPOS* project [23] at the collaborative research center for invasive computing explores memory models for invasive computing. This effort targets processors with multiple consistency islands and reuses the elementary operations. Finally, the *Many Threads Operating System* (MyThOS) project researches minimal operating system components for many-core accelerators. While focusing on lightweight thread management for HPC applications, generic system services can be shared with CoKe.

References

1. Mintomic, `http://mintomic.github.io` (accessed: 2014)
2. Scalemp vsmp foundation, `http://www.scalemp.com` (accessed: 2014)
3. Agarwal, A., Levy, M.: The kill rule for multicore. In: 44th ACM/IEEE Design Automation Conference, DAC 2007, pp. 750–753 (June 2007)
4. Amza, C., Cox, A.L., Dwarkadas, S., Keleher, P., Lu, H., Rajamony, R., Yu, W., Zwaenepoel, W.: Treadmarks: Shared memory computing on networks of workstations. Computer 29(2), 18–28 (1996)
5. Boehm, H.: Threads cannot be implemented as a library. ACM Sigplan Notices, 261–268 (2005)
6. Bueno, J., Martorell, X., Badia, R.M., Ayguadé, E., Labarta, J.: Implementing ompss support for regions of data in architectures with multiple address spaces. In: Proceedings of the 27th International ACM Conference on International Conference on Supercomputing, ICS 2013, pp. 359–368. ACM, New York (2013)
7. Carter, J.B.: Design of the munin distributed shared memory system. Journal of Parallel and Distributed Computing 29(2), 219–227 (1995)
8. Carter, J.B., Khandekar, D., Kamb, L.: Distributed shared memory: Where we are and where we should be headed. In: Proceedings of the Fifth Workshop on Hot Topics in Operating Systems (HotOS-V), pp. 119–122. IEEE (1995)
9. Chamberlain, B.L., Callahan, D., Zima, H.P.: Parallel programmability and the chapel language. International Journal of High Performance Computing Applications 21(3), 291–312 (2007)

10. Chapman, B.: Scalable shared memory parallel programming: Will one size fit all? In: 14th Euromicro International Conference on Parallel, Distributed, and Network-Based Processing, PDP 2006, p. 3 (February 2006)
11. Charles, P., Grothoff, C., Saraswat, V., Donawa, C., Kielstra, A., Ebcioglu, K., Von Praun, C., Sarkar, V.: X10: an object-oriented approach to non-uniform cluster computing. ACM Sigplan Notices 40(10), 519–538 (2005)
12. Cordsen, J., Garnatz, T., Sander, M., Gerischer, A., Gubitoso, M.D., Haack, U., Schröder-Preikschat, W.: Vote for peace: Implementation and performance of a parallel operating system. IEEE Concurrency 5(2), 16–27 (1997)
13. Eicker, N., Lippert, T., Moschny, T., Suarez, E.: The deep project - pursuing cluster-computing in the many-core era. In: 2013 42nd International Conference on Parallel Processing (ICPP), pp. 885–892 (October 2013)
14. El-Ghazawi, T., Smith, L.: Upc: uni ed parallel c. In: Proceedings of the 2006 ACM/IEEE conference on Supercomputing (2006), p. 27. ACM (2006)
15. Fleisch, B., Popek, G.: Mirage: A coherent distributed shared memory design. In: Proceedings of the Twelfth ACM Symposium on Operating Systems Principles, SOSP 1989, pp. 211–223. ACM, New York (1989)
16. Göckelmann, R., Schoettner, M., Frenz, S., Schulthess, P.: Plurix, a distributed operating system extending the single system image concept. In: Canadian Conference on Electrical and Computer Engineering, vol. 4, pp. 1985–1988. IEEE (2004)
17. Itzkovitz, A., Schuster, A., Shalev, L.: Thread migration and its appli- cations in distributed shared memory systems. Journal of Systems and Software 42(1), 71–87 (1998)
18. Lankes, S., Reble, P., Sinnen, O., Clauss, C.: Revisiting shared virtual memory systems for non-coherent memory-coupled cores. In: Proceedings of the 2012 International Workshop on Programming Models and Applications for Multicores and Manycores - PMAM 2012, pp. 45–54 (2012)
19. Lauer, H.C., Needham, R.M.: On the duality of operating system struc- tures. SIGOPS Oper. Syst. Rev. 13(2), 3–19 (1979)
20. Li, K.: Ivy: A shared virtual memory system for parallel computing. In: ICPP (2), pp. 94–101 (1988)
21. Martin, M.M.K., Hill, M.D., Sorin, D.J.: Why on-chip cache coherence is here to stay. Commun. ACM 55(7), 78–89 (2012)
22. McKenney, P.E.: Memory barriers: a hardware view for software hackers. Linux Technology Center, IBM Beaverton (2010)
23. Oechslein, B., Schedel, J., Kleinöder, J., Bauer, L., Henkel, J., Lohmann, D., Schröoder-Preikschat, W.: OctoPOS: A parallel operating system for invasive computing. In: Proceedings of the International Workshop on Systems for Future Multi-Core Architectures (SFMA), EuroSys, pp. 9–14 (2011)
24. Ramos, S., Hoefler, T.: Modeling Communication in Cache-Coherent SMP Systems - A Case-Study with Xeon Phi. In: Proceedings of the 22nd International Symposium on High-Performance Parallel and Distributed Computing, pp. 97–108. ACM (June 2013)
25. Saha, B., Mendelson, A., Zhou, X., Chen, H., Gao, Y., Yan, S., Rajagopalan, M., Fang, J., Zhang, P., Ronen, R.: Programming model for a heterogeneous x86 platform. In: Proceedings of the 2009 ACM SIGPLAN conference on Programming language design and implementation - PLDI 2009, p. 431 (2009)
26. Salihundam, P., Jain, S., Jacob, T., Kumar, S., Erraguntla, V., Hoskote, Y., Vangal, S., Ruhl, G., Borkar, N.: A 2 Tb/s 6x4 Mesh Network for a Single-Chip Cloud Computer With DVFS in 45 nm CMOS. IEEE Journal of Solid-State Circuits 46(4), 757–766 (2011)

27. Seiler, L., Carmean, D., Sprangle, E., Forsyth, T., Abrash, M., Dubey, P., Junkins, S., Lake, A., Sugerman, J., Cavin, R., Espasa, R., Grochowski, E., Juan, T., Hanrahan, P.: Larrabee: A many-core x86 architecture for visual computing. In: ACM SIGGRAPH 2008 Papers, SIGGRAPH 2008, pp. 18:1-18:15. ACM, New York (2008)

28. Sewell, P., Sarkar, S., Owens, S., Nardelli, F.Z., Myreen, M.O.: x86-TSO. Communications of the ACM 53(7), 89 (2010)

29. Snir, M.: Shared memory programming on distributed memory systems. In: Proceedings of the Third Conference on Partitioned Global Address Space Programing Models, PGAS 2009, pp. 3:1-3:1. ACM, New York (2009)

30. Swanson, M., Stoller, L., Carter, J.: Making distributed shared memory simple, yet efficient. In: Proceedings of the Third International Workshop on High-Level Parallel Programming Models and Supportive Environments, pp. 2–13. IEEE (1998)

31. Zappa Nardelli, F., Sewell, P., Sevcik, J.: Relaxed memory models must be rigorous. In: Exploiting Concurrency Efficiently and Correctly Workshop (2000)

32. Zheng, Y., Kamil, A., Driscoll, M., Shan, H., Yelick, K.: Upc++: A pgas extension for c++. In: 2014 IEEE 28th International Parallel and Distributed Processing Symposium, pp. 1105–1114 (May 2014)

The PerSyst Monitoring Tool
A Transport System for Performance Data Using Quantiles

Carla Guillen, Wolfram Hesse, and Matthias Brehm

Leibniz Supercomputing Centre, Germany[*]

Abstract. This paper presents a systemwide monitoring and analysis tool for high performance computers with several features aimed at minimizing the transport of performance data along a network of agents. The aim of the tool is to do a preliminary detection of performance bottlenecks on user applications running in HPC systems with a negligible impact on production runs. Continuous systemwide monitoring can lead to large volumes of data, if the data is required to be stored permanently to be available for queries. For system monitoring level we require to store the monitoring data synchronously. We retain the descriptive qualities by using quantiles; an aggregation with respect to the number of cores used by the application at every measuring interval. The optimization of the transport route for the performance data enables us to precisely calculate quantiles as opposed to quantile estimation.

1 Introduction

In order to have a running machine used as efficiently as possible we identified the need to do systemwide monitoring at application level. Inefficient applications prevent a petaflop system from producing more scientific results compared to an efficient used supercomputer. The preliminary detection of inefficient applications running in a petaflop system enables us to select the applications which need to be optimized. Thus, acquiring performance data of a supercomputer is necessary. Nevertheless, not all the performance data is necessary for analyzing performance; it is sufficient to retain a descriptive measure per application. The PerSyst Monitoring tool uses a fixed number of quantiles for performance monitoring. Quantiles have proven to be sufficient to retain the quality of the performance data for bottleneck detection [7]. The tool also features system level measurements. Thus, the synchronization of the measurements throughout the entire machine was required. The tool copes with a systemwide synchronization and extraction of data from a petaflop system. This is achieved with two main ideas: firstly, by using a tree agent hierarchy which extracts data with optimized routes; and secondly, by using statistical aggregation of data. Performance data is correlated with the job[1] information provided by the resource manager. The

---

[*] This work has been funded by the BMBF, grant 01IH13009A (the FEPA project).
[1] A job is a scheduled application that runs in a supercomputer.

L. Lopes et al. (Eds.): Euro-Par 2014 Workshops, Part II, LNCS 8806, pp. 363–374, 2014.

job information and topology determines how data will be optimally extracted from the transport system. The reduction of the amount of data is done by aggregating at the application level using a fixed number of quantiles. We retain the descriptive qualities by calculating the quantiles with respect to the number of cores used by the application. Given that the number of quantiles is fixed, it is not necessary to store data ranges or histogram bins. By doing this we have a data agnostic database as we do not require previous knowledge of the ranges where the data lies. The percentiles adjust to the range of data available at a given monitoring interval.

Depending on the job size, we may use the tree topology partially and in the most efficient way. System level monitoring is possible by having the distribution of all the jobs together with the monitoring data from unused cores. The aggregations can then be performed for a monitoring interval at system level.

Jobs are assigned to agents that gather the performance data such that the distribution among these agents is as balanced as possible and take into consideration the topological closest distance to the entire job. If job information is collected centrally, calculating the accumulated frequency can be done without estimations.

Jobs that can't be handled at one collector are distributed to the nearest collectors in the tree of agents. These jobs will require an estimation of quantiles based on quantile data obtained at each collecting agent. The calculated quantile subsets are pushed upwards in the topology network using, only in this case, the already existing solutions of a reduction network. The monitoring system has already been deployed in an Itanium IA2 architecture based SGI supercomputer system with 9728 cores, in a BladeCenter HX5 supercomputer based on Intel Xeon architecture with 8200 cores, and has been adapted at a IBM System x iDataPlex Sandy Bridge-EP Supercomputer with 147,456 Cores.

In Section 2 related work is described. Section 3 deals the details of the PerSyst Monitoring tool's transport system. Estimation of quantiles is explained in Section 4. The approach for collecting performance data of jobs is explained in Section 5. Results of the Sandy Bridge-EP system are described in Section 6. We finally conclude in Section 7 and give a brief outlook of the tool.

2   Related Work

There are other tools which have a tree hierarchy architecture for extracting and/or storing data. The Multicast Reduction Network tool (MRNet) is a tool for parallel applications enabling high-throughput communications [10]. Although MRNet is not, per se, a performance measuring tool it can be used for these purposes [2]. MRNet uses the principle of a hierarchy of software in a tree topology, also referred to as a tree-based overlay network, for scaling to hundreds of thousands of cores. Multicast is done from the frontend downwards through the tree, until the command reaches the leaves of the tree-topology. Transport of data is done with a bottom-up logic, i.e. from the leaves of the tree to the frontend. Aggregation can be implemented via customisable filters to aggregate data packets. The filters, however, can aggregate data only from piece-wise continuous aggregation functions. The NWPerf tool [9] uses a hierarchical structure to extract performance data without statistical aggregation. This tool provides systemwide monitoring of performance counters for high performance computers. Periscope [5] is a scalable tool for analyzing the performance of a single application. It enables a distributed on-line search for performance metrics based on hardware counters as well as metrics for MPI and OpenMP [6]. Periscope uses a hierarchy of agents to extract information and to send commands to the leaves of the tree hierarchy. Distributed hierarchical storage also use the idea of a tree structure to query performance data [3].

The PerSyst Monitoring tool has been developed as an overlay of distributed software with a tree agent hierarchy. Using a tree structure we overcome many scalability problems, just like other existing tools. However, data collection and extraction is done differently, making it a distinct tool from other tree overlay network tools. We exploit the topology of the running jobs to optimize the extraction of performance data on a large cluster. The storage of the performance data is done as close as possible to the measurement source, instead of sending the information through the entire tree of agents. A difference to other hierarchical tools is that the collecting agents of a job will have a common and smaller subtree whose root node will finally process the job instead of the frontend thereby avoiding the usage of the entire tree topology.

3   The Transport System

The PerSyst Monitoring tool has three types of agents. These are the synchronization agent, or *SyncAgent*; the *Collector Agent*; and the *PerSyst Agent*, as shown in Figure 1. The main functionality of the SyncAgent is to synchronize measurement, the Collector Agent collects the performance data, and the PerSyst Agent performs the measurements. Every type of agent has a core framework that implements the communication and the basic functionality. The framework provides interfaces which allow the use of ad-hoc delegates. The delegates interact with batch schedulers and system measuring interfaces. This ensures the portability of the tool.

The PerSyst Agents measure at the synchronized command of the frontend. The frontend is the SyncAgent at the root node and orchestrates the rest of the tree. The communication protocol used is TCP/IP, a reliable communication protocol compared to the UDP protocol. While the SyncAgents can only perform estimation of quantiles, the layer of Collector agents performs exact calculations of quantiles. If the collection of performance data is needed at a SyncAgent, the Collector and SyncAgents involved respect the parent-child relation of the original tree configuration. The PerSyst Agents, conversely, send the performance data to an optimized route in the agent tree.

The aggregation of subsets of percentiles is not possible using the definition and can only be done using estimations, thus two types of aggregations are

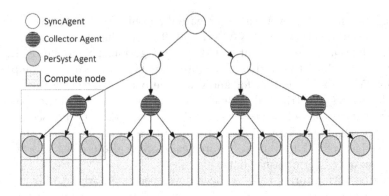

Fig. 1. Agent hierarchy

necessary at different levels of the hierarchy tree. Brim et al. [2] use the same aggregations function (or filters according to their terminology) among the software components which we changed to avoid estimations as much as possible. The top-down control of agents was kept, by sending the command through the tree structure of the agents, just like other hierarchical tools. However, the response of the PerSyst Agents is not necessarily directed to their Collector parent.

4   Estimation of Quantiles

For practical purposes, the definition and implications of using percentiles will be used hereafter. Other quantiles (for example quintiles, quartiles, or deciles) can be adapted to the definitions and usage.

The standard definition [4,8] is the kth percentile P_k is a value within the range of x, say x_k, which divides the data set into two groups. The fraction of the observation specified by the percentile falls below and its complement falls above. Thus, it is necessary to obtain the empirial cumulative distribution function, hereafter *cdf*, of the variate x to calculate any given percentile. To calculate the kth percentile of a distribution, P_k, the value of x_k which corresponds to the element position $\frac{Nk}{100}$ in the cdf is taken, where N is the sample size. When $\frac{Nk}{100}$ is not an integral value the linear interpolation of the cdf between the value corresponding to $\lfloor\frac{Nk}{100}\rfloor$ in the cdf and the next value corresponding to the cdf (i.e. ($\lfloor\frac{Nk}{100}\rfloor + 1$)) is calculated.

A feature of monitoring systems with tree topologies is that they can be configured to perform meta-aggregations[2]. If percentiles are used, estimations are required when an application requires the use of the entire tree topology, i.e. to apply meta-aggregation of percentiles. The percentiles per job are collected

---

[2] The term meta-aggregation refers to performing aggregations of aggregated sets. For example, calculating averages from the averages of multiple sets.

within an agent that aggregates subsets of percentiles. These percentiles are collected and estimated at each common parent of the Collectors. At each common parent the estimates are done by inferring the population of each Collector per job. For example, take

$$P_1 = \{p_0^1, p_1^1, ..., p_{100}^1\} \tag{1}$$

as the percentiles from Collector 1, C_1 and

$$P_2 = \{p_0^2, p_1^2, ..., p_{100}^2\} \tag{2}$$

as the percentiles from Collector 2, C_2. Both P_1 and P_2 belong to the same job such that the new percentiles need to be estimated from both of them. Given that a distribution is not known a priori, the entire set of observations from P_1 and from P_2 is estimated assuming a uniform random distribution between each percentile P_k and P_{k+1}. As seen in Figure 2, uniform random distribution assumes that the data between two deciles is uniformly increasing and curves in the cdf are replaced with a line joining two deciles. The percentile values themselves do not need to be changed; they are part of the newly recreated set. For example:

$$S_1 = \{p_0^1, r_1^1, r_2^1, ..., p_1^1, r_n^1 ..., p_{100}^1\} \tag{3}$$

and

$$S_2 = \{p_0^2, r_1^2, r_2^2, ..., p_1^2, r_n^2 ..., p_{100}^2\} \tag{4}$$

where r are the random values, and S_1 and S_2 are the recreated sets. The new estimated set is then $S = S_1 \cup S_2$. The random values are produced in such a way that they lie within the range of two neighboring percentiles, thus the value r_i lies between $p_k \leq r_i \leq p_{k+1}$. The number of random values $R(k, k+1)$ between two neighbouring percentiles, k and $k+1$, where $k \geq 1$ is

$$R(k, k+1) = \frac{N_o}{n_p} - 1 \tag{5}$$

where N_o is the total number of observations and n_p is the number of percentiles (example: $n_p = 100$ when all percentiles are used, and $n_p = 10$ when only deciles are used). This formula applies except for the first interval, given that

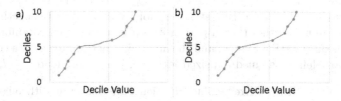

Fig. 2. Example of approximating a population with uniform distribution. Graph a) represents the real distribution. Graph b) represents an estimation using uniform distribution.

the minimum (considered to be the percentile zero) is in this range, there is one less random value to produce:

$$R(0,1) = N_o/n_p - 2 \qquad (6)$$

Both sets S_1 and S_2 are grouped together and they form the estimated observations of the collectors $C_1 \cup C_2$. The cdf is calculated from S, the estimated population. The percentiles are then determined from the estimated population. Analogously, this method can be applied to more than two sets, i.e. percentiles coming from more than two Collectors. Once all the estimated sets are joined together an estimated but complete population is obtained whose cdf can be determined as well as its global percentiles.

5   Collection of Jobs

The decision as to where and at what point the information will be processed is calculated by a job balancer which is integrated in the frontend of the collection system. For every measuring interval, the job balancer will assign the jobs to a collection route (in a large cluster new jobs may appear, while other jobs are terminated and removed). This also ensures that a same job which is reassigned to other nodes will also be reassigned to a new collection route[3].

The PerSyst Agents do not have knowledge of all of the available collectors only of their parent Collector. When the measuring command arrives they also receive information of the route in the tree where they should send the data. The route specifies either the Collector to whom they should send the performance data or if the agent itself can aggregate the performance data and perform the output. After the measurement cycle is completed this information is then lost. The only information kept is the communication address of the parent. Algorithm 1 is the main algorithm which performs this balancing.

When the job size fits exactly in one compute node[4], the job is processed locally. Requests that exceed the capacity of a database, or file system, or any other storage method, will create a bottleneck. Thus, if these requests are exceeding the limits imposed by the storage medium, the jobs are sent through the network tree. l_j and l_{max} are called loads, and the terms represent the amount of performance data of a job l_j or the maximum amount of performance data a Collector can take l_{max}. For jobs where $l_j \leq l_{max}$, it is only necessary to use one Collector and not the entire tree structure for extracting and collecting data. Using the entire tree rather than a part of it implies using more communication. l_{max} depends on the HPC System and the amount of performance data collected. These jobs are defined as medium sized jobs (i.e, jobs whose load $l_j \leq l_{max}$ and

---

[3] The tool would, therefore, redistribute the job collection even with migration of computations to another hardware architecture, if the new job placement information is made available by the batch scheduler.

[4] A compute node refers to an operating system instance which runs on one or more cores with shared memory.

Algorithm 1. Algorithm to distribute jobs to collectors.

Require:

$$\left\lceil \frac{\sum_J l_j}{l_{max}} \right\rceil \leq C \tag{7}$$

Where C is the set of collectors and l_j is the amount of performance data, or load, from job j and J is the set of all jobs at a measuring interval. l_{max} is the maximum performance data amount a Collector can take.

1: Sort jobs J in descending order of load l_j {A job j is running on different compute nodes monitored by agents A_j.}
2: Initialize all collectors in C:
3: **for all** load l_c of $c \in C$ **do**
4:    $l_c \leftarrow 0$
5: **end for**
6: Set loads from jobs to collectors:
7: **for all** $j \in J$ **do**
8:    **if** $l_j = 1$ **then**
9:        Mark j to be processed directly at A_j
10:        Continue to next j in the for-loop
11:    **end if**
12:    $c \leftarrow$ FindBestCollector(C, A_j)
13:    $l_{temp} \leftarrow l_j + l_c$.
14:    **if** $l_{temp} > l_{max}$ **then**
15:        DistributeLoadOnCollectors(C, l_j, A_j)
16:    **else**
17:        Assign $l_c \leftarrow l_{temp}$
18:    **end if**
19: **end for**

---

which run in more than one compute node). Medium sized jobs are collected at one Collector and the aggregation is done with a precise calculation of the percentiles. In this case applying Algorithm 1 with the `FindBestCollector` algorithm (Algorithm 3) will be sufficient to determine where the job should be sent to.

The `FindBestCollector` Algorithm finds the Collector with the minimum assigned performance data load (l_c in Algorithm 1). When minima are found the algorithm considers also the topological distance of a Collector and a PerSyst agent so jobs will be sent to their closest Collector. The topological distance, td, of two tree nodes (leaves or nodes) has been defined to be the longest distance between each node and their common collection node, i.e. the longest distance that the data has to travel such that it is collected centrally at the root of the smallest sub-tree. As described in Algorithm 2, the jobs are distributed to their closest Collector or Collectors. The closest Collector to a job is defined as the Collector with the minimum total td of itself with respect to all the PerSyst Agent nodes were the job is running. By calculating the td, the algorithm

Algorithm 2. Algorithm to find Collector with minimum load and minimum topological distance.

1: Algorithm FindBestCollector(C, A)
2: $C' \leftarrow$ all c_i with minimum load.
3: **if** $|C'| > 1$ **then**
4:     **for all** $c' \in C'$ **do**
5:         Set $d \leftarrow 0$ where d is the topological distance from c to a.
6:         **for all** $a \in A$ **do**
7:             $d \leftarrow d+$ TopologicalDistance(c, a)
8:         **end for**
9:         Insert c' and d in Collector-Distance ordered map. {$c' \in C'$ is mapped to the total distance $d_{c'} \in D$ with $f(c') \mapsto d_{c'}$ with a surjective mapping $f : C' \mapsto D$ }
10:    **end for**
11:    return c'' {where $c'' = f^{-1}(min(D))$, i.e. the collector with minimum distance If $|f^{-1}(min(D))| > 1$, ie more than one collector, only the first one is returned.}
12: **else**
13:    return c' {where $c' \in C'$ with minimum load.}
14: **end if**

---

guarantees that the normal parent-child relations are used as much as possible. This avoids sending additional Collector information to the PerSyst Agents more than necessary.

When $l_j > l_{max}$ the job size is handled with percentile estimation and use the tree partially to fit the collection in the lowest possible number of collectors to extract the information; these jobs are called for convenience big jobs. Algorithm 3 shows how this distribution is done. The idea is to use the tree structure only when it is necessary, otherwise aggregate with exact calculations and store information as quickly and as closest to the source as possible.

The `DistributeLoadOnCollectors` algorithm is similar to the previous algorithm `FindBestCollector`. The main difference is that the number of collectors n_c where the job will be collected is determined. Once the algorithm determines which Collectors will be used, the remaining load is distributed among them. The last remaining task is to calculate the common collection node among the SyncAgents of an entire job. With tree operations the agent responsible for big jobs can be determined. Medium sized jobs finish their collection at one Collector. One-node jobs finish their collection at the PerSyst agent in charge of monitoring it's node. Figure 3 shows the different possibilities of retrieving a job.

The algorithm that calculates the topological distance is not shown but has a time complexity of $O(log(n))$ as it reduces to a tree search. The complexity of the calling algorithm, including all the calls, is therefore $O(n^2 log(n))$, where n is the number of the measuring agents.

Even though the measurements are done synchronously, the collection is done asynchronously, i.e. which ever process finishes collecting a job's data will start

Algorithm 3. Algorithm to distribute performance data load in several collectors.

1: Algorithm DistributeLoadOnCollectors(C, l_j, A_j)

2:
$$n_c \leftarrow ceiling(\frac{l_j}{l_{dist}}) \tag{8}$$

{where n_c is the number of Collectors that will receive the job performance data, also referred to as load, from all agents A_j. l_{dist} refers to a defined distribution load the Collectors will take, thus $l_{dist} < l_{max}$}

3: iter $\leftarrow$ 0

4: $A'_j \leftarrow A_j$ where A'_j is a temporary variable for agents of a job.

5: **while** iter $< n_c$ **do**

6:     $c \leftarrow$ FindBestCollector(C, A'_j)

7:     insert c in C' set.

8:     Child agents of c allocate their load in c

9:     Remove all agents a which are children of c from A'_j

10:     $iter \leftarrow iter + 1$

11: **end while**

12: Place the rest of the load on the first n_c Collectors found.

13: **for all** $a \in A'_j$ **do**

14:     $c \leftarrow$ FindBestCollector(C', A_j)

15:     place load of a in c:

16:     $l_c \leftarrow l_a$

17: **end for**

---

performing the output. The measurements are associated to the synchronized measuring interval. The collection of the performance data asynchronously alleviates the amount of synchronized communication of extracted data on a large cluster.

Extremely big jobs, like those which take up an entire petaflop system, are also handled. The solution is to collect them like the typical procedure other hierarchical tools would do, having aggregation at the middleware of the tree topology that provide's quantile estimations.

6   Results

The PerSyst Monitoring Tool runs currently in production mode in an IBM X Series Cluster system, hereafter SuperMUC, which is based on Intel Sandy Bridge-EP processors and Mellanox FDR-10 Infiniband technology. SuperMUC comprises 18 thin node islands, among other systems. Each thin island has 516 nodes each having two Sandy Bridge-EP Intel Xeon E5-2680 processors with a total of 16 cores per node (a Sandy Bridge-EP processor has 8 cores). A thin island consists of 512 nodes (8256 cores). All individual islands are connected internally via a fully non-blocking infiniband network. SuperMUC has, thus, 9,216 nodes with a total of 148,608 cores in the thin islands. Faster interconnects are available at the level of the island. The batch scheduler does not allow users

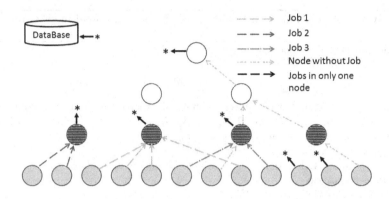

Fig. 3. Example of retrieval of performance data

to share a compute node, thus, a compute node is taken exclusively for a job. There are four job classes; each allows submissions with a different range of job sizes.

The PerSyst Monitoring tool was configured to run as one instance (one tree of agents with one frontend) on SuperMUC. The fanout of the tree hierarchy consisted on one SyncAgent as a frontend, 12 SyncAgents as a middle layer, 216 Collectors, and 9288 PerSyst Agents at every compute node. The 13 SyncAgents were placed at an external node which is used for administrative tasks. Six Collectors per island were placed having each 43 PerSyst Agents (child agents). Parent-child relations among Collectors and PerSyst Agents were placed in the same island. Thus, the tree agent topology exploited the faster interconnects with these placements. The tool was configured to run and aggregate using deciles (10 percentiles). Table 1 shows the collection of jobs at the different levels and the average values from 10 measurements of the job sizes running at the same time. The collection per job at a single point for percentile aggregation is done only at the Collector Agent level and at the PerSyst Agent level. The estimation of percentiles is on average 91% circumvented.

The topology network can be used fully when all the jobs travel to the frontend and are processed at each tree node. The alternative is to try to collect at selected

Table 1. Distribution of jobs in agent tree. Taken from 10 measurements in 10 days.

Tree level	Average number of Jobs	Percentage
Frontend	4.8	2.59%
SyncAgents	11.8	6.37%
Collector Agents	157.5	85%
PerSyst Agents	11.2	6.04%
Total number of jobs	185.3	100%

Table 2. Usage of the topology network for 58 measurements taken during a week

Job retrieving method	Average number of nodes used
Jobs travel through established topology connections until frontend	905.81
Jobs travel to selected nodes with job load balancing algorithm	217.59

Table 3. Collection time from PerSyst Agents to Collectors at a measuring interval

	Performance data one Collector	Performance data of SuperMUC
Bytes	204,426	44,156,016
Average time [s]	0.85	0.85
Used bandwidth [MiB/s]	0.22	49.54

nodes with the job load balancing algorithm (described in Section 5) and perform the output when the job has been collected. Table 2 shows the topology network usage with these two different methods.

The results show that the usage of the topology nodes is more than a factor of four with the traditional bottom-up retrieval of job information. To obtain the time it took to transmit the performance data, nine islands were measured and the average per Collector Agent was taken. Note that the transmission through the network interconnect between nodes includes measurement times and processing times within the PerSyst Agents. As soon as a performance datum is available, depending on the available data, it is sent in groups to the Collectors. This is done in order to not congest the network with performance data and explains the low bandwidths obtained.

By using deciles, we are able to reduce the amount of data more than 91% of the total amount of performance data in a week. No matter how big the job is, its information is compressed to 13 data points per monitoring interval: the deciles, the minimum (considered decile zero), the number of observations, and the average.

7   Conclusions

Percentiles have proven to be effective in data reduction. Due to the use of percentiles, two different kinds of aggregations are needed that produce exact calculations at certain nodes and other type of aggregations that estimate the new set of percentiles from meta-aggregation. In order to avoid meta-aggregation of percentiles, the transport systems adapts to the jobs' topological placement in the supercomputer. Not only the estimations are avoided, but the extraction of data is optimized compared to the traditional extraction that uses the entire tree topology.

Future work includes using a PerSyst Agent also as a Collector for doing collecting tasks in order to further optimize the amount of resources deployed in the supercomputer. Furthermore, optimizations in the algorithms presented will be carried out in order to reduce the time complexity of the job balancer.

References

1. Benedict, S., Brehm, M., Gerndt, M., Guillen, C., Hesse, W., Petkov, V.: Automatic performance analysis of large scale simulations. In: Lin, H.-X., Alexander, M., Forsell, M., Knüpfer, A., Prodan, R., Sousa, L., Stroit, A. (eds.) Euro-Par 2009. LNCS, vol. 6043, pp. 199–207. Springer, Heidelberg (2010)
2. Brim, M.J., DeRose, L., Miller, B.P., Olichandran, R., Roth, P.C.: Mrnet: A scalable infrastructure for development of parallel tools and applications. In: Cray User Group 2010 Proceedings (2010)
3. Focht, E., Jeutter, A.: AggMon: Scalable Hierarchical Cluster Monitoring. In: Proceedings of the Joint Workshop on High Performance Computing on Vector Systems (2012)
4. Frank, I.E., Todeschini, R.: The data analysis handbook, vol. 14. Elsevier Science B.V (1994)
5. Gerndt, M., Fuerlinger, K.: Automatic performance analysis with periscope. In: Journal: Concurrency and Computation: Practice and Experience, Wiley Inter-Science. John Wiley & Sons, Ltd. (2009)
6. Gerndt, M., Fuerlinger, K., Kereku, E.: Periscope: Advanced techniques for performance analysis, parallel computing: Current & future issues of high-end computing. In: International Conference ParCo 2005. NIC Series, vol. 33 (2006) ISBN 3-00-017352-8
7. Guillen, C., Hesse, W., Brehm, M.: A new scalable monitoring tool using performance properties of hpc systems. In: Bischof, C., Hegering, H.-G., Nagel, W.E., Wittum, G. (eds.) Competence in High Performance Computing 2010, pp. 51–60. Springer, Heidelberg (2012) 10.1007/978-3-642-24025-6.5
8. Mendenhall, W., Sincich, T.: Statistics for engineering and the sciences, 4th edn. Prentice-Hall International, Inc. (1995) ISBN 0-13-181017-0
9. Mooney, R., Schmidt, K.P., Studham, R.S.: NWPerf: a system wide performance monitoring tool for large Linux clusters. In: IEEE International Conference on Cluster Computing, pp. 379–389. IEEE Computer Society, Los Alamitos (2004)
10. Roth, P.C., Arnold, D.C., Miller, B.P.: Mrnet: A software-based multicast/reduction network for scalable tools. In: Proc. IEEE/ACM Supercomputing (2003)

A Cloudification Methodology
for Numerical Simulations

Silvina Caíno-Lores, Alberto García,
Félix García-Carballeira, and Jesús Carretero

Universidad Carlos III de Madrid,
Department of Computer Science and Engineering,
Computer Architecture Group,
Leganés, Madrid, Spain
{scaino,agarcia,fgarcia,jcarrete}@arcos.inf.uc3m.es

Abstract. Many scientific areas make extensive use of computer simulations to study complex real-world processes. These computations are typically very resource-intensive and present scalability issues as experiments get larger, even in dedicated clusters since they are limited by their own hardware resources. Cloud computing raises as an option to move forward into the ideal unlimited scalability by providing virtually infinite resources, yet applications must be adapted to this new paradigm. We propose a generalist cloudification method based in the MapReduce paradigm to migrate numerical simulations into the cloud to provide greater scalability. We analysed its viability by applying it to a real-world simulation and running the resulting implementation on Hadoop YARN over Amazons EC2. Our tests show that the cloudified application is highly scalable and there is still a large margin to improve the theoretical model and its implementations, and also to extend it to a wider range of simulations.

1 Introduction

Scientific simulations constitute a major set of applications that attempt to reproduce real-world phenomena in a wide range of areas such as engineering, physics, mathematics and biology. Their complexity usually yields a significant resource usage regarding CPU, memory, I/O or a combination of them.

In order to properly scale the application it can be distributed to a cluster or grid. While these approaches have proved successful, they often rely on heavy hardware investment and they are tightly conditioned by its capabilities, which de facto limits actual scalability and the addressable simulation size. Since sharing resources across multiple clusters implies several limitations, cluster applications cannot be considered sustainable, because their scalability is strongly dependant on the cluster size.

Despite scientific simulations will likely benefit from the upcoming exascale infrastructures [1], the challenges that must be overcome –power consumption, processing speed and data locality, for instance [2]– will probably rise again in

L. Lopes et al. (Eds.): Euro-Par 2014 Workshops, Part II, LNCS 8806, pp. 375–386, 2014.

the future as applications become more complex; therefore, the ideal situation of unlimited scalability seems difficult to reach with this approach.

Moreover, recent advances in cloud interoperability and cloud federations can contribute to separate application scalability from datacenter size [7, 12]. From that point of view, applications would become more sustainable, i.e. they can be operated in a more flexible way through heterogeneous hardware, cross-domain interactions and shared infrastructures.

Another recent option is cloud computing, which has been increasingly studied as an alternative to traditional grid and high-performance distributed environments for resource-demanding and data-intensive scientific simulations [15]. Cloud computing emerged with the idea of virtual unlimited resources obtainable on-demand with minimal management effort [11]. It would enable the execution of large simulations with virtual hardware properly tailored to fit specific use cases like memory-bound simulations, CPU dependent computations or data-intensive analysis. It holds further advantages, such as elasticity, automatic scalability and instance resource selectivity which, along with its so-called pay-as-you-go model, allow to adjust the required instances to the particular test case size while cutting-down the resulting costs.

There are several issues that can be tackled in order to develop a sustainable application, such as:

- Virtual unlimited scalability can be achieved by eliminating architectural bottlenecks such as network communications or master node dependences. This minimises the added overhead of working with more nodes, making a better use of the available resources.
- By making the application platform independent, we can aggregate computational resources possibly located in different places, hence local data center size would not be a limitation. Moreover, we can exploit cluster and cloud resources simultaneously following an hybrid scheme.
- A flexible application could scale up or down easily according to instantaneous user needs, thus adapting computing resources to specific simulation sizes and deadlines.
- If the application already exists and has to be adapted, it is desirable to minimize the impact on the original code, thus performing the minimal modifications needed to achieve the aforementioned objectives.

Given the former, we suggest a paradigm shift from multi-thread computations to a data-centric model that would distribute the simulation load across a set of virtual instances. This paper focuses on resource-intensive numerical simulations which hold potential scalability issues on large cases, since standalone and cluster hardware may not satisfy simulation requirements under such stress circumstances, and it proposes a generic methodology to transform numerical simulations into a cloud-suitable data-centric scheme via the MapReduce framework.

This process is illustrated by means of a real production application, a simulator which calculates power consumption on railway installations. This simulator, starting from the train movements (train position and consumption), calculates the instantaneous power demand (taking into account all railway elements such as tracks, overhead lines, and external consumers) indicating whether the power provisioned by power stations is enough or not. Simulator internals consist on composing the electric circuit on each instant, and solving that circuit using modified nodal analysis. The starting version of the simulator, based on multi-threading, is memory bounded, strongly limited by the number of instants to be simulated simultaneously (and therefore by the number of threads). The resulting performance is evaluated on Amazon Elastic Compute Cloud running Hadoop YARN MapReduce.

The rest of this paper is organized as follows: Section 2 discusses related works, Section 3 describes our proposed methodology, Section 4 illustrates the cloudification transformation method on a particular use case, Section 5 evaluates how the resulting design implementation on Hadoop MapReduce 1.1.2 (MRv1) and Hadoop YARN Mapreduce 2.2.0 (MRv2) behaves on both a cluster and Amazon Elastic Compute Cloud (EC2) and, finally, Section 6 provides key ideas as conclusions and some insight in future work.

2   Related Work

Scientific applications and their adaptability to new computing paradigms have been dragging increasing attention from the scientific community in the last few years. The applicability of the MapReduce scheme for scientific analysis has been notably studied, specially for data-intensive applications, resulting in an overall increased scalability for large data sets, even for tightly coupled applications [6].

The possibility to run such simulations in the cloud in terms of cost and performance was studied in [10], concluding that performance in the Abe HPC cluster and Amazon EC2 is similar –besides the virtualization overhead and high-speed connectivity loss in the cloud– and that clouds are a viable alternative for scientific applications. Hill [9] investigated the trade-off between the resulting performance and achieved scalability on the cloud versus commodity clusters; despite at the time of this work the cloud could not properly compete against HPC clusters, its low maintenance and cost made it a viable option for small scale clusters with a minimum performance loss.

The relationship between Apache Hadoop MapReduce and the cloud for scientific applications has also been tackled in [8], which establishes that performance and scalability tests results are similar between traditional clusters and virtualized infrastructures.

In this context, trends are naturally evolving to migrate applications to the cloud by means of several techniques, and this includes scientific simulations as well. D'Angelo [4] describes a Simulation-as-a-Service schema in which parallel and distributed simulations could be executed transparently, which requires dealing with model partitioning, data distribution and synchronization. He concludes that the potential challenges concerning hardware, performance, usability and cost that could arise could be overcome and optimized with the proper simulation model partitioning.

In [13], Srirama, Jakovits and Vainikko study how some scientific algorithms could be adapted to the cloud by means of the Hadoop MapReduce framework. They establish a classification of algorithms according to the structure of the MapReduce schema these would be transformed to and suggest that not all of them would be optimally adapted by their selected MapReduce implementation, yet they would suit other similar platforms such as Twister or Spark. They focus on the transformation of particular algorithms to MapReduce by redesigning the algorithms themselves, and not by wrapping them into a cloudification framework as we propose.

Finally, in [14] we find interesting efforts to move desktop simulation applications to the cloud via virtualized bundled images that run in a transparent multi-tenant fashion from the end user's point of view, while minimizing costs. As previously discussed, we believe the virtualization middleware might affect performance since it does not take into account any structural characteristics of the model, which could be exploited to minimize cloudification effects or drastically affect execution times or resource consumption.

Our work focuses in providing a general methodology to transform numerical simulations into a cloud-suitable execution framework with minimal impact to the original code, while exploiting simulation model features that inherently aid with partitioning and performance optimization. A related approach is the so-called *parameter sweep* [3], in which the same simulation kernel is executed multiple times with different input parameters, thus providing task independence. However, in our approach we transform a single simulation into several autonomous tasks through any independent variable that belongs to the simulation domain, not only input parameters. Domain decompositions and transformations can be used in applications where task independence is not so evident; therefore, task independence is a result of our methodology, not a means.

3   Methodology Description

The MapReduce paradigm consists of two user-defined operations: *map* and *reduce*. The former takes the input and produces a set of intermediate (*key, value*) pairs that will be organized by key by the framework so that every reducer gets a set of values that correspond to a particular key [5].

As a data-centric paradigm, in which large amounts of information can be potentially processed, these operations run independently and only rely upon the input data they are fed with. Thus, several instances can run simultaneously with no further interdependence. Moreover, data can be spread across as many nodes as needed to deal with scalability issues.

Simulations, however, are usually resource-intensive in terms of CPU or memory usage, so their scalability is limited to hardware restrictions, even in large clusters. Our goal is to exploit the data-centric paradigm to achieve a virtually infinite scalability so that large numeric simulations can be executed independently of the underlying hardware resources, with minimal effects to the original simulation code. From this point of view, numeric simulations would become

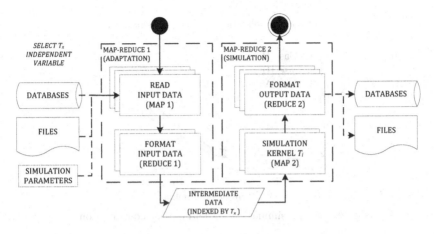

Fig. 1. Methodology overview

more sustainable, allowing us to spread simulation scenarios of different sizes in a more flexible way, using heterogeneous hardware, and taking advantage of shared inter-domain infrastructures.

To achieve this, we will take advantage of MapReduce's lack of task interdependence and data-centric design, this will allow to disseminate the simulation's original input to distribute its load among the available nodes, which will yield the scalability we aim for. The steps involved in our proposed methodology are described in the following sections.

3.1 Application Analysis

Our purpose is to divide the application into smaller simulations that can run with the same simulation kernel but on a fragment of the full partitioned data set, so that we can parallelise the executions and lower the hardware requirements for each.

Hence, we must analyse the original simulation domain in order to find an independent variable $-T_x$ in Fig. 1– that can act as index for the partitioned input data and the following procedures. This independent variable would be present either in the input data or the simulation parameters and it could represent, for example, independent time-domain steps, spatial divisions or a range of simulation parameters.

3.2 Cloudification Process Design

Once the application is shown suitable for the process, it can be transformed by matching the input data and independent variables with the elements in Fig. 1, thus resulting in the two MapReduce jobs described below:

- **Adaptation stage:** reads the input files in the *map* phase and indexes all the necessary parameters by T_x for every execution as intermediate output. The

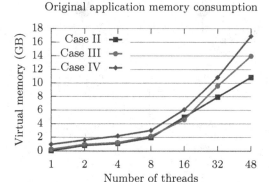

Fig. 2. Original simulation kernel memory consumption

Table 1. Test cases definition

Experiment	Simulated time (hours)	Input size (MB)
I	1	1.7
II	33	170
III	177	1228.8
IV	224	5324.8

Table 2. Execution environments

Configuration	Platform	Underlying infrastructure
1	Multi-thread	Cluster node
2	MRv1	Cluster node
3	MRv2	Cluster node
4	MRv2	EC2

original data must be partitioned so that subsequent simulations can run autonomously with all the necessary data centralized in a unique $(T_x,$ *parameters*) entry.

- **Simulation stage:** runs the simulation kernel for each value of the independent variable along with the necessary data that was mapped to them in the previous stage, plus the required simulation parameters that are common for every partition. Since simulations might generate several output files, mappers would organize the output by means of file identifier numbers as keys, so as reducers could be able to gather all the output and provide final results as the original application.

4   Case Study

To illustrate how this methodology works on a real-world use case, we applied it to transform a memory-bound railway electric power consumption simulation.

Four test cases were considered with variations on the simulation's initial and final time and, consequently, input data volume and memory consumption. A description of these simulations is provided in Table 1. Cases I and II should

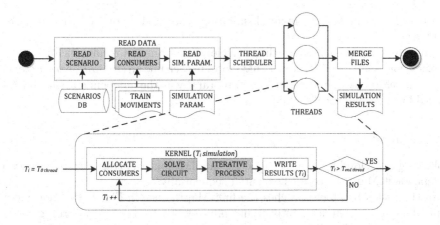

Fig. 3. Case study original simulation structure

not yield any significant load, yet simulation III is expected to show some differences, while the biggest experiment, case IV, should reveal the platforms' actual behaviour and limitations as simulations become larger, if any. These tests are meant to indicate the performance of the cloudified adaptation versus the original application under an increasing amount of input data and simulation time.

As seen in Fig. 2, this application does not scale well for large test cases in terms of memory usage in a standalone environment (Configuration 1, see Sec. 5.1 for further details). We believe we can achieve greater scalability by cloudifying the application, since we can distribute the simulation load across several nodes. It would also disperse memory usage so that we could always add a new node in case we need to tackle a larger case. To show its feasibility, next we will apply the method described in Section 3.

4.1 Analysis

The structure of the selected application is shown in Fig. 3. It consists of a preparation phase in which all the required input data is read and fragmented to be executed in a predefined number of threads. Each of the resulting threads then perform the actual simulation by means of an electric iterative algorithm, storing in shared memory the results that will be merged in the main thread to constitute the final output files.

This simulator, starting from the train movements –that describe train position and power consumption– and infrastructure design –tracks, power stations, among others– calculates the instantaneous power demand taking into account all railway elements such as tracks, overhead lines, and external consumers, indicating whether the power provisioned by power stations is sufficient or not. Simulator internals consist on composing the electric circuit on each instant, and solving that circuit using modified nodal analysis. The initial version of the simulator, based on multi-threading, is memory bounded, strongly limited by the number of instants to be simulated simultaneously, and therefore by the number of threads.

The key to adapt such algorithm to a cloud environment resides its input files, for they hold an indexed structure that stores in each line an $(instant, parameters)$ pair. Therefore, we can consider the temporal key as the independent variable required for the theoretical model.

4.2 Cloudification

Following the cloudification schema, the application was transformed into two independent MapReduce jobs executed sequentially.

In the first job, which matches the first MapReduce in Fig. 1, the movement input files, I_{I_0}, are divided into input splits by the framework according to its configuration. Each split is then assigned to a mapper, which reads each line and emits $(key, value)$ pairs where the key is the instant t_i and the value is the corresponding set of parameters for such instant; the intention is to provide reducers with a list of movement parameters per instant $I_n, \ldots, I_m$ –each element representing the movement of one of the trains involved in the overall system for a particular t_i– to concatenate and write to the output files, so that the simulation kernel can be executed once per instant with all the required data.

As described in Fig. 1, the output of the previous job is used as input to the mapper tasks by parsing each line in order to get the data corresponding to the instant being processed, which is passed to the electric algorithm itself along with the scenario information obtained from the infrastructure file that is also read by the mapper. The mappers' output is compounded by an output file identifier F_j as key and the actual content as value.

Reducers simply act as mergers gathering and concatenating mappers' output organized by file identifier and instant as a secondary key injected in the value content; this arranges the algorithm's output so that the full simulation results are shown as in the original application, in which each output file contains the results for the whole temporal interval of the simulation.

5 Evaluation

In order to asses the application's performance we compared its execution times on both a cluster and the cloud. The following sections describe the utilized resources and a discussion on the obtained outcome.

5.1 Execution Environments

Table 2 summarizes the infrastructures and software platforms on which the tests were conducted.

In a first place, we tested the original multi-thread application's memory consumption and performance on a cluster node consisting of a 24 Xeon E7 cores and 110GB of RAM (Configuration 1).

This node was also used to test the resulting cloudfied application to avoid variations that may arise from heterogeneous configuration, resource differences, or network latency in case of the MapReduce application [10]. This isolation favours the multi-thread application, which is especially designed to perform in standalone environments, yet it allows to focus on the actual limiting factors that may affect scalability in large test cases like I/O, memory consumption and CPU usage. Both Hadoop versions –MRv1 and MRv2– were installed and configured on the single-node cluster to benchmark their performance against the original application (Configurations 2 and 3, respectively).

MRv2 was chosen to be deployed on EC2 given its improved resource management options and better overall performance (Configuration 4). The cloud infrastructure consisted of a general purpose *m1.medium* node as dedicated master and several memory optimized *m2.xlarge* machines as slaves, with 2 CPUs and 17.1GB of RAM each. Tests on EC2 have been conducted using a variable number of slaves in order to check if scalability issues arise as the number of nodes increases.

5.2   Results Discussion

As we already discussed in Section 4, the original multi-thread application's memory usage suggests a lack of scalability in a cluster environment. We will now analyse whether the cloudified simulation behaves as expected in relation to performance and scalability by examining its execution times on several execution environments, which are shown in Fig. 4. This figure shows the time measurements obtained on the configurations in Tab. 2, in which the EC2 cluster is constituted by five slaves –graphs (a), (b) and (c)–. The EC2 values also served as baseline for the scalability study shown in (d).

(a) **Cloudification phase**
   The data adaptation phase –graph (b)– is 65% slower on EC2 compared to the same MapReduce version in the local cluster, for the largest experiment. This is a result of the selected EC2 instances' characteristics, since memory optimised machines are meant to favour the memory-bound kernel execution phase. This stage would benefit from compute optimised instances, since a large number of cores would allow the execution of more mappers simultaneously.

(b) **Kernel execution**
   The algorithm execution stage, (c), is the most determinant phase in the whole process, ranging from the 48% of the whole execution time, in case I on EC2, to an 89%, in case II in the same environment. The total resources held by the physical cluster in terms of memory make a substantial difference in this stage, resulting in simulation times 2.1 times lower than EC2, in average. Cloud's virtualization and communication overhead could also affect the simulation execution and the shuffle of the mapper's output, respectively, degrading performance against the single-node environment.

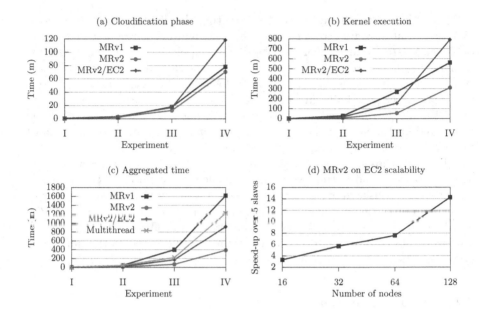

Fig. 4. Evaluation results

(c) Aggregated time

In (c) we observe the overall execution time for the application including both MapReduce jobs and input data upload, which must be considered given that replication and balance must be achieved by the platform to distribute load evenly. The graph indicates that the obtained performance with MapReduce on Yarn in both the single-node cluster and the elastic cloud is remarkably better than the original multi-thread application –68% and 25% less total simulation time for the largest experiment, respectively–. The shared memory simulator's results might be caused by the bottleneck constituted by the physical memory and the disk; the latter is particularly critical, as all threads write their results to disk while they perform their computations in the original simulator.

The smallest experiment is an interesting exception, with execution times ten times greater than the original application in all the platforms. This reflects how the MapReduce framework's overhead significantly affects the time taken to complete such a small simulation compared to the original application benchmark.

(d) Scalability study

Finally, in (d) we observe the speed-up obtained on EC2 running YARN when the number of slaves is increased. The speed-up shown in the figure is related to the execution times commented in the previous paragraphs, which were obtained in a five-slave cluster. As the figure indicates, increasing the number of slaves decreases the total simulation time. However, the performance does not scale up linearly with the number of nodes: while with 16 nodes the speed-up is 3.3, with 64 nodes it is only 7.6. The reason behind this result is that the problem size becomes small for the cluster size as more nodes are added, hence less data is assigned to each slave and some resources become underutilised. Moreover, as we mentioned in the previous paragraph, in very small experiments the measured execution time is mostly spent in the platform's task preparation and scheduling, and not in the actual simulation, resulting in degraded performance due to platform overhead. Therefore, it is necessary to increase the problem size as well as the number of slave nodes in order to achieve linear scalability.

6   Conclusions

As the cloud is increasingly shown as a viable alternative to traditional computing paradigms for high-performance applications and resource-intensive simulations, we propose a general methodology to transform numeric simulations into a highly scalable MapReduce application that re-uses the same simulation kernel while distributing the simulation load across as many nodes are desired in a virtual cluster running on the cloud.

The procedure requires an application analysis phase in which at least one independent variable must be found, since this element will act as index for the cloudification phase. The cloud adaptation stage transforms the original input into a set of partitions indexed by the the previous variable by means of a MapReduce job; these partitions are fed to a second MapReduce job that executes the simulation kernel independently for each, merging the final results as well.

This methodology performs a paradigm shift from resource-bound applications to a data-centric model; such cloudification mechanism provides effective cloud migration of simulation kernels with minimal impact on the original code and achieves great scalability since limiting factors are scattered. Therefore, it provides a way to increase application's sustainability, breaking the dependence on local infrastructure, and allowing to spread simulation scenarios of different sizes in a more flexible way, using heterogeneous hardware, and taking advantage of shared inter-domain infrastructures.

Future works are strongly focused on extending the current methodology to a generalized framework which would allow to cloudify any scientific application. With this aim, several issues have to be solved:

- The behaviour of the methodology should be analysed when other different kinds of applications (CPU or network intensive) are cloudified. Currently we are cloudifying a classic MPI application such as the $n-$bodies problem, in order to assure performance even in cluster-oriented applications.
- Parameter extraction and application analysis is currently performed manually by the user, who is accountable for selecting an independent variable T_x. Current development is also oriented to ease this tasks through creating

data definitions which would allow the adaptation phase to select and split the input data automatically.

References

1. Ashby, S., Beckman, P., Chen, J., Colella, P., Collins, B., Crawford, D., Dongarra, J., Kothe, D., Lusk, R., Messina, P.: et al.: The opportunities and challenges of exascale computing. Summary Report of the Advanced Scientific Computing Advisory Committee (ASCAC) Subcommittee (November 2010)
2. Bergman, K., Borkar, S., Campbell, D., Carlson, W., Dally, W., Denneau, M., Franzon, P., Harrod, W., Hill, K., Hiller, J., et al.: Exascale computing study: Technology challenges in achieving exascale systems. Defense Advanced Research Projects Agency Information Processing Techniques Office (DARPA IPTO), Tech. Rep 15 (2008)
3. Casanova, H., Legrand, A., Zagorodnov, D., Berman, F.: Heuristics for scheduling parameter sweep applications in grid environments. In: Proceedings of the 9th Heterogeneous Computing Workshop (HCW 2000), pp. 349–363. IEEE (2000)
4. D'Angelo, G.: Parallel and distributed simulation from many cores to the public cloud. In: 2011 International Conference on High Performance Computing and Simulation (HPCS), pp. 14–23 (July 2011)
5. Dean, J., Ghemawat, S.: Mapreduce: simplified data processing on large clusters. Communications of the ACM 51(1), 107–113 (2008)
6. Ekanayake, J., Pallickara, S., Fox, G.: Mapreduce for data intensive scientific analyses. In: IEEE Fourth International Conference on eScience 2008, pp. 277–284 (December 2008)
7. Grozev, N., Buyya, R.: Inter-cloud architectures and application brokering: taxonomy and survey. Software: Practice and Experience (2012)
8. Gunarathne, T., Wu, T.L., Qiu, J., Fox, G.: Mapreduce in the clouds for science. In: 2010 IEEE Second International Conference on Cloud Computing Technology and Science (CloudCom), pp. 565–572 (November 2010)
9. Hill, Z., Humphrey, M.: A quantitative analysis of high performance computing with amazon's ec2 infrastructure: The death of the local cluster? In: 2009 10th IEEE/ACM International Conference on Grid Computing, pp. 26–33 (October 2009)
10. Juve, G., Deelman, E., Vahi, K., Mehta, G., Berriman, B., Berman, B., Maechling, P.: Scientific workflow applications on amazon ec2. In: 2009 5th IEEE International Conference on E-Science Workshops, pp. 59–66 (December 2009)
11. Mell, P., Grance, T.: The nist definition of cloud computing. National Institute of Standards and Technology 53(6), 50 (2009)
12. Petcu, D., Macariu, G., Panica, S., Crăciun, C.: Portable cloud applications—from theory to practice. Future Generation Computer Systems 29(6), 1417–1430 (2013)
13. Srirama, S.N., Jakovits, P., Vainikko, E.: Adapting scientific computing problems to clouds using mapreduce. Future Generation Computer Systems 28(1), 184–192 (2012)
14. Srirama, S.N., Ivanistsev, V., Jakovits, P., Willmore, C.: Direct migration of scientific computing experiments to the cloud. In: 2013 International Conference on High Performance Computing and Simulation (HPCS), pp. 27–34 (July 2013)
15. Yelick, K., Coghlan, S., Draney, B., Canon, R.S., et al.: The magellan report on cloud computing for science. US Department of Energy, Washington DC, USA, Tech. Rep. (2011)

Paralldroid: Performance Analysis of GPU Executions

Alejandro Acosta and Francisco Almeida

Dept. de Informática
La Laguna University, Spain
aacostad@ull.edu.es

Abstract. The popularity of the handheld systems (smartphones, tablets, ...) and their great computational capability open a new era in parallel computing terms. The efficient use of such devices is still a challenge. The heterogeneity of the SoCs and MPSocs is demanding very specific knowledge of the devices, what represents a very high learning curve for general purpose programmers. To ease the development task we present Paralldroid, a development framework oriented to general purpose programmers for mobile devices. Paralldroid presents a programming model that unifies the different programming models of Android and allows for the automatic generation of parallel code. The developer just implements an object oriented Java application and introduces a set of Paralldroid annotations in the sections of code to be optimized. The annotations used are based on the OpenMP 4.0 specification. The Paralldroid system then automatically generates the native C or Renderscript code required to take advantage of the underlying platform. The Renderscript generated code allows the execution in the GPU. The computational experience proves that the results are quite promising. The code generated by Paralldroid takes advantage of the GPU and offers good performances with a very low cost of development, so it contributes to increase the productivity when developing efficient code.

1 Introduction

The evolution of many of today's ubiquitous technologies, such as Internet, mobile wireless technology, and high definition television have been possible due to the Systems on Chip (SOCs) technology. The information technology age, in turn, has fuelled a global communications revolution. As a result of this revolution, the computing power of the mobile devices has been increased. The technologies available in desktop computers are now implemented in embedded and mobile devices. In this scenario, we can find that new processors integrating multicore architectures GPUs and DSPs are being developed for this market. The Nvidia Tegra, the Qualcomm snapdragon and the Samsung Exynos are platforms that go in this direction.

Regarding to the software development, many frameworks have been developed to support the building of software for such devices. The main companies in

L. Lopes et al. (Eds.): Euro-Par 2014 Workshops, Part II, LNCS 8806, pp. 387–399, 2014.

this software market have their own platforms: Windows phone from Microsoft, iOS from Apple and Android from Google are contenders in the smartphone market. Developing of applications for such devices is now easier. Besides to the problem of creating energy-efficient hardware, we stumbled on the difficult task of creating efficient, maintainable programs to run on them [1].

Conceptually, the architectural model can be viewed as a traditional heterogeneous CPU/GPU system where memory is shared between the CPU and GPU and acts as a high bandwidth communication channel. In the non-unified memory architectures, it was common to have only a subset of the actual memory addressable by the GPU. Technologies like Algorithmic Memory, GPUDirect and UVA from Nvidia and HSA from AMD are going in the direction of an unified memory system for CPUs and GPUs in the traditional memory architectures. Memory performance continues to be outpaced by the ever increasing demand of faster processors, multiprocessor cores and parallel architectures.

Given the high heterogeneity level of these devices is mandatory the development of tools to keep the mobile device sustainability in terms of programmability. Under this scenario, we find a strong divorce among traditional mobile software developers and parallel programmers, the first tend to use high level frameworks like Eclipse or Android Studio for the development of Java programs, without any knowledge of parallel programming (Android: Eclipse + Java, Windows: Visual Studio + C#, IOS: XCode + Objective C), and the latter that use to work on Linux, doing their programs directly in OpenCL closer to the metal. The first take the advantage of the high level expressiveness while the latter assume the challenge of the high performance programming. Paralldroid tries to help bring these to worlds.

We propose Paralldroid, a development framework that allows the automatic development of Native, Renderscript applications for mobile devices (Smartphones, Tablets, ...). The developer fills and annotates, using the sequential high level language, the sections on a template that will be executed in native and Renderscript language. Paralldroid uses the information provided by the annotations to generate a new program that incorporates the code sections to run over the CPU or GPU. In [2] a comparative between the different Android programming models was presented. The authors show the advantages of each programming model and highlight the importance of creating an unified model. Paralldroid unifies the different programming models of Android.

In this paper we present a performance analysis executions of code generated by a new implementation of Paralldroid over the GPU of the mobile device. Paralldroid can be seen as a proof of concept where we show the benefits of using generation patterns to abstract the developers from the complexity inherent to parallel programs.

Several are the main contributions of the paper are:

- A new implementation of the Paralldroid framework is presented. It extends the OpenJDK compiler to generate new ASTs (Abstract Syntax Trees). Under the Android Development Model, the Renderscript and Native codes are not executed in standalone mode, they must be harnessed to a sequential

Java code to be launched. The technique we use not only allows to generate the new Renderscript and Native ASTs but also modifies the original one, to allow the harnessing, in a process that is hidden to the end user.

– To extend the set of annotations to be used under the object oriented paradigm. Most of the Android developers are Java programmers that apply the object oriented paradigm. Classical OpenMP annotations for C++, for example, handle the directives in an imperative mode to the methods of classes. The object oriented paradigm is not really supported. Paralldroid introduces the annotations to classes and methods trying to be closer to the developers object oriented mode programming style.

– The Paralldroid framework and the target architecture chosen are contributions by themselves. The heterogeneity of the Android programming models allows the programmer to obtain the best performance, implementing each section of the application using the programming model that better fits to his/her code. Paralldroid allows to generate code for each programming model, facilitating the development of efficient heterogeneous applications.

– We analyse the performance over different configurations of CPUs and GPU+ CPU to prove the benefits of our tool. The results obtained show that the Paralldroid framework is a useful tool to increase the programmability and exploits the compute-power available on Android devices.

Some tools that generate parallel code form an extension of Java code were presented in [3,4]. In these cases the Java syntax is modified to introduce new syntactic elements into the language. The main disadvantage of these proposals is that the new elements are not compatible with the Java definition, so the standard Java compiler does not compile the source code with these extensions. The Paralldroid definition does not modify the Java syntax definitions, it just introduces a set of annotations. The standard Java compiler can compile the Java code and ignore the Paralldroid annotations. In [5] the authors present a Domain-Specic Language (DSL) to generate Renderscript code. This DSL is specific for image processing algorithms therefore, the users have to learn a new language. Our framework is based on the main language of Android and our target users know this language.

The paper is structured as follows, in section 2 we introduce the development models in Android and the different alternatives to exploit the devices, some of the difficulties associated to the development models are shown. In section 3 we present the Paralldroid Framework, the performance of Paralldroid is validated in section 4 using five different applications, transform a image to grayscale, convolve 3x3 and 5x5, levels and a general convolve implementation. We execute each application in multiple configurations of CPUs+GPU. The results obtained are compared. The computational results prove the increase of performance provided by Paralldroid at a low cost of development. We finish the paper with some conclusions and future lines of research.

2   The Development Model in Android

Android is a Linux based operating system mainly designed for mobile devices
such as smartphones and tablet devices. Android applications are written in
Java, and the Android Software Development Kit (SDK) provides the API libraries and developer tools necessary to build, test, and debug applications. The
central section of Figure 1(a) shows the compilation and execution model of
a Java Android application. The compilation model converts the Java .java
files to Dalvik-compatible .dex (Dalvik Executable) files. The application runs
in a Dalvik virtual machine (Dalvik VM) that manages the system resources
allocated to this application (through the Linux kernel).

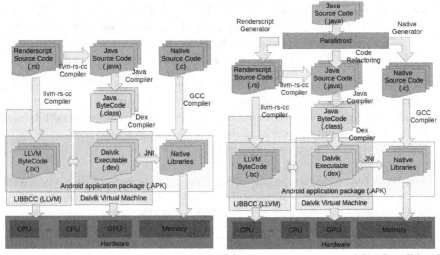

(a) Compilation and execution model of
an application in Android

(b) The development model in Paralldroid

Fig. 1. Compilation and execution model of an application in Android and Paralldroid

Besides the development of Java applications, Android provides packages of
development tools and libraries to develop Native applications, the Native Development Kit (NDK). The NDK enables to implement parts of the application
running in the Dalvik VM using native-code languages such as C and C++.
This native code is executed using the Java Native Interface (JNI) provided by
Java. The right-hand section of Figure 1(a) shows the compilation and execution model of an application where part of the code has been written using the
NDK. The Native .c is compiled using the GNU compiler (GCC). Note that
using native code does not result in an automatic performance increase, but always increases application complexity, its use is recommended in CPU-intensive
operations that don't allocate much memory, such as signal processing, physics

simulation, and so on. Native code is useful to port an existing native code to Android, not for speeding up parts of an Android application.

To exploit the high computational capabilities on current devices, Android provides Renderscript, it is a high performance computation API at the native level and a programming C language (C99 standard). Renderscript allows the execution of parallel applications under several types of processors such as the CPU, GPU or DSP, performing an automatic distribution of the workload across the available processing cores on the device. The left-hand section of Figure 1(a) shows the compilation and execution model used by Renderscript. Renderscript (.rs files) codes are compiled using a LLVM compiler based on Clang, moreover, it generates a set of Java classes wrapper around the Renderscript code. Again, the use of Renderscript code does not result in an automatic performance increasing. It is useful for applications that do image processing, mathematical modelling, or any operations that require lots of mathematical computation.

3   Paralldroid

Paralldroid is designed to ease the development of parallel applications on Android platforms. We assume that the mobile platforms will be provided with a classical CPU and other kind of *co-processor* like a GPU that can be exploited thorough Renderscript. First implementations of Paralldroid were presented in [6,7]. In the proposed translation model, the developers define their problem as Java code in the Android SDK and add a set of directives. These directives are an extension of OpenMP 4.0 [8] that includes directives for accelerators.

The Object Oriented Programming (OOP) is a programming paradigm that represents concepts as objects that include data fields and methods [9] together. Java is a object oriented language and their programmers are familiarized with this paradigm. The first implementation of Paralldroid defines their annotations as Java comments, following the idea of the compiler directives in the C OpenMP definition. It does not take into account the object oriented paradigm and can be difficult to use by the standard Java programmers. For this reason we developed a new implementation of Paralldroid where the programmers use the Java annotations system [10] to define the Paralldroid directives.

OpenMP can be used in object oriented languages, like C++. But the directives used are not a well integrated in the Object Oriented paradigm. The directives are just used in an imperative mode into methods of classes. They only work with object types but do not have the possibility to define this directives directly in the object. In the new implementation of Paralldroid, we present a new methodology that intends to adapt some of the OpenMP directives to the object oriented paradigm. This new definition of directives is based on the OpenMP 4.0 specification but we apply it to the object elements (class, field and method). Paralldroid supports polymorfism and dynamic binding but, at this moment, it doesn't support inheritance of an annotated class. We only used a reduced set of directives, but the same idea can be extended to many others.

A diagram representing the new implementation can be seen in Figure 2. In the first step, we use the OpenJDK parser to create a Java Abstract Syntax

Tree (Java AST) from the Java Code. With this new parser we do not depend of the Java Development Tool library (JDT) used on the previous version. And so the translator is independent from the eclipse libraries. The Java AST is analysed looking for directives (Annotations detector). These directives are defined using the Java annotations specification. The generation process is based on AST transformations. The `NativeTreeTranslator` and `RSTreeTranslator` transform the Java AST to a new AST that represents the Native and Renderscript code respectively. The `JavaAST Translator` modifies the Java AST to access to the code generated by the Native and Renderscript translators. The `CreateNativeCode`, `CreateRenderscriptCode` and `CreateJavaCode` modules transform the AST representations to the corresponding code.

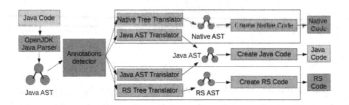

Fig. 2. AST Paralldroid transformation process

In Figure 1(b) you can see as the process of generation is integrated in the Android execution model (Figure 1(a)). The Paralldroid generation process is in the top level and analyzes the Java code looking for directives. The files that do not contain directives are compiled directly (central section). If Paralldroid finds a directive for Native code generation, this code is generated and the Java code is modified to access to generated Native code (right section). The same process is used to generate Renderscript code (left section). The increment of productivity under this approach is clear, moreover when considering that Paralldroid not only generates the Renderscript code but the Native C JNI implementation.

The set of directives supported by Paralldroid are:

@Target creates a device data environment. This directive is responsible for mapping the data to the context of the device. This directive is applied to the class definitions. In this case the elements inside the class (fields and methods) are created into the context of the device. The fields are mapped to the device following the idea of the OpenMP `target data` directive. The methods are executed into the device context and their parameters are mapped, like in the OpenMP `target` directive. To indicate the target language (Renderscript or Native) this directive has the parameter `lang`. The constructor of the class is modified to create the target context, allocate the memory and initialize the field values into the device context. Paralldroid generates a finalized method. This method is a special method in Java and is called when the Java garbage collector destroy the instance of this class. This method frees the memory of the device context and destroy the target context created in the constructor.

@Map is responsible for map a variable from the current Java environment to the target data environment. It is applied to definitions of fields and method parameters. The directive has a parameter to indicate the type of mapping (Alloc, To, From, ToFrom). In field definitions, Paralldroid generates a set of the Setter and Getter methods according to the type of mapping.

@Declare specifies that the element has to be declared in the device context. It is applied to the definition of fields and methods. These fields and methods only are defined into the device context. If the field is initialized, the corresponding variable in the device context is initialized with the same value.

@Parallel specifies a method to be executed in parallel. It is applied to the definition of methods. Currently, it is only supported by the Renderscript target.

@Input and @Output are an extension to the OpenMP standard and specify the input and output vectors in the Renderscript parallel execution. They are applied to definitions of method parameters.

@Index is an extension to the OpenMP standard and specifies the variable used as index in the Renderscript parallel execution. The value of this variable is assigned in runtime. It is applied to definitions of method parameters.

Note that, directives **@Map**, **@Declare** and **@Parallel** should be used in the context of a **@Target** directive. Similarity, directives **@Input**, **@Output** and **@Index** should be used in the context of a **@Parallel** directive

Listing 1.1. GrayScale implementation using Paralldroid and Object Oriented Programming

```
1   @Target(RENDERSCRIPT)
2   public class GrayScaleRS {
3       @Declare
4       private float gMonoMult[] = {0.299f, 0.587f, 0.114f};
5       @Map(TO)
6       private int width;
7       @Map(TO)
8       private int height;
9
10      public GrayScaleRS(Activity act, int width, int height) {
11          this.width = width;
12          this.height = height;
13      }
14      @Parallel
15      public void test(@Input int scr[], @Output int out[], @Index int x){
16          int acc;
17          acc = (int)(((scr[x]) & 0xff) * gMonoMult[0]);
18          acc += (int)(((scr[x] >> 8 ) & 0xff) * gMonoMult[1]);
19          acc += (int)(((scr[x] >> 16) & 0xff) * gMonoMult[2]);
20          out[x] = (acc) + (acc << 8) + (acc << 16) + (scr[x] << 24);
21      }
22  }
```

Listing 1.1 shows a Java class implementation for the grayScale problem with the Paralldroid directives. The `Target` directive (line 1) specifies that the class has to create a Renderscript context definition and the elements of the class have to be defined in this Renderscript context. Lines 3 to 8 define the fields. The `Declare` directive specifies that the `gMonoMult` field has to be defined into the Renderscript context. In this case the field is initialized, so it has to be initialized in the Renderscript context too. The `Map(To)` directive is similar to the `Declare` directive but in this case Paralldroid generates the corresponding setter methods. These methods allow the programmers to modify the values of these fields. The constructor method is defined in lines 10-13. The parameter `Activity act` is necessary to create the Renderscript context. It is a obligatory parameter when the Target is Renderscript. The method `test` (lines 15-21) defines the algorithm to transform an image to grayscale. The `Parallel` directive specifies that this method will be executed in parallel. The `Input` and `Output` directives indicate input and output vectors used by Renderscript in the parallel executions. In this case, these vectors contain the input and output images. The `Index` directive specifies the index used in the parallel execution and it is used to access to the elements of the input vector. The value of this variable is assigned by Renderscript in runtime. Note that, the annotations used are perfectly suited to the object programming definition. The programmer does not need a deep knowledge of the OpenMP standard. It just have to know the meaning of the annotations and where must be applied the annotations into the class definition.

Listing 1.2. Generated Java code by Paralldroid and Object Oriented Programming

```
1   public class GrayScaleRS {
2       private ScriptC_GrayScaleRS script;
3       private RenderScript mRS;
4       private Allocation gMonoMultAllocation;
5       private float[] gMonoMult = {0.299F, 0.587F, 0.114F};
6       private int width;
7       private int height;
8
9       public GrayScaleRS(Activity act, int width, int height) {
10          this.width = width;
11          this.height = height;
12          // Create Renderscript Context
13          // Allocate Renderscript memory form field
14          // Copy field to Renderscript
15      }
16      public void test(int[] scr, int[] out, int x) {
17          // Allocate Renderscript memory form parameter
18          // Copy parameter to Renderscript
19          // Call Renderscript function
20          // Copy parameter from Renderscript
21          // Free Renderscript memory from parameter
22      }
23      public void setWidth(int width) {
24          // Set value to Renderscript
25      }
26
27      ...
28      protected void finalize() {
29          // Free Renderscript memory form field
30          // Destroy Renderscript context
31      }
32   }
```

Listing 1.2 shows the Java class generated by Paralldroid. This class is based on the Java class defined in Listing 1.1. In line 2-3 a set of fields were added. These fields are used to create the Renderscript context and allocate the memory.

This process is done in the constructor method (lines 12-14). The **test** method is modified (lines 17-21). The function allocates the memory of the parameters and calls to the Renderscript function. This function transforms the image to grayscale. In lines 23-26 the setter methods are generated. The **finalize** method frees the Renderscript memory used and destroys the context created.

Listing 1.3. Generated Renderscript version of GrayScale problem.

```
1   #pragma version(1)
2   #pragma rs java_package_name (...)
3   rs_allocation gMonoMult;
4   int width;
5   int height;
6   rs_allocation scrPxsTest;
7   rs_allocation outPxsTest;
8
9   void root(const int *v_in, int *v_out, uint32_t x) {
10      // Code executed in parallel
11  }
```

Listing 1.3 shows the Renderscript code generated by Paralldroid. The fields and parameters mapped by the **target** class are defined in the Renderscript context (lines 3-7). The function **test** is replaced by a root function that will be executed in parallel, the input/output vector and index are used as parameters.

4   Computational Results

Leaving aside to future researches some peculiarities associated to the real time requirements of the smartphones and tables (e.g., power management, network management), we validate the performance of the code generated by Paralldroid using five different applications. Four of these applications are based on the Renderscript image-Processing benchmark [11] (transforming a image to grayscale, to levels and convolve with convolve window of sizes 3x3 and 5x5) and the other one is an additional general convolve implementation developed by ourselves. In all cases, we implemented five versions of code, the ad-hoc version from a Java developer, an ad-hoc Native C implementation, and ad-hoc Renderscript implementations, and the Renderscript version automatically generated by Paralldroid. We executed these codes over a Nexus 7 2013. This device is composed of a Qualcomm Snapdragon S4 Pro holding a Quad-core ARM Cortex-A15 processor (15000MHz), 2GB of RAM memory and a GPU Adreno 320. The Nexus 7 device runs the Android system version 4.4. This device supports GPU Renderscript and the GPU is used as accelerator. For the image processing problems we used a image of size 1600×1067.

To prove the performance obtained with the generated code, we analysed the execution time of each problem. The results obtained by the generated code are compared to the ad-hoc versions. Furthermore, we studied the impact in terms of performance of varying the number of CPUs and also the effect of enabling the GPU. These experiments allow to analyse the differences between the generated code and the ad-hoc code.

4.1   Performance Analysis in the Android Programming Models

To analyse the performance obtained with the different Android programming
models, we compare the execution times obtained with each problem proposed.
The different characteristics of each problem allow us to analyse the behaviour
of the programming models in different situations.

Table 1. Execution times for the Renderscript benchmark problems (AOSP) and general convolve implementation

Implementation	Execution times (ms)							
	GrayScale	Levels	Convolve		General Convolve			
			3x3	5x5	3x3	5x5	7x7	9x9
Java	269	585	2157	4928	2167	4942	9166	15890
Native	104	238	696	1756	679	1352	2491	4013
Renderscript	62	65	91	188	132	195	316	447

Table 1 shows the execution times in milliseconds for the Renderscript benchmark problems (AOSP) and for the General Convolve implementations. The
Ad-hoc Java implementation provides an overview of each problem's granularity. We use the term granularity as the execution time spend by each problem to
compute an image of a particular size. We can see how the GrayScale problem
has the finest granularity. For the convolve problems the granularity increases
when the convolve window size is higher. The Renderscript implementation gets
the best results for all problems.

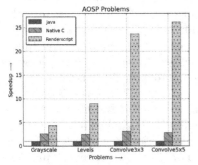
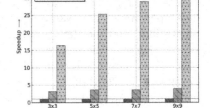

(a) Speedup for AOSP problems   (b) Speedup for General Convolve problem

Fig. 3. Speedup obtained with different Android programming models

Figure 3 shows clearly the differences among the various Android programming models. The speedup showed is relative to the ad-hoc Java versions. The

Ad-hoc Native implementations improve the Ad-hoc Java versions in all cases, showing and speedup that is constant for all problems. In the Renderscript executions, the computational load of the instances solved involves an important impact in the performance, problems with more computational load get a better speedup. When the granularity of the problems increases, the Renderscript implementations obtain better results.

4.2 Performance Analysis on CPU and CPU+GPU Executions

To show the performance obtained with the generated code in different situations. We executed the proposed testing problems under different CPU and GPU configurations. The efficiency of the generated code is analysed.

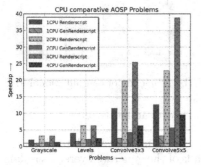

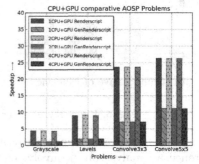

(a) CPU analysis for AOSP problems   (b) CPU+GPU analysis for AOSP problems

Fig. 4. Speedup for the Renderscript codes varying number of CPUs and CPUs+GPU

Figure 4(a) shows the speedup obtained by the ad-hoc and generated Renderscript implementations. Again, the speedup showed is relative to the ad-hoc Java version. We compared the performance according to the number of CPUs used. It can be observed that, for coarse granularity problems the speedup increases when the number of CPUs increases. When the granularity is smaller (Grayscale and levels), the results obtained with 4 CPUs do not improve results with 2 CPUs. For the general convolve implementations similar results were obtained. Regarding to the comparative between ad-hoc and generated Renderscript implementations, as expected, the ad-hoc versions obtain the best results in all cases. These are optimized versions that use vector operations. Currently, Paralldroid does not obtain this level of optimization but it provides a positive speedup at a low development effort.

The speedup obtained with the GPU executions are showed in Figure 4(b), these speedups are also relative to the ad-hoc Java versions. We analysed the results obtained for the different CPU configurations when the GPU execution is enabled. In this case we do not found differences when we vary the number of CPUs. That makes us to think that the problems are executed only in the GPU. Again, the ad-hoc implementations get the best speedups. Comparing the results obtained with (Figure 4(a)) and without GPU (Figure 4(b)). The ad-hoc implementations get better results using the GPU when the problems have a fine granularity. When the granularity increases the best option is to use the 4 CPUs disabling the GPU. For generated implementations the best results are obtained using the GPU in all case.

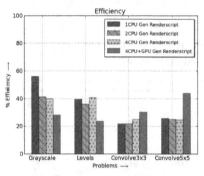 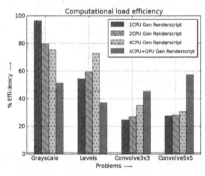

(a) Comparative of Efficiency   (b) Efficiency of computational load

Fig. 5. Efficiency of generated code over ad-hoc code

Ad-hoc and generated Renderscript implementations have a high performance difference, an analysis on the involved overheads of the generated versions is done in Figure 5. It shows the efficiency obtained by the generated codes relative to the ad-hoc Renderscript corresponding versions. The generated versions show an important loss of performance compared with the ad-hoc implementations (Figure 5(a)) due to the following reasons:

- The optimizations of the generated code: The ad-hoc codes are optimized and use vector operations. Currently the generated codes do not use any vector operations. This mainly affect to the coarse granularity problems.
- The overhead on transformed types: For the set of problems considered, the ad-hoc versions used a bitmap object that represents the image. Currently, the generated versions do not manage object types and this bitmap object must be transformed into an array of pixels. This mainly affects to the finest granularity problems.

According to it. Figure 5(b) shows the efficiency obtained if we do not consider the time spent transforming types. As expected, the problems with less computational load improve their efficiency. When the computational load increase, the optimization of the code has a higher impact in the performance.

5   Conclusion

Paralldroid is a framework that simplifies the automatic generation of Native C or Renderscript on Android devices. The user annotates the sequential Java classes definition and Paralldroid automatically transforms these definitions in a Native C or Renderscript implementation. The new Paralldroid specification simplifies the definition of annotations and is more easy to understand for the Java programmers. The validation tests performed on five different problems prove that the results are quite promising. The code generated by Paralldroid can be executed over the CPU or GPU and the implementation details are hidden to the developer. The results show that the GPU executions equal and in some case improve the results obtained by the parallel CPU executions. In the Ad-hoc versions the parallel CPU executions improve in some case the results achieved with the GPU. However, the ad-hoc implementations achieved better results that the generated implementations in all cases. Nevertheless, there is still opportunity for future optimization in terms of the memory transfer among the different devices in the use of vector operations.

Acknowledgment. This work has been supported by the EC (FEDER) and the Spanish MEC with the I+D+I contract number: TIN2011-24598.

References

1. Reid, A.D., Flautner, K., Grimley-Evans, E., Lin, Y.: SoC-C: efficient programming abstractions for heterogeneous multicore systems on chip. In: Altman, E.R. (ed.) Proceedings of the 2008 International Conference on Compilers, Architecture, and Synthesis for Embedded Systems, CASES 2008, pp. 95–104. ACM, Atlanta (2008)
2. Qian, X., Zhu, G., Li, X.-F.: Comparison and analysis of the three programming models in google android. In: First Asia-Pacific Programming Languages and Compilers Workshop (APPLC) (June 2012)
3. Valentin, C., Christian, S., Pierre, K., François, K.P., Jean-François, R.: Parallel object programming with java, http://gridgroup.hefr.ch/popj/doku.php
4. Viry, P.: Ateji px for java-parallel programming made simple. Ateji White Paper (2010)
5. Membarth, R., Reiche, O., Hannig, F., Teich, J.: Code generation for embedded heterogeneous architectures on android. In: DATE, pp. 1–6 (2014)
6. Acosta, A., Almeida, F.: Towards an unified heterogeneous development model in android. In: Eleventh International Workshop HeteroPar 2013: Algorithms, Models and Tools for Parallel Computing on Heterogeneous Platforms (2013)
7. Acosta, A., Almeida, F.: Performance analysis of paralldroid generated programs. In: 2014 22nd Euromicro International Conference on Parallel, Distributed, and Network-Based Processing, pp. 60–67 (2014)
8. OpenMP: The OpenMP API specification for parallel programming, http://openmp.org/wp/openmp-specifications/
9. Lewis, J., Loftus, W.: Java Software Solutions: Foundations of Program Design, 6th edn. Addison-Wesley Publishing Company, USA (2008)
10. Oracle: Java annotations specification, http://docs.oracle.com/javase/1.5.0/ docs/guide/language/annotations.html
11. AOSP: Android Open Source Project, http://source.android.com/

Accurate Blind Predictions of OpenFOAM Energy Consumption Using the LBM Prediction Model

Davide Morelli and Antonio Cisternino

Computer Science Department, University of Pisa
Largo Bruno Pontecorvo 3, 56127, Pisa, Italy
davide.morelli@unipi.it,
cisterni@di.unipi.it

Abstract. The ability to predict the energy consumption of an HPC task, varying the number of assigned nodes, can lead to the ability to assign the correct number of nodes to tasks, saving large amount of energy.

In this paper we present LBM, a model capable of predicting the resource usage (applicable to different resources, such as completion time and energy consumption) of programs, following a black box approach, where only passive measures of the running program are used to build the prediction model, without requiring its source code, or static analysis of the binary. LBM builds the predicting model using other programs as benchmarks. We tested LBM predicting the energy consumption of *pitzDaily*, a case of the OpenFOAM CFD suite, using a very low number of benchmarks (3), obtaining extremely precise predictions.

1 Introduction

The efficiency of the HPC scheduler can benefit in many ways from the ability to predict the amount of resources a job will require to complete. In HPC completion time has traditionally been the most important resource to save, but in the last years we are witnessing a rising interest in reducing energy consumption.

Because of communication time, the number of nodes that will minimize the completion time is not necessarily the highest, i.e. we will have a minimum. When we try to minimize energy consumption we could have a different minimum than the one found when minimizing completion time. A scheduler should be able to predict the correct number of nodes that will minimize the consumption of the resource of interest, usually it will have a limited number of measures at its disposal (as the number of compute nodes varies).

We propose a linear model that leverages on measures taken on a few benchmarks running on a variable number of nodes to predict the resource consumption of a target program, as the number of compute nodes changes.

As shown in [7,11,15,14] a resource can be used to predict other resources (i.e. performance counters can be used to predict energy consumption). Our effort is

L. Lopes et al. (Eds.): Euro-Par 2014 Workshops, Part II, LNCS 8806, pp. 400–411, 2014.

to unify existing approaches dedicated to different resources (in particular, but not limiting to, completion time and energy), creating a more abstract model that can to characterize programs behavior in a more general sense, predicting different resources from the ones used to build a prediction model. Energy characterization and prediction could then take advantage of the vast literature in performance prediction of software.

Prediction models usually require instrumentation of the system, and involve simulation and other complex computationally intensive tasks [4,8]. Resource usage prediction should be performed without knowledge of the program's source code, as in most of the real world scenarios source code is not known. The resource usage prediction model should be able to rely only on data that can be measured running the programs, implementing a *blind* approach. Characterization and prediction should be performed relying only on the informations about running programs that are usually available to the operative system, without the need of additional hardware or manipulations of the binary. For this reason we decided to test our linear prediction model only using information easily available in an HPC cluster (completion time and instant power through the PDU).

The resource prediction model should also be as abstract as possible, avoiding relying on a specific micro architecture or resource kind (as in [10]), as the model would become obsolete before it could become widely used. For a program's descriptive and predictive model to be useful, it should be portable on different hardware from the one where the model was built.

The models that achieve a low prediction error are very narrow, focusing on a particular micro architecture [18,6,17,13], resource (i.e. completion time, energy consumption), even programming language [18,5], they also usually model execution down to the single instruction level of detail [16,13], hiding the interaction between instructions that changes from architecture to architecture, making it difficult to abstract the results to a different architecture.

We developed a simple linear model that leverages on resource usage measures to predict the usage of other resources, the model was designed to be as simple as possible, capable of predicting and describing resource consumption of both hardware and software, not focusing on particular architectures or resources. The model is black-box, it does not require the source code of the program being measured. Because it relies on measures of benchmarks (non linear regressors) it can capture non linear phenomena even if based on linear regression.

We validated our model predicting the energy consumed by a cases of the OpenFOAM suite, using a very limited set of measures of other 3 cases used as benchmarks, running on 1, 2 or 3 compute nodes (24, 48 or 72 processors).

2   The LBM Model

Benchmarking is currently more an art than a science where the performance of a system S is measured against a particular test T in order to characterize the performance of S with respect to T. If T captures a particular feature of a program P we may infer that if T performs well on S then P will follow the same pattern. Moreover, by varying either S or T it is possible to compare different systems against a benchmark or different benchmark against a given system. The quality of a benchmark T is given by the implicit power of capturing a predictive aspect, though what prediction means is often hinted without formal specification.

As witnessed by [12], benchmarking is largely driven by industry and practitioners rather than a well defined theory, this is due to the fact that it is difficult to relate a particular program P with a particular test T.

We propose LBM (Linear Benchmarking Model), a model designed to describe the relation between a set of benchmarks and a program.

LBM is a generalization of [18,7,17,15], designed to be resource agnostic, it can be used to characterize both hardware and software as shown in [9], and can predict the completion time as well as the energy consumption, the allocated memory, the number of cache misses, etc. The contribution of LBM lies in its capability of dealing with measures of different resources, without requiring access to source code or binary instrumentation nor simulation. LBM is also a simple and straightforward model, that allows intuitive interpretations of the surrogate built with it, using linear combinations of predictors.

Resource consumption of programs is known to be a non linear phenomenon, therefore using linear regression could seem a wrong approach. LBM uses other programs as regressors (non linear), hence combining them linearly we still will be able to describe the non linear behavior of the target program.

2.1 Definitions

In this section we provide the definition for terms used in the rest of the paper for presenting the case study.

Definition 1 (program). *A program is a particular and defined sequence of instructions.*

The same *program* can be run on different micro architectures, even if will generate different low level sequence of processor instructions, it will still be considered the same *program*. When called to process different input sizes, because the sequence of high level instructions will considerably change, it will be considered a different program. The *target program* is the program whose resource consumption we are interested in predicting.

Definition 2 (computational environment). *A computational environment is any computational system that can execute programs.*

Examples of *computational environments* are embedded computers, smart phones, PCs with different micro-architectures, clusters. We consider part of the *computational environment* the hardware as well as the operative system and all the software running on the machine at the same time as the *program* being measured.

Definition 3 (resource). *A resource is a finite asset of the computational environment that is used by programs to run.*

The energy used by a computer, or the time used to complete a *program* are examples of *resources*. The same resource on different *computational environments* are considered different *resources*: e.g. completion time on computer A and completion time on computer B are different *resources*.

Not every *resource* can be used in our model, it needs to provide measures that have the following properties: non negativity ($\forall x \; \mu(x) \geq 0$), null empty set ($\mu(\varnothing) = 0$) and countable additivity ($\mu(\cup x_i) = \sum \mu(x_i)$).

Examples of valid resources are processor time, completion time, memory allocations, energy. Examples of invalid resources are % processor time (it may decrease), active memory (memory could be deallocated), power (instant power could decrease). Usually invalid resources can be made valid combining them with time.

An interesting example is power that is not a valid *resource*. Let's consider a program X that is composed of 2 *programs* A and B executed sequentially: $X = \{A; B\}$

if P_a the average power during the execution of A is higher than P_b the average power during the execution of B, then P_x the average power during the execution of X will be $P_b \leq P_x \leq P_a$. This violates the required countable additivity property (the power used by a part of a *program* is higher than the power used by the whole *program*). On the other hand, because both average power and completion time are always positive quantities, countable additivity holds for energy: $E_x = E_a + E_b = P_a T_a + P_b T_b$, $E_x \geq E_a$, $E_x \geq E_b$ (where T_a and T_b are completion times for A and B).

Definition 4 (target resource). *The target resource is the resource that we want to predict for the target program.*

Definition 5 (target program). *The target program is the program that we want to model in terms of the benchmarks, whose target resource we are interested in predicting.*

Definition 6 (measure). *A measure is a positive real number that describes the quantity of resource used by a certain program to run on a certain computational environment.*

A *measure* always refers to both a *program* and a *resource* (therefore a *computational environment*), i.e. a *measure* quantifies the usage of a particular resource on a particular *computational environment* by a *program*.

Definition 7 (target measure). *The target measure is the measure of the target resource and the target program that we want to predict.*

Definition 8 (computational pattern). *A computational pattern is an ideal program the exhibits a peculiar resource consumption.*

Examples of *computational patterns* are: a *program* made in its entirety by floating point operations; or a *program* that triggers a cache miss at every instruction. *Computational patterns* are orthogonal to each other. *Computational patterns* are usually ideal *programs*, real *programs* can not consist only of a single *computational pattern*. At most synthetic *benchmarks* can approximate particular *computational patterns*. Some *computational pattern* could be reasonably be guessed (in some case even designed), but in general they are unknown, and may arise when new micro-architectures are created: a novel micro-architecture could expose a peculiar resource usage when used by a certain sequence of instructions.

The model assumes that all *programs* can ideally be decomposed in sequences of *computational patterns*. The *computational patterns* form a basis of the resource consumption space (because they are orthogonal with respect to resource consumption). Any program, including both the *benchmark* and the *target program*, can be written as a linear combination of the *computational patterns*. If every *computational pattern* used by the *target program* is contained at least in one of the *benchmarks*, and if the *benchmarks* are not linearly dependent, we can operate a change of basis and express the *target program* as a linear combination of the *benchmarks*. If the *target program* contains *computational patterns* that are not contained in any *benchmark*, then the change of basis will lose information.

Definition 9 (benchmark). *A benchmark is a program used to predict the measure of the target resource and the target program.*

Definition 10 (surrogate). *A surrogate is a linear combination of benchmarks used as a model to predict the resource consumption of the target program.*

The surrogate does not depend on the *target resource* or *computational environment*.

Definition 11 (solver). *A solver is an algorithm that, given a set of measures of the benchmarks and the target program, creates a surrogate for it.*

In this work we use linear regression as the solver.

2.2   Model Definition

Given a set of benchmarks and resources **A**, LBM defines the relation between a program p_t and **A**. Every benchmark is characterized by a set of measurements, each relating with one of the model's resources. A combination of benchmarks and resources defines an LBM model.

More precisely measures, resources, benchmarks, target program, target resource and target measure are organized as follows:

– **A** is a matrix that contains the measures of the resources used by the benchmarks, this matrix does not contain the target resource. Each row of **A** contains the measures relative to a resource, each column contains the measures relative to a benchmark.

- **b** is a vector that contains the measures of the resources used by the target program. This vector contains measures relative to the same resources used to build **A**: b_i is the measure of the target program usage of the same resource measured by the values contained in the ith row **A**.
- **c** is the vector that contains measures of the resource that we want to predict used by the benchmarks. This vector contains measures relative to the same benchmarks used to build **A**: c_i is the measure of the target resource used by the benchmark whose values are contained in the ith column of **A**.
- **x** is the surrogate of the target program with respect to the benchmarks.
- μ_t is the target measure.

A, **b**, **c**, **x** and μ_t are linked by the following equations:

$$\mathbf{Ax} = \mathbf{b} \tag{1}$$

$$\mathbf{cx} = \mu_t \tag{2}$$

LBM models can be used to predict target resources: given a set of measures of resources for a set of benchmarks and a target program p_t, we can express p_t as a linear combination of the benchmarks: using equation 1 we can find x. We can add a resource (called target resource) for which we have measures for the benchmarks but not for the target program, LBM can predict the measure of the target resource for the target program (called target measure), using equation 2.

Consider the following example: we have 3 different subset of nodes of a uniform cluster S_1, S_2 and S_3, we have measured the energy consumption of a CPU bound program b_1 and a communication bound program b_2 on all the subsets, we have also measured a program p_t on S_1 and S_2, and we want to predict the energy consumption of p_t on S_3. Energy consumption on S_1, S_2 and S_3 are resources, with S_3 being the target resource; p_t is the target program, the measure of the energy consumption of p_t on S_3 is the target measure. The measures (μ) of b_1 and b_2 on S_1 and S_2 will form A:

$$\mathbf{A} = \begin{pmatrix} \mu(b_1, S_1) & \mu(b_2, S_1) \\ \mu(b_1, S_2) & \mu(b_2, S_2) \end{pmatrix}$$

The measures we have for the target program p_t will form vector **b**, with the same resources and in the same order as in **A**:

$$\mathbf{b} = \begin{pmatrix} \mu(p, S_1) & \mu(p, S_2) \end{pmatrix}$$

The measures for the target resource for the benchmarks (b_1 and b_2) will form vector **c**, with the same programs and in the same order as in **A**:

$$\mathbf{c} = \begin{pmatrix} \mu(b_1, S_3) & \mu(b_2, S_3) \end{pmatrix}$$

μ_t is the target measure: the energy consumption of the target program p_t on S_3.

The surrogate x not only is a tool to predict the target measure μ_t, also provides information about the target program, with respect of the benchmarks. In this example it will estimate the composition of the target program p_t in terms of *CPU bound* vs *communication bound*.

2.3   Limits of LBM

LBM is an extremely generic model that can be applied to different hardware architectures and different types of programs, without instrumentation or source code access.

We believe that LBM can handle measures coming from heterogeneous micro-architectures, actually a desirable scenario because the same program running on different architectures will contain different CPU level instructions, but it will still be composed of the same *computational patterns* (therefore the surrogate does not change when we change *computational environment*), and the different low level behavior will allow a more precise characterization of the surrogate. However the experimental setting presented in this paper is limited to a single architecture (all the compute nodes are uniform), therefore we can not claim yet that the model can successfully operate with heterogeneous architectures.

LBM treats the same program running on different input sizes as different programs. This assumption simplifies the formulation of the model. We have an extension of the model that handles multiple input sizes for the same program as the same program, but for sake of brevity we do not introduce it in this paper.

The *benchmarks* constitute the knowledge base that the *solver* has when it creates the *surrogate*, if the *benchmarks* do not contain most of the *computational patterns* contained in the *target program*, the *surrogate* will not be able to capture the important factors that model the behavior of the *target program*, e.g. if our *target program* is memory bound, and no *benchmark* makes large use of memory, it's very unlikely that linear regression will be able to create a good fit, and the predictions made with LBM will have a large error. To be able to successfully express the *target program* as a linear combination of the *benchmarks*, **b** needs to be in the column span of **A**. To avoid numeric errors in the linear regression, or even **A** not being full rank, the *benchmarks* should not have a similar behavior, i.e. columns of **A** should have low correlation. The *benchmarks* set should therefore be variegate, containing several different algorithms, that exhibit very different behavior.

3   Predicting OpenFOAM Energy Consumption and Completion Time

OpenFOAM is an open source Computational Fluid Dynamics (CFD) and structural analysis tool, widely used in HPC clusters.

To demonstrate the potential of our approach we limited the resources to completion time and energy (we could have used performance resources) and a limited number of benchmarks as predictors.

We tested our model measuring the completion time and energy consumption of 4 cases of the tutorials included in the OpenFOAM CFD suite, running on an enclosure in the IT Center data center at the University of Pisa, with 4 compute nodes, each node equipped with 12 Intel(R) Xeon(R) X5670 CPUs (2.93GHz), hyper threading enabled. We prepared a simple ammeter using a cheap Phidgets [3] component, one compute node was running Windows HPC server 2008 with the measurement framework we wrote [1] to control the experiment and measure the energy consumed by the enclosure. The remaining 3 compute nodes were installed with CentOS, Kernel 2.6.32, we installed OpenFOAM from the RHEL RPM package available on [2]. We modified 4 of the tutorials as follows:

1. case *cavity* with the *icoFoam* solver, augmenting the mesh density 900 times, 100 iterations
2. case *pitzDaily* with the *adjointShapeOptimizationFoam* solver, augmenting the mesh density 400 times, 10 iterations
3. case *squareBump* with the *shallowWaterFoam* solver, augmenting the mesh density 6400 times, 90 iterations
4. case *mixerVesselAMI2D* with the *pimpleDyMFoam* solver, augmenting the mesh density 1000 times, 10 iterations

We measured the completion time (elapsed time from the start of the job to its completion on all nodes) and energy consumed (as the product of average instant power, as measured by the ammeter at PDU level, and completion time) by the 4 cases running on 1 (24 cores), 2 (48 cores) and 3 nodes (72 cores).

To test the prediction accuracy of LBM we measured *cavity*, *mixerVesselAMI2D*, *squareBump* on 1, 2 and 3 nodes; then we measured *pitzDaily* on running on 1 and on 3 nodes and tried to predict its energy consumption running on 2 nodes. We did the following test:

1. matrix **A** is made by the measures of the completion time and energy consumption of programs *cavity*, *mixerVesselAMI2D*, and *squareBump* running on 24 and 72 cores
2. vector **c** is made by the measures of the energy consumption of programs *cavity*, *mixerVesselAMI2D*, and *squareBump* running on 48 cores
3. vector **b** is made by the measures of the completion time and the energy consumption of *pitzDaily* running on 24 and 72 cores
4. our target measure is the energy consumption of *pitzDaily* on 48 cores

The motivation to try to predict the energetic performance of a case with an intermediate number of cores is that the number of cores that will minimize the energy consumption is not likely to be an extreme value, as can be seen in table 1: *cavity* and *squareBump* have a minimum for the intermediate number of cores, *pitzDaily* has the minimum for the lower number of cores.

3.1   Prediction Results

The measures taken to prepare the prediction are reported in table 1, we measured the cases used as benchmarks running on 24, 48 and 72 cores, and measured the target program on 24 and 72 cores (and tried to predict the performance for 48 cores). We also measured each case running in serial.

Table 1. Measures taken to prepare the prediction

Case	Cores	Energy consumed	Completion time	Average Power
cavity	24	269919.72J	706.42s	382.09W
cavity	48	251975.76J	418.78s	601.68W
cavity	72	660199.18J	773.38s	853.64W
mixerVesselAMI2D	24	157951.17J	525.41s	300.61W
mixerVesselAMI2D	48	238653.37J	530.57s	449.80W
mixerVesselAMI2D	72	520949.26J	695.95s	748.54W
squareBump	24	214286.62J	614.60s	348.65W
squareBump	48	190538.20J	375.23s	507.78W
squareBump	72	203057.01J	308.66s	657.86W
pitzDaily	24	201251.53J	661.82s	304.08W
pitzDaily	72	530366.40J	818.13s	648.25W

To prepare the prediction we build **A**, **b**, **c** and **c** using completion time and energy consumption (power is not a valid resource):

$$\mathbf{A} = \begin{pmatrix} 269919.72 & 157951.17 & 214286.62 \\ 660199.18 & 520949.26 & 203057.01 \\ 706.42 & 525.41 & 614.60 \\ 773.38 & 695.95 & 308.66 \end{pmatrix}$$

$$\mathbf{c} = \begin{pmatrix} 251975.76 & 238653.37 & 190538.20 \end{pmatrix}$$

$$\mathbf{b} = \begin{pmatrix} 201251.53 \\ 530366.40 \\ 661.82 \\ 818.13 \end{pmatrix}$$

LBM finds the following surrogate for *pitzDaily*:

$$\mathbf{x} = \begin{pmatrix} -0.40 \\ 1.35 \\ 0.45 \end{pmatrix}$$

The surrogate **x** tells us that, given the information we had when the model was built, *pitzDaily* can be expressed as linear combination of *cavity*, *mixerVesselAMI2D* and *squareBump*, where *mixerVesselAMI2D* is dominant with respect to the other programs.

The prediction of the energy consumption of *pitzDaily* on 48 cores is calculated multiplying **c** by **x** which gives 307586.91J. The measured energy consumption of *pitzDaily* on 48 cores is actually 308195.18J, LBM predicted the energy consumption of the target program running on 48 cores with a -0.19% error.

Similarly we predicted the completion time (setting completion time as our target resource when creating **c**): LBM predicted 719.73s, the actual value is 675.70s, with a -6.51% prediction error.

The prediction provided by LBM is more accurate than the obvious interpolation that can be calculated by the energy consumption on 24 and 72 nodes (365808J); similarly, the prediction regarding completion time provided by LBM is better than the simple interpolation (739,5s), proving that LBM was able to extract useful information from the *benchmarks*.

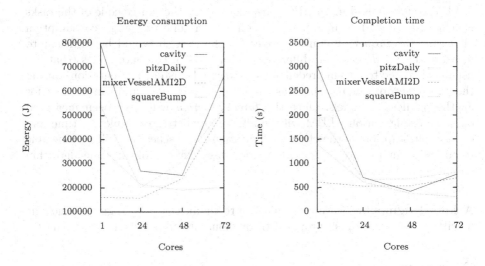

Fig. 1. Resource consumption of programs, changing degree of parallelism

Figure 1 shows the measures of all the experiments used in this paper. We can see how different programs (with certain input) exhibit different behavior as the degree of parallelism grows, now always the degree of parallelism that optimizes the completion time also optimizes the energy consumption, i.e. *squareBump* consumes the less energy with 48 cores, but the completion time is the lowest with 72 cores. Also a small increase in completion time can lead to a considerable increase in energy consumption, i.e. *cavity*, *pitzDaily* and *mixerVesselAMI2D*. LBM can be useful to estimate the optimal degree of parallelism that will minimize the usage of the resource we want to save.

4 Conclusions

This paper presents LBM, a model that can predict resources (the resource consumption of programs) using a black box approach, using a different set of resources (not necessarily of the same kind of the one being predicted) and a set of benchmarks (programs) used to build a surrogate of the target program as a linear combination of benchmarks. This model can be applied to different kind of resources, including energy consumption, completion time, memory, etc.

To the best of our knowledge there is no other black box predictive model achieves the same precision, allowing the usage of measures of different resources.

We tested the model using 4 cases from the OpenFOAM suite, predicting the completion time and energy consumption of one program, using the other 3 as predictors, with a low error. LBM can also be used to characterize the behavior of a program, only using measures of the resources, and it is computationally inexpensive (once the surrogate has been built).

LBM could be used in an HPC scheduler (where the source code of the tasks is seldom available) to minimize the completion time or energy consumption allocating the proper amount of nodes for the task. It would be sufficient to measure the *benchmarks* on different possible sets of compute nodes (that are usually allocated to jobs in predefined sets to avoid cluster fragmentation) during the cluster setup, this measure has to be taken only once, and can be used for all the prediction models. Once the *target program* will have been measured on some configurations, LBM will be able to predict the completion time and energy consumption on the other configurations. The scheduler will then be able to minimize the resource consumption for subsequent run of the same algorithm (running on similar inputs).

Acknowledgments. Authors would like to thank Distretto Ligure Tecnologie Marittime for the support provided throughout the preparation of this paper.

References

1. Energon - a framework for measurement of energy consumption of software, https://github.com/vslab/Energon
2. The OpenFOAM foundation, http://www.openfoam.org
3. Phidgets - Products for USB Sensing and Control
4. Annavaram, M., Rakvic, R., Polito, M., Bouguet, J.-Y., Hankins, R.A., Davies, B.: The fuzzy correlation between code and performance predictability. In: Proceedings of the 37th Annual IEEE/ACM International Symposium on Microarchitecture, pp. 93–104. IEEE Computer Society (2004)
5. Arnold, M., Hind, M., Ryder, B.G.: Online feedback-directed optimization of java. In: Proceedings of the 17th ACM SIGPLAN Conference on Object-oriented Programming, Systems, Languages, and Applications, OOPSLA 2002, pp. 111–129. ACM, New York (2002)
6. Brooks, D., Tiwari, V., Martonosi, M.: Wattch: a framework for architectural-level power analysis and optimizations. In: Proceedings of the 27th Annual International Symposium on Computer Architecture, ISCA 2000, pp. 83–94. ACM, New York (2000)

7. Hoste, K., Phansalkar, A., Eeckhout, L., Georges, A., John, L.K., Bosschere, K.D.: Performance prediction based on inherent program similarity. In: Proceedings of the 15th International Conference on Parallel Architectures and Compilation Techniques, PACT 2006, pp. 114–122. ACM, New York (2006)

8. Lau, J., Sampson, J., Perelman, E., Hamerly, G., Calder The, B.: strong correlation between code signatures and performance. In: IEEE International Symposium on Performance Analysis of Systems and Software, ISPASS 2005, pp. 236–247. IEEE (2005)

9. Morelli, D., Cisternino, A.: A compositional model to characterize software and hardware from their resource usage. In: Jones, A.V. (ed.) 2012 Imperial College Computing Student Workshop. OpenAccess Series in Informatics (OASIcs), vol. 28, pp. 95–101. Schloss Dagstuhl Leibniz-Zentrum fuer Informatik, Dagstuhl (2012)

10. Neugebauer, R., Mcauley, D.: Energy is just another resource: energy accounting and energy pricing in the nemesis OS. In: Proceedings of the Eighth Workshop on Hot Topics in Operating Systems, pp. 67–72 (May 2001)

11. Phansalkar, A., Joshi, A., Eeckhout, L., John, L.K.: Measuring program similarity: Experiments with SPEC CPU benchmark suites. In: Proceedings of the IEEE International Symposium on Performance Analysis of Systems and Software, pp. 10–20. IEEE Computer Society, Washington, DC (2005)

12. Rivoire, S.M.: Models and metrics for energy-efficient computer systems. PhD thesis, Stanford University, Stanford, CA, USA, AAI3313649 (2008)

13. Russell, J.T., Jacome, M.F.: Software power estimation and optimization for high performance, 32-bit embedded processors. In: Proceedings of the International Conference on Computer Design: VLSI in Computers and Processors, ICCD 1998, pp. 328–333 (October 1998)

14. Sankaran, S., Sridhar, R.: Energy modeling for mobile devices using performance counters. In: 2013 IEEE 56th International Midwest Symposium on Circuits and Systems (MWSCAS), pp. 441–444 (August 2013)

15. Sharkawi, S., DeSota, D., Panda, R., Indukuru, R., Stevens, S., Taylor, V.: Xingfu Wu. Performance projection of HPC applications using SPEC CFP2006 benchmarks. In: IEEE International Symposium on Parallel Distributed Processing, IPDPS 2009, pp. 1–12 (2009)

16. Sinha, A., Chandrakasan, A.P.: JouleTrack - a web based tool for software energy profiling. In: Design Automation Conference, pp. 220–225 (2001)

17. Snavely, A., Wolter, N., Carrington, L.: Modeling application performance by convolving machine signatures with application profiles. In: 2001 IEEE International Workshop on Workload Characterization, WWC-4, pp. 149–156 (2001)

18. Tiwari, V., Malik, S., Wolfe, A.: Power analysis of embedded software: a first step towards software power minimization. In: Proceedings of the 1994 IEEE/ACM International Conference on Computer-Aided Design, ICCAD 1994, pp. 384–390. IEEE Computer Society Press, Los Alamitos (1994)

High-Level Topology-Oblivious Optimization of MPI Broadcast Algorithms on Extreme-Scale Platforms

Khalid Hasanov[1], Jean-Noël Quintin[2], and Alexey Lastovetsky[1]

[1] University College Dublin
Belfield, Dublin 4, Ireland
khalid.hasanov@ucdconnecte.ie,
Alexey.Lastovetsky@ucd.ie
[2] Extreme Computing R&D, Bull SAS,
Paris, France
jean-noel.quintin@bull.net

Abstract. There has been a significant research in collective communication operations, in particular in MPI broadcast, on distributed memory platforms. Most of the research works are done to optimize the collective operations for particular architectures by taking into account either their topology or platform parameters. In this work we propose a very simple and at the same time general approach to optimize legacy MPI broadcast algorithms, which are widely used in MPICH and OpenMPI. Theoretical analysis and experimental results on IBM BlueGene/P and a cluster of Grid'5000 platform are presented.

Keywords: MPI, Broadcast, BlueGene, Grid'5000, Extreme-Scale, Communication, Hierarchy.

1 Introduction

Collective communication operations in the Message Passing Interface (MPI) [1] are very important building blocks for many scientific applications. In particular, MPI broadcast is used in a variety of algorithms and applications such as parallel matrix-matrix multiplication, LU factorization and so on. During a broadcast the root process sends a message to all other processes in the specified group of processes. The implementations of the broadcast operation in MPICH [2] and OpenMPI [3] are typically based on linear, binary, binomial and pipelined algorithms [5]. The linear algorithms are not good for a large number of processes, the binary and binomial algorithms are not efficient for large data sizes. On the other hand, pipelined algorithms try to be efficient for large numbers of processes and data sizes. Other widely used broadcast algorithms are scatter-ring-allgather and scatter-recursive-doubling-allgather [6], which have been implemented in MPICH.

In addition, there has been a significant research in optimizing MPI broadcast for some specific platforms. The research work in [9] present efficient implementations of MPI broadcast with native Infiniband multicast. The Cheetah framework

L. Lopes et al. (Eds.): Euro-Par 2014 Workshops, Part II, LNCS 8806, pp. 412–424, 2014.

offers a hierarchical collective communication framework that takes advantage of hardware-specific data-access mechanisms [10]. IBM BlueGene comes with its own platform specific optimizations of MPI collectives [12]. The research work in [11] gives a comprehensive overview of optimization techniques for collectives on heterogeneous HPC platforms using broadcast as a use case.

Theoretically optimal MPI broadcast algorithms have been an active research subject as well. One of the early results in this area is the spanning binomial tree algorithm proposed by Jonson and Ho [7]. Later, the research work in [8] introduced another theoretically optimal broadcast algorithm based on fractional trees. The work in [13] is similar to the algorithm of Jonson and Ho when the number of processes is a power of two and extends it to an arbitrary number of processes.

The number of processors in HPC systems has increased by three orders of magnitude over the past two decades. This in turn raises the cost of coordination and interaction of processes, namely, the communication cost in traditional message-passing data-parallel applications. Meanwhile, a lot of research in optimization of the communication cost of scientific algorithms and applications is going on. Very often such research works focus on specific platforms and propose a redesign of the existing scientific algorithms suitable for these platforms. In contrast to this approach, the goal of our work, which is inspired by our previous study of parallel matrix multiplication on large-scale distributed memory platforms [14], is to provide a simple and general technique to optimize the legacy scientific applications without redesigning them. In this paper, this idea is applied to the MPI broadcast operation as an initial step to achieve this goal.

The contributions of this work are as follows:

- A simple and general hierarchical technique to optimize the MPI broadcast operation, which can be applied to any legacy applications using MPI broadcast with a marginal code modification.
- Theoretical and experimental study of the hierarchical modifications of eight existing broadcast algorithms in MPICH and OpenMPI.

2   Preliminaries and Previous Work

In the rest of this paper the amount of data to be broadcast and the number of MPI processes will be denoted by m and p respectively. It is assumed that the network is fully connected, bidirectional and homogeneous. A process can simultaneously send and receive a message in $\alpha + m \times \beta$ time. Here α is the startup cost or latency, while β is the reciprocal bandwidth.

2.1   Previous Work

This section briefly summarizes the theoretical analysis of the performance of all the general-purpose MPI broadcast algorithms implemented in MPICH and OpenMPI. Namely, we recall the theoretical costs of linear, chain, pipelined, binary, split-binary, scatter-ring-allgather, scatter-recursive-doubling-allgather and binomial tree broadcast algorithms. The first five and the binomial tree algorithm are implemented in OpenMPI and the last three algorithms are implemented in MPICH. Because of space limitation derivations of these algorithms are not provided in this work but can be found in [15].

- Flat tree broadcast algorithm.
  This is the simplest MPI broadcast algorithm, in which the root node sends the same message to all the nodes participating in the broadcast operation. This algorithm does not scale well for large communicators. By using the simple linear communication model its cost can be derived as follows:

$$(p - 1) \times (\alpha + m \times \beta) \ . \tag{1}$$

- Linear tree broadcast algorithm.
  In this algorithm each node sends or receives at most one message. Since the root does not receive the message it is called chain algorithm sometimes. Theoretically its cost is the same as the flat tree algorithm:

$$(p - 1) \times (\alpha + m \times \beta) \ . \tag{2}$$

- Pipelined linear tree broadcast algorithm.
  By splitting and pipelining the message in the linear tree algorithm its performance can be improved. In this case each process can start sending a part of the message after it received the first part of the message.

$$(X + p - 2) \times \left(\alpha + \frac{m}{X} \times \beta\right) \ . \tag{3}$$

Here it is assumed that a broadcast message of size m is split into X segments and in one step of the algorithm a segment of size $\frac{m}{X}$ is broadcast among p processes.
- Binary and binomial tree broadcast algorithms.

$$\log_2 (p) \times (\alpha + m \times \beta) \ . \tag{4}$$

Binary and binomial tree broadcast algorithms theoretically have the same cost. However, in practice, the binomial tree algorithm is more balanced than a binary tree broadcast.
- Scatter-ring-allgather broadcast algorithm.

$$(\log_2 (p) + p - 1) \times \alpha + 2\frac{p - 1}{p} \times m \times \beta \ . \tag{5}$$

This algorithm has two main phases: scatter and allgather. The message is scattered by a binomial tree algorithm in the first phase, and in the next phase a ring algorithm for allgather is used to collect all segments from all processes. It is used in MPICH for large message sizes.

- Scatter-recursive-doubling-allgather broadcast algorithm.

$$2 \times \log_2{(p)} \times \alpha + 2\frac{p-1}{p} \times m \times \beta \ . \tag{6}$$

This algorithm is very similar to the previous one except the allgather uses a recursive doubling algorithm. It is used in MPICH for medium-size messages. However, the ring algorithm is more efficient than this for large message sizes because of its nearest-neighbor communication pattern [4].
- Split-binary tree broadcast algorithm [15].
  The split-binary tree algorithm splits the original message into two segments and the segments are broadcast separately in two different binary trees. Finally, each process in both trees exchanges its message with the corresponding pair process from the other tree.

$$2 \times (\log_2{(p+1)} - 2) \times (\alpha + m \times \beta) + \alpha + \frac{m}{2} \times \beta \ . \tag{7}$$

3   Hierarchical Optimization of MPI Broadcast Algorithms

This section introduces a simple but at the same time general optimization of the MPI broadcast algorithms. The idea was inspired by our previous study on the optimization of the communication cost of parallel matrix multiplication on large-scale distributed memory platforms [14].

The proposed optimization technique is based on the arrangement of the p processes participating in the broadcast into logical groups. For simplicity it is assumed that the number of groups divides the number of MPI processes and can change between one and p. Let G be the number of groups. Then there will be $\frac{p}{G}$ MPI processes per group. Figure 2 shows an arrangement of 12 processes in the original linear way and their hierarchical grouping into 3 groups of 4 processes. The hierarchical optimization has two steps: in the first step a group leader is selected for each group and the broadcast is performed between the group leaders (see Figure 1 in red), and in the next step the leaders start broadcasting inside their own group (in this example among 4 processes). The grouping can be done by taking the topology into account as well. However, in this work the grouping is topology-oblivious and the first process in each group is selected as the group leader. The broadcasts inside different groups happen in parallel. In general different algorithms can be used for broadcast operations between group leaders and within each group. This work focuses on the case where the same algorithm is employed for all broadcast operations. Algorithm 1 shows the pseudocode of the hierarchically modified broadcast algorithm. Line 4 calculates the root for the broadcast inside the groups. Then line 5 creates a sub-communicator of G processes among the groups and line 6 creates a sub-communicator of $\frac{p}{G}$ processes inside the groups. Our implementation uses the MPI_Comm_split MPI routine to create new sub-communicators.

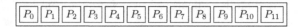

Fig. 1. Arrangement of processes in broadcast

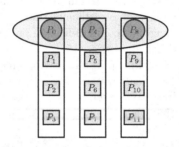

Fig. 2. Arrangement of processes in hierarchical broadcast. Processes in the ellipses are the group leaders. The rectangles show the processes inside groups. In the first step the broadcast is performed among the group leaders and in the next step it is performed among the processes inside each group.

Algorithm 1. Hierarchical modification of an MPI broadcast algorithm

---

Data: p - Number of processes
Data: G - Number of groups
Data: buf - Message buffer
Data: $count$ - Number of entries in buffer (integer)
Data: $datatype$ - Data type of buffer
Data: $root$ - Rank of broadcast root
Data: $comm$ - MPI Communicator
Result: All the processes have the message of size m
begin

1	`MPI_Comm comm_outer` /* communicator among the groups */
2	`MPI_Comm comm_inner` /* communicator inside the groups */
3	`int root_inner` /* root of broadcast inside the groups */
4	`root_inner = Calculate_Root_Inner(`G`, `p`, `$root$`, `$comm$`)`
5	`comm_outer = Create_Comm_Between_Groups(`G`, `p`, `$root$`, `$comm$`)`
6	`comm_inner = Create_Comm_Inside_Groups(`G`, `p`, `$root\_inner$`, `$comm$`)`
7	`MPI_Bcast(`buf`, `$count$`, `$datatype$`, `$root\_outer$`, `$comm\_outer$`)`
8	`MPI_Bcast(`buf`, `$count$`, `$datatype$`, `$root\_inner$`, `$comm\_inner$`)`

3.1 Hierarchical Flat and Linear Tree Broadcast

If we group the processes in the hierarchical way and apply the flat or linear tree broadcast algorithm among G groups and inside the groups among $\frac{p}{G}$ processes then the overall broadcast cost will be equal to their sum:

$$F(G) = (G-1) \times (\alpha + m \times \beta) + (\frac{p}{G} - 1) \times (\alpha + m \times \beta) = (G + \frac{p}{G} - 2) \times (\alpha + m \times \beta) \ . \tag{8}$$

Formula 8 is a function of G for a fixed p. Its derivative will be as follows:

$$F'(G) = \left(1 - \frac{p}{G^2}\right) \times (\alpha + m \times \beta) \ . \tag{9}$$

We can see that $G = \sqrt{p}$ is the minimum of the function $F(G)$ as in the interval $(1, \sqrt{p})$ the function decreases, and in the interval $(\sqrt{p}, p)$ it increases. If we consider $G = \sqrt{p}$ in formula 8 the optimal value of the broadcast will be as follows:

$$F(\sqrt{p}) = (2\sqrt{p} - 2) \times (\alpha + m \times \beta) \ . \tag{10}$$

3.2 Hierarchical Pipelined Linear Tree Broadcast

In the same way, if we add two pipelined linear tree broadcast costs among G groups and inside the groups among $\frac{p}{G}$ processes then the overall communication cost for the hierarchical pipelined linear tree will be as follows:

$$F(G) = \left(2X + G + \frac{p}{G} - 4\right) \times \left(\alpha + \frac{m}{X} \times \beta\right) \tag{11}$$

It can be shown that $G = \sqrt{p}$ is the minimum point again.

3.3 Hierarchical Binary and Binomial Tree Broadcast

Let us apply formula 4 among G groups and inside the groups among $\frac{p}{G}$ processes. The cost of either the binary or the binomial broadcast algorithm among G groups and inside the groups will be $\log_2(G) \times (\alpha + m \times \beta)$ and $\log_2(\frac{p}{G}) \times (\alpha + m \times \beta)$ respectively. If we add these two costs together and consider that $\log_2 \left(\frac{p}{G}\right) = \log_2 (p) - \log_2 (G)$ then the cost of the hierarchical binary/binomial broadcast algorithm will be the same as that of the corresponding non-hierarchical broadcast algorithm.

3.4 Hierarchical Scatter-Ring-Allgather Broadcast

If we apply formula 5 in the same way we can get the following formula:

$$F(G) = \left(log_2(p) + G + \frac{p}{G} - 2\right) \times \alpha + 2 \times m \times \left(2 - \frac{1}{G} - \frac{G}{p}\right) \times \beta \ . \tag{12}$$

Let us find the optimal value of the $F(G)$ function.

$$F'(G) = \frac{g^2 - p}{G^2} \times \left(\alpha - \frac{2m\beta}{p}\right) . \tag{13}$$

Formula 13 shows that if

$$\frac{\alpha}{\beta} > \frac{2m}{p} \tag{14}$$

then $G = \sqrt{p}$ is the minimum point of the $F(G)$ function in the interval $(1, p)$. The value of the function at this point will be as follows:

$$F(\sqrt{p}) = (log_2(p) + 2\sqrt{p} - 2) \times \alpha + 2 \times m \times (2 - \frac{2}{\sqrt{p}}) \times \beta . \tag{15}$$

3.5   Hierarchical Scatter-Recursive-Doubling-Allgather Broadcast

$$F(G) = 2 \times log_2(p) \times \alpha + 2 \times m \times (2 - \frac{1}{G} - \frac{G}{p}) \times \beta . \tag{16}$$

The hierarchical modification of this algorithm has higher theoretical cost compared to the cost of the original algorithm (formula 6): the latency term is increased two times and the bandwidth term is increased as well.

3.6   Hierarchical Split-Binary Tree Broadcast

We take $p+1 \approx p$ in formula 7 to derive the cost of its hierarchical transformation. It can be shown that the overall cost will be slightly worse than that of the original algorithm itself (see formula 7):

$$2 \times (log_2(p) + X - 4) \times (\alpha + \beta \times \frac{m}{X}) + 2 \times (\alpha + \beta \times \frac{m}{2}) . \tag{17}$$

3.7   Summary of Theoretical Analysis

This section can be summarized as follows: the hierarchical transformations of the flat, chain, pipeline and scatter-ring-allgather algorithms theoretically reduce the communication cost of the corresponding original algorithms. The communication costs of the binary, binomial, scatter-recursive-doubling-allgather and split-binary tree algorithms either do not change or slightly increase by a constant factor after the hierarchical transformation.

4   Experiments

4.1   Experiments on BlueGene/P

Some of our experiments were carried out on the Shaheen BlueGene/P at the Supercomputing Laboratory at King Abdullah University of Science&Technology

(KAUST) in Thuwal, Saudi Arabia. Shaheen has 16 racks with a total of 16384 nodes. Each node is equipped with four 32-bit, 850 Mhz PowerPC 450 cores and 4GB DDR memory. The BlueGene/P (BG/P) architecture provides a three-dimensional point-to-point BlueGene/P torus network which interconnects all compute nodes and global networks for collective and interrupt operations. Use of this network is integrated into the BG/P MPI implementation. BlueGene/P MPI implementation is based on MPICH. It is known that MPI broadcast operation in MPICH uses three different broadcast algorithms depending on the message size and the number of processes in a broadcast operation [4]:

– binomial tree algorithm - when the message size is less than 12kB or when the number of processes is less than eight.
– scatter-recursive-doubling-allgather algortihm - when the message size is less than 512kB and the number of processes is a power-of-two.
– scatter-ring-allgather algorithm (we will call it SRGA)- in all other cases, for long messages greater than or equal to 512kB or with non power-of-two number of processes.

Despite the referenced paper was published more than a decade ago it still reflects the current version of MPI broadcast operation implemented in MPICH according to its source code.

In this work we only present experiments with the corresponding hierarchical modifications of the scatter-ring-allgather algorithm. Experiments with the binomial and scatter-recursive-doubling-allgather algorithms showed only slight fluctuations which are expected theoretically. In addition to the algorithms in MPICH, the broadcast operation on BG/P uses different communication protocols and broadcast algorithms: if the communicator is MPI_COMM_WORLD then it uses the BG/P collective tree network and otherwise depending on the communicator shape either a rectangular broadcast algorithm or MPICH are used [12]. However, MPI_COMM_WORLD is not used in computational libraries. On the other hand the rectangular broadcast is used only for rectangular shaped sub-communicators. Depending on the allocated BG/P partition and the mapping of the processes into the physical topology, sub-communicators can be arbitrary shaped. On the other hand, the proposed optimization in this work is more general and topology-oblivious.

Performance modeling and analysis of the BG/P specific broadcast algorithms and optimizations are beyond the scope of this paper. However, we also present experiments with the default BG/P broadcast operation as an initial research in that direction. The experiments have been done with different configurations, message sizes from 1kB up to 16MB and the number of MPI processes from 8 up to 5000. Here we used less number of MPI processes than the allocated BG/P nodes as we created sub-communicators to avoid the case with MPI_COMM_WORLD. Because of space restrictions we provide the results only for 2048 and 5000 processes and message sizes 512kB and 2MB. It is worth mentioning that BG/P is quite stable in terms of reproducibility if the configuration

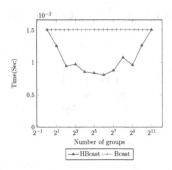

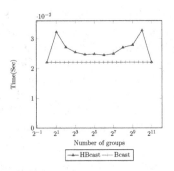

Fig. 3. Hierarchical SRGA bcast on BG/P. m=512kB and p=2048.

Fig. 4. Hierarchical SRGA bcast on BG/P. m=2MB and p=2048.

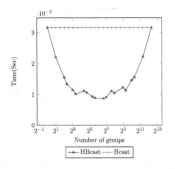

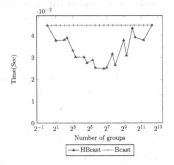

Fig. 5. Hierarchical SRGA bcast on BG/P. m=512kB and p=5000.

Fig. 6. Hierarchical SRGA bcast on BG/P. m=2MB and p=5000.

is kept the same. The allocated BG/P shapes were 2x1x2 and 2x3x2 in the the experiments with 2048 and 5000 processes respectively. Figure 3 and Figure 4 show experiments with the scatter-ring-allgather broadcast with message sizes of 512kB and 2MB respectively. The improvement with 512kB on 2048 nodes is 1.87 times, however with a message size of 2MB there is a performance drop. On the other hand, according to formula 14 (i.e. $\frac{\alpha}{\beta} > \frac{2m}{p}$) if we fix the message size, for a larger number of nodes the hierarchical transformation should improve the performance. This is validated with the experiments: Figure 5 shows that the performance with the message size 512kB increases up to 3.67 times on 5000 nodes. Moreover, Figure 6 shows that on 5000 nodes the hierarchical algorithm is better even with the message size of 2MB. In addition, if we put the platform and algorithm parameters in formula 12 the plots of the hierarchical algorithm will be parabola-like as well (Figure 7 and Figure 8). Figure 9 and Figure 10 show the experiments with the default BG/P MPI broadcast.

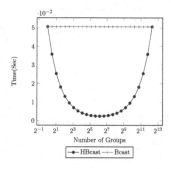

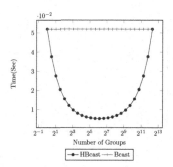

Fig. 7. Theoretical plot of SRGA bcast. m=512kB and p=5000.

Fig. 8. Theoretical plot of SRGA bcast. m=2MB and p=5000.

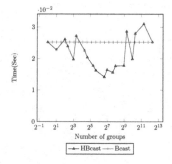

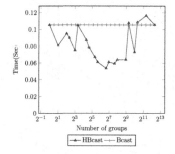

Fig. 9. Hierarchical bcast on BG/P. m=512kB and p=5000.

Fig. 10. Hierarchical bcast on BG/P. m=2MB and p=5000.

4.2 Experiments on Grid'5000

The next part of the experiments was carried out on the Graphene cluster of Nancy site of the Grid'5000 infrastructure in France. The platform consists of 20 clusters distributed over 9 sites in France and one in Luxembourg. The Grid'5000 web site (http://www.grid5000.fr) provides more comprehensive information about the platform.

The experiments on Grid'5000 have been done with OpenMPI 1.4.5 which provides a few broadcast implementations. Among those implementations there are several general broadcast algorithms such as flat, chain(linear), pipelined, binary, binomial, split-binary tree and platform/architecture specific algorithms some of which are broadcast algorithms for Infiniband networks, and the Cheetah framework for multicore architectures. In this work we do not consider the broadcast algorithms for the specific platforms. Furthermore, experiments with the binary and binomial tree broadcasts are not presented here because of space restrictions. Because of the same reason we present experiments only with 128 nodes (one process per node). We have used the same approach as presented in MPIBlib [16] to benchmark the performance.

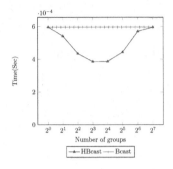

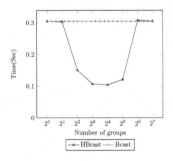

Fig. 11. Hierarchical chain broadcast on Grid'5000. m=16kB and p=128.

Fig. 12. Hierarchical chain broadcast on Grid'5000. m=16MB and p=128.

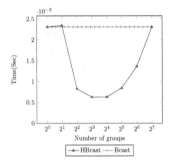

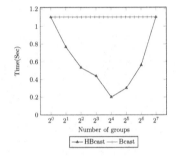

Fig. 13. Hierarchical pipeline broadcast on Grid'5000. m=16kB and p=128.

Fig. 14. Hierarchical pipeline broadcast on Grid'5000. m=16MB and p=128

Figure 11 and Figure 12 represent experiments with the chain broadcast algorithm and its hierarchical transformation with message sizes 16kB and 16MB respectively. The speedup with the message size 16MB is three times and with 16kB is 1.5 times. During the experiments with smaller message sizes up to 1kB the overhead from the two MPI_Comm_split operations were higher than the chain broadcasts itself. Still, an implementation of the algorithm could check the message size beforehand and fall back to use the regular MPI_Bcast for short messages to reduce the overhead even further. Figure 14 and Figure 13 show experiments with the pipeline broadcast algorithm and its hierarchical transformation. The trend is similar to the chain algorithm. This time the improvement is even higher, 5.5 times with the message size 16MB and 3.69 times with the message size 16kB.

5   Conclusion

Our hierarchical approach to optimize MPI broadcast algorithms is more general and simpler than many existing broadcast optimizations. The idea itself does not break up any existing broadcast algorithms, is not limited to some specific platforms and can be used as a standalone library on top of any MPI implementations. Some broadcast algorithms have been improved more than five times even on a relatively small number of processors.

This work presents the application of the proposed technique to general MPI broadcast algorithms implemented in MPICH and OpenMPI. Among these algorithms there are the two most used algorithms: scatter-ring-allgather and pipelined algorithms. Our initial observation showed that BlueGene/P default broadcast operation can be optimized by the hierarchical transformation as well. Therefore, one of our future plans is to study the hierarchical modifications of the broadcast algorithms optimized for IBM BlueGene/P and Infiniband networks. A similar kind of approach can also be applied to other MPI collective operations.

We are working on a software library/tool which can be incorporated into any application which uses MPI broadcast. The software will let users easily transform any broadcast algorithm into a two-level hierarchy and predict their performance.

Acknowledgements. This work has emanated from research conducted with the financial support of IRCSET (Irish Research Council for Science, Engineering and Technology) and IBM, grant number EPSG/2011/188 and Science Foundation Ireland, grant number 08/IN.1/I2054.

Some of the experiments presented in this publication were carried out using the Grid'5000 experimental testbed, being developed under the INRIA ALADDIN development action with support from CNRS, RENATER and several Universities as well as other funding bodies (see https://www.grid5000.fr)

Another part of the experiments were carried out using the resources of the Supercomputing Laboratory at King Abdullah University of Science&Technology (KAUST) in Thuwal, Saudi Arabia.

References

1. Message passing interface forum, http://www.mpi-forum.org/
2. MPICH-A Portable Implementation of MPI, http://www.mpich.org/
3. Gabriel, E., Fagg, G., Bosilca, G., Angskun, T., Dongarra, J., Squyres, J., Sahay, V., Kambadur, P., Barrett, B., Lumsdaine, A., Castain, R., Daniel, D., Graham, R., Woodall, T.: Open MPI: goals, concept, and design of a next generation MPI implementation. In: Proceedings of the 11th European PVM/MPI Users' Group Meeting, pp. 97–104 (2004)
4. Thakur, R., Gropp, W.D.: Improving the Performance of Collective Operations in MPICH. In: Dongarra, J., Laforenza, D., Orlando, S. (eds.) EuroPVM/MPI 2003. LNCS, vol. 2840, pp. 257–267. Springer, Heidelberg (2003)
5. Watts, J., Van de Geijn, R.: A Pipelined Broadcast for Multidimensional Meshes Parallel Processing Letters 05, 281 (1995)
6. Barnett, M., Gupta, S., Payne, D., Shuler, L., Van de Geijn, R., Watts, J.: Interprocessor collective communication library (InterCom). In: Proceedings of the Scalable High Performance Computing Conference, pp. 357–364. IEEE (1994)

7. Johnsson, S.L., Ho, C.-T.: Optimum Broadcasting and Personalized Communication in Hypercubes. IEEE Transactions on Computers 38(9), 1249–1268 (1989)
8. Sanders, P., Sibeyn, J.F.: A bandwidth latency tradeoff for broadcast and reduction. Information Processing Letters 86(1), 33–38 (2003)
9. Hoefler, T., Siebert, C., Rehm, W.: A practically constant-time MPI Broadcast Algorithm for large-scale InfiniBand Clusters with Multicast. In: Proceedings of the 21st IEEE International Parallel and Distributed Processing Symposium, vol. 232 (March 2007)
10. Graham, R., Venkata, M.G., Ladd, J., Shamis, P., Rabinovitz, I., Filipov, V., Shainer, G.: Cheetah: a framework for scalable hierarchical collective operations. In: Proceedings of CCGrid, pp. 73–83 (2011)
11. Dichev, K., Lastovetsky, A.: Optimization of collective communication for heterogeneous HPC platforms. In: High-Performance Computing on Complex Environments, Wiley, pp. 95–114. Wiley (2014)
12. Kumar, S., Dozsa, G., Almasi, G., Heidelberger, P., Chen, D., Giampapa, M.E., Blocksome, M., Faraj, A., Parker, J., Ratterman, J., Smith, B., Archer, C.J.: The deep computing messaging framework: generalized scalable message passing on the Blue Gene/P supercomputer. In: Proceedings of the 22nd Annual International Conference on Supercomputing (ICS), pp. 94–103 (2008)
13. Träff, J.L., Ripke, A.: Optimal Broadcast for Fully Connected Processor-node Networks. Journal of Parallel Distributed Computing 7(68), 887–901 (2008)
14. Hasanov, K., Quintin, J., Lastovetsky, A.: Hierarchical Approach to Optimization of Parallel Matrix Multiplication on Large-Scale Platforms. The Journal of Supercomputing 24 (2014)
15. Pješivac-Grbović, J.: Towards Automatic and Adaptive Optimizations of MPI Collective Operations. PhD Thesis, University of Tennessee, Knoxville (2007)
16. Lastovetsky, A., Rychkov, V., O'Flynn, M.: MPIBlib: Benchmarking MPI communications for parallel computing on homogeneous and heterogeneous clusters. In: Lastovetsky, A., Kechadi, T., Dongarra, J. (eds.) EuroPVM/MPI 2008. LNCS, vol. 5205, pp. 227–238. Springer, Heidelberg (2008)

Improving Node-Level MapReduce Performance Using Processing-in-Memory Technologies

Mahzabeen Islam[1], Marko Scrbak[1], Krishna M. Kavi[1],
Mike Ignatowski[2], and Nuwan Jayasena[2]

[1] University of North Texas, USA
{mahzabeenislam,markoscrbak}@my.unt.edu,krishna.kavi@unt.edu
[2] AMD Research - Advanced Micro Devices, Inc., USA
{mike.ignatowski,nuwan.jayasena}@amd.com

Abstract. Processing-in-Memory (PIM) is the concept of moving computation as close as possible to memory. This decreases the need for the movement of data between central processor and memory system, hence improves energy efficiency from the reduced memory traffic. In this paper we present our approach on how to embed processing cores in 3D stacked memories, and evaluate the use of such a system for Big Data analytics. We present a simple server architecture, which employs several energy efficient PIM cores in multiple 3D-DRAM units where the server acts as a node of a cluster for Big Data analyses utilizing MapReduce programming framework. Our preliminary analyses show that on a single node up to 23% energy savings on the processing units can be achieved while reducing execution time by up to 8.8%. Additional energy savings can result from simplifying the system memory buses. We believe such energy efficient systems with PIM capability will become viable in the near future because of the potential to scale the memory wall.

Keywords: Processing-in-Memory, 3D-DRAM, Big Data, MapReduce.

1 Introduction

While the idea of moving processing to memory (i.e., Processing-in-Memory, PIM) is not new [13,19,6,10] the advent of 3D-stacked DRAMs [2,4,9] which include dedicated logic dies within a DRAM package, have generated renewed interest in PIMs [19,20,12,15]. Current research shows that enough free silicon area is available within the logic layer to permit the inclusion of computational units. PIM architectures are particularly beneficial for data intensive and memory bounded applications that do not necessarily benefit from the conventional cache hierarchy [26]. PIM cores can access memory using faster, high bandwidth TSVs (Through Silicon Via) [15,20,24] instead of conventional or specialized high bandwidth memory buses that consume significant energy for transferring data between DRAM and off-chip processing cores [4]. Because of this observation we favor PIMs over a heterogeneous multicore system where a number of small cores (or GPUs) are integrated with powerful main CPUs since they require excessive amounts of data transferred from/to off-chip DRAM units. Nonetheless,

L. Lopes et al. (Eds.): Euro-Par 2014 Workshops, Part II, LNCS 8806, pp. 425–437, 2014.

several challenges remain. Among the key issues to investigate include the types of computing cores and how many of them to include in the logic layer to fully utilize available (3D) DRAM bandwidth while not exceeding power budgets.

In this paper, we propose a new server architecture with a number of simple in-order single-issue cores as PIM cores. We describe the roles and responsibilities of the main processor and PIM cores and our assumptions about the memory. We also propose modifications to MapReduce framework in order to optimize this unconventional architecture specifically for Big Data processing. In Big Data analysis, generally clusters of large number of commodity machines are used in conjunction with a standard MapReduce framework [5,1]. A cluster of small number of our proposed servers and the modified MapReduce framework will be able to provide better performance with lower energy consumption than existing large commodity cluster systems.

Phoenix++ [18] is a highly optimized MapReduce framework for large-scale shared memory CMP (Chip Multiprocessor)/SMP (Symmetric Multiprocessing) systems. We find that single node performance of Phoenix++ is better than that of Hadoop. This is also true for similar shared memory MapReduce library [11]. We propose a two level MapReduce framework: inter-node and intra-node level. The inter-node level execution flow will be similar to a standard MapReduce framework (e.g., Hadoop). In this paper we focus on intra-node level MapReduce execution flow. We start with Phoenix++ and optimize it for our PIM architecture. The intra-node level reduce phase performs local (node-level) optimization before sending the results for inter-node level reduce phase i.e. global reduction. Our preliminary analyses show that a single node with proposed model can obtain up to 23% energy savings on the processing units and 8.8% reduced execution time as compared to Phoenix++ running on an SMP system for several Big Data workloads.

The rest of the paper is organized as follows. Section 2 includes the background and related work. Section 3 describes the new PIM architecture and system organization. Section 4 describes MapReduce as a use case for the PIM architecture and shows the modifications in the MapReduce workflow. In Sect. 5 we discuss experimental results. Section 6 concludes and discusses future steps.

2   Background and Related Work

3D-stacked DRAM is an emerging memory organization providing larger capacity with lower latency, higher bandwidth and lower energy than existing 2D-DRAM technologies [2,23]. 3D-DRAM package is composed of several layers of DRAM cells stacked on top of a logic layer containing the necessary peripheral circuitry for the DRAM. There are several prototypes, including the Hybrid Memory Cube (HMC) [4] and the High Bandwidth Memory (HBM) DRAM [9]. The logic layer can accommodate additional processing capabilities [19,20,12,15]. Processing-in-Memory is the concept of moving computation closer to memory that was investigated a decade ago [13,19,6,10]. Researchers explored how to integrate logic with memory for various applications.

MapReduce framework for large-scale data processing on clusters of commodity machines was first developed by Google [5]. It involves three major phases: map, reduce and merge. The user supplies the map() and reduce() functions and the MapReduce runtime manages parallelization. Several different types of frameworks are available for MapReduce, including Google MapReduce [5], Apache Hadoop [1], MRMPI [14] for commodity clusters, Phoenix++ [18], Metis [11], Ostrich [3] for shared memory systems, Mars [8], GPMR [17] for systems using GPUs. We model our PIM architecture as a shared memory system, albeit with Non-Uniform Memory Access (NUMA). Thus we rely on shared memory MapReduce frameworks.

The Phoenix system [18,16] and others [11,3] provide MapReduce framework for conventional large-scale shared memory CMP and SMP systems. We use Phoenix++ [18], the most recent and highly optimized MapReduce framework with NUMA-awareness for our study and propose changes to adapt it to our PIM architecture. The architecture and MapReduce framework we propose differ from the Phoenix++ system presented by Talbot et al. [18]. We also diverge from Google MapReduce [5] and Hadoop [1] in node-level task execution.

Recently proposed Near Data Computing (NDC) architecture [15] provides a similar idea to our study and assumes 3D-DRAMs embedded with processing cores. However the NDC study works with in-memory MapReduce workloads where the entire input for computation is assumed to reside in the system memory. We do not make such assumptions but consider conventional storage systems (e.g. Hard Disk Drive-HDD, Solid State Drive-SSD) as the source of input. This difference significantly changes how we approach the Map and Reduce functions using PIM cores.

3 Proposed PIM Architecture

PIM architectures could prove beneficial for data intensive and memory bounded applications that may not necessarily benefit from a cache hierarchy [26]. PIM cores can access memory using faster, high bandwidth, lower power TSVs [15,20,24]. Therefore moving the computation from the main processor closer to the memory is a better choice for such applications. We base our server architecture on the model proposed by Zhang et al. [20]. The server consists of a host multi-core processor. The host is connected to four 3D-stacked DRAM Memory Units (3DMUs). The host views the entire memory as a single physical memory distributed among the 3DMUs. Figure 1 depicts the proposed PIM architecture.

Each 3DMU has several dedicated Processing-in-Memory cores (PIM cores) embedded in its logic layer. Each PIM core is a simple in-order, single-issue, energy efficient processing unit operating at a lower clock frequency than that of the host cores. The system memory for the host and PIM cores is comprised of the DRAM layers in the 3DMUs. We also assume that each PIM core has its own small instruction and data caches. The execution of the threads running on PIM cores is controlled by a manager process running on a host core. The threads can access any physical address residing in any 3DMUs which are part

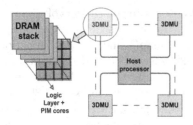 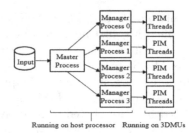

Fig. 1. Proposed Hardware Architecture   **Fig. 2.** Proposed Programming Model

of its manager process address space. However, accesses to data in other 3DMUs should be limited to avoid performance losses due to NUMA.

For our initial analyses we assume 8GB memory and 16 PIM cores in each of the four 3DMUs. In section 5 we justify the number of PIM cores per 3DMU and argue about a good number depending on the system usage. Note that the number of PIM cores in the logic layer should be small enough not to exceed the 10W TDP of the logic layer [24]. Different architectural choices for the PIM cores also play a big role, in terms of both performance and energy consumption. At this time we assume ARM-like processing cores [21] as PIM cores. The proposed server architecture can be used as a node in a cluster configuration for dealing with very large amounts of data.

4   MapReduce Using PIM

MapReduce workloads are memory intensive and do not benefit much from conventional deep cache hierarchies [26]. Our goal is to optimize node level performance of a MapReduce cluster by parallelizing the different phases with the help of PIM cores. Our proposed MapReduce framework consists of two levels, one is inter-node level (using processing nodes of a cluster) and the other is intra-node level. The inter-node level execution flow can be similar to a standard MapReduce framework like Hadoop [1]. The intra-node level reduce phase performs local (node-level) optimization before sending the results for inter-node level reduce phase i.e. global reduction.

Since the server architecture proposed here is a special case of hierarchical multi-core system with NUMA shared-memory (from the PIM cores point of view), we have used Phoenix++ [18], a MapReduce framework designed for large-scale SMP systems that exhibit NUMA behavior, as our base. We pay particular interest to the structures for the intermediate <key, value> stores. Because of these structures we can use PIM cores to efficiently parallelize map, reduce as well as part of the merge phase. Additionally, we propose changes in the actual Phoenix++ MapReduce flow, where we overlap the reading of the input from storage with the actual map phase. The key issues related to MapReduce applications, when executed on shared memory systems, are to ensure the locality of map phase, selection of efficient intermediate data structures, decrease remote memory access during the reduce phase and to use an efficient memory allocator [18,11].

4.1   Intra-node MapReduce Using PIM

Execution Flow of the Intra-node MapReduce Framework. We assume that any process running on a host core can request the runtime system to allocate physical memory in any specific 3DMU, and thus aware of the location of the data for the purpose of spawning PIM tasks on that memory unit. This is a valid assumption because HSA (Heterogeneous System Architecture) Foundation [7] is advocating such an organization. We next describe the MapReduce runtime on a node level with respect to the architecture shown in Fig. 1. There is one master process, which creates 4 manager processes (corresponding to 4 3DMUs) and each manager process creates 16 worker threads on the 16 PIM cores of a certain 3DMU. Inter-process communication is achieved through shared memory. We label the 3DMUs and the manager processes from 0-3 so that each manager corresponds to a 3DMU respectively. Figure 2 depicts the model.

Map and Combine Phase. In Phoenix++, the library reads the input data from disk and keeps it in a single memory buffer prior to starting the map phase. However, in order to obtain maximum parallelism we will overlap these two phases. We next describe the overlapping process using the aforementioned numbered labels for better understanding. The master process reads 16 input splits at a time from the disk and places them in a shared memory buffer residing in 3DMU-0. The master process then starts reading the next 16 input splits into 3DMU-1. In parallel, the manager process-0, which manages the 16 PIM core threads of 3DMU-0, allocates necessary memory in 3DMU-0 for the PIM threads to generate the intermediate output and then hands the execution over to them. Each thread will start processing one input split with the provided map function. This process is repeated until all of the input is processed.

Reduce and Merge Phase. The reduce phase across the 3DMUs is assumed to be completed by the manger processes running on the host processor either independently or with the help of PIM threads. The reduce phase can potentially benefit from the parallel reduction on sets of unique keys. Initial stages of the merge phase can be performed by the PIM cores in parallel as well.

5   Experiments and Results

5.1   Experiments

In order to evaluate the proposed architecture, we use a conventional server as our baseline system. The configuration is provided in Table 1. This baseline system runs Phoenix++ library [16] with its standard setup. In Table 1, we summarize the new system configuration we envision, which will be running the modified MapReduce framework described here.

Table 1. Baseline and New System Configuration

	Baseline System Configuration	New System Configuration	
		Host Processor	PIM Cores
Processing Units	2 × Xeon E5-2640 6 cores/processor, 2 HT/core Out-of-order 4-wide issue	1 × Xeon E5-2640 6 cores, 2 HT/core Out-of-order 4-wide issue	64 (4 × 16) ARM Cortex-A5 In-order Single-issue
Clock Speed	2.5 GHz	2.5 GHz	1 GHz
LL Cache	15 MB/processor	15 MB	32 KB I, D/core
Memory BW	42.6 GB/s per processor	42.6 GB/s	1.33 GB/s per core
Power	TDP = 95 W/processor Low-power = 15 W/processor	TDP = 95 W	80 mW/core (5.12 W for 64)
Memory	32 GB (8 × 4GB DIMM DDR3)	32 GB (4 × 8GB 3DMU)	
Storage	1 TB HDD, SATA3, PERC H710	1 TB HDD, SATA3, PERC H710	
MapReduce	Phoenix++ Framework	Proposed Framework (Sect. 4)	

Table 2. MapReduce workload execution time (in seconds) for baseline system

Workload	IP Size	$t_{baseline}$ (s)	t_{read} (s)	t_{map} (s)	t_{reduce} (s)	t_{merge} (s)
word_count	16 GB	176.67	162	14.6	0.05	0.02
histogram	1.3 GB	13.254	12.9	0.35	0.002	0.002
string_match	16 GB	186.61	181	5.6	0.01	0.0
linear_regression	16 GB	185.61	181	4.6	0.01	0.0

Table 3. $t_{transfer\_unit}$

Storage Technology	$t_{transfer\_unit}$
HDD	10.42 ms
SSD	2.17 ms

Table 4. $t_{map\_unit\_host}$

Workload	$t_{map\_unit\_host}$
word_count	25 ms
histogram	7 ms
string_match	12 ms
linear_regression	7 ms

We use Phoenix++ to obtain the execution times for the baseline system and to estimate the execution times for the proposed MapReduce framework running on the PIM architecture. The total execution time of a MapReduce workload on the baseline system can be expressed as:

$$t_{baseline} = t_{read} + t_{map} + t_{reduce} + t_{merge} . \tag{1}$$

In the baseline configuration there are 24 threads and 16 map tasks per thread (total 384 map tasks). We ran different workloads on the baseline system for different input sizes from 100MB up to 16GB and Table 2 shows execution times for a specific input size. From the collected statistics we compute the following two parameters: $t_{transfer\_unit}$, time to read one input split (1MB) from storage into memory (Table 3) and $t_{map\_unit\_host}$, time to process an input split (1MB) by one map task running on the host (Table 4). In the baseline system we also have used Samsung PM830 SSD as storage and run the benchmarks. In this case we observed around 4.8 times speedup in reading the input as compared to HDD storage as implied by Table 3 data. We also run them with input sizes larger than the physical memory (32GB), the results are discussed in Sect. 5.4.

5.2 Performance Analysis

The execution time benefit of the proposed MapReduce model lies in the overlapping of map tasks with the reading of input from storage to memory. As long as the PIM cores do not sit idle waiting for input buffers to get filled, we believe that this approach delivers performance improvements over a serialized process where all of the input is first read before starting map tasks.

For the baseline system, from (1) the total execution time is $t_{baseline} = t_{read} + t_{map} + t_{reduce} + t_{merge}$. For different workloads we find that when the input size is smaller than that of available physical memory then, $t_{read} > t_{map} + t_{reduce} + t_{merge}$. We discuss the case when the input is larger than available physical memory in Sect 5.4. To reduce the total execution time we overlap the read and map phases in our MapReduce framework. Hence the total execution time for the proposed PIM based system is:

$$t_{new} = t_{read} + t_{reduce} + t_{merge} . \tag{2}$$

In order to achieve (2), we must ensure:

$$t_{map} \leq t_{read} . \tag{3}$$

thereby t_{map} is completely overlapped with t_{read}.

Another important fact is that the processing speed of PIM cores will be slower than the host processor since PIM cores operate at lower clock rate and use in-order single-issue execution. On the other hand, PIM cores are sitting closer to memory so memory accesses are faster for them. We performed a simulation using gem5 [25], and compared the execution time of a map function running on an OoO X86 and an In-Order ARMv7 CPU model. The simulation parameters were picked to mimic the actual CPU specifications in Table 1. We find that the PIM cores would run approximately 4 times slower (i.e., slowdown factor, $s = 4$) than the host cores.

Initially we proposed a server with four 3DMUs each with 16 PIM cores. The following analysis will explain why we choose 16 PIM cores per 3DMU. We wanted to know the minimum number of PIM cores needed on each of the 3DMUs in order to satisfy (3). Each PIM core runs one thread and processes one input split at a time. In our case, following must hold for (3) to be true,

$$s \times t_{map\_unit\_host} \leq 4 \times n \times t_{transfer\_unit} . \tag{4}$$

In (4), s is the slowdown factor ≥ 1, $t_{map\_unit\_host}$ is the time to process an input split (1MB) by one map task running on the host core, 4 is the number of 3DMUs in the server, n is the number of PIM cores in each 3DMU and $t_{transfer\_unit}$ is the time to read one input split (1 MB) from storage into memory.

Here we want the time taken by a group of PIM cores to process the input splits to be smaller than, or equal, to the time taken by the host to fill in the buffers in each of the 3DMUs.

We observe two cases, depending on how fast the PIM cores can process the input in Fig. 3 (a) and (b). The host keeps reading input splits from storage as long as there is more input. As soon as the input is available in a 3DMU, the PIM cores in that 3DMU start the map tasks. In Fig. 3(a) the PIM cores are processing the input at a much higher rate than the host can fill in the buffers. In Fig. 3(b) the PIM cores in each 3DMU are busy processing the input almost up to the point of time when the next set of input splits becomes available.

To achieve full utilization of the PIM cores following must hold,

$$s \times t_{\text{map\_unit\_host}} = 4 \times n \times t_{\text{transfer\_unit}} \ . \tag{5}$$

We solve (5) to find the minimum n (number of PIM cores per 3DMU) for each of the workload independently. We use data from Table 3 and 4, and compute n for a range of slowdown factors s. Figure 4 shows the required number of PIM cores per 3DMU for different slowdown factors for different workloads.

Analyzing the graphs in Fig. 4 for two different storage technologies and four different workloads one can conservatively estimate (choosing the closest greater or equal integer which is a power of two) the number of PIM cores needed per 3DMU as 16 when estimated 4 times slower execution ($s=4$) of the map tasks on a PIM core. Our study allows one to decide on the minimum number of PIM cores per 3DMU needed so that t_{map} is completely overlapped with t_{read}. One can use more PIM cores than the minimum, but their utilization will drop.

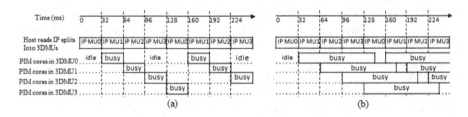

Fig. 3. (a) PIM core utilization is low (b) PIM core utilization is high

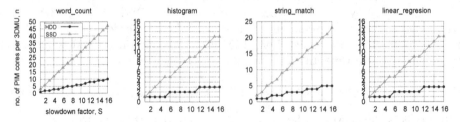

Fig. 4. Each graph shows the number of PIM cores required per 3DMU (Y axis) for different slowdown factors (X axis) for 2 different storage technologies, HDD and SSD

We also analyze the area and power overhead of placing 16 PIM cores in the logic layer of each 3DMU with ARM Cortex-A5 core as PIM core. Each such core, with 32KB data and 32KB instruction cache, has an area of 0.80mm^2 in 40nm technology [21]. So 16 PIM cores in the logic layer have an area overhead of 11.9% [15] when HMC [4] is used as 3DMU. Furthermore, accumulated power consumption of the 16 PIM cores will be 1.28W [21] which is only 12.8% of allowable 10W TDP of logic layer per stack [24]. Therefore we claim that integrating 16 PIM cores in the logic layer of each 3DMU is feasible.

We conclude that the total execution time in the proposed model, t_{new} is faster than total execution time in the baseline system, $t_{baseline}$ by t_{map}. Figure 5 shows t_{new} normalized to $t_{baseline}$ for different workloads. We use data from Table 2 for $t_{baseline}$, for t_{new} we have used (2), and we take the estimated slowdown factor of 4. We observe that the overall execution time for the proposed model is reduced by 2.5% to 8.8% when compared to the baseline system for different Big Data workloads. This evaluation includes only the performance gain for the map phase; additional speedup may be achieved by parallelizing reduce and merge (partially) phases on the PIM cores.

5.3   Energy Consumption

The total energy consumption of running a Big Data workload in the proposed system is reduced by using lower power cores as well as decreasing the overall execution time. We define $E_{baseline}$ and E_{new} as the total energy consumed by the processing elements of the baseline and the new system respectively. The baseline system consists of two Xeon processors (Table 1). To make our analyses fair, and even favor the baseline, while computing $E_{baseline}$, we assume that only one of the processors in the baseline is active while reading the input i.e. during the time t_{read} the second processor will be placed in low power state consuming 15W. For the other phases both processors are fully active. While computing E_{new}, we assume that the host processor and all the 64 PIM cores (Table 1) are active during the entire processing. We calculate the energy consumption of the processing units for the baseline and the new system as follows.

$$E_{baseline} = [(TDP + P_{low\_power\_state}) \times t_{read}]$$
$$+ [2 \times TDP \times (t_{map} + t_{reduce} + t_{merge})] . \qquad (6)$$

$$E_{new} = [TDP + (64 \times P_{PIM\_core})] \times (t_{read} + t_{reduce} + t_{merge}) . \qquad (7)$$

The power specifications for baseline and new system are listed in Table 1 and the execution times of the different phases are given in Table 2. Figure 6 shows that, for processing part, relative energy savings of one node range from 12% to 23% as compared to the baseline system. The absolute energy savings range from 80J to 2045J, depending on the workload.

5.4   Input Exceeding Physical Memory Capacity

If the input is larger than the available physical memory, we observe a non-linear increase in map phase execution time (t_{map}) for our baseline. This happens because by the time map phase starts, all the starting pages containing the input are swapped out and there will be a large number of page faults. In some cases we even have $t_{\mathrm{map}} > t_{\mathrm{read}}$ (e.g. word_count in Table 5). This would not happen if the input splits, on which the map tasks will work, were in the memory. In our proposed model we handle such cases by bringing input splits into memory and performing map tasks on them in an incremental fashion.

Table 5 shows the execution times for workloads in the baseline system (Table 1) for input size larger than the physical memory. In such cases, with our proposed model, one can achieve up to 56% reduction in execution time and up to 71% energy savings on the processing units compared to the baseline system, as calculated by (2) and (7) respectively. Note that here we get these numbers for stand alone server performance. But in such cases, where the input is larger than physical memory, one may choose to use a cluster of such nodes and for each node we may get statistics as Table 2 and obtain gains as presented in Sects. 5.2 and 5.3.

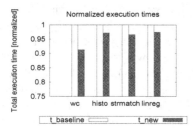

Fig. 5. Normalized execution times for 16 PIM cores per 3DMU with slowdown factor of 4, as compared to the baseline. The total execution time is reduced by 2.5% to 8.8%.

Fig. 6. Energy consumption of processing units of the PIM model compared to the baseline. Energy savings range from 80J to 2045J (12% to 23%).

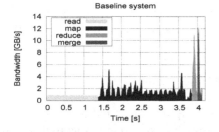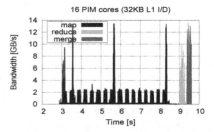

Fig. 7. Bandwidth consumption when running word_count on two different systems

Table 5. Execution time for baseline system when input is larger than physical memory

Workload	IP Size	$t_{baseline}$ (s)	t_{read} (s)	t_{map} (s)	t_{reduce} (s)	t_{merge} (s)
word_count	32.5 GB	801.358	349.981	449.731	1.605	0.041
string_match	32.4 GB	538.346	348.127	190.198	0.021	0.0
linear_regression	32.5 GB	466.538	365.959	100.559	0.02	0.0

5.5 Bandwidth Utilization and Link Power

Figure 7 shows the actual bandwidth consumption of word_count for different MapReduce phases when running on different systems. Interestingly, the bandwidth consumed by the baseline system does not exceed 15GB/s. PIM cores show higher bandwidth utilization at lower power consumption. For our proposed PIM server we can have low bandwidth links between the host processor and the 3DMUs and thereby reduce power consumption. Note that during the map phase the peak bandwidth required will depend on whether or not the intermediate data structures fit in the PIM core caches. 3DMUs provide memory bandwidth of up to 320GB/s within the memory stack [4,23]. The same bandwidth is available to the host processor via 8 high speed SerDes links [4], each of which provides bandwidth of 40GB/s with average power consumption of 5W [23]. We believe that PIM architectures are more energy efficient than traditional heterogeneous multi/many core architectures because they utilize the bandwidth available within the memory stack and do not need the power hungry SerDes links. The bandwidth consumed by the 16 PIM cores in one 3DMU will not exceed 22GB/s [22] which is well below the 320GB/s available in the unit. However, 64 PIM cores in four 3DMUs will have an effective peak bandwidth consumption of 88GB/s. In order to support the same bandwidth for the system with off the 3D-DRAM chip heterogeneous cores, we would need at least 3 SerDes links, consuming three times more energy on the links.

The bandwidth utilized within each 3DMU can be further increased by increasing the number of PIM cores per 3DMU, however at the expense of higher power consumption and possibly lower utilization. To fully utilize the 320GB/s bandwidth, more than 200 PIM cores are needed, but then the power consumption will exceed the constraint of 10W TDP for the logic layer of a 3DMU [24].

6 Conclusion and Future Work

In this paper we outlined our ideas about using simple cores embedded within the logic layer of 3D-DRAMs for running MapReduce applications. We overlap input reading and map phases. We also propose to utilize locality of data for assigning tasks to PIM cores. Our preliminary results show gains in terms of reduced execution time and energy savings for several MapReduce applications.

We intend to extend our preliminary work in several directions. First we want to explore other possible architectures for PIM cores, including GPGPUs, simple RISC cores, FPGA and Dataflow. Second, we want to characterize which emerging workloads, and particularly which functionalities, benefit from a PIM architecture and how to exploit the possible benefits. This includes extensive simulation of memory intensive workloads in a PIM augmented system in order to show the benefits in terms of energy savings as well as performance gains.

Acknowledgments. This work is conducted in part with support from the NSF Net-centric IUCRC and AMD. We acknowledge David Struble's help in making this paper more readable.

References

1. Apache Hadoop, http://hadoop.apache.org/
2. Black, B., Annavaram, M., Brekelbaum, N.: DeVale, et al.: Die stacking (3D) microarchitecture. In: Micro, pp. 469–479. IEEE (2006)
3. Chen, R., Chen, H.: Tiled-MapReduce: Efficient and Flexible MapReduce Processing on Multicore with Tiling. Transactions on Architecture and Code Optimization 10(1), 3 (2013)
4. Hybrid Memory Cube Consortium, http://hybridmemorycube.org/
5. Dean, J., Ghemawat, J., Mapreduce, S.: Simplified data processing on large clusters. In: Proceedings of the Conference on Symposium on OSDI, vol. 6 (2004)
6. Draper, J., Chame, J., Hall, M., et al.: The architecture of the DIVA processing-in-memory chip. In: Proceedings of the Supercomputing, pp. 14–25. ACM (2002)
7. HSA Foundation, http://www.hsafoundation.com/
8. He, B., Fang, W., Luo, Q., et al.: Mars: a MapReduce framework on graphics processors. In: Proceedings of Parallel architectures and compilation techniques, pp. 260-269. ACM, (2008)
9. JEDEC, http://www.jedec.org/category/technology-focus-area/3d-ics-0
10. Rezaei, M., Kavi, K.M.: Intelligent memory manager: Reducing cache pollution due to memory management functions. Journal of Systems Architecture 52(1), 41–55 (2006)
11. Mao, Y., Morris, R., Kaashoek, M.F.: Optimizing MapReduce for multicore architectures. In: CSAIL, Massachusetts Institute of Technology, Tech. Rep. (2010)
12. Loh, G., Jayasena, N., Oskin, M., et al.: A Processing in Memory Taxonomy and a Case for Studying Fixed-function PIM. In: Near-Data Processing Workshop (2013)
13. Patterson, D., Anderson, T., Cardwell, N., et al.: A case for intelligent RAM. Micro. 17(2), 34–44 (1997)
14. Plimpton, S.J., Devine, K.D.: MapReduce in MPI for large-scale graph algorithms. Parallel Computing 37(9), 610–632 (2011)
15. Pugsley, S.H., Jestes, J., Zhang, H.: NDC: Analyzing the Impact of 3D-Stacked Memory+Logic Devices on MapReduce Workloads. In: International Symposium on Performance Analysis of Systems and Software (2014)
16. Phoenix System for MapReduce Program, http://mapreduce.stanford.edu/
17. Stuart, J.A., Owens, J.D.: Multi-GPU MapReduce on GPU clusters. In: Parallel and Distributed Processing Symposium, pp. 1068–1079. IEEE (2011)
18. Talbot, J., Yoo, R.M., Kozyrakis, C.: Phoenix++: modular MapReduce for shared-memory systems. In: Proceedings of the International Workshop on MapReduce and its Applications, pp. 9–16. ACM (2011)

19. Torrellas, J.: FlexRAM: Toward an advanced Intelligent Memory system: A retrospective paper. In: Intl. Conference on Computer Design, pp. 3–4. IEEE (2012)
20. Zhang, D.P., Jayasena, N., Lyashevsky, A., et al.: A new perspective on processing-in-memory architecture design. In: Proceedings of the ACM SIGPLAN Workshop on Memory Systems Performance and Correctness, p. 7. ACM (2013)
21. ARM, http://www.arm.com/products/processors/cortex-a/cortex-a5.php
22. Atmel SAMA5D3, http://www.atmel.com/microsite/sama5d3/highlights.aspx
23. Graham, S.: HMC Overview. In: Memcon Proceedings (2012)
24. Zhang, D., Jayasena, N., Lyashevsky, A., et al.: TOP-PIM: throughput-oriented programmable processing in memory. In: Proceedings of International Symposium on High-Performance Parallel and Distributed Computing, pp. 85–98. ACM (2014)
25. gem5 Simulator System, http://www.m5sim.org
26. Ferdman, M., Adileh, A., Kocberber, O., et al.: A Case for Specialized Processors for Scale-Out Workloads. In: Micro, pp. 31-42. IEEE, (2014)

On Portability, Performance and Scalability of an MPI OpenCL Lattice Boltzmann Code

Enrico Calore[1], Sebastiano Fabio Schifano[2], and Raffaele Tripiccione[3]

[1] Istituto Nazionale di Fisica Nucleare (INFN), Ferrara, Italy
[2] Dip. di Matematica e Informatica, Università di Ferrara and INFN, Ferrara, Italy
[3] Dip. di Fisica e Scienze della Terra, Università di Ferrara and INFN, Ferrara, Italy

Abstract. High performance computing increasingly relies on hetero-geneous systems, based on multi-core CPUs, tightly coupled to accelera-tors: GPUs or many core systems. Programming heterogeneous systems raises new issues: reaching high sustained performances means that one must exploit parallelism at several levels; at the same time the lack of a standard programming environment has an impact on code portability. This paper presents a performance assessment of a *massively parallel* and *portable* Lattice Boltzmann code, based on the Open Computing Lan-guage (OpenCL) and the Message Passing Interface (MPI). Exactly the same code runs on standard clusters of multi-core CPUs, as well as on hy-brid clusters including accelerators. We consider a state-of-the-art Lattice Boltzmann model that accurately reproduces the thermo-hydrodynamics of a fluid in 2 dimensions. This algorithm has a regular structure suitable for accelerator architectures with a large degree of parallelism, but it is not straightforward to obtain a large fraction of the theoretically avail-able performance. In this work we focus on portability of code across several heterogeneous architectures preserving performances and also on techniques to move data between accelerators minimizing overheads of communication latencies. We describe the organization of the code and present and analyze performance and scalability results on a cluster of nodes based on NVIDIA K20 GPUs and Intel Xeon-Phi accelerators.

1 Introduction

High performance computer architectures are becoming more and more heteroge-neous, heavily relying on *accelerators*, which commonly deliver a major fraction (e.g., $\simeq 70\%$) of the full system computing power. Virtually all currently avail-able accelerators (GPUs, many-core CPUs, FPGAs) are independent processing units, connected to commodity CPUs via standard busses, such as PCI-Express. The CPU orchestrates the coarse-grained harness of a complex computation, while accelerators handle compute intensive kernels. In order to use accelerators efficiently, one must partition an algorithm on many processing cores, each core in turn heavily using SIMD features: one is then forced to concurrently exploit several levels of parallelism. Furthermore, accelerators use their own memory hierarchy, so data transfers between host and accelerators have to be carefully

L. Lopes et al. (Eds.): Euro-Par 2014 Workshops, Part II, LNCS 8806, pp. 438–449, 2014.

scheduled. This is an important issue for code performances as also highlighted in [1].

Fortunately enough, several large scale computer codes in the scientific and engineering domain have sufficiently large available parallelism and an algorithmic structure that allows to split the code on the compute elements available on accelerators and to schedule the full computation in a way that tames the problems highlighted above: some handcrafted codes have delivered unexpectedly high performance figures.

An obvious and relevant question is whether a similar level of performance can be obtained using the *same* programming environment and the *same* code for different accelerator architectures and if this approach is also viable when large scale parallelism (involving many nodes with many accelerators) is needed.

In this paper we address this problem, using OpenCL, a software framework able to provide a common abstraction over the underlying computing resources, and MPI, a de-facto standard for multi-node parallel processing. We consider a fluid-dynamics code based on a state-of-the-art massively parallel Lattice-Boltzmann method that we have re-written using OpenCL and MPI. We describe the structure and implementation of the code and present our performance and scaling results on several state-of-the-art heterogeneous architectures, comparing with handcrafted versions of the code for the same algorithm.

We find that the performance of our OpenCL implementation is comparable with that of architecture-specific optimizations, granting, on the other hand, code portability. Moreover, we eventually study the bottlenecks limiting the extent of the scaling window for massively parallel implementations.

Our paper is structured in this way: we first introduce the OpenCL framework and in section 3 we give a short introduction to Lattice Boltzmann methods; section 4 follows, giving details of our implementation and of our optimization results. Section 5 contains an analysis of our performance results, followed by our conclusions and outlook.

2   OpenCL

OpenCL (Open Computing Language) [2] aims to provide a single framework to develop portable code executable across heterogeneous platforms; it is a hardware oblivious open standard, maintained by the non-profit *Kronos Group* and supported by a large set of vendors. OpenCL offers a standard API, providing an extension of the C99 language to write functions that run on heterogeneous platforms (CPUs, GPUs or other accelerators) exploiting a task-based or data-based parallel approach. Manufacturer are responsible for providing an OpenCL API implementation for their devices, following the OpenCL open standard specification. OpenCL codes run on commodity computers, which may or may not host accelerators as GPUs, DSPs (Digital Signal processors), FPGAs (Field-Programmable Gate Arrays), or other processors, in addition to ordinary CPUs. In order to generalize across different architectures, OpenCL provides an abstraction of the actual hardware defining a *platform*, a *memory* and an *execution*

```
__kernel void saxpy( __global double *A, __global double *B,
               __global double *C, const double s) {

   int id = get_global_id (0);  // get global thread ID
   C[id] = s * A[id] + B[id];  // compute the id-th element
}
```

Fig. 1. Sample OpenCL code, computing a saxpy kernel on two vectors

model. How the models map onto the actual hardware is device dependent and is defined by the corresponding implementation; these aspects can be neglected by programmers from the point of view of ensuring program correctness, but they are relevant for performance tuning.

In the OpenCL Platform model, all OpenCL enabled devices in the host are seen as containers of Compute Units (CU); in turn, each CU is made up of different Processing Elements (PE). On the other side, the OpenCL Execution model is made up of two main components: a host program and one or more kernel functions which run on devices. Where each kernel runs depends on the so called OpenCL context, which is defined by the host program as consisting of one or more devices and one or more command queues associated to them. Commands (such as kernel launches or memory transfers) submitted to a command queue may be executed in-order or, optionally, out-of-order; it is possible to define multiple queues for the same device to issue not synchronized commands, which may execute concurrently, if the device is able to do so. The main idea behind OpenCL is the possibility to define an n-dimensional problem domain and then to run a kernel function for each point of it. Each instance, running on each domain point, in the OpenCL taxonomy, is called a work-item and can be thought as a single thread, executing on a processing element within a device. Multiple work-items are commonly grouped in what is called a work-group, which runs on a CU. Each work-item has a global ID and a local ID. The global ID is unique among all work-items of a Kernel. The local ID identifies a work-item within a work-group.

Concerning the OpenCL Memory model, a first distinction is made between the host memory (commonly the host RAM memory) and the device memory (e.g. a GPU memory bank); the device memory in its turn is divided into four address spaces which commonly differ for size and access time. *Global* memory is commonly the largest area; it is visible by all work-items running on the device, but it has the highest access latency. *Constant* memory stores read-only data and is commonly a relatively small cached part of the Global memory. *Local* memory is meant for data sharing by work-items within the same work-group; it is usually faster than Global memory, but smaller and not globally accessible. *Private* memory is accessible only by individual work-items; it is the fastest, but also smallest available storage (e.g. the registers of a CPU).

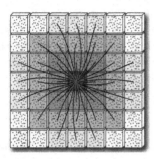
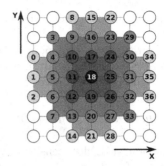

Fig. 2. Left: Velocity vectors for the LB populations in the D2Q37 model. Right: populations labels identify the lattice hop that they perform in the *propagate* phase.

Let us assume that a code is broken down into N_{wg} work-groups and each work-group has N_{wi} work-items. When this code executes on a device with N_{cu} compute units, each able to compute on N_d data items, at any given time $N_{cu} \times N_d$ work-items will execute; iterations will be needed to perform all globally required $N_{wg} \times N_{wi}$ work-items. For example, the Xeon-Phi has 60 physical cores, each supporting up to 4 threads, for a total of 240 virtual cores; it supports AVX 256-bit operations that process 8 double-precision or 16 single-precision floating-point data. In this case, up to 240 work-groups execute on all cores, each core in turn processing up to 8 (or 16) work-items in parallel. Similar mappings of the available parallelism on the computing resources can be worked out for other architectures.

In Fig.1 we show an OpenCL implementation of the *saxpy* operation of the *Basic Linear Algebra Subprogram* (BLAS) set. The parameters of the kernel are three arrays, A, B and C and one double precision number. Pointers to the arrays are marked as __global because they are allocated on the global memory of the device. Each work-item executes the *saxpy* kernel computing just one data-item of the output array: first it computes its unique global identifier id and then uses it to address the id*th* data-item of arrays A, B and C.

3   Lattice Boltzmann Methods

Lattice Boltzmann methods (LB) are widely used in computational fluid dynamics, to describe flows in two and three dimensions. LB methods (see, e.g. [3] for an introduction) are discrete in position and momentum spaces; they are based on the synthetic dynamics of *populations* sitting at the sites of a discrete lattice. At each time step, populations hop from lattice-site to lattice-site and then incoming populations *collide* among one another, that is, they mix and their values change accordingly.

LB models in x dimensions with y populations are labeled as $DxQy$; we consider a state-of-the-art $D2Q37$ model that correctly reproduces the thermo-hydrodynamical equations of motions of a fluid in two dimensions, automatically enforcing the equation of state of a perfect gas $(p = \rho T)$ [4,5]; this model has been extensively used for large scale simulations of convective turbulence (see e.g., [6,7]).

In the algorithm, a set of populations $(f_l(x,t)\ l = 1\cdots 37)$, defined at the points of a discrete and regular lattice and each having a given lattice velocity c_l, evolve in (discrete) time according to the following equation:

$$f_l(\boldsymbol{y}, t + \Delta t) = f_l(\boldsymbol{y} - \boldsymbol{c}_l \Delta t, t) - \frac{\Delta t}{\tau} \left(f_l(\boldsymbol{y} - \boldsymbol{c}_l \Delta t, t) - f_l^{(eq)} \right) \qquad (1)$$

The macroscopic variables, density ρ, velocity $\boldsymbol{u}$ and temperature T are defined in terms of the $f_l(x,t)$ and of the c_ls (D is the number of space dimensions):

$$\rho = \sum_l f_l, \qquad \rho\boldsymbol{u} = \sum_l \boldsymbol{c}_l f_l, \qquad D\rho T = \sum_l |\boldsymbol{c}_l - \boldsymbol{u}|^2 f_l, \qquad (2)$$

and the equilibrium distributions $(f_l^{(eq)})$ are themselves function of these macroscopic quantities [3]. In words, populations drift from different lattice sites (*propagation*), according to the value of their velocities and, on arrival at point y, they change their values according to Eq. 1 (*collision*). One can show that, in suitable limiting cases, the evolution of the macroscopic variables obey the thermo-hydrodynamical equations of motion of the fluid.

An LB code starts with an initial assignment of the populations, in accordance with a given initial condition at $t = 0$ on some spatial domain, and iterates Eq. 1 for each point in the domain and for as many time-steps as needed; boundary-conditions at the edges of the integration domain are enforced at each time-step by appropriately modifying the population values at and close to the boundaries.

The LB approach offers a huge degree of easily identified parallelism. Indeed, Eq. 1 shows that the *propagation* step amounts to gathering the values of the fields f_l from neighboring sites, corresponding to populations drifting towards y with velocity c_l; the following step (*collision*) then performs all mathematical processing needed to compute the quantities appearing in the r.h.s. of Eq. 1, for each point in the grid. Referring again to Eq. (1), one sees immediately that both steps above are completely uncorrelated for different points of the grid, so they can be computed in parallel according to any convenient schedule, if one ensures that for all grid points step 1 is performed before step 2.

In practice, an LB code executes the following three main steps at each iteration of the loop over time:

- propagate moves populations across lattice sites according to the pattern of Fig.2 left, collecting at each site all populations that will interact at the next phase (collide). Consequently, propagate moves blocks of memory locations allocated at sparse addresses, corresponding to populations of neighbor cells. propagate can either use a pull scheme or a push scheme; in the first case populations are gathered at one site as shown in Fig.2; while in the latter case populations are pushed from one lattice-site towards a set of neighbors. Which of the two is best to use depends on the capability of processor memory-controller.

– bc (Boundary Conditions) adjusts the populations at the top and bottom edges of the lattice to enforce appropriate boundary conditions (e.g., a constant given temperature and zero velocity). This is done *after* propagation, since the latter changes the value of the populations close to the boundary points and hence the macroscopic quantities that must be kept constant. At the right and left boundaries, we apply periodic boundary conditions. This is conveniently done by adding *halo* columns at the edges of the lattice, where we copy the 3 (in our case) rightmost and leftmost columns of the lattice before performing the propagate step. Points close to the right/left boundaries can then be processed as those in the bulk. If needed, boundary conditions could be enforced in the same way as done for the top and bottom edges.

– collide performs all the mathematical steps associated to equation 1 and needed to compute the population values at each lattice site at the new time step. Input data for this phase are the populations gathered by the previous propagate phase. This step is the floating point intensive step of the code.

4 Code Implementation

At top level, our code is based on MPI processes, each managing one OpenCL (OpenCL) device. Actual devices are attached to the host nodes of the cluster, so MPI communications are either fully within the host or across a commodity network, such as Infiniband. This is managed transparently and in a uniform way by the MPI run-time support, so our code runs both on single-host and multi-host multi-device systems.

We split a lattice of size $L_x \times L_y$ on N devices along the X dimension; each device allocates a *sub-lattice* of size $L_x/N \times L_y$. On each device the lattice is stored using the SoA (Structure of Arrays) scheme, where arrays of populations are stored in memory one after the other. This allows to exploit data-parallelism and enable data-coalescing in accessing data when executing several work items in parallel. Each array of population is stored in columns-major order, and we keep in memory two copies of it, prv and nxt. Each kernel reads from prv and update results on the nxt copy; nxt and prv swap their roles at each iteration. This solution needs more memory, but it allows to map one work-item per lattice site, and then to process many sites in parallel. The lattice splitting implies a virtual ordering of the MPI-processes along a ring, so each process exchanges its borders of its own sub-lattice with its adjacent processes. One could consider a different decomposition (e.g. $L_y/N \times L_x$, reducing communication overheads if $L_y \geq L_x$); however, since we plan to use our code for physics simulations in a wide range of aspect-ratios (both $L_x > L_y$ and $L_x < L_y$), we arbitrarily select only one of the two possibilities. Moreover, since our lattice is stored in column-major order, splitting along X means that lattice columns are allocated sequentially in memory, improving memory access time when copying halos.

Each device allocates a *sub-lattice* of $NX \times NY$ lattice points, $NX = H_x + L_x + H_x$, and $NY = H_y + L_y + H_y$, including vertical and horizontal halos of size H_x and H_y. Left and right halos keep copies of the three rightmost and

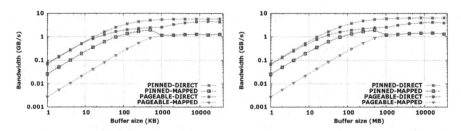

Fig. 3. Bandwidth vs. buffer size for h2d (left) and d2h (right) transfers between host and an NVIDIA K20 GPU device.

leftmost columns of the sub-lattices allocated on the neighbor nodes. This makes the computation uniform for all lattice sites, avoiding divergences of work-items which lead to performance degradation. Bottom and top halos are adjusted to keep memory accesses by work-items aligned, enabling memory coalescing.

Each MPI process runs a loop over time; at each iteration it executes four main-steps: first pbc (Periodic Boundary Conditions) updates the left and right halo columns, and then three kernels – propagate, bc and collide – run on the device to perform the required computational tasks.

Based on previous results in coding with CUDA [8], a language for GPUs not widely different from OpenCL, we configure the OpenCL kernels for propagate, bc and collide as a grid of $(L_y \times L_x)$ work-items; each work-group is a uni-dimensional array of N_{wi} work-items, processing data at successive locations in memory. In this way memory coalescing can be easily exploited.

In the following we describe in details the combination of pbc and propagate, which is critical to scalability when running on multi-device multi-host systems configuration. The key point to consider is that the propagate step for the bulk of the lattice (all lattice points except for three columns at right and left) has no data dependency with pbc (while propagate on the edges depend on fresh data moved to the halos by pbc). Our strategy therefore leverages on i) speeding up data transfers and ii) overlapping as much as possible data transfers with propagate (on the bulk). Let us consider these two points in order. pbc copies the three leftmost and rightmost columns of the lattice respectively into the right and left halos of the neighbor sub-lattices. In a multi-device implementation this implies moving data between OpenCL devices. This task implies the following steps:

1. copy data corresponding to the left and right borders from the device to two host buffers;
2. send data to the previous and the next node in the ring;
3. receive data from neighbors and store them into two host buffers;
4. copy the just received data from host buffers into the halo columns of the device.

All these steps are performance critical, as they use data paths with limited bandwidth and large latency (see later for accurate figures). MPI communi-

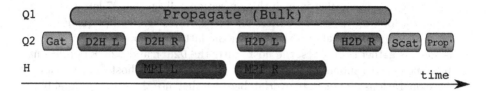

Fig. 4. Concurrent scheduling of the various steps of the propagate and pbc kernels

cations are handled by the MPI run-time support, so there is not much the programmer can do there. On the other hand, OpenCL has several options to allocate memory and to perform device-to-host (d2h) and host-to-device (h2d) copies.

OpenCL has routines to allocate memory in *pageable* or *pinned* mode; the former option is a standard allocation in virtual space that can be swapped out of physical memory by the operating system, while the latter mode forces memory to be always resident in real memory; the OpenCL function clCreateBuffer() function with the CL_MEM_ALLOC_HOST_PTR flag performs this operation. Memory access can be *mapped* or *direct*. In mapped mode, buffers on the device are mapped onto the address space of the host node, while in direct mode, data is moved by specific OpenCL routines such as clEnqueueReadBuffer() to read from the device and clEnqueueWriteBuffer() to write data into it.

We have tested all four combination of allocation and access modes; Fig. 3 shows the bandwidth as a function of the buffer size for h2d and d2h transfers between a host and an NVIDIA GPU K20 device. Perhaps not unexpectedly, one obtains the best performance using *pinned* memory allocation and *direct* memory access. In this case, the transfer time (μsec) as a function of the data block size s (bytes) is well fitted by the following expressions:

$$T_{h2d}(s) = 14.16 + 0.00017 \times s, \qquad T_{d2h}(s) = 14.21 + 0.00015 \times s$$

corresponding to a latency of ≈ 14 μsec (in both directions), and an asymptotic bandwidth of ≈ 6 GB/s for h2d and ≈ 6.6 GB/s for d2h. The asymptotic bandwidth is $\approx 75\%$ of the aggregate raw bandwidth of a 16 lanes (16X) GEN2 PCi-Express bus (8 GB/s). The large value for the latency means that it is useful to gather all data into one block before starting the d2h operation (and scatter back at destination), rather than paying the latency overhead 37 times.

We now consider how to schedule operations in order to overlap (bulk) propagate and pbc. We define two OpenCL queues Q1 and Q2: the first schedules the execution of (bulk) propagate, while Q2 schedules the sequence of operations corresponding to pbc. There is no data dependency between Q1 and Q2, so both queues can in principle fully overlap in time. In practice, we have seen that this option cannot be fully exploited because the execution over the bulk uses all resources of the device; the best it can do is to overlap host-device transfers and computations on the device. According to our measurements the best scheduling is indeed that shown in Fig. 4:

1. the host starts the **gather** kernel; this operation collects the 37 left and right borders into two contiguous buffers allocated on the device (**Q2** queue).
2. the host starts **propagate** on the bulk of the lattice (**Q1** queue)
3. as soon as **gather** completes, the host starts the D2H L and D2H R operations in asynchronous mode to copy the two buffers on the host side memory; these operations do not fully overlap because they use the same channel bus, but the host is not blocked (**Q2** queue);
4. as each of the two D2H transfers finishes the host starts the corresponding MPI communication – first MPI L and then MPI R – to send and receive border data to/from the left and right neighbours;
5. as each MPI communication completes, the host starts the corresponding H2D L or H2D R steps and moves back the buffers onto its device (**Q2** queue);
6. the **scatter** kernel moves the content of the buffers onto the left and right halos (**Q2** queue).
7. **propagate** executes on the lattice columns not handled by Q1, using fresh halo data (Prop', in Fig. 4). This is a **Q2** step, but in practice it does not start before **propagate** on **Q1** finishes.

Inspection of Fig. 4 shows that all data transfer overheads can be hidden behind the execution of (bulk) **propagate**. The effective time for the combined pbc and **propagate** steps on the whole lattice is given by $\max\{T\alpha, T_\beta\}$, where

$$T_\alpha = T_{\mathsf{Gath}} + T_{\mathsf{Prop}} + T_{\mathsf{Scat}} + T_{\mathsf{Prop}'}$$
$$T_\beta = T_{\mathsf{Gath}} + T_{\mathsf{D2h(L)}} + T_{\mathsf{MPI(L)}} + T_{\mathsf{MPI(R)}} + T_{\mathsf{H2d(R)}} + T_{\mathsf{Scat}} + T_{\mathsf{Prop}'}$$

As we split the lattice on more and more devices, **propagate** becomes faster and faster, while data transfers are approximately constant in time, so hiding will be partial. We assess this quantitatively in the next section.

5   Results

We have tested our OpenCL code on the *Eurora* cluster, installed at CINECA (Italy). *Eurora* is a cluster of nodes interconnected through a standard Infiniband network. Each node has two Intel processors of the Xeon-E5 family, based on the Sandybridge micro-architecture, and two accelerators, either two Kepler K20s NVIDIA GPUs or two Intel Xeon-Phi 5100 devices. The double-precision peak

Table 1. Performance comparison of the main critical kernels of the code, using a *common* OpenCL (OCL) code or architecture-specific CUDA and C versions; execution times are in μsec.

	OCL - GPU	CUDA - GPU	OCL - PHI	C - PHI
$T_{\mathsf{Pbc+Prop}}$	17.64	15.40	39.40	37.70
T_{Collide}	104.65	83.33	81.12	79.14

Table 2. Time break-down of all steps of our OpenCL code running on two K20s GPUs for lattice sizes of $L_x \times 2048$. All times are milli-seconds and the lattice is sliced along X-dimension. Values in bold identify the performance limiting factor for scalability.

L_x	3840	1920	960	480	240	120	64	32	16
$T_{\text{Pbc+Prop}}$	17.64	8.93	4.56	2.39	2.07	2.10	2.11	2.03	2.06
T_{Bc}	7.91	3.98	2.02	1.04	0.56	0.30	0.20	0.11	0.11
T_{Collide}	104.65	52.35	26.61	13.15	6.64	3.35	1.82	0.94	0.49
T_{tot}	130.21	65.25	33.19	16.58	9.27	5.74	4.13	3.08	2.66
T_{Gath}	0.07	0.07	0.07	0.07	0.07	0.07	0.07	0.07	0.07
$T_{\text{D2h(L)}}$	0.29	0.29	0.29	0.29	0.29	0.29	0.29	0.29	0.29
$T_{\text{D2h(R)}}$	0.28	0.28	0.28	0.28	0.28	0.28	0.28	0.28	0.28
$T_{\text{MPI(L)}}$	0.70	0.67	0.61	0.60	0.60	0.62	0.64	0.61	0.63
$T_{\text{H2d(L)}}$	0.32	0.32	0.32	0.32	0.32	0.32	0.32	0.32	0.32
$T_{\text{MPI(R)}}$	0.57	0.58	0.58	0.58	0.58	0.58	0.58	0.59	0.59
$T_{\text{H2d(R)}}$	0.32	0.31	0.31	0.31	0.31	0.31	0.31	0.32	0.32
T_{Scat}	0.07	0.07	0.07	0.07	0.07	0.07	0.07	0.07	0.07
$T_{\text{Prop}'}$	0.07	0.07	0.07	0.07	0.07	0.07	0.07	0.07	0.07
T_{Prop}	17.38	8.65	4.31	2.13	1.04	0.50	0.25	0.11	0.04
T_α	**17.60**	**8.86**	**4.53**	**2.35**	1.25	0.71	0.46	0.32	0.25
T_β	2.10	2.06	2.01	2.00	**2.00**	**2.02**	**2.03**	**2.04**	**2.04**

performance of both accelerators is ≈ 1 Tflops. We first assess the performance penalty, if any, of an OpenCL code w.r.t. architecture-optimized codes written using programming languages closer to the specific architecture (i.e. CUDA for GPUs, C and intrinsics for commodity CPUs and Xeon-Phi).

In Table 1 we compare the execution times of the two most critical kernels, propagate and collide, for our OpenCL code and for highly optimized codes written in CUDA for GPUs [10] and C for Xeon-Phis [9]. The GPU CUDA code was compiled using the same configuration options supported by the current NVIDIA OpenCL library. We remark that other options (not supported by the current version of the OpenCL library) allows significantly better performances for the collide kernel [10]. Data is for a lattice large enough (1920 × 2048 per device) that communications are well overlapped with computation. We see that the performances of the *same* OpenCL code are only slightly worse than those of codes specifically optimized for each device. We also notice that the two accelerators have roughly the same performance in the computing intensive kernel (collide), while the PHI processor is slower in the propagate step; this will have an impact on scalability, that we discuss next.

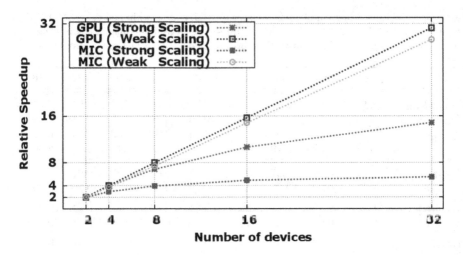

Fig. 5. Weak and strong scalability of our OpenCL code on the EURORA cluster for GPUs and MICs. In the strong regime, the code runs on a lattice of 1024×8192 cells; in the weak regime each device handles a sub-lattice of constant size (256×8192 cells).

Table 2 contains the time break-down of all operations of our OpenCL code on a dual-K20s system (results are qualitatively similar for the Intel Xeon-Phi) as we reduce the value of L_x. The first part shows the execution time of the main steps of our code. $T_{\text{Pbc+Prop}}$ refers to the execution of pbc and propagate scheduled as discussed in the previous section; while T_{tot} is the total execution time of the code. The following section of the table shows the full break down of all steps associated to pbc and propagate, while the last section shows the values of T_α and T_β appearing in the time model of the previous section. Note that our time model describes very well the behavior of $T_{\text{Pbc+Prop}}$ in terms of the contributions of all steps involved. As expected, as we vary the sub-lattice size all operations belonging to Q2 take approximately the same time, as they handle the same amount of data. However, as the sub-lattice size becomes smaller and smaller ($L_x \leq 480$), T_{Prop} for the bulk is too short to successfully hide communication latencies, so violations to scaling start to appear.

Fig. 5 shows scalability results obtained for both GPUs and PHIs. We have measured strong scalability on a lattice of 1024×8192 points. On this purposely small lattice, we see that communications quickly become the major bottlenecks, so there is no real advantage in using more than 32 GPU devices. For PHIs the situation is even worse and we have a performance improvement only up to 16 devices. Here the major bottleneck comes from data transfers between host and PHIs that are slower than for GPUs. For weak scaling we have allocated a lattice of 256×8192 on each device, a typical size for physics simulations. In this case communication overheads are fully overlapped with computation of propagate, and the code enjoys perfect scalability both for GPUs and PHIs in the whole range considered, up to 32 devices.

6   Conclusions and Outlook

An important result of this work is that the same OpenCL code runs on different accelerators, either based on GPUs or MICs, with single-node performance similar to that obtained with programming languages closer to each architecture. This provides an higher portability w.r.t. architecture specific implementations. However, in today heterogeneous cluster architectures, performance scalability of codes is seriously limited by the poor integration at hardware level between accelerators, the host node and the network; this translates to high latencies to move data between accelerators. In our implementation we have shown how computation and commnication can be efficiently overlapped in order to minimize impact of transfer latencies. In a future work we plan to use these results to design and optimize a portable 3D Lattice Boltzmann code using the OpenCL framework, or higher level languages such as OpenACC.

Acknowledgements. This work has been done in the framework of the COKA and Suma projects, supported by INFN. We have used the computing facilities of INFN-CNAF (Bologna, Italy) and CINECA (Bologna, Italy). We thank J. Kraus for useful suggestions and comments.

References

1. Obrecht, C., et al.: Scalable lattice Boltzmann solvers for CUDA GPU clusters. Parallel Computing 39 (2013)
2. Kronos Group, The open standard for parallel programming of heterogeneous systems, http://www.khronos.org/opencl
3. Succi, S.: The Lattice Boltzmann Equation for Fluid Dynamics and Beyond, Oxford University Press (2001)
4. Sbragaglia, M., et al.: Lattice Boltzmann method with self-consistent thermo-hydrodynamic equilibria. J. Fluid Mech. 628, 299–309 (2009), doi:10.1017/S002211200900665X
5. Scagliarini, A., et al.: Lattice Boltzmann methods for thermal flows: Continuum limit and applications to compressible Rayleigh-Taylor systems. Phys. Fluids 22, 055101 (2010), doi:10.1063/1.3392774
6. Biferale, L., et al.: Second-order closure in stratified turbulence: Simulations and modeling of bulk and entrainment regions. Phys. Rev. E 84, 1, 2, 016305 (2011), doi:10.1103/PhysRevE.84.016305
7. Biferale, L., et al.: Reactive Rayleigh-Taylor systems: Front propagation and non-stationarity. EPL 94, 5, 54004 (2011), doi:10.1209/0295-5075/94/54004
8. Biferale, L., et al.: An Optimized D2Q37 Lattice Boltzmann Code on GP-GPUs. Comp. and Fluids 80 (2013), doi:10.1016/j.compfluid.2012.06.003
9. Crimi, G., et al.: Early Experience on Porting and Running a Lattice Boltzmann Code on the Xeon-phi Co-Processor. Proc. Comp. Science 18 (2013), doi:10.1016/j.procs.2013.05.219
10. Kraus, J., et al.: Benchmarking GPUs with a Parallel Lattice-Boltzmann Code. In: Proc. of 25th Int. Symp. on Computer Architecture and High Performance Computing, SBAC-PAD (2013), doi:10.1109/SBAC-PAD.2013.37

Matrix-Free Finite-Element Operator Application on Graphics Processing Units

Karl Ljungkvist

Department of Information Technology, Uppsala University, Sweden
`karl.ljungkvist@it.uu.se`

Abstract. In this paper, methods for efficient utilization of modern accelerator-based hardware for performing high-order finite-element computations are studied. We have implemented several versions of a matrix free finite-element stiffness operator targeting graphics processors. Two different techniques for handling the issue of conflicting updates are investigated; one approach based on CUDA atomics, and a more advanced approach using mesh coloring. These are contrasted to a number of matrix-free CPU-based implementations. A comparison to standard matrix-based implementations for CPU and GPU is also made. The performance of the different approaches are evaluated through a series of benchmarks corresponding to a Poisson model problem. Depending on dimensionality and polynomial order, the best GPU-based implementations performed between four and ten times faster than the fastest CPU-based implementation.

1 Introduction

For applications where the geometry can be expected to be very complicated, methods based on completely unstructured grids, such as finite-element methods, are popular because of their ability to fully capture the geometry. On the other hand, in application fields where solutions also posses a high level of smoothness, such as in micro-scale simulation of viscous fluid, or linear wave propagation in an elastic medium, using a high-order numerical method can give high accuracy and efficiency. However, computational challenges limit the numerical order of a conventional matrix-based finite element-method.

Traditionally, the finite element method, *FEM*, has been seen as consisting of two distinct parts; an assembly of a linear system of equations, and a solution of this system. The system of equations is then typically represented as a sparse matrix, and the solution is found using an iterative Krylov subspace method. However, if high-order basis functions are used, in particular in 3D, the system matrix becomes increasingly less sparse. In order to accurately simulate realistic problems in three dimensions, millions or even billions of degrees of freedom can be required. In such cases, the system matrix can simply be too large to store explicitly in memory, even if a sparse representation is used.

In addition to the problem of storage, an equally important problem is that of memory bandwidth. In most iterative methods, most time is typically spent

L. Lopes et al. (Eds.): Euro-Par 2014 Workshops, Part II, LNCS 8806, pp. 450–461, 2014.

performing sparse matrix-vector products, *SpMV*, with the system matrix [1]. The sparse matrix-vector product has a relatively poor ratio of computations per memory access. On modern computer systems, even the most optimized implementations of this operation will not utilize the computation resources fully and is effectively bound by the memory bandwidth [2].

Matrix-free finite-element methods avoid these issues by merging the assembly and SpMV phases into a single operator application step, thereby removing the need for storing the system matrix explicitly. Since the large system matrix no longer has to be read, the bandwidth footprint is reduced radically. On the other hand, this is traded for additional computations, since the assembly needs to be recomputed at each operator application. For non-linear and time-dependent problems, this is not an issue since reassembly is necessary anyway. In [3], Cantwell et al. perform a comparison of different matrix-based and matrix-free approaches to high-order FEM, concluding that for order one elements, sparse matrices are most efficient, while for orders two and higher, a matrix-free approach yields the best performance. In [4], Kronbichler and Kormann propose a general framework for matrix-free finite element methods.

Due to the increased computational intensity of the matrix-free approach [4], it makes a good candidate for execution on throughput-oriented hardware such as graphics processors. Work on porting high-order FEM code to GPUs include the work by Cecka et al. [5], which compares different methods for performing the assembly of an explicit FEM matrix on GPUs. In [6], Klöckner et al. proposed a GPU implementation of a Discontinuous Galerkin method, which in many ways is similar to finite-element methods. However, there hyperbolic conservation laws were studied, which allows for an explicit time stepping without the need to solve a linear system. In [7], Komatitsch et al. port an earthquake code based on the related spectral element method to GPUs. Also here, the seismic wave equation being studied is hyperbolic and can be integrated explicitly in time.

In this paper, we propose a matrix-free GPU implementation of a finite-element stiffness operator based on CUDA, for future use in a solver for possibly non-linear elliptic and parabolic PDEs. An issue in performing the operator application is how to avoid race conditions when writing partial results to the output. We present two different techniques to handle this; one which uses the intrinsic atomic instruction of CUDA to protect the writes, and a more advanced technique based on mesh coloring to avoid the conflicts. We evaluate the two techniques in benchmarks based on a simple model problem, namely Poisson's equation on a Cartesian mesh in 2D and 3D, for polynomial degrees one to four.

2 A Matrix-Free Finite-Element Method

In the following discussion, the Poisson equation with homogeneous boundary conditions,

$$\nabla^2 u = f \text{ on } \Omega, \tag{1}$$
$$u = 0 \text{ on } \partial\Omega, \tag{2}$$

in two dimensions is studied. This is a simple model problem, however it is still representative of more complex problems as it shares most of their properties. If the equation involves other differential operators than ∇^2, they are typically treated in a similar way. It is readily extensible to three or higher dimensions. If there is a time dependency, a similar time-independent equation is solved at each time step. If the equation is non-linear, it is linearized and a similar linear problem is solved, e.g. throughout a Newton iteration procedure. Non-homogeneous Dirichlet boundary conditions can easily be transformed to homogeneous ones, and the treatment of Neumann conditions or more general Robin conditions leads to similar end results.

By multiplying (1) by a test function v and integrating by parts, the weak form

$$\int_\Omega \nabla v \cdot \nabla u \, dV = \int_\Omega v f \, dV \tag{3}$$

is obtained, where v belongs to the function space V which is chosen to satisfy the boundary conditions (2).

Now, let $\mathcal{K}$ be a quadrilateralization of Ω, i.e. a partitioning of Ω into a set of non-overlapping quadrilaterals Ω_k. Also, let V_h be the finite-dimensional space of all functions v, bi-polynomial of degree p within each element Ω_k, continuous between neighboring elements, and, once again, fulfilling the boundary condition. To find a basis for V_h, we begin by noting that in order to span the space of all p'th order bi-polynomials of an element, $(p+1)^2$ basis functions are needed for that element. To uniquely determine the coefficients of these $(p+1)^2$ element-local basis functions, $(p+1)^2$ *degrees of freedom, (DoFs)* are needed, which are introduced as the function values at $(p+1)^2$ node points on each element. Note that node points on edges and corners will be shared between several elements. The basis is then comprised of the p'th-degree bi-polynomials $\{\psi_i\}_{i=1}^{N_p}$, where basis function ψ_i is equal to unity at precisely node $j = i$, and zero at all other nodes $j \neq i$.

Expanding the solution in this space, $u = \sum_{i=1}^N u_i \psi_i$, and substituting ψ_j as the test functions v, we get

$$\sum_{i=1}^N A_{i,j} u_i = b_j \, , \text{for } j = 1, \ldots, N \, , \tag{4}$$

where

$$A_{i,j} = \int_\Omega \nabla \psi_i \cdot \nabla \psi_j dV \tag{5}$$

$$b_j = \int_\Omega f \psi_j dV \, . \tag{6}$$

This is a linear system in the DoFs u_i, which needs to be solved in order to obtain the approximate solution u to the original problem (1).

Noting that (5) can be writen as a sum over the elements in the mesh $\mathcal{K}$,

$$A_{i,j} = \sum_{k \in \mathcal{K}} \int_{\Omega_k} \nabla \psi_i \cdot \nabla \psi_j \mathrm{d}V \,, \tag{7}$$

we observe that each sub-integral will only be non-zero for very few combinations of basis functions, namely the ones that have a non-zero overlap on element k. If we introduce a local numbering of the DoFs within an element, there will be an element-dependent mapping I^k translating local index j to global index $I^k(j)$, and an associated permutation matrix $P^k{}_{i,j} = \delta_{i,I^k(j)}$. Using this, and introducing ψ_l^k as the l'th basis function on element k, we can write (7) on matrix form as

$$A = \sum_{k \in \mathcal{K}} P^k A^k P^{kT} \,, \tag{8}$$

where the local stiffness matrix A^k is defined as

$$A_{l,m}^k = \int_{\Omega_k} \nabla \psi_l^k \cdot \nabla \psi_m^k \mathrm{d}V \,. \tag{9}$$

2.1 Computation of the Local Matrix

The integral in (9) is usually computed by transforming Ω_k to a reference element, and using numerical quadrature. Typically, Gaussian quadrature is used since polynomials can be integrated exactly.

$$A_{i,j}^k = \sum_q \left[J_k^{-1}(\hat{x}_q)\hat{\nabla}\hat{\psi}_i(\hat{x}_q) \right] \cdot \left[J_k^{-1}(\hat{x}_q)\hat{\nabla}\hat{\psi}_j(\hat{x}_q) \right] |\det J_k(\hat{x}_q)| w_q \,,$$

where J_k is the Jacobian matrix of the transformation from reference element to the k'th real element, $\hat{x}_q$ are the quadrature points of the reference element, and w_q are the quadrature weights.

Now, if the mesh is uniform, i.e. all elements have the same shape and size, J_k will be the same for all k. In this case, also A^k will be independent of k, and a single $\hat{A}$ can be precomputed and stored in memory. For a non-uniform mesh, however, all the A^k will be distinct and a precomputation is unfeasible due to the extensive storage requirement. In such a case, a tensor based approach can be used, as described by Kronbichler and Kormann [4].

2.2 Matrix Free Operator Application

In the case of standard finite-element methods where an explicit matrix is used, (8) is computed once and the resulting matrix is stored, to be used in the subsequent multiplications. To obtain the matrix-free case, we multiply (8) by the vector u and simply rewrite it the following way,

$$Au = \left(\sum_{k \in \mathcal{K}} P^k A^k P^{kT} \right) u \Leftrightarrow Au = \sum_{k \in \mathcal{K}} \left(P^k A^k P^{kT} u \right) \,. \tag{10}$$

Since the permutation matrices merely selects and reorders rows, we have essentially disassembled the operator application from a sparse matrix-vector multiplication into a sum of many, small and dense matrix-vector multiplications, where each such multiplication involves a computation of the local matrix A^k.

2.3   Parallelization

Being made up of many small, independent matrix-vector products and the associated local-matrix computations, the matrix-free operator application in (10) is almost trivially parallelized – the list of elements is simply split into chunks of appropriate size and then all the chunks are processed in parallel. However, a problem arises when assembling the results into the single output vector.

For a given row i of the result, most of the terms in the sum in the right-hand side of (10) will be zero, however, the terms corresponding to all elements to which the i'th DoF belongs will be non-zero. All of these contributions will need to be added to the single memory location at row i of the result. Since these are computed in parallel, care must be taken to avoid race conditions while updating the shared memory location.

Mesh Coloring. As previously stated, only the elements to which a given node i belongs will give a contribution to the i'th row of the result. Conversely, this means that any two elements which do not share a DoF will be free of any conflicting updates, and may thus be processed concurrently.

One way of achieving this, is to use graph coloring. Denote two elements in a mesh as *neighbors* if they do not share any node points, which will hold if they do not share any vertices (see Fig. 1). Then, if all elements in the mesh are colored such that within each color, no two elements are neighbors, then all the elements within a single color can safely be executed in parallel.

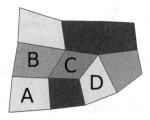

Fig. 1. Elements A and B are neighbors, as are elements A and C, and are thus given different colors. Elements A and D are not neighbors and can be given the same color.

Since not all elements are processed in parallel, there is a reduction of parallelism of $\frac{1}{N_c}$, where N_c is the number of colors needed. For a logically Cartesian mesh, $N_c = 2^d$, where d is the dimensionality of the problem, whereas for an unstructured FEM mesh, $N_c > 2^d$ in general (see Fig. 1). In both cases, however, N_c will be independent of the number of elements of the mesh. Thus, for sufficiently large problems, the overhead will be small enough. For the uniform meshes considered in this paper, the coloring is trivial. For the case of a general mesh, a more advanced graph coloring algorithm must be used, such as the ones of Berger et al. [8], Farhat and Crivelli [9], or Komatitsch et al. [7].

3 Graphics Processors

Recently, graphics processing units (GPUs) have seen an increasing use as general-purpose processors for high-performance computations within science and technology. Computer graphics consists of processing a large number of independent polygon vertices. Tailored for this very parallel and compute-intensive task, the architecture of GPUs is optimized for high throughput rather than low latency, which is the case for CPUs. Because of this, a much larger area of the GPU chip is dedicated to computations compared to a CPU. Also, memory bandwidth is typically considerably higher than on a CPU, whereas the caching system of a CPU aims at achieving low latency. As a consequence of the higher computing power per transistor, GPUs achieve a much higher efficiency, both economically (i.e. Gflops/$) and power-wise (i.e. Gflops/W).

Being comprised of many small similar tasks with a high computational intensity, scientific applications, such as e.g. stencil operations or linear algebra, have in many cases been well suited for the throughput-optimized GPU hardware. However, few applications fit the graphics-tailored GPU architecture perfectly and in practice, issues like the limited support for double precision or the necessity for very high parallelism may limit the utilization of a GPU system.

The first attempts at utilizing commodity graphics hardware for general computations were based on exploiting the programmable vertex and pixel shaders of the graphics pipeline. For a summary of the early endeavors in GPGPU, see the excellent survey by Owens et al. [10]. However, programming the graphics pipeline was difficult, and the real revolution came at the end of 2006, when Nvidia released CUDA, *Compute Unified Device Architecture*. The CUDA platform provides a unified model of the underlying hardware together with a C-based programming environment. The CUDA GPU, or *device*, comprises a number of Streaming Multiprocessors (SMs) which in turn are highly parallel multi-core processors. The threads of the application are then grouped into thread blocks which are executed independently on a single SM. Within a thread block or an SM, there is a piece of shared memory, and a small cache. Finally, synchronization is limited and only possible between threads within a block, except for global barriers. For further details on the CUDA platform, see the CUDA C Programming Guide [11]. Examples of studies based on CUDA include molecular dynamics simulations [12], fluid dynamics [13] and wave propagation [14].

Although CUDA is vendor specific and GPUs have a very specialized architecture, they are both part of a larger movement – that of heterogeneity and increasing use of specialized hardware and accelerators. Thus, developing algorithms and techniques for dedicated accelerators, such as GPUs, is relevant also for the technology of the future.

4   Experiment Code

As part of this research, a small framework for high-order finite-element application in efficient, heavily templated C++/CUDA has been developed. Because of the high accuracy which is needed when solving scientific problems, double precision is used throughout the code. The mesh is stored in an array of points and an array of elements. For the elements, an element struct is used comprising a list of DoF indices. This array-of-structure format was found to perform better than a structure-of-array approach, both for the CPU and the GPU.

We have implemented several different versions of the stiffness-matrix operator. Apart from the matrix-free GPU implementations, we include serial and parallel matrix-free implementations for the CPU, as well as matrix-based implementations for both CPU and GPU, for comparison.

4.1   Matrix-Based Implementations

The matrix-based reference implementation for the CPU, SpM, uses a Compressed Sparse Row (CSR) matrix format, since this performs well during matrix-vector multiplication. For the assembly, a list-of-lists (LIL) format is used, since this has superior performance during incremental construction. After the construction, the LIL matrix is converted to the CSR format, without much overhead. Still, the matrix construction amounts to a significant part of the total execution time (see results under Sect. 5.1). The sparse matrix-vector product is parallelized in OpenMP, by dividing the rows in chunks evenly over the processors. We used four threads, since this gave the best performance.

The corresponding implementation for the GPU, GPU_SpM, uses the efficient SpMV kernel of CUSPARSE, a sparse matrix library released by Nvidia as part of CUDA. The matrix assembly is performed on the CPU identically to the SpM implementation, and then copied to the GPU.

4.2   Matrix-Free Implementations

Our matrix-free implementations follows the idea described in Sect. 2.2. Since a uniform mesh is assumed, the local matrix is the same for all elements and a single copy is precomputed and stored. The serial version is called Mfree.

There are two versions parallelized using OpenMP, both based on computing the contribution from multiple elements in parallel. The main difference between the versions is the technique used to solve the conflict issue described in Sect. 2.3. In the PrivateBuffers implementation, each OpenMP thread writes its result to its own version of the output vector. After all threads have finished computing, a parallel reduction phase sums up the buffers into a single vector, trading off the conflicts for the extra storage and computations. Finally, there is an implementation `Color` which uses the mesh coloring method described in Sect. 2.3 to avoid the conflicts. Once again, four threads are used since this gave the best speedup relative to the serial version.

Much like the matrix-free implementations for the CPU, the ones for the GPU mainly differ in the treatment of conflicts. In all implementations, each thread handles a single element. A block size of 256 threads was chosen since this performed best in the experiments. There is one version, `GPU_Atomic`, which uses the built-in atomic operations of CUDA to protect the conflicting writes. There is also an implementation `GPU_Color` using the more advanced coloring-based treatment of conflicts described in Sect. 2.3. Finally, a version without any protection, `GPU_Max`, is also included to get an upper bound on the performance for an element-wise parallelization of the matrix-free operator application.

5   Numerical Experiments

The performance of the different implementations described above are evaluated through a series of benchmark experiments. These are based on the Poisson problem studied in Sect. 2. The unit square domain is discretized by a Cartesian mesh of quadrilateral elements of order p. A similar problem in 3D is considered, i.e. a unit cube discretized by a Cartesian mesh of p'th-order hexahedral elements. In detail, the experiment consists of the following parts:

1. Setup of data structures for the mesh, the vectors, and the operator.
2. Transfer of data to the appropriate memory location (i.e. device memory for GPU-based implementations).
3. 20 successive applications of the operator.
4. Transfer of data back to main memory.

To evaluate the execution time for the operator application, the time for steps 2–4 is measured, and the time for a single application is calculated by dividing by the number of iterations, i.e. 20. Furthermore, to get more stable results, 20 repetitions of steps 2–4 are performed, and the minimum time is recorded. The experiment is run for all the operator implementations described in Sect. 4, with polynomial degrees of one to four.

All experiments are performed on a server with an Intel Xeon E5-2680 eight-core processor @ 2.70GHz, 64 GB DRAM and an Nvidia Tesla K20c GPU with 2496 cores and 5 GB of ECC-enabled memory. The test system runs Linux 2.6.32, with a GCC compiler of version 4.4, and a CUDA platform of version 5.5.

5.1   Results

Figures 2 and 3 depict the performance of the most important implementations as a function of the number of degrees of freedom, in 2D and 3D respectively.

Firstly, we see that performance increases with the problem size as the parallelism of the hardware is saturated, in particular for the versions for the GPU,

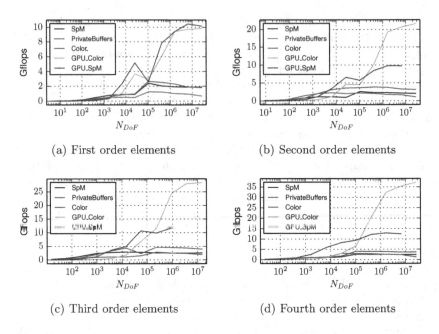

(a) First order elements   (b) Second order elements

(c) Third order elements   (d) Fourth order elements

Fig. 2. Scaling of the performance with the problem size (N_{DoF}), for the 2D experiments

due to its much higher parallelism. Also, it is evident that the GPU versions performed significantly faster than the ones for the CPU. Furthermore, we see that, as the complexity of the elements increases, i.e. as polynomial degree and dimensionality grow, so does the benefit of using a matrix-free approach. Although the matrix-based implementations for CPU and GPU performed on par with the matrix-free ones for element order one, they are outperformed already for second order elements. Moreover, in many cases, as expected, it was simply impossible to use the matrix-based version, since the storage requirement for the matrix exceeded the system memory (indicated by the truncated curves for SpM and GPU_SpM). Finally, as predicted, the setup times were reduced considerably. For the example of fourth-order polynomials in 2D, SpM required 14 seconds for the setup, whereas Color required only 0.2 seconds, a difference that was even larger in 3D. Similar times were recorded for the matrix-based and matrix-free GPU implementations. The performance for the largest problems is presented in more condensed form in Fig. 4 (a) and (b), which display the performance of all implementations at the largest problem size as p varies, for 2D and 3D, respectively.

For the results in 2D (Fig. 4(a)), we begin by noting that the matrix-free GPU versions gave very good speedups over the reference versions (between 5.4 and 10 times versus the fastest CPU version). In fact, the amount of work performed per time by the matrix-free GPU versions grew steadily with the polynomial order, whereas for both the matrix-based GPU implementation and all the CPU imple-

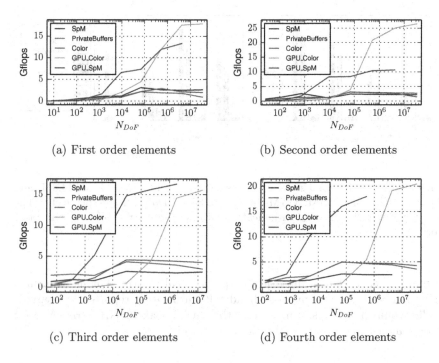

(a) First order elements   (b) Second order elements

(c) Third order elements   (d) Fourth order elements

Fig. 3. Scaling of the performance with the problem size (N_{DoF}), for the 3D experiments

mentations, this stayed roughly constant. Comparing the results of `GPU_Color` and `GPU_Atomic` with the result of version without any protection, `GPU_Max`, we see that there is an overhead of dealing with conflicting updates, but that using a coloring approach was more efficient than using atomic intrinsics.

From the results of the CPU-based matrix-free versions, it is clear that the straightforward implementation using private buffers gave a very poor speedup, due to the overhead of performing the buffer reduction. On the other hand, just as in the case of the GPU implementations, the parallelization based on coloring achieved a good speedup of about 3.5.

Looking at the results for the 3D experiment (see Fig. 4(b)), we see that, once again, using a matrix-free method on the GPU can give large speedups (4.5 – 10×). However, although we still see a speedup over the CPU, there is a significant drop in performance when going to order 3 and 4. An explanation for this can be found by looking at the size of the local matrix, $(p+1)^{(2d)} \cdot 8B$, which for $d = 3$ and $p = 3$ exactly matches the size of the L1 cache available per SM, namely 32kB. Thus, the threads within a block can no longer fetch the local matrix collectively by sharing reads.

Finally, we note that the Gflops numbers in Fig. 2 - 4 are fairly low, and quite far from the theoretical 1.17 double precision Tflops of the K20. However, this is no surprise since the SpMV operation is bandwidth-bound, which is also the case

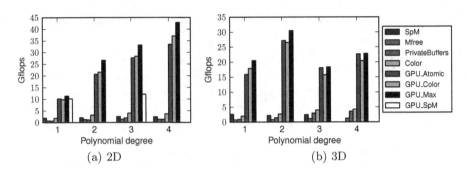

Fig. 4. Performance for the largest problems solved (with 26.2M, 26.2M, 14.8M, and 26.2M DoFs (2D) ; and 33.1M, 33.1M, 14.0M and 33.1M DoFs (3D), respectively). The missing bars for SpM and GPU_SpM indicate a fail, i.e. the matrix did not fit in main memory.

for a matrix-free version using a precomputed local matrix. This is confirmed by the numbers for global memory bandwidth utilization reported by nvprof, which lie around 110 GB/s, compared to the official peak 208GB/s (reported for ECC off), indicating a fairly well utilized bandwidth.

6   Conclusions

Our GPU implementations of the matrix-free stiffness operator achieved speedups of 4.5 and 10 times relative to the fastest CPU-based implementation. The results indicate that as element complexity grows, i.e. if the dimensionality and element degree increases, so does the performance benefit of using the GPU, which is promising for future use in a high-order finite-element method solver of elliptic and parabolic PDEs. Finally, as indicated by our results for the setup times, applications where frequent reassembly is necessary, such as time-dependent or non-linear problems, can benefit substantially from using a matrix-free approach. In addition, with the matrix-free method, we were able to solve problems an order of magnitude larger than with the matrix-based methods.

We saw that for a too large local matrix, performance drops significantly. However, as was pointed out in Sect. 2.1, the strategy based on a local matrix is limited to uniform meshes, meaning that for more realistic problems, other approaches, such as the tensor based technique of Kronbichler and Kormann [4], are necessary anyway. Considering this, the present result suggests that such methods can be favorable also for uniform meshes due to the lower memory footprint, for which the already good speedups can be expected to improve further.

Topics of ongoing research include development of a tensor-based operator implementation, as well as techniques for reduction of the high bandwidth usage, and solution of realistic problems within the field of two-phase flow simulation.

Acknowledgments. The computations were performed on systems provided by the Linnaeus center of excellence UPMARC, Uppsala Programming for Multicore Architectures Research Center.

References

1. Saad, Y.: Iterative Methods for Sparse Linear Systems, vol. 2. Society for Industrial and Applied Mathematics, Philadelphia (2003)
2. Williams, S., Oliker, L., Vuduc, R., Shalf, J., Yelick, K., Demmel, J.: Optimization of sparse matrix-vector multiplication on emerging multicore platforms. In: Proceedings of the 2007 ACM/IEEE Conference on Supercomputing, pp. 1–12 (2007)
3. Cantwell, C.D., Sherwin, S.J., Kirby, R.M., Kelly, P.H.J.: From h to p efficiently: Strategy selection for operator evaluation on hexahedral and tetrahedral elements. Computers & Fluids 43(1, SI), 23–28 (2011)
4. Kronbichler, M., Kormann, K.: A generic interface for parallel cell-based finite element operator application. Computers & Fluids 63, 135–147 (2012)
5. Cecka, C., Lew, A.J., Darve, E.: Assembly of finite element methods on graphics processors. International Journal for Numerical Methods in Engineering 85, 640–669 (2011)
6. Kckner, A., Warburton, T., Bridge, J., Hesthaven, J.S.: Nodal discontinuous Galerkin methods on graphics processors. Journal of Computational Physic 228(21), 7863–7882 (2009)
7. Komatitsch, D., Micha, D., Erlebacher, G.: Porting a high-order finite-element earthquake modeling application to NVIDIA graphics cards using CUDA. Journal of Parallel and Distributed Computing 69(5), 451–460 (2009)
8. Berger, P., Brouaye, P., Syre, J.C.: A mesh coloring method for efficient MIMD processing in finite element problems. In: Proceedings of the International Conference on Parallel Processing, pp. 41–46 (1982)
9. Farhat, C., Crivelli, L.: A General-Approach to Nonlinear Fe Computations on Shared-Memory Multiprocessors. Computer Methods in Applied Mechanics and Engineering 72(2), 153–171 (1989)
10. Owens, J.D., Luebke, D., Govindaraju, N., Harris, M., Krger, J., Lefohn, A., Purcell, T.J.: A Survey of General-Purpose Computation on Graphics Hardware. In: Eurographics 2005, State of the Art Reports, pp. 21–51 (2005)
11. NVIDIA Corporation: NVIDIA CUDA C Programming Guide, Version 5.5 (July 2013)
12. Anderson, J.A., Lorenz, C.D., Travesset, A.: General purpose molecular dynamics simulations fully implemented on graphics processing units. Journal of Computational Physics 227(10), 5342–5359 (2008)
13. Elsen, E., LeGresley, P., Darve, E.: Large calculation of the flow over a hypersonic vehicle using a GPU. Journal of Computational Physics 227(24), 10148–10161 (2008)
14. Micha, D., Komatitsch, D.: Accelerating a three-dimensional finite-difference wave propagation code using GPU graphics cards. Geophysical Journal International 182(1), 389–402 (2010)

Dynamic Load Balancing with Pair Potentials

Jean-Charles Papin[1,2], Christophe Denoual[2],
Laurent Colombet[2], and Raymond Namyst[3]

[1] CMLA, ENS-Cachan, 61 avenue du Prsident Wilson 94235 Cachan, France
[2] CEA, DAM, DIF, F-91297 Arpajon, France
[3] Université de Bordeaux, 351 cours de la Libration, 33400 Talence, France

Abstract. We present a new load balancing algorithm inspired by Molecular Dynamics Simulations. Our main motivation is to anticipate the rising costs of tasks-scheduling caused by the growth of the number of available cores on chips. This algorithm is based on a virtual decomposition of workload in Vorono cells centered around computing units. The method used in this paper allows cores to virtually move in order to change their computing load. Cores displacements are result of forces computation (with pair potential): attractive or repulsive forces between cores are balanced by the cores computing load (total cost of Vorono cell). Over-charged cores are more attractive than under-charged cores (which are then more repulsive). In this paper, we demonstrate the relevance of our approach by experimenting our algorithm with a high number of automatically-generated test cases, ranging from almost stable to quickly-evolving scenarii. In all cases, our algorithm is able to quickly converge to a distribution which maintains good locality properties.

Keywords: Simulation, dynamic load-balancing, tasks, many-core, pair potential.

1 Introduction

In order to reach exascale, current trends in super-computing are on low-energy consumption systems [1], with systems containing an increasing number of energy-aware processors and accelerators [2] [3]. These processors and accelerators offer more computing cores with reduced frequencies, making task optimization very demanding. A common way to extract parallelism from applications is to distribute the main computing flow into a large number of tasks [4]. Numerous run-times [5] [6] [7] actually work this way. In addition, since its third version, OpenMP offers task support in it specification [8].

Accurate task scheduling must provide numerous tasks for one thread, leading to an important scheduler overhead when hundred of cores are considered, mainly due to finding the best queue and inserting the new task. Algorithm to find the best queue is critical (a bad task distribution drives to poor performances) and depends on tasks properties, e.g., average task duration, data amount, etc. Usually, those kinds of difficulties are solved by introducing work-stealing strategies, but finding a victim among thousands of threads is very expensive. Advanced

L. Lopes et al. (Eds.): Euro-Par 2014 Workshops, Part II, LNCS 8806, pp. 462–473, 2014.

schedulers take care about data dependencies and data locality [9]. Tasks with strong data affinity should be scheduled to the same computing unit to prevent from data migrations and improve cache usage. NUMA-aware allocations. One other important aspect of tasks scheduling is the ability to take into account the possible evolution of task load during simulations.

Aiming to propose an efficient task scheduler with NUMA-aware allocations, we use a partition of the simulation domain into boxes of fixed size. Each box is associated to one elementary task and contains a few numbers of elementary calculation element, typically 10 to 100 atoms, finite elements, or finite difference cells. We then gather the boxes around a virtual center by using a Vorono tessellation, and associated each Vorono zone to a thread. In doing so, we ensure that threads are always dealing with a compact set of boxes, which maximize caches usage. Since the CPU cost of a task may vary due to internal evolution of the elementary calculation element, the amount of calculation of a thread could strongly vary during a simulation. Noting that the density of Vorono centers is related to the number of elementary tasks in the Vorono zones (the higher the density the lower the tasks number), we chose to move the Vorono centers to adapt the CPU charge of the threads. In opposition to a "task by task" scheduling, the proposed approach induces a limited fraction of tasks to be re-scheduled during charge adaptation (typically, tasks at thread domain boundary). The method to adapt the thread charge "on the fly" uses an analogy with the dynamic of electrically charged particles.

We will first define the "virtual core" as the center of the Vorono tessellation method, then recall the pair potential theory, and put forward the advantage of this method in tasks scheduling. We then discuss our choice of pair forces and their relevance for load balancing. A large set of test-cases, which present different charge variations (smooth/aggressive), are then proposed to demonstrate the advantages of a dynamic load balancing based on pair potentials. We will then conclude by the evaluation of our scheduler in a real parallel application.

2   Tasks Scheduling with Pair Potentials

We use a 2D grid (see fig. 1) in which every cell represents a task. Each task has a computing load of its own, which can evolve over time. We gather tasks around a virtual core (termed in the following a *vCores*, a virtual representation of the physical computing units) by using a Vorono tessellation[10]. By this way, we maximise per-core data locality. In a shared-memory environment, this guarantees NUMA-aware allocations and better caches usage. In a distributed-memory environment, this reduces inter-node data displacements. The load of a *vCore* is the sum of the computing load of each tasks in its Vorono cell. Thus, real-time tasks cost variations have a direct influence on the *vCores* load.

We then associate to each *vCores* a force and make them *virtually* move over the task domain in response to this force. By moving, a core will change its computing load, which gives the opportunity to re-equilibrates the computing load between *vCore*.

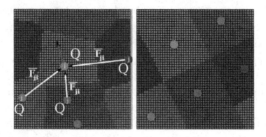

Fig. 1. By introducing pair potentials in task scheduling, a core can move over the tasks domain (red arrow). Q is the local computing load of the core and F_{ij} the applied forces on i. This local computing load modulate the intensity of attractive/repulsive forces between cores. In this case, all tasks have the same computing cost.

Figure (1) gives a representation of the elementary tasks (or cells) the *vCores* and the associated Vorono cells, as colored domains.

In the next section we define a pair potential between *vCores* that would lead to a good load balancing, for any variations of the underlying elementary tasks load.

3   Evolution of a Set Charged Particles

Let us consider the Coulomb force between of two particles i, j separated by a vector $\mathbf{r}_{ij} = \mathbf{x}_i - \mathbf{x}_j$ with charge Q_i, Q_j:

$$\mathbf{F}_{ij} = Q_i Q_j \frac{\mathbf{r}_{ij}}{|\mathbf{r}_{ij}|^3}. \tag{1}$$

Different charge signs lead to attractive forces whereas charges with same sign produce repulsive ones. Pairs interactions of this N-Body system are calculated by exploiting the symmetry of interactions, i.e., $\mathbf{F}_{ij} = -\mathbf{F}_{ji}$. In order to get the relaxed state only, we minimize the potential by using a steepest descent algorithm: $d\mathbf{x}/dt = -\alpha \mathbf{F}_{ij}$ (with α a positive scalar), and by lumping α and time increment into a simple scalar k:

$$\mathbf{x}(t) = \mathbf{x}(t-1) - k \sum_j \mathbf{F}_{ij} \tag{2}$$

We rescale k so that the distance $\mathbf{x}(t) - \mathbf{x}(t-1)$ is a fraction of the verlet box dimension (a task), which ensure convergence to stable or metastable states.

Going on this analogy between charged particles and computing loads, we set the charge of a *vCore* to be the sum of the computing load of each tasks in the Vorono cell q_k:

$$Q_i = \sum_{k \in Vorono(i)} q_k. \tag{3}$$

Preliminary results using this force are discussed in the following section. Enhanced forces expressions are then proposed to improve the load balance, and discussed.

4   Potential Test Cases

Despite its apparent simplicity, minimizing a set of particles interacting by an electric potential could lead to complex behaviors. For example, when homogeneous repulsive charges are considered, the minimization leads to a cubic close-packed lattice with a minimal number of neighboring cells (i.e. 12). Dealing with non-constant loads requires to slightly modify the pair potential, as proposed below, but also to test it on standardized tests cases.

We have developed a *C++* simulator which helps us to select an efficient potential. This simulator generates a grid of tasks (of different charges), and randomly inserts a bunch of *vCores* (see fig. 2). Thanks to this simulator, we have a real-time feedback on the actual load balancing and Vorono cells configuration. Various charge evolutions are supported by our simulator. We can generate a whole new map that leads to strong tasks charge variations, or we can translate the map (smooth tasks charge transitions). The map is based on a Perlin noise [11] generated with the LibNoise [12] library. A stable configuration is reached when the *vCores* are stable (i.e. velocity is null).

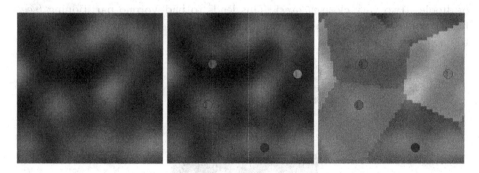

Fig. 2. Simulator used to find an efficient potential for tasks scheduling. From left to right: tasks grid with different loads, *vCores* are positioned on the grid, associated Vorono cell.

4.1   Three Potentials

Our original idea was to use a slightly modified Coulomb potential so that overloaded *vCores* allows their neighboring *vCores* to get closer, whereas underloaded *vCores* are strongly repulsive. Two possible choices are presented. Decreasing repulsive force for increasing load Q can be obtained by considering the force:

$$\mathbf{F}_{ij} = \lambda \frac{\mathbf{r}_{ij}}{|\mathbf{r}_{ij}|^3} \text{ with } \lambda = \frac{1}{Q_i} + \frac{1}{Q_j} . \tag{4}$$

This modified potential is repulsive-only. Preliminary tests show that minimization leads to cubic closed-packed lattice for homogeneous task load, but fails to obtain a reasonably well balanced load for inhomogeneous task repartition. With the objective to define a potential that produce null forces when *vCores* are *optimally* charged, we note that ideal load partitions are obtained when all the charges Q_i are equal to the mean charge m

$$m = \frac{1}{N} \sum_{i=1,N} Q_i \text{ with } N, \text{ the number of VCores.} \tag{5}$$

We then propose to use a potential that leads to null forces when $Q_i - m$.

$$\mathbf{F}_{ij} = \lambda \frac{\mathbf{r}_{ij}}{|\mathbf{r}_{ij}|^3} \text{ with } \lambda = 1 - \frac{Q_i + Q_j}{2m}. \tag{6}$$

In this case, when a pair of *vCores* is globally under-loaded (the λ term is positive), the two *vCores* repulse each other. By this way, its Vorono surface and local load will grow. The reverse behavior occurs when the *vCore* is over-loaded (the λ term is negative): the Vorono surface and the local load decrease thanks to the attractive forces. Even if we have noted good load partitioning (6% to the optimal load distribution), our preliminary simulations show the formation of dipoles (two very close *vCores*). This leads to bad Vorono partitioning (see fig. 3): some *vCores* are no longer in the center of their Voronoi cell, but close to one of the frontier.

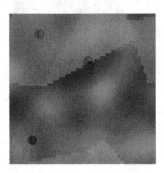

Fig. 3. Dipole formation: in this case (potential (6)) produces a bad Vorono cell splitting. Some *vCores* are too close to each other. The short repulsive term introduced in (7) solves this issue.

To tackle to this problem, we have added a short-distance repulsion to our potential (7). This term ensures that two *vCores* can not be too close to each other.

$$\mathbf{F}_{ij} = \lambda \frac{\mathbf{r}_{ij}}{|\mathbf{r}_{ij}|^3} + \frac{\mathbf{r}_{ij}}{|\mathbf{r}_{ij}|^5} \text{ with } \lambda = 1 - \frac{Q_i + Q_j}{2m}. \tag{7}$$

5 Experiments

In order to evaluate our task scheduling method, we have developed four kinds of test cases (see fig. 4). The simulated domain is a 50×50 grid of tasks, and we arbitrary place 10 *vCores* on the domain (the random position is the same for each test case). A stable configuration is accepted when the variance to the optimal task distribution is below 2. The tests runs on an Intel® Xeon E5-2650.

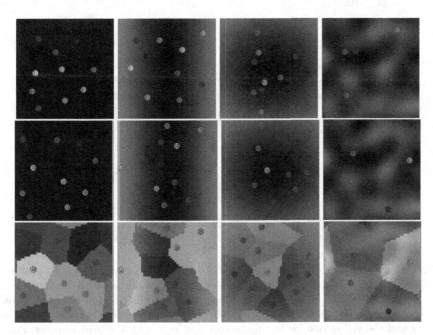

Fig. 4. From left to right: (1) the load is uniform over the domain, (2) the load is distributed over a line, (3) the load is concentrated in a disc, (4) the load is randomly distributed. From top to bottom: the first line presents the load distribution, the second line shows the final *vCores* configuration, and the last line represents the domain of each *vCores*.

5.1 Experimental Results

Static Scheduling. Here, we evaluate the number of computing steps needed to reach a stable *vCore* configuration. Figure 5 shows the convergence curves for our test-cases. The two curves represent the distance to the optimal load per *vCore.* The upper curves (in blue) show the convergence of the most over-loaded *vCore*, and lower curves (in yellow), the convergence of the least under-charged *vCore*. We can observe that tests-cases (2) and (3) are complex to schedule. With the loaded-line, we never reach a good tasks scheduling: we are nearly 25% to the optimal. A solution that may solve this issue is presented in 5.2. In case of the loaded-disc, we reach a good tasks distribution, but with an important number of steps. Cases (1) and (4) reach a good tasks distribution in a reasonable number of steps.

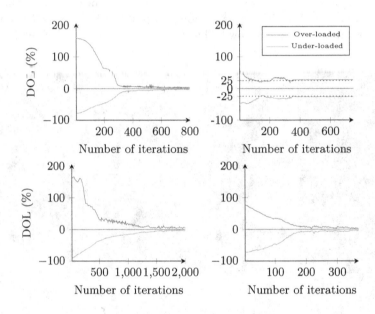

Fig. 5. Convergence of different test-cases. The red horizontal curve represents the optimal per-core load of the domain. The blue and yellow curves show the distance to optimal load (DOL) of *vCores*. This expresses the tasks distribution efficiency (tasks distribution is better when DOL is close to 0). The blue one is for the most overloaded *vCores* and the yellow one for less underloaded *vCores*. **(1)**: the load is uniform over the domain. **(2)** the load is distributed in a line, **(3)**: the load is concentrated in a disc. **(4)**: the load is randomly distributed.

Dynamic Scheduling. For dynamic scheduling, we use two kinds of charge variations. The first one is the LibNoise [12] ability to change the frequency of the generated noise. By this way, we translate the load map over the task domain. The second type of load variation is done by generating a completely new map. We call rough load variation the generation of a new map, and smooth load variation a simple change in frequency of the actual noise. Table 1 summarize the efficiency of our tasks scheduling method. This shows us that reaching a tasks distribution in case of smooth task load variation is nearly 90 times faster than in case of rough load transition.

Table 1. Average number of steps for rough and smooth charge variation over 1000 tests

Transition type	Number of steps			Time (ms)		
	Average	Min	Max	Average	Min	Max
Rough	432.700	27	5115	32.674	3.888	755.744
Smooth	5.238	2	312	0.151	0.144	70.847

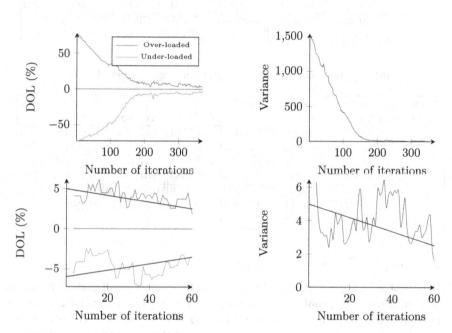

Fig. 6. Left: number of steps needed to converge after a rough (top) or a smooth (bottom) load variation of tasks for the most/least loaded *vCores*. Right: variance variations of the global system (convergence criteria).

Large Number of Cores. Here, we evaluate the ability to find a stable *vCores* configuration for a large number of *vCores*. We use different configurations (i.e. number of tasks, number of *vCores*) to stress our simulations. Tables 2 and 3 compare the number of steps and the time needed to distribute tasks over *vCores*. As expected, the number of *vCores* and tasks impact the number of steps needed to reach an equilibrium. In every cases, reaching a new task distribution after a smooth load variation of tasks is almost-instantaneous.

With an higher number of cores (table 3), the number of compute steps needed is reasonably proportional to the number of *vCores*. Nevertheless, the associated time explodes, due to our Vorono tessellation algorithm. Our implementation has a complexity in $\mathcal{O}(n \times m)$, with n the number of *vCores*, and m the number of tasks in the domain. We are currently looking for graph partitioning optimisation[13] in aim of reducing this computing cost.

Table 2. Dynamic load distribution for a large number of *vCores*

Number of *vCores*	Domain dimensions	Transition type	Number of steps			Time (ms)		
			Average	Min	Max	Average	Min	Max
13	50x50	Rough	578.810	96	1939	138.871	29.005	599.621
	50x50	Smooth	16.229	2	1188	0.624	0.304	374.893
	100x100	Rough	997.230	238	2544	113.442	268.578	2271.620
	100x100	Smooth	26.983	2	1331	10.587	1.306	339.403
	150x150	Rough	1146.040	237	1977	279.070	582.276	4582.276
	150x150	Smooth	101.386	2	1578	68.887	2.866	1073.940

Table 3. Dynamic load distribution for a large number of *vCores*

Number of *vCores*	Domain dimensions	Transition type	Number of steps			Time (ms)		
			Average	Min	Max	Average	Min	Max
72	50x50	Rough	763.321	5	7784	612.415	130.010	1097.750
	50x50	Smooth	62.366	2	4942	2.174	2.068	990.199
	100x100	Rough	2310.150	477	4915	1447.130	301.027	3245.290
	100x100	Smooth	319.010	2	1988	161.877	6.289	125.502
	150x150	Rough	3152.600	803	4968	4138.220	1086.650	6760.730
	150x150	Smooth	414.260	4	1990	173.868	40.390	269.675
	250x250	Smooth	-	-	-			

5.2   Complex Cases

We have seen in the second case in fig. 5 that reaching a good task distribution
can be difficult. The problem is that some *vCores* are heavily over-loaded while
others are strongly under-loaded and are caught by surrounding *vCores*. We are
currently working on a complementary potential that produces only attractive
forces between tasks and *vCores*. By this way, *vCores* will be attracted by the
most costly tasks. Preliminary results show promising configurations (see fig.7).
Nevertheless, with this new interaction, computing time increases dramatically.
We need to compute interaction between *vCores* and tasks. Initial complexity
of the algorithm is in $\mathcal{O}(N^2)$, but with this potential, it increases in $\mathcal{O}(mN^2)$,
with m, the number of tasks.

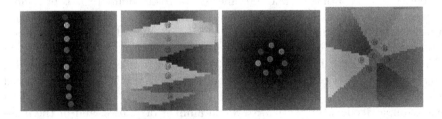

Fig. 7. With the attraction of tasks, the final distribution is better

6   Case Study: Coddex

In order to experiment our scheduler in a real-world application, we have extended the StarPU [5] runtime, which is used by Coddex, a CEA software. Coddex is a Finite Element code dedicated to the modeling of plasticity and phase transition on solid materials. This software is based on the MPI library for inter-node communications and on StarPU for a threads/tasks parallelism inside a computing node. The experimental platform used for our experiments is a double-sockets node (Intel Xeon E5-2650). By using a multi-sockets node, we want to evaluate the ability for our scheduler to minimize the tasks data displacements over the different NUMA nodes. Our scheduler is compiled as

Table 4. Comparison of cache misses (L2_DCM)

		Values (%)		
		Average	Max	Min
Scheduler	Eager	5.0184	16.9964	0.0
	PBS	0.6830	3.6833	0.0
Gain (%)		86.4	78.3	0.0

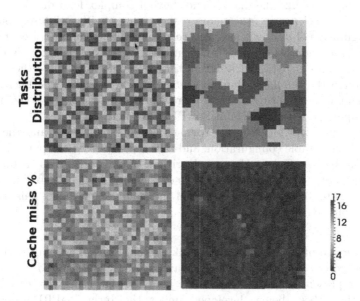

Fig. 8. Average number of L2 data cache misses for a typical Coddex execution (1 MPI node, 32 threads). The left side figures show the results with the default StarPU scheduler (eager), and the right side figures, the results with our scheduler (PBS). On the top of the figure, each color represent a thread (one per thread), while on the bottom on the figure, a color represent a cache miss rate.

a separate library (**P**otential **B**ased **S**cheduler, PBS) and can then be used by several applications. In order to integrate our scheduler inside StarPU, we've add a "meta-scheduler" that calls the PBS library to retrieves the tasks distribution over threads.

In the following, we compare two schedulers : eager [14], the default StarPU scheduler (a simple FIFO list of tasks) and PBS, our scheduler. We measure the average number of data cache misses [1] of each task for each simulation time step. Figure 8 presents the percent of L2 data cache misses for a typical Coddex execution (50K points, 2D domain), and the table 4 shows the cache misses rate reduction. Each square of the figure represents a task (Verlet box), and we can see that the task distributions (top of the figure) over threads (one color per thread). We can notice that the PBS scheduler provides a better memory accesses between our tasks; this is mainly due to a better cache usage, and a better NUMA accesses.

7   Conclusions and Future Work

The Pair-potential approach for task scheduling over a large number of cores produces efficient task distribution, especially in case of dynamic load. Our preliminary experiments show a rapid convergence of task distribution in a close to optimal per-core load. Nevertheless, this distribution can be sometime difficult to reach: cases like the disc of load, have a complex load distribution to be balanced over *vCores*. In other more realistic cases (with a diffused load), a stable configuration of *vCores* is easy and relatively fast to compute. Best results are obtained for smooth load variations. In this case, task scheduling is nearly instantaneous. This is particularly interesting in simulations where the load is *moving* through the simulated domain (eg. shock waves). Our experimentation on a real simulation application shows an real improvement of the cache misses rates in comparison with the default StarPU scheduler.

Our next works will focus on improving the number of steps and the time needed to reach a stable configuration, and thus, by adjusting our potential and by implementing an efficient Vorono algorithm. Some work needs to be done on the removal of some centralized aspects of the current algorithm: our actual potential needs to know the total charge of the simulated domain. This implies communications/synchronizations steps.

Acknowledgements. We wish to thank Julien Roussel for his participation to the forces equation 4, which have strongly accelerated our work. Experiments presented in this paper were carried out using the PLAFRIM experimental testbed, being developed under the Inria PlaFRIM development action with support from LABRI and IMB and other entities: Conseil Rgional d'Aquitaine, FeDER, Universit de Bordeaux and CNRS (see https://plafrim.bordeaux.inria.fr/).

---

[1] We use the PAPI[15] library.

References

1. Hemmert, S.: Green hpc: From nice to necessity. Computing in Science & Engineering 12, 8–10 (2010)
2. Showerman, M., Enos, J., Pant, A., Kindratenko, V., Steffen, C., Pennington, R., Hwu, W.M.: Qp: a heterogeneous multi-accelerator cluster. In: Proc. 10th LCI International Conference on High-Performance Clustered Computing (2009)
3. Kindratenko, V.: Novel computing architectures. Computing in Science and Engineering 11, 54–57 (2009)
4. Turek, J., Schwiegelshohn, U., Wolf, J.L., Yu, P.S.: Scheduling parallel tasks to minimize average response time. In: Proceedings of the Fifth Annual ACM-SIAM Symposium on Discrete Algorithms, Society for Industrial and Applied Mathematics, pp. 112–121 (1994)
5. Augonnet, C., Thibault, S., Namyst, R., Wacrenier, P.A.: StarPU: a unified platform for task scheduling on heterogeneous multicore architectures. Concurrency and Computation: Practice and Experience 23, 187–198 (2011)
6. Kukanov, A., Voss, M.J.: The foundations for scalable multi-core software in intel threading building blocks. Intel Technology Journal 11 (2007)
7. Supercomputing Technologies Group, Massachusetts Institute of Technology Laboratory for Computer Science: Cilk 5.4.6 Reference Manual (2001)
8. OpenMP-Committee: Openmp application program interface 3.0 (Technical report)
9. Augonnet, C., Clet-Ortega, J., Thibault, S., Namyst, R.: Data-Aware Task Scheduling on Multi-Accelerator based Platforms. In: 16th International Conference on Parallel and Distributed Systems, Shangai, Chine (2010)
10. Aurenhammer, F., Klein, R.: Voronoi diagrams. In: Handbook of Computational Geometry, pp. 201–290 (2000)
11. Perlin, K.: Perlin noise is a computer-generated visual effect developed by ken perlin, who won an academy award for technical achievement for inventing it
12. Bevins, J.: Libnoise: a portable, open-source, coherent noise-generating library for c++
13. Chevalier, C., Pellegrini, F.: Pt-scotch: A tool for efficient parallel graph ordering. Parallel Computing 34, 318–331 (2008)
14. Sarmenta, L.F.G., Hirano, S.: Bayanihan: Building and studying web-based volunteer computing systems using java 15, 675–686 (1999)
15. Browne, S., Dongarra, J., Garner, N., Ho, G., Mucci, P.: A portable programming interface for performance evaluation on modern processors. Int. J. High Perform. Comput. Appl. 14, 189–204 (2000)

Analysis of Parallel Applications
on a High Performance–Low Energy Computer

Florina M. Ciorba[1], Thomas Ilsche[1], Elke Franz[2], Stefan Pfennig[2],
Christian Scheunert[3], Ulf Markwardt[1], Joseph Schuchart[1],
Daniel Hackenberg[1], Robert Schöne[1], Andreas Knüpfer[1], Wolfgang E. Nagel[1],
Eduard A. Jorswieck[3], and Matthias S. Müller[4]

[1] Center for Information Sciences and High Performance Computing,
Technische Universität Dresden, Germany
[2] Faculty of Computer Science, Chair of Privacy and Data Security,
Technische Universität Dresden, Germany
[3] Faculty of Electrical Engineering, Chair of Communications Theory,
Technische Universität Dresden, Germany
{firstname.lastname}@tu-dresden.de
[4] Rheinisch-Westfälische Technische Hochschule Aachen, Germany
Chair for Computer Science 12 - High Performance Computing
mueller@itc.rwth-aachen.de

Abstract. In this paper, we propose a holistic approach for the analysis of parallel applications on a high performance–low energy computer (called the HAEC platform). The HAEC platform is currently under design and refers to an architecture in which multiple 3-D stacked massively parallel processor chips are optically interconnected on a single board and multiple parallel boards are interconnected using short-range high-speed wireless links. Although not exclusively targeting high performance computing (HPC), the HAEC platform aims to deliver high performance at low energy costs, which are essential features for future HPC platforms. At the core of the proposed approach is a trace-driven simulator called `haec_sim` which we developed to simulate the behavior of parallel applications running on this hardware. We investigate several mapping layouts to assign the parallel applications to the HAEC platform. We concentrate on analyzing the communication performance of the HAEC platform running parallel applications. The simulator can employ two communication models: dimension order routing (DOR) and practical network coding (PNC). As a first example of the usefulness of the proposed holistic analysis approach, we present simulation results using these communication models on a communication-intensive parallel benchmark. These results highlight the potential of the mapping strategies and communication models for analyzing the performance of various types of parallel applications on the HAEC platform. This work constitutes the first step towards more complex simulations and analyses of performance and energy scenarios than those presented herein.

Keywords: performance, HAEC, simulation, network coding, routing.

L. Lopes et al. (Eds.): Euro-Par 2014 Workshops, Part II, LNCS 8806, pp. 474–485, 2014.

1   Introduction

Energy efficiency is one of the greatest challenges in information and communication technology. A large part of the energy costs can be attributed to the transfer of information. Progress in energy efficient interconnections is necessary to allow high performance computing (HPC) and data centers to manage their energy costs while performing powerful applications. Future computing systems will largely consist of chips with energy efficient interconnects, such as IBM's Holey Optochip [7] or HP's Corona architecture [20].

The highly adaptive energy efficient computing (HAEC) platform [9] is a future computing system design aimed at dynamically adjusting the energy usage according to the workload without compromising on performance. It uses optical on-board [16] and wireless board-to-board [10] connections to mitigate the bandwidth and latency bottlenecks inherent in existing multiprocessor systems. Optical and wireless interconnects provide a wider opportunity for selecting different operation modes such that the energy consumption of individual links can be adjusted according to their load. We use an integrated approach of a highly scalable end-to-end simulation framework combining sufficient details of the application, processor, and network.

Our goal is to analyze the performance of applications executed on a high performance–low energy computer. We are concerned with questions regarding: (i) Modeling of the behavior of the various independent software and hardware components of such a system, (ii) Their integration into a holistic system model, and (iii) The prediction of the performance and energy costs of running applications on the HAEC platform. A more specific challenge on which we concentrate in this work is to predict the performance of the HAEC platform running (communication intensive) parallel applications.

Our approach is holistic and comprises multiple models. The application model is based on event traces obtained from running the parallel applications on existing platforms. This model is mapped onto the HAEC platform model using several mapping strategies. Our simulations employ two communication models to predict the behavior of parallel applications on the HAEC platform. The resulting simulated application traces form the basis for our analysis using state-of-the-art performance measurement and visualization tools.

The main contribution of this work is a holistic approach for analyzing the performance of parallel applications on the HAEC platform. We developed a trace-driven simulation framework (`haec_sim`) that employs three strategies for mapping applications to the target platform. Another major contribution is a novel communication model for the HAEC platform developed using network coding (NC) technology. This model has been implemented in the simulator in addition to standard routing. Even though these communication models do not account for transmission errors, they can easily be extended to address errors. Then, NC will outperform standard routing [1]. Given that the design of the HAEC platform is ongoing, the simulator will account for new aspects of the hardware that may otherwise be hard to capture by existing simulators.

2   Related Work

Topology aware mapping of parallel applications with regular and irregular communication patterns onto supercomputers has been studied in [4]. Mapping is also a very important area of research in network on chip (NoC) systems, where a major challenge in overall system design is to associate the intellectual property (IP) cores implementing tasks of an application with the NoC routers [17].

Many communication models in HPC belong to the LogP model family or the BSP model family [11]. Even though the parameters of these models capture significant characteristics of the underlying hardware, they do not explicitly account for the network topology. Routing [6] and network coding [1] are at a lower abstraction level than the LogP and BSP models and account for the network topology. For multiple concurrent flows, network coding can achieve higher throughput, lower latency, and better energy efficiency than standard routing.

BigSim [19] is a parallel trace-based simulator for predicting the performance of MPI applications on future large scale systems larger than those available today. COTSon [2] is a parallel simulation infrastructure for modeling clusters of multicore CPU nodes, networking, and I/O. It combines functional simulation for the behavior of devices and software, and timing simulators for the timing of all components. Apart from the compute performance, it also enables to simulate the power consumption. Dimemas [14] is a sequential trace-based simulator for predicting the performance of parallel MPI or multithreaded applications. The simulation model uses parameters such as relative processor speeds, network bandwidth and latency within and across nodes, the number of input and output links, and the processor scheduling policy. The network model assumes two-level buses. Existing trace-driven simulation approaches combine only a subset of all the aspects considered in this work, such as performance *or* energy efficiency, and application *or* system modeling.

3   Aspects of Application Analysis on Future Computing Systems

3.1   Simulation and Analysis Workflow

We employ trace-driven simulation to simulate future computing systems, such as the HAEC platform (cf. §3.3), using traces generated with the scalable performance measurement infrastructure for parallel codes Score-P (cf. §3.2). We developed a parallel trace-based simulation framework (haec_sim) for predicting the behavior of applications running on a future computing system (described via hardware and system software abstraction models). The simulation concentrates on maximizing performance, minimizing energy consumption, and optimizing communication. The simulated HAEC platform (cf. §3.3) employs a heterogeneous and adaptive communication model (cf. §4.2) to combine high application performance with high energy efficiency.

The proposed simulation and analysis workflow is illustrated in Fig. 1. The source code of a parallel application of interest represents the first step in the

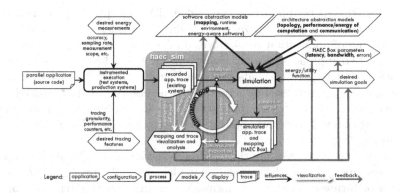

Fig. 1. Proposed trace-driven simulation and analysis workflow

proposed workflow. This is followed by specification of performance and energy features desired to be collected using Score-P [13]. The instrumented application is executed either on an energy measurement test system or on high performance computing production systems. The resulting execution trace forms the input to the simulation. This trace can be visualized and analyzed using Vampir [12]. In addition to the input trace, the simulator (haec_sim) contains and employs various software and architecture abstraction models. The software abstraction models include the mapping of the processes in the input trace to the HAEC platform topology (cf. §4.1), the operating system, and energy-aware software. The architecture abstraction models include the topology of the HAEC platform (cf. §3.3), a model for predicting the energy consumption of running the desired application on the HAEC platform, and a communication model that describes how will communication be carried out over the wireless and optical links of the HAEC platform (cf. §4.2). The HAEC platform parameters refer to latency, bandwidth, and error rates. The desired simulation goals also form an input to the simulator and may include the optimization criteria (or metrics) such as performance (time) or cost (energy). The output of the simulation is an event trace describing the predicted behavior of the initial application if it were executed on the HAEC platform. Similar to the input trace, the output trace can also be visualized and analyzed with Vampir. Simulation-based analysis results in valuable feedback that can be provided to the abstraction models, to tune the target system parameters, and to adjust the desired simulation parameters to gain more insight towards the goals of the analysis.

3.2 Modeling Applications

Modeling and simulation of the performance and energy consumption of parallel applications require a detailed description of their characteristics and their behavior on various computing platforms. This can be provided in several ways, such as via: (i) Expert application knowledge, (ii) Conceptual application models, (iii) Distribution parametrized (or stochastic) models (e.g., profiles), and (iv) Recording of application event traces on existing computing systems.

The first two approaches are not easily amenable to a broad range of parallel applications and require a significant modeling effort. The third one may not provide the fine-grained level of detail that is necessary to capture correlations and interference effects in the application. The last approach is more generic and can be employed to derive application descriptions even for highly complex applications [18].

Discrete event traces capture the runtime behavior of parallel applications on existing systems and form the application model for simulating their performance on target or future computing platforms. Traces preserve the dynamic application behavior and can yield meaningful results even for small changes in the model [10]. An application trace consists of a time-ordered sequence of discrete events including functions execution, communication operations, and management of parallelism [12]. In addition, runtime hardware performance characteristics, including energy measurements, can be recorded. We use Score-P [13] to record the execution of parallel applications in the OTF2 [8] file format.

3.3   Modeling a High Performance–Low Energy Computer

The HAEC platform refers to a new high performance–low energy parallel computer architecture [9]. In this architecture, the compute nodes consist of 3-D stacked processor chips with thousands of 'thin' cores [15] offering massive intra-node parallelism. This parallelism is not modeled explicitly in haec_sim and is abstracted. Thus, a collection of many lightweight application threads are represented as a single coarse-grain application process. Several such processes can run concurrently on a single compute node or across multiple compute nodes and we assume that the 'thin' cores are not oversubscribed.

Multiple compute nodes on a single board are interconnected using optical waveguides [16] and multiple such boards are interconnected using board-to-board high-speed wireless links [10]. The on-board optical links have high data transmission rates, low transmission errors, and their topology is 2-D mesh [16]. The board-to-board wireless links are arranged around a compute node using very large Butler matrices (antenna arrays of 8x8 or 16x16) which correspond to narrow beams. When this is considered for both for transmitter and receiver nodes, the interference decreases significantly and can be neglected [10]. The wireless antennas use a beamforming architecture with phase shifters which enables suppression of signals from directions that are not desired. The placement of the wireless antennas around the compute nodes yields a 1-D mesh topology between neighboring boards. The 3×3×3 HAEC platform topology is schematically illustrated in Fig. 2a.

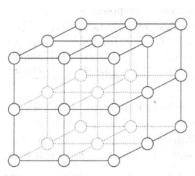

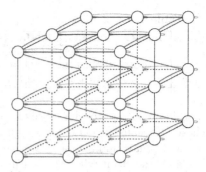

(a) 3×3×3 HAEC platform topology. Circles indicate compute nodes, blue/green lines indicate optical/wireless links, respectively.

(b) *lu.C.81* mapped onto the 3×3×3 HAEC platform using *block xyz* mapping. Color lines denote inter-process logical communications (red: ∼80k, turquoise: ∼160k, green: ∼240k).

Fig. 2. The HAEC platform (a) without and (b) with an assigned application

4   Modeling and Simulation Results

4.1   Mapping Applications to Systems

Simulating the behavior of any parallel application on the HAEC platform requires that the application processes be mapped to the nodes of the HAEC platform topology illustrated in Fig. 2a. High quality mappings increase the likelihood of achieving high performance and low energy consumption. The objectives of mapping application processes to compute nodes are *reducing the overall communication cost* and *maximizing parallelism.*

The *process-to-node* mapping is fixed for the duration of the simulation, i.e., no process is migrated. We compare three single-pass mapping strategies: xyz, block xyz, and random. These strategies are oblivious of the application communication requirements. The *xyz* mapping identifies the compute node to assign to an application process by first increasing the x coordinate of the last assigned node until every node along the x dimension is assigned, then by increasing the y coordinate and, finally, the z coordinate in the same manner. When the number of application processes is larger than the number of nodes in the system, the strategy proceeds in a round-robin fashion. Otherwise, *xyz* is the default mapping strategy. *Block xyz* mapping is similar to *xyz* and maps $\lfloor N/(d_x \cdot d_y \cdot d_z) \rfloor$ application processes to a single compute node, where d_x, d_y, and d_z are the number of nodes in the x, y, and z dimensions, respectively. *Random* mapping assigns application processes to compute nodes in a random fashion, and may result in unassigned system nodes when $N > (d_x \cdot d_y \cdot d_z)$. The three strategies result in different distributions of the application processes to the HAEC platform nodes, which in turn yield different numbers of intra-node and inter-node logical communications.

Table 1. Comparison of three process-to-node mappings for *lu.C.81*

Mapping	IePLC	IaNLC	IeNLC	AVG IeNLC	MIN IeNLC	MAX IeNLC
xyz		0	11,639,408	228,223	161,658	242,490
block xyz	11,639,408	**4,364,778**	7,274,630	173,205	80,829	242,488
random		646,633	10,992,775	99,934	80,829	242,488

To evaluate our approach we use the *lu* benchmark from the NPB 3.3 suite [3]. We chose *lu* because it performs a high number of point-to-point (unicast) messages and a small number of collective (multicast) messages. We use problem class C and execute it with 81 MPI processes (denoted *lu.C.81*) on 6 compute nodes of our current HPC production system[1].

In preparation for the simulations described in §4.2, we used the above strategies to map *lu.C.81* to the 27 nodes of the HAEC platform. The number of interprocess logical unicast communications (IePLC) of the benchmark is 11,639,408. These communications are illustrated in Fig. 2b where *lu.C.81* is mapped to the HAEC platform using *block xyz*. As comparison metrics (cf. Table 1), we use the number of intra-node logical communications (IaNLC), number of internode logical communications (IeNLC), and the average, minimum, and maximum number of IeNLC between any node pair. The *block xyz* strategy yields the smallest IeNLC value, which results in the largest IaNLC value. Thus, it is expected that *block xyz* results in the best overall simulated performance.

In reality, a single MPI process of *lu* represents more than single 'thin' core parallelism (e.g., as it is the case in the multi-zone version of this benchmark). In our approach, we abstract this parallelism and consider that a single MPI process partially or entirely exploits the available intra-node parallelism. When multiple MPI processes are mapped to the same compute node, we assume that they equally share the 'thin' cores of the node. In this work we concentrate on the inter-node communication requirements of applications mapped to the HAEC platform, and model them explicitly.

4.2   Application Performance for Different Communication Models

It is possible that the HAEC platform topology dynamically changes at runtime given the presence of wireless links. To accurately model the communication behavior of applications running on the HAEC platform, the communication models must account for the shape and characteristics of the interconnection network topology. Hence, we consider routing and network coding as alternative communication models. For the scope of this work the topology is assumed to be fixed (a 3-D mesh illustrated in Fig. 2a).

In standard routing, data packets are forwarded by intermediate nodes in a first come first serve manner. Network Coding (NC) [1] allows to increase throughput, energy efficiency, and robustness of data transmission in comparison to standard routing. These benefits result from the basic concept of NC to compute linear combinations of data packets instead of simply forwarding them.

---

[1] https://doc.zih.tu-dresden.de/hpc-wiki/bin/view/Compendium/SystemTaurus

The min-cut max-flow (the number of packets that can simultaneously be transmitted by a sender) of a network can be achieved using NC in unicast scenarios (a single sender transmits data to a single receiver) as well as in multicast scenarios (one or more senders transmit data to multiple receivers). NC can also be beneficial due to enhanced transmission robustness against node/link failures. Receivers require sufficient linear independent data packets to be able to decode by solving a system of linear equations, hence, the loss of single data packets can be mitigated.

To study the benefits of network coding versus routing in the context of the HAEC platform, we implemented both models in the simulator. The routing model is based on *dimension order routing* (DOR) [6]. Using DOR in a 3-D mesh (such as the one in Fig. 2b), packets are first routed in the x dimension, then in the y dimension, and lastly in the z dimension. The network coding approach is based on *practical network coding* (PNC, [5]), a practical implementation of random linear network coding. Random refers to the selection of the coefficients needed for computing the linear combinations of the data packets. In view of sending, the data packets are organized into matrices of s_w rows × $(s_w + n_s)$ columns, called generations (or windows), where s_w is the number of data packets per generation, and n_s is the number of data symbols per packet. The data packets are augmented by a global encoding vector that reflects all linear combinations applied to the data packets. Hence, the receiver does not need to know the randomly selected coefficients for decoding the combinations. For each packet, the first s_w columns contain the global encoding vector. In PNC, only data packets from one generation can be combined. PNC employs the same path selection between (sender,receiver) pairs as DOR.

At the moment, both communication models address only unicast communication. In unicast communication, NC is beneficial in case of packet loss caused by errors or attacks. In the simulations reported below, communication is assumed to be error-free. Thus NC will not outperform routing. However, integrating NC as a communication model in the simulator enables future evaluations in which certain packet loss rates will be considered.

Using NC for communication requires accounting for additional associated costs. In our case, the forwarding nodes are not burdened with additional computational effort for receiving the linear combinations of packets and for forwarding them. However, both sender and receiver nodes must perform additional operations, such as computing linear combinations or solving a system of linear equations. We assume that the nodes of the HAEC platform have sufficient computational resources; thus the additional operations will not significantly decrease efficiency. Analysis of the energy consumption of these operation will be conducted in future work. Regarding communication overhead, the fact that some additional information is transmitted (e.g., global encoding vector and generation identifier) needs to be considered. In comparison to the payload, which in our context refers to the amount of data symbols per packet, the cost of transmitting this additional information is also negligible.

Table 2. Parameters used in the simulation

Parameter	Notation	DOR	PNC
latency	l		$1\,\mu s$
bandwidth	b		$250\,\text{Gbit/s}$
packet size	s_p		$288\,\text{bytes}$
sending delay	d_{out}		$100\,\text{ns}$
receiving delay	d_{in}		$100\,\text{ns}$
delay per hop	d_h		$d_{out} + s_p/b + l + d_{in}$
acknowledgment processing delay	d_a		$d_{out}/2$
delay intermediate node	d_i		d_a
packet processing delay	d_p		$0.625\,\text{ns}$
finite field size	s_{ff}		$8\,\text{bits}$
window ID	s_{wid}		$4\,\text{bytes}$
delay sender node	d_s	$2 \cdot d_{out}$	$2 \cdot d_{out} + s_w \cdot d_p$
delay recv. node	d_r	$2 \cdot d_{out}$	$2 \cdot d_{out} + s_w^2 \cdot d_p$
payload/packet	L_p	$s_p - s_{wid}$	$s_p - s_w \cdot s_{ff} - s_{wid}$

Within our evaluations, we focus on comparing the transfer times of messages of applications running on the HAEC platform. To enable comparison between DOR and PNC, we assume that data packets are organized in windows of the same size as the generations. After sending one window (or generation) of data packets, the sender waits for the acknowledgment of receipt from the receiver before sending the next window of data packets. Given a payload L_p per data packet, sending a message of size m requires sending $n_p = \lceil m/L_p \rceil$ data packets and, hence, sending $n_w = \lfloor n_p/s_w \rfloor$ full windows (or generations) containing s_w data packets and a non-full window containing the remaining $n_r = n_p - s_w \cdot n_w$ data packets (if any). For the tests reported in the following, we set s_w to 5. Other parameters and their notation and values are given in Table 2.

Assuming the delay caused by sending a message over one hop (d_h) exceeds both the delay associated with preparing the data to be sent by the sender (d_s) and the associated delay at the receiver (d_r), the time to transfer x data packets over h hops between sender s and receiver r in the absence of errors is given by:

$$tt(x) = d_s + (h + x - 1) \cdot d_h + (h - 1) \cdot d_i + d_r, \tag{1}$$

where d_i denotes the delay associated with processing data packets at the intermediate nodes. When s and r are mapped to the same node, we assume $tt(x) = (d_s + d_r)/2$. The time needed for transmitting all data packets of message m is given by:

$$T(n_p) = tt(s_w) \cdot n_w + tt(n_r) + h \cdot (n_w + 1) \cdot (d_h + d_a), \tag{2}$$

where d_a refers to the delay associated with processing of an acknowledgment and $tt(s_w)$ is given by Eq. (1). Both DOR and PNC employ Eq. (1) and (2) with different payloads L_p and delays d_s and d_r (cf. Table 2). This holds for the error-free case.

The instrumented *lu.C.81* benchmark (cf. Sec. 4.1) ran in 41.8 s and resulted in a trace of 1.4 GiB. This trace was given as input to haec_sim. We conducted six simulations: one for each of the three mapping strategies, and for each mapping we employed DOR and PNC as communication models. Each simulation was

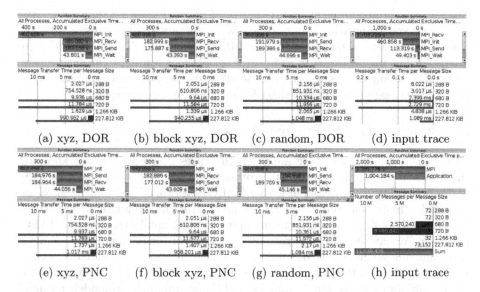

Fig. 3. Function and message statistics of the simulated *lu.C.81* running on the 3×3×3 HAEC platform. (d) shows function and message statistics of the input trace while (h) shows function groups statistics and message counts per message size of the input trace. Visualization with Vampir [12].

conducted in parallel on 6 compute nodes using 81 simulation processes, and completed in 675 seconds. The duration of the simulated *lu.C.81* benchmark on the HAEC platform was between 23.7 s to 24.1 s for the different mappings using DOR and PNC (Fig. 3). Two types of statistics are shown for each simulated trace: (1) the accumulated exclusive time spent in MPI functions and (2) the average transfer times for the different message sizes. The following statistics are shown additionally for the input trace: (3) accumulated exclusive time spent in functions of group Application (green bar) and MPI (red bar) and (4) the number of messages grouped by message size. The original trace is shown only for illustration and not for comparison against the simulated traces.

The choice of mapping or communication model has no impact on the duration of the simulated benchmark, even though most of the time is spent in MPI functions in the input trace (cf. Fig. 3d). Note that the communication models only alter the duration of the following MPI functions: Send, Recv, Wait, and Irecv. Time spent in all other functions is the same in both input and simulated traces. There are differences in the times spent in these four MPI functions and in the transfer times per message sizes among the three mappings and the two communication models.

From a mapping strategy perspective, less time is spent in send, recv, and wait for *block xyz* mapping using DOR and PNC, than in any other case. From a communication model perspective, more time is spent in send and wait using PNC than DOR for all mappings. This confirms our expectation, given that the simulation assumed an error-free HAEC platform and knowing that use of NC for unicast communication is only beneficial in the presence of errors or attacks. However, less time is spent in recv using PNC than DOR. This may be due to indirect balancing effects, such as faster transmissions leading to longer waiting times on subsequent messages. Also, the effect of mapping and communication model on message transmission time depends on the message size.

5   Conclusion and Future Work

This paper presents a holistic approach that uses a trace-driven workflow to simulate and analyze the performance of parallel applications running on a high performance–low energy computer (the HAEC platform). We have presented an application model based on event traces, an abstract model for the HAEC platform, as well as three strategies for mapping parallel applications to the HAEC platform. We have developed a trace-driven simulator (haec_sim) which employs two communication models: dimension order routing and practical network coding. The simulation results conducted on a well known parallel benchmark show the potential of the mapping strategies and the communication models for analyzing the performance of various parallel applications on the HAEC platform.

There are multiple future work directions. Immediate directions include: simulation experiments on various parallel applications from the scientific community; development of energy consumption models for computation and communication operations; development of mapping strategies that take into account the communication patterns of the application; modeling of unicast communication in the presence of errors/attacks; and modeling of HAEC platform (compute and communication) resources management in order to address, e.g., congestion over communication links. Longer-term work directions include: modeling of multicast communications; development of support for migration of tasks across compute nodes to increase performance or decrease energy costs; development of a hybrid communication model that supports dynamic latency, bandwidth, and topology.

Acknowledgements. This work is supported by the German Research Foundation (DFG) in the Collaborative Research Center 912 "Highly Adaptive Energy-Efficient Computing". The authors thank Mario Bielert and Miriam Debus for contibution in simulator implementation and visualization.

References

1. Ahlswede, R., Cai, N., Li, S.-Y.R., Yeung, R.W.: Network information flow. IEEE Trans. on Inf. Theory 46(4), 1204–1216 (2000)
2. Argollo, E., Falcón, A., Faraboschi, P., Monchiero, M., Ortega, D.: COTSon: Infrastructure for full system simulation. SIGOPS Op. Sys. Review 43(1) (2009)
3. Bailey, D., Barszcz, E., Barton, J., Browning, D., Carter, R., Dagum, L., Fatoohi, R., Fineberg, S., Frederickson, P., Lasinski, T., Schreiber, R., Simon, H., Venkatakrishnan, V., Weeratunga, S.: The NAS parallel benchmarks. RNR Technical Report RNR-94-007, NASA (March 1994)

4. Bhatele, A.: Automatic Topology Aware Mapping for Supercomputers. PhD thesis, University of Illinois at Urbana-Champaign (2010)
5. Chou, P.A., Wu, Y., Jain, K.: Practical network coding. In: Proc. Annual Allerton Conf. on Comm., Control, and Computing (2003)
6. Dally, W.J., Towles, B.: Principles and Practices of Interconnection Networks. Morgan Kaufmann (2004)
7. Doany, F.E., Lee, B., Rylyakov, A., Kuchta, D.M., Baks, C., Jahnes, C., Libsch, F., Schow, C.: Terabit/sec VCSEL-based parallel optical module based on Holey CMOS transceiver IC. In: Optical Fiber Communication Conf. and Expo. and the National Fiber Optic Engineers Conf. (2012)
8. Eschweiler, D., Wagner, M., Geimer, M., Knüpfer, A., Nagel, W.E., Wolf, F.: Open Trace Format 2: The next generation of scalable trace formats and support libraries. In: Applications, Tools and Techniques on the Road to Exascale Computing. Advances in Par. Co, vol. 22, pp. 481–490 (2012)
9. Fettweis, G., Nagel, W.E., Lehner, W.: Pathways to servers of the future. In: Design, Automation, Test in Europe, pp. 1161–1166 (2012)
10. Israel, J., Martinovic, J., Fischer, A., Jenning, M., Landau, L.: Optimal antenna positioning for wireless board-to-board communication using a butler matrix beamforming network. In: 17th Int'l ITG Workshop on Smart Antennas, pp. 1–7. VDE (2013)
11. Kielmann, T., Gorlatch, S.: Bandwidth-latency models (BSP, LogP). In: Padua, D. (ed.) Encycl. of Par. Co., pp. 107–112. Springer, US (2011)
12. Knüpfer, A., Brunst, H., Doleschal, J., Jurenz, M., Lieber, M., Mickler, H., Müller, M.S., Nagel, W.E.: The Vampir performance analysis tool-set. In: Resch, M.M., Keller, R., Himmler, V., Krammer, B., Schulz, A. (eds.) Tools for High Perf. Comp, pp. 139–155. Springer (2008)
13. Knüpfer, A., Rössel, C., Mey, D., Biersdorff, S., Diethelm, K., Eschweiler, D., Geimer, M., Gerndt, M., Lorenz, D., Malony, A., Nagel, W.E., Oleynik, Y., Philippen, P., Saviankou, P., Schmidl, D., Shende, S., Tschüter, R., Wagner, M., Wesarg, B., Wolf, F.: Score-P: A joint performance measurement run-time infrastructure for Periscope, Scalasca, TAU, and Vampir. In: Brunst, H., Müller, M.S., Nagel, W.E., Resch, M.M. (eds.) Tools for High Perf. Comp, pp. 79–91. Springer, Heidelberg (2012)
14. Labarta, J., Girona, S., Cortes, T.: Analyzing scheduling policies using Dimemas. Par. Co. 23(1-2), 23–34 (1997)
15. Marowka, A.: Back to thin-core massively parallel processors. Computer 44(12), 49–54 (2011)
16. Nieweglowski, K., Rieske, R., Henker, R., Schöniger, D., Ellinger, F., Wolter, K.-J.: Optical interconnects for adaptive high performance computing. In: IEEE Workshop Photonics and Microsys. (July 2013)
17. Sahu, P.K., Chattopadhyay, S.: A survey on application mapping strategies for network-on-chip design. J. Syst. Archit. 59(1), 60–76 (2013)
18. Sherman, S.W., Browne, J.C.: Trace driven modeling: Review and overview. In: 1st Symp. on Simul. of Computer Sys., pp. 200–207. IEEE Press (1973)
19. Totoni, E., Bhatele, A., Bohm, E.J., Jain, N., Mendes, C.L., Mokos, R.M., Zheng, G.,, L.: V Kale. Simulation-based performance analysis and tuning for a two-level directly connected system. In: 17th IEEE Intl. Conf. on Par. and Dist. Sys., pp. 340–347 (2011)
20. Vantrease, D., Schreiber, R., Monchiero, M., McLaren, M., Jouppi, N.P., Fiorentino, M., Davis, A., Binkert, N., Beausoleil, R.G., Ahn, J.H.: Corona: System implications of emerging nanophotonic technology. In: IEEE Intl. Conf. on Progr. Comprehension, pp. 153–164 (June 2008)

Migration Techniques in HPC Environments

Simon Pickartz[1,*], Ramy Gad[2,*], Stefan Lankes[1], Lars Nagel[2,*], Tim Süß[2], André Brinkmann[2], and Stephan Krempel[3]

[1] Institute for Automation of Complex Power Systems,
E.ON Energy Research Center, RWTH Aachen University, Aachen, Germany
`{spickartz,slankes}@eonerc.rwth-aachen.de`
[2] Zentrum für Datenverarbeitung, Johannes Gutenberg Universität, Mainz, Germany
`{gad,nagell,suesst,brinkman}@uni-mainz.de`
[3] ParTec Cluster Competence Center GmbH, Munich, Germany
`krempel@par-tec.com`

Abstract. Process migration is an important feature in modern computing centers as it allows for a more efficient use and maintenance of hardware. Especially in virtualized infrastructures it is successfully exploited by schemes for load balancing and energy efficiency. One can divide the tools and techniques into three groups: Process-level migration, virtual machine migration, and container-based migration.

This paper presents a qualitative and quantitative investigation of the different migration types for their application in High-Performance Computing (HPC). In addition to an overhead analysis of the various migration frameworks, our performance indicators include the migration time. The overall analysis suggests that VM migration has the most advantages and can even compete performance-wise.

The results are applied in the research project FAST addressing the problem of process scheduling in exascale environments. It is assumed that a shift in hardware architectures will result in a growing gap between the performance of CPUs and that of other resources like I/O. To avoid that these resources become bottlenecks, we suggest to monitor key performance indicators and, if conducive, trigger local amendments to the schedule requiring the efficient migration of jobs so that the downtime is reduced to a minimum.

1 Introduction

The fastest computers listed in the *Top 500* are able to execute 10^{16} FLOPS. The next generation of computer clusters will move into new dimensions and be a hundred times faster. Such *exascale computers* will not have significantly more nodes, but considerably more cores per node. It is predicted that this increase of CPU performance will not be matched by other resources resulting in an imbalance between CPU performance on the one hand and I/O performance on the other hand [1].

* Supported by the Federal Ministry of Education and Research (BMBF) under Grant 01IH13004B (Project FAST).

L. Lopes et al. (Eds.): Euro-Par 2014 Workshops, Part II, LNCS 8806, pp. 486–497, 2014.

The FAST[1] project develops dynamic scheduling strategies balancing the system's load such that resource bottlenecks are avoided. It is assumed that the exclusive assignment of jobs to nodes or vice versa will be inefficient, if not impossible, for computing centers of the exascale area. In fact, it will be necessary to schedule (sub-)jobs subject to their resource requirements. The approach in FAST is twofold: (1) an initial placement of the jobs provided by a global scheduler, (2) local adjustments by the migration of jobs to other nodes during the applications' runtime.

In this paper we present an investigation of migration techniques that can be part of the solution to the second problem. We discuss their qualitative and quantitative properties and determine virtualization as the solution most suitable for FAST. Generally, there are three types of migration, namely process-level, virtual machine, and container-based migration. The first is supposed to have the least overhead, as it restricts the migrating only to the process and its context. Yet, the gathering of the context can be a problem and is certainly easier when most of it is already wrapped into a VM or container. Other advantages of Virtual Machines (VMs) and containers are the support of live migration and the ability to run on basically any system, while existing tools for process-level migration do not offer live migration and usually require a homogenous cluster. Finally, the decisive factors pro virtualization are (1) that in contrast to containers a more flexible range of application is provided, e. g., guest and host do not necessarily have to use equivalent operating systems, and (2) that the experiments conducted reveal a competitive performance of virtualization including the migration itself compared to the other approaches.

The rest of the paper is structured as follows: First we explain the different types of migration in Section 2, display their pros and cons, and give a detailed survey of the related work. In Section 3 we describe the experiments and analyze their results. Section 4 concludes the paper with a summary and future work.

2   Process Migration in HPC Environments

In this section we discuss three different approaches for the realization of process migration. The first, process-level migration, achieves minimal overhead by restricting the transferred data to the process and its context. Virtual machine migration provides more flexibility and a migration framework that can be integrated more easily. Finally, container-based migration is discussed depicting a compromise between these two approaches.

2.1   Process-Level Migration

Migration on the process-level is the operation of moving a process, i. e., the execution context of a running program including registers and physical memory addresses, from one node to another. Process-level migration can be regarded as a

---

[1] Find a Suitable Topology for Exascale Applications (FAST) is a project funded by Germany's Federal Ministry of Education and Research (BMBF).

special kind of Checkpoint/Restart (C/R) operation where a checkpoint is copied to another node before it is restarted [2]. While C/R mechanisms are intended to recover long-running applications in case of node failures, process migration techniques may have other motivations. Besides the prevention of application interruptions due to node failures [3], they can also be used for the conductance of readjustments to the cluster's workload to improve energy efficiency or balance the load more evenly, like in FAST.

There are several C/R implementations available such as Condor's checkpoint library, the libckpt library, and Berkley Lab Checkpoint/Restart (BLCR) [4–6]. We use BLCR for the evaluation of process-level migration because the open source tool was specifically designed for HPC applications. It targets at CPU and memory intensive batch-scheduled parallel jobs and consists of two components: a kernel module performing the C/R operations inside the Linux kernel and a shared library enabling the access to user-space data [7]. This library needs to be loaded with the application to activate the support for checkpointing. Applications using sockets, block devices, or SystemV IPC mechanisms are not natively supported by BLCR. However, Sankaran et al. developed in [8] an extension to LAM/MPI with a callback interface enabling any library or application code to cooperate in the C/R procedure. This allows for closing communication channels prior to the migration and restoring them afterwards [7]. Meanwhile, the callback interface is availabe for LAM/MPI 7.x, MPICH, and Open MPI [8,9].

For the evaluation of process-level migration, we chose Open MPI 1.7 and its BLCR plug-in. Migrations are initiated by the *ompi-checkpoint* command creating a checkpoint of the running MPI job on the source nodes. After killing the job and all its processes, the checkpoint file containing their states is copied to the destination nodes, and the job is restarted by calling *ompi-restart*. The successful restoration of the job demands all libraries and files required for its execution to be present in exactly the same version on all nodes participating in the migration and prelinking of shared libraries has to be disabled. Prelinking is a feature which is used by some Linux distributions to perform a relocation of library code in advance of its execution. This technique accelerates the startup of applications by the assignment of fixed addresses to shared libraries. Furthermore, the source and destination nodes should have the same kernel version and hardware architecture. A successful migration of a process to a remote node is only possible if all resources that were allocated at the origin, i. e., the *residual dependencies*, are provided by the migration target as well [10]. With resources like communication channels, open files, or subprocesses this is not possible, as the respective file descriptors would not be valid on the target host and had to be closed in advance of the migration. This restriction could require a non-transparent migration from the application's point of view.

2.2   Virtual Machine Migration

As an alternative to process-level migration we investigate the deployment of VMs which reduce the aforementioned problem of residual dependencies [11]. Open files and virtual I/O devices do not cause any problems as the according descriptors are still valid within the resumed VM on the target node. The only residual dependencies that remain are the Instruction Set Architecture (ISA) as well as the hardware state of the virtualized devices. Since most hardware can be virtualized efficiently, these dependencies generally do not cause any issues. If the origin and target Virtual Machine Monitor (VMM) have the same hardware configuration, the latter only needs to receive the guest memory state and the guest device model state in order to start the VM on the new host. Thus, a migration transparent to the application can be realized.

I/O Virtualization. In contrast to CPUs and memory components of VMs, the virtualization of I/O devices may result in an unacceptable performance degradation. The emulation of high-performance networks like InfiniBand with native performance is still not possible. For this reason virtualization has mostly been disregarded in the area of HPC in the last years [12]. However, progress in this field of research accompanied by new hardware technologies changed this situation [13]. Driven by industry, a shift to cloud computing approaches can be observed in the area of HPC [14].

With Intel VT-d extensions it is possible to perform a physical device pass-through to a VM while providing DMA and interrupt isolation [15]. This technology gives I/O devices direct access to the memory space of a VM. The VM, in turn, is able to control the device by accessing the according hardware registers without intervention by the host system. However, this solution suffers from scalability issues as one physical device can only be assigned to exactly one VM at a time. Hence, if a single VM was used per high-performance process, one physical Host Channel Adapter (HCA) would be required per process. Such a setup would dramatically reduce the maximal amount of processes per node within a cluster.

A solution to this issue is addressed by the Peripheral Component Interconnect Special Interest Group (PCI-SIG) with the Single Root I/O Virtualization (SR-IOV) specification. This technology enables the native sharing of I/O devices by a replication of all necessary resources for each VM [16]. For this purpose, two new PCIe function types are introduced, namely Physical Functions (PFs) and Virtual Functions (VFs). An I/O device supporting SR-IOV may be configured to appear in the PCI configuration as multiple functions including one and only one PF. This function covers all PCIe capabilities including SR-IOV. Furthermore, there may be several VFs covering the necessary capabilities for data movement. Each of these VFs may then be assigned to one VM with the mechanisms described above. Although the VMs get the impression of possessing the I/O device exclusively, they share the same physical device with nearly native performance.

Hypervisor. There is a variety of virtualization techniques and tools today including Xen and KVM [17, 18]. Although the former has been the tool of choice in the open source world in the past, KVM is taking over this status more and more [14]. While Xen is a bare-metal hypervisor, KVM is integrated into Linux as kernel-module, and hence benefits from existing resources like the scheduler, the memory management, etc. The tight integration into the upstream Linux kernel with version 2.6.20 in 2007 allows KVM to take advantage of the kernels evolution [19]. Bugfixes and improvements within the kernel code will automatically apply to KVM-based systems using the current kernel version. In contrast, Xen is still not part of the Linux kernel and patches have to be applied explicitly. These facts led to the decision to focus on KVM as basis for the virtualization approach. It was further supported by performance evaluations showing that KVM is at least as good as other hypervisors [14].

KVM is providing full virtualization on x86 hardware depending on the VT-x or AMD-V hardware extensions [20, 21]. A VM is started as an ordinary Linux process that can be scheduled by the host system. If the VM is configured with more than one virtual CPU, one thread is created for each of them so that they can be scheduled individually. Furthermore, a migration framework supporting cold as well as live migration is already provided. Hence, KVM would allow for the realization of a first prototype of the migration framework within a narrow time frame.

2.3   Container-Based Migration

Traditional virtualiziation solutions like KVM result in multiple kernel instances running on one node. A light-weight alternative is *Container-based Virtualization* (or *Operating System Virtualization*) using the host-sytem kernel for the managment of so-called virtual containers as well. This concept aims at the provision of an isolation similar to full virtualization, but promises a better utilization and less overhead. An application running within a container can use standard system calls to interact with the server system but does not have to use hypercalls, e. g., when accessing virtualized I/O devices. However, this virtualization approach comes along with a certain inflexibility. It is not possible to run different operating systems on the same hardware and a crash of the kernel would halt the complete system, since it is shared among all instances.

OpenVZ[2] and LinuX Containers (LXC)[3] are typical representatives of this virtualization technique. In contrast to LXC, OpenVZ is not part of the vanilla Linux kernel, although efforts have been made to add their container functionality to LXC. Regola and Ducom conducted an analysis of OpenVZ with respect to its application in HPC and could show that some container-based virtualization solutions offer near native CPU and I/O performance [22]. Yet, since OpenVZ comes with its own kernel, which does not support our new InfiniBand adapters from Mellanox, we did not analyze OpenVZ more deeply. It would complicate the integration of new hardware. Figure 1 vizualizes the difference between container-based and full virtualization in the case of LXC and KVM, respectively. Both examples present a setup with two VMs und two containers, respectively. It is visible that container-based virtualization provides lower overhead as only one kernel instance is required for the host and all containers.

---

[2] https://openvz.org
[3] http://www.linuxcontainers.org

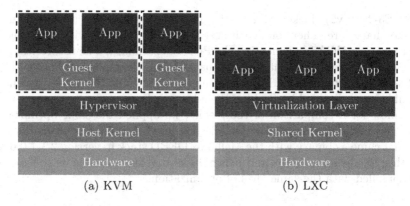

Fig. 1. Comparison of KVM- and LXC-based Virtualization

With Checkpoint/Restore In Userspace (CRIU)[4], there exists a mechanism similar to BLCR for LXC and OpenVZ. Yet, in contrast to BLCR, CRIU allows live migration[5] which can be valuable for many applications. Currently, CRIU offers no support for checkpointing of applications using file locks, block devices, or System V IPC mechanisms.

Our test system is based on Centos 6.5 constituting an extremely stable system. Yet, the LXC part of CentOS is not up to date and it is not possible to pass through general character devices from the host to the guest. Without this feature, which is supported by newer versions of LXC, it is not possible to use InfiniBand in LXC guests. The situation is similar concerning CRIU, which requires Linux kernel version 3.11 or newer. For these reasons, the quantative evaluation of LXC and CRIU was postponed.

3   Evaluation

The focus of this paper is a comprehensive evaluation of process-level and VM migration. Besides a qualitative comparison of these two approaches, a quantitative evaluation is indispensable to make an informed decision. Here, two key figures are important, namely the general overhead imposed by the respective migration technique on the application's performance and the characteristics of the migration itself in terms of the time needed to transfer a process from one node to the other.

All benchmarks were performed on an InfiniBand-based cluster comprising four NUMA nodes exposing 32 virtual cores, each on two sockets with 8 physical cores. While the hardware assembly is generally equal to all of the systems, two nodes are equipped with Intel SandyBridge CPUs (E5-2650) clocked at 2 GHz. The other two host systems are supplied with newer generation Intel IvyBridge

---

[4] http://criu.org/Main_Page
[5] http://criu.org/Live_migration

CPUs (E5-2650 v2) clocked at 2.6 GHz. The InfiniBand fabric is built by using Mellanox hardware. Therefore, each host system is equipped with a ConnectX-3 VPI two-port HCA implementing the PCIe 3.0 standard. The theoretical peak throughput for point-to-point connections is at 56 Gbit/s in accordance with the FDR signaling rate and the HCAs implement the SR-IOV technology which can be enabled and disabled by flashing the adapter's firmware.

To allow for a comparison of the results, we applied the same optimization techniques in the test scenarios. On the one hand, low-level benchmarks were used that came as binary with the Mellanox OFED stack in version 2.1-1.0.6. On the other hand, applications and benchmarks that are avaiable as source code were compiled with the same level of optimization.

3.1 Overhead

In order to see the impact of either migration technique on the runtime of our test application, we started with a general analysis of the overhead caused by them without actually performing a migration. In case of process-level migration with BLCR, the requirement of disabling the prelinking feature might have a negative impact on the application's performance. In contrast, the VM approach does not demand any modifications of the executed code. However, the additional software layer may introduce a certain overhead even if full virtualization is applied. The VM runs in *guest-mode* on x86 hardware with virtualization support. On the execution of a privileged instruction, i. e., an instruction that traps if the CPU is in user-mode while it does not trap in kernel-mode, the CPU switches to *host-mode* returning control back to the hypervisor. Moreover, an additional overhead might be introduced by the SR-IOV technology. Despite its realization on the hardware layer, the logic for the multiplexing of the VFs to the hardware consumes time that might result in performance penalties.

Microbenchmarks. For the investigation of the influence of the respective migration technique on the communication performance, a microbenchmark analysis was performed in terms of throughput and latency measurements. Therefore, we compared the results when using one of the two approaches with those obtained by native execution on the host systems. This was done on the MPI layer by using a self-written PingPong application and Open MPI 1.7 with BLCR support. For the measurement of the throughput and latency on the InfiniBand layer the `ib_write_bw` and `ib_write_lat` tools were used that come with the OFED stack.

The latencies on the InfiniBand layer in Table 1 reveal a slight impact of the SR-IOV technology. Although increased by roughly 27 % compared to native host execution, the communication latency between two guests equipped with passed-through VFs is only at 1.16 μs. As the pure pass-through of the InfiniBand hardware does not have any influence on the latencies, this difference must be caused by the SR-IOV technology itself. The additional software layer in terms of the Open MPI results in a further increase of the latency. With 1.48 μs the

Table 1. Latencies in µs (RTT/2)

Layer	Native	Pass-Through	SR-IOV	BLCR
InfiniBand	0.91	0.90	1.16	–
Open MPI	1.19	1.21	1.48	1.61

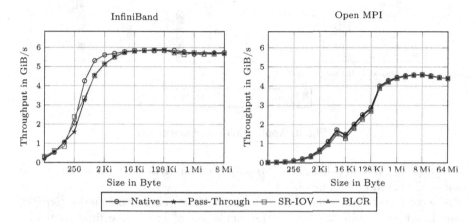

Fig. 2. Throughput Results

VM approach still performs slightly better than the native host execution while having the BLCR feature enabled.

The throughput results (see Fig. 2) show a similar trend. For small message sizes the SR-IOV technology as well as the BLCR framework have a marginal influence on the achievable performance. Larger messages instead can be transferred at nearly native performance. However, the results of the microbenchmark analysis are so close in all cases that they do not allow to make a decision for either of the frameworks.

Application Benchmarks. One reference application in the FAST project is mpiBLAST [23]. This is a parallelization of the BLAST algorithm applied in biological research that searches in a short query sequence of DNA or amino acids for similarities within a database of longer sequences.

Like in the previous section, an overhead analysis was conducted comparing the application runtime with the different frameworks. The left part of Figure 3 summarizes the results of different runs with 8 to 32 processes. A comparison between the native environment and execution with enabled BLCR yields a slight increase of the runtime in the order of 1 %. This increase is rather negligible and affiliates BLCR good performance characteristics in this application scenario. In contrast, the execution of the same scenario within a virtualized environment decelerates the runtime by 7 % to 8 %. This certainly constitutes an important performance degradation compared to BLCR and native execution, however it

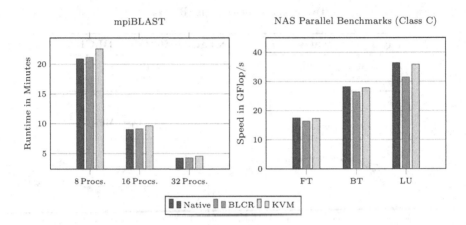

Fig. 3. Application Benchmarks

should be kept in mind that there has only been put little effort in the optimization of the KVM environment.

A second test was performed with the NAS Parallel Benchmarks (NPBs). This benchmark suite targets at the emulation of large-scale fluid dynamics applications [24]. We used the FT kernel calculating a discrete 3D Fast Fourier Transformation as well as the two pseudo applications, BT and LU, which are solvers for linear equation systems. The results were obtained by starting the benchmarks with 16 processes on two hosts, i.e., NUMA effects do not have to be considered as all processes on one host could be pinned to the same socket. Here, the results are quite different from the mpiBLAST evaluation. In fact, the virtualization layer reduces the performance by only 1 % outperforming BLCR which, in turn, generates an overhead of 6 % to 14 %. We think that this overhead is not caused by the BLCR but rather by the implementation of the callback interface inside Open MPI in order to support checkpointing with BLCR.

These results lead to the conclusion that the actual overhead generated by the particular approach is highly application dependent. Both solutions exhibit fairly good performance results compared to native execution. While BLCR shows better results for mpiBLAST, though with decreasing advance for higher process counts, the virtualization approach has the edge over process-level migration for the NPBs while offering more flexibility as discussed before.

3.2 Migration Time

Finally, an investigation of the migration time was performed. This is a key value particular important for the evaluation of the differen migration techniques. In this timeframe the nodes participating in the migration are not responsive and these phases depict an overhead that has to be compensated by sophisticated scheduling strategies to improve the overall utilization of the cluster. To perform this evaluation, the following scenario was conducted.

An mpiBLAST job with three processes on two different nodes was started, i. e., on one node a single process was launched while the other holded two processes. The single process was then migrated to a third node not yet participating in the execution. For the evaluation of the virtualization approach with KVM, two VMs were launched on the origin nodes. Instead of moving the mpiBLAST process to a remote node, the VM holding this process was then transferred to the same remote node.

We started with an evaluation of the *overall* migration time from initiating the migration command until its successful return. With the BLCR framework we were able to migrate the MPI process within 0.51 s averaged over multiple runs. In contrast, the VM migration required 2.87 s constituting an important overhead. The VMs were configured with 256 MiB of RAM. Although a lightweight CentOS 6.5 installation was used for the guest systems, the migration time might be reduced by the usage of a minimal kernel only providing the necessary environment for executing MPI jobs (e. g. a system configured with Buildroot). We could observe a dependency between the migration time and the assigned memory when migrating a KVM guest. Hence, a kernel optimized to memory utlization might improve the results presented above. However, this dependency has to be further investigated in this context. As we used the libvirt tool set to access the KVM hypervisor, time is not only consumed by the migration itself but also by preparatory tasks like establishing connections to the daemons on the respective host systems. Moreover, the process representing the VM on the source host has to be properly removed subsequent to the successful migration.

To get an impression of the *real* downtime of the VM, we wrote a socket-based PingPong application using the UDP protocol. The server was started on the VM being migrated. It listens for incoming UDP packets on a dedicated port and directly responds to the sender. The client was started on one of the cluster nodes not participating in the migration. This runs two threads, a sender and a receiver thread. The first posts with a fixed interval of 500 µs UDP packets containing a sequence number while the receiver thread constantly listens for the responses from the server running in the VM. This benchmarks allows for the determination of packet losses due to unresponsiveness of the VM during migration. The actual downtime may then be determined by multiplying the amount of packets that were not answered with the time interval the packets have been transmitted.

For the mpiBLAST scenario described above we captured a downtime of about 1.2 s reducing the previously measured advantage of process-level migration. With KVM it would even be possible to perform a *live-migration*, i. e., not stopping the VM during migration. Hu et al. could show that this technique allows for a considerable decrease of the downtime to the order of 0.2 s in the best case [25]. Furthermore, it should be noted that the current implementation of BLCR requires *all* process to be halted in advance of the migration. Within the VM approach applications may benefit from the fact that only those process have to be freezed at some point in time that are situated within the migrated VM.

4   Conclusion

In this paper two migration techniques have been examined, namely process-level migration using BLCR and virtual machine migration on top of KVM. We have conducted a qualitative and a quantitative comparison of these two techniques. In particular, we have studied the overhead on the application's performance imposed by each solution and the characteristics of the migration itself in terms of the time needed to transfer a process from one node to the other. In accordance with the presented results, we favor virtual machine migration over process-level migration for the FAST project. The overhead imposed by the virtualization layer is acceptable and offers more flexibility in terms of a greater application range.

In the near future, we will further investigate LXC as a complement to our migration framework. Although it imposes some restrictions compared to full virtualization (e. g., host and guest cannot use different kernels), it might have a better performance which may be more important than flexibility in some cases. Should it be possible to support both virtualization techniques in FAST, we will offer them and let end-users choose the one more suitable for their domain. Besides the implementation of the migration framework, future tasks in FAST include the development of an agent-based monitoring system and a scheduler on top of it, which triggers process migrations based on the resource utilization.

References

1. Dongarra, J.: Impact of Architecture and Technology for Extreme Scale on Software and Algorithm Design. Presented at the Department of Energy Workshop on Cross-cutting Technologies for Computing at the Exascale (February 2010)
2. Roman, E.: A Survey of Checkpoint/Restart Implementations. Technical report, Lawrence Berkeley National Laboratory, Tech (2002)
3. Wang, C., Mueller, F., Engelmann, C., Scott, S.: Proactive process-level live migration in hpc environments. In: International Conference for High Performance Computing, Networking, Storage and Analysis, SC 2008, pp. 1–12 (November 2008)
4. Litzkow, M., Tannenbaum, T., Basney, J., Livny, M.: Checkpoint and Migration of UNIX Processes in the Condor Distributed Processing System. Technical Report UW-CS-TR-1346, University of Wisconsin – Madison Computer Sciences Department (April 1997)
5. Plank, J.S., Beck, M., Kingsley, G., Li, K.: Libckpt: Transparent Checkpointing under Unix (1995)
6. Duell, J.: The Design and Implementation of Berkeley Lab's Linux Checkpoint/Restart. Technical report, Lawrence Berkeley National Laboratory (2003)
7. Hargrove, P.H., Duell, J.C.: Berkeley Lab Checkpoint/Restart (BLCR) for Linux Clusters. Journal of Physics: Conference Series 46(1), 494 (2006)
8. Sankaran, S., Squyres, J.M., Barrett, B., Lumsdaine, A.: The LAM/MPI Checkpoint/Restart Framework: System-Initiated Checkpointing. In: Proceedings of LACSI Symposium, Sante Fe, pp. 479–493 (2003)
9. Hursey, J., Squyres, J.M., Lumsdaine, A.: A Checkpoint and Restart Service Specification for Open MPI. Technical Report TR635, Indiana University, Bloomington, Indiana, USA (July 2006)

10. Milojičić, D.S., Douglis, F., Paindaveine, Y., Wheeler, R., Zhou, S.: Process migration. ACM Computing Surveys (CSUR) 32(3), 241–299 (2000)
11. Clark, C., Fraser, K., Hand, S., Hansen, J.G., Jul, E., Limpach, C., Pratt, I., Warfield, A.: Live Migration of Virtual Machines. In: Proceedings of the 2nd Conference on Symposium on Networked Systems Design & Implementation, NSDI 2005, vol. 2 (2005)
12. Ranadive, A., Kesavan, M., Gavrilovska, A., Schwan, K.: Performance implications of virtualizing multicore cluster machines. In: Proceedings of the 2nd Workshop on System-level Virtualization for High Performance Computing, HPCVirt 2008, pp. 1–8. ACM, New York (2008)
13. Birkenheuer, G., Brinkmann, A., Kaiser, J., Keller, A., Keller, M., Kleineweber, C., Konersmann, C., Niehörster, O., Schäfer, T., Simon, J., Wilhelm, M.: Virtualized HPC: a contradiction in terms?. Softw., Pract. Exper. 42(4), 485–500 (2012)
14. Younge, A.J., Henschel, R., Brown, J.T., von Laszewski, G., Qiu, J., Fox, G.C.: Analysis of Virtualization Technologies for High Performance Computing Environments. In: Proceedings of 2011 IEEE International Conference on Cloud Computing (CLOUD), pp. 9–16. IEEE (2011)
15. Intel Virtualization Technology for Directed I/O. Technical report, Intel Corporation (2013)
16. Intel LAN Access Division: PCI-SIG SR-IOV Primer. Technical Report 2.5, Intel Corporation (January 2011)
17. Barham, P., Dragovic, B., Fraser, K., Hand, S., Harris, T., Ho, A., Neugebauer, R., Pratt, I., Warfield, A.: Xen and the Art of Virtualization. SIGOPS Oper. Syst. Rev. 37(5), 164–177 (2003)
18. Kivity, A., Kamay, Y., Laor, D., Lublin, U.: kvm: the Linux Virtual Machine Monitor. In: Proceedings of the Linux Symposium, vol. 1, Ottawa, Ontario, Canada, pp. 225–230 (June 2007)
19. Nussbaum, L., Anhalt, F., Mornard, O., Gelas, J.P.: Linux-based virtualization for HPC clusters. In: Proceedings of the Linux Symposium (July 2009)
20. Uhlig, R., Neiger, G., Rodgers, D., Santoni, A.L., Martins, F.C.M., Anderson, A.V., Bennett, S.M., Kagi, A., Leung, F.H., Smith, L.: Intel Virtualization Technology. Computer 38(5), 48–56 (2005)
21. Virtualization, A.: Secure Virtual Machine Architecture Reference Manual. AMD Publication (2005)
22. Regola, N., Ducom, J.C.: Recommendations for Virtualization Technologies in High Performance Computing. In: Proceedings of 2nd IEEE International Conference on Cloud Computing Technology and Science (CloudCom), pp. 409–416 (November 2010)
23. Darling, A., Carey, L., Feng, W.: The design, implementation, and evaluation of mpiBLAST. In: Proceedings of ClusterWorld (2003)
24. Bailey, D.H., Barszcz, E., Barton, J.T., Browning, D.S., Carter, R.L., Dagum, L., Fatoohi, R.A., Frederickson, P.O., Lasinski, T.A., Schreiber, R.S., Simon, H.D., Venkatakrishnan, V., Weeratunga, S.K.: The NAS Parallel Benchmarks. International Journal of High Performance Computing Applications 5(3), 63–73 (1991)
25. Hu, W., Hicks, A., Zhang, L., Dow, E.M., Soni, V., Jiang, H., Bull, R., Matthews, J.N.: A quantitative study of virtual machine live migration (August 2013)

Planning Live-Migrations to Prepare Servers
for Maintenance

Vincent Kherbache[1], Eric Madelaine[1], and Fabien Hermenier[2]

[1] INRIA Sophia Antipolis, France
vincent.kherbache@inria.fr, eric.madelaine@inria.fr
[2] University Nice Sophia Antipolis, CNRS, I3S, UMR 7271, France
fabien.hermenier@unice.fr

Abstract. In a virtualized data center, server maintenance is a common
but still critical operation. A prerequisite is indeed to relocate elsewhere
the Virtual Machines (VMs) running on the production servers to prepare
them for the maintenance. When the maintenance focuses several servers,
this may lead to a costly relocation of several VMs so the migration plan
must be chose wisely. This however implies to master numerous human,
technical, and economical aspects that play a role in the design of a
quality migration plan.

In this paper, we study migration plans that can be decided by an
operator to prepare for an hardware upgrade or a server refresh on multiple servers. We exhibit performance bottleneck and pitfalls that reduce
the plan efficiency. We then discuss and validate possible improvements
deduced from the knowledge of the environment peculiarities.

1 Introduction

In data centres, virtualization has become a cornerstone. On one side, it raised
the hosting capabilities thanks to performance isolation [2] and consolidation
techniques [19,12]. On the other side, live migration [5] permitted the operators
to perform server maintenance more easily. Indeed, maintenance operations such
as server updating, hardware or software upgrade are critical tasks to perform on
production servers. It is then recommended to operate on idle or offline servers to
prevent any failure or mis-configuration to alter client virtual machines (VMs).
Thanks to live migration, it is now possible to prepare the servers by migrating
their VMs elsewhere in prior, with a negligible downtime for the VMs.

Maintenance tasks can occur at the level of a single server as well at the scale
of an entire blade-center or rack. With the ever increasing number of servers and
VMs per server in a data center, planning efficiently numerous migrations over
multiple servers becomes problematic [17]. Indeed the notion of efficiency has
many facets: an operator may expect short completion times, small migration
durations or low energy usage for example. However, many technical, environ-
mental or even human aspects dictate these optimisation criteria and today, all
these parameters but also their interactions must be mastered to design migration plans of quality.

L. Lopes et al. (Eds.): Euro-Par 2014 Workshops, Part II, LNCS 8806, pp. 498–507, 2014.
© Springer International Publishing Switzerland 2014

In this paper we analyze different realistic migration plans to exhibit common pitfalls and discuss some levers to improve their quality. Our results are derived from experiments on a real testbed involving up to 45 servers connected through a hierarchical network. In both scenarios we compare two migration strategies that consist to execute all the tasks in parallel or sequentially. We analyze the pros and cons of both approaches with regards to performance, energy efficiency and duration optimization criteria. Finally, we discuss and validate possible improvements that consider the infrastructure and the workload properties.

The rest of this paper is organized as follows. Section 2 presents related works. Section 3 presents our experimental analysis of migrations plans. Section 4 discusses possible solutions to improve the plan efficiency. Finally, Section 5 presents our conclusions and future research directions.

2   Related Works

Live Migrations Efficiency. Many efforts have been made to improve the live migration efficiency and many research papers proved that the network speed and the VM's dirty page rate are the main factors affecting the live migrations behavior in pre-copy migration architecture. Based on these findings, Sherif et al. [1] offer good predictions of the duration and the workload service interruptions arising from live migrations. Also, to help administrators at making optimal migrations decisions, Liu et al. [14] define a performance model to predict the energy consumed by a live migration at different transmission rates. Although being linked to our work, these work study the migration of a single VM while we focus on issues related to the concurrent migration of multiple VMs.

Accordingly, several works have been conducted to improve the performance of multiple live migrations. Among the studies that most closely match our work, Kejiang et al. [20] consider the live migration efficiency of multiple VMs with different strategies (sequential / parallel migrations) by investigating resources reservation methods on target servers. Nevertheless their study does not include network management or information about the topology which are the preeminent aspects that we consider in this paper. Sarker et al. [16] propose an algorithm to schedule the migrations of a given set of VMs by minimizing the total migration time and the VMs downtime. The novelty of their approach is to take into account the network topology and the inter-VM data dependencies. In this paper we also focus on the need to reduce individual migration durations and energy consumption. Furthermore, despite all their experiments were performed in a simulated environment, we focus exclusively on a real testbed. Deshpande et al. [7] introduce Live gang migration of VMs to speed up the parallel migration of co-located VMs to the same destination server thanks to memory deduplication. Nevertheless the proposed technique requires a deep modification of the underlying hypervisor and does not address the migration of VMs over a complex network topology. Zheng et al. [22] propose a centralized architecture to coordinate the migration of multi-tiers applications between distant sites inter-connected through a slow network path. The objectives are to ensure the convergence of all migrations and to minimize the impact of inter-VMs communications on migrations duration. In contrast, in this paper we consider an isolated network dedicated to migrations within the same data-centre, which greatly reduces the impact of inter-VMs communications on the migrations performance.

Maintenance operations in virtualized data centers: The new considerations related to the virtualization for management operations in data centers have been introduced in [17]. The authors explain that the management operations constitute themselves a workload over the applications running in VMs and becomes more and more critical with increasing multi-core architectures. They analyze 5 common management tasks in virtualized data centres, although they do not investigate the blade-center maintenance or server upgrading scenarios which are the main interests of this paper.

In the best of our knowledge, our work is the first study to tackle multiple migrations plans in the context of critical maintenance operations such as replacing a whole blade-center in a real infrastructure, and to propose solutions to automate these operations with the aim to facilitate the work of administrators.

3   Analysis of Migrations Plans

In this section, we experiment on a testbed the effects of 2 intuitive migration plans in the case of a blade-center maintenance or a server upgrading. In practice, we evaluate the impact of the migration plans on the completion time, the individual migration duration, the instantaneous power and the energy consumption.

3.1   Environment

The experimental testbed is composed of three Bullx B500 blade-centers. Each blade-center consists of 15 servers with 2 Intel quad-core Xeon E5520 2.27 GHz processors and 24 GB RAM each. All servers run Debian Wheezy with a Linux 3.2.0-4 amd64 kernel and the KVM/Qemu hypervisor 1.7.50. The testbed hosts 60 VMs. Every single VM uses 2 VCPUs, 2 GB RAM and runs a Ubuntu 13.10 desktop distribution. Each VCPU is mapped to a dedicated physical core.

Figure 1 depicts a testbed fragment. In a single blade-center, each server is connected to a switch through a Gigabit Ethernet interface. The bandwidth between the blade-centers is however limited to 3 Gb/s by an aggregation of 3 Gigabit links. All the servers are also connected to a 10 Gb/s Infiniband network that share the VM disk images exported by a dedicated NFS server. To only analyze the migration related traffic, only the live migrations operate over the Ethernet network.

The VM workload is generated by the Web server benchmark tool `httperf` [15]. Inside each VM, the benchmark repeatedly retrieves a static Web page from a local Apache Web server. Two workloads, equally distributed between the VMs, retrieve the Web page at a rate of 100 or 200 requests per second.

During experiments, the power consumption of each server is retrieved every second from a remote dedicated server through its management board.

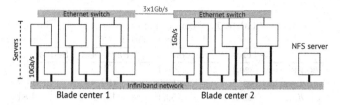

Fig. 1. Testbed design

3.2 Experiments

We consider two maintenance scenarios that reflect common situations:

Scenario 1 - Blade-Center Maintenance. This scenario simulates the preparation of a maintenance on a whole blade-center that need to be powered down. The 60 VMs are relocated to a spare blade-center having the same hardware specification. The spare servers are initially offline to save power. Each server to put into maintenance hosts 4 VMs. All the VMs of a source server are migrated to a specific destination server (see Figure 2a).

Scenario 2 - Server Upgrading. This scenario simulates the replacement of two out-dated blade-centers by a single one that is more powerful. Each deprecated server has 4 cores while each new server has 8. Initially, each deprecated server hosted 2 VMs while each new server will host 4 VMs (see Figure 2b). Initially the servers in the new blade-center are offline. Once the migration terminated, the old blade-center is shut down. To simulate the low performance of the out-dated servers, half the cores are disabled using linux `procfs`.

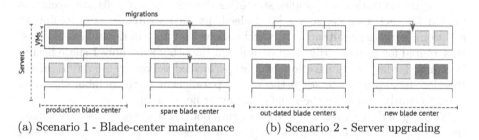

(a) Scenario 1 - Blade-center maintenance   (b) Scenario 2 - Server upgrading

Fig. 2. Experimental scenarios

In both scenarios, we evaluated 2 migration strategies that can be inferred naturally by an operator. The first strategy launches all the migrations sequentially. This has the benefits of being safe and easily trackable. The second strategy launches all the migrations in parallel to reduce the completion time, a common objective of reconfiguration algorithms to increase their reactivity [12,22,19]. Table 1 shows the experimental results.

We observe that with parallel strategies, the average VM migration duration is about 15 times longer, but also less stable, than with the sequential strategies.

Table 1. Scenarios comparison

	Scenario 1		Scenario 2	
Metrics	Sequential	Parallel	Sequential	Parallel
Time to completion (sec.)	2871	446	3467	384
Mean migration duration (sec.)	12.2	192.9	11.2	158.0
standard deviation	5.41	45.12	4.81	52.97
Server boot time (sec.)	113.1	116.5	114.9	115.0
Server shutdown duration (sec.)	29.5	28.8	32.2	32.1
Energy consumption (kWh)	2098.4	366.4	3317.5	548.1
Max. peak power (kW)	2.70	4.47	4.24	6.05

This difference is explained by the network interlink that restricts the throughput between the blade-centers to 3 Gb/s when the maximum rate could be up to 15 Gb/s. In contrast, the interlink bandwidth is under-utilized in sequential strategies as the maximum throughput between the two blade-centers equals 1 Gb/s. In practice, long migration durations are not desirable as they lead to performance issues. Indeed, a migration consumes resources on the involved servers and this additional load reduce the VM performance. Furthermore, the links aggregation that composes the interlink does not balance the traffic fairly. Indeed, the negotiation protocol distributes the traffic with a XOR hash-based on the source and the destination MAC addresses. As a consequence in parallel strategies, multiples migrations can share a single 1 Gb link while others will have a dedicated one. Therefore the main issue of parallel strategies is related to the network overload but also the network topologies. Both must be carefully investigated to use them to their best.

Another limitation of parallel strategies occurs when a software license is needed for each running server [4]. Indeed, parallel strategies bring online 15 additional servers simultaneously, which means that 15 additional licenses must be acquired for a short utilisation period. On the other side, only 1 spare license is required when the migration plan is performed server by server. It might therefore be important to adapt the level of parallelism, so the number of servers simultaneously online, to the number of server licenses [6].

We observe that with sequential strategies, booting a server (respectively shutting down) is about 10 times longer (resp. 3 times) than the average migration duration. As each action is executed sequentially, the time spent to boot and shutdown the servers is not used to migrate VMs. In the scenario 1, 2139 sec. or 74.5 % of the completion time is then wasted waiting for power switching actions (boot and shutdown of 15 servers). It is usually not desirable to have long standing critical operations as the operator in charge must be continuously available to fix potential failures. It is then important to parallelize as much as possible the power-switching actions to reduce the waiting time to a minimum. Likewise, the longest completion times in scenario 2 are essentially due to the time spent to shutdown the 15 additional servers.

We finally observe a higher energy consumption in the scenario 2 due to the higher number of servers. More important, we observe significant power consumption peaks in the parallel strategies. These peaks occur at the beginning of each experiment during the simultaneous boot of all the destination servers. This situation is problematic when the energy is a scarce or expensive resource. For example, when the energy price market is volatile [18] or when the data center is partially powered by renewable energies [13,9]. In these cases, a solution is to delay some boot actions to more *energy-friendly* periods. Such a delay must however be considered carefully with regards to the priority of the maintenance operation. These results demonstrate the need to control the energy consumption during the maintenance task to be adaptive to external energy constraints. One of the consequences will be to choose the best sequence of power switching actions.

4   Toward Smarter Migration Plans

Experiments exhibited that pure parallel and pure sequential strategies have their own benefits and drawbacks. Pure parallel strategies provide short completion time but long migrations while pure sequential strategies provide the opposite. In practice, the efficiency of each approach is strongly related to the environment and the workload peculiarities. This advocates for a smart composition of both approaches to provide finer migration plans. In this section, we explore hybrid strategies to prepare servers for a blade-center maintenance according to the network and the workload peculiarities and verify their effectiveness.

Table 2. Optimisations according to the network interlink peculiarities

Metrics	Scenario A1	Scenario A2	Scenario A3
Mean migration duration (sec.)	284.2	63.66	50.62
standard deviation	251.78	33.15	23.17
Time spent to migrate (sec.)	604	213	148
Energy consumption (kWh)	286.27	156.35	132.52

The first experiment considers the network interlink in a testbed reduced to 6 servers per blade-center. We chose this smaller and more manageable set of servers to easily analyze the behavior of the 3 links aggregation. In all subsequent experiments, httperf is configured at a rate of 200 requests per second for all VMs. Table 2 shows the results. In Scenario A1, all the VMs are migrated in parallel. Similarly to previous experiments, we observe long and unstable migration due to the interlink saturation. Furthermore, some migrations did not complete in live. This happens when the dirty page rate of a VM is greater than the bandwidth available for the migration. In this case, KVM cannot guarantee a VM downtime lesser than 30 ms, the maximum allowed by default. It then suspends the VM after 10 minutes for a possible long period to terminate the migration. We note that this behavior does not occur in the previous scenarios involving a whole blade-center, this is mainly explained by the less intensive workloads on VMs. In Scenario A2, the source servers are freed 3 by 3. We then observe the migration time is 4 time faster and the completion time is 3 times shorter. This is explained by the interlink that is no longer saturated as each server has in theory a 1Gbit/s bandwidth to migrate its VMs. Dirty-pages are then send faster and the number of rounds to synchronize the memory is reduced. We however reported in Section 3 that the link aggregation protocol is not fair. In Scenario A3, we then decided to probe the interlink topology using `iperf` to choose for each source server, a destination server reachable through a dedicated Gigabit link. This micro-optimisation reduced again the total migration time by 65 sec. and the average migration duration by 13 sec. This experiments reveals that a fine grain optimisation of the level of parallelism between the migration of different servers allows to reduce by up to 4 the time spent to migrate but also by 5 the average migration duration. We also observe that the energy consumption is lower in connection with the reduced completion time.

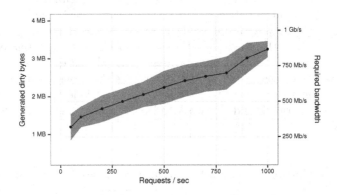

Fig. 3. Dirty pages generated by `httperf` in 30 ms (95% confidence interval)

We finally refines the migration plan according to the workload peculiarity. With regard to results in Section 3, we observe the average migration duration is 7 times longer and less stable than when migrations are performed sequentially. This reveals despite the network interlink is not saturated, the parallel migration of 4 VMs on a single Gigabit link still saturates the network. According to the pre-copy algorithm used in Qemu, a bandwidth below a certain threshold causes the re-transmission of the set of dirty pages that are quickly updated, named `Writable Working Set` (WWS) [5]. The minimum bandwidth that guarantee the termination of a migration depends therefore of the WWS size and the memory dirtying rate. Figure 3 shows the number of pages that are made dirty by `httperf` in 30 ms depending on the request rate. This indicates that with a 200 requests per second rate, at most 2 VMs should be migrated simultaneously on a Gigabit link to ensure their termination. We verified this assumption in an experiment that varies the number of VMs migrated simultaneously on a Gigabit link. It consists to migrate the VMs of 3 servers from a server to another. The servers were selected to ensure an equitable sharing of the 3 Gb/s interlink between them.

Table 3. Optimisations according to the workload peculiarities

Metrics	Scenario B1	Scenario B2	Scenario B3
Mean migration duration (sec.)	49.51	15.41	7.66
standard deviation	34.51	0.47	0.45
Time spent to migrate (sec.)	94	31	31
Energy consumption (kWh)	46.36	33.49	33.28

Table 3 shows the results. In Scenario B1, the 4 VMs on each server are migrated in parallel. In Scenario B2, the VMs are migrated 2 by 2. With regard to Scenario B1, the migration duration is 3 times shorter and stable. This indicates the network is no longer saturated and the bandwidth available for the migration is sufficient to prevent a repetitive copy of the dirty pages. In Scenario B3, the VMs are migrated one at a time. With regard to Scenario B2, the migration duration has been only divided by 2 while the completion time remains unchanged. The last two scenarios ensure then a fully effective migration management by dealing with workloads and network specificities. We were able to reduce by up to 7 the average migration duration and by up to 3 the time spent to migrate. However, it may be judicious to prefer Scenario B3 over Scenario B2 depending on the VMs peculiarities. For example, when a group of VMs communicates extensively, it is preferable to migrate the VMs in parallel and synchronize the migration terminations to restrict the amount of data exchanged over a high-latency interlink [22]. In contrast, when the VMs are independent, it is wise to migrate the VMs one by one to reduce the average migration duration so the impact on the workload.

5 Conclusion and Future Work

Server maintenance is a common but still critical operation that must be prepared by operators. It requires to plan the migration of numerous VMs but also the management of the server state. With the ever increasing complexity of the datacenter infrastructure, it becomes difficult to define plans that are fast, reliable or simply fitting the environment peculiarities.

In this paper, we experimented migration plans involving up to 45 servers. This exhibited performance bottlenecks but also evaluation metrics to qualify the quality of a migration plan. We then show how the knowledge of the environment peculiarities can improve the migration plan quality. In practice, we adapted the number of migrations to perform in parallel between the servers, but also inside each server. These decisions were applied manually from the knowledge of the network topologies, and the workload particularities.

As future work, we then want to automatize the creation of efficient plans. We first need to model the aspects that qualify a migration plan. Based on the experiments, we conclude our model must consider the workload characteristics such as the dirty page rate and the estimated migration durations, the network topology but also external and possible evolving side constraints such as a possible power budget, a completion deadline or a server licensing policy. We already patched Qemu to retrieve the VM dirty page rate but we also planned to use an approach similar to Pacer [21] to predict the duration of a live migration. With regards to the network, it is possible to extract the network topology using standard monitoring tools. In addition, dynamic aspects such as the practical decomposition of the traffic made by an aggregation protocol can be observed from benchmarks. We plan to implement this model over the VM manager Btr-Place [10,11]. BtrPlace is an extensible VM manager that can be customized to augment its inferring capabilities. It provides a composable VM placement algorithm that has already been used to address energy-efficiency [8], or scheduling concerns such as the continuous respect of server licensing policies [6]. The use of BtrPlace might also be beneficial to support side constraints that have to be expressed by the operators. It already provides a support for configuration scripts to state easily constraints over servers and VMs. Furthermore, the implementation of the constraints is usually short.

We also want to investigate on another common maintenance operation that is the usage of anti-virus over VM disk images, a very storage intensive operation that must be planned carefully to maintain the performance of the storage layer. More generally, we think that while advanced algorithms have been proposed to optimize the datacenter usage, there is a large pace for innovation to assist operators at doing their job. Typically, how to automatically improve the preparation of maintenance operations from high-level expectations while hiding the complex technical peculiarities that are today required to be mastered.

Acknowledgments. This work has been carried out within the European Project DC4Cities (FP7-ICT-2013.6.2). Experiments presented in this paper were carried out using the Grid'5000 experimental testbed [3][1], being developed by INRIA with support from CNRS, RENATER and several universities as well as other funding bodies.

References

1. Akoush, S., Sohan, R., Rice, A., Moore, A.W., Hopper, A.: Predicting the performance of virtual machine migration. In: MASCOTS. IEEE (2010)
2. Barham, P., Dragovic, B., Fraser, K., Hand, S., Harris, T., Ho, A., Neugebauer, R., Pratt, I., Warfield, A.: Xen and the art of virtualization. In: 19th SOSP (2003)
3. Bolze, R., Cappello, F., Caron, E., Daydé, M., Desprez, F., Jeannot, E., Jégou, Y., Lanteri, S., Leduc, J., Melab, N., Mornet, G., Namyst, R., Primet, P., Quetier, B., Richard, O., Talbi, E.G., Touche, I.: Grid'5000: A Large Scale And Highly Reconfigurable Experimental Grid Testbed. Int. Journal of High Performance Computing Applications 20(4) (November 2006)
4. Citrix store, http://store.citrix.com
5. Clark, C., Fraser, K., Hand, S., Hansen, J.G., Jul, E., Limpach, C., Pratt, I., Warfield, A.: Live migration of virtual machines. In: Proceedings of the 2nd NSDI. USENIX Association (2005)

---

[1] https://www.grid5000.fr

6. Dang, H.T., Hermenier, F.: Higher SLA Satisfaction in Datacenters with Continuous VM Placement Constraints. In: Proceedings of the 9th Workshop on Hot Topics in Dependable Systems. HotDep 2013. ACM, New York (2013)
7. Deshpande, U., Wang, X., Gopalan, K.: Live gang migration of virtual machines. In: Maccabe, A.B., Thain, D. (eds.) HPDC. ACM (2011)
8. Dupont, C., Schulze, T., Giuliani, G., Somov, A., Hermenier, F.: An energy aware framework for virtual machine placement in cloud federated data centres. In: Proceedings of the 3rd International Conference E-energy. ACM, NY (2012)
9. Goiri, I.: n., Katsak, W., Le, K., Nguyen, T.D., Bianchini, R.: Parasol and GreenSwitch: Managing Datacenters Powered by Renewable Energy. In: Proceedings of the Eighteenth International Conference on Architectural Support for Programming Languages and Operating Systems. ASPLOS 2013. ACM, NY (2013)
10. Hermenier, F., Demassey, S., Lorca, X.: Bin repacking scheduling in virtualized datacenters. Principles and Practice of Constraint Programming (2011)
11. Hermenier, F., Lawall, J., Muller, G.: BtrPlace: A Flexible Consolidation Manager for Highly Available Applications. IEEE Transactions on Dependable and Secure Computing 10(5) (2013)
12. Hermenier, F., Lorca, X., Menaud, J.M., Muller, G., Lawall, J.: Entropy: a Consolidation Manager for Clusters. In: Proceedings of the ACM SIGPLAN/SIGOPS Intl. Conference on Virtual Execution Environments. ACM, NY (2009)
13. Li, C., Qouneh, A., Li, T.: iSwitch: Coordinating and optimizing renewable energy powered server clusters. In: 39th Annual International Symposium on Computer Architecture (ISCA) (June 2012)
14. Liu, H., Jin, H., Xu, C.Z., Liao, X.: Performance and energy modeling for live migration of virtual machines. Cluster Computing 16(2) (2013)
15. Mosberger, D., Jin, T.: httperf - a Tool for Measuring Web Server Performance. SIGMETRICS Performance Evaluation Review 26(3) (1998)
16. Sarker, T., Tang, M.: Performance-driven live migration of multiple virtual machines in datacenters. In: IEEE International Conference on Granular Computing (2013)
17. Soundararajan, V., Anderson, J.M.: The Impact of Management Operations on the Virtualized Datacenter. SIGARCH Comput 38(3) (2010)
18. U.S. Energy Information Administration: Wholesale Electricity and Natural Gas Market Data (May 2014), http://www.eia.gov/electricity/wholesale/
19. Verma, A., Ahuja, P., Neogi, A.: pMapper: Power and migration cost aware application placement in virtualized systems. In: Issarny, V., Schantz, R. (eds.) Middleware 2008. LNCS, vol. 5346, pp. 243–264. Springer, Heidelberg (2008)
20. Ye, K., Jiang, X., Huang, D., Chen, J., Wang, B.: Live migration of multiple virtual machines with resource reservation in cloud computing environments. In: Liu, L., Parashar, M. (eds.) IEEE CLOUD. IEEE (2011)
21. Zheng, J., Eugene Ng, T.S., Sripanidkulchai, K., Liu, Z.: Pacer: A Progress Management System for Live Virtual Machine Migration in Cloud Computing. IEEE Transactions on Network and Service Management 10(4) (December 2013)
22. Zheng, J., Ng, T.S.E., Sripanidkulchai, K., Liu, Z.: COMMA: Coordinating the Migration of Multi-tier Applications. In: Proceedings of the 10th ACM SIGPLAN/SIGOPS International Conference on Virtual Execution Environments, VEE 2014. ACM, New York (2014)

Virtual Cluster Deployment with Dynamically Detachable Remote Shared Storage

Yusuke Tanimura and Takahiro Hamanishi

National Institute of Advanced Industrial Science and Technology (AIST), Japan
{yusuke.tanimura,t-hamanishi}@aist.go.jp

Abstract. Efficient management of virtual machine (VM) images is important for the HPC Cloud where many VMs are provisioned and released by individual users who run parallel applications. Although existing VM deployment methods achieve high efficiency by thin-provisioning on the shared storage with caching on the VM hosting nodes, unexpected interruption and unstable performance of the shared storage are still of concern for HPC applications. This paper presents a novel method to resolve these concerns by detaching the remote shared storage dynamically after a base image of the virtual disk is transferred from the shared storage to a local disk of the VM hosting nodes. The dynamic detachment achieves both a fast boot and isolation from the shared storage, and the delayed image transfer by multicast, at a low, controlled speed, successfully minimizes negative performance impact on the running VMs.

Keywords: virtual machine deployment, storage management, offline caching, high performance computing, cloud computing.

1 Introduction

A virtualized HPC environment on the cloud is increasingly being adopted due to users' demands for more flexible usability [9,1]. Unlike traditional non-virtualized systems, the users can build their own application development and execution environment without compromising with others for software versions, dependencies, configurations, etc. These environments can be instantly scaled, shrunk, or moved through system-wide resource coordination. However, for such an 'HPC Cloud,' one of the remaining issues is efficient management of users' virtual machines (VMs) and their virtual disk images. As many HPC applications run in parallel over multiple servers, numerous VMs must be provisioned or released in a short time period without keeping the users waiting for interaction. Then, once the users start their applications on the VMs, fast access to the virtual disk should be available for the applications. Hence, the virtual disk images should be efficiently and scalably stored and provided to the VM instances.

At present, the above demand for VM image management is mainly responded by two techniques, thin-provisioning on remote shared storage and taking an advantage of local disks attached to host nodes, as shown in Figure 1. The former technique achieves fast bootup of VMs because only necessary data for

L. Lopes et al. (Eds.): Euro-Par 2014 Workshops, Part II, LNCS 8806, pp. 508–518, 2014.

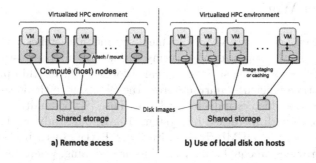

Fig. 1. Techniques for hosting VM disk images

the boot, which are mostly small, are transferred to the VMs. Storage space is saved by eliminating duplicate stores of the image data as a capability of the shared storage. However, I/O performance might be influenced by other VMs, in particular when too many VMs concurrently access the shared storage, due to I/O contention on the storage and on the network between the host nodes and the storage. For the latter technique, the local disks on the host nodes are used as a staging area for the VM image but the boot after copy from the shared storage takes a significantly longer time than the remote boot, and the same issue exists for stage-out. A combined method using the local disks as a cache for the shared storage is sometimes used for reducing I/O requests to the shared storage, which would cover the shortcomings of both techniques. However, the problem of using the shared storage is still a concern involving the HPC cluster use case. The reason is that HPC applications usually run in parallel, demand a much higher performance requirement than other applications, and take a longer time for execution. Therefore, any interruption and/or performance decrease of the remotely shared storage service could possibly cause a serious problem.

This paper proposes a novel method to resolve the above concern by detaching the remote shared storage dynamically after the boot of the virtual cluster (i.e., a set of VMs). In this method, the same benefit mentioned for the combined method is provided and furthermore, an ability to be independent from the shared storage is available. When a user considers if it is beneficial and makes a request, the whole VM image is gradually transferred without much effect on performance of the running VMs, and eventually staged onto the local disk which may be either devoted to the VM or less competitive with other VMs. The detachment would be more valuable when the cluster runs for longer time, like the HPC use case. Our proposed method is implemented for the cloud infrastructure built with QEMU/KVM [6], RADOS [12] and RBD (RADOS Block Device) [8], and evaluated to examine I/O performance of the VM instance before and after the detachment, and performance of the cluster deployment, including interference effects between I/O access and the delayed but controlled image transfer.

2   Related Work

Nicolae, et al. propose a lazy VM deployment scheme that fetches VM image content as needed by the application executing on the VM [5]. They use cloning and shadowing of their scalable storage system, BlobSeer [4], for thin-provisioning. The image is then efficiently mirrored from the BlobSeer to the local disk on an on-demand basis, which is implemented with Fuse [2]. Schmidt, et al. study a similar approach with a stacked file-system [10]. In our study, we have setup a copy-on-write mode of QEMU/KVM with RBD/RADOS as a backend storage. Since RBD provides an equal ability for thin-provisioning, when the RBD cache is enabled, the image hosting manner is close to their approaches. In a later section, a comparison of the results of I/O performance measured on the VM instance between this similar method and our proposed method is shown.

Razavi, et al. study VM image caching in front of a remote network-attached storage system like NFS for fast bootup of multiple VMs [7]. Since the boot data is cached on a local disk or in main memory on host machines, VMs can boot quickly without performing the bulk image transfer. Their approach can be applied to a heterogeneous environment where each VM image is largely different. Zhao, et al. also use a caching technique for VM image deployment on a WAN-based, grid computing infrastructure [13].

Our proposed method is different from the above work, in the point of dynamically and completely switching use of remote storage to use of local storage devices, after the VMs start. Our goal is to eliminate any interruption and shared use concerns during execution of HPC applications on the deployed virtual cluster, while maximally keeping fast VMs deployment by using the remote storage.

3   Our Proposed Method

Our proposed method is designed taking into account two observations. The first observation is that each VM needs a small fraction of its total disk image at the boot time. The amount of read data in our traced boot of CentOS 6.3 was about 86MB. According to a similar experiment shown in the paper [7] mentioned above, the required size would be at most 200MB. In addition, I/O time during the boot is short enough measured against the total boot time. These indicate that booting from remote storage is clearly superior to booting after the VM image is staged onto a host node. The second observation is that most VM images forming the same HPC cluster are similar because parallel applications (e.g., MPI programs) mostly assume a homogeneous environment. As long as all VMs in the cluster use the same software versions and do not store so much unique data on their virtual disks, the difference among the images would be kept to a minimum. This characteristic is useful not only for saving the storage space on the shared storage, but also for reducing the total data transfer size between host nodes and the shared storage.

We now present an outline of our method as follows, with illustrations in Figure 2. At the initial deployment of a), a set of VM disk images for the virtual

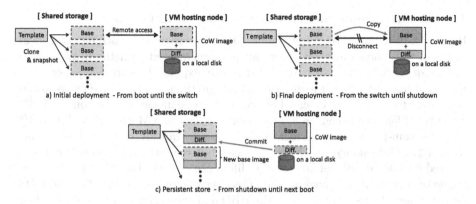

Fig. 2. Outline of our proposed method

cluster is created from the same template by using the clone and snapshot functions of shared storage. Subsequently, a copy-on-write (CoW) image is created for each node and every VM boots with the CoW mode. The CoW mode uses the shared storage for remotely reading a base image and a local disk on a host node for writing any updates (diff.), during the boot process. After the entire cluster has booted, users can start to use the cluster with this CoW mode. Upon the users' request after the boot, the base image transfer to the local disk of all of the host nodes is launched in the background. The transfer is performed by using multicast with a controlled bandwidth so that any impact on the performance of the running VMs can be managed to be smaller. Then, each VM switches the base image on the remote storage to its own just copied one on the local disk, which is the final deployment shown in b). At the shutdown of the cluster, each difference image (diff.), in which all updates on the VM are written, is committed to the remote storage, as shown in c).

The procedure on and after the second time boot is almost the same as the first one, except that a unique part of the base image for each VM is separately read by each host node. The read operations are performed in parallel after the common part is transferred by multicast. Then, the unique part and the common part are merged to form the base image on each host node, before switching the base image. At the shutdown, for every VM, any new diff. from the last commit is committed to the corresponding base image on the remote storage.

4 Implementation

We have implemented our proposed method as Skilfish, which provides a deployment service for a virtual cluster. Skilfish uses RADOS [12] as a backend storage system through the RBD [8] interface, and deploys the QEMU/KVM [6] based VMs by efficiently using the remote shared storage and local disks on host nodes. In order to clarify a distinctive feature of Skilfish, we first introduce how the existing CoW method, which also uses both remote and local storage, can be implemented with RBD and QEMU/KVM, and then explain Skilfish.

4.1 Use of Remote Shared Storage with Local Caching

Hosting a disk image by using remote shared storage with caching on a local disk is a well-known method. This can be implemented with the qcow2 image format of QEMU. We call it CoW-LR in our explanations in this paper. The qcow2 format supports copy-on-write, where each incremental difference is stored separately from the base image. Therefore, the base image is placed on the RBD while the difference is kept in a local cache during the VM execution. The RBD provides thin-provisioning, which allows users to quickly create a base image from a template image by clone and snapshot operations. A qcow2 image is created on a local disk for storing the difference, associating this with the base image on the RBD as a backing file. Thus, write operations from the guest OS do not require transferring data to the RBD and the performance would be close to that of the local disk. In addition, read operations can benefit from the cache function of the RBD. When the VM is shut down and it will not be booted on the same host again, the difference is committed to the base image. Since the qemu-img command does not support direct commit to an image on the RBD, the commit operation is executed through rbd-fuse, which exposes RBD images as files by Fuse. When the VM is booted again but on another host node, a new qcow2 file is created from the last updated base image, and subsequently the VM is booted in the same manner.

Although Nicolae, et al. [5] mentioned several drawbacks of using qcow2, such as complexity of managing multiple image snapshots, image portability, and performance. We assume that the complexity will be reduced by committing updated data to the base image on the RBD after every shutdown of the VM. Moreover, at least in our operation case, conversion of the VM image format of the virtual cluster would not be a strong requirement. One remaining issue for the performance is discussed with our experiment results in Section 5.

4.2 Skilfish: Providing Delayed Transfer and Dynamic Switching of the Base Image

Skilfish extends the above CoW-LR method, as Figure 3 illustrates the implementation. In Skilfish, a base image, which is a backing file of a qcow2 image, is always accessed through the Fuse [2] module. The module confirms completion of reception of the entire base image from the RBD, so that the image can be safely switched and the VM can be disconnected from the RBD. Due to the Fuse function, it is not necessary to modify the qcow2 implementation at all.

A common part of the base image is transferred by a set of one UDPcast [11] sender and its multiple receivers. The sender is normally launched on one of the host nodes, and one receiver is launched on each host node. They synchronize after launched, and then the sender carries out a read of the common part from the RBD and sends it to the receivers by multicast. This image transmission is triggered by a user's request after the entire cluster boots, and the transfer speed is controlled by the MAX bit rate parameter of the UDPcast. If a unique part for each VM exists, it will be read by each host via the RBD, and merged into the common part to reconstruct the base image before the final deployment.

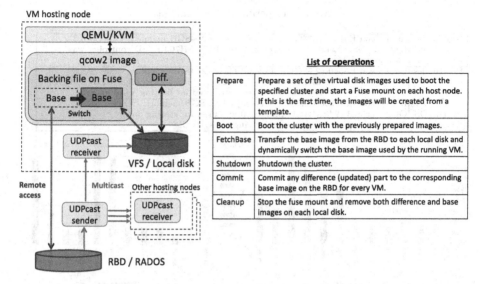

Fig. 3. Implementation of Skilfish

Skilfish supports 'sparse' file. The sparse nature of the imported image is preserved in the RBD/RADOS. When the image is distributed to the host nodes, Skilfish uses the pipe option of UDPcast to compress/decompress data by lzop [3] on the fly. Thus the amount of transferred data can be kept smaller. The copied base image files are also stored in sparse form on the host nodes.

For the virtual cluster users and the upper cloud management software, Skilfish implements a set of operations to manage the cluster deployment, in the command line interface shown on the right of Figure 3. Development of a more sophisticated interface, for example, like that of the RESTful API, which can be easily integrated into the cloud management software, is one of our future tasks.

5   Evaluation

We have evaluated Skilfish, in terms of the I/O performance of the VM instance deployed by Skilfish and the performance of the virtual cluster deployment with using the distinctive features of Skilfish.

5.1   Experiment Setup

The experiment was conducted with the machines shown in Table 1. There were two types of hosting nodes; one used SSD and the other used HDD. All the host nodes were connected to a 10GbE switch and all RADOS OSD servers were connected to another 10GbE switch. Both of the switches were connected by a single 10GbE cable. QEMU/KVM v1.6.2 was used for virtualization, and each VM instance used 256MB memory and Virtio to access its virtual disk with the 'cache=writethrough' option. We disabled the cache on the disks and the RAID

Table 1. Experiment environment

Host nodes /w SSD	Intel Xeon E5540 (2.54GHz, 4 cores) CPU×2, 48GB memory, CentOS 6.3. Intel 520 SSD (240GB) connected to the PERC H700 RAID controller was used for hosting VM images.
Host nodes /w HDD	Intel Xeon E5540 (2.53GHz, 4 cores) CPU×2, 48GB memory, CentOS 6.3. 2×Seagate Savvio 10K (SAS-HDD, 300GB), which were configured to be RAID-1 by the PERC H700 RAID controller, were used for hosting VM images.
OSD servers of RADOS	Intel Xeon E3-1230 (3.2GHz, 4 cores) CPU, 8GB memory, CentOS 6.2. OCZ Vertex3 (240GB) via SATA 2.0 was used for storing data. Each OSD used XFS as its underlying file system.

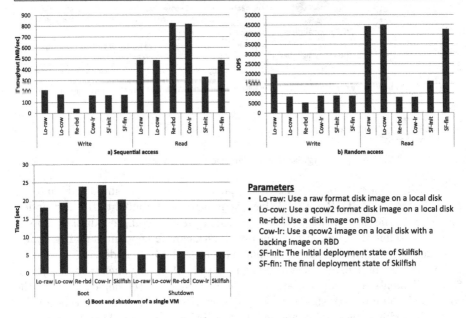

Fig. 4. I/O performance of the VM instance

controllers and flushed the cache of the file system on the host OS, guest OS and OSD servers before every benchmark execution, in order to minimize cache effects. Ceph v0.72.2 was used for the RBD/RADOS system and configured with default parameters, in which 2 replicas were created for each object.

5.2 I/O Performance of the VM Instance

Figure 4-a) and -b) show I/O performance on a deployed VM by Skilfish (SF) and other VMs whose disk images were provided in 4 different ways. Cow-lr in the figure is the CoW-LR type mentioned in Section 4.1. In the read test with the qcow2 modes (Lo-cow, Cow-lr and SF), data was read from a backing file. The experiment was performed using the host node with SSD in Table 1.

In the results, the write performance of SF is almost equal to Lo-cow, which indicates the difference between SF and Lo-raw mostly comes from the qcow2 overhead. Since SF and Cow-lr write data on a fast local disk, the performance is clearly higher than Re-rbd. On the other hand, SF neither provides enough sequential read throughput compared with RBD (See Re-rbd and Cow-lr.) nor IOPS for random read compared with a local disk (See Lo-raw and Lo-cow.). In our investigation, the overhead would be caused mainly by the Fuse layer and it would appear significantly in the fast storage backends such as SSD and RADOS. However, since read cache is available in multiple layers: page cache on both guest and host OS, OSD servers, etc., read performance would certainly be improved. In additional tests, when data were on cache, the measured read performance was comparable among Lo-raw, Lo-cow and SF, and higher than others. In a comparison of the two deployment states of Skilfish, SF-fin achieves equal or higher performance than SF-init in both sequential and random accesses.

Figure 4-c) shows the boot and shutdown time of a single VM by using Skilfish and the other four methods of providing the disk image. The boot with Skilfish took just a few seconds longer than the boot from a local image, and the shutdown with Skilfish was comparable with the other methods.

5.3   Performance of the Virtual Cluster Deployment

Performance of the virtual cluster deployment by using Skilfish has been evaluated in terms of the cluster size, the advantages of the controlled image transfer, and the image size of the virtual disk. All the experiments were performed on up to 16 host nodes with HDD, and only one VM was allocated to one host node so that the VM could occupy a local disk. In the experiment of the I/O interference, the results of HDD and SSD are compared.

Scalability of Cluster Size. Figure 5-a) shows execution time of the Skilfish operations for deployment, against the number of VMs. Each VM was simply booted, switched to the final deployment state and then shut down without running any user applications. The operation time was measured from command execution until the operation was completed for the entire cluster. The actual size of the template disk image was 2.06GB though the virtual image size seen by the VM instance was 4GB. In this experiment, the base image was transferred without the LZO compression. In Figure 5-a), Skilfish provides acceptable scalability such that a user can start to use a 16-node cluster within 24 seconds after executing the Boot operation, and can shut down the cluster within 6 seconds. The FetchBase and Commit operations have been investigated further next.

Effect of Controlled Image Transfer. When a virtual disk image is transferred at a low bit rate, the transfer time takes longer, but the I/O performance of the VM instance is less affected by the background transfer workload. Figure 5-b) shows such interference effects in cases where the bit rate was limited to less than 40MB/s, which is approximately 30% of the sustained write performance for the HDD we used, and 16% for the SSD. In this experiment, only one VM was booted and switched, and its actual size of the base image was 3.06GB. The LZO compression was enabled in the image transfer. On the left in Figure 5-b), the increase ratio of the image transfer (FetchBase) time during I/O

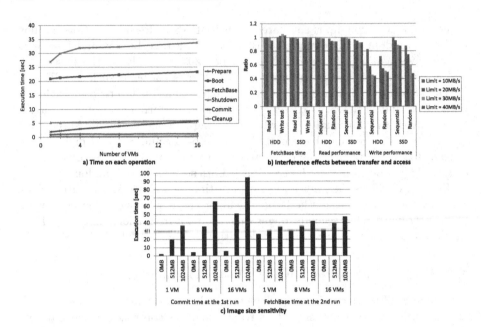

a) Time on each operation

b) Interference effects between transfer and access

c) Image size sensitivity

Fig. 5. Performance of the virtual cluster deployment by using Skilfish

benchmarks is shown. The result indicates that the transfer time is not affected
much by the I/O benchmark execution. On the right, the decrease ratio of the
I/O performance during the image transfer is shown. For read access, the performance dropped at most 7.6%, which was caused by the interference between
the RBD access and the image transfer. For write access, a significant decrease
was seen for the HDD access and random I/O to the SSD. However, when the
transfer speed is limited to 10MB/s, the decrease stayed at 27.5% for the HDD
and 12.5% for the SSD. This implies that the speed control capability of Skilfish
is useful for not affecting much on the I/O performance of the running VM.

Image Size Sensitivity. Figure 5-c) shows the performance of the FetchBase
and Commit operations against the image size. In this experiment, first, we
booted a VM, wrote some data on that VM, shut it down and committed the
update to the image on the RBD. Then we booted the VM again and executed
the FetchBase, in which the last update must be transferred to a local disk
separately from the multicast transfer of the common part. The LZO compression
was disabled in the image transfer. In the measurement of the operation time, we
tried three patterns, 0, 512 or 1024MB, for the amount of write data at the first
run. In each case, the commit size was 80, 614 or 1126MB respectively. We also
compared the operation time among another three patterns for the number of
VMs. The results show that the Commit operation time increases linearly as the
amount of update, which is multiplied by the size and the number of VMs, scales
up. For the FetchBase operation at the second boot, the time increase is smaller

than the Commit. This implies that improvement of the Commit operation speed would be a primary task to support larger-scale cluster deployment.

6 Conclusion

This paper presents a virtual cluster deployment method, which boots a set of VMs from a remote shared storage system and later switches the base of the virtual disk images to the copies on an ephemeral local disk attached to the host nodes, upon the user's request. The method eliminates risks of outage, faults, and interference issues of the remote shared storage so that users can run HPC applications just by using allocated hosting nodes from that time forth, while the method still provides a quick boot of the virtual cluster. Through our experiments with Skilfish, it has been confirmed that the base images can be transferred at a controlled, low speed, in the background, so that the I/O performance of the running VMs will not be affected much. Write performance on the VM instance deployed by Skilfish is comparable to the instance which directly accesses the local disk, but sequential read performance from the remote storage should be improved by reducing the overhead in the switching layer.

In the future, we would like to investigate further about the I/O performance of the deployed VM instance and the deployment scalability in a larger environment, including comparison with the use of other cluster storage systems, and improve the implementation (e.g., in consideration of direct access without Fuse). We also plan to integrate Skilfish into a cloud management platform.

References

1. Ekanayake, J., Fox, G.: High Performance Parallel Computing with Clouds and Cloud Technologies. In: Proceedings of CloudComp, pp. 20–38 (2009)
2. Filesystem in Userspace, http://fuse.sourceforge.net/
3. lzop, http://www.lzop.org/
4. Nicolae, B., Antoniu, G., Bogué, L., Moise, D., Carpen-Amarie, A.: BlobSeer: Next Generation Data Management for Large Scale Infrastructures. Journal of Parallel and Distributed Computing 71(2), 169–184 (2011)
5. Nicolae, B., Bresnahan, J., Keahey, K.: Going Back and Forth: Efficient Multi-deployment and Multisnapshotting on Clouds. In: Proceedings of the 20th International Symposium on High Performance Distributed Computing (HPDC 2011), pp. 147–158 (2011)
6. QEMU/KVM, http://wiki.qemu.org/KVM
7. Razavi, K., Kielmann, T.: Scalable Virtual Machine Deployment Using VM Image Caches. In: Proceedings of the International Conference for High Performance Computing, Networking, Storage and Analysis (SC 2013), vol. 12, pp. 65:1–65:12 (2013)
8. RADOS Block Devices, http://ceph.com/docs/master/rbd/rbd/
9. Rehr, J.J., Vila, F.D., Gardner, J.P., Svec, L., Prange, M.: Scientific Computing in the Cloud. Computing in Science and Engineering 12(3), 34–43 (2010)

10. Schmidt, M., Fallenbeck, N., Smith, M., Freisleben, B.: Efficient Distribution of Virtual Machines for Cloud Computing. In: Proceedings of the 18th Euromicro Conference on Parallel, Distributed and Network-based Processing (PDP 2010), pp. 567–574 (2010)
11. UDPcast, http://www.udpcast.linux.lu/
12. Weil, S.A., Leung, A.W., Brandt, S.A., Maltzahn, C.: RADOS: A Scalable, Reliable Storage Service for Petabyte-scale Storage Clusters. In: Proceedings of the 2nd International Workshop on Petascale Data Storage, pp. 35–44 (2007)
13. Zhao, M., Zhang, J., Figueiredo, R.: Distributed File System Support for Virtual Machines in Grid Computing. In: Proceedings of the 13th International Symposium on High Performance Distributed Computing (HPDC 2004), pp. 202–211 (2004)

Hecatonchire: Towards Multi-host Virtual Machines by Server Disaggregation

Petter Svärd[1], Benoit Hudzia[2], Johan Tordsson[1], and Erik Elmroth[1]

[1] Dept of Computing Science, Umeå University, Sweden
[2] Stratoscale, Belfast, UK

Abstract. Horizontal elasticity through scale-out is the current dogma for scaling cloud applications but requires a particular application architecture. Vertical elasticity is transparent to applications but less used as scale-up is limited by the size of a single physical server. In this paper, we propose a novel approach, server disaggregation, that aggregates memory, compute and I/O resources from multiple physical machines in resource pools. From these pools, virtual machines can be seamlessly provisioned with the right amount of resources for each application and more resources can be added to vertically scale a virtual machine as needed, regardless of the bound of any single physical machine. We present our proposed architecture and implement key functionality such as transparent memory scale-out and cloud management integration. Our approach is validated by a demonstration using benchmarks and a real-world big-data application and results indicate a low overhead in using memory scale-out in both test cases.

1 Introduction

Large peta-byte, and soon exa-byte, data collections are becoming more common [17], with data emanating from transactional enterprise applications, energy grids, social web services, weather sensors or mobile devices. To work upon these large data sets, large amounts of scalable computing resources are required. Today's cloud is designed to provide scalability via the main two scaling methods: horizontal and vertical elasticity. Horizontal elasticity involves allocating more Virtual Machines, *VMs*, to run an application while vertical on the other hand means adding more resources like CPU and memory to an existing VM.

Vertical elasticity is well suited to scale resource demanding business-critical applications such as large databases, ERP systems and big data analytics. It should therefore be a part of cloud platforms in order to enable applications and infrastructure to work together to provide the scalability they need. However, current virtualization technologies are ill-equipped to deliver vertical elasticity as they were primarily built for sharing of individual servers.

In this contribution we introduce the concept of Server Disaggregation to address these shortcomings by enabling cloud infrastructure to lift the physical limitations traditionally associated with memory, compute and I/O resources.

L. Lopes et al. (Eds.): Euro-Par 2014 Workshops, Part II, LNCS 8806, pp. 519–529, 2014.

Server Disaggregation allows cloud platforms to aggregate and manipulate resources more freely, for example scaling up by adding more hardware resources to a VM, regardless of the limitations of the server where it is deployed. As computer prices drop and performance continues to increase, low cost *commodity* systems are the perfect fit for the Server Disaggregation approach as they be configured in large clusters to aggregate computing power. In the paper we present the Hecatonchire, or *Heca* for short, approach to Server Disaggregation and a part-implementation of the concept, namely scale-out of memory and a proof-of-concept integration of memory scale-out into OpenStack. We validate our findings by means of a performance study of memory scale-out for a benchmark appliction and the SAP HANA in-memory database.

2   Vision and General Approach

The goal of the Heca project is to provide a true utility service by disassociating servers from their core resources and relaxing the coupling between VMs and their physical hosts, thereby creating a radically new delivery model for IaaS platforms. Today, CPU development no longer follows Moores law [7] and instead, the industry has moved towards parallelism with processors featuring more cores. The same applies to RAM and disk where, relative to CPU performance, disk performance has actually become slower over the past 30 years [15]. In contrast, network bandwidth continues to increase rapidly. Interfaces such as Infiniband provide interconnect speeds that are approaching internal bus speeds [15] and techniques like Remote Direct Memory Access, RDMA, enable fast access to remote memory. This means that the performance overhead for using resources on remote servers is decreasing.

In a Heca-enabled datacenter, a VM can use resources from multiple servers. Aggregated Memory, compute, and I/O resources are made available in separate pools from which a VM can dynamically consume the aggregated resources to meet changes in application requirements at runtime. This effectively frees the cloud system from some of the constraints of the underlying physical infrastructure and also means that larger VMs than can fit on a single server can be provisioned.

2.1   Server Disaggregation

Server Disaggregation constitutes a major shift in the evolution of data centers and serves as a key enabler for providing a complete scaling solution for platforms on the cloud. Compared to traditional IaaS platforms, the technique has several potential benefits, which we enumerate in this section.

Superior Scalability. For large memory workloads, vertical elasticity is often the most suitable scaling approach. However, there are limits on maximum memory size for commodity hardware and typically a large memory size has to be traded for reduced memory bandwidth, e.g., lower frequency DIMMs. Very often, an additional storage hierarchy that relies on SSDs or disks as a temporary data store is introduced, with severe impact on performance. In contrast, distributed memory aggregation over high-speed interconnects across servers provides a cost-effective, high-performance, alternative as it enables applications to leverage the memory of multiple systems. Server Disaggregation thus combines a cost-effective virtual x86 platform running on commodity hardware with a large shared memory thereby enabling provisioning of resource-intensive VMs.

Improved Resource Utilization. Scheduling of VMs to achieve maximum hardware utilization is known to be an NP-hard problem [18], e.g., provisioning a lot of memory-bound VMs can lead to underutilized CPUs, etc. Using resource aggregation technology, VMs can be deployed independent of single server boundaries, to simplify scheduling and improve resource utilization. Also, fewer but larger nodes mean reduced cluster complexity and reduced fragmentation of the resources. For example, financial organizations run up to thousands of simulations at once, and a common deployment involves hundreds of servers, where each node is running a simulation application at 80% utilization. By using resource aggregation to create fewer larger nodes, every four aggregated systems can run another copy of the application, in theory approaching 100% utilization.

Better Performance. When I/O, computing and memory resources are separated into purpose-built nodes, servers can be better optimized to the requirements of the hosted applications. For compute-intense workloads, proprietary shared-memory systems have traditionally been used. Systems such as the SGI Ultraviolet [14] or the Cray XMT [5] come with significantly larger memory sizes but they are comparatively expensive. Aggregation technology benefits from the local memory bandwidth across servers, as opposed to traditional SMP [16] or, to a lesser extent, NUMA architecture, where memory bandwidth decreases as the machine scales out. Solutions based on resource aggregation can thus show close-to-linear memory bandwidth scaling, thereby delivering excellent performance in particular for many-threaded applications, e.g., graph analysis, or memory bandwidth bound ones, such as computational fluid dynamics simulations.

Easier Use and Administration. Traditionally, using distributed memory across several servers requires that the application is developed for an explicit memory distribution model which require highly skilled, domain-aware software developers using custom software libraries [11]. Having a single virtual system to manage is also simpler compared to the complexities involved in managing a cluster with respect to software installation and synchronization. Furthermore, aggregation technology also simplifies the I/O architecture by consolidating each individual server's network and storage interfaces. The administrator gets fewer I/O devices to manage leading to increased availability, higher utilization, better resiliency, and runtime scalability of I/O resources.

Improved Economics. Thanks to improved scalability, hardware utilization and performance and simplified administration, aggregation technologies show great potential for cost savings in data center operations. Server Disaggregation also provides a cost-effective x86 alternative to expensive and proprietary shared memory systems.

3   Heca Architecture and Implementation

The Heca architecture, outlined in Figure 1, decouples virtual resource management from physical resources by providing the capability to mediate between applications and servers in real-time. This decoupling is achieved by aggregating and managing server resources in a datacenter. Each resource type is exposed to the overall cloud platform via an independent mediation layer that arbitrates the allocation of resources between multiple applications, creating a distributed and shared physical resources layer. The architecture is composed of three layers,

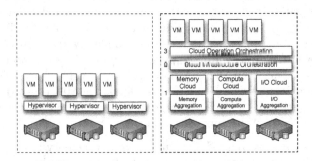

Fig. 1. Traditional (left) vs Heca (right) Virtualization

the *Cloud Resource Aggregation* layer, marked as 1 in Figure 1, provides access to and management for the aggregated resources, i.e. Memory Cloud, Compute Cloud and I/O Cloud. The *Cloud Infrastructure Orchestration* layer, marked as 2, provides the ability to compose logical virtual servers with a level of service assurance that guarantees resources and performance provided by the resource aggregation layer. It also exposes extended features enabled by the decoupled resource layers. The *Cloud Operation Orchestration* layer, marked as 3, provides service life cycle management. It enables provisioning of self-configuring, self-healing, self-optimizing services that can be composed to create self-managed business workflows that are independent of the physical infrastructure.

3.1   Transparent Memory Scale-out

To enable *transparent memory scale-out*, Heca makes it possible for a VM to allocate memory on multiple servers. The server that hosts the VM to be scaled-up is termed a *memory demander*. The application is transparently scaled vertically by using memory provided by other hosts in the cluster, denoted *memory sponsors*. Figure 2 depicts memory scale-out, with a memory demander running an application, and several memory sponsors. The memory sponsors are VMs whose sole purpose is to provide memory to its demanders. Note that a server can host both memory sponsors and demanders at the same time.

All hosts run a modified Linux kernel, including a Heca kernel module, and also include a modified version of the QEMU hypervisor. On a higher level the kernel module fits in Layer 1 in Figure 1, while the modified hypervisor belongs to Layer 2 in the same figure. The kernel module handles the operations during scale-out and the transfer of memory content to and from remote hosts. The hypervisor enables full transparency as it communicates cluster setup to the kernel module, and applications run unchanged on top of it. It also generates specialized system calls, *ioctls*, to the kernel module, passing relevant parameters needed to set up the memory scale-out. The behavior of the kernel module differs between memory sponsors and demanders. On the memory demander, the VM's RAM is partitioned into address ranges. Each address range is registered as sponsored by a memory sponsor. Appropriate page table entries, *PTEs*, are put in place. Each memory sponsor allocates enough memory in its VM to sponsor one address range on the memory demander. Besides that, memory sponsors can continue to operate as usual.

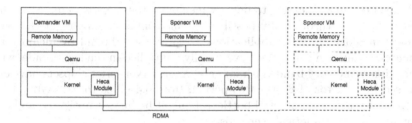

Fig. 2. High-level architecture of a memory scale-out

The partitioning of memory into address spaces is determined by the parameters passed to the VMs during provisioning. Therefore, when setting-up the memory scale-out each address range is created in accordance with a corresponding amount of physical memory provided by a memory sponsor. When the VM faults on an address, the kernel identifies the modified PTE and passes execution to the kernel module. The module requests the memory page from the memory sponsor, and the page fault is resolved. If the kernel later decides to swap out the page, its contents are re-sent to the memory sponsor, and the PTE is updated. Our solution achieves transparency as the application runs in a VM, unaware of the scale-out operation. Also, application performance is good as most memory operations are carried out in kernel space, beneath the I/O layer. Use of a virtual stack also enables integration with cloud platforms such as OpenStack [12], managing a cluster of VMs. This simple approach reflects a trade-off however, and on the downside, it binds the approach to a virtualization stack, in our case KVM.

Resilience and Fault-Tolerance. The Heca approach can provide resilience by preparing memory sponsors with twice the available memory, compared to the requirements of the memory demander. Arguments are passed to the VMs reflecting that each address space is sponsored by two memory sponsors. The hypervisors pass that information on to the kernel module. When the kernel module faults on an address, it sends the request to both memory sponsors, sponsoring its address space. The first arriving response is used. When the kernel module swaps a page out, it sends it to both memory sponsors, and waits for validation that both of them stored the content, before discarding the page. The biggest advantage of this approach is zero-downtime failover of memory sponsors. If one sponsor fails, the other sponsor continues responding to the memory demander's requests for memory content. Furthermore, the memory demander can identify the fault (trusting the remote kernel module, and the underlying networking fabric), and disconnect from the sponsor. Another host can later join the system, taking up the role of the failed sponsor.

However, there are a few disadvantages with this approach. First of all, it consumes twice the amount of memory, compared to a non-resilient scheme. Our mirroring approach also doubles the required bandwidth, an increase that previous generations of networking fabrics could not support [8]. However, today's fabrics can handle much higher loads. With bandwidths exceeding 100 Gb/s this would require the application to be very memory intensive, swapping more than 50 Gb/s, yet it is theoretically possible. In this context we highlight that even the most memory-intensive applications are practically bound by memory bus capacities. Infiniband capacities have rapidly multiplied in the last decade, while the maximum memory bandwidth for Intel Xeon server series chipsets have only increased by a factor of 8 over this period, from 6.4 Gbps to 51.2 Gbps [4]. If this trend persists, the potential bottleneck might be further mitigated and even eliminated in most practical scenarios.

Other resiliency approaches, such as RAID-5, are more conservative in memory and bandwidth requirements. Yet such approaches require a lengthy computation process to recover from a fault, in which lost data is re-built. This prevents them from ensuring zero-downtime failover. Additionally, such approaches may incur a performance penalty on the scale-out operation, as computation of parity bits is required when swapping pages out.

We highlight that this discussion does not deal with fault tolerance for the main host running the application, the memory demander. This issue is beyond the scope of this paper, as it is not a scale-out challenge, but rather a generic challenge of fault tolerance for VMs.

3.2   Cloud Management Integration

To simplify the use of memory scale-out we have integrated resource disaggregation of VMs into OpenStack. If the VM is too large to fit on any host, our modified OpenStack scheduler splits the VM into sponsors and a demander. The feature is enabled by setting a flag in an OpenStack VM flavor.

The launch of a VM instance in OpenStack starts with the cloud controller receiving a request to deploy an instance via the Compute API (Step 1 in Figure 3). The instance is given an instance ID and the message is forwarded to the scheduler which selects a suitable worker to run the instance (Steps 2 and 3) and passes the message to it (Step 4). The compute worker sends a message to the network controller to get an IP for the instance (Steps 5-8) and continues provisioning of the instance.

To provision the VMs correctly as demander and sponsors, extra information must be passed to the hypervisor. These parameters include a heca mode, *sponsor* or *demander*, two heca process identifiers, TCP ports for control and memory transfer, and RDMA IP addresses for both demander and sponsors. The start address and size of the shared memory region is also needed and is given by how much more memory the VM requests than maximum free on any host. Figure 3 illustrates how OpenStack allocates the instance before it is sent to the scheduler, which also performs the actual deployment in an asynchronous manner. This creates an issue as the sponsor and demander both need each others RDMA IP addresses at the time of creation. Our pragmatic solution is to perform a "pre-scheduling" round to determine the placement of the VMs without actually provisioning them. The instances are then sent to the scheduler again, using scheduler hints to achieve the desired placement. To pass these parameters to qemu-kvm our modified OpenStack constructs a `<qemu:commandline>` block that is added to the instance.xml file. On instance creation, instance.xml is fed to the libvirt API that passes the Heca parameters to the qemu-kvm hypervisor.

4   Experimental Demonstration of Heca functionality

To verify the memory scale-out functionality we deploy an 8 GB VM to an OpenStack cloud with a controller node and three compute nodes, see Table 1. We present performance results for two deployments, with and without memory scale-out enabled. The outcome of the two deployments are shown in Figure 4.

Table 1. Testbed Description.

Node	CPU	RAM	Free RAM	Network	Kernel
Controller	i5@3 GHz	4 GB	N/A	Gb Ethernet	Linux Heca 3.6
Compute A,B,C	i5@3 GHz	8 GB	4,3,5 GB	iWARP	Linux Heca 3.6

In the first deployment, the VM is provisioned on the host with the most amount of RAM available. As overbooking of resources is enabled in OpenStack, virtual memory is used to account for the overbooked RAM. In the second deployment, the modified OpenStack avoids using virtual memory by memory scale-out and provisions the memory demander on Node B and a memory sponsor on Node A.

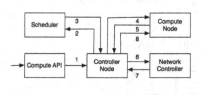

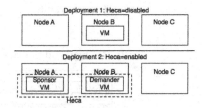

Fig. 3. OpenStack deployment   **Fig. 4.** Deployment outcome

Remote Memory Performance. To evaluate the relative performance of using remote memory we made four comparisons using the Linux *MBW* [9] tool
that allocates two arrays and copies the first to the second using memcopy. We
ran MBW with an array size of 3 GB which means it allocated 6 GB of RAM.
In Figure 5, for the baseline case, marked as *bare-metal*, MBW was run non-
virtualized with more than 6 GB of free RAM. In the second case, *virtualized* in
Figure 5, MBW was run in an 8 GB VM, with more than 6 GB of free RAM.
For the third experiment, *overcommitted* in the same figure, the second experiment was repeated but the amount of free memory on the host was restricted
to 4 GB meaning that the host is overcommitted. In the fourth experiment,
marked as *memory scale-out*, MBW was run on a demander-sponsor VM pair
with 2 GB scaled out to the sponsor. All other conditions were identical to the
overcommitted case. An overall observation is that virtualized is 6% slower than
bare-metal and memory scale-out is 6% slower than virtualized. The results of
the overcommitted case vary greatly between iterations due to swapping.

To further evaluate the memory scale-out functionality we performed an experiment with a real-world, big data application, SAP HANA [13], which is an
in-memory database. The application was run on a 40 vCPU VM on a 4 socket,
10 core Intel Xeon West Mere cluster with 1 TB RAM, connected by a 40 Gbps
Infiniband network. The experiment was performed with a set of 18 different
queries against a 2.5 TB OLAP dataset. Between tests, we varied the number
of simultaneous users running the query sets. The complete test was performed
twice, the second time 512 GB of the VMs RAM was scaled out to a memory
sponsor. The results are shown in Figure 6. In all runs, the overhead in query
response time with 50% remote memory was around 3% compared to running
virtualized with no remote memory.

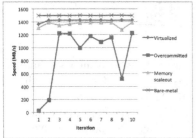
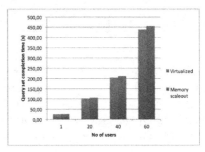

Fig. 5. Memcopy speed test results   **Fig. 6.** Overhead per query set

Table 2. Overhead per query set with 80 HANA users

Demander : Sponsor A : Sponsor B	Overhead
1 GB : 2 GB : -	4%
1 GB : 3 GB : -	5.6%
2 GB : 1 GB : 1 GB	0.9%
1 GB : 1 GB : 1 GB	2%

To investigate the overhead when using remote memory in more detail, we present the result from a test running HANA on a smaller VM, this time with 80 users but varying the amount of remote memory. We ran the experiment with one and two sponsors, varying the distribution of memory between the demander and sponsors as shown in Table 2. The table also shows that the overhead increases with the amount of remote memory and that distributing the remote memory over several sponsors improves performance, due to the increased bandwidth.

5   Related Work

Han et al. advocate a datacenter architecture in which the resources within a server are disaggregated and the datacenter is architected as a collection of standalone resources [3]. However, they do not implement anything but rather investigate the feasibility of such an approach.

The Oracle Transcendent Memory project makes unused memory on a node available to other nodes through the use of an API [6]. The main difference from Heca is that guest OS changes are explicitly required in order to use the shared memory using the Oracle approach. Also, there is no guarantee that memory that is currently idle will not eventually be needed as the future working set size of a VM cannot be accurately predicted. Another similar approach is VMware DRS which enables managing a cluster containing many potentially-heterogeneous hosts as if it were a single pool of resources [2]. The main difference between the DRS and the Heca approaches is that the DRS approach splits a cluster into smaller groups. A number of VMs attached to a group can then share the CPU and Memory resources in the group among them. Dragojevic et al. propose their Fast Remote Memory, *FaRM*, approach which exposes remote memory over RDMA as a shared address space [1], consisting of 2 GB memory regions. In contrast to Heca, the FaRM approach does not use a virtualization stack, but the shared memory is made available trough a programming model.

Sharing of resources is also provided by XtreemOS, which is a distributed Linux distribution that aggregates resources from compute resources in a cluster [10]. However, as the system is perceived as one single computer this approach can be cumbersome when running many applications in parallel. This means that XtreemOS is more suited for the Grid use-case.

6   Conclusion

We propose a solution to enable vertical elasticity, beyond the capacity limitations of individual servers, by aggregating CPU, memory, and I/O resources into reusable pools that can be used to provision VMs independent of limitations of the underlying hardware. The core concepts of our outlined architecture is implemented as a kernel module and a modified Qemu-KVM hypervisor integrated into OpenStack. Our approach is validated by provisioning multi-host VMs and a performing an evaluation of memory scale-out. The results indicate that our server disaggregation concept is feasible, with as little as 6% overhead compared to single-host virtualization as well as simplified administration, thus enabling a broader range of applications to take advantage of the cloud.

Acknowledgments. The authors thank Steve Walsh and Aidan Shribman for their valuable contributions to this project as well as SAP (UK) Limited, Belfast, where much of this work was performed. Financial support has been provided in part by the Swedish Governments strategic effort eSSENCE and the Swedish Research Council (VR) under contract number C0590801 for the project Cloud Control.

References

1. Dragojević, A., Narayanan, D., Hodson, O., Castro, M.: FaRM: fast remote memory. In: NSDI 2014. USENIX (2014)
2. Gulati, A., Holler, A., Ji, M., Shanmuganathan, G., Waldspurger, C., Zhu, X.: Vmware distributed resource management: Design, implementation, and lessons learned. VMware Technical Journal 1(1), 45–64 (2012)
3. Han, S., Egi, N., Panda, A., Ratnasamy, S., Shi, G., Shenker, S.: Network support for resource disaggregation in next-generation datacenters. In: HOTNETS 2013: The Twelfth ACM Workshop on Hot Topics in Networks, pp. 10:1–10:7. ACM (2013)
4. Intel. Microprocessor quick reference guide, http://www.intel.com/pressroom/kits/quickrefyr.htm (Visited on April 27, 2014)
5. Konecny, P.: Introducing the Cray XMT. In: CUG 2007: The 2007 Cray User Group meeting (2007)
6. Magenheimer, D., Mason, C., McCracken, D., Hackel, K.: Transcendent memory and linux. In: Proceedings of the Linux Symposium, pp. 191–200 (2009)
7. Mann, C.C.: The end of Moores law. Technology Review 103(3), 42–48 (2000)
8. Markatos, E., LeBlanc, T.: Using processor affinity in loop scheduling on shared-memory multiprocessors. IEEE Transactions on Parallel and Distributed Systems 5(4), 379–400 (1994)
9. MBW. MBW: Memory bandwidth benchmark (2010), http://manpages.ubuntu.com/manpages/lucid/man1/mbw.1.html (Visited on January 2, 2014)
10. Morin, C.X.: A grid operating system making your computer ready for participating in virtual organizations. In: ISORC 2007: 10th IEEE International Symposium on Object and Component-Oriented Real-Time Distributed Computing, pp. 393–402 (2007)
11. Nussle, M., Scherer, M., Bruning, U.: A resource optimized remote-memory-access architecture for low-latency communication. In: ICPP 2009: The 2009 International Conference on Parallel Processing, pp. 220–227. IEEE (2009)
12. OpenStack. OpenStack Cloud OS, https://www.openstack.org (Visited on April 27, 2014)
13. SAP. SAP HANA (2014), http://bit.ly/GKZkDy (Visited on April 27, 2014)
14. SGI. Technical Advances in the SGI UVTM Architecture, http://www.sgi.com/pdfs/4192.pdf (visited on April 27, 2014)

15. Subramoni, H., Koop, M., Panda, D.: Designing next generation clusters: Evaluation of InfiniBand DDR/QDR on Intel computing platforms. In: HOTI 2009: The 2009 IEEE Symposium on High Performance Interconnects, pp. 112–120 (2009)
16. Tipparaju, V., Nieplocha, J., Panda, D.: Fast collective operations using shared and remote memory access protocols on clusters. In: IPDPS 2003: The 2003 International Parallel and Distributed Processing Symposium, p. 10. IEEE (2003)
17. Trelles, O., Prins, P., Snir, M., Jansen, R.C.: Big data, but are we ready? Nature Reviews Genetics 12(3), 224–224 (2011)
18. Wood, T., Shenoy, P.J., Venkataramani, A., Yousif, M.S.: Black-box and gray-box strategies for virtual machine migration. In: NSDI, vol. 7, pp. 229–242 (2007)

EXA-DUNE: Flexible PDE Solvers, Numerical Methods and Applications

Peter Bastian[1], Christian Engwer[2], Dominik Göddeke[3], Oleg Iliev[4],
Olaf Ippisch[5], Mario Ohlberger[2], Stefan Turek[3], Jorrit Fahlke[2],
Sven Kaulmann[2], Steffen Müthing[1], and Dirk Ribbrock[3]

[1] Interdisciplinary Center for Scientific Computing, Heidelberg University,
Im Neuenheimer Feld 368, D-69120 Heidelberg, Germany
[2] Institute for Computational and Applied Mathematics, University of Münster
Orleans-Ring 10, D-48149 Münster, Germany
[3] Department of Mathematics, TU Dortmund,
Vogelpothsweg 87, D-44227 Dortmund, Germany
[4] Fraunhofer Institute for Industrial Mathematics ITWM
Fraunhofer-Platz 1, D-67663 Kaiserslautern, Germany
[5] Institut für Mathematik, TU Clausthal-Zellerfeld,
Erzstr. 1, D-38678 Clausthal-Zellerfeld, Germany

Abstract. In the EXA-DUNE project we strive to (i) develop and implement numerical algorithms for solving PDE problems efficiently on heterogeneous architectures, (ii) provide corresponding domain-specific abstractions that allow application scientists to effectively use these methods, and (iii) demonstrate performance on porous media flow problems. In this paper, we present first results on the hybrid parallelisation of sparse linear algebra, system and RHS assembly, the implementation of multiscale finite element methods and the SIMD performance of high-order discontinuous Galerkin methods within an application scenario.

1 The EXA-DUNE Project

Many processes from science and engineering can be modelled with stochastic or parameterised partial differential equations (PDEs). Despite increasing computational capacities, many of these problems are still only solvable with severe simplifications. This is particularly true if not only single forward problems are considered, but rather uncertainty quantification, parameter estimation or optimisation in engineering applications are investigated.

Within the EXA-DUNE[1] project we pursue three different routes to make progress towards exascale: (i) we develop new computational algorithms and implementations for solving PDEs that are highly suitable to better exploit the performance offered by prospective exascale hardware, (ii) we provide domain-specific abstractions that allow mathematicians and application scientists to exploit (exascale) hardware with reasonable effort in terms of programmers' time (a metric that we consider highly important) and (iii) we showcase our methodology to solve complex application problems of flow in porous media.

---

[1] http://www.sppexa.de/general-information/projects.html#EXADUNE

L. Lopes et al. (Eds.): Euro-Par 2014 Workshops, Part II, LNCS 8806, pp. 530–541, 2014.

Software development, in the scope of our work for the numerical solution of a wide range of PDE problems, faces contradictory challenges. On the one hand, users and developers prefer flexibility and generality, on the other hand, the continously changing hardware landscape requires algorithmic adaptation and specialisation to be able to exploit a large fraction of peak performance.

A framework approach for entire application domains rather than distinct problem instances facilitates code reuse and thus substantially reduces development time. In contrast to the more conventional approach of developing in a 'bottom-up' fashion starting with only a limited set of problems and solution methods (likely a single problem/method), frameworks are designed from the beginning with flexibility and general applicability in mind so that new physics and new mathematical methods can be incorporated more easily. In a software framework the generic code of the framework is extended by the user to provide application specific code instead of just calling functions from a library. Template meta-programming in C++ supports this extension step in a very efficient way, performing the fusion of framework and user code at compile time which reduces granularity effects and enables a much wider range of optimisations by the compiler. In this project we strive to redesign components of the DUNE framework [3,2] in such a way that hardware-specific adaptations based on the experience acquired within the FEAST project [15] can be exploited in a transparent way without affecting user code.

Future exascale systems are characterised by a massive increase in node-level parallelism, heterogeneity and non-uniform access to memory. Current examples include nodes with multiple conventional CPU cores arranged in different sockets. GPUs require much more fine-grained parallelism, and Intel's Xeon Phi design shares similarities with both these extremes. One important common feature of all these architectures is that reasonable performance can only be achieved by explicitly using their (wide-) SIMD capabilities. The situation becomes more complicated as different programming models, APIs and language extensions are needed, which lack performance portability. Instead, different data structures and memory layouts are often required for different architectures. In addition, it is no longer possible to view the available off-chip DRAM memory within one node as globally shared in terms of performance. Accelerators are typically equipped with dedicated memory, which improves accelerator-local latency and bandwidth substantially, but at the same time suffers from a (relatively) slow connection to the host. Due to NUMA (non-uniform memory access) effects, a similar (albeit less dramatic in absolute numbers) imbalance can already be observed on multi-socket multi-core CPU systems. There is common agreement in the community that the existing MPI-only programming model has reached its limits. The most prominent successor will likely be 'MPI+X', so that MPI can still be used for coarse-grained communication, while some kind of shared memory abstraction is used within MPI processes at the UMA level.

Our work within the EXA-DUNE project currently targets pilot applications in the field of porous media flow. These problems are characterised by coupled elliptic/parabolic-hyperbolic PDEs with strongly varying coefficients and highly anisotropic meshes. The elliptic part mandates robust solvers and thus does not lend itself to the current trend in HPC towards matrix-free methods with their beneficial properties in terms of memory bandwidth and/or FLOPs/DOF ratio; typical matrix-free techniques like stencil-based geometric multigrid are not suited to those types of problems. For that reason, we aim at algebraic multigrid (AMG) preconditioners known to work well in this context, and work towards further improving their scalability and (hardware) performance. Discontinuous Galerkin (DG) methods are employed to increase data locality and arithmetic intensity. Matrix-free techniques are investigated for the hyperbolic/parabolic parts.

In this paper we report on the current state of the EXA-DUNE project. As message passing parallelism is well established in DUNE (as documented by the inclusion of DUNE's solver library in the High Q Club[2]), we concentrate on core/node level performance. Regarding the three 'exa-avenues' identified in the project, implementations of multiscale reduced basis and high-order spectral DG methods are treated in Sections 3 and 4, hybrid parallelisation of finite element assembly and sparse linear algebra is covered in Section 2 and preliminary results for density-driven flow in porous media are shown in Section 4.

2   Hybrid Parallelism in DUNE

In the following, we introduce the 'virtual UMA node' concept at the heart of our hybrid parallelisation strategy, and ongoing current steps to incorporate this concept into the assembly and solver stages of our framework.

2.1   UMA Concept

Current and upcoming HPC systems are characterised by two trends which greatly increase the complexity of efficient node-level programming: (i) A massive increase in the degree of parallelism restricts the amount of memory and bandwidth available to each compute unit, and (ii) the node architecture becomes increasingly heterogeneous. Consequently, on modern multi-socket nodes the memory performance depends on the location of the memory in relation to the compute core (NUMA). The problem becomes even more pronounced in the presence of accelerators like MICs or GPUs, for which memory accesses might have to traverse the PCIe bus, severely limiting bandwidth and latency. To illustrate this issue, we consider the relative runtime of an iterative linear solver (Krylov-DG), as shown in Table 1: An identical problem is solved with different mappings to MPI processes and threads, on a representative 4-socket server with AMD Opteron 6172 12-core processors and 128 GB RAM. On this architecture, a UMA domain comprises half a socket (6 cores), and thus, (explicit or implicit) multi-threading beyond 6 cores actually yields slowdowns. This experiment validates our design decision to regard heterogeneous nodes as a collection of 'virtual

---

[2] http://www.fz-juelich.de/ias/jsc/EN/Expertise/High-Q-Club/_node.html

Table 1. Poisson on the unit cube, discretised by the DG-SIPG method, timings for 100 Krylov iterations. Comparison of different MPI / shared memory mappings for varying polynomial degree p of the DG discretisation and mesh width h. Timings $t_{M/T}$ and speedups for varying numbers of MPI processes M and threads per process T.

p	h^{-1}	$t_{48/1}[s]$	$t_{8/6}[s]$	$\frac{t_{48/1}}{t_{8/6}}$	$t_{4/12}[s]$	$\frac{t_{48/1}}{t_{4/12}}$	$t_{1/48}[s]$	$\frac{t_{48/1}}{t_{1/48}}$
1	256	645.1	600.2	1.07	1483.3	0.43	2491.7	0.26
2	128	999.5	785.7	1.27	1320.7	0.76	2619.0	0.38
3	64	709.6	502.9	1.41	1237.2	0.57	1958.2	0.36

UMA nodes' on the MPI level: Internal uniform memory access characteristics are exploited by shared-memory parallelism, while off-node communication is handled via (classical/existing) message passing.

2.2 Finite Element Assembly

Assembling the finite element operator or the residual vector typically involves two user-level inputs: The assembler iterates through the grid cells of a given mesh, and for each grid cell a local operator is evaluated, which computes the local contributions to the global stiffness matrix or the residual vector. Following DUNE's general approach, we implement threading and vectorisation on top of the existing grid abstraction.

Globally the grid is partitioned using the existing MPI layer. Within each UMA node system threads are used to share the workload among all cores. For a user-defined number of concurrent threads the grid is locally partitioned such that each thread handles the same amount of work. On the finest level vectorisation (SIMD, ILP) is required to fully exploit the hardware. SIMD has the largest impact in the local operator which also poses the biggest challenge, as this is user code. The resulting requirement of fully exploiting SIMD in that setting without exposing users to the details of vectorisation presents an additional problem compared to the linear algebra, where the number of kernels is much smaller.

Multi-threading support is implemented on top of the existing grid interface, thus we can easily compare different strategies for the local partitioning of a mesh $\mathcal{T}(\Omega)$. Experiments are carried out on an Intel Xeon E7-4850 with 10 cores (20 hyperthreads), 2 GHz and 12 GB RAM and on an Intel Xeon Phi 5110P, with 60 cores (240 hyperthreads), 1 GHz and 8 GB RAM. Many bottlenecks for multi-threading only become visible on many-core systems like the Xeon Phi. SIMD experiments are carried out on an Intel Core i5-3340M with 2 cores (4 hyperthreads), 2.7 GHz and 8 GB RAM and a 256-bit SIMD unit (AVX). See [5] for more details. Our experiments indicate that the additional complexity of partitioning the node-local mesh into per-thread blocks that optimise properties like surface-to-volume ratio, e.g. using graph partitioning libraries like METIS or SCOTCH, does not pay off; those approaches impose prohibitive setup and memory penalties. Instead, a *ranged* partitioning strategy showed the best overall

Table 2. Comparison of different polynomial degrees k, number of threads P, and hardware X. Time per DOF t_P^X [μs] and efficiency E_P^X of the Jacobian assembly using ranged partitioning and entity-wise locking. We see a clear benefit from higher order discretisations, due to the increased algorithmic intensity.

k	CPU t_1	CPU t_{10}	CPU t_{20}	CPU E_{10}	CPU E_{20}	PHI t_1	PHI t_{60}	PHI t_{120}	PHI t_{240}	PHI E_{60}	PHI E_{120}	PHI E_{240}
0	4.59	0.74	0.54	62%	42%	59.57	1.33	1.17	1.20	75%	43%	21%
1	1.38	0.22	0.17	62%	42%	18.92	0.37	0.27	0.26	84%	57%	30%
2	1.10	0.15	0.12	72%	46%	17.12	0.32	0.21	0.19	90%	69%	38%
3	1.29	0.16	0.13	79%	50%	19.84	0.36	0.23	0.20	92%	72%	41%
4	1.52	0.18	0.15	87%	49%							
5	1.81	0.21	0.18	88%	51%							

performance. We define consecutive iterator ranges of the size $|\mathcal{T}|/P$. This is efficiently implemented using entry points in the form of begin and end iterators. The memory requirement is $O(P)$ and thus will not strain the bandwidth.

Data access is critical during the assembly, as different local vectors and local matrices contribute to the same global entries. Two approaches are possible to avoid race conditions: locking and colouring. *Entity-wise locks* are expected to give very good performance, as they correspond to the granularity of the critical sections. The downside is the additional memory requirement of $O(|\mathcal{T}|)$. With a ranged partitioning and entity-wise locking, or with colouring, we obtain good performance on multi-core CPUs and on many-core systems alike. The performance gain from colouring is negligible, but increases code complexity, so that this approach is less favourable.

Timings for ranged partitioning and entity-wise locking are presented in Table 2. As a benchmark we consider the assembly of the Jacobian and measure strong scalability. Discretisations using different polynomial orders are evaluated and the problem sizes are chosen such that the global number of unknowns is roughly the same. The results indicate the benefit of higher order trial and test functions, due to the increased arithmetic intensity in the local operator. The absolute timings show a significant issue for the Xeon Phi, which can only exhibit its full performance if the code is able to use the 512-bit wide SIMD instructions.

Vectorising computations in the local operator requires pursuing different avenues depending on the number of local DOFs / quadrature points: For high-order discretisations, good performance can be achieved by simply unrolling / vectorising the existing loops (cf. results in Sec. 4). For low-order methods this approach is only feasible if the number of DOFs / quadrature points is a multiple of the SIMD width, limiting the applicability of this technique. We thus follow a different approach to transparently add SIMD parallelism at the level of the local operator and vectorise over N elements, operating on the same local function space, and encapsulate data in a packed C++ data type. This approach is inspired by [7]; their Vc library is also used for the presented preliminary results. The packed data consists of a vector of N doubles. Using operator overloading an arithmetic operation $a \odot b$ is mapped to the component-wise evaluation $a_i \odot b_i$.

All interfaces providing local information of the N cells are now vectorised as well as the residual vector and the local matrix. In particular, information like the Jacobian of the geometric mapping and the determinant of the Jacobian are now provided for all N elements.

We investigate a 3D Q_2 discretisation of the Poisson problem with 262 144 cells and benchmark the assembly of the residual and the Jacobian on a structured grid on a single core. First results show a speedup of 1.8 (SSE, 2 lanes) and 2.6 (AVX, 4 lanes) for the Jacobian and 1.7 (SSE) and 2.3 (AVX) for the residual. This is measured without the scatter operation into the global matrix as this is not yet optimised — if we include scattering in the timing the speedup is, e.g., 1.7 for the Jacobian and AVX. Even without scattering some operations are not vectorised yet, so we do not obtain the full speedup, but we can show that it is possible to add SIMD parallelism to the local operator with only minimal restrictions for the user.

2.3   Sparse Linear Algebra and Solvers

Designing effcient implementations and realisations of solvers effectively boils down to (i) a suitable choice of data structures for sparse matrix-vector multiply, and (ii) numerical components of the solver, i.e., preconditioners.

DUNE's current matrix format, (block) compressed row storage, is ill-suited for modern hardware and SIMD, as there is no way to efficiently and generally expose a block structure that fits the size of the SIMD units. We have thus extended the SELL-C-σ matrix format introduced in [8] which is a tuned variant of the sorted ELL format known from GPUs, to be able to efficiently handle block structures [11].

As we mostly focus on solvers for DG discretisations, which lend themselves to block-structured matrices, this is a valid and generalisable decision. The standard approach of requiring matrix block sizes that are multiples of the SIMD size is not applicable in our case because the matrix block size is a direct consequence of the chosen discretisation. In order to support arbitrary block sizes, we interleave the data from N matrix blocks given a vector unit of size N, an approach introduced in [4]. This allows us to easily vectorise existing scalar algorithms by having them operate on multiple blocks in parallel, an approach that works as long as there are no data-dependent branches in the original algorithm. Sparse linear algebra is typically memory bandwidth bound, and thus, the main advantage of the block format is the reduced number of column block indices that need to be stored (as only a single index is required per block). With growing block size, this bandwidth advantage quickly approaches 50% of the overall required bandwidth.

So far, we have implemented the SELL-C-σ building blocks (vectors, matrices), and a (block) Jacobi preconditioner which fully inverts the corresponding subsystem; for all target architectures (CPU, MIC, CUDA). Moreover, there is an implementation of the blocked version for multi-threaded CPUs and MICs. While the GPU version is implemented as a set of CUDA kernels, we have not used any intrinsics for the standard CPU and the MIC – instead we rely on the

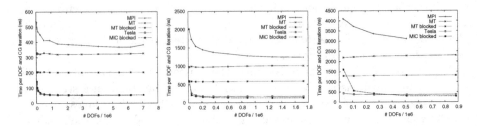

Fig. 1. Normalised execution time of the (block) Jacobi preconditioned CG solver for polynomial degrees $p = 1, 2, 3$ (left to right) of the DG discretisation. The multithreaded (MT) and MIC versions use a SIMD block size of 8. Missing data points indicate insufficient memory.

auto-vectorisation features of modern compilers without performance penalty [11]. Due to the abstract interfaces in our solver packages, all other components like the iterative solvers can work with the new data format without any changes. Finally, a new backend for our high-level PDE discretisation package enables a direct assembly into the new containers, avoiding the overhead of a separate conversion step. Consequently, users can transparently benefit from our improvements through a simple C++ typedef.

We demonstrate the benefits of our approach for a linear system generated by a 3D stationary diffusion problem on the unit cube with unit permeability, discretised using a weighted SIPG DG scheme [6]. Timings of 100 iterations of a CG solver using a (block) Jacobi preconditioner on a single-socket Intel Sandy Bridge machine (8 GB DDR3-1333 RAM, 2 GHz 4-core Intel Core i7-2635QM, no hyper-threading) which supports 256-bit wide SIMD using AVX instructions, on a NVIDIA Tesla C2070 for the GPU measurements and on a Intel Xeon Phi 7120P, are presented in Figure 1, normalised per iteration and DOF.

As can be seen, switching from MPI to threading affords moderate improvements due to the better surface-to-volume ratio of the threading approach, but we cannot expect very large gains because the required memory bandwidth is essentially identical. Accordingly, switching to the blocked SELL-C-σ format consistently yields good improvements due to the lower number of column indices that need to be loaded, an effect that becomes more pronounced as the polynomial degree grows due to larger matrix block sizes. Finally, the GPU and the MIC provide a further speedup of 2.5–5 as is to be expected given the relative peak memory bandwidth figures of the respective architectures, demonstrating that our code manages to attain a constant fraction of the theoretically available memory bandwidth across all target architectures.

3   Multiscale Methods

Our software concept for numerical multi-scale methods in a parameterised setting is based on the general model reduction framework for multi-scale problems presented in [12]. The framework covers a large class of numerical multi-scale approaches based on an additive splitting of function spaces into macroscopic and fine scale contributions combined with a tensor decomposition of function spaces in the context of multi query applications. Numerical multi-scale methods make use of a possible separation of scales in the underlying problem. The approximation spaces for the macroscopic and the fine scale are usually defined a priori. Typically, piecewise polynomial functions are chosen on a relatively coarse and on a fine partition of the computational domain. Based on such discrete function spaces, an additive decomposition of the fine scale space into coarse parts and fine scale corrections is the basis for the derivation of large classes of numerical multi-scale methods. A variety of numerical multi-scale methods can be recovered by appropriate selection of decomposed trial and test functions, the specific localisations of the function space for the fine scale correctors, and the corresponding localised corrector operators.

To efficiently cope with multi-scale problems in multi-query scenarios, we add a further tensor type decomposition of function spaces that can be derived as a generalisation of the classical projection based reduced basis approach. Suppose that in a first step a small number of snapshots have been computed with some numerical multi-scale method for suitable parameters, e.g., chosen by a greedy algorithm based on efficient a posteriori error estimates. As a generalisation of the classical reduced basis approach, we then define a reduced approximation space as a non-linear combination of the computed snaphots. As a particular example we focus on tensor product type approximation spaces spanned by products of coarse scale functions and precomputed snapshots. A reduced multi-scale scheme is then obtained by suitable projection of the original problem onto such function spaces. A particular realisation of this approach is, e.g., the localised reduced basis multi-scale method [1].

Within EXA-DUNE we develop a unified interface-based software framework that mimics the mathematical concept for numerical multiscale methods in multi-query scenarios. Particular implementations of this framework are pursued for the multiscale finite element method as a representative of classical numerical multiscale methods and for the localised reduced basis multiscale method as a representative of the generalised model reduction approach.

Concerning the structure of the solution spaces and the resulting discrete approximation schemes, in all the above mentioned methods the global solution is decomposed into dense local solutions on coarse grid blocks, and blockwise sparse global solutions. Therefore, the general structure of approximation spaces, discrete operators and solvers is similar as for DG schemes with locally high polynomial degrees. Thus, for an efficient implementation in heterogeneous parallel environments, we can directly build upon concepts developed, e.g., for DG schemes. The realisation of the parallel multiscale methods is based on the DUNE-Multiscale module[3] and on the DUNE-gdt module[4] and builds upon the hybrid parallelism in DUNE as discussed in Section 2.

---

[3] http://users.dune-project.org/projects/dune-multiscale

[4] http://users.dune-project.org/projects/dune-gdt

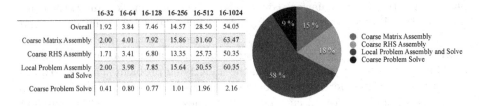

	16-32	16-64	16-128	16-256	16-512	16-1024
Overall	1.92	3.84	7.46	14.57	28.50	54.05
Coarse Matrix Assembly	2.00	4.01	7.92	15.86	31.60	63.47
Coarse RHS Assembly	1.71	3.41	6.80	13.35	25.73	50.35
Local Problem Assembly and Solve	2.00	3.98	7.85	15.64	30.55	60.35
Coarse Problem Solve	0.41	0.80	0.77	1.01	1.96	2.16

Fig. 2. Left: Strong scaling factors for different parts of the multiscale finite element (msfem) method from 16 to N cores. Right: Distribution of wall time amongst 4 heaviest callers (accounting for 99% of overall runtime) during msfem method on 1024 Cores.

In the hybrid setting, the computational grid associated with the coarse solution space is decomposed into patches (of varying size) that are then distributed to the processes using the MPI-based parallel communication interface of DUNE. On each coarse patch, a virtual local grid refinement is constructed. This locally structured grid then serves as computational mesh for the derivation of the fine scale corrections. Using the virtual grid refinement allows for fully unstructured meshes on the coarse scale while avoiding memory and bandwidth limitations on the fine scale. The fine-scale correction assembly and solve phases can then be further distributed via shared-memory parallelisation within one UMA-node using the techniques from Section 2.

In Figure 2 we demonstrate the scaling capabilities of the multiscale finite element method using an artificial 3D benchmark problem on 32768 coarse cubes, each subdivided into 4096 fine cubes. We test strong scaling on 16 to 1024 cores of our local PALMA cluster at the University of Münster. Most parts of our code show promising scaling, except for the coarse scale system solve which necessitates MPI-communication in each step of the iterative solver and therefore is inefficient for the relatively small coarse problem. Bigger meshes stemming from real-world applications will show better scaling on this part, too.

4   A First Porous Medium Flow Application

As a prototypical example for flows in porous media we consider density driven flow in a three-dimensional domain $\Omega = (0,1)^3$ given by an elliptic equation for pressure $p(x, y, z, t)$ coupled to a parabolic equation for concentration $c(x, y, z, t)$:

$$- \nabla \cdot (\nabla p - c\mathbf{1}_z) = 0, \tag{1}$$

$$\partial_t c - \nabla \cdot \left((\nabla p - c\mathbf{1}_z)c + \frac{1}{Ra}\nabla c \right) = 0. \tag{2}$$

Boundary conditions for the pressure equation are $p = 0$ at $z = 0$ and 'no flow' at all other boundaries. Boundary conditions for the concentration equation are $c = 1$ for $z = 1$, 'no flow' at lateral boundaries and 'inflow/outflow' at $z = 0$. Initial condition is $c = 0$. This system serves as a model for the dissolution of a CO_2 phase in brine, where the unstable flow behaviour leads to enhanced

Fig. 3. Density driven flow in a porous medium in three space dimensions for $Ra = 8000$. Left: concentration at $t = 2.25$ after the onset of instability, right: concentration at $t = 4.8$ in the nonlinear regime where persistent fingers have developed.

dissolution. The system is formulated in non-dimensional form with the Raleigh number Ra as the only governing parameter. For details we refer to [13].

The system (1), (2) is solved in a decoupled fashion resulting, after discretisation in space and time, in a large and sparse linear system which is solved by algebraic multigrid and a system of ordinary differential equations. The pressure equation (1) is discretised using the cell centered finite volume (CCFV) method with two-point flux approximation on a structured, equidistant mesh. The velocity field $v = -(\nabla p - c\mathbf{1}_z)$ required in the transport equation is then reconstructed from the finite volume fluxes with lowest order Raviart-Thomas (RT$_0$) elements. The transport equation (2) is discretised in space with the symmetric weighted interior penalty DG finite element method [6]. For the Raleigh number and mesh sizes utilised below the grid Peclet number is of order 1 and explicit time stepping schemes for the transport equation are efficient. Using strong stability preserving explicit Runge-Kutta methods [14] we can exploit the increased arithmetic intensity of a matrix-free implementation. Figure 3 shows results of a 3D simulation on 8 Xeon E5-2680v2 10-core processors, mesh size 240^3, Q_2 DG elements ($373 \cdot 10^6$ DOF) and 16000 time steps. One time step takes $14s$.

DG methods are popular in the porous media flow community due to their local mass conservation properties, the ability to handle full diffusion tensors and unstructured, nonconforming meshes as well as the simple way to implement upwinding for convection dominated flows. The efficient implementation of high order 'spectral' DG methods relies on a tensor product structure of the polynomial basis functions and the quadrature rules on cuboid elements. At each element the following three steps are performed: (i) evaluate the finite element function and gradient at quadrature points, (ii) evaluate PDE coefficients and geometric transformation at quadrature points, and (iii) evaluate the bilinear form for all test functions. The computational complexity of steps (i) and (iii) is reduced from $O(p^{2d})$, $p - 1$ being the polynomial degree and d the space dimension, to $O(dp^{d+1})$ with the sum factorisation technique, see [9,10]. This can be implemented with matrix-matrix products, albeit with small matrix

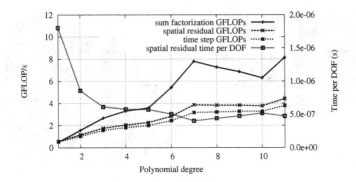

Fig. 4. Single core performance for various components of the DG method

dimensions. For the face terms, the complexity is reduced from $O(p^{2d-1})$ to $O(3dp^d)$. For practical polynomial degrees, $p \leq 10$, the face terms dominate the overall computation time, resulting in the time per degree of freedom (DOF) to be independent of the polynomial degree. This is illustrated by the finely dotted curve in Figure 4. We employ a nodal basis on Gauß-Lobatto points with under-integration on the Gauß-Lobatto points for the temporal bilinear form leading to a diagonal mass matrix. Gauß-Legendre quadrature is used for the spatial bilinear form.

Figure 4 presents performance results of the sum factorisation based 3D DG code on a single core of a Xeon E5-2680v2 for varying polynomial degree. The stand-alone sum factorisation kernel (solid line) achieves up to 8 GFLOP/s corresponding to 40% peak performance. The performance peaks at Q_7/Q_{11} with 8/12 basis functions per direction show that vectorisation is effective. The performance for the complete spatial residual evaluation and a complete time step peak at 4 GFLOP/s. These results clearly illustrate that high order methods can take advantage of modern multicore architectures and their SIMD capabilities.

5   Conclusion

This paper reports first results on introducing hybrid parallelisation and hardware-orientation into the DUNE framework. In the finite element assembly process we obtain promising results for low order methods by vectorising over several elements while for high polynomial degree good performance can also be achieved by loop auto-vectorisation. In ongoing work both approaches will be combined. On the sparse linear algebra level shared memory parallelisation and vectorisation is based on the SELL-C-σ matrix format and additionally exploits the matrix block structure. These components have already been used to speed up a multiscale finite element and a density driven flow solver.

Acknowledgements. This research was funded by the DFG SPP 1648 'Software for Exascale Computing'.

References

1. Albrecht, F., Haasdonk, B., Kaulmann, S., Ohlberger, M.: The localized reduced basis multiscale method. In: Proceedings of Algoritmy 2012, Conference on Scientific Computing, Vysoke Tatry, Podbanske, September 9-14, pp. 393–403 (2012)
2. Bastian, P., Blatt, M., Dedner, A., Engwer, C., Klöfkorn, R., Kornhuber, R., Ohlberger, M., Sander, O.: A generic grid interface for parallel and adaptive scientific computing. part II: Implementation and tests in DUNE. Computing 82(2-3), 121–138 (2008)
3. Bastian, P., Blatt, M., Dedner, A., Engwer, C., Klöfkorn, R., Ohlberger, M., Sander, O.: A generic grid interface for parallel and adaptive scientific computing. part I: Abstract framework. Computing 82(2-3), 103–119 (2008)
4. Choi, J., Singh, A., Vuduc, R.: Model-driven autotuning of sparse matrix-vector multiply on GPUs. In: Principles and Practice of Parallel Programming, pp. 115–126 (2010)
5. Engwer, C., Fahlke, J.: Scalable hybrid parallelization strategies for the DUNE grid interface. In: Proceedings of ENUMATH 2013 (2014)
6. Ern, A., Stephansen, A., Zunino, P.: A discontinuous Galerkin method with weighted averages for advection-diffusion equations with locally small and anisotropic diffusivity. IMA Journal of Numerical Analysis 29(2), 235–256 (2009)
7. Kretz, M., Lindenstruth, V.: Vc: A C++ library for explicit vectorization. Software: Practice and Experience 42(11), 1409–1430 (2012)
8. Kreutzer, M., Hager, G., Wellein, G., Fehske, H., Bishop, A.R.: A unified sparse matrix data format for modern processors with wide SIMD units. SIAM Journal on Scientific Computing 36(5), C401–C423 (2014)
9. Kronbichler, M., Kormann, K.: A generic interface for parallel cell-based finite element operator application. Computers & Fluids 63, 135–147 (2012)
10. Melenk, J., Gerdes, K., Schwab, C.: Fully discrete hp-finite elements: fast quadrature. Computer Methods in Applied Mechanics and Engineering 190(32-33), 4339–4364 (2001)
11. Müthing, S., Ribbrock, D., Göddeke, D.: Integrating multi-threading and accelerators into DUNE-ISTL. In: Proceedings of ENUMATH 2013 (2014)
12. Ohlberger, M.: Error control based model reduction for multiscale problems. In: Proceedings of Algoritmy 2012, Conference on Scientific Computing, Vysoke Tatry, Podbanske, September 9-14, pp. 1–10. Slovak University of Technology in Bratislava, Publishing House of STU (2012)
13. Riaz, A., Hesse, M., Tchelepi, H., Orr, F.: Onset of convection in a gravitationally unstable diffusive boundary layer in porous media. Journal of Fluid Mechanics 548, 87–111 (2006)
14. Shu, C.: Total-variation-diminishing time discretizations. SIAM Journal on Scientific and Statistical Computing 9, 1073–1084 (1988)
15. Turek, S., Göddeke, D., Becker, C., Buijssen, S., Wobker, S.: FEAST – Realisation of hardware-oriented numerics for HPC simulations with finite elements. Concurrency and Computation: Practice and Experience 22(6), 2247–2265 (2010)

DASH: Data Structures and Algorithms with Support for Hierarchical Locality

Karl Fürlinger[1], Colin Glass[2], Jose Gracia[2], Andreas Knüpfer[4], Jie Tao[3], Denis Hünich[4], Kamran Idrees[2], Matthias Maiterth[1], Yousri Mhedheb[3], and Huan Zhou[2]

[1] Ludwig-Maximilians-Universität (LMU) Munich
Computer Science Department, MNM Team
Oettingenstr. 67, 80538 Munich, Germany
[2] High Performance Computing Center Stuttgart
University of Stuttgart, Germany
[3] Steinbuch Center for Computing
Karlsruhe Institute of Technology, Germany
[4] Center for Information Services and High Performance Computing (ZIH)
TU Dresden, Germany

Abstract. DASH is a realization of the PGAS (partitioned global address space) model in the form of a C++ template library. Operator overloading is used to provide global-view PGAS semantics without the need for a custom PGAS (pre-)compiler. The DASH library is implemented on top of our runtime system DART, which provides an abstraction layer on top of existing one-sided communication substrates. DART contains methods to allocate memory in the global address space as well as collective and one-sided communication primitives. To support the development of applications that exploit a hierarchical organization, either on the algorithmic or on the hardware level, DASH features the notion of teams that are arranged in a hierarchy. Based on a team hierarchy, the DASH data structures support locality iterators as a generalization of the conventional local/global distinction found in many PGAS approaches.

1 Introduction

High performance computing systems are getting bigger and bigger in terms of the number of cores they are composed of and the degree of parallelism that needs to be exploited to successfully use them is becoming higher and higher. Billion-way parallelism is envisioned for Exascale-class machines [22] and one of the consequences of this trend is that data movement is becoming a more significant contributor to computing cost (in terms of time and energy) than the arithmetic operations performed on the data [8].

At the same time, while data comes to the fore in many areas of science, technology, and industry in the form of data-intensive science and big data, the programming models in use today are still largely compute-centric and do not support a data-centric viewpoint well. Consequently, programming parallel systems is difficult and will only get more complex as the Exascale era approaches.

L. Lopes et al. (Eds.): Euro-Par 2014 Workshops, Part II, LNCS 8806, pp. 542–552, 2014.

PGAS (partitioned global address space) languages have long been proposed as a solution to simplifying the process of developing parallel software, but traditional PGAS solutions are ill equipped to address the two trends outlined above. First, most PGAS approaches offer only the differentiation between local and global data, a more fine-grained differentiation that corresponds to hierarchical machine models often envisioned for Exascale computing is not straightforward. Second, many existing PGAS solutions only offer basic data structures of built-in data types such as one-dimensional arrays and users have to develop more complex abstractions from scratch.

To address some of these issues, we are developing DASH, a PGAS approach that comes in the form of a C++ template library, supports hierarchical locality, and focuses on data structures and programmer productivity. The rest of this paper gives an overview of the project and its current status and is organized as follows: In Sect. 2 we start with the discussion of the high-level layered structure of our project. Sect. 3 describes the foundation of the project, the DART runtime layer and its interface to the C++ template library, in some detail. In Sect. 4 we describe how the abstractions of DASH can be used by an application developer. In Sect. 5 we discuss research projects that are related to DASH and in Sect. 6 we summarize the current status and discuss the further direction for our project.

2   An Overview of DASH

DASH [9] is a data-structure oriented C++ template library under development in the context of SPPEXA [23], the priority program for software for Exascale computing funded by the German research foundation (DFG). The DASH project consortium consists of the authors' four German partner institutions and the Center for Earth Observation and Digital Earth (CEODE) in Beijing, China. The layered structure of the project is shown in Fig. 1; each project partner is leading the efforts for one of the layers.

A DASH-enabled application makes use of the data structures, algorithms, and additional abstractions (such as the hierarchical team construct) that are provided in the form of a C++ template library. DASH relies on a one-sided communication mechanism to exchange data, residing in the memory of multiple separate nodes, in the background, while providing the programmer with a convenient, local view.

As an example, Fig. 2 shows a simple stand-alone *hello world* DASH programme that allocates a small 1D array of integer keys and stores them over all available nodes. DASH follows the SPMD (single program, multiple data) model and the execution environment is initialized by the `dash::init()` call in line 3. Subsequently, `size` gives the number of participants in the program (denoted units) and `myid` identifies an individual unit. As an extra benefit of using DASH, rather than a local container such as an STL vector or array, the storage space is not limited by the locally available memory, but is extensible by adding more resources in a distributed memory setting. In the example code (Fig. 2), the DASH array allocated in line 8 is used to communicate a single integer key from unit 0 to every other unit in the application. The communication

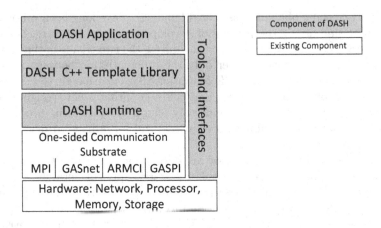

Fig. 1. The layered structure of the DASH project

is accomplished by overloading the subscript (`[]`) operator of the `dash::array` container and in lines 11–13 unit 0 stores the key at every (distributed) memory location of the array. The default layout for DASH one-dimensional arrays is blocks of elements over the available units. In our example this mapping implies that `key[`i`]` is stored on unit i and hence the access in line 18 (`key[myid]`) does not generate a communication event, since every unit reads its own local data item.

DASH builds upon existing one-sided communication substrates. A variety of one-sided communication solutions such as GASNet [4], ARMCI [18], OpenSH-MEM [21], GASPI [12], and MPI exist, each with various features, restrictions and levels of maturity. DART (the DASH runtime), aims at abstracting away the specifics of a given substrate and provides services to the upper levels of the DASH stack. Most importantly, global memory allocation and referencing, as well as one-sided puts and gets, are provided by DART. In principle, any communication substrate can form the basis for DASH. However, since interoperability with existing MPI applications is among our design considerations, we chose MPI-3 one-sided (RMA, remote memory access) operations as the foundation for our scalable runtime implementation.

A DASH-enabled application can use the data structures and programming mechanisms provided by DASH. An application can be written from scratch using DASH, but we envision that more commonly existing applications will be ported to DASH, one data-structure at a time. In our project, two application case studies guide the development of the features of DASH. One application is a remote sensing Geoscience application from CEODE (China), the other is a molecular applications code contributed by HLRS Stuttgart. Finally, the tools and interfaces layer in Fig. 1 encompasses the integration of parallel I/O directly to and from the data structures as well as the inclusion of a tools interface to facilitate debugging and performance analysis of DASH programs.

```
#include <libdash.h>                                        1
                                                            2
int main(int argc, char* argv[]) {                          3
   dash::init(&argc, &argv);                                4
                                                            5
   int myid = dash::myid();                                 6
   int size = dash::size();                                 7
                                                            8
   dash::array<int> key(size);                              9
                                                           10
   if(myid==0) {                                           11
      for(i=0; i<size; i++) key[i]=compute_key(...);       12
   }                                                       13
                                                           14
   dash::barrier();                                        15
                                                           16
   cout<<"Hello from unit "<<myid<<" of "                  17
      <<size<<" my key is "<<key[myid]<<endl;              18
                                                           19
   dash::finalize();                                       20
}                                                          21
```

Fig. 2. A *hello world* stand-alone DASH program that makes use of a small, shared 1D array for passing an integer key from unit 0 to all units in the program.

3 DART: The DASH Runtime Layer

DART is a plain-C based runtime that defines and implements central abstractions governing the development and usage of the DASH library and DASH applications. This section describes some of the key concepts that have been included in the first realization (v1.0) of the DART interface. In this first iteration of the interface we have been intentionally conservative and have limited ourselves to the necessities required to implement a functional version of the DASH library. A future iteration of the DART interface is likely to relax some of the restrictions and allow for a more expressive execution model. Specifically, DART v1.0 does not contain a tasking or explicit code execution model. Instead, data can be transparently accessed and computed on by regular operating system threads. Work is currently in progress to identify the requirements for extending DART to GPUs and in the context of this work a DART task execution model will be developed.

In the DART execution model, the individual participants of a DASH/DART program are called *units*. The generic name unit was chosen because other related terms such as process or thread already have a specific meaning in a variety of contexts and with DART we would like to have the conceptual freedom to map a unit onto any operating or runtime system concept that fits our requirements. A DASH application follows the SPMD programming model and the total number of units that exist is fixed at program start and does not change in the course of the program execution. Units are organized into *teams* and one team is referred to as DART_TEAM_ALL, comprising all existing units. Every unit in a team has an integer identifier (ID) which remains unchanged throughout the lifetime of the team; a unit's ID with respect to DART_TEAM_ALL is referred to as the unit's *global ID*. Like units, teams are identified by integer IDs, but teams can be created and destroyed dynamically. A unit's ID with in a team other than DART_TEAM_ALL is referred to as a local id.

A new team in DART is formed by specifying a subset of an existing parent team. The team creation routine dart_team_create() is a collective operation on the parent team and returns an integer identifier for the new team. Since we want to support large hierarchical machines and a localized sub-team creation that requires the involvement of the whole application would be prohibitively expensive, the new team ID does not have to be globally unique. However, the following localized uniqueness guarantees are provided:

- The same team ID is returned to all units that are members of the new team.
- The team ID is unique with respect to the parent team.
- If a unit is participating in two teams, t_1 and t_2, then it is guaranteed that t_1 and t_2 will receive different identifiers.

Teams are a mechanism for representing the hierarchical structure of algorithms and machines in a program [16]. An example for a team hierarchy representing the machine hierarchy of a system like SuperMUC (which has the notion of interconnected *islands* [24]) is shown in Fig. 3. Clearly it is not desirable for every team creation operation to require global synchronization – creating the sub-teams of team $t1$ (island 1) should only involve team $t1$ and not require any involvement from the rest of the machine. A straightforward algorithm that we use in our implementation to guarantee the above requirements, while avoiding global communication, keeps a unit-local *next_team_id* counter and performs a maximum reduction among all members of the parent team. After creating the new team, the *next_team_id* counter on all units of the new team is set to $max + 1$.

An important abstraction provided by DART is the virtual global memory space and a mechanism to refer to data items residing in it (i.e., a global pointer). A DART global pointer is a structure of 128 bits which has a 32 bit field for identifying the unit providing the memory, a 64 bit offset or local address field and 32 bits for flags and a segment identifier. Importantly, the global pointer on the DART level has no phase information associated with it. However, a similar construct is provided on the C++ (DASH) level, which then does contain appropriate phase information needed to decide when to switch between units.

The DART virtual global memory space is composed of the memory segments contributed by the units of an application on demand. Visibility of and accessibility to memory is based on the team concept. The team-collective operation dart_team_memalloc_aligned(t, nbytes) allocates nbytes in the memory of every unit in team t. This memory is accessible only by the members of team t and

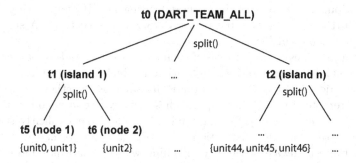

Fig. 3. An example team hierarchy for an execution of an application on a machine like SuperMUC, with a hierarchical interconnect architecture

is said to be *team-aligned* and *symmetric*. Symmetric refers to the property that all units allocate the same amount of memory, while team-aligned denotes that every unit can compute the global pointer to any location in the global memory by simple arithmetic. A second memory allocation function supported in DART is dart_memalloc, which allocates a "local global" memory that is accessible by any unit (the memory has implicit associativity with DART_TEAM_ALL), but the call is local. The two memory allocation functions are depicted in Fig. 4.

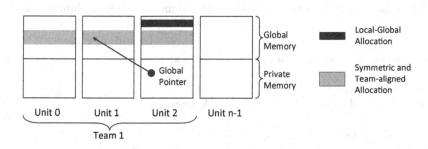

Fig. 4. The two types of memory allocation functions supported by DART

4   Using DASH in Applications

The overall goal of DASH is to provide a programmer with data structures that can be used productively on large, parallel machines. C++ was chosen as a host language for our project, because it is used in an increasingly large number of HPC and data-science applications [27] and it has powerful features that allow us to realize PGAS semantics efficiently. Specifically, we use templates to provide efficient implementations of containers for user defined types and operator overloading, thus achieving a PGAS abstraction without relying on a custom compiler.

Applications can be written from scratch using DASH and existing applications can furthermore be adapted to use DASH data structures. A stand-alone application is shown in Fig. 2.

PGAS approaches are often classified into local-view and global-view solutions, where global-view describes a situation in which the programming entities are global objects and it is not syntactically obvious, whether accessed data is local or remote. In local-view approaches, this syntactic visibility is always guaranteed, often in the form of an explicit co-index that explicitly states the location of data. Since this distinction is important for performance and energy efficiency, there is always some way of telling whether data is remote or local (say, by computing an affinity expression), but global-view does not force this differentiation to be syntactic.

With DASH we largely follow the global-view approach. The constructors of our data containers are collective operations on a team and every participating unit receives an object representing the entire data structure. In several cases, this global-view approach allows us to use a DASH container (instead of a standard STL container) in a straightforward manner. An example is shown in Fig. 5. A 1D array, stored over several units, is used in combination with the standard library's sort algorithm in line 11. Naturally, this approach has several drawbacks: `std::sort()` is a sequential sorting procedure that only engages one unit at a time, resulting in fine-grained communication, as the sorting algorithm fetches data items to compare with. However, despite these drawbacks, we envision that the ability to seamlessly replace STL with DASH containers can be useful in some situations for prototyping and removing memory limitations.

```
// split the units into 8 teams (e.g., one per node)        1
dash::team nodeteam = dash::TeamAll.split(8);                2
                                                             3
// allocate an array over the node team                      4
dash::array<double> b(100000, nodeteam);                     5
                                                             6
// use the DASH container in place of an STL container        7
// note sequential sort and perf. implications               8
int myid=nodeteam.myID();                                     9
if(myid==0) {                                                10
  std::sort(b.begin(), b.end());                             11
}                                                            12
                                                             13
// to use containers with standard algorithms in parallel    14
// local iterators lbegin(), lend() are provided             15
// this fills the array in parallel (aka. 'owner computes    16
   ')
std::fill(b.lbegin(), b.lend(), 23+myid);                    17
```

Fig. 5. A small example that shows teams and DASH containers used with global-view and local-view semantics

Accompanying the DASH data structures, we are investigating algorithms analogous to those found in the STL to take into account data distribution and parallelism (i.e., a parallel `dash::sort()`). Additionally, the standard *owner-computes* paradigm is supported by DASH in the form of local iterators (`lbegin()`, `lend()`), as shown in line 17 of Fig. 5. These local iterators allow each unit to access its local portion of the data and they correspond to the classic two-level affinity model (local/remote) of PGAS. As a generalization of this concept we are investigating hierarchical locality iterators by leveraging the hierarchical team concept in the DASH data containers.

5 Related Work

A number of realizations of the PGAS concept exist. UPC [26] is an ANSI C dialect that extends C with the ability to declare shared pointers and data items. The portable Berkeley UPC implementation relies on GASNet [4] for communication, while some vendors directly target their own low-level interconnect API. Co-array Fortran [20,17] extends the notion of standard Fortran arrays with a co-index to specify the process holding the array. The molecular dynamics application has already been ported to UPC which can be used for performance comparison with DASH porting in future [14]. The DARPA sponsored HPCS (High Productivity Computing Systems) languages X10 [7], Fortress [1], and Chapel [6] followed the PGAS model, of which Chapel remains the most actively developed and used.

PGAS has been realized in the form of a library in the past. Global Arrays [19] is an early example of an API for shared memory programming on distributed memory machines, primarily used in the context of quantum chemistry applications. GASPI [12] is an effort to standardize an API for PGAS programming developed by Fraunhofer, it features support for fault tolerance, by supporting timeouts for all non-local operations. OpenSHMEM [21] is a community effort to standardize the various dialects of SHMEM, which provides a strongly typed API for shared memory programming on distributed memory machines.

Recently, C++ has been used as a vehicle for realizing a PGAS approach in the UPC++ [29] and Co-array C++ [15] projects. While the DASH runtime is based on MPI, UPC++ is based on GASNet. Porting an existing MPI application will therefore be more straightforward using DASH. Co-array C++ follows a strict local-view programming approach and is somewhat more restricted than DASH and UPC++ in the sense that it has no concept of teams.

STAPL [5,13,25] is a C++ template library for distributed data structures supporting a "shared view" programming model that shares several goals with DASH. The library provides a local view on data, while it can be physically spread over several nodes. The authors of STAPL mention PGAS as related work, but don't seem to consider their own work a PGAS solution. STAPL does provide a large set of data containers and places a lot of emphasis on extensibility and configurability – it does however not seem to be intended for classic HPC applications.

Hierarchical computation and data structure layout have been explored in several approaches before. Sequoia [10,2] is a programming approach (language, compiler, and runtime system) for exploiting the memory hierarchy of modern machines in a portable way. Sequoia provides tasks that are restricted to access only local memory and the only supported way of communication between tasks is through parameters passed to tasks and the return values. Thus, a programmer expresses an application as a hierarchy of tasks, and this abstract hierarchy is later mapped to a concrete machine hierarchy. In Sequoia this mapping is done by the compiler, in Hierarchical Place Trees (HPT) [28] the mapping is done by the runtime. HPT are an extension to the flat place concept of X10. Hierarchically Tiled Arrays (HTA) [3,11] are data structures that enable locality and parallelism of array intensive computations, by using a block-recursive storage scheme. Several implementations of HTA exist, including one for C++. Finally, the work of Kamil et al. [16] explores additions and modifications to the SPDM programming model to support a hierarchical concept of teams. The DASH concept for hierarchical teams is inspired by his work.

6   Conclusion and Future Work

We have presented an overview of the DASH project. One goal of DASH is to make the PGAS (partitioned global address space) concept available to a wider range of application developers. PGAS languages often suffer from limited acceptance, because existing applications have to be ported to the new language as a whole. With DASH we offer a way to port C++ MPI applications incrementally (one data structure at a time). DASH has the advantage that it is not a new language to learn and does not require a custom compiler or pre-processor. Instead, DASH is realized as a C++ template library and operator overloading is used to provide the PGAS semantics on the data containers.

As high performance computing machines are getting bigger and more hierarchical on the way to Exascale, we plan to exploit the flexibility of the library-based approach DASH to address this trend and include support for hierarchical locality in our data structures. To this end, we are supporting the concept of hierarchical teams. Teams determine visibility and accessibility of the DASH data structures and allow for the realization of hierarchical locality iterators.

We are presently in the process of putting together a first public release of our DASH software stack. This first release will contain a generic 1D distributed array as the basic data structure, and it will be based on the first realization of our MPI-based DART runtime. The next steps for the projects will be to include additional data structures, such as multi-dimensional arrays, and distributed lists. We will continue our work on flexible data layout mappings and explore concepts to support hierarchical locality. With these data structures and concepts in place, work on the DASH-enabled molecular dynamics and remote sensing applications can proceed and thereby guide the next iteration of DASH features.

Acknowledgments. The authors gratefully acknowledge funding by the German Research Foundation (DFG) through the German Priority Programme 1648 Software for Exascale Computing (SPPEXA).

References

1. Allen, E., Chase, D., Hallett, J., Luchangco, V., Maessen, J.-W., Ryu, S., Steele Jr., G.L., Tobin-Hochstadt, S.: The fortress language specification. sun microsystems. Sun Microsystems (September 2006)
2. Bauer, M., Clark, J., Schkufza, E., Aiken, A.: Programming the memory hierarchy revisited: Supporting irregular parallelism in Sequoia. In: Proceedings of the 16th ACM SIGPLAN Symposium on Principles and Practice of Parallel Programming (PPoPP 2011), pp. 13–24 (2011)
3. Bikshandi, G., Guo, J., Hoeflinger, D., Almasi, G., Fraguela, B.B., Garzarán, M.J., Padua, D., von Praun, C.: Programming for parallelism and locality with hierarchically tiled arrays. In: Proceedings of the 11th ACM SIGPLAN Symposium on Principles and Practice of Parallel Programming (PPoPP 2006), pp. 48–57. ACM (2006)
4. Bonachea, D.: GASNet specification, v1. Univ. California, Berkeley, Tech. Rep. UCB/CSD-02-1207 (2002)
5. Buss, A., Papadopoulos, I., Pearce, O., Smith, T., Tanase, G., Thomas, N., Xu, X., Bianco, M., Amato, N.M., Rauchwerger, L., et al.: STAPL: standard template adaptive parallel library. In: Proceedings of the 3rd Annual Haifa Experimental Systems Conference, p. 14. ACM (2010)
6. Chamberlain, B.L., Callahan, D., Zima, H.P.: Parallel programmability and the Chapel language. International Journal of High Performance Computing Applications 21, 291–312 (2007)
7. Charles, P., Grothoff, C., Saraswat, V., Donawa, C., Kielstra, A., Ebcioglu, K., Von Praun, C., Sarkar, V.: X10: an object-oriented approach to non-uniform cluster computing. ACM Sigplan Notices 40(10), 519–538 (2005)
8. Dally, B.: Power, programmability, and granularity: The challenges of exascale computing. In: IPDPS 2011 Keynote Address (2011)
9. DASH project webpage, http://www.dash-project.org/
10. Fatahalian, K., Knight, T.J., Houston, M., Erez, M., Horn, D.R., Leem, L., Park, J.Y., Ren, M., Aiken, A., Dally, W.J., Hanrahan, P.: Sequoia: Programming the memory hierarchy. In: Proceedings of the 2006 International Conference for High Performance Computing, Networking, Storage and Analysis (SC 2006) (2006)
11. Fraguela, B.B., Bikshandi, G., Guo, J., Garzarán, M.J., Padua, D., Von Praun, C.: Optimization techniques for efficient HTA programs. Parallel Comput. 38(9), 465–484 (2012)
12. Grünewald, D., Simmendinger, C.: The GASPI API specification and its implementation GPI 2.0. In: 7th International Conference on PGAS Programming Models, Edinburgh, Scotland (2013)
13. Fidel, H.A., Amato, N.M., Rauchwerger, L.: The STAPL parallel graph library. In: LCPC, pp. 46–60 (2012)
14. Idrees, K., Niethammer, C., Esposito, A., Glass, C.W.: Evaluation of unified parallel C for molecular dynamics. In: Proceedings of the Seventh Conference on Partitioned Global Address Space Programing Models (PGAS 2013), ACM, New York (2013)

15. Johnson, T.A.: Coarray C++. In: 7th International Conference on PGAS Programming Models, Edinburgh, Scotland (2013)
16. Kamil, A.A., Yelick, K.A.: Hierarchical additions to the SPMD programming model. Technical Report UCB/EECS-2012-20, EECS Department, University of California, Berkeley (February 2012)
17. Mellor-Crummey, J., Adhianto, L., Scherer, W.N., Jin, G.: A new vision for coarray Fortran. In: Proceedings of the Third Conference on Partitioned Global Address Space Programing Models (PGAS 2009). ACM, New York (2009)
18. Nieplocha, J., Carpenter, B.: ARMCI: A portable remote memory copy library for distributed array libraries and compiler run-time systems. In: Rolim, J.D.P., et al. (eds.) IPPS-WS 1999 and SPDP-WS 1999. LNCS, vol. 1586, pp. 533–546. Springer, Heidelberg (1999)
19. Nieplocha, J., Harrison, R.J., Littlefield, R.J.: Global arrays: A nonuniform memory access programming model for high performance computers. The Journal of Supercomputing 10, 169 189 (1996)
20. Numrich, R.W., Reid, J.: Co-array Fortran for parallel programming. SIGPLAN Fortran Forum 17(2), 1–31 (1998)
21. Poole, S.W., Hernandez, O., Kuehn, J.A., Shipman, G.M., Curtis, A., Feind, K.: OpenSHMEM - Toward a unified RMA model. In: Padua, D. (ed.) Encyclopedia of Parallel Computing, pp. 1379–1391. Springer, US (2011)
22. Shalf, J., Dosanjh, S., Morrison, J.: Exascale computing technology challenges. In: Palma, J.M.L.M., Daydé, M., Marques, O., Lopes, J.C. (eds.) VECPAR 2010. LNCS, vol. 6449, pp. 1–25. Springer, Heidelberg (2011)
23. SPPEXA webpage, http://www.sppexa.de/.
24. SuperMUC system description, http://www.lrz.de/services/compute/supermuc/systemdescription/
25. Tanase, G., Buss, A.A., Fidel, A., Harshvardhan, Papadopoulos, I., Pearce, O., Smith, T.G., Thomas, N., Xu, X., Mourad, N., Vu, J., Bianco, M., Amato, N.M., Rauchwerger, L.: The STAPL parallel container framework. In: Proceedings of the 16th ACM SIGPLAN Symposium on Principles and Practice of Parallel Programming (PPoPP 2011), pp. 235–246 (February 2011)
26. UPC Consortium. UPC language specifications, v1.2. Tech Report LBNL-59208, Lawrence Berkeley National Lab (2005)
27. Wong, S., Stojiljkovic, G.D., Erotokritou, S., Tsouloupas, G., Manninen, P., Horak, D., Prangov, G.: PRACE training and education survey. Technical report, PRACE (December 2011), http://prace-ri.eu/IMG/zip/d4.1_2.zip
28. Yan, Y., Zhao, J., Guo, Y., Sarkar, V.: Hierarchical Place Trees: A Portable Abstraction for Task Parallelism and Data Movement. In: Gao, G.R., Pollock, L.L., Cavazos, J., Li, X. (eds.) LCPC 2009. LNCS, vol. 5898, pp. 172–187. Springer, Heidelberg (2010)
29. Zheng, Y., Kamil, A., Driscoll, M.B., Shan, H., Yelick, K.: UPC++: A PGAS extension for C++. In: 28th IEEE International Parallel & Distributed Processing Symposium (2014)

ExaStencils: Advanced Stencil-Code Engineering

Christian Lengauer[1], Sven Apel[1], Matthias Bolten[2], Armin Größlinger[1],
Frank Hannig[3], Harald Köstler[3], Ulrich Rüde[3], Jürgen Teich[3],
Alexander Grebhahn[1], Stefan Kronawitter[1], Sebastian Kuckuk[3],
Hannah Rittich[2], and Christian Schmitt[3]

[1] Faculty of Computer Science and Mathematics,
University of Passau, Passau, Germany
[2] Department of Mathematics and Science,
University of Wuppertal, Wuppertal, Germany
[3] Department of Computer Science,
Friedrich-Alexander University Erlangen-Nürnberg (FAU), Germany

Abstract. Project ExaStencils pursues a radically new approach to
stencil-code engineering. Present-day stencil codes are implemented in
general-purpose programming languages, such as Fortran, C, or Java,
or derivates thereof, and harnesses for parallelism, such as OpenMP,
OpenCL or MPI. ExaStencils favors a much more domain-specific approach with languages at several layers of abstraction, the most abstract
being the mathematical formulation, the most concrete the optimized
target code. At every layer, the corresponding language expresses not
only computational directives but also domain knowledge of the problem
and platform to be leveraged for optimization. This approach will enable
a highly automated code generation at all layers and has been demonstrated successfully before in the U.S. projects FFTW and SPIRAL for
certain linear transforms.

1   The Challenges of Exascale Computing

The performance of supercomputers is on the way from petascale to exascale.
Software technology for high-performance computing has been struggling to keep
up with the advances in computing power, from terascale in 1997 to petascale in
2008 on to exascale, now being only a factor of 30 away and predicted for the end
of the present decade.[1] So far, traditional host languages, such as Fortran and
C, being equipped with harnesses for parallelism, such as MPI and OpenMP,
have taken most of the burden, and they are being developed further with some
new abstractions, notably the partitioned global address space (PGAS) memory
model [1] in the languages Coarray Fortran [30], Chapel [9], Fortress [38], Unified
Parallel C [8] or X10 [10]. Yet, the sequential host languages remain general-
purpose: Fortran or C or, if object orientation is desired, C++ or Java.

The step from petascale to exascale performance challenges present-day software technology much more than the advances from gigascale to terascale and
terascale to petascale have. The reason is the explicit treatment of the massive

---

[1] http://www.top500.org

L. Lopes et al. (Eds.): Euro-Par 2014 Workshops, Part II, LNCS 8806, pp. 553–564, 2014.

parallelism inside one node of a high-performance cluster cannot be avoided any longer. That is, the cluster nodes must be manycores with high numbers of cores. The reorientation of the computer market from single cores to multicores and manycores has been observed with concern [29]. In the high-performance market, the situation is somewhat alleviated by the fact that the additional cycles that large numbers of cores provide are actually being yearned for. But, the question of how to exploit them with efficient and robust software remains.

While the potential for massive parallelism on and off the chip is the single most serious challenge to exascale software technology, other challenges take on a high priority and are frequently being mentioned, such as power consumption, fault tolerance and heterogeneity of the execution platform [2]. At best, one would strive for performance portability, i.e., the ability to switch the software with ease from one platform, when it is being decommissioned, to the next, while maintaining highest performance.

2   ExaStencils Application Domain: Stencil Codes

Stencil codes have extremely high value for a significant community of scientific-computing experts in academia and industry. They see wide-spread use in solving the systems arising form a discretization of partial differential equations (PDE) and systems composed of such equations. For the implementation of scalable stencil codes, the foremost requirement is the use of efficient solution algorithms, i.e., iterative solvers that rely on the application of a stencil and that provide good convergence properties. Major application areas are the natural sciences and engineering.

Stencil codes are algorithms with a pleasantly high regularity: the data structures are higher-dimensional grids, and the computations follow a static, locally contained dependence pattern and are typically arranged in nested loops with linearly affine bounds. This invites massive parallelism and raises the hope for easily achieved high performance. However, serious challenges remain:

- Because of the large numbers and varieties of stencil code implementations, deriving each of them individually—even if by code modification from one another—is not practical. Not even the use of program libraries is practical because they do not cover unforeseen variants that may be required by future technology; instead, a domain-specific metaprogramming approach is needed.
- High parallel efficiency is impaired by the low *computational intensity*, i.e., the low ratio of computation steps to data transfers of stencil codes.
- An unsuitable use of the execution platform may act as a performance brake.

3   ExaStencils Approach: Domain-Specific Optimization

With project ExaStencils, we propose a radical departure from the traditional way of developing stencil codes. To this end, we make two major decisions.

3.1   Domain-Specific Source Languages

The first decision is to liberate ourselves from the traditional, general-purpose source languages that have historically been dominating high-performance software development, and to move to much easier languages that cater to a specific application domain. This has a serious consequence. The language technology that ensues has great power but for a, in current thinking, shockingly small domain of programs. The most striking example is FFTW (the Fastest Fourier Transform in the West) [17], which is a highly powerful optimizing compiler for essentially one problem: the fast Fourier transform. An optimizing compiler with a somewhat larger domain has been SPIRAL [34], which addresses also a number of (but not all) other linear transforms.

Domain-specific programming has become quite popular recently, and many languages (DSLs), and their compilers, have been proposed and used for specific domains [40,27]. Alone for the domain of stencil computations, there are, e.g., Liszt [13] (or the newer DeLite), Pochoir [39], and PATUS [11]. Each one of these is pursuing specific goals: Liszt adds abstractions to Java to make stencils programming easier, also for unstructured problems; Pochoir employs a divide-and-conquer skeleton on top of the parallel C extension Cilk to make stencil computations cache-oblivious; PATUS achieves performance by auto-tuning. ExaStencils seeks highest performance via a second radical decision, which we describe next.

3.2   Domain-Specific Optimization at Every Refinement Step

None of the approaches just mentioned has the explicit goal of reaching exascale performance. This is our goal for the domain of stencil codes (thus, the name of our project: ExaStencils). In order to reach it, we insist not only on the freedom to choose or craft the DSL. Rather, we demand also the freedom to choose one dedicated language at every one of a small number of refinement steps, from the first, abstract, executable formulation of the stencil computation down to the target code actually running on the platform of our choice. With every refinement step also comes its own, dedicated, highly automated optimization technology, which exploits the domain-specific knowledge available and useful at this step.

Roughly, the ExaStencils project follows Wirth's notion of stepwise refinement [42] and Parnas' approach of program design, which has later been condensed in the paradigm of model-driven software development [35], and Parnas' notion of program families [33]. The idea is to traverse a path of refinement steps from the mathematical statement of the stencil computation to the target code to be executed on the platform at hand. In every step, choices are made that specialize the solution. These choices are governed by the implementation goals to be reached – different implementation goals, different choices. The overall goal will be the same: exascale performance! But, for different stencil computations and different execution platforms, it may be reached by different choices. By developing a variability model, we hope to achieve performance portability.

The novel contribution of ExaStencils, beyond the notions of stepwise refinement, model-driven software development, and program families, is the representation, aggregation, and employment of a knowledge base of conditions and rules concerning stencil codes and the platforms on which they run. ExaStencils makes choices at different layers of abstraction, which form work areas in the project. Let us discuss them in turn.

4 ExaStencils Workflow

The workflow of a stencil-code generation à la ExaStencils is illustrated in Fig. 1. In a first step, a stencil algorithm is engineered by a mathematician. The solution is put into a first executable form via a cooperation of the mathematician with a software engineer. In the ExaStencils approach, the software description names a set of algorithmic and platform choices, each made from a number of options and alternatives. Then, an implementation is "woven" automatically. The weaving algorithm is capable of applying optimizations customized for the specific choices made. One powerful model exploited in ExaStencils is the polyhedron model for automatic loop parallelization. In a final step, some low-level fine-tuning for the platform at hand takes place. The target code can be in any language—or, indeed, mix of languages—that is suitable. In a preliminary code generator, this is C++ (see Subsect. 4.5). In the following subsections, we expand further on these development steps.

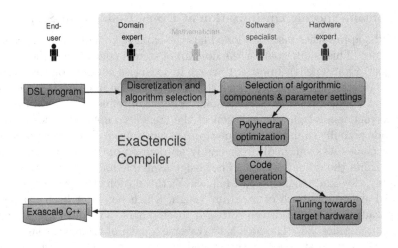

Fig. 1. The workflow of the ExaStencils programming paradigm: the ExaSencils compiler builds on the combined knowledge of domain experts, mathematicians, and software and hardware specialists to generate high-performance target code.

4.1 Algorithmic Engineering

The domain of ExaStencils is multigrid stencil codes on (semi-)structured grids. In many applications, a large, structured, linear system consisting of hundreds of millions of unknowns or more must be solved, whose system matrix can be described compactly, memory-efficiently by one or more stencils. Multigrid methods are *asymptotically optimal* solvers for elliptic PDEs, i.e., they belong to the few algorithms that qualify as starting point to implement scalable parallel solvers. Thus, multigrid methods are widely used on massively parallel computers, and different parallel implementations are available that scale on current supercomputer architectures [3,4,5,14,15,21]. Multigrid methods involve stencil computations on a hierarchy of very fine to successively coarser grids. On the coarser grids, less processing power is required and communication dominates. A multigrid method is characterized by two strategies: (1) a smoothing strategy, which is used to smooth the sampling error of the grid at hand, and (2) a coarsening strategy, which transfers data from one grid to the next coarser grid. Once one arrives at the coarsest level, one refines the grid again via some form of interpolation. This cycle of coarsening and refining is called a V-cycle. Various cycling strategies are commonly used. For instance, an F-cycle multigrid method consists of a sequence of progressively deeper V-cycles (Fig. 2). The technology for the efficient implementation and a systematic performance engineering of parallel multigrid methods is a major current research topic [18].

Most of the computational effort in multigrid methods is spent in the smoother, which in simple cases can be a point relaxation, such as Gauss-Seidel or Jacobi. This results in a low ratio of computation to memory load and store operations, limiting the performance that can be achieved on modern architectures, as is typical for applications limited by memory bandwidth [24]. Furthermore, scaling to

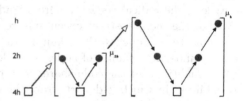

Fig. 2. An F-cycle as a succession of V-cycles

very high numbers of processors can suffer from a higher number of levels. For the latter, aggressive coarsening can be a viable option, while the number of computation steps that are necessary can be raised by pipelining of multiple steps of the iterative smoothing procedure, by using polynomial smoothers or by the use of block smoothers. These techniques typically result in a better smoothing factor yielding an overall improved convergence rate.

The performance of multigrid methods depends on the choice of algorithmic components for discretization, grid transfer, cycling strategy, and smoothing. They do influence the total run time, on the one hand, by their influence on the convergence rate, that is the reduction of the error per iteration, and, on the other hand, by the execution time of the individual components on a given architecture. While the former is independent of the target architecture, the latter is influenced strongly by specific hardware properties such as the cache size, the size of the vector units, if present, etc. The convergence rate can be predicted by Local Fourier Analysis (LFA), a mathematical tool that analyzes a given iterative method by freezing coefficients and neglecting boundary conditions. The LFA is used widely in the multigrid community [28,41]. We have begun to extend the technique to deal with block-smoothers and aggressive coarsening in addition to the standard LFA techniques [6]. The LFA tool developed will then be used to determine the convergence rate of a multigrid method in terms of the expected convergence rate a priori, i.e., without building and running the actual multigrid method. The combination with a performance model for stencil computations, in general, and the specific requirements of multigrid methods, in particular, enable a prediction of the overall run time of the method without actually running it on the target architecture. This will massively speed up the optimization process used later in the code-generation workflow.

4.2   Domain-Specific Representation and Modelling

Multigrid solvers come in thousands of variants, which differ in the shape of the stencil and the grid, the coarsening and smoothing strategy, the boundary conditions, the communication patterns, and many other conceptual and implementation-level aspects. For example, there are the special strategies necessary to exploit the resources of the execution platform at hand, e.g., caching and load balancing.

One of the radical departures from tradition in our approach happens at the layer of the most abstract executable representation of our problem solution, i.e., our stencil code: Rather than as an individual, we will consider the code as a member of a family of codes. Our domain-specific program pinpoints the commonalities that the code shares with the other codes of the family, and the variabilities in which it departs from the other codes. Each point of variability comes with a number of options or alternatives.

Domain-specific language elements will be our devices for specifying the choices of individual configuration options and their combinations. A review of different technologies for the implementation of DSLs [36] led us to choose Scala [31] as the host language. We favored its modern features, such as object-oriented and functional programming, an expressive static type system, parser combinators, and pattern matching. Actually, we will use four DSLs at decreasingly abstract layers of abstraction (Fig. 3), all hosted by a common parsing and transformation framework. Layers 1–2 address the concerns of application scientists, Layers 2–3 those of mathematicians, and Layers 3–4 those of computer scientists. The workflow depicted in Fig. 1 represents the ideal situation in which only the application scientists interact with the system and code at the lower levels is generated automatically. This is the vision of project ExaStencils.

At present, we are finalizing a prototype generator that will handle input code written in our DSLs.

4.3   Domain-Specific Optimization and Generation

Which configuration options (i.e., which choices of algorithmic components, alternatives of data structures, and parameter values) contribute to maximal performance is obvious in some cases and very surprising in others. To make matters

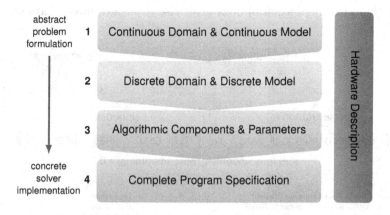

Fig. 3. The DSL hierarchy of ExaStencils

worse, certain combinations of options can interfere with each other with respect to performance in subtle ways (which is an instance of the feature-interaction problem [7,37]). To make this problem tractable, ExaStencils will provide a capability of recommending suitable combinations of configuration option, based on a machine-learning approach. The objective is to make sufficiently accurate performance predictions on the basis of performance measurements of only a small number of concrete stencil-code variants. The latest innovation here emerged from recent work on automated software configuration [37]: The key idea is to detect and handle explicitly interactions among configurations options—even among numeric parameters, rather than simply using black-box auto-tuning [12] or machine-learning approach [22].

We started experiments with the Highly Scalable Multigrid Solver [26]. This solver tolerates a limited lack of structure in the grid by considering so-called hierarchical hybrid grids, as depicted in Fig. 4. At the coarsest level, on the left, the grid is unstructured, but refinements of each segment (middle and right) must be homogeneous, though each segment may exhibit a different structure.

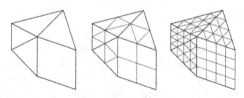

Fig. 4. Successive refinement of a hierarchical hybrid grid

Commonalities and variabilities are usually specified in terms of a *variability model*. The variability model for the Highly Scalable Multigrid Solver is illustrated in Fig. 5. Each node denotes a *configuration option*—in our case, the choice of a coarse grid solver, a smoother, and pre- and post-smoothing parameter values which must satisfy the condition that their sum is greater than zero.

A selection of configuration options gives rise to an executable variant of the stencil code.

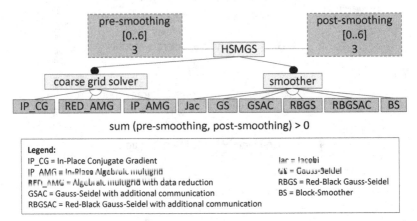

Fig. 5. Concrete variability model for the Highly Scalable Multigrid Solver (HSMGS).

First experiments have demonstrated already that a machine-learning approach based on the explicit detection and treatment of configuration-option interactions can predict the performance of individual stencil-code variants with a high accuracy [19]. We are only just beginning to exploit domain knowledge but obtained promising results in a first pass even without it. With domain knowledge, notably about already-know configuration-option interactions, we will be able to reduce the number of measurements needed for the prediction further.

In the treatment of values of numerical parameters, we employ a function-learning approach: We deduce one polynomial function for each pair or binary option and numerical parameter. Again, so far, we did not exploit domain knowledge, such as the degree of the function that describes the contribution of the parameter values best. Measurements of 10.2% of all stencil-code variants resulted in performance predictions of an accuracy of 89%, on average.

4.4 Loop Parallelization

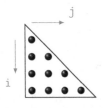

Fig. 6. Triangular grid

Stencil codes are highly iterative. Since nested iterations exhibit a high potential of a speed gain, loop parallelization is a promising technique for the optimization of stencil codes. This issue is address at DSL Layer 4.

The polyhedron model for automatic loop parallelization [16] is a powerful platform for static, i.e., compile-time program optimization. However, it comes with some restrictions that are easily violated by stencil codes. Most importantly, it requires the linear affinity of the loop bounds and the array index expressions.

For example, consider the following code for an update of a linearized triangular grid, as depicted in Figure 6:

```
for (int i = 0; i < n; ++i)
  for (int j = 1; j < i; ++j)
    A[(i*i+i)/2+j] = 0.5 * (B[(i*i-i)/2+j] + B[(i*i+i)/2+j-1]);
```

The linearization avoids memory waste that would occur with the use of a two-dimensional, rectangular array. However, this is relevant only in the final target code. During the optimization, one can work with the domain-specific knowledge of the triangularity of the two-dimensional grid and let the polyhedron model loose on the corresponding code, whose two-dimensional accesses are affine:

```
for (int i = 0; i < n; ++i)
  for (int j = 1; j < i; ++j)
    A[i][j] = 0.5 * (B[i-1][j] + B[i][j-1]);
```

Another concern is to optimize reductions in stencil codes effectively. An iterative reduction via a scalar accumulator leads to flow dependences which prevent a direct parallelization. But, with the domain-specific knowledge that the reduction operator is associative and commutative, a corresponding extension to the polyhedron model makes a multitude of optimizations available, such as loop splitting, fusing, or blocking.

The restriction to the domain of stencil codes allows us to perform suitable optimizations, such as temporal or spatial blocking or a combination of both, according to the target architecture [25]. Here, the use of the polyhedron model also ensures a correct boundary handling, regardless of its complexity caused by the combination of different transformations.

Table 1. A variability model for the preliminary Scala prototype. Variabilities in italics must be specified by the application expert, all others can be derived from them.

Variability	Layer	Options
Computational domain	DSL 1	UnitSquare, UnitCube
Operator	DSL 1	Laplacian, ComplexDiffusion
Boundary conditions	DSL 1	Dirichlet, Neumann
Location of grid points	DSL 2	node-based, cell-centered
Discretization	DSL 2	finite differences, finite volumes
Data type	DSL 2	single/double accuracy, complex numbers
Multigrid smoother	DSL 3	ω-Jacobi, ω-Gauss-Seidel, red-black
Multigrid inter-grid transfer	DSL 3	constant + linear interpolation + restriction
Multigrid coarsening	DSL 3	direct (re-discretization)
Multigrid parameters	DSL 3	various
Platform	Hardware	CPU, GPU
Parallelization	Hardware	serial, OpenMP

4.5   Preliminary Code Generator

The ExaStencils vision that a wide range of stencil codes can be engineered with the same automatic tool –even only that target code for them can be generated with the same code generator– has been met with disbelief. Thus, we decided to give an immediate proof of concept with a preliminary prototypical code generator written in Scala [23]. It lacks many features expected of a mature code generator, and it is completely unoptimized. However, it is already able to generate code for a non-trivial configuration space, as summarized in Table 1.

The first three DSL layers offer variabilities and appear in the table. The idea is that application scientists, and the ExaStencils compiler and run-time system, choose suitable options from these variabilities – and no more has to be specified to obtain a custom-optimized implementation.

The preliminary code generator produces code in C++ with OpenMP and CUDA. We are presently working on a more serious version of the code generator that produces C++ code with MPI and OpenMP. Our experiments on large-scale supercomputers like the Blue Gene/Q in Jülich [26] yielded feasible results for this scenario. ExaStencils aims at generating stand-alone code only. That is, it does not come with a dedicated library but may make use of standard libraries. The code generated is for a specific grid size. The grid size is a variability in the performance model and, thus, influences the choice of the different algorithmic components.

5   Conclusions

The overall goal of project ExaStencils is to provide proof of the application relevance of the ExaStencils paradigm of domain-specific stencil code engineering and to encourage experts of other suitable domains to take a similar approach.

Acknowledgements. Funded by the DFG in programme *Software for Exascale Computing (SPPEXA)*.

References

1. Almasi, G. (PGAS) Partitioned global address space languages. In: Padua, et al. (eds.) [32], pp. 1539–1545
2. Ashby, S., Beckman, P., Chen, J., Colella, P., Collins, B., Crawford, D., Dongarra, J., Kothe, D., Lusk, R., Messina, P., Mezzacappa, T., Moin, P., Norman, M., Rosner, R., Sarkar, V., Siegel, A., Streitz, F., White, A., Wright, M.: The opportunities and challenges of exascale computing – Summary report of the advanced scientific computing advisory committee (ASCAC) subcommittee. Tech. rep., Office of Science, U.S. Department of Energy Fall (2010)
3. Bergen, B., Gradl, T., Hülsemann, F., Rüde, U.: A massively parallel multigrid method for finite elements. Computing in Science and Engineering 8(6), 56–62 (2006)

4. Bolten, M.: Multigrid Methods for Structured Grids and their Application in Particle Simulation. Ph.D. thesis, Bergische Universität Wuppertal (2008)
5. Bolten, M.: Evaluation of a multigrid solver for 3-level Toeplitz and circulant matrices on Blue Gene/Q. In: Binder, K., Münster, G., Kremer, M. (eds.) Proc. NIC Symp. NIC Series, vol. 47, pp. 345–352. John von Neumann Institute for Computing (2014)
6. Bolten, M., Kahl, K.: Using block smoothers in multigrid methods. Proc. Appl. Math. Mech. 12(1), 645–646 (2012)
7. Calder, M., Kolberg, M., Magill, E., Reiff-Marganiec, S.: Feature Interaction: A Critical Review and Considered Forecast. Computer Networks 41(1), 115–141 (2003)
8. Carlson, W., Merkey, P.: UPC. In: Padua, et al. (eds.) [32], pp. 2118–2124
9. Chamberlain, B.L.: Chapel. In: Padua, et al. (eds.) [32], pp. 249–256
10. Charles, P., Grothoff, C., Saraswat, V.A., Donawa, C., Kielstra, A., Ebcioglu, K., von Praun, C., Sarkar, V.: X10: An object-oriented approach to non-uniform cluster computing. In: Proc. 20th Ann. ACM SIGPLAN Conf. on Object-Oriented Programming, Systems, Languages, and Applications (OOPSLA), pp. 519–538 (2005)
11. Christen, M., Schenk, O., Burkhart, H.: PATUS: A code generation and autotuning framework for parallel iterative stencil computations on modern microarchitectures. In: Proc. IEEE Int. Parallel & Distributed Processing Symp (IPDPS), pp. 676–687. IEEE (2011)
12. Datta, K.: Auto-tuning Stencil Codes for Cache-Based Multicore Platforms. Ph.D. thesis, EECS Department, University of California, Berkeley (2009)
13. DeVito, Z., Joubert, N., Palaciosy, F., Oakleyz, S., Medinaz, M., Barrientos, M., Elsenz, E., Hamz, F., Aiken, A., Duraisamy, K., Darvez, E., Alonso, J., Hanrahan, P.: Liszt: A domain specific language for building portable mesh-based PDE solvers. In: Proc. Conf. High Performance Computing Networking, Storage and Analysis (SC 2011), paper 9, 2p. ACM (2011)
14. Falgout, R.D., Jones, J.E., Yang, U.M.: The design and implementation of hypre, a library of parallel high performance preconditioners. In: Bruaset, A.M., Tveito, A. (eds.) Numerical Solution of Partial Differential Equations on Parallel Computers, ch. 8. LNCSE, vol. 51, pp. 267–294. Springer, Heidelberg (2006)
15. Falgout, R.D., Meier Yang, U.: *hypre*: A library of high performance preconditioners. In: Sloot, P.M.A., Tan, C.J.K., Dongarra, J., Hoekstra, A.G. (eds.) ICCS-ComputSci 2002, Part III. LNCS, vol. 2331, pp. 632–641. Springer, Heidelberg (2002)
16. Feautrier, P., Lengauer, C.: Polyhedron model. In: Padua, et al. (eds.) [32], pp. 1581–1592
17. Frigo, M., Johnson, S.G.: The design and implementation of FFTW3. Proc. IEEE 93(2), 216–231 (2005)
18. Gmeiner, B., Köstler, H., Stürmer, M., Rüde, U.: Parallel multigrid on hierarchical hybrid grids: A performance study on current high performance computing clusters. Concurrency and Computation: Practice and Experience 26(1), 217–240 (2014)
19. Grebhahn, A., Siegmund, N., Apel, S., Kuckuk, S., Schmitt, C., Köstler, H.: Optimizing performance of stencil code with SPL Conqueror. In: Größlinger, Köstler (eds.) [20], pp. 7–14
20. Größlinger, A., Köstler, H. (eds.): Proc. Int. Workshop on High-Performance Stencil Computations (HiStencils) (January 2014), www.epubli.de

21. Hülsemann, F., Kowarschik, M., Mohr, M., Rüde, U.: Parallel geometric multigrid. In: Bruaset, A.M., Tveito, A. (eds.) Numerical Solution of Partial Differential Equations on Parallel Computers. LNCSE, vol. 51, pp. 165–208. Springer, Heidelberg (2006)

22. Hutter, F., Hoos, H.H., Leyton-Brown, K., Stützle, T.: J. Artificial Intelligence Research 36, 267–306 (2009)

23. Köstler, H., Schmitt, C., Kuckuk, S., Hannig, F., Teich, J., Rüde, U.: A Scala Prototype to Generate Multigrid Solver Implementations for Different Problems and Target Multi-Core Platforms. Computing Research Repository (CoRR), arXiv:1406.5369, 18 (June 2014),

24. Kowarschik, M., Rüde, U., Weiss, C., Karl, W.: Cache-aware multigrid methods for solving Poisson's equation in two dimensions. Computing 64(4), 381–399 (2000)

25. Kronawitter, S., Lengauer, C.: Optimization of two Jacobi smoother kernels by domain-specific program transformation. In: Größlinger, Köstler (eds.) [20], pp. 75–80

26. Kuckuk, S., Gmeiner, B., Köstler, H., Rüde, U.: A generic prototype to benchmark algorithms and data structures for hierarchical hybrid grids. In: Proc. Int. Conf. on Parallel Computing (ParCo), pp. 813–822. IOS Press (2013)

27. Lengauer, C., Batory, D., Blum, A., Odersky, M. (eds.): Domain-Specific Program Generation. LNCS, vol. 3016. Springer, Heidelberg (2004)

28. MacLachlan, S.P., Oosterlee, C.W.: Local Fourier analysis for multigrid with overlapping smoothers applied to systems of PDEs. Num. Lin. Alg. Appl. 18, 751–774 (2011)

29. Manferdelli, J.L., Govindaraju, N.K., Crall, C.: Challenges and opportunities in many-core computing. Proc. IEEE 96(5), 808–815 (2008)

30. Numrich, R.W.: Coarray Fortran. In: Padua, et al. (eds.) [32], pp. 304–310

31. Odersky, M., Spoon, L., Venners, B.: Programming in Scala. Artima Press (2010)

32. Padua, D.A., et al. (eds.): Encyclopedia of Parallel Computing. Springer (2011)

33. Parnas, D.L.: On the design and development of program families. IEEE Trans. on Software Engineering (TSE) SE 2(1), 1–9 (1976)

34. Püschel, M., Franchetti, F., Voronenko, Y.: Spiral. In: Padua, et al. (eds.) [32], pp. 1920–1933

35. Schmidt, D.C.: Model-driven engineering. Computer 39(2), 25–31 (2006)

36. Schmitt, C., Kuckuk, S., Köstler, H., Hannig, F., Teich, J.: An evaluation of domain-specific language technologies for code generation. In: Proc. Int. Conf. on Computational Science and its Applications (ICCSA), pp. 18–26. IEEE Computer Society Press (June-July 2014)

37. Siegmund, N., Kolesnikov, S., Kästner, C., Apel, S., Batory, D., Rosenmüller, M., Saake, G.: Predicting Performance via Automated Feature-Interaction Detection. In: Proc. Int. Conf. on Software Engineering (ICSE), pp. 167–177. IEEE (2012)

38. Steele Jr., G.L., Allen, E.E., Chase, D., Flood, C.H., Luchangco, V., Maessen, J.W., Ryu, S.: Fortress. In: Padua, et al. (eds.) [32], pp. 718–735

39. Tang, Y., Chowdhury, R.A., Kuszmaul, B.C., Luk, C.K., Leiserson, C.E.: The Pochoir stencil compiler. In: Proc. 23rd ACM Symp. on Parallelism in Algorithms and Architectures (SPAA), pp. 117–128. ACM Press (2011)

40. van Deursen, A., Klint, P., Visser, J.: Domain-specific languages. In: Kent, A., Williams, J.G. (eds.) Encyclopedia of Microcomputers, pp. 53–68. Marcel Dekker (2002)

41. Wienands, R., Joppich, W.: Practical Fourier Analysis for Multigrid Methods, Numerical Insights, vol. 4. Chapman and Hall (2004)

42. Wirth, N.: Program development by stepwise refinement. Comm. ACM 14(4), 221–227 (1971)

EXAHD: An Exa-scalable Two-Level Sparse Grid Approach for Higher-Dimensional Problems in Plasma Physics and Beyond

Dirk Pflüger[1], Hans-Joachim Bungartz[2], Michael Griebel[3],
Frank Jenko[4], Tilman Dannert[5], Mario Heene[1], Christoph Kowitz[2],
Alfredo Parra Hinojosa[2], and Peter Zaspel[3]

[1] Institute for Parallel and Distributed Systems, University of Stuttgart, Germany
[2] Chair of Scientific Computing, Technische Universität München, Germany
[3] Institute for Numerical Simulation, University of Bonn, Germany
[4] Max Planck Institute for Plasma Physics, Germany
[5] Computing Centre of the Max Planck Society
and the MPI for Plasma Physics, Germany

Abstract. High-dimensional problems pose a challenge for tomorrow's supercomputing. Problems that require the joint discretization of more dimensions than space and time are among the most compute-hungry ones and thus standard candidates for exascale computing and even beyond. This project tackles such problems by a hierarchical extrapolation approach, the sparse grid combination technique. The method not only enables their treatment in the first place. The hierarchical approach also provides novel ways to deal with central problems in high-performance computing such as scalability and resilience: Global communication can be avoided and reduced to a small subset, and faults can be compensated for without the need for recomputations or checkpoint-restart. As an exemplary prototype for high-dimensional problems, turbulence simulations in plasma physics are studied.

1 Introduction

The emergence of future exascale systems requires the development of new algorithms and software to harness the computational power that will be available in the near future. Classical parallelizations that scale even up to petaflop systems will encounter limits on these "mega-node kilo-core giga-Hertz" architectures [15], and the rise of accelerator cards in HPC further increases the hardware complexity. On these future systems, three main challenges will be scalability, resilience, and load balancing, which are addressed in this project.

High-dimensional mesh-based problems require the joint discretization of more than the classical four dimensions, space and time. Straightforward approaches fully suffer the so-called curse of dimensionality: requiring M degrees of freedom in each dimension, M^d unknowns are required in d dimensions. The effort grows exponentially in the dimensionality, and the need for at least exascale computing becomes obvious even for moderate $d > 3$.

L. Lopes et al. (Eds.): Euro-Par 2014 Workshops, Part II, LNCS 8806, pp. 565–576, 2014.

This project exemplarily considers turbulence simulations of hot fusion plasmas, where in the gyrokinetic formulation five dimensions plus time have to be dealt with. Fusion energy is one of the most attractive options to meet the growing global electricity demands in a sustainable and carbon-free way. To achieve this in a controlled way, 100 million degree hot plasma has to be kept away from the reactor walls by means of a strong magnetic field. On the way to the international ITER project, one of the most challenging scientific endeavors ever undertaken in an international joint effort, plasma turbulence simulations play a key role. In our project, time-dependent problems and eigenvalue problems are studied based on the gyrokinetic simulation code GENE.

For high-dimensional problems, a hierarchical approach comes to the rescue, the sparse grid combination technique [6]. It mitigates the curse of dimensionality on the one hand and reduces the number of unknowns in the discretisation significantly. On the other hand, it allows one to deal with the exascale challenges mentioned above in a novel, compelling way. It decouples the overal problem into multiple problems of reduced size and breaks the demand for global communication, reducing the synchronization bottleneck significantly. A second level of parallelism is introduced, which offers new approaches to load balancing, and a hierarchical superposition can be exploited to deal with faults.

To achieve the goals of this project, new algorithmic and numerical approaches have to be developed. First, we give a short overview on the problem and the numerical method in Sect. 2. In Sect. 3, which is the core of this work, we describe the state of the art and current developments in our project, followed by an outlook on next steps in Sect. 4.

2   Plasma Physics and the Combination Technique

Besides a description by means of magnetohydrodynamics, plasmas can also be modelled kinetically by the six-dimensional Vlasov equation

$$\frac{\partial g}{\partial t} + \boldsymbol{v} \cdot \frac{\partial g}{\partial \boldsymbol{x}} + \frac{q}{m}(\boldsymbol{E} + \boldsymbol{v} \times \boldsymbol{B}) \cdot \frac{\partial g}{\partial \boldsymbol{v}} = C(g). \tag{1}$$

Due to the restricted movement of the plasma particles of charge q and mass m around the magnetic field-lines (gyration), these equations can be reduced to the five-dimensional set of gyrokinetic equations with g representing the distribution in 5D phase-space consisting of three spatial coordinates (x, y and z) and two velocity coordinates $v_\parallel$ (velocity parallel to the magnetic field line) and μ (the magnetic moment). The collisions operator C governs the interaction of particles by collision, which is usually weak compared to the forces induced by the electric and magnetic fields $\boldsymbol{E}$ and $\boldsymbol{B}$ and will thus be neglected.

The gyrokinetic simulation code GENE discretizes the gyrokinetic equations by an Eulerian approach. A five-dimensional Cartesian grid is spanned throughout the domain, where the x and y coordinates are transformed to Fourier space. After discretization and other approximations, the equations implemented in GENE roughly have the structure $\frac{\partial g}{\partial t} = \mathcal{L}(g) + \mathcal{N}(g)$, with g representing the

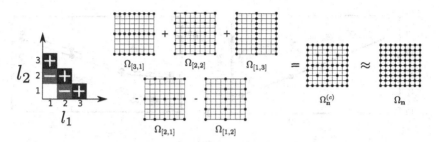

Fig. 1. The combination technique for a two-dimensional problem with $n = [3, 3]^T$ and $l_{\min} = [1, 1]^T$

distribution function discretized on the Cartesian grid. The operators $\mathcal{L}$ and $\mathcal{N}$ act on this vector and comprise all linear and non-linear terms, respectively. For an extensive description of the equations implemented in GENE, we refer to [3]. The linear operator $\mathcal{L}$ already describes the basic behavior of the plasma and allows studies of instabilities and estimates of turbulent transport. It will be used for the tests of the combination technique in this paper.

The combination technique [6] computes a sparse grid approximation of a function f_n defined on a regular Cartesian grid Ω_n. In general, an anisotropic grid Ω_l can be defined by a level-vector l that determines the uniform mesh-width 2^{-l_k} in dimension $k = 1, \ldots, d$. The combination technique approximation $f_n^{(c)} \approx f_n$ can then be written as a sum of m full anisotropic Cartesian grids of smaller size, where each grid is weighted with its combination coefficient c_l,

$$f_n^{(c)}(x) = \sum_{l \in \mathcal{I}} c_l f_l(x), \tag{2}$$

with $\mathcal{I}$ being the set of level-vectors of the grids used for the combination, see Fig. 1 for an illustration. Here, we consider the space of piecewise d-linear functions and thus interpolate d-linear between the grid points. Different approaches to determine the appropriate combination coefficients c and index set $\mathcal{I}$ exist [12], with

$$f_n^{(c)}(x) = \sum_{q=0}^{d-1}(-1)^q \binom{d-1}{q} \sum_{l \in \mathcal{I}_{n,q}} f_l(x) \tag{3}$$

being the classical combination technique with the index set [6]

$$\mathcal{I}_{n,q} = \{l \in \mathbb{N}^d : |l|_1 = |l_{\min}|_1 + c - q : n \geq l \geq l_{\min}\}, \tag{4}$$

where $l_{\min} = n - c \cdot 1$, $c \in \mathbb{N}_0$ s.th. $l_{\min} \geq 1$, specifies a minimal resolution level in each direction. The hierarchical sparse grid approach thus decomposes a single problem (discretized on a full grid with a high resolution) into multiple smaller, anisotropic problems that can be computed independently and in parallel, and standard solvers working on anisotropic grids can be employed.

Bringing the combination technique and GENE together required only minor modifications of GENE, specifically, slightly shifting and stretching the original

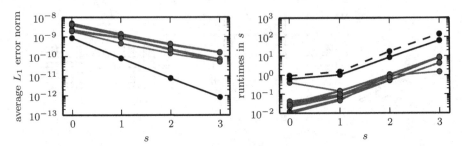

Fig. 2. Left: the error of the combined solution $f_n^{(c)}$ compared to the reference solution f_n (*black*) and the GENE results f_l computed on Ω_l with $l \in \mathcal{I}_n$ (*gray*). The error is the norm of the L_1 error normalized by the number of unknowns. **Right**: the computation time of the combined solution (*black*), of each partial solution (*gray*) and of the full grid solution (*dashed*). Obtaining the combined solution only requires half of the time compared to the full grid solution.

GENE grid in each dimension. We apply the combination technique separately for the real part and the imaginary part of GENE's complex-valued output.

GENE provides test cases of typical application scenarios, the simplest being the linear simulation of an unstable ion-temperature-gradient (ITG) mode [18]. To demonstrate the feasibility, we use for each Ω_l the same physical parameters and time-steps and combine the result once in the end, and refer to [16] for other scenarios that we have studied. In order to test the combination technique for different resolutions, we varied $l_{\min}$ and n according to

$$n = l_{\min,s} + [2, 2, 2]^T \quad l_{\min,s} = [2, 3, 2]^T + s \cdot [1, 1, 1]^T \quad s \in \{0, 1, 2, 3\},$$

with l being the level vector for dimensions $(\mu, v_\parallel, z)$. The resolution of x and y was fixed to 1. In Fig. 2 one can see that the combined solution is actually close to the solution on the reference grid Ω_n, and that each of the partial solutions has a much higher error than the combined solution. Already for this rather small setup on a desktop system, the combination technique retrieves an approximation of the reference solution with a diminished runtime. Larger GENE runs are addressed in Sec. 3.1.

3   Exa-Challenges and -Solutions

In the following, we address the challenges that we face towards exascale simulations which will be required for full-scale simulations of the numerical ITER fusion experiment. As the project studies all aspects that are required, this reaches from load balancing, scalability, and resilience via the usage of hybrid parallelizations up to novel numerical schemes.

3.1   Load Balancing

Achieving full scalability with the combination technique on an exascale system requires effective load balancing. The anisotropy in the discretization of the partial solutions influences the convergence rate and stability of the underlying numerical solvers. This results in larger numbers of iterations and enforces smaller time-step sizes for very anisotropic discretizations compared to more isotropic ones. For our application code GENE, the anisotropy additionally influences the efficiency of the parallelization. We measured a difference in execution time of more than a factor of three for partial solutions computed with GENE with roughly the same number of unknowns.

The combination technique enables two levels of parallelization: on the coarse level, the individual partial solutions can be computed independently of each other in parallel. On the fine level, each partial solution can be solved in parallel using the parallelization concept of the application, see Sect. 3.4 for the latter one. In order to exploit the two-level parallelization, we use a manager-worker concept to distribute the partial solutions onto the available number of nodes of an HPC system. This concept has already successfully been used for the combination technique in [5]. A manager process distributes the partial solutions to a number of process groups using MPI.

In order to minimize the total runtime by optimally distributing the partial solutions onto the process groups, we have developed a load model [9] which predicts the execution time of a partial solution. The two parameters used for the model are the number of unknowns of the partial solution, $N := 2^{|l|_1}$, and the anisotropy s_l, with $s_{l,i} = \frac{l_i}{|l|_1}$, of the corresponding grid Ω_l. It holds $|s_l|_1 = 1$. Thus, a high value in one dimension will result in a low value in at least one of the other dimensions. For a perfectly isotropic grid it holds $s_{l,i} = \frac{1}{d}$. With this notation we can express the anisotropy of the grid completely decoupled from the number of grid points. Our load model then has the form

$$t(l) = t(N, s_l) = r(N)h(s_l). \tag{5}$$

The function $r(N)$ models the dependence of the execution time of a partial solution on the number of unknowns. The value provided by $r(N)$ is scaled by the function $h(s_l)$, which solely depends on the anisotropy of the discretization. The parameters of $r(N)$ and $h(s_l)$ are determined by fitting the functions to measurement data in the least squares sense.

Figure 3 shows, for different numbers of process groups, the predicted parallel efficiency E_p for the anisotropy model (AM) in comparison to a simple linear model (LM) that depends only on the number of unknowns. The predictions are based on measured execution times of other partial solutions. In this experiment, a process group that computes one partial solution at a time, corresponds to one node of Hermit (HLRS). We used the ITG test case described in Sec. 2 with $n = [17, 17, 17, 17]^T$ and $l_{\min} = [3, 3, 3, 3]^T$ for $(\mu, v_\parallel, z, x)$. The resolution of y was fixed to 1. Thus, the test case consisted of 425 partial solutions in essentially four dimensions. For LM, we have $t(l) = 2^{|l|_1}$ and only consider the number of unknowns, but not the anisotropy. Furthermore, Fig. 3 includes

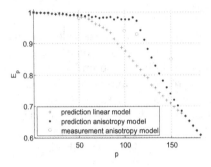
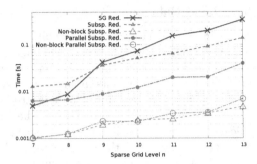

Fig. 3. Parallel efficiency E_p over the number p of process groups

Fig. 4. Communication time for a 5-dimensional SG on 456 nodes of Hermit [13]

actual measurements using the AM in our manager-worker concept. The parallel efficiency $E_p = T_1/(pT_p)$ is predicted to decrease significantly above $p = 50$ using the LM, which is confirmed in practice. The anisotropic model, in contrast, predicts more than 97% until $p = 113$ solutions are computed in parallel. While the measurements fit well to the predictions for $p = 50$ and are a bit optimistic for $p = 100$ and $p = 113$, the model is slightly too pessimistic for a large degree of parallelism and works much better than it's own prediction. Eventually, E_p has to decrease, of course, as not more process groups can be spent than partial solutions exist.

3.2   Global Communication

The hierarchical approach allows one to decouple a single problem with global dependencies into independent partial problems. For initial value computations with the combination technique, it is furthermore necessary to combine the partial solutions every several time steps and to distribute the combination solution back to avoid divergence. This gather-scatter step is the remaining synchronization bottleneck. Therefore, we have developed global communication schemes for the combination technique, which minimize the communication time by exploiting the hierarchical structure of the combination solution [13].

The combination is assembled in the hierarchical sparse grid function space, not in the full grid nodal basis, see [14] for details. The idea of the communication scheme *Sparse Grid Reduce (SGR)* is to transform each partial solution to the sparse grid space and to sum them up according to the combination coefficients. This is the straightforward approach and will serve as the baseline. The summation can be expressed as a standard reduce operation like *MPI_Allreduce* on a set of vectors containing the sparse grids' coefficients. Note that each partial solution includes only a subset of the hierarchical subspaces of the sparse grid solution. Thus, the transformation has to interpolate the others in the hierarchical basis, which corresponds to a fill-in with zeros. This results in a high overhead of communicated data not containing any information.

A new *Subspace Reduce (SubR)* scheme avoids this overhead and communicates only the minimum necessary amount of data. The idea of this method is to reduce the hierarchical subspaces individually by using an efficient standard implementation like *MPI_Allreduce*. When reducing a particular hierarchical subspace, only the nodes actually containing this subspace contribute to the reduce operation. Thus, we do not need to communicate any data that contains no information, but the number of messages sent increases significantly compared to *SGR*, which only requires one reduce operation. If the sets of nodes contributing to the reduce operation of two particular subspaces are disjoint, the subspaces can be reduced in parallel. *Parallel Subspace Reduce (ParSubR)* further improves the run time by reducing the hierarchical subspaces in an order that enables a higher degree of parallelism than *SubR*.

We were able to significantly speed up *SubR* on Hermit by using the non-blocking *MPI_Iallreduce* of the MPI 3.0 standard (*Non-blocking Subspace Reduce (NB-SubR)*). This enables the MPI system to rearrange the substeps of the reduction operations on a fine granular level. This resulted in significantly lower run times than we were able to achieve by just rearranging the order of the library calls in *ParSubR*. Using the non-blocking operations for *ParSubR* resulted in a similar, though not systematically better, performance.

Figure 4 shows the run time of the communication step for dimension $d = 5$ and different discretization levels n. The experiments were done on 456 nodes of the supercomputer Hermit (HLRS). *SGR* is only faster than *SubR* for low n since the overhead is small. However, with increasing n the total communicated volume becomes the dominating factor and *SubR* is faster. Reordering the reduction operations with *ParSubR* significantly improved the performance of *SubR*. For $n = 13$, *ParSubR* was 8.5 times faster than *SGR*. An even larger speed up was achieved using non-blocking collective operations. For $n = 13$, *NB-SubR* was 72 times faster than *SGR*.

3.3   Fault Tolerance

Large scale simulations require large computation times. If we assume one hardware failure each week on current HPC systems, we will be down to failure rates in the range of minutes on future exascale systems. And this does not even take into account that smaller hardware integration will lead to higher failure rates. Thus it will be a necessity to deal with faults. In the context of the combination technique, this means that some of the component grids will not be computed successfully, and one cannot carry out the combination step properly. Recalculating the solutions on those grids in case of failures would require the rescheduling of tasks, which can increase the overall computation time and fool the load balancing schemes.

We therefore opt for an algorithm-based fault tolerant (ABFT) approach to overcome this problem. Several methods have been developed that attempt to recover the combined sparse grid solution in the case of processor failure [17,7,8] without checkpoint-restart. One of the most promising modifies the set of successfully calculated partial solutions and combines them with new coefficients,

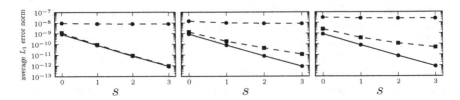

Fig. 5. Left: The error of the usual combination solution (*solid, circles*, no faults), the error with one grid missing on the highest level (*dashed, circles*), and the error after the recovery scheme has been applied (*dashed, squares*). **Middle:** the same as **Left,** but with two missing grids: one on the highest level, and one on the level below. **Right:** we added one more fault on the second level (3 faults in total).

following existing ideas from adaptive sparse grids [10]. More sophisticated approaches involve inter- and extrapolation, and some error bounds for the different approaches are detailed in [8].

We carried out several tests on GENE with simulated faults. Our recovery strategy approximates the lost partial solutions by a linear combination of available ones. This simple approach already reveals promising features, as illustrated in Fig. 5, where we repeated the simulations from Sec. 2, now including faults. All combination schemes involve 10 grids, and we simulated one, two, and three faults on different levels. Note that in the last scenario 30% of all computations fail, but these can be compensated incredibly well and without the need for further (re)computations. We expect that more sophisticated approaches further reduce the recombination error.

3.4   GPU Computing

Many of the actual supercomputers are of heterogeneous type. Usually they are large Linux-based compute clusters where some or all nodes are equipped with an additional accelerator card, mainly of the GPU or Intel Xeon Phi type. To fully use the amazing performance of these accelerated cluster systems, a first attempt to port GENE to GPUs was carried out. We focused on the computation of the non-linear part $\mathcal{N}$ in (2) in a global (full-torus) simulation [2], since this part takes around half of the total runtime of the time loop. Therefore, it is a promising candidate for acceleration. The non-linear part consists of the following steps: Transposition to exchange the x and k_y directions, extension of the k_y direction for dealiasing, Fourier transform in the k_y direction, and multiplication of two extended, transposed, and transformed arrays to get the nonlinear term. The latter is then processed the same way backwards. For the Fourier transform, we used the cuFFT library which is part of CUDA, while all other operations had to be written as CUDA-C kernels, nearly doubling the number of code lines.

First performance comparisons of older Nehalem CPU cores with older Nvidia Fermi cards were promising, as they showed a speedup (always defined as the reduction of runtime of the optimized code on a whole CPU socket with GPU to the runtime on a whole CPU socket without GPU) of 4–5 for the nonlinearity.

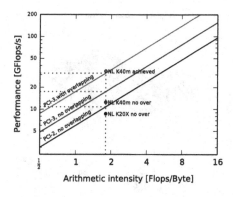

	1 SNB	2 SNB
CPU only	4.4s	2.1s
Fermi M2090	7.4s	3.5s
Kepler K20X	4.1s	2.3s

Fig. 6. Left: part of the roofline model of a Kepler GPU with respect to floating point performance and transfer bandwidth for low arithmetic intensity. **Right**: performance of the nonlinearity with GPU acceleration.

Figure 6 (right) shows a more recent comparison of new architectures. On the CPU side, an 8-core SandyBridge socket and on the GPU side, a Kepler K20X card, did not hold these nice performance results. In the end, we found that the 8-core CPU alone performs as powerful as the CPU-GPU combination.

Investigating this result with the help of the "roofline model" [19], we could identify the slow PCIexpress 2.0 bus in combination with the relatively low arithmetic intensity (defined as the number of floating point operations per amount of data transferred via PCIexpress bus to the GPU), which is only 0.38 flops/byte for the nonlinearity, as the key to understanding the low performance. Since the transfer is slow, the computing power of the GPU cannot be fully exploited while waiting for the transferred data. As a remedy, one could increase the amount of computation per data transfer by porting the whole right-hand side computation to the GPU. From the roofline model, for the whole right-hand side we expect then again a factor 4–5 of performance gain, depending on the problem size and the quality of the kernel implementations.

A second possibility to speed up the CPU-GPU performance is to use a faster bus between host and device. This can be achieved in the simplest case by using the PCIexpress gen. 3 bus, which nominally doubles the bandwidth. A computationally similar (around 8% faster) K40m Nvidia GPU has been used, which has more memory and can use the faster bus in combination with an Ivybridge CPU. We measured 4.4s on the CPU and 3.1s with the Kepler K40m.

Figure 6 (left) shows a roofline plot including the results. The two bandwidth ceilings for pure PCI-2 and PCI-3 are shown as black and blue lines, together with the achieved performance for the nonlinearity (black and blue data points) if overlapping of computation and transfer is switched off. If two streams are used and the work is distributed over these streams, one can overlap part of the transfer by computation on the GPU. This can be taken as a kind of increased bandwidth as the idle time where only transfer occurs decreases. The red ceiling represents the improved bandwidth when the overlapping is switched on. Hence,

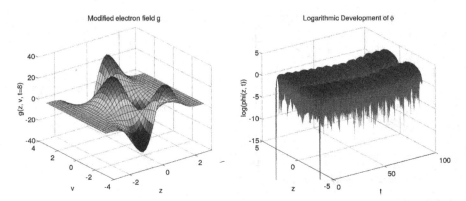

Fig. 7. Left: Initial value runs of the $(1+1)$D simplified Vlasov-model with the modified electron field g at $t = 8.0$. **Right:** the electrostatic potential ϕ over time are small model problems for full 5D Vlasov simulations.

we see a significant improvement with a faster transfer, but still the gain of roughly 30% compared to a pure-CPU implementation is not worth the effort.

3.5 Numerics

In addition to the standard sparse grid combination technique, an iterated version of the classical and optimized combination technique [11] is under investigation for Vlasov initial value and eigenvalue problems. It will guarantee convergence of the standard combination technique to the corresponding sparse grid solution for complex PDEs. The iterated combination technique applies a residual correction method [4]. It is a second way to deal with errors at almost no additional cost.

To examine our method, we introduced a set of small-scale model problems that run independently of the large-scale simulation code GENE, including the Poisson problem and the Poisson eigenvalue problem. As a small-scale version of the full Vlasov equations, a driftkinetic version of the Vlasov-Maxwell equations in $(1+1)$D phase space is considered, see [1]. It can be used both as an initial value problem and an eigenvalue problem if the spatial operator is analysed for its spectral structure. An efficient GPU implementation is available. Simulation runs, see Fig. 7, were validated against results from the literature.

The classical combination technique was applied both to the Poisson problem and the small-scale Vlasov initial value problem leading to numerical reference solutions. Next, the iterated combination technique was analysed for the Poisson problem. The resulting numerical scheme converges to a fixpoint, cf. Fig. 8. We are currently assessing the quality of this solution and developing a new sparse grid residual evaluation scheme constructed by subspace problems.

In addition to the initial value problem, iterative correction methods for eigenvalue problems are under investigation. As a simplified model, the Poisson eigenvalue problem was first considered. An operator-based sparse grid combination technique is proposed, which avoids the evaluation of the Rayleigh quotient and

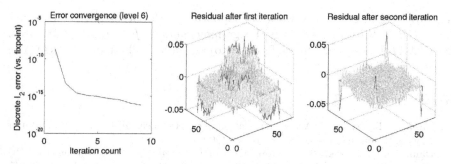

Fig. 8. Left: the iterated sparse grid combination technique converges to a fixpoint, **Middle, Right**: with some structure in the iterates of the residual

the eigenvalue identification problem available in previous approaches. This is done by applying the combination technique to the discrete operator instead of the generated eigenvalue/eigenvector pairs. First tests comparing numerical results of the Poisson eingenvalue problem with the numerically known eigenvalues of the Poisson operator are very promising. They suggest that the new scheme converges for a subset of the full-grid Poisson eigenvalue problem. Replacing interpolation in the operator-based sparse grid combination technique by a discrete l_2-projection allows to further improve convergence.

4 Conclusions and Future Work

To successfully solve high-dimensional problems on future exascale systems, novel algorithms, implementations, and numerical schemes have been developed. The hierarchical discretization scheme, which reduces the number of unknowns and will make full-scale high-resolution simulations possible on tomorrow's HPC systems, provides new methods to deal with the exa-challenges of scalability (breaking the need for global communication), resilience (without checkpoint-restart) and load balancing (due to a second, coarse-grain level of parallelism). We have shown the feasibility of our approach for turbulence simulations in plasma physics, presented new load models, communication schemes, first approaches to fault tolerance, and results on a hybrid implementation, as well as sketches of new iterative numerical schemes.

The next steps include a load model generated at runtime and refined as soon as new runtime data is available, also extendable to non-linear and eigenvalue runs. For our communication schemes, the transformation of the partial solutions into the hierarchical basis (required for the gather-scatter step) has to be done in a distributed way, at latest if the size of the overall solution exceeds the memory available on a single node. To deal with faults, we will examine whether it pays off to precompute partial solutions from additional, coarser discretization levels to speed up the recovery algorithms. Considering numerics, the iterated operator-based sparse grid eigenvalue problem will be considered and extended to full GENE runs. We will develop new numerical schemes in a simplified test-bed by extracting and analyzing the linear operator of GENE as a matrix.

Acknowledgements. This work was supported by the German Research Foundation (DFG) through the Priority Programme *Software for Exascale Computing (SPPEXA)*. The author Alfredo Parra Hinojosa additionally thanks CONACYT, Mexico.

References

1. Dannert, T., Jenko, F.: Vlasov simulation of kinetic shear alfvén waves. Computer Physics Communications 163(2), 67–78 (2004)
2. Dannert, T., Marek, A., Rampp, M.: Porting large HPC applications to GPU clusters: The codes GENE and VERTEX. Parallel Computing: Accelerating CSE. Advances in Parallel Computing 25, 305–314 (2014)
3. Görler, T.: Multiscale effects in plasma microturbulence. Ph.D. thesis, Universität Ulm (2009)
4. Griebel, M.: A domain decomposition method using sparse grids. In: Contemporary Mathematics, DDM6, vol. 157, pp. 255–261. Am. Math. Soc (1994)
5. Griebel, M., Huber, W., Rüde, U., Störtkuhl, T.: The combination technique for parallel sparse-grid-preconditioning or -solution of PDEs on workstation networks. In: Parallel Processing: CONPAR 92 VAPP V, LNCS, vol. 634 (1992)
6. Griebel, M., Schneider, M., Zenger, C.: A combination technique for the solution of sparse grid problems. In: Iterative Methods in Lin. Alg, pp. 263–281 (1992)
7. Harding, B., Hegland, M.: A robust combination technique. In: CTAC-2012. ANZIAM J., vol. 54, pp. 394–411 (August 2013)
8. Harding, B., Hegland, M.: Robust solutions to PDEs with multiple grids. In: Garcke, J., Pfluger, D. (eds.) Sparse Grids and Applications 2012. LNCISE, vol. 97, pp. 171–193. Springer, Heidelberg (2014)
9. Heene, M., Kowitz, C., Pflüger, D.: Load balancing for massively parallel computations with the sparse grid combination technique. In: Parallel Computing: Accelerating CSE. Advances in Parallel Computing, vol. 25, pp. 574–583 (2014)
10. Hegland, M.: Adaptive sparse grids. In: Proc. of 10th Computational Techniques and Applications Conference CTAC-2001., vol. 44, pp. C335–C353 (2003)
11. Hegland, M., Garcke, J., Challis, V.: The combination technique and some generalisations. Linear Algebra and its Applications 420(2–3), 249–275 (2007)
12. Hegland, M.: Adaptive sparse grids. ANZIAM Journal 44, C335–C353 (2003)
13. Hupp, P., Heene, M., Jacob, R., Pflüger, D.: Global communication schemes for the numerical solution of high-dimensional PDEs. Parallel Computing (submitted)
14. Hupp, P., Jacob, R., Heene, M., Pflüger, D., Hegland, M.: Global communication schemes for the sparse grid combination technique. Parallel Computing: Accelerating CSE. Advances in Parallel Computing 25, 564–573 (2014)
15. Keyes, D.E.: Exaflop/s: The why and the how. Comptes Rendus Mcanique 339(2–3), 70–77 (2011)
16. Kowitz, C., Pflüger, D., Jenko, F., Hegland, M.: The Combination Technique for the Initial Value Problem in Linear Gyrokinetics. In: Garcke, J., Griebel, M. (eds.) Sparse Grids and Applications. LNCSE, vol. 88, pp. 205–222. Springer, Heidelberg (2013)
17. Larson, J., Hegland, M., et al.: Fault-tolerant grid-based solvers: Combining concepts from sparse grids and mapreduce. Proc. Comp. Science 18, 130–139 (2013)
18. Wesson, J., Campbell, D.: Tokamaks. International Series of Monographs on Physics. OUP Oxford (2011)
19. Williams, S., Waterman, A., Patterson, D.: Roofline: an insightful visual performance model for multicore architectures. Comm. of the ACM 52(4), 65–76 (2009)

ESSEX: Equipping Sparse Solvers for Exascale

Andreas Alvermann[1], Achim Basermann[2], Holger Fehske[1], Martin Galgon[3],
Georg Hager[4], Moritz Kreutzer[4], Lukas Krämer[3], Bruno Lang[3], Andreas Pieper[1],
Melven Röhrig-Zöllner[2], Faisal Shahzad[4], Jonas Thies[2], and Gerhard Wellein[4]

[1] Ernst-Moritz-Arndt-Universität Greifswald, Greifswald, Germany
[2] German Aerospace Center, Köln, Germany
[3] Bergische Universität Wuppertal, Wuppertal, Germany
[4] Friedrich-Alexander-Universität Erlangen-Nürnberg, Erlangen, Germany

Abstract. The ESSEX project investigates computational issues arising at exascale for large-scale sparse eigenvalue problems and develops programming concepts and numerical methods for their solution. The project pursues a coherent
co-design of all software layers where a holistic performance engineering process
guides code development across the classic boundaries of application, numerical
method, and basic kernel library. Within ESSEX the numerical methods cover
widely applicable solvers such as classic Krylov, Jacobi-Davidson, or the recent
FEAST methods, as well as domain-specific iterative schemes relevant for the
ESSEX quantum physics application. This report introduces the project structure
and presents selected results which demonstrate the potential impact of ESSEX
for efficient sparse solvers on highly scalable heterogeneous supercomputers.

1 Sparse Solvers for Exascale Computing

Energy-efficient execution, fault tolerance (FT), and exploiting extreme levels of parallelism of hierarchical and heterogeneous hardware structures are widely considered to
be the basic requirements for application software to run on future exascale systems.
Specific hardware structures and best programming models for the exascale systems
are, however, not yet accessible, let alone settled. Thus, development of exascale applications can be considered as a research project on its own. Existing software structures,
numerical methods, and conventional programming and optimization approaches need
to be reconsidered. New techniques such as FT or parallel execution on heterogeneous
hardware have to be developed.

A wide range of sparse linear algebra applications from quantum physics to fluid dynamics have already identified urgent problems which can only be solved with exascale
computers. The relevant sparse linear solvers are typically based on iterative subspace
methods, including advanced preconditioners. At the lowest level, large sparse matrix-
vector multiplications (spMVM) and vector-vector operations are frequently the most
time-consuming building blocks. Most of the available sparse linear (solver) packages
were designed in the early 1990s for moderately parallel, homogeneous, and reliable
computers (e.g., PETSc [1] or (P)ARPACK [2]) or with a strong focus on object orientation and abstraction (e.g., Anasazi [3]). Numerically intensive kernels are still encapsulated in independently developed libraries (see LAMA [4,5] for a recent project), which

L. Lopes et al. (Eds.): Euro-Par 2014 Workshops, Part II, LNCS 8806, pp. 577–588, 2014.

rules out the opportunity for coherent performance-aware and fault-tolerant co-design throughout all software layers up to and including the application. For the same reason this approach makes it difficult to accommodate new hardware architectures (see, e.g., the status of GPGPU support in PETSc [1]) and programming models, which is critical in view of the unknown shape of hardware and software environments for exascale systems. Autotuning approaches such as, e.g., pOSKI [6], try to relieve the developer from the tedious task of finding the problem- and hardware-specific optimization opportunities. While this may seem attractive, it does not generate true insight into the real performance issues, and shares the main problems of all encapsulated libraries.

These observations raise doubts about the fitness of existing sparse matrix applications for future exascale environments: (i) The problem of *optimal performance* and *energy efficiency* on highly parallel, heterogeneous node architectures is far from being solved. When the ESSEX project started, sparse data formats were strongly hardware-dependent, which was a major obstacle for software development and code efficiency on strongly heterogeneous systems. (ii) Existing sparse linear algebra frameworks use a strictly data-parallel approach, ignoring the need for additional levels of parallelism. These would allow for the concurrent execution of, e.g., several independent building blocks, asynchronous communication, or FT schemes. (iii) The standard solution for FT is classic synchronous file-based checkpoint/restart, which will lead to severe problems on exascale. Multi-level checkpointing [7] has recently been proposed as an alternative but it is not clear if those hierarchical disk systems will be affordable in terms of energy consumption at exascale. There is very little work on automatic FT approaches with minimal or no file system involvement beyond long-known "RAID-like" ideas [8].

The need for a complete re-design of existing large-scale application software with these exascale challenges in mind has been recognized by research activities in dense linear algebra [9]. The sparse linear algebra community still lacks such an initiative, in particular with respect to the co-design of all software layers, including basic building blocks, numerical methods, and application layers. Focusing on sparse linear eigenproblems from quantum physics, the ESSEX project is an attempt to close this gap. It will deliver methods and programming techniques that can serve as blueprints for other exascale initiatives in the sparse linear algebra community.

2   ESSEX Project Overview

The ESSEX project addresses the three fundamental software layers of computational science and engineering: basic building blocks, algorithms, and applications. The need for coherent FT approaches and energy efficiency are strongly integrating components which drive the tight exchange between the classic layers (see Fig. 1). Both vertical pillars share the important constraint of minimal time to solution. For a more detailed analysis of the relevance of code optimization for energy efficiency see [10]. Thus, the complete project is embedded in a structured holistic performance engineering process, which detects and guides performance potentials across the classic layers. This process is driven by the activities at the building blocks and successively integrates topics above them.

At the **application layer**, the ESSEX project is motivated by large-scale eigen-value problems from quantum physics, including highly relevant application fields such as graphene and topological insulators. Determining the relevant static and dynamic physical properties requires addressing various aspects of an eigenvalue problem that involves extremely sparse matrices with dimensions between 10^9 and 10^{14}: The computation of (i) the minimal and the maximal eigenvalue, (ii) a block of eigenpairs at the lower end or at the middle of the spectrum, and (iii) high quality approximations to the complete eigenvalue spectrum. All these aspects are of general interest, and not restricted to the applications considered in this project.

The **algorithms layer** has identified appropriate numerical schemes to determine blocks of eigenpairs including both classic schemes (Lanczos and Jacobi-Davidson [JADA]) with relevant preconditioners and the recently introduced FEAST [11] algorithm. The kernel polynomial method (KPM) [12] and related polynomial expansion schemes (ChebTP [13,14],CFET [15]) are employed to compute the density of states, excitation spectra, and dynamical properties.

Figure 2 demonstrates how the numerical methods in ESSEX map to the physical properties to be computed. Enabling these popular algorithms for exascale is of broad interest. Even the KPM, which has been application-specific for quantum physics and chemistry for a long time, has recently gained wider attention [16,17].

The **basic building block layer** provides a collection of all relevant basic operations (such as parallel spMVM, vector-vector operations, and global reductions) and efficient FT strategies, all tailored to the needs of the other two layers. The major design goals for these building blocks are: (i) "Optimal" performance, in the sense that a suitable performance model is available that describes the relevant execution bottlenecks, and that the implementation operates at these bottlenecks. (ii) Minimum impact of FT overhead on time to solution.

Although there is a huge variety of potential programming models to choose from, the project consistently follows an "MPI+X" approach, where "X" addresses parallelism on the compute node level, be it multiple cores or accelerators. CUDA, OpenMP, and POSIX threads are typical choices for "X" in our project.

The major challenges addressed at this layer are, e.g., developing optimized data structures for all available hardware architectures, obtaining high parallel performance when executing on heterogeneous compute nodes (using standard CPUs, GPGPUs, and Intel Xeon Phi concurrently), or hiding the costs of FT schemes based on checkpoint-restart strategies. Performance engineering, used as a well-defined process targeting

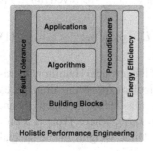

Fig. 1. Basic structure of the ESSEX project. The vertical activities are driven by a holistic performance engineering process and span the classic boundaries of application, algorithms and basic building blocks.

Fig. 2. The ESSEX research addresses the eigenproblem with classic and new eigensolvers (Krylov, JADA, FEAST) and preconditioners, established Chebyshev techniques (KPM, ChebTP) and novel implementations (CFET). The implemented methods will be part of the Exascale Sparse Solver Repository (ESSR).

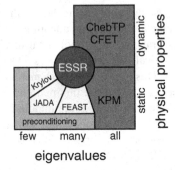

"optimal" performance, starts at the basic blocks and is instrumental for developing insights into the relevant performance-limiting bottlenecks. Since it extends into the algorithms and application layers, it breaks up abstraction boundaries and enables optimizations that would be impossible in a pure library-based approach, where building blocks and algorithms are abstracted and inaccessibly wrapped in libraries.

The developments of all layers will eventually contribute to the Exascale Sparse Solver Repository (ESSR), which will become publicly available.

3   Results and Work in Progress

This section presents selected results and current work in progress. The topics have been chosen so as to demonstrate the broad range of activities and the potential general impact of the ESSEX project.

3.1   Applications

Quantum physics and quantum chemistry applications rely on a variety of numerical linear algebra techniques. Coming from the application side we can broadly classify the possible algorithmic choices by whether only a few eigenvalues are needed—such as for the computation of low-energy properties or ground states—, or whether all eigenvalues contribute—such as for the computation of spectral functions or dynamical properties (see Fig. 2).

To illustrate this concept we briefly develop the central computational ideas underlying one particular application scenario, the computation of the electronic properties of graphene samples [18,19]. At the core of the computation are energy-resolved functions

$$X(\omega) = \frac{1}{N}\mathrm{tr}[\delta(\omega - H)X] = \frac{1}{N}\sum_{n=1}^{N}\delta(\omega - E_n)\langle\psi_n, X\psi_n\rangle \qquad (1)$$

of an observable X. Here, H is the matrix representation of the physical Hamilton operator, with N eigenvalues E_n and eigenstates ψ_n. In this particular expression, all matrices are symmetric (or Hermitian). Physical quantities such as the electric conductivity are now obtained as a weighted mean of the form $\int X(\omega)f(\omega)d\omega$, where $f(\omega)$ is a prescribed scalar function such as the Boltzmann or Fermi-Dirac weight. In the special

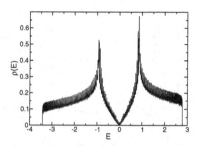

Fig. 3. Density of states (DOS) of a graphene nano-ribbon [20], computed with the KPM-DOS method (see Alg. 1)

case $X = I$ and $f(\omega) \equiv 1$, the above function gives the density of states (DOS), which counts the number of eigenvalues in a given interval (see Fig. 3).

3.2 Algorithms

In (1) all eigenpairs of H contribute, but explicit computation of a substantial fraction or even of all eigenpairs is not feasible. It is now the application that further dictates the algorithmic choice.

FEAST algorithm For very narrow $f(\omega)$, which occurs for instance at low temperatures, we can compute the eigenpairs selected by $f(\omega)$ with the FEAST algorithm. Typically about 200 to 400 eigenpairs are requested. FEAST has not yet reached the algorithmic maturity of JADA and other well-established iterative eigensolvers (cf., e.g., [21]). Therefore, performance optimization for FEAST must be accompanied, and preceded, by enhancements of the basic scheme in order to improve its robustness and numerical efficiency. Recent methodological progress and first numerical results for graphene nano-ribbon models are reported in [20,22].

Chebyshev polynomial expansion schemes If more eigenvalues contribute in the sum (1) for broader $f(\omega)$ we compute a polynomial approximation to the entire function $X(\omega)$ with the KPM. In this way, explicit computation of eigenpairs can be avoided. The KPM is based on the recurrence relation

$$|v_0\rangle = |v\rangle \,, |v_1\rangle = \tilde{H}|v_0\rangle \,, |v_{m+1}\rangle = 2\tilde{H}|v_m\rangle - |v_{m-1}\rangle \qquad (2)$$

for vectors $|v_m\rangle = T_m[\tilde{H}]|v\rangle$, where the $T_m(x)$ are the Chebyshev polynomials of the first kind. Note that the original matrix has been rescaled to $\tilde{H} = a(H - b)$ such that all eigenvalues lie in the definition range $[-1, 1]$ of the $T_m(x)$. To this end, an approximation to the minimum and maximum eigenvalues is computed initially, for which the Lanczos algorithm can be used. The corresponding Chebyshev moments $\mu_m = \int X(\omega)T_m(\omega)d\omega$ of $X(\omega)$ are obtained from the scalar products

$$\mu_m = \langle v|T_m(\tilde{H})X|v\rangle = \langle v_m|X|v_0\rangle. \qquad (3)$$

From these moments, the function $X(\omega)$ is reconstructed as a Fourier transform. The full trace tr$[\ldots]$ in (1) is replaced by a stochastic sum over several random starting vectors $|v\rangle$. For more details see our KPM review [12].

Several computational steps can now be identified in the above scheme: spMVM, vector-vector operations, scalar products, and an outer loop over random vectors.

Fig. 4. Performance of block spMVM for various numbers of vectors (n_b) involved in the vector block. Measurements have been performed on a single Intel Xeon E5-2660 v2 processor (fixed clock speed of 2.2 GHz). The matrix has approximately 10^7 rows and an average number of non-zero entries per row of $N_{nzr} = 14$.

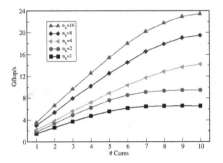

A straightforward implementation of these steps leads to the KPM-DOS algorithm discussed below (Alg. 1). Performance engineering, which exploits the specific combination in which the individual computational steps occur together with the different levels of parallelism, results in a highly efficient algorithm (cf. Sect. 3.4) that is tailored to achieve best performance for the KPM-DOS application class represented by Fig. 3.

In this way application-specific information enters at all stages of the development cycle, which is characteristic for the strong vertical integration that we pursue in the ES-SEX project. It applies equally to the other applications and algorithms addressed. For instance in the graphene application, specifically in the computation of time-resolved electron dynamics, the above FEAST/KPM steps are complemented by computations of the matrix exponential e^{-iHt}, for which we use again Chebyshev techniques.

Parallel block JADA Many quantum physics applications, such as strongly correlated systems, require the computation of a few extremal eigenvalues of a symmetric matrix, for which we use the classic JADA algorithm. The implementation of iterative JADA solvers relies on spMVM and (block) vector-vector operations. Hence, a functional interface to the basic building blocks library GHOST (see Sect. 3.3) has been developed. In order to increase the impact of our new JADA implementation, we also implement this interface for other linear algebra packages such as the Trilinos[1] project. On the other hand, the abstraction introduced here allows us to exploit the work of others and makes GHOST compatible with, e.g., the "tall skinny QR" factorization (TSQR), block Krylov-Schur and communication-avoiding GMRES in Trilinos.

Two JADA variants have been implemented: A single-vector method as a reference solver and an experimental pipelined block method that performs as key operations a block spMVM (spMVM applied to multiple vectors) and a block orthogonalization step [23]. Block spMVM reduces overall main memory data traffic as compared to an equivalent series of standard spMVMs. Using an highly optimized block spMVM routine (from the GHOST library) based on a row-wise storage scheme for the vector block, a performance gain of almost four can be typically achieved on a full socket basis (cf. Fig. 4). In a set of representative experiments this advantage outweighed the increase in floating point operations due to the blocked JADA algorithm in almost all cases so that an overall speed-up of blocked JADA of around 50% is achieved on the socket level for recent Intel processors. The performance advantage continues into the parallel region as demonstrated by first measurements using a moderately sized test

---

[1] http://trilinos.sandia.gov

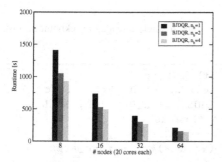

Fig. 5. Hybrid-parallel (MPI+OpenMP) execution times of the block JADA solver for up to 64 nodes (1280 cores) of a Infiniband cluster using the compute nodes specified in Fig. 4, i.e. each node carries 20 physical cores. The matrix has about 1.6×10^8 rows and 2.6×10^9 non-zero entries.

matrix (see Fig. 5). Note that in the block variant the average message size increases (at constant overall communication volume) and we have furthermore eliminated global synchronization points wherever possible.

In the current package, JADA uses a pipelined block GMRES method without further preconditioning for the solution of the correction equation. In the future we will integrate advanced preconditioning techniques to accelerate convergence. Furthermore, algorithmic overlapping of communication and computation will be made possible by exploiting the GHOST task queueing system, which will enable, e.g., overlapping spMVM communication with numerical operations in other JADA or GMRES loops. Another focus of future work will be to include GPGPUs in all JADA operations, which is already possible with GHOST, but not fully implemented in our interface.

3.3 Basic Building Blocks

As a first step towards a flexible repository of basic building blocks, multi-threaded low-level routines for basic operations such as spMVM, vector-vector operations, etc., were developed. Naturally, the spMVM has received special attention since it is the hot spot in most of the algorithms employed in the project. OpenMP and CUDA were chosen as the "X" programming model in order to address the most popular computing devices in modern, heterogeneous clusters. On the distributed-memory level, the MPI implementation allows for a simple MPI-only model as well as for hybrid approaches where each process owns multiple threads, possibly dedicated to the separate tasks of communication and computation. This makes it possible to achieve an explicit overlap between computation and communication, even if the underlying MPI implementation does not support truly asynchronous point-to-point transfers for large messages.

The FT aspect of the building blocks layer was initially addressed by an implementation of checkpointing for a lattice-Boltzmann flow solver using dedicated checkpoint threads [24], by which we could demonstrate the feasibility of asynchronous checkpointing and its low overhead on modern commodity systems. In order to get a more complete view of available checkpointing techniques, several existing solutions were investigated and compared [25,26]. However, checkpoint/restart is only the most basic FT technique. Future systems will not be able to sustain the continuous I/O load caused by checkpoint/restart when the job-level mean time between failure is of the order of minutes. Hence, research is going on in many directions in search for fault-tolerant programming models which enable applications to continue running even if a

Listing 1.1. Spawning a multi-threaded computation and a single-threaded checkpointing task using GHOST.

```
// define task: checkpointing with 1 thread
ghost_task_create(&chkpTask, 1, curTask->LD, &chkp_func, \
      (void *)&chkp_func_args, GHOST_TASK_DEFAULT, NULL, 0);
// define task: compute with N-1 threads
ghost_task_create(&compTask, curTask->nThreads-1, \
      curTask->LD, &comp_func, (void *)&comp_func_args, \
      GHOST_TASK_DEFAULT, NULL, 0);
// initiate tasks
ghost_task_enqueue(chkpTask); ghost_task_enqueue(compTask);
// wait for completion
ghost_task_wait(chkpTask); ghost_task_wait(compTask);
```

node fails. Since the MPI standard does not yet contain any such features today, we have first ported a distributed-memory spMVM operation to GPI [27]. GPI[2] is an open source implementation of the GASPI PGAS standard, and explicitly supports continuous execution after hardware failures. Work is ongoing to test these facilities using the KPM-DOS application.

Taking as much complexity as possible out of the developer's hands without sacrificing full control over performance and execution modes (such as affinity, threading, functional parallelism) were conflicting goals in the development of the basic blocks layer. We have addressed this challenge by developing GHOST (General Hybrid Optimized Sparse Toolkit). GHOST is a library that can be used from C/C++ and Fortran programs. It implements a flexible thread-tasking model on the process level, providing the required affinity and resource management functions to support functional parallelism as needed by all project layers. For instance, a background task for parallel checkpointing can be initiated with a single function call, while another task is executing a sparse MVM (see Listing 1.1).

Addressing heterogeneity, especially when dealing with sparse matrices, requires more than a proper choice of programming model. The optimal format for storing sparse matrices was, up until recently, highly hardware-dependent: On standard cache-based processors the compressed row storage (CRS) format usually leads to best performance, while GPGPUs require the fundamentally different ELLPACK or one of its derivatives [28]. On vector computers, the jagged diagonals storage (JDS) is most suitable since it leads to long, easily vectorizable inner loops, while the optimal format for the new Intel Xeon Phi architecture was yet to be found. In the basic building blocks layer we have developed SELL-C-σ, a sparse matrix storage format that yields best or competitive performance on all modern computer architectures (see Fig. 6), with the added benefit of saving memory compared to the popular ELLPACK-based variants on GPGPUs [29]. This format facilitates the programming of heterogeneous hardware, since

[2] http://www.gpi-site.com

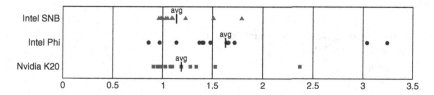

Fig. 6. Relative performance benefit of the unified SELL-32-σ format over the vendor-supplied library spMVM performance for twelve "non-pathological" test cases in the UoF matrix collection (see [29] for details) on Intel Sandy Bridge ("SNB"), Intel Xeon Phi, and Nvidia K20. A format similar to SELL-C-σ will be supported in a future release of the Intel Math Kernel Library [32].

load balancing and FT features do not have to take format conversions into account. Furthermore it will greatly ease the development of efficient code on upcoming unified memory architectures, where the host CPU and the accelerator hardware share memory. SELL-C-σ has immediately been taken up and adapted to special needs by several research groups [30,31].

3.4 Holistic Performance Engineering

The performance optimization process applied to the computation of the DOS with the KPM (KPM-DOS, for $X = I$ in (1)) is a simple but very instructive example for the advantages of a holistic view on the complete software stack.

A standard scheme for computing the Chebyshev moments $\{\mu_m; m = 0, \ldots, M\}$ for a given M is shown in Alg. 1 (middle loop over m). In terms of computational complexity the relevant step is the construction of the vectors $|v_m\rangle = T_m[\tilde{H}]|v\rangle$ through the recurrence (2). Note that, using the relation $T_{m+n}(x) = 2T_m(x)T_n(x) - T_{m-n}(x)$, the algorithm can be formulated as presented, delivering two moments ($\mu_{2m} = 2\eta_{2m} - \mu_0, \mu_{2m+1} = 2\eta_{2m+1} - \mu_1$) per spMVM operation.

The Chebyshev scheme requires a spMVM routine involving the original matrix H and various vector-vector operations including a scalar product as basic building blocks. Typically, highly optimized subroutines are provided by an external low-level library and are called in the order shown. As a consequence, besides the spMVM, eight vectors of matrix dimension have to be loaded and four stored from/to main memory, generating data traffic which can be as high as in the spMVM alone. Extending the optimization scope to the algorithmic layer allows to define a tailored spMVM routine that eliminates all data transfers for the vector-vector operations. Those operations are performed in the spMVM step when the relevant data is available in registers or in the L1 cache. Thus, the overall data traffic is reduced to a single basic spMVM step (see Alg. 2). Further performance potential becomes accessible if the optimization scope also includes the application problem, which is the KPM-DOS computation. Here, the outer loop runs over a set of random vectors for which the Chebyshev moments are computed independently, loading the full matrix in each iteration. Applying the tailored spMVM to a block of random vectors can add the substantial performance gains demonstrated in Fig. 4 to our application scenario. The optimal number of vectors in the block is set by

for $r = 0$ *to* $R - 1$ **do**
   | $|v\rangle = |\mathrm{rand}()\rangle$;
   | Initialization steps and computation of μ_0, μ_1
   | **for** $m = 1$ *to* $M/2$ **do**
   | | $\mathrm{swap}(|w\rangle, |v\rangle)$;
   | | $|u\rangle \quad = \qquad H|v\rangle$;
   | | $|u\rangle \quad = \quad |u\rangle - b|v\rangle$;
   | | $|w\rangle \quad = \qquad -|w\rangle$;
   | | $|w\rangle \quad = |w\rangle + 2a|u\rangle$;
   | | $\eta_{2m} \quad = \qquad \langle v|v\rangle$;
   | | $\eta_{2m+1} = \qquad \langle w|v\rangle$;
   | **end**
end

Algorithm 1: Basic scheme to compute the Chebyshev moments (KPM-DOS) for a set of R random vectors $\{|\mathrm{rand}()\rangle\}$ using the standard spMVM operation

a subtle interplay of matrix dimension, matrix bandwidth, and cache size, and is subject to current research in ESSEX. For the benchmarks presented below, eight vectors per block are chosen, which reduces the overall data traffic for loading matrix information accordingly. Note that the use of block vectors is only possible if KPM is applied to compute the density of states. If a static excitation spectrum is determined there is no outer loop in the scheme.

For the test matrix and a single socket of the compute node used in Fig. 4, the two successive optimizations have improved the performance from 5.5 GF/s (basic version) to 8.3 GF/s (tailored spMVM) to finally 21.6 GF/s (blocked tailored spMVM). Though the matrix is rather small, the KPM scheme is still completely memory bound. Hence, considering all software layers in the optimization process results in an almost $4\times$ speed-up. Note that in the basic version each of the different subroutines had been individually well optimized: The basic spMVM step runs at a performance of 6.5 GF/s, indicating a very good utilization of the memory bandwidth bottleneck (45 GB/s read-only bandwidth for the test system) according to the spMVM performance model presented in [29].

for $r = 0$ *to* $R - 1$ **do**
   | $|v\rangle = |\mathrm{rand}()\rangle$;
   | $|w\rangle = a(H - b)|v\rangle$ & $\mu_0 = \langle v|v\rangle$ & $\mu_1 = \langle w|v\rangle$;
   | **for** $m = 1$ *to* $M/2$ **do**
   | | $\mathrm{swap}(|w\rangle, |v\rangle)$;
   | | $|w\rangle = 2a(H - b)|v\rangle - |w\rangle$ & $\eta_{2m} = \langle v|v\rangle$ & $\eta_{2m+1} = \langle w|v\rangle$;
   | **end**
end

Algorithm 2: Improved computation of Chebyshev moments (KPM-DOS) with a tailored spMVM operation. Operations chained by "&" in a single line do not cause main memory traffic as they are performed in the spMVM operation.

4 Conclusions

In the first 18 months the ESSEX project has made substantial contributions to the sparse linear algebra community reaching far beyond its application area. Other groups have already picked up several results, and new collaborations with projects both within SPPEXA and beyond have been established. A preliminary version of the Exascale Sparse Solver Repository (ESSR) will be released by the end of 2014.

Acknowledgments. This work is supported by the German Research Foundation (DFG) through the Priority Programme 1648 "Software for Exascale Computing" (SPPEXA) under project ESSEX.

References

1. Threading and GPGPU support in PETSc, http://www.mcs.anl.gov/petsc/features/
2. Parallel Arnoldi package (PARPACK) homepage,
   http://www.caam.rice.edu/~kristyn/parpack_home.html
3. Anasazi package homepage, http://trilinos.sandia.gov/packages/anasazi/
4. LAMA — Library for Accelerated Math Applications, http://www.libama.org
5. Förster, M., Kraus, J.: Scalable parallel AMG on ccNUMA machines with OpenMP. Computer Science - Research and Development 26, 221–228 (2011) ISSN 1865-2034
6. pOSKI: parallel optimized sparse kernel interface,
   http://bebop.cs.berkeley.edu/poski
7. Bautista-Gomez, L., Tsuboi, S., Komatitsch, D., Cappello, F., Maruyama, N., Matsuoka, S.: FTI: high performance fault tolerance interface for hybrid systems. In: Proceedings of 2011 International Conference for High Performance Computing, Networking, Storage and Analysis, SC 2011, pp. 32:1–32:32. ACM, New York (2011)
8. Plank, J.S., Kim, Y., Dongarra, J.J.: Algorithm-based diskless checkpointing for fault-tolerant matrix operations. In: Proceedings of the Twenty-Fifth International Symposium on Fault-Tolerant Computing, FTCS 1995, pp. 351–360. IEEE Computer Society, Washington, DC (1995)
9. Horton, M., Tomov, S., Dongarra, J.: A class of hybrid LAPACK algorithms for multicore and GPU architectures. In: Symposium on Application Accelerators in High-Performance Computing, pp. 150–158. IEEE Computer Society, Los Alamitos (2011)
10. Hager, G., Treibig, J., Habich, J., Wellein, G.: Exploring performance and power properties of modern multicore chips via simple machine models. Concurrency Computat. Pract. Exper. (2013), doi:10.1002/cpe.3180
11. Polizzi, E.: Density-matrix-based algorithm for solving eigenvalue problems. Phys. Rev. B 79, 115112 (2009)
12. Weiße, A., Wellein, G., Alvermann, A., Fehske, H.: The kernel polynomial method. Rev. Mod. Phys. 78, 275 (2006)
13. Tal-Ezer, H., Kosloff, R.: An accurate and efficient scheme for propagating the time dependent Schrödinger equation. J. Chem. Phys. 81, 3967 (1984)
14. Fehske, H., Schleede, J., Schubert, G., Wellein, G., Filinov, V.S., Bishop, A.R.: Numerical approaches to time evolution of complex quantum systems. Phys. Lett. A 373, 2182 (2009)
15. Alvermann, A., Fehske, H.: High-order commutator-free exponential time-propagation of driven quantum systems. J. Comp. Phys. 230, 5930 (2011)
16. di Napoli, E., Polizzi, E., Saad, Y.: Efficient estimation of eigenvalue counts in an interval, Preprint arXiv:1308.4275 (2013)

17. Bhardwaj, O., Ineichen, Y., Bekas, C., Curioni, A.: Highly scalable linear time estimation of spectrograms - a tool for very large scale data analysis. Poster at 2013 ACM/IEEE International Conference on High Performance Computing Networking, Storage and Analysis (2013)
18. Pieper, A., Schubert, G., Wellein, G., Fehske, H.: Effects of disorder and contacts on transport through graphene nanoribbons. Phys. Rev. B 88, 195409 (2013)
19. Pieper, A., Heinisch, R.L., Wellein, G., Fehske, H.: Dot-bound and dispersive states in graphene quantum dot superlattices. Phys. Rev. B 89, 165121 (2014)
20. Krämer, L., Galgon, M., Lang, B., Alvermann, A., Fehske, H., Pieper, A.: Improving robustness of the FEAST algorithm and solving eigenvalue problems from graphene nanoribbons (Submitted to PAMM 2014)
21. Krämer, L., Di Napoli, E., Galgon, M., Lang, B., Bientinesi, P.: Dissecting the FEAST algorithm for generalized eigenproblems. J. Comput. Appl. Math. 244, 1–9 (2013)
22. Krämer, L.: Integration Based Solvers for Standard and Generalized Eigenvalue Problems. Ph.D. thesis, Bergische Universität Wuppertal (2014)
23. Röhrig-Zöllner, M., Thies, J., Kreutzer, M., Alvermann, A., Pieper, A., Basermann, A., Hager, G., Wellein, G., Fehske, H.: Increasing the performance of the Jacobi-Davidson method by blocking. SIAM J. Sci. Comput. (Submitted)
24. Shahzad, F., Wittmann, M., Zeiser, T., Wellein, G.: Asynchronous checkpointing by dedicated checkpoint threads. In: Träff, J.L., Benkner, S., Dongarra, J.J. (eds.) EuroMPI 2012. LNCS, vol. 7490, pp. 289–290. Springer, Heidelberg (2012)
25. Shahzad, F., Wittmann, M., Kreutzer, M., Zeiser, T., Hager, G., Wellein, G.: A survey of checkpoint/restart techniques on distributed memory systems. Parallel Processing Letters 23(04), 13400111–134001120 (2013)
26. Shahzad, F., Wittmann, M., Zeiser, T., Hager, G., Wellein, G.: An evaluation of different I/O techniques for checkpoint/restart. In: Proceedings of the 2013 IEEE 27th International Parallel and Distributed Processing Symposium Workshops & PhD Forum (IPDPSW), pp. 1708–1716. IEEE Computer Society (2013)
27. Shahzad, F., Wittmann, M., Kreutzer, M., Zeiser, T., Hager, G., Wellein, G.: PGAS implementation of SPMVM and LBM with GPI. In: Proceedings of the 7th International Conference on PGAS Programming Models, pp. 172–184 (2013)
28. Bell, N., Garland, M.: Implementing sparse matrix-vector multiplication on throughput-oriented processors. In:Proceedings of the Conference on High Performance Computing Networking, Storage and Analysis, SC 2009, pp. 18:1–18:11. ACM, New York (2009)
29. Kreutzer, M., Hager, G., Wellein, G., Fehske, H., Bishop, A.: A unified sparse matrix data format for efficient general sparse matrix-vector multiplication on modern processors with wide SIMD units. SIAM Journal on Scientific Computing 36(5), C401–C423 (2014)
30. Müthing, S., Ribbrock, D., Göddeke, D.: Integrating multi-threading and accelerators into DUNE-ISTL. In: Proceedings of ENUMATH 2013 (accepted 2014)
31. Anzt, H., Tomov, S., Dongarra, J.: Implementing a sparse matrix vector product for the SELL-C/SELL-C-σ formats on NVIDIA GPUs. Tech. rep. (March 2014), http://www.eecs.utk.edu/resources/library/585
32. Intel Math Kernel Library (MKL), https://software.intel.com/en-us/intel-mkl

Catwalk: A Quick Development Path for Performance Models

Felix Wolf[1,2], Christian Bischof[3], Torsten Hoefler[4], Bernd Mohr[5],
Gabriel Wittum[6], Alexandru Calotoiu[1,2], Christian Iwainsky[1],
Alexandre Strube[5], and Andreas Vogel[6]

[1] German Research School for Simulation Sciences, 52062 Aachen, Germany
[2] RWTH Aachen University, 52056 Aachen, Germany
[3] Technische Universität Darmstadt, 64293 Darmstadt, Germany
[4] ETH Zurich, CH-8092 Zürich, Switzerland
[5] Forschungszentrum Jülich, 52425 Jülich, Germany
[6] Goethe Universität Frankfurt, 60325 Frankfurt am Main, Germany

Abstract. Many parallel applications suffer from latent performance
limitations that may prevent them from scaling to larger machine sizes.
Often, such scalability bugs manifest themselves only when an attempt
to scale the code is actually being made—a point where remediation can
be difficult. However, creating analytical performance models that would
allow such issues to be pinpointed earlier is so laborious that application
developers attempt it at most for a few selected kernels, running the risk
of missing harmful bottlenecks. The objective of the Catwalk project,
which is carried out as part of the DFG Priority Programme 1648 Software for Exascale Computing (SPPEXA), is to automate key activities
of the performance modeling process, making this powerful methodology
easier to use and expanding its coverage. This article gives an overview of
the project objectives, describes the results achieved so far, and outlines
future work.

1 Introduction

When scaling their codes to larger numbers of processors, many HPC application developers face the situation that all of a sudden a part of the program
starts consuming an excessive amount of time. Unfortunately, discovering latent
scalability bottlenecks through experience is painful and expensive. Removing
them requires not only potentially numerous large-scale experiments to track
them down, prolonged by the scalability issue at hand, but often also major
code surgery in the aftermath. All too often, this happens at a moment when
the manpower is needed elsewhere. This is especially true for applications on
the path to exascale, which have to address numerous technical challenges simultaneously, ranging from heterogeneous computing to resilience. Since such
problems usually emerge at a later stage of the development process, dependencies between their source and the rest of the code that have grown over time can
make remediation even harder. One way of finding scalability bottlenecks earlier is through analytical performance modeling. An analytical scalability model

L. Lopes et al. (Eds.): Euro-Par 2014 Workshops, Part II, LNCS 8806, pp. 589–600, 2014.
© Springer International Publishing Switzerland 2014

expresses the execution time or other resources needed to complete the program as a function of the number of processors. Unfortunately, the laws according to which the resources needed by the code change as the number of processors increases are often laborious to infer and may also vary significantly across individual parts of complex modular programs. This is why analytical performance modeling—in spite of its potential—is rarely used to predict the scaling behavior before problems manifest themselves. As a consequence, this technique is still confined to a small community of experts.

If today developers decide to model the scalability of their code, and many shy away from the effort, they first apply both intuition and tests at smaller scales to identify so-called *kernels*, which are those parts of the program that are expected to dominate its performance at larger scales. This step is essential because modeling a full application with hundreds of modules manually is not feasible. Then they apply reasoning in a time-consuming process to create analytical models that describe the scaling behavior of their kernels more precisely. In a way, they have to solve a chicken-and-egg problem: to find the right kernels, they require a pre-existing notion of which parts of the program will dominate its behavior at scale—basically a model of their performance. However, they do not have enough time to develop models for more than a few pre-selected candidate kernels, inevitably exposing themselves to the danger of overlooking unscalable code.

In the Catwalk project, which is part of the DFG Priority Programme 1648 Software for Exascale Computing (SPPEXA), we are developing a novel tool that eliminates this dilemma. Instead of modeling only a small subset of the program manually, we generate an empirical performance model for each part of the target program automatically, significantly increasing not only the coverage of the scalability check but also its speed.

The remainder of the paper is structured as follows. Section 2 describes the empirical performance modeling tool and its applications. Section 3 explains the automatic workflow manager used to run the experiments needed as input for the tool. Section 4 outlines ongoing work of extending the current MPI-centric approach towards OpenMP and hybrid applications. One of the target codes for performance modeling, the library UG4, is discussed in Section 5. Finally, we summarize our results and outline future work in Section 6.

2   Automated Performance Modeling

The primary objective of our approach is the identification of *scalability bugs*. A scalability bug is a part of the program whose scaling behavior is unintentionally poor, that is, much worse than expected. As computing hardware moves towards exascale, developers need early feedback on the scalability of their software design so that they can adapt it to the requirements of larger problem and machine sizes. Our method can be applied to both strong scaling and weak scaling applications. In addition to searching for performance bugs, the models our tool produces also support projections that can be helpful when applying

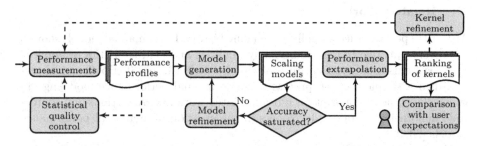

Fig. 1. Workflow of scalability-bug detection. Solid boxes represent actions or transformations, and banners their inputs and outputs. Dashed arrows indicate optional paths taken after user decisions.

for the compute time needed to solve the next larger class of problems. Finally, because we model both execution time and requirements alongside each other, our results can also assist in software-hardware co-design or help uncover growing wait states. Note that although our approach can be easily generalized to cover many programming models, we focus on message passing programs. For a detailed description including modeling results, the reader may refer to [3].

The input of our tool is a set of performance measurements on different processor counts $\{p_1, \ldots, p_{max}\}$ in the form of parallel profiles. The execution of these experiments is supported by a workflow manager, which is described in Section 3. The output of our tool is a list of program regions, ranked by their predicted execution time at a target scale of $p_t > p_{max}$ processors. We call these regions *kernels* because they define the code granularity at which we generate our models.

Figure 1 gives an overview of the different steps necessary to find scalability bugs, whose details we explain further below. To ensure a statistically relevant set of performance data, profile measurements may have to be repeated several times—at least on systems subject to jitter. This is done in the optional statistical quality control step. Once this is accomplished, we apply regression to obtain a coarse performance model for every possible program region. These models then undergo an iterative refinement process until the model quality has reached a saturation point. To arrange the program regions in a ranked list, we extrapolate the performance either to a specific target scale p_t or to infinity, which means we use the asymptotic behavior as the basis of our comparison. A scalability bug can be any region with a model worse than a given threshold, such as anything scaling worse than linearly. Alternatively, a user can compare the model of a kernel with his own expectations to determine if the performance is worse than expected. Finally, if the granularity of our program regions is not sufficient to arrive at an actionable recommendation, performance measurements, and thus the kernels under investigation, can be further refined via more detailed instrumentation.

2.1 Related Work

Analytical performance modeling has a long history. Early manual models showed to be very effective in describing many qualities and characteristics of applications, systems, and even entire tool chains [2, 9, 13, 16, 18]. Hoefler et al. established a simple six-step process to guide manual performance modeling [6], which served as a blueprint for our automated workflow. Assertions and source-code annotations support developers in the creation of analytical performance models [20–22].

Various automated modeling methods exist. Many of these tools focus on learning the performance characteristics automatically using various machine-learning approaches [8, 12]. Zhai, Chen, and Zheng extrapolate single-node performance to complex parallel machines using a trace-driven network simulator [25]. Wu and Müller extrapolate traces to predict communications at larger scale [24]. Carrington et al. choose a model from a set of canonical functions to extrapolate traces of applications at scale [4].

2.2 Model Generation

Model generation forms the core of our method. When generating performance models, we exploit the observation that they are usually composed of a finite number n of predefined terms, involving powers and logarithms of p (or some other parameter):

$$f(p) = \sum_{k=1}^{n} c_k \cdot p^{i_k} \cdot log_2^{j_k}(p) \qquad (1)$$

This representation is, of course, not exhaustive, but works in most practical scenarios since it is a consequence of how most computer algorithms are designed. We call it the *performance model normal form* (PMNF). Moreover, our experience suggests that neither the sets $I, J \subset \mathbb{Q}$ from which the exponents i_k and j_k are chosen nor the number of terms n have to be arbitrarily large or random to achieve a good fit. Thus, instead of deriving the models through reasoning, we only need to make reasonable choices for n, I, and J and then simply try all assignment options one by one. A possible assignment of all i_k and j_k in a PMNF expression is called a *model hypothesis*. Trying all hypotheses one by one means that for each of them we find coefficients c_k with optimal fit. Then we apply cross-validation [17] to select the hypothesis with the best fit across all candidates. In our experiments we use $I = \{0, 0.5, 1, 1.5, 2, 2.5, 3\}$, $J = \{0, 1, 2\}$ and $n = 5$, and we have observed that it is more than sufficient to accurately represent behaviors found in real world applications.

2.3 Evaluation Summary

We analyzed real-world applications such as climate codes, quantum chromodynamics, fluid dynamics and more. We were able to identify a scalability issue in

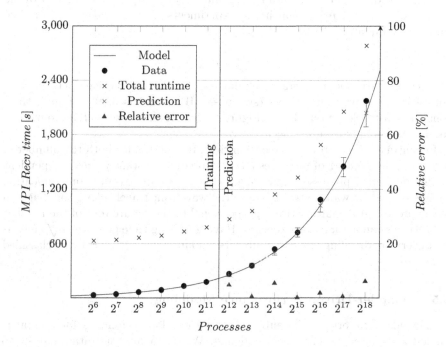

Fig. 2. Measured vs. predicted execution time of the two receive operations involved in the wavefront process of Sweep3D on Juqueen

codes that are known to have such issues (Sweep3D, XNS) and not identify any scalability issue in codes that are known to have none (MILC, UG4). Moreover, we were able to identify two scalability issues in a code that was thought to have only one (HOMME).

2.4 Case Study

In this example, we show how our tool helps identify and explain a scalability problem, providing a first impression of the user experience. The Sweep3D benchmark [10] is a compact application that solves a 1-group time-independent discrete ordinates neutron transport problem. It was extracted from a real ASCI code. The literature mentions accurate models [7, 23] that describe the performance behavior of wavefront processes as they occur in Sweep3D on various architectures. The LogGP model reported in [7] characterizes the communication time as follows:

$$t^{comm} = [2(p_x + p_y - 2) + 4(n_{sweep} - 1)] \cdot t_{msg} \qquad (2)$$

p_x and p_y denote the lengths of the process-grid edges, n_{sweep} the number of wavefronts to be computed, and t_{msg} the time needed for a one-way nearest-neighbor communication. Given that both n_{sweep} and t_{msg} are largely independent of the number of processes p and that in our experiments $p_x = p_y$ and $p = p_x \cdot p_y$, we can rewrite Equation (2) as:

$$t^{comm} = c \cdot \sqrt{p} \tag{3}$$

The (combined) model generated by our tool for the two receive operations involved in the wavefront process (sweep $\to$ MPI_Recv) is $3.99 \cdot \sqrt{p}$ and, thus, consistent with Equation (3). As Figure 2 illustrates, it also matches our measurements on Juqueen quite accurately.

In contrast to the growing execution time, the models for both the number of bytes and the number of messages received predict constant values independent of the number of processes. This suggests that any increase in communication time is caused by wait states. Because the wavefront travels along the diagonal of the process grid, waiting times proportional to the square root of the number of processes can actually be expected. Having waiting time grow with $\sqrt{p}$ means that every quadrupling of p will double its amount, which can hardly be classified as scalable.

2.5   Compiler-Driven Performance Modeling

In a similar but orthogonal subproject, we develop techniques for compiler-guided automated performance modeling. We use a mix of static analysis to count loop iterations and assess the theoretical scaling and parallelizability of practical codes [5] with dynamic multi-parameter performance model generation during runtime [1]. The static analysis instantiates work-depth models of parallel applications. It supports the large class of practically relevant loops with affine update functions and generates additional parameters for other expressions. The method can be used to determine whether the theoretically maximum parallelism is exposed in a practical implementation of a problem. The scheme over-approximates the performance of programs if loops are not affine or guards cannot be determined automatically. The dynamic approach under-approximates the program's behavior by analyzing particular executions. PEMOGEN, our compilation and modeling framework, automatically instruments applications to generate performance models during program execution. We used PEMOGEN to automatically detect 3,370 kernels from fifteen NAS and Mantevo applications and model their execution times. Both schemes were implemented in the Low Level Virtual Machine (LLVM) compiler framework [11].

This work is a first step towards full automation of the model generation. Open problems include non-linear combinations of different parameters as well as improved statistical techniques for model generation.

3   Workflow Manager

As illustrated in Figure 1, the identification of scalability bugs demands multiple executions of performance measurements, both with different and with identical

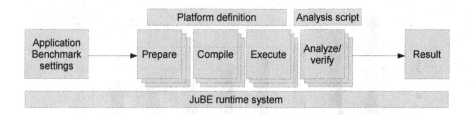

Fig. 3. JuBE workflow

input parameters, the latter to minimize the impact of jitter on shared machines. To automate this process, we use the Jülich Benchmarking Environment (JuBE) developed by Forschungszentrum Jülich. The steps carried out by JuBE are shown in Figure 3. The stacked boxes for preparation, compilation, execution, and analysis mean that these steps of the workflow might exist multiple times.

When running JuBE, it will perform the aforementioned steps in sequence. It is important to note that JuBE is able to easily create combinatorial runs of multiple parameters. For example, in a scaling experiment, one can simply specify multiple numbers of processes, and/or multiple threads per process, and JuBE will create one experiment for each possible combination, submit all of them to the resource manager, collect all results, and display them together.

4 Modeling OpenMP Performance

While scalability bugs are known issues for MPI applications and an MPI performance modeling methodology exists, it has not been applied to OpenMP and the interactions with MPI. As OpenMP represents the de-facto standard for exploiting manycore architectures, it will become of higher importance to exascale systems. Historically, multithreading and hence OpenMP usually did not require modeling, as it was easily possible to experimentally tests applications due to the limited amount of parallelism. With the ongoing trend of integrating more cores into CPUs, the level of parallelism rises and will most likely continue to rise well into the exascale era. Therefore, modeling OpenMP performance and detecting scalability bugs becomes important. Also understanding OpenMP modeling will enable to address hybrid applications, i.e., application using both MPI and OpenMP, which have to strike a careful balance distributing available compute resources between MPI processes and per-process OpenMP threads. Performance modeling could provide an answer to this question, indicating the sweet spot—without the need to experimentally test all possible thread and process combinations.

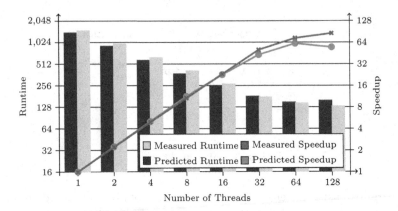

Fig. 4. OpenMP CG solver: comparison of measurements with the model

First OpenMP Modeling Experience

To determine possible model parameters and to ascertain precision, we analyzed a best effort implementation of a conjugate-gradient (CG) solver implementation from a recent OpenMP tuning study. In contrast to pure MPI applications, the regions required to sufficiently model the core are much smaller - typically comprising only the extent of single OpenMP constructs. On the other hand, the impact of resource limitations, such as memory bandwidth, and the impact of additional parallelism on the available resources is much more difficult to account for.

For our test code, we were able to manually create a fairly accurate model of the runtime using existing standard benchmarks. For this we measured memory bandwidth using the STREAM TRIAD benchmark and the runtime overhead of OpenMP constructs for each possible thread count on our test system, the BCS System of the RWTH Aachen University. We then combined these measurement results with an analytical model of the remaining computational parts to obtain the times shown in Figure 4 [19]. Our measurement results of an optimized kernel implementation were relatively close to the predicted runtimes, with some leeway owed to peculiarities of the STREAM memory benchmark. As this benchmark does not exhibit exactly the same memory access pattern as the CG solver, its measurements can only approximate the bandwidth used by the CG solver. As a result, especially for the first eight threads of the deployed eight-socket system and for the close to saturation levels at the peak capacity of the system (128 threads), the memory bandwidth available to each thread deviates more substantially, causing a higher deviation of the model from the predicted runtime. A better memory model would most certainly have reduced these effects. Overall, however, our experience shows that by combining per-thread measurements of memory bandwidth and OpenMP construct overhead with partial analytical modeling of the application a model of OpenMP performance can be constructed.

5   Scalability of the Multigrid Solver in UG4

A real-world application code for the performance analysis within the project is the UG4 software library. It is a general-purpose simulation framework for the grid-based solution of partial differential equations using finite element or finite volume methods and actively developed at the Goethe Center for Scientific Computing of University of Frankfurt. It is used to address a broad variety of problems arising in natural sciences such as biology, neuroscience, physics and engineering, including drug diffusion through human skin, signal transport in neurons, and several kinds of flow problems like Navier-Stokes flow or subsurface flow in porous media.

Because it is a relevant application from computational biology, we are focusing in this project on the drug transport through the human skin. The medicine diffusion is modeled in a 3d tetrakaidekahedra-based grid, resolving lipid bilayers and corneocyte cell components of the stratum corneum in detail [14, 15]. To get an idea, consider the simplified 2d brick-and-mortar model shown in Figure 5. While the transport is faster within the lipid bilayers, also the transport through the corneocytes is analyzed. To resolve the biological setting in detail, a 3d tetrakaidekahedral grid must be used. These delicate geometries need high resolutions and therefore require massively parallel computation.

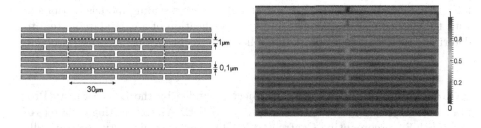

Fig. 5. Illustration of skin permeation. Left: The stratum corneum is build up by corneocyte cells (yellow) and lipid bilayers (channels). Right: medicine concentration diffusing from top to bottom.

Within a simulation, large sparse matrix systems arise that must be inverted. This part is not only one of the most time-consuming kernels of the application but also an algorithm that is hard to parallelize. We chose a geometric multigrid algorithm, since these are known to be of optimal complexity, i.e., its computational effort only increases linearly with the problem size, which makes it a promising candidate to achieve good weak-scaling results.

To generate performance models of the solver implementation, we performed weak-scaling runs for a diffusion problem on the Juqueen supercomputer using five identical runs for each process number to account for run-to-run variation. The analysis showed that no kernel in the application exhibited more than $O(log(p))$ growths in runtime. Hence, no scalability bugs were detected. This is also in agreement with weak scaling studies performed on process configurations larger than the ones used to generate the models. This is a good starting point for a more complex and in-depth analysis in the future where we plan to analyze different matrix solver types and setups. In addition we want to analyze other metrics such as floating-point rates or message sizes, and apply the model generator to different physical settings.

6   Conclusion

In the Catwalk project, we have already made significant progress towards our original goal of automating key activities of the performance modeling process. Now, a lightweight tool exists that can be used to generate useful scalability models for arbitrarily complex MPI codes. Tests on a range of applications confirmed models reported in the literature in cases where such models existed, and also helped uncover a previously unknown scalability issue in another case.

In the future, we want to apply our approach to the co-design of exascale software and hardware. Co-designing applications with systems is a powerful technique to ensure early and sustained productivity as well as good system design. We want to assist this process by automating many of the back-of-the-envelope calculations involved in co-design with a lightweight requirements analysis for scalable parallel applications. We want to generate empirical models that allow projections not only for different numbers of processes but also for different problem sizes. System designers then can use the process-scaling models in tandem with the problem-scaling models and the specification of a candidate system to determine the resource usage of an application execution with a certain problem size.

Acknowledgment. The Catwalk project is funded by the DFG Priority Program 1648 *Software for Exascale Computing* (SPPEXA). Computing resources of the Jülich Supercomputing Centre and RWTH Aachen University are gratefully acknowledged.

References

1. Bhattacharyya, A., Hoefler, T.: PEMOGEN: Automatic Adaptive Performance Modeling during Program Runtime. In: To appear in Proc. of the 23rd Intl. Conference on Parallel Architectures and Compilation Techniques (PACT 2014). ACM (August 2014)
2. Boyd, E.L., Azeem, W., Lee, H.H., Shih, T.P., Hung, S.H., Davidson, E.S.: A hierarchical approach to modeling and improving the performance of scientific applications on the ksr1. In: Proc. of the Intl. Conference on Parallel Processing (ICPP), pp. 188–192. IEEE Computer Society (1994),
http://dx.doi.org/10.1109/ICPP.1994.30
3. Calotoiu, A., Hoefler, T., Poke, M., Wolf, F.: Using automated performance modeling to find scalability bugs in complex codes. In: Proc. of the ACM/IEEE Conference on Supercomputing (SC 2013). ACM, Denver (November 2013)

4. Carrington, L., Laurenzano, M., Tiwari, A.: Characterizing large-scale hpc applications through trace extrapolation. Parallel Processing Letters 23(4) (2013)
5. Hoefler, T., Kwasniewski, G.: Automatic Complexity Analysis of Explicitly Parallel Programs. In: To appear in Proc. of the 26th ACM Symposium on Parallelism in Algorithms and Architectures (SPAA 2014). ACM (June 2014)
6. Hoefler, T., Gropp, W., Kramer, W., Snir, M.: Performance modeling for systematic performance tuning. In: State of the Practice Reports, SC 2011, pp. 6:1–6:12. ACM (2011), http://doi.acm.org/10.1145/2063348.2063356
7. Hoisie, A., Lubeck, O.M., Wasserman, H.J.: Performance analysis of wavefront algorithms on very-large scale distributed systems. In: Cooperman, G., Jessen, E., Michler, G. (eds.) Workshop on Wide Area Networks and High Performance Computing. LNCIS, vol. 249, pp. 171–187. Springer, Heidelberg (1999), http://dl.acm.org/citation.cfm?id=647259.720937
8. Ipek, E., de Supinski, B.R., Schulz, M., McKee, S.A.: An approach to performance prediction for parallel applications. In: Cunha, J.C., Medeiros, P.D. (eds.) Euro-Par 2005. LNCS, vol. 3648, pp. 196–205. Springer, Heidelberg (2005)
9. Kerbyson, D.J., Alme, H.J., Hoisie, A., Petrini, F., Wasserman, H.J., Gittings, M.: Predictive performance and scalability modeling of a large-scale application. In: Proc. of the ACM/IEEE Conference on Supercomputing (SC 2001), p. 37. ACM (2001)
10. Los Alamos National Laboratory: ASCI SWEEP3D v2.2b: Three-dimensional discrete ordinates neutron transport benchmark (1995), http://wwwc3.lanl.gov/pal/software/sweep3d/
11. Lattner, C., Adve, V.: Llvm: A compilation framework for lifelong program analysis & transformation. In: Proc. of the Intl. Symposium on Code Generation and Optimization: Feedback-directed and Runtime Optimization CGO 2004, p. 75. IEEE Computer Society, Washington, DC (2004), http://dl.acm.org/citation.cfm?id=977395.977673
12. Lee, B.C., Brooks, D.M., de Supinski, B.R., Schulz, M., Singh, K., McKee, S.A.: Methods of inference and learning for performance modeling of parallel applications. In: Proc. of the 12th ACM SIGPLAN Symposium on Principles and Practice of Parallel Programming (PPoPP 2007), pp. 249–258. ACM (2007), http://doi.acm.org/10.1145/1229428.1229479
13. Mathis, M.M., Amato, N.M., Adams, M.L.: A general performance model for parallel sweeps on orthogonal grids for particle transport calculations. Tech. rep., College Station, TX, USA (2000)
14. Nägel, A., Heisig, M., Wittum, G.: The state of the art in computational modelling of skin permeation. Advanced Drug Delivery Systems (2012)
15. Nägel, A., Heisig, M., Wittum, G.: A comparison of two-and three-dimensional models for the simulation of the permeability of human stratum corneum. European Journal of Pharmaceutics and Biopharmaceutics 72(2), 332–338 (2009)
16. Petrini, F., Kerbyson, D.J., Pakin, S.: The case of the missing supercomputer performance: Achieving optimal performance on the 8,192 processors of ASCI Q. In: Proc. of the ACM/IEEE Conference on Supercomputing (SC 2003), p. 55. ACM (2003), http://doi.acm.org/10.1145/1048935.1050204
17. Picard, R.R., Cook, R.D.: Cross-validation of regression models. Journal of the American Statistical Association 79(387), 575–583 (1984), http://www.tandfonline.com/doi/abs/10.1080/01621459.1984.10478083

18. Pllana, S., Brandic, I., Benkner, S.: Performance modeling and prediction of parallel and distributed computing systems: A survey of the state of the art. In: Proc. of the 1st Intl. Conference on Complex, Intelligent and Software Intensive Systems (CISIS), pp. 279–284 (2007)

19. Schmidl, D., Terboven, C., Iwainsky, C., Bischof, C., Müller, M.S.: Towards a performance engineering workflow for OpenMP 4.0. In: Performance Engineering MS bei ParCo 2013, Munich (2013)

20. Spafford, K., Vetter, J.S.: Aspen: a domain specific language for performance modeling. In: Proc. of the ACM/IEEE Conference on Supercomputing (SC 2012), p. 84 (2012), http://dl.acm.org/citation.cfm?id=2389110

21. Tallent, N.R., Hoisie, A.: Palm: easing the burden of analytical performance modeling. In: Proc. of the International Conference on Supercomputing (ICS), pp. 221–230 (2014), http://doi.acm.org/10.1145/2597652.2597683

22. Vetter, J.S., Worley, P.H.: Asserting performance expectations. In: Proc. of the ACM/IEEE Conference on Supercomputing (SC 2002), pp. 1–13 (2002), http://doi.acm.org/10.1145/762761.762809

23. Wasserman, H., Hoisie, A., Lubeck, O., Lubeck, O.: Performance and scalability analysis of teraflop-scale parallel architectures using multidimensional wavefront applications. The Intl. Journal of High Performance Computing Applications 14, 330–346 (2000)

24. Wu, X., Mueller, F.: ScalaExtrap: trace-based communication extrapolation for SPMD programs. In: Proc. of the 16th ACM symposium on Principles and practice of parallel programming, PPoPP 2011, pp. 113–122. ACM, New York (2011), http://doi.acm.org/10.1145/1941553.1941569

25. Lee, B.C., Brooks, D.M., de Supinski, B.R., Schulz, M., Singh, K., McKee, S.A.: Methods of inference and learning for performance modeling of parallel applications. In: Proc. of the 12th ACM SIGPLAN Symposium on Principles and Practice of Parallel Programming (PPoPP 2007), pp. 249–258. ACM (2007), http://doi.acm.org/10.1145/1229428.1229479

Task-Based Programming with OmpSs and Its Application

Alejandro Fernández[1], Vicenç Beltran[1], Xavier Martorell[1,3], Rosa M. Badia[1,2], Eduard Ayguadé[1,3], and Jesus Labarta[1,3]

[1] Barcelona Supercomputing Center - Centro Nacional de Supercomputación (BSC-CNS), Spain
{alejandro.fernandez,vicenc.beltran,xavier.martorell,
rosa.m.badia,eduard.ayguade,jesus.labarta}@bsc.es,
[2] Artificial Intelligence Research Institute (IIIA),
Spanish Council for Scientific Research (CSIC), Spain
[3] Universitat Politècnica de Catalunya, Spain

Abstract. OmpSs is a task-based programming model that aims to provide portability and flexibility for sequential codes while the performance is achieved by the dynamic exploitation of the parallelism at task level. OmpSs targets the programming of heterogeneous and multi-core architectures and offers asynchronous parallelism in the execution of the tasks. The main extension of OmpSs, now incorporated in the recent OpenMP 4.0 standard, is the concept of data dependences between tasks.

Tasks in OmpSs are annotated with data directionality clauses that specify the data used by it, and how it will be used (read, write or read&write). This information is used during the execution by the underlying OmpSs runtime to control the synchronization of the different instances of tasks by creating a dependence graph that guarantees the proper order of execution. This mechanism provides a simple way to express the order in which tasks must be executed, without the need of adding explicit synchronization.

Additionally, OmpSs syntax offers the flexibility to express that given tasks can be executed on heterogeneous target architectures (i.e., regular processors, GPUs, or FPGAs). The runtime is able to schedule and run these tasks, taking care of the required data transfers and synchronizations. OmpSs is a promising programming model for future exascale systems, with the potential to exploit unprecedented amounts of parallelism while coping with memory latency, network latency and load imbalance.

The paper covers the basics of OmpSs and some recent new developments to support a family of embedded DSLs (eDSLs) on top of the compiler and runtime, including an prototype implementation of a Partial Differential Equations DSL.

1 Introduction

During the last decades, the number of available transistors inside a chip has continuously increased as predicted by the well known Moore's law [12]. The

L. Lopes et al. (Eds.): Euro-Par 2014 Workshops, Part II, LNCS 8806, pp. 601–612, 2014.
© Springer International Publishing Switzerland 2014

extra transistors provided by each successive processor generation have been traditionally used to increase the complexity of the processors and the size of the cache memories. However, due to the memory and power walls, this trend has halted and replaced by the multi-core and heterogeneous era.

Multi-core processors and heterogeneous architectures are still quite complex, with several functional units in them, including floating point units and vector units. Also, the ability to place other accelerators in the same chip or connected through the PCI express bus resulted in heterogeneous computing nodes. Examples of these architectures are the Xeon Phi processor or general purpose processors with GPU cards. While this trend has been observed for about a decade now, the difficulty to program such architectures still represents a challenge.

Additionally, the interface to program a processor has increasingly been complicated with specific instructions for vector units, specific languages for accelerators which include calls to APIs for data allocation and management (i.e. CUDA or OpenCL), APIs for offloading computation, etc.

All this specific code requirements have made the life of programmers increasingly more difficult, forcing them to mix application logic with specialized instructions. Such code complexity is inversely proportional to code readability and maintainability, thus resulting in an undesired trade-off between productivity and performance. Moreover, these programs are hardly portable: every time a new architecture appears, a new version of the code is necessary. For example, a large number of applications has recently been adapted to enable their execution in nodes with GPUs.

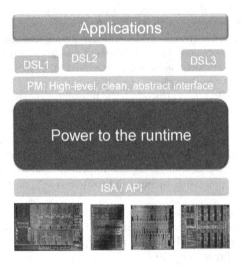

Fig. 1. Software stack in the BSC vision

In this situation, strategies to offer higher levels of abstraction to application developers are necessary. The specifics of the different architectures and hardware organization (architecture-dependent instructions, APIs, separate memory spaces, etc.) should be hidden from the application developers, enabling them to focus on the logic of the application rather than on the low-level performance aspects.

Figure 1 illustrates this idea where a higher level interface in the form of a programming model is offered to the applications. With this layer, a cleaner, more abstract interface results in clean programs without hardware-specific details. Such abstraction is possible thanks to an underlying compiler and/or runtime infrastructure which is the responsible for dealing with the APIs and specific features of the hardware.

In the case of the Barcelona Supercomputing Center (BSC), the programming model considered is StarSs[1], a task-based programming model with tasks' data dependencies taken into account at execution time, building a task dependence graph which defines a partial execution order of the tasks. While the sequential programming paradigm with information about the tasks and the directionality of its parameters is the user interface[2], applications are executed in parallel thanks to the information about the potential parallelism that is derived from the task graph. Another feature of the StarSs programming model is that it enables the application to be unaware of the underlying computing platform. For example, in StarSs instances tailored for distributed computing, the runtime will be responsible for the corresponding data transfers required between computing nodes, performing these activities in a way transparent to the application.

Additionally, in order to offer an even higher level of abstraction, the construction of a high performance framework for a family of Domain-Specific Languages (DSLs) on top of the programming model is currently being considered. DSLs are a promising approach to hide the complexity of hardware systems and boost programmers' productivity. However, the huge cost and complexity of implementing efficient and scalable DSLs, specially for complex platforms such as HPC systems, is hindering their adoption for most domains. For this reason, the strategy adopted at BSC has been to divide the complexity of building such a programming interface by building a DSL development infrastructure on top of one of the implementations of the StarSs programming model. Each instance of this DSL family can focus on a different domain and can be of a different level of complexity (different sizes of DSLs boxes in Figure 1 represent this heterogeneity).

This paper will review the current status of one of the StarSs implementations, the OmpSs project, as well as present an overview of the recent developments towards DSLs for HPC environments. The rest of the paper is structured as follows:

---

[1] StarSs stands for Star superscalar, since most of the ideas behind this programming model are inspired by the field of computer architecture and superscalar processors.

[2] By directionality we mean, input when the parameter is read, or output when the parameter is written. This information is used at runtime to derive the data-dependences between tasks.

First, Section 2 presents the StarSs programming model and its instance, OmpSs. Then, Section 3 presents the OmpSs programming model. Next, Section 4 presents the DSL family developed on top of the OmpSs infrastructure and Section 5 concludes the paper.

2   StarSs Overview

StarSs is a family of programming models recently developed at BSC. The main characteristics of these programming models are: task–based programming with indication of data directionality, flat single logical address space, and a dynamic behaviour addressed by a runtime that takes care of functions such as generation of a task-dependence graph, task scheduling, driven by the partial order defined by this graph, resource selection, automatic data transfers, etc.

Several prototype implementations of these programming models have been developed to test main ideas in different computing platforms and to make progress in research topics, the more relevant being: GRIDSs [3] for grid computing, CellSs [14] for the Cell processor, SMPSs [13] for shared memory systems, and GPUSs [2] for heterogeneous nodes with GPUs.

BSC efforts currently focus in two implementations: OmpSs [7], for HPC (multicore and heterogeneous computing), and COMPSs [19] for distributed computing and cloud computing.

This paper focuses in the OmpSs implementation, which merges the OpenMP standard [1] with the StarSs extensions. OmpSs has been used to promote the StarSs ideas (tasking, dependences, support to heterogeneity) into the OpenMP standard. Achievements of the BSC team in this aspect have been the inclusion of the tasking model (version 3.0) and dependences in tasks (version 4.0). However, OmpSs does not intend to be a reference implementation of OpenMP, but a long term research project where new ideas can be evaluated.

Currently OmpSs features which do not have a match in the OpenMP standard include the support of non-contiguous/strided regions in their dependence detection and data-management mechanisms. The OpenMP dependence mechanism uses the initial address of a region to detect dependences between tasks and therefore dependences between partially overlapping regions or strided regions cannot be detected [6].

Support of heterogeneity in OpenMP 4.0 and in OmpSs is significantly different and complementary. While OmpSs extensions to support heterogeneous environments are designed to simplify the synchronization and data transfers required between host and accelerator codes, OpenMP tries to generate parallel kernels from annotated sequential code that can efficiently run on accelerators. While both OpenMP and OmpSs specifications include a `target device` clause, this clause has a different semantics in OpenMP and OmpSs. In OmpSs, the options of clause `target device` are, for example, `cuda` or `opencl`, while in OpenMP the clause takes a numeric parameter, e.g., `target device (3)`, which represents a device. In OmpSs, the programmer needs to provide the code of the kernel in CUDA or OpenCL, but this code can be part of a task, and therefore it will be independently scheduled and executed asynchronously on a device [7], [9]. The support provided by OmpSs includes the ability to schedule tasks in multiple GPUs independently of the code and automatic data transfers (including awareness of the data locality to reduce the number of transfers). In OpenMP, the compiler translates the C code to the language required by the device (i.e. CUDA), but the code is bound to a given device specified statically in the clause, and the programmer is responsible for finding the identifier of the device. In terms of scheduling, the code embedded in a `target device` clause in OpenMP is executed synchronously, and in case it is embedded in a task which will enable the asynchronous execution, the programmer needs to guarantee the exclusive access to the device at every moment since no support is provided by the OpenMP scheduling.

Another support of scheduling in OmpSs is the possibility of providing more than one implementation (version) of a given task through the `implements` clause. The versions can target one or more devices. At runtime, the scheduler will decide which version should be scheduled taking into account parameters such as execution time or locality of the data. Even more, if slower devices are idling, a few tasks can be scheduled there [15].

The OmpSs runtime is able to target heterogeneous devices not only of a single node, but also of several nodes in a cluster [5]. In this case, the OmpSs scheduler distributes the tasks to the different nodes. As in the case of the GPUs, the required data transfers are performed transparently by the runtime. The runtime keeps a directory with information of the locations of the data regions in the cluster. This directory comes with a software cache policy implemented in each memory space (both memory nodes and GPU memory spaces). Concerning programming methodology, while there are no specific requirements for these architectures, organizing the applications in nested tasks improves the performance. With nested tasks, first level tasks are generated by the main program and scheduled in nodes of the cluster. The node responsible for executing this task will generate the children tasks which are naturally scheduled on the node, including both CPU and GPU tasks.

With regard to the hybrid version of OmpSs with MPI, the strategy goes beyond the traditional parallelization at the node level with OmpSs using MPI for the communication between nodes: with MPI/OmpSs, MPI communications are wrapped into OmpSs tasks which are then automatically included in the task dependence graph. With this approach, overlapping of communication and computation is naturally achieved, since computations that do not hold any dependence with the communication tasks may be executed earlier or together with the communication tasks. Additionally, this implementation presents better sensibility to OS noise and jitter [20].

To further improve the behaviour of MPI/OmpSs applications, DLB is a dynamic library designed to speed up hybrid applications with nested parallelism by improving the load balance each computational node [10]. In general, DLB will redistribute the computational resources of the second level of parallelism (OmpSs) to improve the load balance of the outer level of parallelism (MPI).

This is achieved by dynamically and automatically lending threads between MPI processes sharing the same node.

3   OmpSs Development Environment

OmpSs infrastructure is composed of two main components: Mercurium, the compiler, and Nanos++, the runtime. Mercurium is a source to source compiler that supports C99, C++ 2003 and Fortran 95 and also (an increasing) set of features of C 2011, C++ 2011 and Fortran 2003/2008 and extensions of GNU C/C++/Fortran (see Figure 2). The goal of Mercurium is to provide a sufficiently powerful framework for high-level transformations and analyses in source code in order to support research in parallel and high performance programming models.

In order to support heterogeneous computing, Mercurium supports multi-file processing, that is, from a single source file Mercurium can generate several source files which can be combined at the link step. Compiler phases can reintroduce new files into the compilation pipeline and new files may use a different compilation pipeline.

Mercurium processes the OmpSs pragmas and inserts the corresponding calls to the Nanos++ interface. Mercurium also parses CUDA and OpenCL and emits this code unchanged.

After the compiler phase, the corresponding back-end compiler is invoked. This can be configured to use different compilers (i.e., gcc or icc for C code). For the case of CUDA, the NVIDIA compiler is later invoked. For OpenCL, the

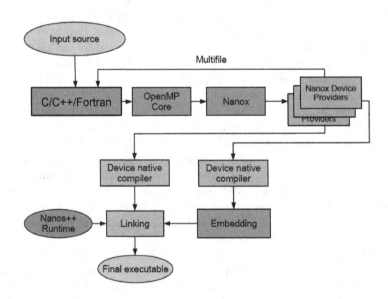

Fig. 2. Mercurium compiler structure

code is processed at execution time by the selected OpenCL runtime. Finally, all objects are linked and embedded into a single binary.

Nanos++ is the OmpSs runtime (see Figure 3). This piece of software is organized in components, each of them responsible for a given behaviour: thread management, task management, dependence checking, cache management, etc. Several of these components are configurable, such as the scheduling policy, the throttle policy or the dependence checker. The runtime also has specific components for the supported devices: SMP, GPU, Cluster, Tasksim (an architecture simulator [16]), etc.

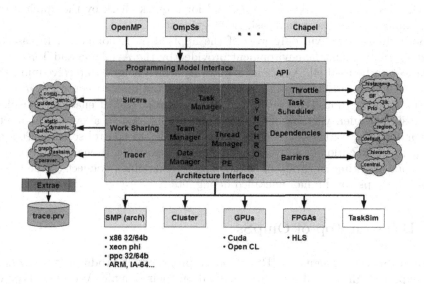

Fig. 3. Nanos++ runtime structure

The runtime can be compiled in different flavours: performance, debug, and instrumentation. While the performance flavour would be the default version to use, the debug version can be used for debugging purposes. The instrumented version is used for several purposes: trace file generation, task graph generation, and debug with Temanejo [18].

The trace file generation emits a time stamped event list ordered by time with information about what happened at execution time. The format of this trace file conforms to the Paraver format (in fact, the Extrae instrumentation library, provided to generate Paraver trace files is called by Nanos++) [11]. Paraver is a very powerful performance visualization and analysis tool based on traces that can be used to analyse any information that is expressed on its input trace format. Its analysis power is based on two main pillars. First, its trace format has no semantics; extending the tool to support new performance data or new programming models requires no changes to the visualizer, just to capture such data in a Paraver trace. The second pillar is that the metrics are not hard-wired in the tool but programmed. To compute them, the tool offers a large set of time functions, a filter module, and a mechanism to combine two time lines. This approach allows displaying a huge number of metrics with the available data. To be able to analyse OmpSs programs, a set of configuration files is provided with the OmpSs distribution that enable to visualize meaningful views (i.e., view of tasks executed in each thread, communications between host and GPU when running on a GPU node, etc), while each programmer/developer can build up her own configuration files with specific purposes.

Another alternative when running with the instrumentation library is to generate an image of the task dependency graph, which can be later visualized with a PDF viewer. This option is very useful for a quick check by the application programmer about the actual task graph generated.

Both these views will only work if the application is not faulty. In case of a faulty application, the environment provided by the Ayudame and Temanejo libraries can be used [4]. Ayudame is a library which is used to receive information (events) from the Nanos++ runtime system and to exert control over it by issuing requests to it. Temanejo is the graphical front end. It enables to display the task dependency graph of OmpSs applications, and to allow simple interaction with the Nanos++ runtime system in order to control some aspects of the parallel execution of a given application. For example, it enables to execute tasks one at a time or group of tasks, define breakpoints, connect to the GNU debugger to perform a more detailed debug, etc.

4   DSLs on Top of OmpSs

Domain Specific Languages (DSLs) boost programmer productivity by offering experts high level abstractions focused on their domain. With this type of languages, mapping and solving a domain problem becomes extremely easy. Additionally, due to the clarity of the code, applications are easily maintained and extended.

However, developing a DSL is expensive and complex, and therefore it would be only justified when a large community is behind. With this idea in mind, the strategy of the BSC Computer Science department has been to develop a framework that can be shared by several DSLs.

This framework is composed of a HPC compiler framework and a runtime system. The compiler framework is based on Lightweight Modular Staging (LMS) [17] (see Figure 4), a Scala library for embedding DSL compilers together with DSL applications, thus reusing the Scala features to define new languages. LMS is a technique for embedding DSLs as libraries into Scala as a host language, while enabling domain specific optimizations and code generation.

As an intermediate language between the actual DSL and the OmpSs compiler, the Data Flow Language (DFL) [8] has been defined. DFL provides a data-flow model based on four concepts: buffers, tasks, kernels and high-level operations. Buffers abstract the concept of data, while tasks and kernels represent computations written in C++ and OpenCL on a multi-core or accelerator,

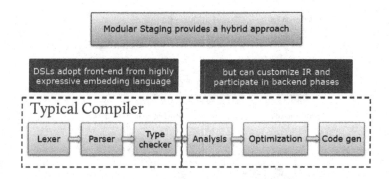

Fig. 4. LMS library design idea

respectively. With these features DFL provides a powerful abstraction to implement HPC DSLs that run on machines composed of CPUs and accelerators.

With the collaboration of the BSC CASE department, Saiph, a DSL for solving Convection-Diffusion-Reaction (CDR) equations has been defined. In this DSL, the programmer first specifies a physical geometry and a set of boundary conditions on that geometry. Then, the initial state of the system is specified by means of functions. Afterwards, the equation to simulate is specified, and the DSL generates DFL and OpenCL code to automatically run the simulation on a multi-GPU architecture.

In addition, some data post process can be specified in order to visualize the output or convert it to a scientific format for analysis tools. An example application of the DSL for CDR equations is shown in Listing 5.

```
1   // Defining preprocess
2   val pre = PreProcess(waveSource1, waveSource2, waveSource3)
3
4   // Defining equation
5   val wavePropagation = c*c * lapla(pressure) - dt2(pressure)
6
7   // Defining postprocess
8   val post = PostProcess(snapshoot each 10 steps)(VTK)
9
10  solve(pre)(post) equation wavePropagation to "wave"
```

Fig. 5. Sample DSL code for a CDR equation

From this input code, the environment generates (see Figure 6) a set of OpenCL kernels that solve the equations and a DFL application that calls the kernels. The DFL application is finally translated to an OmpSs application.

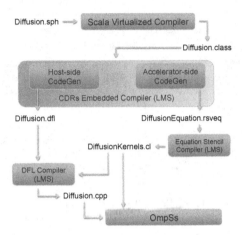

Fig. 6. DSL framework structure

A prototype implementation of this entire framework has been implemented at BSC.

5   Conclusions

This paper has reviewed the current state of the OmpSs programming model, including new developments in the design and implementation of a family of DSLs. While OmpSs offers a reasonable programming interface to average to advanced programmers, more specialized languages will increase the productivity of computational scientists in general. The goal is to achieve high programming productivity with efficient execution in an HPC system.

Acknowledgements. This work has been developed with the support of the grant SEV-2011-00067 of the Severo Ochoa Program, awarded by the Spanish Government, by the Spanish Ministry of Science and Innovation (contracts TIN2012–34557, and CAC2007–00052) and by the Generalitat de Catalunya (contract 2014–SGR-1051).

References

1. OpenMP architecture review board, OpenMP 4.0 specification,
   http://www.openmp.org
2. Ayguadé, E., Badia, R.M., Igual, F.D., Labarta, J., Mayo, R., Quintana-Ortí, E.S.: An extension of the starSs programming model for platforms with multiple gPUs. In: Sips, H., Epema, D., Lin, H.-X. (eds.) Euro-Par 2009. LNCS, vol. 5704, pp. 851–862. Springer, Heidelberg (2009)
3. Badia, R.M., Labarta, J., Sirvent, R., Pérez, J.M., Cela, J.M., Grima, R.: Programming grid applications with grid superscalar. Journal of Grid Computing 1(2), 151–170 (2003)

4. Brinkmann, S., Niethammer, C., Gracia, J., Keller, R.: TEMANEJO - a debugger for task based parallel programming models. In: Proceedings of the ParCO2011 Conference, pp. 639–645 (2011)
5. Bueno, J., Martinell, L., Duran, A., Farreras, M., Martorell, X., Badia, R.M., Ayguade, E., Labarta, J.: Productive Cluster Programming with OmpSs. In: Jeannot, E., Namyst, R., Roman, J. (eds.) Euro-Par 2011, Part I. LNCS, vol. 6852, pp. 555–566. Springer, Heidelberg (2011)
6. Bueno, J., Martorell, X., Badia, R.M., Ayguadé, E., Labarta, J.: Implementing ompss support for regions of data in architectures with multiple address spaces. In: Proceedings of the 27th International ACM Conference on International Conference on Supercomputing, ICS 2013, pp. 359–368. ACM, New York (2013)
7. Duran, A., Ayguadé, E., Badia, R.M., Labarta, J., Martinell, L., Martorell, X., Planas, J.: OmpSs: a proposal for programming heterogeneous multi-core architectures. Parallel Processing Letters 21(02), 173–193 (2011)
8. Fernández, A., Beltran, V., Mateo, S., Patejko, T., Ayguadé, E.: A Data Flow Language to Develop High Performance Computing DSLs. In: Proceedings of the Fourth International Workshop on Domain-Specific Languages and High-Level Frameworks for High Performance Computing, SC 2014, IEEE Computer Society, New Orleans (2014)
9. Ferrer, R., Planas, J., Bellens, P., Duran, A., Gonzalez, M., Martorell, X., Badia, R., Ayguade, E., Labarta, J.: Optimizing the exploitation of multicore processors and gpus with openmp and opencl. In: Cooper, K., Mellor-Crummey, J., Sarkar, V. (eds.) LCPC 2010. LNCS, vol. 6548, pp. 215–229. Springer, Heidelberg (2011)
10. Garcia, M., Labarta, J., Corbalán, J.: Hints to improve automatic load balancing with lewi for hybrid applications. J. Parallel Distrib. Comput. 74(9), 2781–2794 (2014)
11. Labarta, J., Girona, S., Pillet, V., Cortes, T., Gregoris, L.: DiP: A parallel program development environment. In: Fraigniaud, P., Mignotte, A., Robert, Y., Bougé, L. (eds.) Euro-Par 1996. LNCS, vol. 1124, pp. 665–674. Springer, Heidelberg (1996)
12. Moore, G.E.: Cramming more components onto integrated circuits. Electronics 38(8) (April 1965)
13. Perez, J.M., Badia, R.M., Labarta, J.: A dependency-aware task-based programming environment for multi-core architectures. IEEE Int. Conference on Cluster Computing, 142–151 (September 2008)
14. Perez, J.M., Bellens, P., Badia, R.M., Labarta, J.: CellSs: Making it easier to program the Cell Broadband Engine processor. IBM Journal of Research and Development 51(5), 593–604 (2007)
15. Planas, J., Badia, R.M., Ayguadé, E., Labarta, J.: Self-adaptive ompss tasks in heterogeneous environments. In: 27th IEEE International Symposium on Parallel and Distributed Processing, IPDPS 2013, Cambridge, MA, USA, May 20-24, pp. 138–149 (2013)
16. Rico, A., Duran, A., Cabarcas, F., Etsion, Y., Ramírez, A., Valero, M.: Trace-driven simulation of multithreaded applications. In: IEEE International Symposium on Performance Analysis of Systems and Software, ISPASS, Austin, TX, USA, April 10-12, pp. 87–96 (2011)
17. Rompf, T., Odersky, M.: Lightweight modular staging: A pragmatic approach to runtime code generation and compiled DSLs. In: Proceedings of the Ninth International Conference on Generative Programming and Component Engineering, GPCE 2010, pp. 127–136. ACM, New York (2010)

18. Subotic, V., Brinkmann, S., Marjanovic, V., Badia, R.M., Gracia, J., Niethammer, C., Ayguadé, E., Labarta, J., Valero, M.: Programmability and portability for exascale: Top down programming methodology and tools with starss. J. Comput. Science 4(6), 450–456 (2013)
19. Tejedor, E., Badia, R.M.: Comp superscalar: Bringing grid superscalar and gcm together. In: 8th IEEE International Symposium on Cluster Computing and the Grid, CCGRID 2008, pp. 185–193. IEEE (2008)
20. Ayguadé, V.M.J.L.E., Valero, M.: Effective communication and computation overlap with hybrid mpi/smpss. In: Proceedings of the 15th ACM SIGPLAN Symposium on Principles and Practice of Parallel Programming, PPoPP 2010. ACM, New York (2010)

Author Index